DIGITAL CRIME AND DIGITAL TERRORISM

Second Edition

DIGITAL CRIME AND DIGITAL TERRORISM

Robert W. Taylor
Eric J. Fritsch
John Liederbach
Thomas J. Holt

Prentice Hall

Boston   Columbus   Indianapolis   New York   San Francisco   Upper Saddle River
Amsterdam   Cape Town   Dubai   London   Madrid   Milan   Munich   Paris   Montreal   Toronto
Delhi   Mexico City   Sao Paulo   Sydney   Hong Kong   Seoul   Singapore   Taipei   Tokyo

Editor in Chief: Vernon R. Anthony
Acquisitions Editor: Tim Peyton
Editorial Assistant: Lynda Cramer
Director of Marketing: David Gesell
Senior Marketing Manager: Adam Kloza
Senior Marketing Coordinator: Alicia Dysert
Marketing Assistant: Les Roberts
Senior Managing Editor: JoEllen Gohr
Senior Production Editor: Steve Robb

Project Manager: Susun Hannahs
Senior Art Director: Jayne Conte
Cover Designer: Suzanne Duda
Cover Art: SuperStock
Full-Service Project Management: Hemalatha, Integra Software Services, Ltd.
Composition: Integra Software Services, Ltd
Text and Cover Printer/Bindery: Edwards Brothers Malloy
Text Font: 10/12, Minion

Credits and acknowledgments borrowed from other sources and reproduced, with permission, in this textbook appear on appropriate page within text.

Library of Congress Cataloging-in-Publication Data

Digital crime and digital terrorism / Robert W. Taylor . . . [et al.].
  p. cm.
Includes index.
ISBN-13: 978-0-13-700877-3 (alk. paper)
ISBN-10: 0-13-700877-5 (alk. paper)
 1. Computer crimes.   2. Cyberterrorism.   3. Computer hackers.
4. Computer crimes—Investigation—United States.   5. Computer crimes—United States—Prevention.   I. Taylor, Robert W.
HV6773.D54 2011
364.16'8—dc22

2010000680

10 9 8 7 6

Prentice Hall
is an imprint of

PEARSON

www.pearsonhighered.com

ISBN 10:   0-13-700877-5
ISBN 13: 978-0-13-700877-3

For my beautiful grandchildren: Madison, Olivia, and August
RWT

For Cheryl, Jerod, Jacob, Joley, and Jadyn
EJF

For Allyson and Ben
JL

For Bruce, Ginger, Melissa, and Mike: The greatest support that I know
TJH

CONTENTS

Section III   Controlling Digital Crime: Legislation, Law Enforcement, and Investigation   212

NEW TO THIS EDITION

Chapter 1 Introduction and Overview of Digital Crime and Digital Terrorism

- Updated statistics, trends, and patterns relating to digital crime and digital terrorism
- New material on social networking Web sites such as Facebook, Myspace, and Twitter; cyber-crime victimization; information warfare; and use of the computer in criminal enterprises
- Updated content about insider theft of pirated material

Chapter 2 Digital Terrorism

- New material on the Internet as a tool for social and political activism
- Discussion of President Obama's new "Cyberspace Policy Review" presented in 2009
- Significant additional coverage relating to the use of electronic communication and the Internet by terrorist groups, both domestically and internationally
- More content on attacks by foreign countries, especially China's Titan Rain attack in 2003 and the other attempts to gain access to critical infrastructure in the United States in 2009

Chapter 3 The Criminology of Computer Crime

- Updated theoretical research relating to computer crime
- Significant enhancement of content on Choice, Deterrence, Psychological, General Strain, Subcultural, Social Learning, and Social Control theories

Chapter 4 Digital Criminals and Hackers

- A comprehensive rewrite of the chapter, with new material on who and what is a hacker and new material on the various categories of hackers
- Completely new sections on the "Origins and History of Hacking" and on the "Hacker Subculture"

Chapter 5 White-Collar Crimes

- Updated statistical information regarding white-collar crime in the United States
- New material on contemporary white-collar crimes
- New section on "phishing"

Chapter 6 Viruses and Malicious Code

- Significantly updated statistical information on trends relating to viruses and malicious code, as well as restructuring of the entire chapter
- New section on "The Language of Malicious Software"
- New content on Program Sub7, Pinch, and other well-known Trojan horses

- New discussion on viruses and malicious code attacks, with updated information regarding attack trends, vulnerability trends, malicious code trends, and spam trends
- Significant new material entitled "Bank Failures, Mergers and Takeovers: A "Phisherman's" Special"
- Extensive new discussion summarizing malicious software creation and Trojan horse development at the end of the chapter

Chapter 7 Sex Crimes, Victimization, and Obscenity on the World Wide Web

- Updated statistical information on incidents and victimization online
- Updated Table 7.2, Risky Online Behavior
- Completely new section on cyberbullying including common issues observed on Facebook, Twitter, and MySpace
- Completely new material on "Sexting"
- New discussion on cyberstalking including
- New material on "Pedophilia and Child Pornography"
- Complete new section on "Prostitution and the Sex Trade"

Chapter 8 Anarchy and Hate on the World Wide Web

- New discussion of right-wing hate groups, focusing on stormfront.org and the "New Saxon" (a social networking site for people of Northern European descent)
- Updated coverage of the Animal Liberation Front (ALF), focusing on the FBI's 2006 arrest of several ALF leaders
- New section on the Reauthorized PATRIOT Act (2006)

Chapter 9 Digital Laws and Legislation

- Modest update of this very stable and contemporary chapter
- New material and section on the "Family Entertainment and Copyright Act"

Chapter 10 Law Enforcement Roles and Responses

- Complete restructuring of the chapter to reflect the major changes in federal law enforcement since 9/11 and the massive shuffle of federal agencies under President Bush in 2002.
- Significant new material on the expanded role of various federal departments and agencies in combating computer crime
- Reorganization of material relevant to the development of the U.S. Department of Homeland Security

Chapter 11 The Investigation of Computer-Related Crime

- New material on handheld devises and networking equipment
- New sections on "Handling Ongoing Activity," "Examining the Crime Scene," and "Challenges to Forensic Analysis Strategies"

Chapter 12 Digital Forensics

- New material relating to Vista

Chapter 13 Information Security and Infrastructure Protection

- New material on Wireless Networks and Security, including discussion on WiFi connections, and WEPs, and on cyber home users and attacks

Chapter 14 Digital Crime and Terrorism: A Forecast of Trends and Policy Implications

- Updated statistical information and new research regarding patterns and trends in computer crime
- New opening discussion relating to the changes already observed in the technological area that are forcing change in the nature, scope, and patterns of digital crime and digital terrorism
- Expanded Forecast 4's warning that computer hacker groups will emerge in developing countries, increasing the threat of malice attacks motivated by religion, politics, and money
- Expanded Forecast 5 to reflect the fact that the global penetration of the Internet is changing the landscape of hacking
- Expanded discussion on increased electronic crime

PREFACE

It is the authors' shared experience that there is little in the way of introductory textbooks covering the issues of digital crime and digital terrorism. We have found numerous books covering the details of the technical side of these issues and others that cover the legal side. However, there are very few works that attempt to provide a summary introduction and overview of these issues. In this vein, we have tried to approach the various topics covered in this book in a nontechnical and nonjargon style. Criminal justice students and practitioners will find the technical components quite readable and understandable. Computer science students and practitioners will find the criminal justice material bereft of jargon and written in a readable and understandable style as well. In sum, we specifically tried to bridge the gap between criminal justice knowledge and competence and the technical issues that arise during investigations of the crimes and terrorist acts we cover. It is our fervent hope that the techie will get as much out of this book as the criminal justice student.

Digital Crime and Digital Terrorism is written for students and practitioners with a beginning interest in studying crimes and terrorist acts committed using digital technology. The text is written in a user-friendly fashion, designed to be understandable by even the most technologically challenged reader. Issues addressed in the book include descriptions of the types of crimes and terrorist acts committed using computer technology, theories addressing hackers and other types of digital criminals, an overview of the legal strategies and tactics targeting this type of crime, and in-depth coverage of investigating and researching digital crime and digital terrorism. Readers will find a conversational tone to the writing designed to convey complex technical issues as understandable concepts and issues. Additionally, upon completion of the text, readers should find themselves better prepared for further study into the growing problem of crime and terrorism being committed using computer technology.

The first section of the book covers the etiology of the digital crime and digital terrorism problem. The focus in this section is on the types of crimes and acts of terrorism that are committed using computers, networks, and the Internet. Additionally, the reasons why offenders commit these types of crimes are examined in relation to current criminological theories and explanations. As the reader will find, applying criminological theory to digital crime and terrorism is a relatively recent endeavor. Finally, the section concludes with a chapter on digital criminals and hackers. Chapter 1 provides an introduction and overview of computer crime. In particular, a categorization of computer crimes is presented. Chapter 2 provides a definition and overview of two key areas of concern in regard to computer crimes, specifically "information warfare" and "cyberterrorism." Chapter 3 reviews criminological theories that can explain digital crime. Since few theories have been applied directly to digital crime, this chapter focuses on the criminological theories that can be applied to digital crime. In other words, the theories explained in this chapter were developed to explain crime in general, not digital crime specifically. Finally, Chapter 4 presents an overview of hackers.

The second section of the book details the various types of crimes that are committed using digital technology. Chapter 5 describes the ways in which the computer revolution has altered the techniques used to commit some of the most common white-collar offenses, including embezzlement, corporate espionage, money laundering, and fraud. In addition to these traditional white-collar offenses, the chapter provides an overview of the emerging area of identity theft crimes. Chapter 6 discusses viruses and other types of malicious code. The chapter takes an etiological approach with an emphasis on description, examples, and categorical analysis of these various threats. Chapter 7 focuses on crimes against persons committed over the Internet, including exploitation, stalking, and obscenity. The chapter goes into detail on the etiology of these types of offenses and the offenders who commit them. Finally, Chapter 8 provides the reader with an introduction to the issues surrounding the growth of the Internet and the dissemination of extremist ideologies over the World Wide Web.

The third section of the book discusses the law, law enforcement, and investigation of digital crime and digital terrorism. Chapter 9 reviews the law and legislation as it applies to the collection of evidence and prosecution of digital crime. First, search and seizure law for digital evidence is discussed, including searches with warrants and numerous searches without warrants. Second, the major federal statutes governing the collection of digital evidence, especially electronic surveillance law, are discussed along with federal criminal statutes that forbid certain types of computer crime. Third, issues related to the admission of digital evidence at trial, including authentication and hearsay, are reviewed. Finally, significant U.S. Supreme Court cases in the area of digital crime are discussed. Chapter 10 then discusses the primary role of the many federal agencies involved in detecting and enforcing computer crimes. The chapter continues with a discussion concerning the role of local agencies, with an emphasis on detailing the myriad of limitations associated with the local agencies' response to computer crime. Chapter 11 highlights the role that investigators play in the enforcement of digital crime laws. Techniques for acquiring investigative information are presented in this chapter, along with conceptual tools that allow an investigator to communicate with computer experts. Finally, Chapter 12 reviews the collection of evidence and evidentiary issues related to digital crime and terrorism.

The final section of the book covers prevention of digital crime and terrorism and an overview of what the future might hold in these areas. Chapter 13 presents the problems associated with information security and infrastructure protection. The chapter discusses at length the problems and prospects presented by the USA PATRIOT Act as well as other laws designed to protect the information infrastructure. Chapter 14 uses research developed by Carter and Katz as a framework to present an analysis of what the future of digital crime and digital terrorism might look like. The results of the research led to the development of eight forecasts for the future. Each prediction is accompanied by examples, trends, and analysis of what the future may hold.

RWT

EJF

JL

TJH

ACKNOWLEDGMENTS

First and foremost, we want to thank our wives, children, extended family, and friends for their support and patience with all of us as we compiled the second edition of this book. As is the case with many of these types of projects, we locked ourselves in our offices, missed family functions, and, in general, put out our loved ones while writing this book. Thank you for your love, patience, and support during these times.

Since our first edition, time has presented us with a new set of authors. Dr. D. Kall Loper has left academia to pursue a career as an expert in digital forensics, a field that he helped found and develop. And quite sadly, our good friend and colleague Dr. Tory J. Caeti was killed in a terrible traffic accident in August 2006 while serving as a consultant with Bob Taylor to the U.S. Department of State Anti-Terrorism Assistance Program in Kenya. Tory and Bob were to present material to the Kenyan National Police on digital terrorism. We will miss Tory, and he will be forever in our thoughts as we continue our "quest for world domination!" We were fortunate to have our newest team member, Dr. Tom Holt, join us for this edition. He has conducted exceptional work in the area of digital crime and digital terrorism and was a perfect fit for our team, although I am sure that he wished our timing had been a little better. Tom moved from Charlotte, North Carolina, to assume his new position at Michigan State University during the course of writing this edition. Welcome aboard, Tom.

We also express our sincere appreciation to our editorial staff at Pearson. Tim Peyton's guidance and assistance was instrumental in getting this book to press, and Lynda Cramer was outstanding at coordinating and presenting our effort. We also want to thank all other Pearson staff involved in this project. They epitomize patience and understanding in dealing with slow academics who take forever to return phone calls and e-mails.

Last, but not least, we thank the reviewer of the manuscript, Cecile Van de Voorde at John Jay College of Criminal Justice (CUNY), who provided invaluable insight and suggestions for the final version of this manuscript.

CHAPTER 1

Introduction and Overview of Digital Crime and Digital Terrorism

CHAPTER OBJECTIVES

After completing this chapter, you should be able to

- Describe the current issues, trends, and problems in the areas of digital crime and digital terrorism.
- Understand the intended audience, purpose, and scope of this text.
- Be able to discuss how cyber victimization has changed in the recent history of digital crime.
- Be able to describe the four primary categorizations of computer crime.

INTRODUCTION

Viruses destroying data and shutting down the Internet, computer thieves stealing credit card and Social Security numbers, millions of people becoming victims of identity theft, terrorists laundering money and using the Internet to coordinate their attacks, and nation states using the Internet to attack other countries—all of these scenarios are endemic to the growing problems of digital crime and digital terrorism. Worsening this situation is the perception that law enforcement and governmental officials are ill-equipped to deal with these crimes and attacks. Digital crimes inspire fear in consumers and lead to a lack of trust in the security and safety of conducting business online. Our reliance on computers and networks for military operations, financial transactions, communications, utilities, and mass transit inspires fear that an attack on our information structure would cripple our society. In 2003, images of thousands of people walking home from work due to a power problem that began in Canada and quickly spread to the United States led many to believe that terrorists had attacked the nation's power grid. Recent descriptions of both Chinese and Russian hacker intrusions into power grids in the United States continue to concern citizens and government alike. In sum, the areas of digital crime and digital terrorism are marked by perhaps more misperception and fear than by actual threat. Nonetheless, these problems are real and present unique challenges to law enforcement and other governmental officials.

The first electronic computer was completed in 1945, and the first long-distance electronic communication on the Internet was sent in 1969.[1] Until the creation of the personal computer, computers and the Internet were the exclusive tools of society's scientific elite and the military and were housed at major university campuses, military bases, and corporate research parks. In fact, the coming "information society" would become increasingly dependent on computers and networks to keep our society operational. Computers are now fixtures of everyday life, and almost every form of interaction and communication between people relies on computers and network systems in some fashion. The Internet has truly made the world a smaller place. Students can register for or drop classes in real time from their homes while sitting in front of a keyboard. Individuals are able to swiftly and conveniently withdraw money from bank accounts at any time by using automated teller machines (ATMs). Friends use satellite transmissions linked across vast computer networks to "instant message" one another. Social networking Web sites like Facebook, Myspace, and Twitter allow individuals to connect, communicate, and update the world about their attitudes and activities in real time. Stock transactions, flight schedules, reference libraries, online commerce, the latest news, and innumerable other resources are all available with a few clicks of the mouse.

The advancement of computer technology and networking rapidly expanded communications and information markets, but this progress comes with costs, both social and economic. The same technology that provides useful services has also been perverted for criminal and terrorist purposes. The advancing technology provides criminals and terrorists with a variety of new tools and opportunities to conduct their activities. The Internet is, in essence, a lawless frontier where bullies, deviants, criminals, and terrorists can roam freely with reckless abandon. Computers and networks advanced so rapidly, and without adequate regulation and monitoring, that the law of the jungle prevailed. Lawmakers and police officials are still playing catch-up to this day.

New Threats in the Information Age

Now, computers are also used to perform many traditional criminal acts, most prominently the production and distribution of child pornography, financial crimes, information and corporate espionage, exploitation, stalking, and identity theft. The openness of the Internet expanded the scope of criminal opportunities and has spawned whole new categories of crimes and criminals, including "hackers," who seek to invade our computer networks, and virus writers, who develop tools that can damage and destroy computer systems. The opportunities to commit computer crimes and the technical competence of the criminals have expanded faster than we can control them.

Currently, there are over 625 million named hosts on the Internet, with each host representing a network of up to one billion computers.[2] The expansion and sheer amount of Internet traffic has already exceeded the estimates predicted by experts and commentators a few years ago. Perhaps the most feared online crime is the interception of privileged information, such as credit card numbers or passwords, perhaps leading to identity theft. Abuses associated with the issuance of credit have reached epidemic proportions. In fact, a small group of hackers compromised the financial database of the TJX Corporation in 2005, causing over $1 billion in fraud and bank losses.[3] Theft of intellectual property ranging from trade secrets to illegal reproduction of copyrighted consumer materials such as music and movies has an incalculable cost. The Motion Picture Association of America (MPAA) reported fiscal losses upward of $6 billion in 2005 from movie piracy in the United States alone. Over 40 percent of these reported losses were argued to be a result of university students in the United States.[4] Trading and selling illicit information on the Internet is a recurring problem and instills fear in online consumers.

While identity theft is probably the most feared online crime, it is not the only threat to Internet consumers. The other category of digital crime that inspires the most fear and disdain is virus writing and other types of malicious software, or malware. Any time an average user has a problem with his or her computer, the person is likely to have a knee-jerk response, blaming the problem on a virus. The virus protection industry is now a multimillion dollar business, selling and proffering security online. Consumer fear is, however, not unfounded, as a recent study by the security company PandaLabs found: Almost 25 percent of personal computers with some sort of protective software around the world were infected with malicious software, compared to 33.2 percent of systems without protection.[5] Beyond these dangers, threats from would-be terrorists and politically motivated "hactivists" threaten the functioning of our government, commerce, and military operations. Recent studies indicate that many corporations, government agencies, and utility companies are highly vulnerable to computer attacks from outsiders, who in some cases may be able to seriously affect large segments of the population through a single organization's computer system. This threat cannot be taken lightly, and the Federal Bureau of Investigation (FBI) and the Department of Homeland Security both conclude that the potential exists for serious harm emanating from attempts to tamper with the information infrastructure.

Purpose and Scope of This Book

This text is primarily intended to be an introduction to the problems of digital crime and digital terrorism. A special emphasis is placed on being decidedly nontechnical in our writing and explanations; however, some technical terms and issues are inevitable in this field of study. We hope that we have described the technical jargon in sufficient detail such that the casual reader will not be lost in the shuffle. The intended audience is anyone interested in learning more about the etiology of digital crime and digital terrorism. The average criminal justice student may have a solid knowledge of the law, criminology, and criminal justice systems, yet possess little knowledge of the complexities of digital crime and victimization. Computer science students well versed in the technical aspects of computers and networks may have little knowledge of the legal aspects of their field and issues of criminality and victimization. Further, practitioners in both the criminal justice field and the computer science field typically have limited knowledge of each other's occupations. Finally, many students and casual readers may simply wish to become better educated in this area. This text is written with all of these groups in mind.

The ambition of the authors was to bring aspects of both of these fields together in a readable, nontechnical text designed to increase knowledge about the problems of digital crime and digital terrorism. Anyone with a little knowledge about computers and the criminal justice system should find merit in the topics covered in this text. We have also consciously focused on common digital crimes and common computer systems, as these will be most familiar to the neophyte. The text is decidedly focused on Microsoft-based systems, common Internet systems, and the most typical types of digital crime and digital terrorism. As such, certain types of digital crimes and certain operating systems/software are beyond our scope and intent. Again, a decided effort was made to explain the more technical parts of this book in a "user-friendly" tone; however, readers who know very little about computers might have some difficulty with some of the details and level of description.

The first section of this book covers the etiology of digital crime and digital terrorism and includes a discussion of the criminology of these types of crimes and potential offenders. Who are the digital terrorists and digital hackers, and why do they commit their crimes and acts of aggression? The second section addresses the various types of digital crimes and covers the nature, extent, and offender groups in each of the chapters. Chapters on white-collar crime, viruses and malicious code, exploitation, and hate are all covered in this section. The third section covers the law, enforcement, and investigation of digital crimes and terrorism. Included in this section are chapters on the laws and legislation covering digital crime and digital terrorism, the agencies charged with enforcing these laws, and the investigative and forensic aspects of this area. Finally, the book concludes with chapters on preventing these types of crimes and threats and discusses what the future might hold.

DIGITAL CRIME AND DIGITAL TERRORISM[6]

Computer-related crime has increased dramatically in recent years—indeed, both the character and nature of these offenses and their frequency of occurrence have changed notably since about 1995, when the Internet experienced explosive growth.[7] One simply needs to search the phrase "computer crime" on LEXIS-NEXIS® or an Internet news site to find a plethora of incidents and commentaries on the problem. How much computer crime is occurring? It is simply unknown. Not only is there significant inconsistency in defining computer crime offenses, there is an absence of any attempt to collect offense data systematically.

Offenses vary in character from clear criminality (e.g., theft, fraud, or destruction of data files) to acts where criminal culpability is less clear, such as violations of privacy (e.g., unauthorized access to credit reports or medical records). Similarly, types of criminal behavior by computer users also vary (e.g., pornography, extortion, cyberstalking, or gambling). This situation is complicated by the global character of networking offenses—transactions and behavioral interactions can occur between people worldwide from their homes with no scrutiny by immigration, customs, or other government entity. The gravity of the problem is illustrated by international estimates that place the costs of cybercrime at as much as $50 million a year.[8]

Since data are not collected to document the nature, trends, and extent of computer crime, it is difficult to develop a clear image of the problem and to predict future trends. Pragmatically, the utility of having good data would be to serve as the basis of law and policy related to cyber-criminality. Prevention programs, resource allocation for investigation and prosecution, as well as risk management can all be more effectively designed and employed if data that provides insights on the character and extent of the crime problem existed. Hence, perhaps the first problem is how to get an accurate picture of the crime problem and the nature and extent of digital crime and digital terrorism.

A Developmental Perspective on the Growing Problem

Since the introduction of the microcomputer on the public market, personal computing and the Internet have grown substantially. Technological development of memory capacity, processing speed, software capabilities, and remote communications via computer (i.e., networking) grew geometrically. Similarly, there was rapid integration of computing, telecommunications, multimedia, and information archiving technologies. With the public's embrace of the Internet and its staggering growth since 1995—Sky Dayton, founder of the Earthlink Network, has described 1995 as "pre-historic" in networking terms[9]—the need for network security became obvious. Certainly there were some early efforts in exploring the idea of computer crime and recognition of it as a criminal problem. These inquiries were groundbreaking yet limited, just as the technology was.

One of the earliest publications on computer crime was by Parker,[10] discussing the feasibility and potential of cybercriminality. Parker's foresight recognized the potential for such criminality even in systems that were, in comparison to today, archaic. Despite this, Parker noted the potential for abusing information that was in a compact, easily accessible form. In the late 1970s, the Bureau of Justice Statistics focused on the issue through a series of publications that included an overview of computer crime issues,[11] computer security,[12] and crimes related to electronic fund transfers.[13] These monographs focused on the potential for cybercriminality and considered issues of law, investigation, case development, and possible criminal strategies. This research was groundbreaking, and many of the methodologies still have applications to operational aspects of security and crime control today. Yet, the reports contain very limited documentation of actual criminality and do not include discussion of cybercriminals, per se. In the 1980s, a few more publications emerged on the topic, predominantly dealing with logistical issues associated with computer-related criminality. Several publications discussed methods to prevent computer crimes.[14] Others explored practices for effectively investigating and prosecuting a computer crime case.[15]

As research developed on the problems of computer crime, several common themes emerged. Some research offered classifications for the emerging crime problem,[16] which are now largely dated as a result of the significant changes in computing capabilities (such as digital imaging) and networking. Scholars began documenting cases of computer-related fraud that occurred in government agencies (nearly all of which were cases of trust violations)[17] and discussed the capabilities of hackers in the early days of Bitnet (the Internet "predecessor").[18] Other research began to call for the creation of dedicated computer crime units.[19]

A new industry emerged with many publications and products directed at various aspects of computer security. Firewalls, encryption systems, operations security, virtual private networks (VPNs), physical security, access controls, and biometric security developments are all illustrations of the issues explored. Nearly all of the publications employ the same methodology: describe the security issue, offer options for a solution, and provide technological procedural alternatives for each potential solution. Behavioral approaches and descriptions of problems and trends are virtually nonexistent. One exception is Icove et al.,[20] who not only comprehensively focus on security and investigation but also offer some interesting insights about motivations and behaviors. Moreover, the behavioral implications provide some guidance; however, they are limited to observations from a small number of investigations rather than a scientific study of trends or patterns.

Other publications about cybercrime are found in the popular press. Case studies such as *The Cuckoo's Egg*[21] and *Takedown*[22] look at specific instances of network incursion. Stoll[23] documents the case of a computer hacker from Germany who penetrated a wide range of U.S. academic and military computers seeking information to steal and sell on the global national security market. Shimomura[24] describes the investigation, arrest, and prosecution of Kevin Mitnik, perhaps the most well known of all hackers, who was released in early 2000 from federal prison for computer crime violations. Both publications provide interesting and unique insights about the capacity to commit cybercrimes as well as the difficulty of investigating these offenses. However, as case studies, they offer information about specific offenders, not generalizations about trends in cybercriminality or patterns of offending.

A great deal of effort continues to be dedicated to all forms of computer security, ranging from firewalls to encryption to access control to virus prevention, because of growing problems in hacking/cracking and the use of malicious software. Interestingly, the computer security industry has grown rapidly without fully understanding the nature of cybercrimes and criminals. The effect of this rapid change was that cybercrime, per se, was largely ignored—both by policy makers and the research community.

Increases in Cybervictimization

As computers become increasingly integrated in day-to-day lives and as more people use the Internet, cybervictimization will continue to increase. Furthermore, the ease of finding technical documentation on creating viruses and hacking techniques will lead to larger numbers of technically competent criminals. In short, anyone with a computer and a cause can become a cybercriminal. Therefore, most research in this area focuses on the mechanisms and techniques used rather than on the etiology of the offenders and the offenses they commit. According to Parker, the lack of attention paid to computer crime historically is no accident. "In 1970, a number of researchers concluded that the problem was merely a small part of the effect of technology on society and not worthy of specific explicit research."[25] However, Parker went on to note that "the increase in substantial losses associated with intentional acts involving computers proved the fallacy of this view."[26] The irony is that Parker's observations were made a decade ago, yet there is little substantial progress in understanding and addressing the problem from criminological and investigative perspectives. Furthermore, when Parker's early observations were made, most computing was the province of big business, government, and academe. Today, personal computing has changed the entire face of the computer industry.

While there is some debate about who poses the greatest risk as a cybercriminal, the fact remains that anyone who has computing skills may pose a criminal threat.[27] This fact is exacerbated by easy Web access to hacking tools and Web sites devoted to writing viruses and cracking into systems. In the mid-1980s, Van Duyn observed that "insiders pose a far greater threat to the organization's computer security than outside 'electronic invaders' possibly could."[28] His reasoning was that "insiders are familiar with their employers' data processing operations and the type of data each system and application is storing and processing" and therefore know exactly where to look for information. Certainly this logic still has merit. However, the emergence of networking, expansive growth of easily adapted databases integrated with Web pages, and user-friendly protocols are changing this balance.

Many experts conclude that vulnerability from within an organization is the most dangerous and poses the most serious threat. In fact, "one study estimated that 90% of economic computer crimes were committed by employees of the victimized companies." A more recent study conducted in North America and Europe found that 73 percent of the risk to computer security was from internal sources, while only 23 percent was attributable to external sources.[29] Unlike "outsiders" attempting to break into a system, "insiders" are oftentimes able to more easily circumvent safeguards, reducing their chances of being detected. Moreover, if the employee has authorized access to the information, but chooses to steal or destroy it, then detection is even more difficult. While insider theft remains an important issue, the pervasive advent of networking, personal computing, and e-commerce has changed this significantly, bringing more threats from "outsiders." "Insiders" also have a distinct advantage, for not only do they often know immediately where to look for the data, but, if in doubt, "they can reference the systems documentation which usually includes programming specifications, file and record layouts, a data element dictionary, and so on."[30]

In terms of general assessments of cybervictimization, there appears to be a connection between industrialization, Internet connectivity, and victimization. A study comparing reporting of cybercrime victimization in eight industrialized nations across the globe from 1999 to 2001 found that computer security incidents were on the rise, particularly in Canada, Australia, the United Kingdom, and the United States.[31] In fact, the United States had the highest victimization rate overall, followed by the United Kingdom and Japan. These findings would suggest that the risk of victimization increases with time and the penetration of computers and the Internet in a society.

The Changing Character of Cybervictimization

From a descriptive perspective, Barrett[32] offers insights about the wide range of cybercriminality that can occur. He provides a foundation about the capacity of computers to be used as criminal instruments as well as instruments of warfare. Interestingly, the dynamics and processes are virtually the same; hence, the integrated discussion of criminality and national security is becoming an increasingly prevalent theme in the literature. In many ways, inferences from the National Infrastructure Protection Center data[33] can be made that digital crime and digital terrorism are on parallel tracks. This is reinforced by the January 1999 experience of simultaneous attacks on U.S. Defense Department computer systems originating in Russia. Similar tactics were used by Russian organized crime groups against banks.[34] Other attacks, such as those perpetrated by Chinese hackers, utilize the same techniques and tools as in coordinated attacks against private citizens and financial industries.[35]

One project conducted by the American Bar Association (ABA) in 1987 found that of the 300 corporations and government agencies surveyed, 72 (24 percent) claimed to have been the victim of a computer-related crime in the 12 months prior to the survey.[36] The estimated losses from these crimes ranged from $145 million to $730 million over the one-year period. The broad range of estimates shows that not only is it difficult to identify and document these crimes, it is even more difficult to place a monetary value on the loss of intellectual property wherein the actual value may not be known for months or years.

The Florida Department of Law Enforcement (FDLE) surveyed 898 public and private sector organizations that conducted business by computer. Of the 403 (44.9 percent) respondents, 25 percent reported they had been victimized by computer criminals.[37] The Florida study found embezzlement of funds by employees to be a major source of the crimes; however, no attempt to estimate losses was made because, according to one of the researchers interviewed, "losses would have been nothing more than a guess." Many experts believe that the true level of computer crime is severely underreported because companies handle these matters internally. This is due primarily to a desire to limit the public's perceptions of the vulnerability of companies to these types of crimes and intrusions.

In perhaps one of the most comprehensive studies on computer security threats and crimes, a survey conducted in 1991 of 3,000 Virtual Address Extension (VAX) sites in Canada, Europe, and the United States found that 72 percent of the respondents reported a security incident had occurred within the previous 12 months and 43 percent reported the incident was criminal in nature.[38] By far the greatest security threats came from employees or people who had access to the computers; however, a number of external security breaches from hackers telephoning into the systems or accessing via networks were also reported. The ABA and FDLE studies scarcely mentioned this "external threat" and gave little attention to it as a growing problem. This is not surprising, since networking in the late 1980s was comparatively limited, and networking technology was both more expensive and more cumbersome. However, a 1991 United Nations study suggested that external threats via remote access were a problem that would grow in the years to come.

Carter and Katz[39] show a trend of victimization that increased significantly over previous studies, with 98.5 percent of the respondents reporting they had been victimized—43.3 percent reported being victimized more than 25 times. While these numbers seem dramatic, security professionals with whom these results were discussed stated they were surprised at the frequency of admitted victimization, not actual victimization. One respondent stated, "Do we know the national or even local scope of the computer crime threat? Probably not; but it has to be higher than anyone wants to admit."

The 1998 joint survey by the FBI and Computer Security Institute found that for the third year in a row, corporate security directors reported an increase of computer system penetration by outsiders. This represented a 20 percent increase of successful system incursions since 1996.[40] In fact, their 2007 data suggest that most directors believe that less than 40 percent of their security incidents are due to insiders.[41] Collectively, these data provide empirical support for the anecdotal evidence: Not only is unauthorized access to and theft from computer systems increasing, but so does the number of system incursions committed by "outsiders".

Hacking and thefts are the best documented offenses, but other forms of cybercriminality are emerging. Fraud through investment Web sites, theft of identity, and telecommunications are all examples of expanding areas of criminality.[42] Cybercrime is not limited to crimes against property. A recent initiative by the U.S. Department of Justice (DOJ) explored the problem of cyberstalking, noting the rapidly increasing nature of the problem, which is aggravated by the increasing amount of personal information available on the Internet.[43] While largely anecdotal information has been collected on these crimes, little is known about offense patterns and offender characteristics.

TYPES OF COMPUTER CRIME

Defining computer crime sufficiently is a daunting and difficult task. Nevertheless there are, generally, four categories of computer crime, including (1) the computer as a target, (2) the computer as an instrument of the crime, (3) the computer as incidental to crime, and (4) crimes associated with the prevalence of computers. Definitions can become rapidly outdated, as new technology has consistently bred new offenses and victimizations.

The Computer as a Target

Crimes where the computer itself is the target include the denial of expected service or the alteration of data. In other words, the attack seeks to deny the legitimate user or owner of the system access to their data or computer. Network intruders target the server and may cause harm to the network owner or the operation of their business.

Data alteration and denial directly target the computer by attacking the useful information stored or processed by the computer. Altered data may affect business decisions made by the company or may directly impact individuals by altering their records. Further, this activity, in some circumstances, results in the expenditure of great resources to recover the data. Although malicious network intruders may alter critical data, the most common source of such damage is an employee of the affected company. The primary difference between data alteration and network intrusion is the intent of the intruder. By reading or "browsing" through confidential files, the intruder actually creates a copy of the file. Thus, mere browsing may be theft, but it does not deprive the owner of the data or the user of the data. This makes the distinction between data alteration and intrusion more meaningful.

The story of Kevin Mitnick (perhaps the poster boy of hackers) perfectly exemplifies this distinction, as he wreaked havoc on countless systems during his hacking career. The prosecution of Mitnick relied on estimates of the value of software he downloaded but did not alter. Several major corporations placed a total value of hundreds of millions of dollars on the software Mitnick obtained. This amount was determined by a method suggested by the FBI: They directed the companies to estimate the total development costs of the software. This amount was questioned at various stages in Mitnick's trial. Since Mitnick did not deprive the companies of the product of their research and development, it seems that the actual economic harm caused would be less than the total cost. This contention was supported by the failure of any of the corporation on the list of Mitnick's victims to report such a loss to the Securities and Exchange Commission, as required for losses suffered by a company that sells stock.

When intrusion is discovered, it often requires the owner or administrator of the affected system to question the integrity, accuracy, and authenticity of data on the network. Although the legitimate user of the system and data is not denied access to either, there is no reasonable certainty of the data's security in the system. Security measures often require the removal of Web-based resources and restoration of data from, hopefully, unaffected backup copies.

More direct than the subtleties of a network intruder, the denial of service leaves little room for argument of a negative effect. Although any resource may be denied to the rightful user, the most prominent example of this crime targeting the computer is the network denial-of-service attack. For example, on February 7, 2000, the Web site of Yahoo! was subjected to an unprecedented attack that effectively removed the site from the Internet for three hours. The initial reaction of law enforcement, security, and even hackers was shock that a site as large as Yahoo could be overwhelmed.[44] Subsequent investigation showed that the attacks had been aimed at choke points that funneled the majority of the site's traffic through a few routers. While not as bad as first suspected, the attack showed that even the largest sites on the Internet were not safe.

The significance of denial-of-service attacks was also demonstrated in the recent conflict between Russia and Estonia, which was caused by the removal of a Russian war monument from a memorial garden in Estonia[45] Russian citizens in Estonia and elsewhere were enraged by this action, leading to protests and violence in the streets of both Estonia and Russia. Computer-based attacks quickly ensued against government and private resources in both nations by computer hackers and citizens alike. In particular, Russian hackers so severely limited access to Estonian government and financial systems that the government had to temporarily host files on servers in the United States to continue business without interruption.[46] The damage the denial-of-service attacks caused to the Estonian economy was so severe that the country was crippled as a result.

Computer vandalism also falls under the category of crimes where the computer is a target. When an intruder removes valuable information from a computer system, the intruder denies the legitimate user or owner access to that information. This could represent a substantial loss of expected revenue. If the data are for direct sale, like a computer program or music, it may be possible to estimate the value of the lost data. However, it is more likely that data disrupted will be provided to the public for goodwill, to generate advertising income, or for no commercial purpose.

Even though a dollar value cannot be attached to the data, the owner still has a right to present the intended message and be free from disruption. Many organizations, like the University of Cambridge, maintain a Web presence for no apparent commercial purpose. In this case, the University of Cambridge has the distinction of owning the last defaced Web page to be archived at Attrition.org. On May 13, 2001, the Web camera at the University of Cambridge was replaced with the calling card of a computer vandal. The vandal wished to express nothing more important than "Ne0tz owned u!"[47] In another example of computer vandalism, a group named "Hacking for Girlies" defaced the *New York Times* Web site. The defacement caused the *New York Times* embarrassment and the loss of advertising revenue for their free Web-based service. Some defacements, however, allow individuals to express their perspectives about a political or religious agenda. For example, when a U.S. spy plane crashed in China in 2001, a small war erupted between hackers in these countries over the rights to the plane and the reasons the jet was flying in the first place. The defacements contained political messages such as "Fuck the U.S.A." and "China is Wrong!" and affected Web sites owned by the government, academia, and the private sector.[48] The consequences of computer vandalism are similar to data alteration or denial of service; many instances of computer vandalism also include network intrusion. All of these offenses target the computer.

The Computer as an Instrument of a Crime

Unlike crimes targeting the computer, using the computer as the instrument of the crime means that the computer is used to gain some other criminal objective. In other words, a burglar uses crowbars and lock picks as the instruments of crime in a fashion similar to the cybercriminal using computers and networks for crimes such as theft, theft of service, fraud, exploitation, and threats or harassment.

Theft is defined as the taking of property with the intent of permanently depriving the owners of their property or service. In an environment where data are more easily copied than deleted, depriving the owner of the property permanently is relatively rare. However, theft can also mean taking property with the intent to deprive the owner of the value of the property or stealing securities. Parker, creator of the first computer crime typology, notes that market-sensitive proprietary information, financial information, trade secrets, process technology information, human resources information, customer information, information products, transitory information, and security information can all have value to the owner.[49] To some degree, each of these forms of information requires that the owner either maintain confidence in the integrity of the information or control the distribution of the information to maintain its value.

Other, more blatant, examples of computerized theft do actually deprive the legitimate owner of a tangible asset. The salami slice technique is a money crime; it is an automated means of stealing assets from a large number of transactions. In the round-down salami technique, the computer is used to round calculated dollar amounts down to the nearest cent. By always rounding down and diverting that amount to a special account, the criminal deprives both merchant and consumer of assets; however, the amounts are often trivial, similar to a slice taken from a salami, too thin to produce a noticeable effect, unless millions of transactions are involved.

Some thefts specifically involve theft of service. Although many services available on the Internet are free, some data and services are considered proprietary. This means the users must pay to use the data or service. The use of these proprietary services without payment is theft. For example, many service providers invest in the ability to meet demand for their service. In the mid-1990s, Internet service provider America Online (AOL) failed to anticipate demand for Internet access. As a result, many customers were not able to connect to AOL servers. To remedy this situation, AOL invested significant amounts of money in increasing their capacity. The amount of the increase was carefully planned to avoid spending too much. The damage from theft of service occurs when the criminal use of service forces the owner to invest in greater capacity to meet the projected needs of legitimate users.

Computers can also be used as instruments to commit fraud. Fraud committed by using a computer exploits the trust, which is guaranteed by law, in a business transaction. The buyer, seller, or peer in a transaction can perpetrate fraud. Shopping cart fraud is an example of consumer fraud against a business. Once purchases are selected, the computer criminal saves a copy of the purchase page and alters the prices. Once the altered prices are in place, the criminal submits the page as normal. Some merchants do not discover the fraud until they match inventory to purchases—possibly a month or more after the merchandise is shipped. Although basic security procedures or well-designed shopping cart programs would prevent this, many online merchants do not use either.

Other varieties of fraud found online are simply high-tech variants of older methods. Old scams have found entirely new audiences of victims on the Internet. Pyramid schemes have found a new source of legitimacy with professional-appearing Web sites and official-sounding Web addresses. In fact, virtually every tired bunko scheme has found new life through the Internet. Perhaps the most common one recently is the Nigerian bank scheme, where unsuspecting victims send their bank account numbers overseas with the dreams of getting millions in return. New forms of whole cloth fraud have also developed online, such as phishing. This offense involves victims being tricked into providing their financial information to a criminal through the use of convincing and extremely accurate fraudulent Web sites.[50]

Computers are now often used as instruments to make threats or harass individuals. The U.S. DOJ maintains a Web site that details a range of threatening behaviors conducted on the Internet. In an early case of cyberstalking, a Maryland man, Warren Gray, pled guilty to sending five e-mail messages that graphically threatened the life of his victim and the victim's family. At the same time, Gray slashed the victim's car tires and left a hatchet in the victim's office. In this case, cyberstalking coincided with real-world stalking, but the conviction under federal law came from the use of "interstate wires" to transmit the threat.

Even schoolyard bullying has moved to the Internet through the use of social networking Web sites and instant messaging services. Children can easily post messages that attempt to poke fun or humiliate another individual. In fact, a recent case of bullying through the social networking Web site Myspace led a young woman named Megan Meier to commit suicide after receiving cruel and harassing messages from a young man named Josh Evans. In reality, Evans was a fictitious identity created by Lori Drew, the mother of one of Megan's friends.[51] Drew created this identity as a means to humiliate Megan as retribution for slighting her daughter. Unfortunately, this event highlights the severity of cyberbullying.

The Computer as Incidental to a Crime

Carter characterizes the computer as incidental to other crimes when "a pattern or incident of criminality uses a computer simply for ease in maintaining the efficacy of criminal transactions."[52] In this category, the computer is not the primary instrument of the crime; it simply facilitates it. These crimes include money laundering, criminal enterprise, child pornography, and luring victims into compromising situations.

Money laundering is needed to provide criminals with the ability to spend their money. Funds can be divided into groups that are too small to be noticed and "smurfed"[53] out of the country to be assembled later in an offshore bank. Coordinating such a complex scheme is greatly facilitated by using computers.[54] Banks or casinos are closely regulated and heavily penalized for money laundering; however, the enormous volume of financial transactions in the United States makes it difficult for regulators to identify even relatively large questionable transactions. These types of transactions have increased with the growth of electronic payment systems, such as e-gold, which allow individuals to make and accept payments in foreign countries without any regulation.[55]

Criminal enterprises also use computers as incident to the crimes that they commit. Computers appeal to criminal enterprises or businesses for many of the same reasons they appeal to others: They are quick, reliable, very accurate, and perform many business-related tasks far faster than if done manually. Thus, they are used to support many different types of criminal enterprises, including loan-sharking and drug rings. A number of prostitution rings have been found using computers to keep track of customers and payroll. The customers of prostitutes have also developed Web sites that enable discussion and reviews of the services provided by a sex worker.[56] This sort of Internet-based information sharing helps to facilitate the sex trade in the real world.

The production and distribution of child pornography have also benefited from the computer revolution. The Internet has been the key communication medium for the sale and exchange of child pornography on both international and domestic bases. In September 1998, the largest single child pornography sting operation in history occurred, resulting in the arrest of over 200 people in 21 countries.[57] Code named "Operation Cathedral," British police coordinated raids in Europe, Australia, and the United States, confiscating more than 100,000 indecent images of children. Most of the images were being traded between child pornographers over the Internet. While most of those arrested were men, some were women who also belonged to exclusive child pornography clubs throughout the world. One U.S.-based club, called "Wonderland," had images for sale depicting children as young as two years of age. The sheer size of the pornography network shocked the police as well as the general public. The United Nations called for a worldwide offensive to curb the exchange of pedophilia on the Internet—a very difficult task considering the vast number of jurisdictions and judicial systems present in the international community.[58]

Some crimes of violence are facilitated through the use of a computer. For example, the Internet has been used to lure victims to pedophiles. Adult users of chat rooms may use the supposed anonymity of the Internet to pose as teenagers to establish a rapport with their intended victim. Numerous "sting" operations have placed law enforcement officers in these same chat rooms posing as children. In fact, a recent study found that these sorts of proactive investigations comprised 25 percent of all arrests for Internet sex crimes against minors and produced a high rate of guilty pleas and generally successful prosecutions.[59]

Crimes Associated with the Prevalence of Computers

Targets of these types of crimes are mainly the industry itself, but also include its customers and even people who have avoided information technology. These crimes include intellectual property violations, component theft, counterfeiting, identity theft, and a variety of corporate offenses. Intellectual property violations are often described as piracy. The music trading service Napster has recently caused music piracy to replace software piracy in the public mind as the leading example of this crime. Large-scale software piracy began in Asia. The Business Software Alliance reports that just one person selling unauthorized copies of some 40 different popular programs in Singapore may have made several million dollars, even though he charged as little as $15 for copies of programs that retailed for as much as $600.[60] Violation of American copyright laws in China—particularly piracy of software, videotaped entertainment, and music—led the United States in early 1995 to announce that it would place a 100 percent tariff on all products entering this country from China unless the Chinese government took action to eliminate such violations.

Extensive software piracy now exists worldwide and is facilitated by the Internet. Dutch bulletin boards[61] provided the nexus of "cracked" games and software during the 1980s. Today, piracy groups continue the tradition by racing to provide the first cracked edition of new software, music, and movies for download through Web sites and resources around the world, often before it is released officially. In fact, a movie reviewer for Fox News online was fired for reviewing a pirated copy of the movie *X-Men Origins: Wolverine,* which he obtained through a piracy group a few months before its official release in the theater.[62] This sort of rapid and large-scale piracy is engendered by the growth of file-sharing programs such as Bit Torrent and Rapidshare, which enable individuals to quickly capture data hosted on multiple computers around the world.

The theft of desktop and laptop computers, monitors, printers, scanners, modems, and other computer components has also become a problem due to the increased portability of computer systems and the potential for sensitive information to be contained on the system files. In 2007, the theft of laptops and mobile devices accounted for 50 percent of the incidents reported by business and industry security professionals.[63] Though the value of laptops have decreased due to dropping prices of computer technology, the information contained on their hard drives, such as documents and passwords, have significant monetary value. Theft of proprietary information accounts for over $3 million in losses within the private sector.[64]

The full extent of computer theft is unknown because many thefts go unreported and because many police departments consider theft of computer hardware as just another stolen-property crime. Some computer owners do not even know what they own and therefore cannot provide the police with an accurate description, let alone the serial numbers. This is a problem compounded by the inability of some police officers to accurately differentiate among computer equipment and peripherals. Furthermore, the massive growth in small portable devices like iPods, Blackberry devices, and other personal computers and their perceived value make them attractive targets for thieves due to their value and popularity.

Identity theft has become a major concern for both the public and members of the law enforcement community. Although identity theft can occur without the aid of a computer, the anonymity of the Internet and access to vast numbers of personal information have fundamentally changed the nature of this crime. In a fairly common case, almost 40 people employed by a San Diego pharmaceutical company had their identities stolen by a laboratory aide who had discovered unprotected personnel records at the firm. Before being caught, the thief obtained 75 credit cards, $100,000 in merchandise, 20 cellular phones, and rented three apartments.

Identity theft is also significantly enabled by hackers who can gain access to sensitive databases of information. Once inside of a large repository of credit cards, personal information, and other files, hackers can parse out this information and sell it in open markets for a profit. In fact, an individual named Kenneth Flurry obtained stolen debit card numbers with personal information from hackers in Russia and Asia and used the information to create fraudulent ATM cards. He obtained over $380,000 from ATMs over a three-week period using these cards and was arrested and subsequently prosecuted in the U.S. federal court system.

The expanded use of the Social Security number is the primary reason for the ease of identity theft. Three major credit reporting bureaus control the information on all persons applying for credit in the United States: Equifax, Trans Union, and Experian. These companies allow anyone with a name and Social Security number to access credit histories. Credit card companies make the process of credit application little more complicated than supplying this information.

Various corporate crimes also appear to be on the rise as computer use has expanded. The rapid growth of the computer industry has caused many questionable business practices to be developed. Examples of these questionable practices include rebate fraud, grossly one-sided end user license agreements (EULAs), misleading advertising, component swapping, reselling refurbished components in "new" systems, simple fraud, and many others. The Federal Trade Commission (FTC) has become involved in actions against several companies that promised mail-in rebates, but could not deliver. Although rebates are a common practice in the industry, the first case to draw widespread attention was the Iomega Zip Drive.[TM] With the unprecedented demand for the Zip Drive, the rebate fulfillment center contracted to handle the processing of rebates was overwhelmed. A large number of rebates were simply lost, and delays of a year or more were common. Interestingly, with the advancement of rewritable computer disks (CDs) and CD/DVD burners, and their subsequent affordability to the general public, the demand for "zip drives" has decreased significantly over the past two years.

EULAs are contracts that specify the rights of the consumer when purchasing a license[65] to use software. Originally intended to prevent people from reselling copies of their software, EULAs have become so one-sided as to violate common tenets of contract law and consumer protection legislation. Common elements of the EULAs include a stipulation that the software licensed need not function for any particular purpose, even if that function is advertised. Although it is legal to require an EULA, the terms of that contract do not automatically supercede false advertising legislation. There is also an assumption that an item sold is fit for use.

An excellent example of a problem resulting from EULAs is the Sony Music Trojan, which was revealed in 2005. The Sony Corporation placed a program called XCP, or Extended Copy Protection, onto its music CDs to limit the ability of the consumer to make copies of the disk. The functionality of the program and its presence were not fully elaborated in the EULA.[66] Though the program did nothing malicious, many consumers and artists were embarrassed and outraged that the company felt it appropriate to micromanage customer computer activity.

Summary

Attempts to categorize and label specific types of computer crime have followed traditional methodologies, looking at the computer as a target or instrumentality of the crime as applied to other types of existing legislation. Unfortunately, these types of categorizations and labeling exercises often fall short in grasping the overall milieu in which computer crime is observed. Additionally, they often fail to take into account the behavioral and criminological aspects of digital crime. This may be particularly true when the crime touches some aspect of the Internet or involves a new type of white-collar scam or sophisticated corporate fraud.

Categorizations do help us sort out and define more commonly observed criminal incidents where computers are used. We would like to fit all sorts of different and varied criminal methodologies that involve computers into discrete boxes. Certainly, society has accomplished this task for traditional crime by defining the elements necessary to commit a specific crime. There is a new challenge posed by computer crime: Specific incidents may well fit into a criminal violation and hence meet the basic elements of a crime, while other, more sophisticated criminalities may not. The difficulty in specifically and accurately defining each type and incident of computer crime will continue to plague successful prosecution of those misusing computers.

However, and much more important, the nature of digital crime is so expansive as to include ominous and catastrophic events that cripple our critical infrastructure and threaten national security and cause international conflict. In the post-9/11 era, terrorism has become a real threat to our society and to our way of life. We have attempted to secure ourselves through the use of physical searches for weapons, the employment of new technological sensing devices in critical areas, more visible signs of police and security presence, and a stepped-up military offensive against those in foreign countries who may pose threats. Trying to engage the police in the "war on terrorism" may be futile, as the criminal justice system (and particularly the police) is designed to address crime. The people who pose significant terrorist dangers are often motivated by ideologies that are really not criminal in the traditional sense of the word. They seek destruction and devastation as part of war. The police and the criminal justice system are ill-equipped to handle such threats. Sometimes, these terrorists pose significant threats to computer and information systems by targeting our critical infrastructure. Designing a system that will be secure, yet provide easy accessibility to needed data and information, will be a trick. Indeed, securing our information infrastructure may well be one of the most challenging tasks of the future.

Review Questions

1. What factors led to the explosive growth of digital crime over the past few decades?
2. Describe some of the most common forms of digital crime.
3. What gaps exist in our understanding of digital crime? What can be done to address these gaps?
4. Why is the number of cybervictims growing?
5. Why is computer crime severely underreported?
6. What are the four categories of computer crime? Give examples of the types of crimes that fall under each category.

Endnotes

1. LEINER, B.M., et al. (February 1997). "The Past and Future History of the Internet." *Communications of the ACM* 40(2): 102–108.
2. Internet Software Consortium (January 2001). *Internet Domain Survey.* Redwood City, CA.
3. GOODIN, D. (2007). "TJX Breach Was Twice As Big As Admitted, Banks Say." *The Register.* Retrieved March 27, 2008 from *http://www.theregister.co.uk/2007/10/24/tjx_breach_estimate_grows/*
4. Motion Picture Association of America, see: http://www.mpaa.org (June 25, 2009).
5. Pandalabs (2007). "Malware Infections in Protected Systems." Retrieved November 1, 2007 from *http://research.pandasecurity.com/blogs/images/wp_pb_malware_infections_in_protected_systems.pdf*
6. The material in this first section was adapted from an original paper developed by Carter and Katz-Bannister (2003). The remainder of the material is presented in Chapter 14.
7. PARKER, D. (1999). *Fighting Computer Crime: A New Framework for the Protection of Information.* New York: John Wiley & Sons, Inc.
8. HALE, C. (2002). "Cybercrime: Facts & Figures Concerning the Global Dilemma." *Crime & Justice International* 18(65): 5–6, 24–26.
9. See *www.earthlink.net/bLink*
10. PARKER, D. (1979). *Crime by Computer.* New York: Charles Scribner and Sons.
11. Bureau of Justice Statistics (1979). *Computer Crime: Criminal Justice Resource Manual.* Washington, DC: U.S. Department of Justice.

12. Bureau of Justice Statistics (1980). *Computer Security Techniques.* Washington, DC: U.S. Department of Justice.

13. Bureau of Justice Statistics (1982). *Electronic Fund Transfer Systems and Crime.* Washington, DC: U.S. Department of Justice.

14. Bequai, A. (1983). *How to Prevent Computer Crime.* New York: John Wiley & Sons; Cooper, J.A. (1984). *Computer Security Technology.* Lexington, MA: D.C. Heath and Company; Roache, J.Y. (1986). "Computer Crime Deterrence." *American Journal of Criminal Law* 13(2): 391; Carroll, J.M. (1987). *Computer Security.* Boston, MA: Butterworth Publishing; Gallery, S. (ed.) (1987). *Computer Security.* Boston, MA: Butterworth Publishing Company; Arkin, S. (ed.) (1988). *Prevention and Prosecution of Computer and High Technology Crime.* Oakland, CA: Matthew Bender.

15. Thackery, G. (1985). "Problems of Computer Evidence." In *The Practical Prosecutor,* Vol. 2. Houston, TX: National College of District Attorneys; Rostoker, M., and Rines, R. (1986). *Computer Jurisprudence.* New York: Oceana Publications; Arkin, *Prevention and Prosecution of Computer and High Technology Crime*; Conser, J.A., Carsone, L.P., and Snyder, R. (1988). "Investigating Computer-Related Crimes Involving Small Computer Systems." In M. Palmiotto (ed.), *Critical Issues in Computer Investigations,* 2nd ed. Cincinnati, OH: Anderson Publishing Company; Hollinger, R.C., and Lanza-Kaduce, L. (1988). "The Process of Criminalization: The Case of Computer Crime Laws." *Criminology* 26(1): 101; Conly, C.H. (1989). *Organizing for Computer Crime Investigation and Prosecution.* Cambridge, MA: Abt Associates.

16. Bequai, A. (1987). *Technocrimes.* Lexington, MA: D.C. Heath and Company.

17. Kusserow, R.P. (1983). *Computer-Related Fraud and Abuse in U.S. Government Agencies.* Washington, DC: U.S. Department of Health and Human Services.

18. Landreth, B. (1985). *Out of the Inner Circle: A Hacker's Guide to Computer Security.* Bellevue, WA: Microsoft Press.

19. McEwen, T. (1989). *Dedicated Computer Crime Units.* Washington, DC: National Institute of Justice.

20. Icove, D., Seger, K., and VonStorch, W. (1995). *Computer Crime: A Crimefighter's Handbook.* Sebastopol, CA: O'Reilly & Associates, Inc.

21. Stoll, C. (1988). *The Cuckoo's Egg.* New York: Bantam Books.

22. Shimomura, T. (1996). *Takedown.* New York: Hyperion Books.

23. Stoll, *The Cuckoo's Egg.*

24. Shimomura, *Takedown.*

25. Parker, D. (1989). *Fighting Computer Crime.* New York: Charles Scribner and Sons.

26. *Ibid.*

27. Carter, D.L., and Katz, A.J. (1999). "Computer Applications by International Organized Crime Groups." In L. Moriarity and D.L. Carter (eds.), *Criminal Justice Technology in the 21st Century.* Springfield, IL: Charles C Thomas, Publisher.

28. Van Duyn, J. (1985). *The Human Factor in Computer Crime.* Princeton, NJ: Petrocelli Books, Inc.

29. U.N. Commission on Crime and Criminal Justice (1995). *United Nations Manual on the Prevention and Control of Computer-Related Crime.* New York: United Nations.

30. Van Duyn, *The Human Factor in Computer Crime.*

31. Holt, T.J. (2003). "Examining a Transnational Problem: An Analysis of Computer Crime Victimization in Eight Countries from 1999 to 2001." *International Journal of Comparative and Applied Criminal Justice* 27: 199–220.

32. Barrett, N. (1997). *Digital Crime.* London: Kogan Page.

33. See *www.calea.org/online/newsletter/No75/The%20National%20Infrastructure%20Protection%20Center.htm, www.cert.org* and *www.fbi.gov*

34. Sinuraya, T. (June 1999). "The Cyber Crime Problem Increases." *Crime and Justice International,* pp. 1–10, 32.

35. Henderson, S.J. (2007). *The Dark Visitor.* Scott Henderson.

36. American Bar Association (1987). *Report on Computer Crime.* Chicago, IL: American Bar Association.

37. Florida Department of Law Enforcement (1989). "Computer Crime in Florida." An unpublished report prepared by the Florida Department of Law Enforcement, Tallahassee, FL.

38. U.N. Commission on Crime and Criminal Justice (1995). *United Nations Manual on the Prevention and Control of Computer-Related Crime.* New York: United Nations.

39. Carter, D.L., and Katz, A.J. (1998). "Computer Crime Victimization: An Assessment of

Criminality in Cyberspace." *Police Research Quarterly* 1(1).

40. Computer Security Institute (1999). *Issues and Trends: 1999 CSI/FBI Computer Crime and Security Survey.* San Francisco, CA: Computer Security Institute.

41. Computer Security Institute (2007). *2007 CSI/FBI Computer Crime and Security Survey.* San Francisco, CA: Computer Security Institute.

42. Public Interest Research Group (1999). "Identity Theft II: Return to the Consumer X-Files."

43. U.S. Department of Justice (1999). "Cyberstalking: A New Challenge for Law Enforcement and Industry." A report to the Vice-President, *http://www.justice.gov/criminal/cybercrime/cyberstalking.htm*

44. EUNJUNG CHA, A., and SCHWARTZ, J. (February 8, 2000). "Hackers Disrupt Yahoo Web Site." *Washington Post.*

45. BRENNER, S.W. (2008). *Cyberthreats: The Emerging Fault Lines of the Nation State.* New York: Oxford University Press; JAFFE, G. (2006). "Gates Urges NATO Ministers to Defend Against Cyber Attacks." *The Wall Street Journal.*

46. *Ibid.*

47. Attrition.org (May 13, 2001). "Video cam: University of Cambridge" [defaced Web page]. Retrieved August 30, 2001 from the World Wide Web: *http://www.attrition.org/mirror/attrition/2001/05/13/video.cbcu.cam.ac.uk/*

48. DENNING, D.E. (2001). "Activism, Hacktivism, and Cyberterrorism: The Internet as a Tool for Influencing Foreign Policy." In JOHN ARQUILLA and DAVID F. RONFELDT (eds.), *Networks and Netwars: The Future of Terror, Crime, and Militancy.* Santa Monica, CA: Rand, pp. 239–288.

49. PARKER, D. (1998). *Fighting Computer Crime: A New Framework for Protecting Information.* New York: John Wiley & Sons, Inc.

50. JAMES, L. (2005). *Phishing Exposed.* Rockland, MA: Syngress.

51. CATHCART, R. (2008). "MySpace Is Said to Draw Subpoena in Hoax Case." *The New York Times.*

52. CARTER, D.L., and BANNISTER, A.J. (2000). "Computer Crime: A Forecast of Emerging Trends." Presented at the Academy of Criminal Justice Sciences Annual Meeting in New Orleans, LA.

53. Smurfing in money laundering should not be confused with smurfing in denial of service attacks.

54. ZAGARIS, B., and MCDONALD, S.D. (1992). "Money Laundering, Financial Fraud and Technology: The Perils of an Instant Economy." *George Washington Journal of International Law and Economics* 26(1): 61–90.

55. Department of Justice (2007). "Digital Currency Business E-Gold Indicted for Money Laundering and Illegal Money Transmitting." United States Department of Justice. Retrieved December 25, 2008 from *http://www.usdoj.gov/opa/pr/2007/April/07_crm_301.html*

56. HOLT, T.J., and BLEVINS, K.R. (2007). "Examining Sex Work from the Client's Perspective: Assessing Johns Using Online Data." *Deviant Behavior* 28: 333–354.

57. SERJEANT, J. (September 2, 1998). "Police Raid Global Internet Child Porn Club." Reuters.

58. *Ibid.*

59. MITCHELL, K.J., WOLAK, J., and FINKELHOR, D. (2005). "Police Posing as Juveniles Online to Catch Sex Offenders: Is It Working?" *Sexual Abuse: A Journal of Research and Treatment,* 17(3): 241–267.

60. Anonymous (February–March 1992). "Stalking Asian Software Pirates." *Technology Review* 95(2): 15.

61. The telephone-based electronic bulletin board systems (BBS) was the primary method for most computer users to communicate and exchange software before Internet access became widely available.

62. SIEGEL, T. (2009). "Fox Fired Up Over 'Wolverine' Review." *Variety.* Retrieved May 25, 2009 from *http://www.variety.com/VR1118002128.html*

63. POWERS, R. (ed.) (2007). *2007 CSI/FBI Computer Crime and Security Survey.* San Francisco, CA: Computer Security Institute.

64. *Ibid.*

65. Software licenses grant the purchaser limited rights to use the compiled version, but not to reverse engineer or sell copies. Thus, the purchaser does not buy the software; he or she buys the right to use it.

66. MCMILLAN, R. (2005). "Sony is loading spyware into users' PCs." *Techworld.* Retrieved May 15, 2007 from *http://www.techworld.com/security/features/index.cfm?featureid=1931*

CHAPTER 2

Digital Terrorism

CHAPTER OBJECTIVES

After completing this chapter, you should be able to

- Define the concepts of "information warfare" and "cyberterrorism."
- List the four categories of attacks that encompass cyberterrorism and/or information warfare.
- Identify various elements of our critical infrastructure that are potentially vulnerable to cyberterrorism and/or information warfare.
- Define and describe an information attack.
- Describe some of the tactics used in cyberspace to share information and promote terrorist ideologies between and within terrorist groups.
- Define the words "stenography" and "cryptography" and relate their use in information warfare and cyberterrorism.
- Explain the active role of China and al Qaeda in recent cyber attacks against the United States.

INTRODUCTION

Since the beginning of history, warfare has evolved parallel to the development of tools, weapons, and technology. In the twentieth century, warfare developed from hand-to-hand and small weapons combat to sophisticated air combat, and now to the development of electronic "smart" bombs that are programmed to destroy their targets. Traditional means of warfare have been further distorted through the means of technology and also by the escalating events of international terrorist activity. Before September 11, 2001, few would have considered that America's civil aircraft would have been used as weaponry against America itself. However, al Qaeda operatives did just that, killing over 2,840 people in a few short hours. It should not be a surprise, then, that military and guerrilla offensives could be waged on many fronts, from the skyscrapers of Manhattan to the digital networks that coordinate our critical infrastructure (e.g., the Internet, computer networks, telephone systems, and electricity and water supplies).

In fact, the Internet is a critical tool for political and social movements of all types around the world. Groups have employed a range of tactics depending on the severity of the perceived injustice or wrong that have been performed. Often, these virtual efforts develop in tandem with real-world protests and demonstrations. For example, the native peoples, called Zapatistas, in Chiapas, Mexico, used the Internet to post information and mobilize supporters for their cause against governmental repression.[1] Politically driven groups have also employed hacking techniques to engage in more serious strikes against governments and political organizations.[2] Members of a hacktivist group called the Electronic Disturbance Theater developed an attack tool called FloodNet that overloaded Web servers and kept others from being able to access their services. FloodNet was used against the Pentagon as well as other government and business targets as a means of protest against their activities and policies.[3] Even entrenched and stable organized terrorist groups like Sri Lanka's Tamil Tigers have engaged in acts of cyberterrorism to disrupt or damage Sri Lankan government computer networks.[4]

Few among the American population have considered a situation involving an attack on our infrastructure. However, this type of attack became a frightening possibility when the lights went out across the northeastern United States on Friday, August 15, 2003. During the initial hours of the blackout, which affected New York City, parts of Connecticut, Vermont, Ohio, and Canada, confusion reigned, and many newscasters covering the outage speculated that it could be a terrorist act. By evening, that scenario had been ruled out and the outage was eventually traced to a power grid failure in Ohio. Regardless, the American public had now seen a glimpse of the very real consequences of such an attack—the cities affected had ground to a virtual halt, oil prices began to rise almost instantly, and panic among the population was evident, especially in the first hours after the outage.

DEFINING THE CONCEPTS

Even though the protection of our national infrastructure is a large part of the national strategy for homeland security,[5] most individuals take for granted that such entities are secure. Perhaps the notion of information warfare or cyberterrorism is not at the forefront of our national public consciousness because it is somewhat nebulous. Information warfare and cyberterrorism are actually very broad concepts that, depending on who is defining them, can encompass a range of activity by a variety of different people. They are also two conceptually different events: Cyberterrorism is a component of information warfare, but information warfare is not necessarily cyberterrorism. For this reason, it is necessary to define these topics as separate entities.

Buzzwords: Information Warfare and Cyberterrorism

Information warfare is an overarching concept that actually encompasses cyberterrorism. Essentially, information warfare is the gathering or use of information to gain an advantage over another party. More specifically, John Alger, the dean of the School of Information Warfare and Strategy at the National Defense University, defines information warfare as "those actions intended to protect, exploit, corrupt, deny or destroy information or information resources in order to achieve a significant advantage, objective or victory over an adversary."[6] Still another definition states that information warfare is the "coherent and synchronized blending of physical and virtual actions to have countries, organizations, and individuals perform, or not perform, actions so that your goals and objectives are attained and maintained while simultaneously preventing competitors from doing the same to you."[7]

Information warfare consists of six components: psychological operations, electronic warfare, military deception, physical destruction, security measures, and information attacks.[8]

Psychological operations (or psy-ops, in popular military lingo) use information to affect the state of mind of the adversary. This could include propaganda, or the spreading of information intended to convince people to subscribe to a certain cause or doctrine. The Internet is a perfect tool for this objective.[9]

Electronic warfare is the denial of information or accurate information to an adversary. This is a tool widely used by terrorist organizations, political hackers, and rival countries via the Internet. Military deception is an age-old attack that generally misleads an adversary about military capabilities or intentions. This type of information warfare does not require that the Internet even exist—it can be carried out by more traditional media.[10]

Physical information warfare involves a physical attack on an information system. Security measures are the methods of protecting an information system so that an adversary cannot breach it. Finally, an information attack is the direct corruption of information without actually changing the physical structure in which it is located.[11]

This should make it clear, then, that information warfare is not limited to those things that can be done with computers. In fact, information warfare is the exploitation or strategic protection of a number of things: telephones, radio signals, radar, electronic devices—anything that can be manipulated in order to control or influence the actions of a decision maker. A more practical definition is that information warfare is any sort of strike or protective measure against an information system, whatever the means. Implanting a virus into a military computer is an information warfare tactic. On the other end of the spectrum, blowing up a cellular phone tower could also be considered information warfare.

In contrast, terrorism is defined as the actual or threatened use of violence by an individual or group motivated by ideological or political objectives. The goal of terrorism is to intimidate or coerce a government or its people.[12] Cyberterrorism, however, cannot be as concretely defined and has spurred significant debate over exactly what it means. The fact is that the word "cyberterrorism" has been misrepresented in both academic circles and the media at large. A panel of experts on cyberterrorism was convened in March of 2003, with one stating that "Dropping ATM networks and shutting down e-mail is not terrorism. If I can't get to my e-mail for a few days, I am not terrorized."[13] This illustrates the common misperception that a network disruption is an act of cyberterrorism. This would be considered more of an act of information warfare.

Cyberterrorism is also not defined by the group perpetrating it. Terrorist groups, such as al Qaeda, may use the Internet to further their propaganda, hide their secrets, or recruit new members. However, none of this is considered to be inherently terroristic and, again, may be considered more of an act of information warfare.[14] According to one definition, "terrorism is defined by the nature of the act, not by the identity of the perpetrators or the nature of their cause."[15]

Cyberterrorism is specifically a premeditated, politically or ideologically motivated attack or threat of attack against information, computer systems, computer programs, and data that can result in violence against civilian targets.[16] According to Barry Collin of the Institute for Security and Intelligence, cyberterrorism is "hacking with a body count."[17] A 2001 assessment by RAND's National Research Defense Institute concluded that cyberterrorism may also include attacks motivated by political or ideological objectives that can cause serious harm, such as a prolonged loss of infrastructure, like electricity or water.[18] A similarly broad definition of cyberterrorism was developed and presented by the National Institute of Justice in 2001, recognizing any "premeditated, politically motivated attack against information systems, computer programs and data . . . to disrupt the political, social, or physical infrastructure of the target."[19] Yet another

BOX 2.1
A Short History of Warfare

In a popular futuristic and thought-provoking book, *The Third Wave,* Alvin Toffler discusses a specific approach to the history of warfare. He describes and explains the development of warfare in three different and separate epochs or waves.

The first, or agrarian, wave produced the first known effective change (or revolution) in the history of humankind. Humans began to settle in specific areas and grow food rather than forage and roam large expanses of the land. During the agrarian wave, societies developed and the production of goods and commerce began. Tools were relatively rudimentary, and weapons were designed more for personal protection against wild animals and hunting, rather than specifically for killing people. The value of the goods and/or the rapidly increasing value of property (soil) created new conflicts among people—the first cause of war.

The second, or industrial wave, marked a significant departure from the manufacturing of simple weapons. Industrial and technological improvement allowed the first weapons for the destruction of multiple persons and buildings (infrastructure). Indeed, this era witnessed the defeat of agrarian-based societies to more advanced industrialized people. Landowners had become industrialized nations. Most importantly, war and defense had become a means for justifying the production of more advanced weaponry, including weapons of mass destruction (e.g., nuclear, chemical,

and biological). Arbitrary and loosely defined armies had become well structured and highly mechanized forces. Nations were now capable of delivering lethal attacks against entire societies of people, leaving behind large expanses of scorched and uninhabitable land.

The third wave, the information wave, reveals societies based on the rapid exchange of vital and critical information. Accurate and timely communication characterizes successful, thriving, and global societies. War also emulates information importance and is focused on the destruction of critical infrastructure within societies, hence *information warfare*. High-tech weapons "invade" computer systems and networks with the aim of destroying the ability of a nation to operate. Interestingly, the large sophisticated armies of the industrial period are relatively useless when communication and transportation systems, logistical support, targeting systems, defense networks, and the like succumb to electronic attack.

Most importantly, the third wave points to the vulnerability of large information-based nations and suggests how a relatively small, unorganized yet knowledgeable group of individuals could wreak havoc on such a society. Quite prophetic, considering that the book was written more than 25 years ago, in 1984!

Source: TOFFLER, ALVIN. (1984). *The Third Wave.* New York: Bantam Books.

definition includes severe economic loss as a qualifier for cyberterrorism: If economic loss is harsh enough, a destabilization may occur that can result in serious harm to a society.[20]

Because of the obvious semantic problems presented by the misuse of the terms "information warfare" and "cyberterrorism," it is important to keep these definitions in mind when reviewing the threats that terrorist groups or hostile nations pose to the cyber security of the United States. Four categories of attacks that encompass acts of cyberterrorism and/or information warfare will be discussed. These categories include ***infrastructure attacks,*** or those attacks designed to destroy a system that includes critical data; ***information attacks,*** or attacks focused on demolishing or altering the content of electronic files or computer systems; ***technological facilitation,*** or the use of cyber communication to distribute and coordinate plans for a terrorist attack, incite an attack, or otherwise assist in the facilitation of terrorism; and ***promotion,*** which includes fundraising, solicitation, and recruitment.[21]

RISK AND CRITICAL INFRASTRUCTURE ATTACKS

Given that most parts of the world now have access to the Internet, almost any country can fall victim to some form of cyberterrorism or information warfare. In fact, Russian factions have engaged in cyber attacks with Estonia in 2007 and Georgia in 2008, which caused the citizens of these countries to face significant economic harm.[22] These conflicts developed from real-world events, notably the removal of a statue in Estonia and an attempted seccession in Georgia. However, the virtual attacks that ensued forced financial and government Web sites offline in these countries, and the amount of Internet connectivity taken up by malicious Web traffic kept individuals from being able to access regular resources like e-mail. Thus, this chapter and discussion will emphasize events that can or have taken place in the United States, but it is important to recognize that some of the conditions we discuss can apply to many other industrialized nations in the world.

The United States is at a particular risk for cyber attack, whether related to information warfare or cyberterrorism, because of several factors. The first is that the United States continues to occupy a precarious position regarding the Middle East. Several fundamentalist and radical Islamic groups (e.g., al Qaeda, Hezbollah, and the Muslim Brotherhood) perceive the United States to be evil. Indeed, much of their radical philosophy attacks modernity itself, characterizing complex communication systems, energy use, and computer networks as threats to fundamental Islam. To make matters worse, recent activities by the United States within the Israeli–Palestinian conflict, in Iraq since 2003, and in Afghanistan after the events of September 11, 2001, have all contributed to anti-American sentiment within the radical Muslim world. Many of these groups have significant experience in launching cyber attacks.[23]

Muslim fundamental and radical groups aren't the only threat to the United States' cyber security. Anticapitalist movements, such as those observed in China and North Korea, have also shown their prowess at engaging American targets in cyber attack. Either type of group could levy a great amount of damage on commercial or government interests using techniques that they have already employed in different cyber realms.[24] Indeed, our country has already suffered very sophisticated attacks from such entities. The question, of course, is whether these attacks were state supported. Is it a single hacker or a group acting alone, or might they have been given some incentive by the military or government? Are they using equipment and resources that they obtained or those that have been provided by a covert military group? What resources are they attacking, and how might they benefit a nation more than an individual? In the often confusing and murky world of cyberterrorism and information warfare, the answers to these types of questions are often blurred, as might be expected when secret agencies and spy services are employed.

The second factor that causes significant concern to the United States is the country's significant reliance upon a national information infrastructure. Information infrastructure is composed of five essential components: communications networks, such as those used for phones, satellites and cable networks; equipment used for the provision of information, including televisions, radios, computers and phones; information resources, which might consist of educational or medical programs or databases; applications, like those used for electronic commerce or digital libraries; and people.[25]

The United States, which has identified itself as the most infrastructure reliant of any nation on earth, is also possibly the most at risk for an infrastructure attack.[26] Critical infrastructure is a particularly attractive target to terrorists, due to the large-scale economic and operational damage that would occur with any major shutdown.[27] The Clinton administration identified eight areas of infrastructure that constitute a virtual national life support system: telecommunications, banking and finance, electrical power, oil and gas distribution and storage, water supply, transportation, emergency services, and government services.[28] The plan presented by former president Bush in his *National Strategy for Homeland Security* further identified and characterized the need for critical infrastructure protection.[29] Many of these areas are interdependent on each other, magnifying the potential effects of a breach of one system.[30] President Obama has laid out a similar plan arrayed along the same lines in a document referred to as the "Cyberspace Policy Review."[31] This document also suggests a need for increased cooperation between the government and private industry in order to secure critical infrastructure from cyber attack.

Banking and financial institutions are also vulnerable to infrastructure attack, as they depend heavily on networks. If one system is breached by an attacker, then all connecting systems can be severely impacted. However, most banking or financial networks tend to be private, with little external access. This helps to mitigate somewhat vulnerability in this sector. At the same time, a severe attack against a resource such as the stock exchange or a military bank could cause significant harm to multiple sectors of the country's economy.

Electrical power and water supply systems rely heavily on electronic sensors that maintain safe levels and aid engineers in shutting off supplies if something were to go wrong. Manipulation of these remote sensors by network intrusion is a threat, especially by those who have legitimately gained access in the past. In fact, "malicious insiders," or those who have been given access to a system for a valid reason, such as employment or research, are the greatest threat to infrastructure. Such an insider would have specialized knowledge of a system, as well as access.[32] However, individual hackers in Russia and China have begun to access these systems remotely, emphasizing the threat goes far beyond that of insiders.[33]

Transportation infrastructure, particularly related to civil air traffic control, is also a concern, particularly after the events of September 11, 2001. The systems used specifically for civil aviation have in the past been largely custom designed, which isolates civil aviation systems from most direct attacks. Today, as more and more tasks, including aircraft maintenance, parts manufacturing, and flight management systems, are slowly being replaced by commercial-off-the-shelf software, civil aviation systems are very well protected.[34] Security for both new and old systems is generally elaborate, with layers of administrative controls that could thwart even the most technologically sophisticated intruder. Furthermore, most civil aviation technology is designed to withstand system failure or breakdown through the use of redundant systems or separate subsystems, which are designed to pick up where the main system left off.[35] The Achilles' heel of civil aviation security is its heavy reliance on other types of infrastructure. Air traffic control centers depend on electricity, communications systems, and government services, such as the Federal Aviation Administration. For example, radar operates through simple, dedicated telephone lines. If those telephone lines were to be compromised, the impact could be catastrophic.[36]

The potential severity of an electronic attack against critical infrastructure has led some individuals to use the term "electronic pearl harbor" to refer to such an event.[37] This is a reference to the notion that the attack will take citizens and the government by surprise and devastate the population. However, there have already been attacks against the United States' critical infrastructure involving many of these systems. For the most part, these have been perpetrated by juvenile hackers, seeking a new thrill or acting as pranksters. None have been directly linked to or proven to be the act of any terrorist organization or foreign country. For example, in March 1997, a teenager hacked into a telephone company computer that serviced the Worcester Airport, located in Massachusetts. Telephone service to the control tower, the airport fire department, airport security, and various other departments was out for more than six hours. The attack caused a ripple effect of delayed and cancelled flights across the country, leading to serious financial losses to the airport and several airlines.[38]

In another infrastructure attack, a disgruntled former Chevron employee disabled the firm's alert system by hacking into the company computers. The attack was not discovered until the system failed to notify engineers of a release of noxious chemicals into the air at a plant in Richmond, California. This event put millions of people in the western United States and Canada at risk.[39]

These two attacks were potentially deadly and costly, but were perpetrated by people without political or terrorist agenda. One was motivated by ego, the other by pure revenge. It is particularly disconcerting to think of what someone with a deep-rooted ideological hatred for the United States could do if a cocky teenager can shut down an airport for no specific reason. Possibilities put forth in academic literature include the most heinous visions of disaster:[40]

- Penetration of an air traffic control system in order to send misleading signals to aircraft, causing midair collisions.
- Taking advantage of the United States' increasing reliance on telemedicine by intruding into hospital computers and changing prescription dosages, resulting in patient death.
- Entering into computerized commuter and freight train routing systems, causing passenger trains to collide or hazardous materials to be released.
- Destroying government computer systems that process tax returns.

What is the risk of an attack on the U.S. critical infrastructure by a terrorist group or rival nation? Unfortunately, no one really knows how vulnerable our critical infrastructure is. Consider this April 23, 2003, testimony before the U.S. House of Representatives from Michael Vatis, Director of the Institute for Security Technology Studies at Dartmouth College:[41]

> . . . to say that cyber networks are vulnerable does not mean that the critical infra-structures that rely on those networks—such as electrical power, grids, pipelines, telecommunications switching nodes, hospitals, etcetera—are necessarily vulnerable, or that a cyber attack would have a sufficiently long-lasting destructive impact to achieve a terrorist or nation-state's military or political objectives. We still do not actually know the full extent of our critical infrastructure's vulnerabilities to various types of cyber attacks and the extent of their potential impact.

In her testimony before the same group in October 2001, Terry Benzel, the vice president of advanced security research for Network Associates, Inc., stated that she was unaware of any analysis of infrastructure that identified its weaknesses or even the extent to which systems are codepen-dent. Benzel referenced a 1997 exercise designed to identify vulnerabilities against infrastructure.[42] Using only hacking tools available on the Internet, National Security Agency hackers successfully gained access to a number of military and infrastructure systems. However, specific vulnerabilities were never disclosed—only the assertion that the United States is at risk on some level for such an attack.[43] Benzel recommended an in-depth study and analysis of infrastructure to the House, to culminate in suggestions and solutions to shore up vulnerabili-ties.[44] Even after the devastation of 9/11 and the identification of significant national threats, her advice has still not been fully implemented.

INFORMATION ATTACKS

Both information warfare and cyberterrorism create a host of scenarios for cyber attacks. Attacks on infrastructure have already been discussed. There are less destructive forms of cyber attack that terrorist groups or adversarial nations could employ to achieve information warfare objectives.

These information attacks are focused on destroying or altering content within a system, and while information may be corrupted and temporarily lost, physical and virtual systems are still preserved. This means that the attack is much less destructive and more disruptive in nature. However, such an attack can (and most likely would) cause major economic damage and loss.[45] The following sections present examples of these types of attack.

Web site Defacement

India and Pakistan have been feuding over a relatively small strip of land known as Kashmir for over half a century. Cyber attacks are a more recent development in the history of this conflict, and the most visible of these attacks have been perpetrated by pro-Pakistan hacker groups. Since 1995, over 500 Web defacements on Indian sites have taken place, and all have been either political or highly visible to the public. For instance, sites representing the Indian parliament, television networks, newspapers, and academic institutions have all been defaced at some point. These Web sites have been defaced with anti-India images and slogans, with some automatically redirecting Web traffic to pro-Pakistani sites, or in some cases, to Web sites containing pornographic or generally offensive material.[46] This technique has also been used by both Israeli and Palestinian groups, often coinciding with specific political events in the region.[47] Domestically, the White House and the FBI Web sites have both been attacked by single-issue terrorist groups such as the Earth Liberation Front and right-wing hate groups such as the Aryan Nation.

Private industry has also become a regular target for Web defacements by political or religiously motivated hackers. For example, a Danish newspaper published a cartoon featuring the prophet Muhammad with a bomb in his turban in 2005.[48] This image was deemed offensive by the Muslim community, and the newspapers' Web site was defaced repeatedly along with any other site that featured the cartoon. Thousands of Web sites were hacked or defaced by Turkish hackers, who in turn received a great deal of attention from the press for their efforts.[49]

Cyberplagues: Viruses and Worms

The terms "viruses" and "worms" are often used synonymously to describe malevolent computer programs that are capable of running and duplicating themselves. However, there is a subtle difference between the two. A virus is actually a piece of code that attaches itself to other instructions within a computer, like software application codes or booting systems. When the user takes an action to make these host instructions run, the virus starts to run as well. The virus then performs a function and lets the host resume control.[50] Meanwhile, the virus has implanted itself into the memory of the computer, where it searches for new hosts. Each time it finds a new host, it inserts itself and then executes its payload, or function, which may be anything from displaying a smiley face on screen to completely wiping the files from a hard drive.[51] The ILOVEYOU virus, which affected Web development and multimedia files and was spread through Microsoft Outlook address books, hit tens of millions of computer users who opened a seemingly innocuous attachment in their email entitled "Love Letter." The total cost of that virus was over a billion dollars.[52] For more detailed information on viruses and malicious code, please refer to Chapter 6.

The ILOVEYOU virus was eventually traced to a college student, but there have been indications that foreign governments have explored viruses as a means of offensive information warfare. A report from the U.S. Defense Intelligence Agency in 1995 warned that the Cuban military was developing a program to propagate viruses against civilian computers in the United States. China has also developed programs to spread computer viruses.[53]

A worm is a program that reproduces itself over a computer network by breaking into computers much like a virtual hacker. Worms do not need the assistance of an unwitting computer user to be unleashed—rather, they find computers that they are able to penetrate, carry out their attack, and then transfer a replica of their code to the next target.[54] Worms run off of weaknesses in popular software in order to reproduce quickly and can have the results of a virus. However, they generally spread much faster, affecting tens of thousands of computers in as little as two to three hours. Estimated costs of worm attacks parallel those of many viruses, with an estimate from a recent attack (Blaster) topping a billion dollars in damage.[55] The Code Red worm in 2001 specifically targeted the White House computer systems that were running on commercial off-the-shelf software.[56] Although this particular attack was not tied to any type of terrorism or specific information warfare agenda, others as noted were.

Distributed Denial-of-Service Attacks

The denial-of-service (DoS) attack is an attempt by a cyber attacker to prevent legitimate usage of service. DoS attacks generally take the following forms: destruction or alteration of configuration information for a system, expenditure of resources needed for legitimate operation, and the actual physical modification of network elements. The result of any of these three types of DoS attacks is that a system becomes unavailable for a period of time until the system can be brought back under control.[57]

One of the more common types of DoS attack is the flood attack. In this type of action, the attacker starts the process of establishing a connection to another machine. The connection is never completed, but data structures within the victim computer have been reserved to meet the requirements of that connection. As a result, no legitimate connection may be made while the victim machine is waiting to complete the original phony connection. The DoS instigator can take over other computers and use them to establish a simultaneous attack of bogus connections of one victim computer.[58] DoS attacks have been used against government and defense computers, as well as in the largest attack on e-commerce ever recorded. This attack, in February 2000, shut down the giants of e-commerce, including eBay, Amazon, and Yahoo, for nearly a full day. The economic impact of this attack was astounding.[59] Once again, the attack was not related to any terror or political objectives.

In 2006, however, a tool called Electronic Jihad Program was found that easily enables DoS attacks against a variety of targets.[60] The tool is linked with a forum and chat room and coordinates attacks and targets a specific site each day. Using a simple-to-use interface, this resource was used in variety of attacks against Web sites around the world. Thus, DoS attacks are an important resource in the terrorist community.

Unauthorized Intrusions

Intrusions are "any set of actions that attempt to compromise the integrity, confidentiality or availability of a computer resource."[61] Theft of classified government information is of particular interest to terror groups or adversarial nations. The consequences of such an attack could have wide-ranging implications. However, this type of attack is very difficult to identify once it has occurred. Unless data have been altered, or administrators are specifically looking for an intrusion, such an attack may go undetected forever.[62] In April of 1998, a group of hackers composed of people from around the globe announced that they had stolen programs off of U.S. Department of Defense computers that essentially ran U.S. military networks and satellites. The software was taken off of a Windows NT server in the Defense Information Systems Agency with the

Department of Defense. The hackers claimed that the software could be used to virtually shut down U.S. military operations. The group also claimed to have penetrated National Aeronautics and Space Administration (NASA) computers, as well as Pentagon computer systems.[63] The group claimed that their attack was merely an act of public service—a kind of wake-up call for the United States to realize that if a group of simple hackers could gain access to sensitive information, so too could terrorist groups willing to use that information to their advantage. Detailed information relating to the event is difficult to acquire, which heightens anxiety and leads to paranoid visions of extreme national vulnerability.

Similarly, a coordinated series of attacks against government and private industry contractor systems occurred in 2003. The attacks, referred to as "Titan Rain," appeared to come from Chinese systems operated by very skilled hackers.[64] Evidence suggests they were able to steal massive amounts of files from NASA, Lockheed Martin, and Sandia National Laboratories in as little as 10–30 minutes, leaving no traces behind. Though little information is available, this example clearly demonstrates that intrusions are a serious and very real threat to critical infrastructure and networked systems.

CYBER AND TECHNOLOGICAL FACILITATION

These final categories of cyber attack are less a physical attack and more of a tactic in information warfare. Facilitation of attack can encompass such things as communication via the Internet by terrorist groups, while promotion of terror might be as simple as recruitment and propaganda.

Facilitation of Attack

Information technology has played a great role in the emergence of networked terrorist groups, such as al Qaeda and Jemmah Islamiyiah. Technology has allowed for reduced transmission time in communication, so that members of an organization all over the globe may coordinate their tasks.[65] Information technology has also reduced the cost of communication. In the past, terrorist networks have had to centralize their major activities to reduce detection resulting from direct travel and telephone communication. This made them more vulnerable to discovery, and their operations could effectively be wiped out with just one major raid. However, information technology has allowed these organizations to disperse throughout the world, decentralizing their operations and thereby safeguarding them.[66]

Developments in information technology have also allowed for more complex information sharing among terrorist groups. Organizations now have access to computer conferencing, chatting, and Web sites that allow for quick and direct communication.[67] Domestic right-wing groups have historically used Web sites for recruitment and advancement of their philosophies. In fact, a range of Web forums and social networking sites exist for neo-Nazi groups and other racist organizations to connect and discuss their positions.

The emergence of the Internet and cellular communications devices has also engendered the development of so-called **flash mobs** or **smart mobs**.[68] These terms refer to mass formations of individuals in one place and time, coordinated through the use of text or instant messaging, e-mails, and other Web-based communications. This technology enables protests, civil unrest, and violence with some organization. In 2005, for example, the French police were investigating a break-in at a construction site in a largely Muslim and African community, where they found several teenagers.[69] The teens began to run, though it is not clear if they were being chased by police, and climbed into an electrical power substation where two died as a consequence of severe electric shock. These deaths incited local tensions, leading to weeks of rioting, during which buildings and cars were burned, police assaulted, bus stations destroyed, and several killed. The youths involved in these riots are said to have used text messaging and e-mails to coordinate their attacks and avoid law enforcement.[70]

Data Hiding

Also known as stenography, data hiding includes an assortment of methods for secret communication that can conceal the fact that a message even exists at all. Most practically, data hiding refers to the act of taking a piece of information and hiding it within another piece of data, such as an image, sound recording, or word-processing file.[71] Data hiding is based upon two main principles: The first is that files that contain digital images or recordings may be altered without losing their functionality, and secondly, files may be altered without the effects ever being perceived by the human eye or ear.[72] After the events of September 11, 2001, reports surfaced that revealed that al Qaeda had been transmitting hidden data over the Internet. Hidden maps of terrorist targets and instructions were posted in sports chat rooms and pornographic sites, which could be accessed by anyone with an Internet connection.[73] Data hiding is fairly easy to do, given the availability of free programs on the Internet and commercially available software, and is complex enough that it would take an impossible amount of time and energy to find hidden data in every Internet file. It is for these reasons that data hiding is such a valuable tool for terrorists or adversarial nations.

Cryptography

For the most part, cryptography is discussed as a methodology to secure and protect information from unwanted eyes and unauthorized use. The same technology can be used to secure communication between terrorist groups. Cryptography is generally used in conjunction with data hiding. An encryption program scrambles information in a controlled manner through the use of a cryptographic key. Only those with access to the key can read the encoded material. Couriers for the terrorist group al Qaeda have been intercepted while carrying encrypted diskettes. Ramzi Yousef, convicted of the 1993 World Trade Center bombing, had encrypted plans to destroy 11 American airliners. This was discovered only after FBI agents spent over a year decoding files found in Yousef's Manila apartment in 1995.[74] Similarly, a tool called Mujahedeen Secrets has circulated among Middle Eastern hacker groups as a means of encrypting e-mail communications with some ease.[75] This free tool was created by Ekhlass Network, Global Islamic Media Front, and allows individuals to encrypt files and messages, compress them, and securely destroy them.

PROPAGANDA AND PROMOTION

Terrorist organizations and adversarial nations have also used the Internet for purposes of propaganda and recruitment. The Internet is the best tool available for these purposes, mainly because it remains largely unregulated and has the potential to reach so many. Organizations can influence public opinion and generate funding through the use of Web sites, which can offer even greater control over a message than TV or print, due to the interactive nature of the Internet and the direct link between a group and its webmaster.

Recruitment and mobilization is an important part of terrorist Web presence. Individuals not directly affiliated with a terrorist group, but who support their agenda, may be tapped through the Internet to provide hacking tools, funds, or merely "spread the word." During the al-Aqsa Intifada, Israeli and Palestinian groups each employed this technique to encourage sympathizers to download hacking tools and use them against whichever side they opposed.[76] In addition, a young hacker named Irhabi 007, who was active in a number of Web forums devoted to jihad, or holy war, against the West, hacked into an FTP site operated by the Arkansas Highway and Transportation Department in 2004.[77] He used the site to post 70 terrorist-related files, including audio and video messages encouraging war and hacking methods, and advertised the hacked site in forums across the world to encourage and spread the message of jihad.

Recruiting is made easier by tracking which propaganda is accessed most on a Web site and tailoring messages to fit that particular audience. Terrorist groups can also capture information about those who peruse their Web sites and later contact them. Chat rooms and cyber cafes can also serve as forums to recruit interested members of the public, especially the young. It is no surprise, then, that nearly all terrorist groups have an official presence on the Internet. Even the Palestinian Resistance Movement (Hamas, responsible for literally hundreds of suicide bombings in Israel) can be accessed at *http://en.wikipedia.org/wiki/Hamas* Hizbollah, a Lebanese Shiite group known best for its involvement in the 1983 bombing of the U.S. marine barracks in Beirut, has a site at *http://english.moqawama.org/.*[78] Again, on the domestic front, literally hundreds of sites exist for right-wing hate groups and single-issue terrorist groups. At one point during the late 1990s, there were over 250 sites dedicated just to the emergence and development of state militia groups.

CYBERTERRORISM AS AN ADJUNCT ATTACK

As illustrated previously, not many can agree on exactly what threats cyberterror or information warfare pose to the United States. However, one common theme throughout the literature on this topic is that the threat of cyberterror is at its greatest when considered in conjunction with other terrorist actions. According to testimony of Virginia Governor Jim Gilmore before the House Science Committee in October 2001, "if a cyber attack occurs simultaneously with either a conventional attack or a weapon of mass destruction attack . . . it can compound and enhance the impact of the original attack."[79]

Cyber attacks are potential force multipliers, which in military terms mean that these types of attacks can increase the impact of a terrorist action when combined with more traditional attacks. This is done without escalating the need for manpower or capital on the terrorists' side. For example, if a terrorist organization bombed a building through conventional means, but coupled it with hacking into and disabling 911 systems, the impact of the attack would be exponentially multiplied, as rescue personnel would not be able to respond effectively.[80]

Al Qaeda and Information Technology

Much of the current interest in cyberterrorism and information warfare has sprung from the events of September 11, 2001, and the subsequent discovery of information technology tools used to plan and coordinate those attacks. Al Qaeda, under the direction of Osama bin Laden (and now his son, Saad bin Laden), appears to have a sophisticated system of communication, surveillance, and coordination via computer networks and other information tools. It is widely agreed that members of al Qaeda pose a major threat to the Internet.

In a 2002 interview with *Computerworld*, Sheikh Omar Bakri Muhammed, an Islamic cleric with proven ties to bin Laden, said that al Qaeda was actively planning a "cyber jihad," or holy war, against the United States and its allies. Bakri identified the stock market as a major target and described how the fundamentalist Islamic groups are assembling cadres of computer science students sympathetic to al Qaeda's cause in places like Pakistan and Malaysia.[81]

In late 2001, the FBI noted a series of network intrusions into emergency telephone and electrical generation systems, water storage facilities, nuclear power plants and gas facilities. Each of the probes had been routed through telecommunications centers in Saudi Arabia, Pakistan, and Indonesia—all known operational centers for al Qaeda. In 2002, al Qaeda computers seized in Afghanistan contained information yielded from these probes.[82]

U.S. officials found evidence on these computers that al Qaeda operatives spent considerable time on Web sites that offer software and programming instructions for the digital switches that run critical infrastructure such as transportation and power grids. Because the switches are not meant for public access, they have few security safeguards built into them. An attack using these switches could yield devastating results. When questioned, some captured al Qaeda operatives admitted that they had large-scale intentions to use that information in attacks on the United States.[83] This information is further confirmed by reports from the FBI (in 2003) that directly point to al Qaeda targeting of commuter rail systems within the United States.

Simple hacking tools, such as LOphtCrack, were also found on al Qaeda computers. LOphtCrack allows a hacker to run combinations of characters at lightning speed in order to try and replicate a password. Other more sophisticated information technology tools, such as data hiding and encryption, were also a common theme in al Qaeda caches.[84] Additionally, terrorist groups have developed hacker tools to engage in credit card theft and rootkits that would allow hackers to remotely command victim machines. These resources are available for download through a range of Web sites, including a resource titled the "al_Qaeda University for Jihad Studies."[85] This page provides access to propaganda, hacker tools, and instructional materials to train new generations of hackers to continue the mission of this terror network.

Al Qaeda uses this technology so effectively, partly because of the structure of the organization. Bin Laden is part of an inner circle that has reverted to using nonelectronic means of communication recently due to the sophistication of U.S. and allied interception. However, outside of this core group exists a loose network of operators who coordinate using the sophisticated information technology already described. These operators are able to participate in the exchange of ideas, information, and plans related to the planning and targeting of attacks against the United States and/or its allies. It is this community of terrorists, residing all over the globe and with varying technological knowledge, that poses such a great threat to the United States.[86]

China and Information Warfare

The People's Republic of China is probably not the first threat that comes to mind when discussing information warfare or cyberterrorism. However, tensions between the United States and China remain high, and China is one of the few countries in the world eager to adopt the concept of information warfare. In fact, cyber warfare has been almost totally incorporated into the military lexicon, training, and organization in China.[87] Consider this excerpt from the official Chinese military science handbook:

> "In the near future, information warfare will control the form and future of war. We recognize this developmental trend of information warfare and see it as a driving force in the modernization of China's military and combat readiness. This trend will be highly critical to achieving victory in future wars."[88]

The Chinese government has assembled special hacker forces to engage the United States in online or cyber warfare and has apparently already used them. In the spring of 2001, a hack into the California power grid was traced back to the Guangdong province in China, where several malicious worms and Trojan horse attacks had also originated. Department of Defense officials did not think that was a coincidence. Although no proof was ever found that directly implicated the Chinese government or military, conventional wisdom suggests that these attacks had been "ordered."[89] Evidence also emerged in 2009 concerning repeated penetrations into American electrical grids by Chinese hackers.[90] A recent study using covert research methods also found that Chinese computers comprise the largest percentage of machines on the Internet actively scanning for electrical grid communications.[91] This information, coupled with the previously described Titan Rain incidents, suggests that the Chinese are heavily engaged in attempts to access critical infrastructure in the United States.

Further, on April 1, 2001, an American spy plane and a Chinese fighter aircraft collided in midair, leading to the capture of the American plane by the Chinese. The political conflict that followed was accompanied by a wave of attacks on U.S. Web sites by Chinese hacker groups. Approximately 1,200 sites, including those of the White House, the Air Force, and the Department of Energy, were targeted via defacement or DoS attacks. Again, this was never directly proven to be the work of the Chinese government. However, the attacks were highly visible, and China took no action to sanction those who perpetrated them. The attacks were at least tolerated by the Chinese government; however, given their hard-line stance on crime in China, it seems more likely that the government directly supported such action.[92]

Summary

China, al Qaeda, domestic right-wing hate groups, and numerous other terrorist or nation-state entities all have access to the Internet and have the tools to perpetrate a variety of cyber attacks against the United States and/or its allies. By the very nature of these technological attacks, our critical infrastructure is most vulnerable. As a result, a great deal of attention has been focused on the topic. Scholars, government officials, and reporters alike have speculated on the vulnerabilities of the United States to cyber attacks, as well as to the "types" of attacks that may be implemented.

As illustrated throughout this discussion, there is a great deal of confusion as to what the threats against U.S. information systems really are.

Clearly, there is a tremendous range of domestic and international terror groups, unfriendly nations, and criminals attempting to or successfully subverting U.S. critical and economic infrastructure. Such attacks could cause untold damage, though it is difficult to document the scope of the problem. It is, however, obvious that the Internet is now a critical component of information warfare and terror activities.

Review Questions

1. Define the concepts of information warfare and cyberterrorism.
2. What are the six components of information warfare?
3. What are the four major categories of cyberterrorism and/or information warfare?
4. Define critical infrastructure, and give some specific examples of the types of systems vulnerable to

cyberterrorism and information warfare within the United States.
5. Name and describe various types of information attacks.
6. What are stenography and cryptography?
7. What has the role of China been in recent cyber attacks against the United States?

Endnotes

1. CERE, RINELLA. (2003). "Digital Counter-Cultures and the Nature of Electronic Social and Political Movements." In YVONNE JEWKES (ed.), *Dot.cons: Crime, Deviance and Identity on the Internet.* Portland, OR: Willan Publishing, pp. 147–163.

2. FURNELL, STEVEN. (2002). *Cybercrime: Vandalizing the Information Society.* Boston, MA: Addison Wesley.

3. *Ibid.*

4. DENNING, D.E. (2001). "Activism, Hacktivism, and Cyberterrorism: The Internet as a Tool for Influencing Foreign Policy." In JOHN ARQUILLA and DAVID F. RONFELDT (eds.), *Networks and Netwars: The Future of Terror, Crime, and Militancy.* Santa Monica, CA: Rand, pp. 239–288.

5. See *National Strategy for Homeland Security* (2002). Office of the President: U.S. Government Printing Office.

6. SCHWARTEAU, WINN. (1996). *Information Warfare.* New York: Thundersmouth Press, p. 12.

7. JONES, ANDY, KOVACICH, GERALD L., and LUZWICK, PERRY G. (2002). *Global Information Warfare: How Businesses, Governments and Others Achieve Objectives and Attain Competitive Advantages.* New York: Auerbach Publication, p. 5. For further information on definitions, refer to DENNING, DOROTHY E. (1999). *Information Warfare and Security.* New York: ACM Press.

8. United States Air Force. "Cornerstones of Information Warfare." See *http://www.af.mil/lib/corner.html*

9. See JONES, KOVACICH, and LUZWICK, "*Global Information Warfare,*" p. 394.

10. See United States Air Force.

11. *Ibid.*

12. DENNING, DOROTHY. (1999). *Information Warfare and Security.* Reading, MA: Addison-Wesley, p. 68.

13. "Cyberterror Threat Overblown, Say Experts." *Computerworld,* March 14, 2003.

14. EMBAR-SEDDON, AYN. (February 2002). "Cyberterrorism: Are We Under Siege?" *American Behavioral Scientist* 45(6): 1036.

15. THACKRAH, R. (1987). "Terrorism: A Definitional Problem," *Contemporary Research on Terrorism.* Aberdeen, Scotland: Aberdeen University Press, p. 1043.

16. POLLITT, MARK. (October 25, 1997). "Cyberterrorism—Fact or Fancy?" *Proceedings of the 20th National Information Systems Security Conference,* pp. 285–289

17. GROSSMAN, M. (February 15, 1999). "Cyberterrorism." See *http://www.mgrossmanlaw.com/articles/1999.cyberterrorism.htm*

18. *Ibid.*, p. 4.

19. STAMBAUGH, HOLLIS, BEAUPRE, DAVID S., ICOVE, DAVID J., BAKER, RICHARD, CASSADY, WAYNE, and WILLIAMS, WAYNE P. (2001). *Electronic Crime Needs Assessment for State and Local Law Enforcement.* Washington, DC: National Institute of Justice. NCJ 186276.

20. DENNING, DOROTHY E. "Cyberterrorism." See *http://www.cs.georgetown.edu/~denning/infosec/cyberterror-GD.doc*

21. BALLARD, J. DAVID, HORNIK, JOSEPH G., and MCKENZIE, DOUGLAS. (February 2002). "Technological Facilitation of Terrorism." *American Behavioral Scientist* 45(6): 1009.

22. LANDLER, MARK, and MARKOFF, JOHN. (2008). "Digital Fears Emerge After Data Siege in Estonia." *The New York Times.* Retrieved May 24, 2007 from *www.nytimes.com/2007/05/29/technology/29estonia.html*

23. Institute for Security Technology Studies at Dartmouth College (September 22, 2001). "Cyber Attacks During the War on Terrorism: A Predictive Analysis," pp. 1–9.

24. *Ibid.*

25. See JONES, KOVACICH, and LUZWICK, "*Global Information Warfare,*" pp. 56–57.

26. *Ibid.*, p. 67.

27. Testimony of JIM GILMORE, Virginia Governor, before the House Science Committee on October 17, 2001.

28. See DENNING, "Cyberterrorism."

29. See *National Strategy for Homeland Security.*

30. See JONES, KOVACICH, and LUZWICK, "*Global Information Warfare,*" p. 71.

31. MCCULLAGH, D. (2009). "A Cybersecurity Quiz: Can You Tell Obama from Bush?" *Cnet News.* Retrieved May 29, 2009 from *http://news.cnet.com/8301-13578_3-10252263-38.html*

32. See Institute for Security Technology Studies, "Cyber Attacks During the War on Terrorism," p. 17.

33. GORMAN, S. (2009). "Electricity Grid in U.S. Penetrated by Spies." *Wall Street Journal.*

34. GOODMAN, SEYMOUR. (2001). "The Civil Aviation Analogy: International Cooperation to Protect Civil Aviation Against Cyber Crime and Terrorism." In A.D. SOFAER and S.E. GOODMAN (eds.), *Transnational Dimensions of Cyber Crime and Terrorism*. Stanford, CA: Hoover Institution Press, pp. 77–80.

35. *Ibid.*, p. 78.

36. *Ibid.*, p. 79.

37. *Ibid.*, p. 2.

38. See DENNING, "Cyberterrorism."

39. *Ibid.*

40. See JONES, KOVACICH, and LUZWICK, "*Global Information Warfare*," p. 112.

41. Testimony of MICHAEL A. VARTIS, Director of Institute for Security Technology Studies at Dartmouth College, before the House Science Committee on April 8, 2003.

42. Testimony of TERRY BENZEL, vice-president of advanced security research for Network Associates, Inc., before the House Science Committee on October 10, 2001.

43. See DENNING, *Information Warfare and Security*, pp. 75–76.

44. See Testimony of TERRY BENZEL.

45. ZANINI, M., and EDWARDS, S. (2001). "The Networking of Terror in the Information Age." In J. ARQUILLA and D. RONFELDT (eds.), *Networks and Netwars*. Pittsburgh: RAND, p. 44.

46. See Institute for Security Technology Studies, "Cyber Attacks During the War on Terrorism," p. 5.

47. *Ibid.*, p. 6.

48. [24] WARD, M. (February 8, 2006). "Anti-Cartoon Protests Go Online," *BBC News*. http://news.bbc.co.uk/2/hi/technology/4692518.stm; DANCHEV, D. (August 25, 2008). "Hundreds of Dutch web sites hacked by Islamic hackers," *ZDNet*. http://blogs.zdnet.com/security/?p=1788

49. *Ibid.*

50. See DENNING, *Information Warfare and Security*, p. 270.

51. *Ibid.*

52. See DENNING, "Cyberterrorism."

53. See DENNING, *Information Warfare and Security*, p. 275.

54. *Ibid.*

55. *Ibid.*

56. See Institute for Security Technology Studies, "Cyber Attacks During the War on Terrorism," p. 10.

57. See JONES, KOVACICH, and LUZWICK, "*Global Information Warfare*," p. 398.

58. *Ibid.*, pp. 398–399.

59. See Institute for Security Technology Studies, "Cyber Attacks During the War on Terrorism," p. 11.

60. DENNING, D. (May 15, 2008). "The Jihadi Cyberterror Threat." Paper presented at the UNCC Interdisciplinary Conference on Cybercrime.

61. *Ibid.*

62. *Ibid.*

63. See DENNING, *Information Warfare and Security*, p. 226.

64. THORNBURG, N. (2005). "Inside the Chinese Hack Attack." *Time.*

65. See ZANINI and EDWARDS, "The Networking of Terror in the Information Age," p. 35.

66. *Ibid.*, p. 36.

67. *Ibid.*

68. CERE, R. (2007). "Digital Undergrounds: Alternative Politics and Civil Society." In Y. JEWKES (ed.), *Crime Online*. Portland, OR: Willan Publishing, pp. 144–159.

69. *Ibid.*

70. *Ibid.*

71. See JONES, KOVACICH, and LUZWICK, "*Global Information Warfare*," p. 389.

72. See BALLARD, HORNIK, and MCKENZIE, "Technological Facilitation of Terrorism," p. 996.

73. See JONES, KOVACICH, and LUZWICK, "*Global Information Warfare*," p. 388.

74. *Ibid.*, pp. 388–389.

75. *Ibid.*, p. 60.

76. See ZANINI and EDWARDS, "The Networking of Terror in the Information Age," p. 42.

77. *Ibid.*, p. 60.

78. See ZANINI and EDWARDS, "The Networking of Terror in the Information Age," p. 43.

79. See Testimony of JIM GILMORE.

80. See EMBAR-SEDDON, "Cyberterrorism," pp. 1038–1039.

81. "Al Qaeda Poses Threat to the Net." *Computerworld*, November 25, 2002.

82. "Cyber-Attacks by Al Qaeda Feared." *Washington Post*, June 27, 2002.

83. *Ibid.*

84. Summarized from Public Broadcasting Station interviews, April 24, 2003. See *www.pbs.org/wgbh/pages/frontline/shows/cyberwar/interviews/*

85. *Ibid.*, p. 60.

86. *Ibid.*

87. HILDRETH, S. (2001). "Cyberwarfare." In J. BLANE (ed.), *Cyberwarfare: Terror at a Click*. Huntington, NY: Novinka Books, p. 14.

88. See JONES, KOVACICH, and LUZWICK, "*Global Information Warfare*," p. 221.

89. "Is China Ground Zero for Hackers?" *ZDNET*, August 28, 2001. See *http://zdnet.com.com/ 2100-1107-504010.html*

90. *Ibid.*, p. 33.

91. KREBS, BRIAN. (2009). "Report: China, Russia Top Sources of Power Grid Probes." *The Washington Post*. Retrieved May 1, 2009 from *http://voices. washingtonpost.com/securityfix/2009/04/report_ china_russia_top_source.html*

92. See Institute for Security Technology Studies, p. 8.

CHAPTER 3

The Criminology of Computer Crime

CHAPTER OBJECTIVES

After completing this chapter, you should be able to

- Discuss the tenets of choice theory, including routine activities theory, and its applicability to digital crimes.
- Describe the assumptions of deterrence theory and its utility.
- Discuss the impact of personality disorders on digital crime.
- Discuss the major social structure theories that apply to digital crime.
- Discuss the learning and social control theories that apply to digital crime.
- Describe the relationship between terrorism and political theory.

INTRODUCTION

This chapter will focus on the causes of digital crime. There are several theories that have been postulated over the past 100 years to explain crime, and there is an emerging body of research attempting to apply these concepts to digital crimes. A theory is an attempt to answer the question "Why?" In this chapter, theories will be presented that attempt to answer the question "Why do individuals commit digital crime?" This chapter will review criminological theories that can explain digital crime, though it is important to note that these theoretical frameworks were developed to explain crime in general, not digital crime specifically. As a result, support for some of these theories is mixed and require a great deal of investigation. The discussion presented here will present the existing body of criminological research with a variety of offending and victimization practices, as well as examples to demonstrate how a particular theory can explain digital crime.

CHOICE THEORY

According to choice theory, an individual commits a crime because he or she makes a rational choice to do so by weighing the risks and benefits of committing the act. If the risks (e.g., apprehension and punishment) outweigh the benefits, then the person will not commit the act. The opposite is also true. Choice theory became popular among criminologists in the late 1970s for three reasons. First, the positive school began to be questioned. The positive school was based on the belief that crime-producing traits and factors could be isolated, and treatment could be administered to eliminate or control the trait/factor. However, it was being argued at the time that these factors and traits had failed to be identified and isolated after almost 100 years of effort.

Individuals became dissatisfied with the positive school and began to offer alternative reasons for why people commit crime. Second, the reported crime rate in the 1960s and 1970s increased significantly. This was evidence to some that what was currently being done to control crime was not working. Therefore, some began to look for other means to control the crime rate besides treatment and rehabilitation. Third, the practice of rehabilitation came under attack.[1] In 1974, Robert Martinson wrote an article reviewing 231 studies of prison programs aimed at rehabilitating inmates. Martinson concluded that "with few and isolated exceptions, the rehabilitative efforts that have been reported so far have had no appreciable effect on recidivism."[2] This finding, which was picked up by the mass media, was used by critics of prison programs to argue against rehabilitation as a primary justification for incarceration. The results of the article are commonly referred to as "nothing works." Since it appeared that the current efforts had failed, many started to call for a change in judicial policy. Many started to emphasize the need for punishment, not rehabilitation, as the primary reason for incarceration.

Based on these reasons, choice theory and its policy implications became popular. Judicial policy started to change focus, on the offense and not the offender. Choice theory argues that since the offender has made a rational choice to commit the offense, the focus should be on the offense committed, not the offender. Policies such as mandatory sentencing and "three strikes and you're out laws" have become popular in recent years and are based on choice theory. The idea is that the way to control crime, including digital crime, is to have offenders fear the punishment and be deterred from committing the act. Since humans are hedonistic, efforts should be placed on making the risks of committing digital crime higher than any benefit derived from committing the offenses. Those who support the use of punishment to control crime assume that the offender is making a choice to commit the act and can be deterred if the risks outweigh the benefits.

Routine Activities

Routine activities theory is based on rational choice. Routine activities theory was developed by Lawrence Cohen and Marcus Felson. Cohen and Felson argue that the motivation to commit crime and the supply of offenders are constant.[3] Many would argue that changes in the crime rates are due to changes in the number of motivated offenders. However, Cohen and Felson argue that there is always a steady supply of offenders who are motivated to commit crime: Changes in crime rates are due to changes in the availability of targets and the absence of capable guardians.[4]

According to Cohen and Felson, crime occurs when there is a convergence in time and space of three factors:

1. A motivated offender (e.g., a hacker)
2. A suitable target (e.g., a vulnerable computer system)
3. The absence of a capable guardian (e.g., inadequate software protection)[5]

All three factors must be present in order for a crime to occur. In sum, when motivated offenders are present, they make rational choices by selecting suitable targets that lack capable guardianship.

This theory can also account for victimization, as they are the other player in a criminal event. Victimization is most likely when individuals are placed in high-risk situations, are in close proximity to motivated offenders, appear to be attractive targets to criminals, and lack a capable guardian.[6] In addition, victims report higher levels of deviant behavior than non-victims and share demographic characteristics with offenders.[7] Similarly, individuals who engage in criminal and deviant behavior are at an increased risk of victimization.[8]

This theory is applicable to digital crime because the rapid expansion of the use of computers and the Internet has increased the number of available targets. The millions of computers online at any point in time are all potential targets for hackers or malicious software writers. In addition, the global nature of the Internet means that an offender in Egypt, for example, could hack into hundreds of computer in the United States without ever leaving home.

In addition, without adequate software protection, there is frequently a lack of capable guardians to protect people from digital crime. Physical guardians are readily available on computer systems through antivirus software and similar programs.[9] These programs are expressly designed to reduce the likelihood of attacks from viruses, worms, and data loss by either scanning and preventing infected files from being introduced to the system or identifying and removing malicious software if it already has infected the system. Thus, physical guardians in cyberspace work similarly to physical guardians in the real world.

One of the first empirical studies testing this theory conducted by Holt and Bossler found that postulates of routine activities theory can be used to account for online harassment.[10] Specifically, routine computer use, including spending more time in online chat rooms increased the odds of online harassment. Physical guardianship measures, through antivirus programs and other software, had little influence on the likelihood of being harassed while chatting online. There was also a significant influence that personal and peer involvement in deviance had on the risk of online harassment. Engaging in digital crime can expose individuals to offenders, thereby increasing their risk of victimization.

A similar test of malicious software infection found that spending more time online engaging in shopping, e-mailing, and chatting did not affect the likelihood of receiving a virus or worm.[11] Individuals engaging in media piracy and viewing pornography were at an increased risk of malware infection, largely because these files are attractive packages that many individuals would want to open. Thus, the findings suggest that the relationship between crime and victimization in the real world may be replicated in online environments. Additionally, computer software that has been created specifically to decrease malware victimization had no significant impact in this study. These initial findings suggest that there may be some considerable utility in the routine activities framework, though greater research is needed to better understand and assess its applicability to digital crime.

DETERRENCE THEORY

Deterrence theory flows directly from choice theory. The idea is that offenders, including digital criminals, commit crime because they make a choice to do so. This choice is based on the perceived risks and benefits of committing the criminal act. If the risks (e.g., apprehension and punishment) outweigh the benefits, then the person will not commit the act. The offender will be deterred from committing the criminal act because of the threat of punishment. There are two types of deterrence: general and specific. **General deterrence** seeks to discourage would-be offenders from committing criminal acts because of the threat of punishment. Therefore, general deterrence occurs when would-be offenders choose not to commit a certain act because they fear the sanction that may be imposed. Sometimes offenders are made an example of in order to keep others from committing the same act. For example, an eighteenth-century judge reportedly told a defendant, "You are to be hanged not because you have stolen a sheep but in order that others may not steal sheep."[12] This is an example of general deterrence. **Specific deterrence** is designed to impose a sanction on a convicted offender in order to prevent him or her from continuing to commit criminal acts in the future. In other words, the sanction should be distasteful to the offender so that he or she does not want to commit any more offense.

There are several assumptions of deterrence theory. First and perhaps the most important assumption is that individuals are rational actors.[13] In other words, offenders weigh the potential risks and benefits of committing a criminal act and then make a conscious decision about whether to commit the offense. As it applies to digital crime, it can be argued that many digital criminals are rational actors, making rational choices to commit a computer crime. Second, offenders must be aware of the penalty for particular crimes.[14] As it applies to computer crime, it is argued that many computer criminals do not know the potential penalties they face for particular crimes. Third, they must view the risks as unpleasant.[15] If a computer criminal does not think apprehension and incarceration is unpleasant, then the criminal will not be deterred. Fourth, in order for deterrence to be effective, it is assumed that the sanction is swift, certain, and severe. The sanction must be imposed quickly to have the greatest deterrent effect, and there must be a high probability that a sanction will be imposed.

It is important to keep in mind that it is not the actual certainty, severity, and swiftness of the sanction that serves as a deterrent but the criminal's perception of the certainty, severity, and swiftness of the sanction. If potential computer criminals believe that the certainty of arrest is high for computer crime, then they will be deterred from committing the offense even if there is little chance of arrest in reality. Likewise, if potential computer criminals perceive prison as a terrible place that they do not want to go to, then they may be deterred from committing offenses. On the other hand, if a computer criminal does not believe that being incarcerated is anything to fear, then the individual is less likely to be deterred. Therefore, if offenders do not believe that the sanctions in court are severe, then they are unlikely to be deterred from committing criminal acts. Likewise, if they do not believe they will be caught, then they perceive a lack of certainty of punishment and thus are likely to commit the crime. The lack of certainty of arrest and punishment is particularly pronounced when it comes to computer crime. There is generally a low risk of apprehension and punishment.

There is minimal evidence to support the argument that the threat of arrest and punishment deters criminals.[16] In fact, evidence supports the contention that informal sanctions from parents and friends serve as more of a deterrent than legal sanctions.[17] In other words, fearing disapproval from your parents and peers for your actions is more likely to keep individuals from committing those acts than the fear of arrest and punishment.

A limited body of research has considered the applicability of deterrence for software and music piracy. Research using samples of college students suggests that the certainty of being caught by an IT administrator or fellow student did not reduce the likelihood of hacking systems without authorization.[18] Severity of punishment, however, helped to reduce the likelihood of hacking activity.[19] The relationship between detection and software piracy is also mixed. For example, one study found that when the certainty of being caught was high, software piracy declined.[20] Though there is not much research in this area, deterrence may have some success in accounting for digital crimes. Further research is needed to better understand this relationship.

PSYCHOLOGICAL THEORIES

There are several psychological theories that have been applied to criminal activity. This section will explore the impact of moral development and personality disorders on crime. Moral development theories support the contention that there are differences between the moral beliefs of criminals and noncriminals, while personality disorders argue that there are certain personality characteristics that are predictive of crime.

BOX 3.1

Hijacking the Al Jazeera Web Site

John William Racine II, a Web site designer from Norco, California, pleaded guilty to felony charges after admitting to federal authorities that he was responsible for the hijacking of Arabic-language news station Al Jazeera's Web site during the war in Iraq. He was charged with wire fraud and unlawful interception of an electronic communication. Al Jazeera Space Channel, based in Doha, Qatar, is an Arabic-language media organization that had registered the domain name *www.Aljazeera.net* through Network Solutions, Inc., in Dulles, Virginia. In addition to its satellite television news service, Al Jazeera provides English- and Arabic-language news through its *www.Aljazeera.net* Web site. Racine diverted the Web site and e-mail traffic for *www.Aljazeera.net* after learning in March 2003 that the Web site contained images of captured American prisoners of war and soldiers killed in action during Operation Iraqi Freedom.

Racine gained control of the *www.Aljazeera. net* domain name by defrauding Network Solutions, where Al Jazeera maintained an account for its domain name and e-mail services. Racine then diverted the Web site traffic to another Web site he had designed featuring an American flag in the shape of the continental United States and the words "Let Freedom Ring." Racine also intercepted approximately 300 e-mail messages destined for the *www.Aljazeera.net* domain and diverted the messages to an e-mail account under his control.

Racine admitted to FBI agents that he had contacted Network Solutions by telephone and e-mail in an attempt to gain control of the *www.Aljazeera.net* domain name. He ultimately created a false photo identification card to impersonate an Al Jazeera systems administrator and forged the systems administrator's signature on a Network Solutions "Statement of Authorization" form. Racine then sent the fraudulent documents to Network Solutions by facsimile and induced Network Solutions to give him control of the Al Jazeera account.

Racine subsequently changed the *www. Aljazeera.net* account settings and redirected all Web traffic through a dynamic domain name service and ultimately to his Web site containing the American flag. In addition, he rerouted all e-mail traffic to an account he had created on MSN Hotmail using the name of the Al Jazeera systems administrator. While Racine maintained control of Al Jazeera's domain name, Internet users were unable to access the Al Jazeera news Web sites and Al Jazeera was unable to receive e-mails sent to the domain. On March 26, Racine contacted agents of the FBI and admitted that he was responsible for hijacking the Web site and intercepting the e-mails sent to *www.Aljazeera.net*.

The plea agreement includes a sentence of three years' probation along with 1,000 hours of community service. Additionally, Racine agreed to pay a fine of $1,500 and full restitution to the victims of the offenses.

Which theory do you think applies best to this case?

Source: http://www.cybercrime.gov/racinePlea.htm

Moral Development and Crime

The relationship between moral development and crime focuses on cognitive development. Cognitive development theory assumes that individuals develop in a sequential manner. The individual passes through one step in development, then another step, then another, and so on. Kohlberg argues that there are sequential stages in moral reasoning that individuals pass through as they develop. At each stage, the decision of what is right and what is wrong is made for different reasons. Crime, including computer crime, can be explained by arrested development of moral reasoning at certain stages. People stop at a certain stage and do not progress any further.

Kohlberg stated that there are six stages of moral development. They are as follows:

Stage 1: Punishment and obedience orientation stage—what is right is obedience to power and rules and avoiding punishment

Stage 2: Hedonistic orientation stage—right corresponds to seeing one's own needs met, taking responsibility for oneself, and allowing others to do the same

Stage 3: Interpersonal concordance stage—right is having good intentions and motives and being concerned for others

Stage 4: Law and order orientation stage—right is doing one's duty to society and others and maintaining the rules of society

Stage 5: Social contract, legalistic orientation stage—right is based on upholding the rules and values agreed upon by society; a social contract

Stage 6: Orientation to universal ethical principles stage—right is an assumed obligation to principles such as justice and equality, which apply to all individuals; the individual recognizes the moral rightness of behavior[21]

The first two stages are usually completed by age 7. Stages 3 and 4 are passed through and completed from preadolescence through adolescence, while the last two stages begin in early adulthood. Where do criminals stop in moral development in comparison to noncriminals? Research has found that criminals frequently fall into stage 1 or 2 of moral development, while noncriminals frequently fall into stage 3 or 4.[22] In stage 1, children comply with authority out of fear. Something is viewed as morally right if punishment is avoided. Individuals who did not progress through this stage will think that their criminal behavior is permissible as long as they are not punished for it. Obviously, this stage of moral development does not take into account other people or an obligation to society. In stage 2, children define what is right as that which satisfies their needs. That is why it is referred to as the hedonistic orientation stage. At this stage, children define something as right if they are not punished for it (i.e., stage 1) and it satisfies their needs. It is easy to see why it is argued that many criminals have stopped their moral development at stage 1 or 2. Their only concern with whether something is right or wrong is whether they get punished and satisfy their needs. It is not until stage 3 that children begin to take into account the feelings of others. Development to stage 3 insulates people from crime because they have become concerned about others, not just their own needs. Therefore, it is clear to see that individuals who proceed to stage 3 and perhaps beyond are far less likely to commit criminal acts.

Personality Disorders

Psychologists argue that certain personality characteristics of an individual may influence crime. Personality refers to the emotional and behavioral attributes of an individual. Attempts have been made to provide support for the belief that individuals with certain personality types are much more likely to commit criminal acts. These attempts have focused on identifying differences in the personalities of criminals and noncriminals. One attempt at identifying these personality characteristics was completed by Sheldon and Eleanor Glueck after they compared 500 delinquent and nondelinquent boys. Personality characteristics that were conducive to crime included extroversion, impulsivity, lack of self-control, hostility, resentment, suspicion of others, destructiveness, less fearful of failure, ambivalence toward authority, assertiveness, and feeling unappreciated.[23]

Frequently the term "psychopath" or "sociopath" is used in describing some offenders. These terms technically refer to a condition known as antisocial personality disorder. According to the *Diagnostic and Statistical Manual of the American Psychiatric Association,* "the essential feature of antisocial personality disorder is a pervasive pattern of disregard for, and violation of, the rights of others that begins in childhood or early adolescence and continues into adulthood."[24] Some of the characteristics of antisocial personality disorder are (1) repeatedly performing acts that are grounds for arrest, (2) deceitfulness, (3) impulsivity, (4) irritability and aggressiveness, (5) reckless disregard for safety of self or others, (6) consistent irresponsibility, and (7) lack of remorse.[25] Although no research to date has been conducted that analyzes the personality characteristics of computer criminals, it can be argued that certain computer criminals may satisfy the criteria of antisocial personality disorder. However, it is argued that the prevalence of antisocial personality disorder is lower among computer criminals than among other criminals.

Pedophiles and Psychological Theory

Many people wonder why pedophiles commit the crimes that they do; what combination of factors leads a person to want to commit sexual offenses against a child? Unfortunately, there are no easy answers. As discussed in Chapter 7, pedophiles commit their crimes for a variety of reasons and go on committing their crimes, with little hope of rehabilitation. Most experts agree that pedophiles develop a sexual interest over a long period of time. Further, there is a variety of reasons and factors that relate to developing pedophilia, none of which fully cause or explain the crime. Most commonly, pedophiles are exposed to some type of sexual abuse or trauma during their childhood. Another common factor is that they have had some type of abuse or other related problem during their sexual development and, as a result, develop an interest in children as sexual objects. Interestingly, the advent of the Internet has led to numerous problems in dealing with and detecting pedophiles.

The Internet serves many purposes for the pedophile of today, the least of which is the dissemination of child pornography. This poses a conundrum for theorists: Which comes first—an interest in computers due to existing pedophiliac interests or an interest in pedophilia as a result of viewing these types of images on the Internet? Some of the pedophiles arrested state that they developed an interest in children as sexual objects as the result of seeing such images on the Internet. Others clearly were pedophiles prior to the advent of the Internet and simply learned another technique for obtaining child pornography. In short, the specific reasons why a person becomes a pedophile aren't immediately or clearly understood. Nonetheless, psychological theories posit that a person's sexual interests and sexual paraphilias develop in much the same way as other interests and our personalities—through a process of learning, cognitive reinforcement, and psychological development. Thus, the specific reasons why a person becomes a pedophile are different from case to case, but the process is relatively common. The best explanation for this interest is psychological and cognitive in nature.

BOX 3.2
Massive Data Theft and Fraud

In 2003, Scott Levine was the controlling owner of a company called Snipermail, Inc., which distributed advertisements via e-mail. He was able to steal more than one billion records containing names, addresses, phone numbers, and other personal information from clients of Acxiom Corporation, which is a repository for personal, financial, and company data, including customer information for other companies. Levine used sophisticated decryption software to illegally obtain passwords and exceed his authorized access to Acxiom databases, which contained information belonging to Acxiom's clients. He also concealed physical evidence relating to the intrusions and thefts of data.

The U.S. attorney for this case, Bud Cummins, said that "At first blush, downloading computer files in the privacy of your office may not seem so terribly serious. But, if you are stealing propriety information worth tens of millions of dollars from a well-established and reputable company, you can expect to be punished accordingly." Levine was found guilty of 120 counts of unauthorized access of a protected computer, two counts of access device fraud, and one count of obstruction of justice in a federal court on August 12, 2005, and received 96 months in court.

Which theory do you think applies best to this case?

_____

Source: http://www.usdoj/gov/criminal/cybercrime/levine Sent.htm

SOCIAL STRUCTURE THEORIES

The first set of social theories that will be discussed in this chapter can be classified as social structure theories. When originally developed, social structure theories focused on why lower-class individuals are more likely to commit crime than middle- and upper-class individuals. However, modifications and expansions of the original theories have moved away from this distinction and have attempted to explain criminal behavior by all social classes (e.g., general strain theory). This is important in the study of digital crime because many offenders come from the middle and upper classes. Traditionally, these theories focus on socioeconomic conditions and cultural values as two prominent factors that impact crime. In this section, two major subtypes of social structure theory will be discussed: strain theory and subculture theory.

Strain Theory

One major type of social structure theory is strain theory. Originally, strain theorists saw crime as a result of a lack of opportunity, in particular economic opportunity. Today, modern-day strain theories are much broader than the original theories. At the time of the development of strain theory, it was argued that U.S. society instills in citizens a desire for financial success but does not provide all individuals equal opportunity to achieve that success. Those who do not have an equal opportunity are strained and thus more likely to be criminal. The most prominent strain theory is the one presented by Robert Merton.

MERTON: STRAIN THEORY   There is a unique combination of cultural goals and the means to obtain them in every society. According to Merton, the cultural goal of American society is economic success.[26] It is argued that the primary goal of citizens in the United States is material wealth. This goal is promulgated through a variety of mechanisms including the media, cultural transmission, and other mechanisms. Along with the goal, there are institutionalized means to obtain the goal such as education, occupation, and deferral of gratification. However, not everyone has equal access to the institutionalized means to obtain financial success. Members of the lower class have less access to education and good jobs than members of the middle and upper class. Strain theory is sometimes referred to as blocked opportunity theory. In other words, people are blocked in their ability to access education and a good job. Therefore, there is a discrepancy between a person's desire to obtain economic success and their ability to do so. These individuals suffer from strain.

If an individual is strained, how do they adapt to the strain? Merton developed five modes of adaptation.[27] The modes of adaptation vary in their acceptance or rejection of the cultural goal of economic success and the institutionalized means to obtain the goal. They also vary in the propensity for criminal behavior. The first mode of adaptation is **conformity.** A conformist both accepts the cultural goal of economic success and accepts the institutionalized means to obtain it. A conformist is highly unlikely to commit criminal acts. It is also the most common mode of adaptation.

The second mode of adaptation is **ritualism.** A ritualist rejects the cultural goal of economic success but accepts the institutionalized means to obtain the cultural goal. One response to strain is to lower your aspirations. This is what a ritualist does. They have lowered their aspiration for financial success but still abide by the means to obtain it, such as employment and education. It is unlikely that a ritualist will commit criminal acts as well.

The third mode of adaptation is **innovation.** An innovator accepts the goal of economic success but rejects the institutionalized means to obtain it. In this instance, the individual engages in innovation to find new means to obtain economic success besides education and employment. One such means is likely to be criminal activity. The innovator may commit such offenses as computer crime, fraud, drug dealing, robbery, burglary, auto theft, bribery, and prostitution, among others in an effort to obtain financial success. This is the mode of adaptation that is most likely to lead to criminal activity and to include computer criminals. Basically, the person wants to be financially successful and will commit criminal acts that help to obtain this goal.

The fourth mode of adaptation is **retreatism.** A retreatist rejects both the cultural goal of economic success and institutionalized means to obtain it. These individuals do not aspire to financial success, nor are they concerned with getting an education and employment. These individuals frequently escape into drug addiction and may commit crimes to support their drug use, but they do not aspire to financial success. Therefore, their strain is reduced by abandoning both the goal and the means to obtain it.

The fifth mode of adaptation is **rebellion.** A rebel rejects both the cultural goal and means but substitutes new goals and means to obtain them. This adaptation is likely to lead to crime and can be represented by some gangs, militias, cults, and countercultures. Criminality is likely to occur with this mode of adaptation, but it will not be as prevalent as criminal activity among innovators.

White-Collar Crime and Strain Theory

White-collar crimes such as money laundering, corporate espionage, and the numerous varieties of Internet fraud schemes described in Chapter 5 fit neatly into the strain theory school of criminology, which suggests that crime and deviance is largely the result of blocked legitimate opportunities. In this sense, individuals who engage in such schemes can be viewed as "innovators" who pursue illegitimate means in order to achieve the conventional goal of material success.

While Merton's original formulation of the theory focused on the blockage of legitimate opportunities experienced predominantly by those in the lower economic classes, contemporary strain theorists have sought to extend strain theory in order to explain the instrumental crimes of middle- and high-class individuals by defining what they have termed the "relative deprivation" experienced by persons of higher economic status. That is, individuals who already enjoy a certain degree of monetary success may engage in instrumental crimes such as money laundering, sespionage, or fraud simply because they *perceive* goal blockage in their attempt to secure ever-increasing wealth. From this perspective, "relative deprivation" offers an explanation as to why crimes such as money laundering and/or corporate espionage are primarily committed by individuals who may already be materially successful.

AGNEW: GENERAL STRAIN THEORY   A more modern version of strain theory is general strain theory. General strain theory was developed by Robert Agnew and tries to explain why individuals who feel stress and strain in their lives are more likely to commit crimes. Agnew's theory does not focus on economic success as the prominent goal in U.S. society, but instead offers a broader explanation of crime than focusing exclusively on the lower class. Agnew argues the crime is due to negative affective states. Negative affective states can include anger, frustration, disappointment, depression, and fear, which are obviously experienced by all classes.[28]

According to Agnew, these negative affective states are caused by several different sources of strain. First, strain can be caused by the failure to achieve positively valued goals. This is similar to the strain discussed by Merton in that it is the result of a disjunction between aspirations (i.e., what one aspires to) and expectations (i.e., what one can expect to achieve). Second, strain can be caused by the disjunction between expectations and achievements. This is different than the first source of strain because it does not focus on aspirations, but on expectations. This disjunction between expectations and achievements frequently occurs when people compare themselves to peers who seem to be doing better than they (e.g., financially or socially). Based on this disjunction, individuals may feel a sense of inequity. Third, strain can be caused by the removal of positively valued stimuli from the individual. This can include the loss of a boyfriend or girlfriend, the death of a relative, the loss of a job, or the divorce of parents, to name a few. Fourth, strain may be due to the presentation of negative stimuli. Examples of negative stimuli include family conflict, school failure, child abuse, and stressful life events. These sources of strain may have a cumulative effect on people in reality. The greater the intensity and frequency strain experiences become for an individual, the more likely the person is to turn to crime.[29]

There are no real empirical assessments of the ways that general strain theory may work to explain digital crimes; there are several offenses where it could fit, especially cyberbullying and stalking. Middle and high school students who feel that they are not as popular or pretty as their peers may choose to gossip or make fun of them through social networking sites like Facebook as a means of dealing with the frustration they experience. For example, a young girl named Piper Smith, in Spanaway, Washington, was horrified to learn that her sixth-grade classmates posted a cartoon on the video-sharing site YouTube titled "Top Six Ways to Kill Piper."[30] The video featured animated images of girls shooting her and poisoning her, although it is unclear why these girls posted the video. This sort of behavior from Piper's classmates is extreme, but could be a direct response to feelings of anger or frustration toward her.

Individuals who are rejected or jilted by a close friend or romantic partner can feel anger over this and find that the way to cope with this strain is to begin to send mean or threatening messages to get back at this person. For example, a young girl in Missouri named Megan Meier committed suicide as a consequence of receiving hurtful instant messages from a young man she

BOX 3.3

Ordering Attacks against Computer Systems

Jason Salah Arabo, aged 19, owned a sportswear company with two Web sites and was convicted of conspiring to conduct attacks against his competitors' Web sites. Arabo met an individual named Jasmine Singh, aged 16, through online communications and found that Singh had covertly infected over 2,000 computers with programs that enabled him to control them remotely. Singh demonstrated that he could use these compromised computers to engage in distributed DoS attacks. Arabo asked Singh to attack his competitors' Web sites to reduce their online sales operations, for which Singh would be compensated with merchandise, including designer sneakers. Singh used his infected machines to crash one of Arabo's competitors' Web sites and the servers hosing the page, leading to unrelated businesses around the globe to be harmed by the attack.

In August 2005, Singh pleaded guilty as an adult to two counts of computer theft and was sentenced to five years in prison and ordered to pay $35,000 in restitution for damage. Arabo pled guilty to one count of conspiracy to cause the transmission of a command that would intentionally cause damage without authorization to a protected computer. Arabo received 30 months in prison for conspiring to conduct highly destructive computer attacks on competitors and was required to make restitution of $504,495 to his victims.

Which theory do you think applies best to this case?

Source: http://www.usdoj.gov/criminal/cybercrime/arabo Sent.htm

met on the social networking site MySpace. They developed a relationship online, and he terminated it by sending Megan a hurful message stating that the "world would be a better place without you in it."[31] These messages were actually sent by the mother of Megan's friend named Lori Drew, who created the fraudulent account as a means of getting retribution for slights against her child. This sort of behavior is another extreme example, but demonstrates that cyberstalking and harassment could be a result of strains.

SOCIAL PROCESS THEORIES

Social process theories focus on the relationship between socialization and crime. In particular, social process theories analyze the impact of certain factors such as peer group relationships, family relationships, and failure in school on crime. All of these factors are related to crime. Individuals who associate with criminal peers are at significant risk of committing crime themselves. Likewise, individuals who were brought up in an unnurturing, dysfunctional family are at greater risk of committing crime. Finally, individuals who drop out of school are also at risk for committing crime. Two branches of social process theory will be discussed in this section: learning theory and the social control theory of low self-control.

Learning Theory

According to learning theory, individuals commit crime, including computer crime, because they learn the attitudes, skills, and rationalizations necessary to commit these acts. Many times this learning takes place in interaction with parents and peers. Criminals are different from noncriminals in the extent to which they have been exposed to definitions and situations that portray criminal acts as appropriate. There are four interrelated learning theories that will be

BOX 3.4
Russian Organized Hacking

On July 25, 2003, Alexei V. Ivanov was sentenced to 48 months of imprisonment to be followed by three years of supervised release. Ivanov had pled guilty to numerous charges of conspiracy, computer intrusion (i.e., "hacking"), computer fraud, credit card fraud, wire fraud, and extortion. The charges stemmed from the activities of Ivanov and others who operated from Russia and hacked into dozens of computers throughout the United States, stealing usernames, passwords, credit card information, and other financial data, and then extorting those victims with the threat of deleting their data and destroying their computer systems. In sentencing Ivanov, the district judge described his participation as a "manager or supervisor" in an "unprecedented, wide-ranging, organized criminal enterprise" that "engaged in numerous acts of fraud, extortion, and intentional damage to the property of others, involving the sophisticated manipulation of computer data, financial information, and credit card numbers." The district judge found that Ivanov was responsible for an aggregate loss of approximately $25 million.

Which theory do you think applies best to this case?

Source: http://www.cybercrime.gov/ivanovSent.htm

discussed: Sutherland's differential association theory, Akers' social learning theory, Sykes and Matza's techniques of neutralization/drift theory, and subcultural theories.

SUTHERLAND: DIFFERENTIAL ASSOCIATION THEORY   The first learning theory to be presented is Sutherland's differential association theory. At the time of Sutherland's work, social structure theories such as strain were popular. However, he argued that criminal behavior is a function of learning, not the inability to obtain economic success. He presented nine formal propositions that demonstrate that social interaction and learning leads to criminal activity:[32]

1. *Criminal behavior is learned.*[33] Sutherland argued that criminality is not a function of a biological or psychological malady or a function of the social structure, but learning.

2. *Criminal behavior is learned in interaction with other persons in a process of communication.*[34] This communication is verbal and involves interaction with others.

3. *The principal part of the learning of criminal behavior occurs with intimate personal groups.*[35] Learning involves interaction with significant others such as parents, siblings, and peers. Therefore, families and peers have the greatest influence on learning criminal behavior and attitudes. Sutherland did not see much of a role for movies and newspapers to serve as a medium to learn criminal behavior. However, Sutherland developed his theory prior to development of television and video games.

4. *When criminal behavior is learned, the learning includes (1) techniques of committing the crime, which are sometimes very complicated, sometimes very simple; and (2) the specific directions of motives, drives, rationalizations, and attitudes.*[36] In the process of learning criminal behavior, an individual will learn how to commit the offense. The individual also learns the attitudes necessary to commit crimes as well as appropriate rationalizations which may justify their behavior.

5. *The specific direction of motives and drives is learned from definitions of the legal codes as favorable or unfavorable.*[37] Sutherland argued that an individual may be surrounded by persons who define the legal codes as rules to be observed. In this case, crime is unlikely because the individual believes the law is something to be followed. However, some individuals associate with

people whose definitions of the legal code are favorable to the violation of the legal codes. Obviously, crime is much more likely in the latter situation.

6. *A person becomes criminal because of an excess of definitions favorable to violation of the law over definitions unfavorable to violation of the law.*[38] This is the principle of differential association. Sutherland argued that people learn definitions favorable and unfavorable to the violation of the law. When an individual, through association with others, has obtained more definitions that are favorable to the violation of the law than unfavorable, then crime is likely to occur. In other words, the individual has learned to commit certain crimes. This principle is important because it can help to explain why criminals may think that some crimes are appropriate while others are not. For example, an individual may think that committing fraud via the Internet is appropriate, but robbery is wrong. How can this be justified? According to Sutherland, the individual has received enough definitions in interaction with others to believe that committing fraud via the Internet is appropriate. On the other hand, the same individual has not received enough definitions to believe that committing robbery is appropriate as well. Think of definitions favorable to violation of the law on one side of a scale while definitions unfavorable to violation of the law are on the other side. If an individual receives enough definitions favorable to the violation of the law, then the balance will be tipped in favor of committing the crime. The balance can vary from offense to offense and action to action, however.

7. *Differential associations may vary in frequency, duration, priority, and intensity.*[39] Differential association varies on the quality and quantity of social interactions. Therefore, associations with criminal and noncriminal behavior vary in those respects. Frequency and duration mean that more attention will be paid by an individual to definitions obtained in interaction with those with whom they have frequent contact and have had contact with for a long period of time. Priority involves the importance of the relationship to the individual and the importance of criminal or noncriminal behavior to the individual. Intensity involves the prestige of the source of a criminal or noncriminal pattern and the emotional reactions related to the associations.[40]

8. *The process of learning criminal behavior by association with criminal and anticriminal patterns involves all of the mechanisms that are involved in any other learning.*[41] In other words, learning criminal behavior is not different from learning any other behavior.

9. *While criminal behavior is an expression of general needs and values, it is not explained by those, since noncriminal behavior is an expression of the same needs and values.*[42] Sutherland argued that thieves steal in order to obtain money, but workers work to obtain money as well. Therefore, one cannot say that an individual committed a criminal act in order to get money, because that is the same reason why another individual works at a restaurant. In other words, the need for money explains lawful as well as unlawful behavior.

Therefore, Sutherland argued that the accumulation of an excess of definitions obtained in interaction with intimate social groups which say it is OK to commit certain criminal acts leads to criminality.

AKERS: SOCIAL LEARNING THEORY   The second learning theory to be presented is Akers' differential reinforcement theory. Sutherland did not apply a learning theory to his theory of differential association. Instead, he stated that criminal behavior is learned like any other behavior. He did not explain how other behavior or criminal behavior is learned.

Akers' social learning model is grounded in four principal components: differential association, definitions, differential reinforcement, and imitation.[43] These concepts are part of a dynamic and interactive process in which the components have effects on each other and reciprocal effects with behavior. The social learning process begins with the relationships individuals have with deviants and nondeviants. Akers defines differential association as, "the process whereby one is exposed to normative definitions that are relatively more favorable or unfavorable to illegal or law-abiding behavior."[44] These interactions with others vary in frequency, duration, priority, and intensity, and are the context in which the other elements play a role. The most essential interactions are those involving intimate personal groups, such as family and friends. Secondary and distant reference groups also affect individual behavior by providing context. Individuals are more likely to commit deviant behavior if their patterns of differential association with these groups are involved in deviant behavior.[45]

As individuals are differentially exposed to others, they develop definitions that support or justify their behavior. Definitions are often viewed as an individual's attitude toward and perception of certain behaviors as either acceptable or unacceptable.[46] Definitions can be derived from moral or religious beliefs, from interaction and imitation of others, and through reinforcement of current beliefs. These definitions include justifications and excuses for deviant behavior that neutralize the potential negative ramifications of deviance. In the context of social learning theory, the more neutralizing and positive definitions an individual has toward deviance, the more likely he or she will be to commit deviance when opportunity is provided.[47]

While definitions support involvement in deviance, the balance between past, present, and expected future reinforcements and punishments shape the likelihood of future deviant behavior. Specifically, behavior is more likely to occur when a reward is given (positive reinforcement) or an unpleasant stimulus is taken away (negative reinforcement). Individuals differentially experience multiple forms of reinforcement and punishment as a consequence of their behavior.[48] Social reinforcements can reward deviance, such as praise and encouragement from peers or changes in social status as a consequence of individual action. Nonsocial reinforcements are also pertinent, encompassing financial gains or losses, legal consequences, and physical harm or gains. Differential reinforcement measures are not frequently included in tests of social learning, though they are related to repeated behavior when measured.[49]

Finally, imitation refers to the commission of behavior after observing someone else committing similar behavior. Whether the person actually imitates a behavior depends on his or her peers, the behavior that he or she observes, and the differential reinforcements observed.[50] Imitation has its strongest role in the initiation stage of behavior and with younger samples. It becomes less influential as the behavior is repeated, as differential reinforcements and definitions play a more important role. Several studies have found strong effects for imitation, though this component is often absent in research to their narrow role in the learning process and empirical overlap with differential association.[51]

Scholars have applied social learning theory to cybercrime with some success in recent years, primarily explaining forms of music or media piracy,[52] as well as a range of offenses including hacking and guessing passwords.[53] In addition, multiple studies have found strong support for a link between having deviant friends, deviant definitions, and piracy.[54]

The significance of differential reinforcement and imitation within the social learning model to account for cybercrime is limited. Research has found mixed results for imitation, as its effects vary based on the type of cybercrime committed. Imitation of family members influenced piracy, while teacher encouragement and electronic bulletin boards increased the likelihood of guessing passwords and other deviant act.[55] These findings suggest that there may be significant value in the social learning theories to account for digital crime.

SYKES AND MATZA: TECHNIQUES OF NEUTRALIZATION/DRIFT THEORY   The third learning theory to be presented is Sykes and Matza's techniques of neutralization/drift theory. Sykes and Matza also argued that the process of becoming a criminal is a learning experience. They posited that most criminals hold conventional values, norms, and beliefs, but must learn to neutralize the values before committing crimes.[56] Most criminals are not committed to a criminal lifestyle and only commit criminal acts on rare occasions. However, these same criminals hold values and beliefs that state that criminal behavior is wrong. How can they commit criminal acts and still hold conventional values? The individuals use techniques of neutralization, which shield them from any sense of guilt. These techniques of neutralization allow individuals to drift into criminality and then back into conventional behavior. That is why this theory is sometimes referred to as drift theory. Sykes and Matza argue that the techniques of neutralization are learned and come before the criminal act. There are five techniques of neutralization:[57]

1. *Denial of responsibility:* This occurs when an individual states that his or her behavior was an accident or resulted from forces beyond his or her control, such as unloving parents, bad companions, or living in a criminogenic neighborhood.[58] Saying "I did not mean to do it" reflects denial of responsibility.

2. *Denial of injury:* This technique of neutralization occurs when an individual denies the wrongfulness of his or her action or believes the offense does not really cause any harm.[59] Saying "I did not really hurt anybody" reflects this technique of neutralization. This technique of neutralization can be applied to many instances of computer crime where the computer criminals do not feel that anybody is truly hurt by their criminal activity. An example can include the propagation of a worm that does not actually damage anything and is more of a nuisance than anything else. The computer criminal may argue that no one really got hurt.

3. *Denial of victim:* This occurs when an individual believes that the victim had it coming or the victim caused the offense to occur.[60] Saying "They had it coming to them" reflects denial of victim. This is certainly reflected in some computer crimes, especially recent malicious attacks on several companies' computers by ex-employees.

4. *Condemnation of the condemners:* This occurs when the individual shifts the blame to others by focusing attention on the motive and behavior of those who disapprove of his or her actions.[61] Basically, the individual is challenging those who are condemning the actions by arguing that the police are corrupt and parents take out their frustrations on their children. Asking "Why is everybody picking on me?" reflects this technique of neutralization.

5. *Appeal to higher loyalties:* This occurs when the individual's peer group takes precedence over the rules of society.[62] Saying "I did not do it for myself, but for my friends" reflects appeal to higher loyalties.

Cressey's classic work, *Other People's Money,* describing the cognitive processes experienced by his sample of convicted embezzlers, compares favorably to Sykes and Matza's attempt to explain youthful deviance in their techniques of neutralization/drift theory. Similar to the "techniques" employed by juveniles in order to escape or "drift" from the norms associated with conventional behavior, Cressey found that many of his sampled embezzlers had successfully "neutralized" their embezzlement prior to committing the actual crime by convincing themselves that they were only temporarily "borrowing" the money, or that he or she was justifiably "owed" the money in exchange for years of underpaid, faithful service to the employer.

Recent research on digital piracy found that those who have developed definitions that support or neutralize responsibility for piracy behavior are more likely to illegally download

---

BOX 3.5

Cyber Harassment

On May 16, 2002, Raymond Blum, the former chief technology officer for Askit.com, a Manhattan-based computer consulting company, was arrested on charges of transmitting threats via the Internet to his former employer at Askit. As chief technology officer, Blum had access to all computer system passwords and information necessary to operate Askit's computer networks. In February 2002, shortly after Blum's departure from the company, Askit began to experience computer and telephone voice mail problems. There was unusual network traffic on its computer system, which caused its computer network to fail. Askit's e-mail servers were flooded with thousands of messages containing pornographic images, and its voice mail system was altered so that certain customers calling the company were directed to a pornographic telephone service.

Following the intrusions directed against their computer and voice mail systems, Askit's chief executive officer and its president began receiving threatening communications in various forms. For example, the president received an e-greeting card containing an image of a box, which, shortly after being displayed on the president's computer screen and accompanied by a creaking sound, opened to display a voodoo doll with skeleton-like features. The doll had pins stuck through various parts of its body and was wearing a name tag that identified it as being the president.

Which theory do you think applies best to this case?

Source: http://www.cybercrime.gov/blumArrest.htm

---

media.[63] Data using college samples have found that those who engage in higher levels of piracy report greater acceptance of beliefs of neutralization focusing on denial of responsibility, injury, and victims.[64] For example, those who believe that it is okay to pirate music because they only want one or two songs from CDs (denial of responsibility) or believe that the creators of music are not going to lose any money (denial of victim) are more likely to engage in piracy.[65] Additionally, those who believe that law enforcement and universities do not care about piracy are also more likely to engage in piracy. Finally, those who strongly support the notion that it is acceptable to engage in piracy to provide materials to family or friends or use the resources to complete schoolwork or projects are much more likely to engage in piracy at extremely high levels.[66]

Similar evidence appears to account for the creation of malicious software and virus writing. Once confronted or apprehended because of their virus-writing activity, virus writers use the same justifications and excuses consistent with techniques of neutralization theory. A common statement by virus writers is that it is the computer user's or system's fault that they were infected, not the virus writer's (blaming the victim). They state that if the victims had their security up to par, they would not have become a victim in the first place. They also note that such neophytes have no business being online or using their computer if they don't know how to protect themselves. In fact, virus writers tend to show disdain for the average "Internet surfer." Another common theme in the comments of virus writers is that they aren't really doing any harm and, in fact, are performing a public service by pointing out the security holes in the software and computer systems (denial of injury/denial of the victim). Some claim that there aren't really any victims of viruses, and that such users are simply ill-prepared to conduct commerce or surf online. Another typical justification is that they are really doing good by showing the greed and incompetence of software vendors (especially Microsoft) and other corporations (condemn the condemners). Finally, many virus writers claim that they really didn't intend to cause any harm by writing their virus. These techniques of neutralization can be seen in several of the anecdotal items contained in Chapter 6, especially the interview with the Dark Avenger. Taken as a whole, the techniques of neutralization may be significantly useful to account for cybercrimes.

Subcultural Theories

A **subculture** is a set of values, norms, and beliefs that differ from the dominant culture. The main tenet of subculture theory is that criminals, including computer criminals, hold values, norms, and beliefs that are in opposition to those held in the dominant culture. These individuals behave in a manner that is consistent with their values, norms, and beliefs, which many times will bring them in conflict with the law. When originally developed, subculture theories attempted to explain gang formation and crime. However, certain types and examples of computer crime can be due to the existence of subcultures. Since there is significant debate over what constitutes a subculture, it may be best to approach the question by determining its main characteristics.

Defined from a broad sociological and criminological perspective, a subculture is any group having certain values, norms, traditions, and rituals that sets them apart from the dominant culture. This includes an emphasis on performing certain behaviors or developing skill sets, like confidence of men learning to steal and bilk money from unsuspecting people.[67] Also, subcultural rules or codes of conduct exist that structure how individuals view and interact with different groups. A special argot or slang is present, as well as some outward symbols of membership like tattoos or informal uniforms.[68] These all provide ways to measure an individual's reputation, status, and adherence to the subculture.

This framework suggests membership in a subculture influences behavior by providing individuals with beliefs, goals, and values that approve of and justify particular types of activities, including crime. In the case of offender subcultures, the transmission of subcultural knowledge increases the likelihood of involvement in criminal behavior despite potential legal consequences for these actions. Thus, this is an important perspective to explain how the values and ideas espoused by members of a criminal subculture affect the behavior of its members.

Different types of subcultural frameworks have been developed and vary based on assumptions about the members' adherence to conventional norms and values. For example, Cohen used strain theory to explain the formation and persistence of gangs in the lower classes.[69] Males who could not achieve status through legitimate means in schools felt strained and rebelled against the middle-class values imposed on them. They established an alternative subculture allowing them to achieve status through the use of illegitimate means, including property and violent crime. Cohen's framework suggests that this subculture held behaviors and values in direct opposition to the middle-class values espoused by groups such as the school. As such, this perspective on subculture assumes an outright rejection of conventional norms and values.

Other frameworks do not require members of a subculture to perfectly adhere to its specific values. For instance, Wolfgang and Ferracuti[70] suggested a subculture of violence exists wherein individuals place great importance on their honor and use violence to defend it. According to their theory, this subculture does not require individuals to accept or approve of its norms for their behaviors to be influenced. Anyone may use lethal violence at any time, so all must be willing to respond to this threat in kind.

A similar argument has been made by Elijah Anderson in the book, *Code of the Street*.[71] He suggests a code exists in inner-city communities that lead individuals to conform to a pattern of violent behavior on the streets in response to slights against their honor. Regardless of one's involvement in street life and its values, many conform to this code of behavior to navigate through their communities. Thus, a contrasting perspective indicates that subcultures can influence behavior without requiring individuals to adhere to its values.

Hackers and Learning Theories

By rejecting the goals and opportunities of the dominant culture, the hacker subculture provides the context in which hackers situate their actions. It forms their ethics and laws distinct from those of the dominant culture. There is strong evidence of the presence of a social scene, slang, and value system that defines boundaries between hackers and others. For example, the act of hacking is illegal under most conditions, yet the skill and ability needed to perform a hack is highly valued among hackers.[72] In addition, many hackers acknowledge their activities are illegal, but legitimize and justify the actions using various rationales, such as that their actions improve computer security. Thus, hackers place emphasis and value on activities directly contradicting the larger culture.

In addition, hackers have adapted the English language to create a unique slang. There also appears to be a hacker "scene," composed of "inside jokes, real world meetings (cons) and hacker magazines ('zines)."[73] Understanding this "scene" is part of the enculturation process of hacker subculture, occurring through exchanges with other hackers either in person or online. Referencing these cultural elements permit individuals to measure their status as a hacker against others. Status can also be determined through a great deal of debate over what constitutes a "hacker" as well as motives for hacking, such as curiosity or revenge.[74] These debates create boundaries between hackers, as well as the general computer using public, based on knowledge, skill, and status.[75]

Research on the hacker subculture has found that there are three consistent ideas or values that guide hacker behavior: technology, secrecy, and mastery. One of the most recognized elements of hacker subculture is its relationship to technology. Both the hack and hacker could not exist without technology, and an intimate connection between the individual and technology facilitates the ability to hack.[76] To generate such a connection, hackers must develop "an easy, if not all-consuming, relationship" with computer and communications technology and a willingness to explore and apply it in new ways.[77]

The more closely an individual is connected to technology, the greater their ability to understand and perform hacks. Those who can perform "true hacks" have a deep comprehension of computers and programming, allowing them to identify and fix security flaws.[78] Conversely, "derivative hacks" involve the use of prewritten scripts or codes to access flaws without actually understanding how the technology works. Less-skilled hackers, especially those called script kiddies, are more likely to perform a "derivative hack." Hence, the hacker's relationship to technology can generate status: those who complete "true hacks" are revered and praised, and the "derivative hack" user is often made fun of or rejected by others.[79]

The importance of technology is also related to the significance of secrecy in hacker subculture. Secrecy is important for several reasons. First, it is a motive for hacking in that many hackers abhor keeping certain types of information private.[80] This fuels many attempts by hackers to remove barriers to certain kinds of information, such as government and technological data. Second, subcultural members place great emphasis on secrecy because hacking is an illegal act. Hacker activities are kept secret to avoid unwanted attention from various parts of the "establishment," including the criminal justice system.[81] Thus, anonymity is indispensable to the subculture and is the reason hackers create virtual identities online via a screen name or "handle."[82] This protects the hacker's actual identity while engaged in hacking.

However, there is also some ambivalence about secrecy in hacker subculture. Successful hacking creates a desire to brag and share accumulated hacking knowledge. This can help an individual gain status within the hacker community, but places them at risk for law enforcement detection.[83] Hackers tread a fine line between sharing information and keeping certain knowledge private. Those who can successfully navigate this line can also gain some status in the hacker community. Demonstrating a commitment to secrecy is a benchmark for how well one lives up to the image and nature of hacking. True hackers are capable of keeping secrets, creating an ideal for hackers to aspire to; thus, secrecy reinforces and maintains boundaries between hackers.[84]

Status is also tied to another important element of the culture: the idea of mastery. Mastery is a complex element that involves continual learning of new skills that individuals demonstrate to their peers.[85] For example, hackers taunt and challenge the ability of others while online. This frequently leads hackers to use their knowledge and skill to gain control over another individual's system, or take "root" in a system.[86]

Such a demonstration of mastery can increase a hacker's status, as can displays of knowledge of hacker subculture. When communicating with other hackers, especially through Web forums, individuals may refer to the history of hacking, use slang, or reference other important parts of the hacking scene.[87] These references appear to illustrate the intensity of individual connections to hacker subculture and their relative status. The agreed-upon values of the hacker community provide the social context for the hacking activities that violate the standards of the normative culture. The disjunction between the morals of the hacker subculture and the morals of normative society helps to define the activities of "criminal hackers."

Virus Writers and Learning Theories

Social process theories are probably best when used to explain the crimes committed by virus writers and those who propagate and spread viruses. The first empirical observation to take into account when examining the phenomenon of why people engage in virus writing is that there is no common profile of a "typical" virus writer. As discussed in Chapter 6, a common misperception is that virus writers are 13-year-old brainiacs that unleash their wrath on society for no apparent reason. In reality, a virus writer could be that kid or a 35-year-old computer programmer looking to increase his or her salary. This tends to limit the explanatory power of social structure theories, because virus writers can come from many walks of life and are typically wealthy enough to afford the computer machinery necessary to practice their trade. Further, not all virus writers are in it for the money or for the fame. The reasons why virus writers write and propagate viruses can be for money, fame, attention, competition, and simply for a perverse sense of fun.

What is undeniable in the development of a virus writer is that a certain level of technical competency is required. While it is true that virus creation tools exist that make it easier to write viruses, one does not become a virus writer overnight. As such, all virus writers must learn how to write and propagate viruses. The learning process that they go through is similar to any other learning process. The learning includes learning how to write the code necessary to create a virus, but as important is learning how to become a good virus writer. In the world of virus writers, competition and bravado play an important role in conditioning the person, as does learning the tools and tactics of the trade. Some writers do so to prove their computer programming capability. Anecdotal, yet unproven, stories of virus writers who have programmed a "quality" virus and found fame and fortune as the result of their prowess abound. Other virus writers achieve fame because their virus infects a large number of computers and makes it into the media spotlight.

However, prior to the fame and supposed fortune of the virus writer, the person goes through a learning and social conditioning process.

When the writer first enters the world of the virus writers, they are treated with disdain and as the newcomer that they are. If they enter chat rooms and exchange information and curiosity about virus writing, they are often ridiculed and subjected to a social conditioning process where they learn the practice through trial and error, and also learn how to be a better virus writer or face ridicule from their peers. Once they have established their reputation, they often engage in banter with other self-proclaimed virus writers. They learn to show their accomplishments and show others how successful their virus is "in the wild." Others receive financial rewards and eventually develop into for-profit virus writers. Still others enjoy the thrill of infecting other people's machines, hacking into secure systems via their Trojan horses, and enjoy reading about their exploits online and in the media.

Nonetheless, they all share a common learning experience in order to ply their trade. This learning experience is unique compared to other forms of criminal learning in that the significant peers that teach them will likely never see them face to face. Most of the learning takes place in chat rooms, on bulletin boards, and via distance learning. As social learning theory posits, the learning is reinforced both positively and negatively over its course, which serves to reinforce the technical competency of the virus writers. Positive reinforcement includes the thrill experienced by propagating the virus and infecting systems; it can also include notoriety and kudos received from their peer group—like graffiti writers, they also love to see their moniker appearing with their work—and, finally, there can be financial rewards. Negative reinforcements include receiving hostility from other virus writers (eventually ending up with an online competition to hack the other's system), receiving ridicule and disdain for their viruses and exploits online, and being sought out by law enforcement. If caught, they may discontinue their activity, but the other forms of negative reinforcement they receive may serve to make them want to become more proficient.

Social Control Theory

Social control theory seeks to answer the question, "Why *don't* individuals commit crime?" Social control theory assumes that people will violate the law. So why don't they? The answer to this question, according to social control theorists, lies in the strength of an individual's ties to conventional individuals and society. Those who have close ties with their families and noncriminal friends as well as those who possess high self-esteem are unlikely to commit criminal acts. These individuals are bonded to the larger society. Individuals who are not bonded to the larger social order are free from constraints to violate the law.

GOTTFREDSON AND HIRSCHI: SELF-CONTROL THEORY In a later control theory, Gottfredson and Hirschi argue that a person's tendency to commit crime can be found in their level of self-control.[88] Self-control involves a person's ability to control their own behavior. Basically, they proposed that individuals who commit crime have limited self-control. These people have a tendency to be impulsive, insensitive, and focused on immediate gratification.

What causes people to have limited self-control? Gottfredson and Hirschi argue that lack of self-control is caused by inadequate child rearing.[89] Self-control, according to Gottfredson and Hirschi, is instilled in people by age eight and is relatively constant thereafter. They suggested that parents must be willing to monitor their child's behavior, to recognize inappropriate behavior when it occurs, and to punish the inappropriate behavior.[90] If this occurs consistently, the child will develop a high level of self-control. Over time, the child will internalize the monitoring by the parents. If the parents are unwilling or unable to do this, then it is likely that their children will lack self-control. When this occurs, criminal activity is likely—however, not guaranteed.

Gottfredson and Hirschi also integrated elements of rational choice theory into the development of their theory. Individuals with low self-control must be presented with the opportunities to commit criminal acts in order for crime to occur. If an individual has low self-control but there is no criminal opportunity, then crime will not take place. On the other hand, if criminal opportunity presents itself to an individual with low self-control, then crime is likely to occur.

Recent cybercrime scholarship has found that individuals with low levels of self-control are more likely to view online pornography.[91] Additionally, researchers have found a significant relationship between low self-control and digital piracy in college student populations.[92] This evidence suggests that college students with low self-control cannot resist the temptation of pirating software and music that they are interested in due to the fact that they do not see the consequences of their behavior.

Preliminary research on self-control in the hacker community finds that this theory may have limited applicability. A study using a sample of active hackers at multiple computer security conferences and in a university setting found that both groups had high levels of self-control.[93] In addition, the active hackers had higher levels of self-control than those inside the university. This may be a reflection of the general traits required to become a skilled hacker, including a capacity to learn, diligence, and forethought as discussed in Chapter 4. In turn, their hacks may be more complex, utilizing persistent and unique attacks against specific targets. As a consequence, it may be that computer hackers have higher levels of self-control than both street and digital criminals.

TERRORISM AND POLITICAL THEORY

The term "terrorism" has been defined in a number of ways by a variety of scholars. For the most part, each definition has yielded a limited understanding of the actual phenomenon. This is particularly true when analyzing the current wave of international and technological situations in contemporary global affairs, such as those occurring in the Middle East and those involving digital crime and digital terrorism. In the popular mind, terrorism is viewed as the illegitimate and violent actions of specific groups that violate the authority of rightfully established political entities.[94] Terrorism, in general, always has a political agenda. This agenda may be motivated by various political ideologies, separatist ethnic movements, or radical religious philosophies, but always the purpose of achievement is a specific set of political objectives. Although vague, as to explaining who terrorists are, this definition does provide a conceptual framework concerning what terrorism is.[95] It can be reduced, simply to a choice among violent means—not a choice between violence and nonviolence, but a manifestation of violence against people to achieve a goal. By extension, terrorists often apply extreme, random acts of violence against the innocent (e.g., attacks on symbolic institutions such as schools, churches, and synagogues; bombings of common gathering places such as cafes, shopping malls, and office buildings; and the killing of individuals that represent legitimate governments such as soldiers, police officers, and political leaders), in an attempt to instill fear in the general population. Thus, terrorism is used as a methodology for political action. As Hoffman argues, terrorism is fundamentally and inherently "political." Terrorism is "ineluctably about power: the pursuit of power, the acquisition of power, and the use of power to achieve political change. Terrorism is thus violence—or, equally important, the threat of violence—used and directed in pursuit of, or in service of, a *political aim*."[96]

BOX 3.6
Time Bomb Attacks by an Insider

William Carl Shea, aged 39, was hired around August 2001 as a programmer and manager for Bay Area Credit Services Inc., in San Jose, California. Shea's position gave him administrative access to and familiarity with the company's computer systems, including the database server. He was notified of poor job performance in 2002 and was given an improvement plan in 2003. He was fired on January 17, 2003, when he failed to show up at work. Around this period, a malicious code "time bomb" was placed on the company network that was set to delete and change data at the end of the month. This malicious software caused financial records to be altered and removed and disrupted the computer networks within the company, affecting more than 50,000 debtor accounts. Shea was sentenced to 12 months and 1 day in prison, 6 months of home confinement with electronic monitoring, and three years of supervised release for his jury conviction.

Which theory do you think applies best to this case?

Source: http://www.usdoj.gov/criminal/cybercrime/shea Sent.htm

The psychological, economic, strategic, and political consequences of violence associated with terrorism is often much more prominent than the attack itself. Short-term effects of terrorism involve an immediate psychological effect on society, but are relatively benign compared to the long-term impact, which includes a widespread realization of vulnerability. In fact, the consequences of terrorism tend to have a higher value as time goes on.[97] For instance, the economic impact of the September 11 attack on the World Trade Center Building (2001) was first estimated at a real cost of just over $10 billion. However, looking at the much more involved secondary costs—such as loss of service, impact on the stock market, declining investor sentiment, economic failure of the airline industry, rebuilding of structures, and loss in tourism dollars to the world and, specifically, New York—the estimated cost exceeds $2 trillion.[98] Essentially, the real impact of terrorist events can be measured in the creation of an atmosphere of chaos, fear, and panic in the target population.

No one understood this phenomenon better than Karl Marx. His early work (in 1887) argued that political change could not be achieved without conflict.[99] Indeed, he believed that epochs of history changed as groups of people bound by loss of status and class revolted against ruling elites. In Marxist thought, successful revolutionary strategy began with a core group of leading individuals dedicated to the cause. This group, the vanguard, represented the frontlines of violent activity. It was the express purpose of the vanguard to violently confront private property owners and wealthy elites with the opposite elements that maintained their ruling status—replace trust, order, and security with chaos, fear, and panic. To the dedicated Marxist, the vanguard represented contemporary terrorist groups. Interestingly, a century and a half later, Franz Fanon argued that no government would willingly give up power and wealth; therefore, this power and wealth had to be taken violently. Fanon suggested that the international act of colonization was in itself an act of violence and thus had to be confronted with violence.[100] Accordingly, governments under attack must respond with stricter measures against the general public (the masses). Since there is no clearly identifiable enemy, governments must resort to more harsh and brutal treatment of the indigenous population in order to ferret out the hardcore vanguard members. Constitutional rights become suspended, unwarranted searches become commonplace, torture replaces interrogation, and innocence gives way to presumption of guilt. At the point that rule of law erodes and the masses react against the ruling government, revolution begins, spurring yet another epoch in human history. To Marx, contemporary terrorists represent the vanguard.[101]

The acts of terrorism aimed at critical information infrastructure (what we call cyberterrorism or digital terrorism) are simply new tactics to accomplish the same end. The modern and complex societies of today are built on information exchange, global processing, and reliance on computerization and telecommunication. What were supposed to be the hallmarks of advanced societies to increase democratic and free thought have now become huge vulnerabilities. Government and business depend on these critically vital systems, making them prize targets for individuals aimed at destroying normalcy. To compound the problem, these systems have been built by information elites that control them. Government and society have been more than happy to place the burden of development and maintenance of computer systems, with a few individuals having narrow educational fields and a keen understanding of complex information systems. Indeed, there has been safety in the fact that few of the masses actually understood much of the critical infrastructure on which our society depended upon for vital existence. All of that changed, however, as the interconnectivity of systems became commonplace through the marvels of the World Wide Web and the Internet. Heretofore closed and secured systems became vulnerable to outside attack, relatively unsophisticated juvenile hackers could close down business enterprise with seeming ease, and the "experts" were mystified in ways to prevent such attacks. Digital terrorism has become a reality as sophisticated terrorists understand new tactics that can render airplanes helpless to navigate, force railroads and commuter trains to stop, make electric and water plants idle, and stop local and global communication. In the past, having a tactic that could do so much damage was relatively closed to terrorist groups. Today, they provide some of the most frightful and devastating scenarios relating not only to specific violent actions but also to the extreme vulnerability of our country and our world. Terrorism that attacks our critical information infrastructure may not only attack our country but also the world in one massive strike. Retrospectively, Karl Marx may well have been correct. It will be through force that revolution is sparked and accomplished; it is specific acts of violence (and terrorism) that will erode safety, security, and peace and substitute chaos, fear, and panic.[102]

Summary

In this chapter, the major criminological theories that can or have been used to explain digital crime have been presented. Several different areas of criminological thought can be used to explain digital crime. First, it can be argued that some computer criminals commit their offenses due to rational choice and a lack of fear of apprehension. Second, it can be argued that restricted moral development and the presentation of a personality disorder may lead a person to commit digital crime. Third, strain and subculture theories can be applied to digital crime. Fourth, learning and social control theories can explain some types of digital crime as well. Fifth, political theory can be used to explain acts of terrorism. Although little theoretical development has occurred in the area of digital crime, several current criminological theories have been applied with some success to this phenomenon, including piracy, hacking, cyberstalking, and harassment.

Review Questions

1. According to choice theory, why do individuals commit digital crime?
2. What are the major assumptions of deterrence theory?
3. Which psychological theories can be applied to digital crime?
4. What are the five modes of adaptation? Which is most likely to lead to the commission of digital crime?
5. What are the nine propositions presented by Sutherland?
6. What are the four elements of Akers' social learning theory?
7. How does self-control affect digital crime?

Endnotes

1. SIEGEL, LARRY J. (1992). *Criminology: Theories, Patterns, and Typologies,* 4th ed. St. Paul, MN: West.
2. MARTINSON, ROBERT. (1974). "What Works? Questions and Answers About Prison Reform." *The Public Interest* 35: 22–54.
3. COHEN, LAWRENCE, and FELSON, MARCUS. (1979). "Social Change and Crime Rate Trends: A Routine Activities Approach." *American Sociological Review* 44: 588–608.
4. *Ibid.*
5. *Ibid.*
6. *Ibid.*
7. SAMPSON, ROBERT J., and LAURITSEN, JANET L. (1990). "Deviant Lifestyles, Proximity to Crime, and the Offender-Victim Link in Personal Violence." *Journal of Research in Crime and Delinquency* 27: 110–139.
8. LAURITSEN, JANET L., LAUB, JOHN H., and SAMPSON, ROBERT J. (1992). "Conventional and Delinquent Activities: Implications for the Prevention of Violent Victimization Among Adolescents." *Violence and Victims* 7: 91–108; ZHANG, LENING, WELTE, JOHN W., and WIECXOREK, WILLIAM F. (2001). "Deviant Lifestyle and Crime Victimization." *Journal of Criminal Justice* 29: 133–143.
9. MELL, P., KENT, K., and NUSBAUM, J. (2005). *Guide to Malware Incident Prevention and Handling: Recommendations of the National Institute of Standards and Technology.* Washington, DC: National Institute of Standards and Technology.
10. HOLT, T.J., and BOSSLER, A.M. (2009). "Examining the Applicability of Lifestyle-Routine Activities Theory for Cybercrime Victimization." *Deviant Behavior* 30(1): 1–25.
11. BOSSLER, A.M., and Holt, T.J. (2008). "Examining the Utility of Routine Activities Theory for Cybercrime." Paper presented at the American Society of Criminology meetings, Atlanta, GA.
12. KADISH, SANFORD H., and PAULSEN, MONRAD G. (1969). *Criminal Law and Its Processes.* Boston, MA: Little, Brown, p. 85.
13. WALKER, SAMUEL. (1998). *Sense and Nonsense About Crime and Drugs: A Policy Guide,* 4th ed. Belmont, CA: West/Wadsworth.
14. *Ibid.*
15. *Ibid.*
16. PATERNOSTER, RAYMOND. (1987). "The Deterrent Effect of Perceived and Severity of Punishment: A Review of the Evidence and Issues." *Justice Quarterly* 42: 173–217.
17. GREEN, DONALD. (1989). "Measures of Illegal Behavior in Individual-Level Deterrence Research." *Journal of Research in Crime and Delinquency* 26: 253–275.
18. HOLLINGER, RICHARD C. (1992). "Crime by Computer: Correlates of Software Piracy and Unauthorized Account Access." *Security Journal* 2(1): 2–12; SKINNER, WILLIAM F., and FREAM, ANNE M. (1997). "A Social Learning Theory Analysis of Computer Crime Among College Students." *Journal of Research in Crime and Delinquency* 34(4): 495–518.
19. *Ibid.*
20. *Ibid.*
21. KOHLBERG, LAWRENCE. (1969). *Stages in the Development of Moral Thought and Action.* New York: Holt, Rinehart and Winston.
22. HENGGELER, SCOTT. (1989). *Delinquency in Adolescence.* Newbury Park, CA: Sage.

23. GLUECK, SHELDON, and GLUECK, ELEANOR. (1950). *Unraveling Juvenile Delinquency.* New York: Commonwealth Fund.

24. America Psychiatric Association (2000). *Diagnostic and Statistical Manual of Mental Disorders,* DSM-IV-TR, 4th ed. New York: American Psychiatric Publishing, p. 645.

25. *Ibid.*

26. MERTON, ROBERT K. (1968). *Social Theory and Social Structure.* Glencoe, IL: The Free Press.

27. *Ibid.*

28. AGNEW, ROBERT. "Foundation for a General Strain Theory of Crime and Delinquency." *Criminology* 30: 47–87.

29. *Ibid.*

30. HAHN, E. (2009). "Girls Post Online Cartoon on How to Kill Classmate." *MSNBC.* Retrieved June 1, 2009 from http://www.msnbc.msn.com/id/30881980/

31. CATHCART, R. (2008). "MySpace Is Said to Draw Subpoena in Hoax Case." *New York Times.*

32. SUTHERLAND, EDWIN H., and CRESSEY, DONALD R. (1978). *Criminology,* 10th ed. Philadelphia, PA: J.B. Lippincott Co., pp. 77–83.

33. *Ibid.*

34. *Ibid.*

35. *Ibid.*

36. *Ibid.*

37. *Ibid.*

38. *Ibid.*

39. *Ibid.*

40. *Ibid.*

41. *Ibid.*

42. *Ibid.*

43. AKERS, RONALD L. (1998). *Social Learning and Social Structure: A General Theory of Crime and Deviance.* Boston, MA: Northeastern University Press.

44. AKERS, RONALD L. (2001). "Social Learning Theory." In RAYMOND PATTERNOSTER and RONET BACHMAN (eds.), *Explaining Criminals and Crime: Essays in Contemporary Criminological Theory.* Los Angeles, CA: Roxbury.

45. AKERS, RONALD L., and JENSEN, GARY F. (2006). "The Empirical Status of Social Learning Theory of Crime and Deviance: The Past, Present, and Future." In FRANCIS T. CULLEN, JOHN PAUL WRIGHT, and KRISTIE R. BLEVINS (eds.), *Taking Stock: The Status of Criminological Theory.* New Brunswick, NJ: Transaction Publishers.

46. *Ibid.,* p. 62.

47. *Ibid.*

48. *Ibid.*

49. *Ibid.*

50. *Ibid.*

51. *Ibid.*

52. HIGGINS, GEORGE E. (2005). "Can Low Self-Control Help with the Understanding of the Software Piracy Problem?" *Deviant Behavior* 26(1): 1–24; HIGGINS, GEORGE E. (2006). "Gender Differences in Software Piracy: The Mediating Roles of Self-Control Theory and Social Learning Theory." *Journal of Economic Crime Management* 4(1): 1–30; HIGGINS, GEORGE E., FELL, BRIAN D., and ABBY L. WILSON. (2006). "Digital Piracy: Assessing the Contributions of an Integrated Self-Control Theory and Social Learning Theory Using Structural Equation Modeling." *Criminal Justice Studies* 19(1): 3–22; HIGGINS, GEORGE E., FELL, BRIAN D., and WILSON, ABBY L. (2007). "Low Self-Control and Social Learning in Understanding Students' Intentions to Pirate Movies in the United States." *Social Science Computer Review* 25(3): 339–357; HIGGINS, GEORGE E., and DAVID A. MAKIN. (2004a). "Self-Control, Deviant Peers, and Software Piracy." *Psychological Reports* 95: 921–931; HIGGINS, GEORGE E., and MAKIN, DAVID A. (2004b). "Does Social Learning Theory Condition the Effects of Low Self-Control on College Students' Software Piracy?" *Journal of Economic Crime Management* 2(2): 1–22; HIGGINS, GEORGE E., and WILSON, ABBY L. (2006). "Low Self-Control, Moral Beliefs, and Social Learning Theory in University Students' Intentions to Pirate Software." *Security Journal* 19: 75–92; HIGGINS and WILSON, "Low Self-Control and Social Learning in Understanding Students' Intentions to Pirate Movies in the United States."

53. *Ibid.,* p. 18.

54. *Ibid.*

55. *Ibid.*

56. SYKES, GRESHAM M., and MATZA, DAVID. (1957). "Techniques of Neutralization: A Theory of Delinquency." *American Sociological Review* 22: 664–670.

57. *Ibid.*

58. *Ibid.*

59. *Ibid.*

60. *Ibid.*

61. *Ibid.*

62. *Ibid.*

63. *Ibid.*, p. 71.

64. For example, see INGRAM, J.R., and HINDUJA, S. (2008). "Neutralizing Music Piracy: An Empirical Examination." *Deviant Behavior* 29: 334–366.

65. *Ibid.*

66. *Ibid.*

67. MAURER, D.W. (1974). *The American Confidence Man.* Springfield, IL: Thomas.

68. SIMMONS, J.L. (1985). "The Nature of Deviant Subcultures." In E. RUBINGTON and M.S. WEINBERG (eds.), *Deviance: The Interactionist Perspective.* New York: Macmillan.

69. COHEN, A.K. (1955). *Delinquent Boys: The Culture of the Gang.* Glencoe, IL: Free Press.

70. WOLFGANG, M.E., and FERRACUTI, F. (1967). *The Subculture of Violence: Towards an Integrated Theory in Criminology.* London: Tavistock Publications.

71. ANDERSON, E. (1999). *Code of the Street.* Philadephia, PA: W. W. Norton.

72. THOMAS, D. (2002). *Hacker Culture.* Minneapolis, MN: University of Minnesota Press; HOLT, T.J. (2007). "Subcultural Evolution? Examining the Influence of On- and Off-Line Experiences on Deviant Subcultures." *Deviant Behavior* 28(2): 171–198.

73. LOPER, D.K. (2000). "The Criminology of Computer Hackers: A Qualitative and Quantitative Qnalysis." (Doctoral Dissertation, Michigan State University, 2000) *Dissertation Abstracts International* 61-08, Section: A, p. 3362.

74. JORDAN, T., and TAYLOR, P. (1998). A Sociology of Hackers. *The Sociological Review* 46(4): 757–780.

75. HOLT, "Subcultural Evolution?"

76. *Ibid.*

77. *Ibid.*, p. 93.

78. *Ibid.*, p. 91.

79. *Ibid.*

80. *Ibid.*, p. 94.

81. *Ibid.*, p. 93.

82. *Ibid.*

83. *Ibid.*, p. 94.

84. *Ibid.*, p. 91.

85. *Ibid.*, p. 94.

86. *Ibid.*, p. 91.

87. *Ibid.*, p. 92.

88. GOTTFREDSON, MICHAEL, and HIRSCHI, TRAVIS. (1990). *A General Theory of Crime.* Stanford, CA: Stanford University Press.

89. *Ibid.*

90. *Ibid.*

91. BUZZELL, B., FOSS, D., and MIDDLETON, Z. (2006). "Explaining Use of Online Pornography: A Test of Self-Control Theory and Opportunities for Deviance." *Journal of Criminal Justice and Popular Culture* 13: 96–116.

92. HIGGINS, "Can Low Self-Control Help with the Understanding of the Software Piracy Problem?"; HIGGINS, FELL, and WILSON, "Digital Piracy"; HIGGINS and MAKIN "Self-Control, Deviant Peers, and Software Piracy."

93. HOLT, T.J., and KILGER, M. (2008). "Techcrafters and Makecrafters: A Comparison of Two Populations of Hackers." Information Security Threats Data Collection and Sharing 2008. WISTDCS '08.

94. TAYLOR, ROBERT W., and VANDEN, HARRY E. (September 1982). "Defining Terrorism in El Salvador: La Matanza." *The Annals of the American Academy of Political and Social Sciences* 463: 1.

95. See SCHULZ, RICHARD. (Spring/Summer 1978). "Conceptualizing Political Terrorism: A Typology." *Journal of International Affairs* 4: 8; and HOFFMAN, BRUCE. (1998). *Inside Terrorism.* New York: Columbia University Press.

96. HOFFMAN, *Inside Terrorism*, p. 2.

97. See CRENSHAW, MARTHA. (1998). "The Logic of Terrorism: Terrorist Behavior as a Product of Strategic Choice." In WALTER REICH (ed.), *Origins of Terrorism: Psychologies, Theologies, and States of Mind.* Princeton, NJ: The Woodrow Wilson International Center for Scholars.

98. Institute for the Analysis of Global Security-IAGS, 2004.

99. MARX, KARL. (1887). *Das Capital.* Moscow: Progress Publishers.

100. See FANON, FRANZ. (1963). *The Wretched of the Earth.* New York: Grove Press; and FANON, FRANZ. (1965). *A Dying Colonialism.* New York: Grove Press.

101. COHEN-AMAGOR, RAPHEL. (Summer 1991). "Foundations of Violence, Terror and War in the Writings of Marx, Engels, and Lenin." *Terrorism and Political Violence* 1(2): 1–24.

102. MARX, KARL. From his speech at Amsterdam in 1872.

CHAPTER 4

Digital Criminals and Hackers

CHAPTER OBJECTIVES

After completing this chapter, you should be able to

- Distinguish between computer crime, criminal hacking, and noncriminal hacking.
- Explain why hackers think that the term "hacker" does not refer to criminals.
- Identify hype and exaggeration of hacking incidents found in the media.
- Recognize the role media hype plays in influencing young hackers.
- Classify hackers into broad categories based on activities and expression of ideas in online communication or statements made in person.
- Describe the role of technology that drives the hacker subculture.
- Explain how subcultural status depends on an understanding of technology achieved by the hacker and his or her knowledge of the ethics and values held by hackers.
- Predict hacker actions based on their type.
- Understand how the perceptions of hacking have changed based on shifts in hacker activity over time.

INTRODUCTION: WHAT IS A HACKER?

At this point in most texts, a reader might expect to see a quick definition of a hacker. In some sense, this entire chapter is the definition of "hacker." Originally, the word "hacker" referred to an unorthodox problem solver and master programmer; in fact, these original hackers made the machines and the programs that are vital to modern society.[1] Recognizing this fact, some media sources have championed terms like "computer cracker" and "black hat" to describe criminal hackers. Some sources even directly equate computer criminals and hackers. The consensus of computer crime experts is that most computer criminals are insiders to the victim organization, not hackers seeking to gain entry.[2] One thing that is clear is that there is no universal agreement as to the meaning of the word "hacker" or "computer criminal." However, there is a *popular* consensus that hackers are bad people who do bad things.[3]

This chapter presents a view of hackers that is intended to assist investigators and law enforcement officer in understanding the way hackers think. Many descriptions of motive and interpretation of hacker actions come directly from hackers themselves. At no time should this chapter be read to condone breaking the law. Although sympathetic to a hacker's sensibilities, it is not sympathetic to harm caused intentionally or through negligence. Hackers have established their own set of values; these values often conflict with the laws and values of the greater society. Rather than simply reaffirm our distaste for the illegal actions of some hackers, this chapter presents the hacker's understanding of these actions in an attempt to help investigators predict, effectively investigate, and appropriately respond to the intention of the criminal, not media-induced hysteria or uninformed prejudice.

Who and What Is a Hacker?

Hackers break into government and military systems around the world, from the U.S. Department of Defense to NORAD, the North American Aerospace Defense Command.[4] Hackers also electronically steal millions of dollars from major banks.[5] It must be noted, however, that not all hackers engage in illegal activity. Basic First Amendment activities like communication and association are probably the most frequent online activities of hackers.[6] Similarly, not all illegal online activities are hacking. Pedophilia and child pornography draw as much disgust from most hackers as they do from law enforcement. Hackers and the law enforcement community come into conflict over activities like system intrusions and subsequent illegal acts.

When discussing hackers, it is critical to note this distinction and recognize the fact that hacking can be a legitimate and perfectly legal action. In fact, one of the best definitions for a hacker identifies this issue, and thus considers him or her to be "an individual with a profound interest in computers and technology that has used this knowledge to access computer systems with or without authorization from the system owners."[7] Authorization is critical because individuals who hack without it are committing a crime. Those with permission, however, are not technically breaking the law.

The hacker population represents individuals with a broad spectrum of personal motivations, skills, and activities.[8] For example, one of the more inclusive definitions from outside the hacking world is from the Jargon File. This text document, which defines and translates hacker slang, provides eight different definitions for a hacker, including those who "enjoy exploring the details of programmable systems and how to stretch their capabilities, as opposed to most users, who prefer to learn only the minimum necessary" as well as those who are a "malicious meddler who tries to discover sensitive information by poking around."[9] The emphasis on gaining unauthorized access to computer systems is key to the notion of hackers that has been spread in the popular media over the last decade. However, researchers suggest there is no real consensus as to what constitutes a hacker.[10]

This may be due in part to the range of activities that hackers engage in, and the legality of their actions depends on authorization from the system owners. For example, some hackers engage in phone phreaking, which involves the manipulation, theft, or use of telephone networks for illegal activities. While some have suggested this behavior constitutes a separate category of computer crime, hackers often break into telephone systems to assist in accomplishing hacks. This was a common practice in the 1980s when telephone systems operated through a variety of switching systems. However, most telephone equipment developed in the last ten years is now indistinguishable from computer networks. Phreakers now operate within these environments,

---

BOX 4.1

Phone Phreaks Bring Technology and Attitude to Hacking

═══

- *Telephone technologies (boxes).* Phone phreaks created devices that produced effects on the phone system. The blue box was used to produce a 2,600-Hz tone, gaining access to the toll network for the placement of calls without charge. The red box simulates the noise of a quarter, nickel, or dime being dropped into a pay phone, allowing free pay phone calls. Other boxes exist or may simply be part of phreak lore. *Note:* These devices no longer work on the North American phone system, but they did during the days of the bedroom hacker.

- *Counterculture of the 1960s and 1970s.* There was an affinity for political subversives and Vietnam War protestors with the phone phreaks. Many freaks were members of the youth culture movements of this period. In fact, one famous phreak, Cheshire Catalyst, edited the Technical Assistance Program (TAP) newsletter founded by Abbie Hoffman.[11]

- *Phone company lore.* Phone phreaks did not restrict themselves to the technology of the Phone Company (there was only one back then[12]). This interest was the beginning of social engineering (see below).

- *Paranoia.* Years of hiding from Bell System security and listening in on phone conversations taught phreaks that privacy was an illusion on the phone system. "Ma" Bell heard everything.

- *"ph"onetic spelling.* Phone phreaks regularly replace the letter "f" with "ph." Phonetic spelling may be the basis of "'leet speek," discussed later in this chapter.

---

using hacking techniques and tools. Thus, the practice of phreaking has changed but is still an important interest in the hacker community.[13]

The same can be said for software cracking, which involves overcoming copy protection devices in electronic media to copy and distribute them.[14] In the 1980s, such materials were called warez or cracks, and the individuals who created the materials were called warez d00dz (pronounced: wârz dōōdz). Initially, warez d00dz actively cracked software and games to quickly and efficiently trade large volumes of what were expensive materials. As computer technology changed, Internet connectivity became extremely common, and digital materials like CDs and laser disks developed, the warez d00dz began to become actively involved in the creation of pirated movies, music, and television. Thus, the contemporary warez scene has expanded to include the following:

- Music and movies
- MP3s (volume counts)
- Digitally compressed movies before they are actually released (zero-day release)
- Cable and satellite descrambling
- DVD decoding
- Peer-to-peer networking
- Console games

However, most of the warez scene does not pursue technology like other forms of hackers. They focus heavily on tools and materials rather than discovering new problems and weaknesses. Warez groups do intersect with the hacker community today, however, as they support the efforts of hackers through the creation of peer-to-peer networking technology that can be used to share files. In particular, pirated materials like Gnutella and programs like BitTorrent allow for file sharing over distributed computers across the Internet.[15] Thus hackers are responsible for the creation, distribution, and facilitation of modern piracy.

Likewise, writing or programming malware software such as viruses and Trojan horse programs is a growing computer crime problem and is directly tied to hackers. These tools can be used to steal money and data, automate attacks, and control systems remotely. The creation of malicious software can be challenging and requires a good deal of skill to successfully develop.[16] Only a small portion of the hacker community can create these tools, though they are used by a wide range of hackers regardless of their level of skill. The problem of malicious software is detailed in Chapter 6 in some detail, giving context to this issue.

Hackers also engage in a form of fraud they refer to as "social engineering." This practice was introduced by phone phreaks; the technique is based on the use of the telephone. The idea is to acquire sensitive information from the human running the machine rather than using advanced computer skills to beat the electronic security. Employees reveal passwords, internal information, and even execute the commands for the hacker. Social engineering is essentially a confidence scam. Additionally, hackers will sometimes engage in dumpster diving, or trashing, as a direct way to obtain information. A person enters a dumpster and looks for useful information, which can include technical manuals, notes, technical bulletins, and a plethora of information useful to a phone phreak. Aside from the direct access to phone technology from castoff manuals, even small scraps of office minutia were highly prized (names, schedules, internal information). Such information could be used to further social engineering.

THE MEDIA'S POINT OF VIEW: THE DANGER OF HACKERS   Since the first public awareness of hackers, a deluge of lurid news stories has blurred the line between hacker and computer criminal. In the 1980s, hackers took control of computer systems and left taunting messages to legitimate users. Hackers became the focus of fear for a society struggling to come to grips with the nascent information age. The previous generation of hackers largely ignored the upstarts but resented the media's use of the word hacker applied to electronic trespassers and vandals. "It was understandable that the journalists covering these stories would refer to the young perps as hackers—after all, that's what the kids called *themselves*."[17] This has continued through today, as the media often focuses on malicious attacks against computer networks and government resources.

BOX 4.2
Social Engineering Tactics

Different tactics are used by social engineers. If one technique fails, it is often possible simply to call back and get a fresh start with a new representative from the company and use any information gained from the failed attempt.

> *Camaraderie:* "Hey, this is Joe out here on a pole. I forgot my order sheet. Can you look up the service on this pair? If I have to drive back to the shop, I'll be behind all day."

> *Bluster:* "This is Supervisor Wilson. I need to reset service flags on this account now . . . Of course I can't do it myself! I'm up a pole trying to fix what your technicians did to this setup."

> *Technical detail:* "Hello, who am I speaking to? . . . Okay Roger, this is Bill at the Tulsa switch. You have a problem with trunk 6. It's okay, we haven't lost calls yet. Go to frame 009 and count up 16 and over 10. That's the bugger as near as we can tell . . . Oh—it has a little pen-shaped device on it? That means that it is being monitored. Let's route around it by switching the pair attached. Here's what you do . . . "

There is also a tendency in the media toward publishing the lurid or frightening aspects of crimes, including hacker crimes.[18] When citing worst-case scenarios for hacking or network intrusion, the alteration of medical records always comes up. In a review of "shockers," author Jonathan Littman reported that a Berkeley researcher discovered a medical facility in the San Francisco Bay Area with open telephone lines to medical records. An examination of medical records will show a great deal of personal information, but beyond the threat to privacy, alteration of those records by a single character can be fatal (in the case of blood type). It is easy to understand why the alteration of medical data has received such attention. The problem is that there has never been a recorded instance of a hacker corrupting medical records and killing a person. The lurid nature of the story and the implied threat to readers changes the threat of hackers from a remote curiosity to an immediate threat, and therefore sells. Unfortunately, aspiring hackers often become acquainted with media portrayals of hacking before they begin to interact with actual hackers.[19]

LAW ENFORCEMENT'S POINT OF VIEW: ILLEGAL ACTIONS AND DAMAGE   Although the fine points of labeling hacker activities will be covered in more depth later in the chapter, for now, general descriptions will suffice. Hackers explore computers. When the computer belongs to the hacker or when the hacker has legitimate access to the computer, there is no crime. When the hacker does not have permission to use the computer or network, the action is called system intrusion. Federal statute makes it a crime to knowingly use false credentials or access devices (which include passwords). Virtually any system intrusion requires that use of such a device.[20] Further, federal statute also makes it a crime to illegally access or damage a "protected" computer.[21] In this case, illegally accessing a computer connected to the Internet is a federal crime. During the process of an intrusion, data may be intentionally or unintentionally altered. Numerous other crimes may be committed, depending on the effects of such data alteration.[22] Worst-case scenarios include damage to financial networks (carrying billions of dollars each day); alteration, deletion, or exposure of health records; and compromise of safety-related systems. The potential for serious economic harm or catastrophic loss of life is very real in computer intrusion when data are altered.

The primary difference between simple network intrusion and data alteration is the intent of the intruder. By reading or "browsing" through confidential files, the intruder actually creates a copy of the file. Thus, mere browsing may be theft, but it does not deprive the owner of the data or the use of the data. To hackers, this makes the distinction between data alteration and intrusion more meaningful. It may be impossible for an investigator to determine if data have been altered. While criminally altered data may be used for fraud, like manipulating stock prices, or simply to deny the expression of the owner's idea, as with Web page defacements, the simple intruder may not cause actual harm. The problem for law enforcement is that it is often hard to determine the intent of an intruder. Substantial effort must be invested in assuring that data have not been altered or that no malicious intent is present. Law enforcement officers and investigators know that malicious intent is not always necessary for a crime to occur. Sometimes simple negligence or innocent mistakes can cause actual harm. Fundamentally, the law does not recognize a hacker's right to explore the systems, confidential data, and computer resources of others. This basic difference in perceptions makes understanding and predicting hacker actions difficult for law enforcement.

THE HACKER'S POINT OF VIEW: PROSOCIAL HACKING   The concept of a hacker subculture was introduced in Chapter 3. Essentially a subculture is a group of individuals within a larger culture. These individuals develop different attitudes and sometimes appearances from the dominant culture. Sometimes members of "deviant" communities define their activities as beneficial or "prosocial."[23] The hacker subculture is a group of like-minded individuals who share a set of values defined in the hacker ethic. It exists through real-world communication but also through common pursuits and common styles in virtual interactions.[24] The subculture's definitions of prosocial hacking define it and differentiate its activities from computer crime. For example, hackers report learning experiences, including creative problem solving and educating others about security vulnerabilities.[25] Hackers understand the crime as a positive action under the "higher" goals supported by the subculture.

DEFINING HACKERS

Although it borders on political correctness for crooks, there is some actual value to understanding the distinctions of a name drawn in the hacker community.[26] Perhaps most important, hackers themselves sometimes use these terms to draw distinctions based on fine points of motivation and action that can be valuable to an investigation. Such information may allow an investigator to include or exclude a suspect from an investigation. There are certain actions that a hacker simply would not perform. For example, a malicious attack that serves only to back up an extortion threat would be very unhackerlike. Other hackers would probably be more cooperative in the investigation of such an incident. On the other hand, an attack that demonstrated technical skill in a novel way and embarrassed law enforcement or corporate interests would create solidarity among hackers and great status for the perpetrator.

Computer Criminals Vs. Hackers

Although a violation of the law is still a crime, juries may be more sympathetic to the motive of exploration versus personal profit. It is also hard to prosecute a "pure" hacker under federal statutes because the sentencing guidelines are driven by financial damages. These facts alone justify recognizing a distinction; this does not mean excusing an illegal action. It simply means recognizing a fundamentally different reality for investigation and prosecution.

There is little said in mainstream analyses that distinguish hackers from computer criminals.[27] In fact, some well-respected computer crime fighters flatly deny that there is a distinction.[28] Others acknowledge the illegality of the actions, but point to a radically different set of motivations.[29] However, in the underground hacker media, the distinction is a subject of primary importance.[30] Emanuel Goldstein, editor of *2600: The Hacker Quarterly*, has addressed the distinction between hackers and computer criminals in three ways. First, he minimized the criminal damage caused by hacking, implying that very little actual harm is caused. Second, he defended the criminal actions of hackers based on their motives and adherence to hacker subcultural values, which were not viewed as criminal by him. Third, he disavowed hackers who commit crimes that violate hacker values, such as crimes of financial gain.[31] Thus, it appears that at least some elements of the hacker subculture do not condone what they define as computer crime.

The majority of hacker online actions are perfectly legal; it is hard to imagine committing a crime with every keystroke. Basic activities like communication and information sharing as well as illegal activities all fall within the range of hacker behavior. All of these behaviors can be called hacking. The distinction between hackers who commit crimes and other computer criminals rests upon the attitudes with which a hacker approaches the activity. For various reasons, the hacker subculture accepts actions that violate law. These actions may be called criminal hacking. However, some actions are not accepted by the subculture. These actions and criminal hacking behaviors may be called computer crime. The point of confusion lies in the fact that criminal

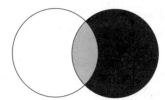

Hacking   Criminal Hacking   Computer Crime

FIGURE 4.1 The relationship between hacking, criminal hacking, and computer crime.

hacking is considered to be computer crime by law enforcement, but perfectly acceptable hacking by the hacker subculture. Figure 4.1 shows the overlap of these concepts.

Definitions of computer crime that equate all hacking with criminal behavior are both offensive to hackers and inaccurate. Similarly, definitions that deny that any meaningful criminal action is committed by hackers are absurd to law enforcement and also inaccurate. This Venn diagram depicts a subset of hacker behavior that is illegal but condoned by the hacker subculture (labeled criminal hacking). The reality of computer crime and obscurity of perpetrator motives makes this abstract system of defining hackers and computer criminals unworkable in the field. As a consequence, less clear-cut labels are often applied.[32]

Crackers

A cracker is a malicious hacker. There is no final authority on who determines when or how a hacker becomes a cracker. There is no clear way to cross the line back to hacker, either.

In response to a computer incident, John Gilmore, cofounder of the Electronic Frontier Foundation, said:

> As usual, the computer underground is doing a service to the country by making it clear just how shallow the government's understanding of computer security is. They are quite curiously refraining from damaging anything in their intrusions but the egos of the bureaucracies involved. As usual, the first response of the Feds is to threaten dire punishment for the messengers. But they are being prodded into actually attempting to keep serious attackers out, a novel idea somewhat overdue for consideration.[33]

Gilmore's recognition of the possible benefit of even vandalous intrusion echoes the hacker community's divergent values. There is no room for this view in the generally accepted concept of property rights, but the hacker community has a different understanding of their actions. Most hackers claim to benefit the systems they intrude upon because they do not destroy data and alert system administrators to security flaws.

Script Kiddies

Script kiddies are often described as a scourge or pestilence on the Internet. A well-administered system with good security policies has little to fear from most script kiddies, but even such a system is vulnerable to a distributed denial-of-service (DoS) attack launched from a point-and-click program. Distributed DoS attacks use unsuspecting, zombie computers to attack a victim. Persons with inoffensive and frankly uninteresting information on their Web sites may become unwitting accomplices in the script kiddies' attack. Unsecured, home computer systems with cable modems provide easy targets for script kiddies. When equipped with a software program called a client or zombie, the system becomes a weapon to be used against more secure sites.[34]

Script kiddies seem to be primarily concerned with bragging and attacking each other or anyone else who draws their wrath. The attacks are often simple exploits of well-known vulnerabilities, but can disrupt Internet Relay Chat (IRC) channels. Chat rooms are often raided by script kiddies who provoke verbal attacks (a process known as trolling) and retaliate by "punting" the user out of the chat room. Web page hacking is also a favorite activity of script kiddies and script kiddie groups. The altered Web pages often contain little more than rants, nonsense, or shoutz to friends and insults to enemies and law enforcement.[35]

The term *script kiddie* comes from their use of premade tools or scripts. Script kiddies do not have enough skill to write their own programs or explore new exploits for themselves. They download an attack program and attempt to get it to run. Many such programs exploit long-known vulnerabilities, but some system administrators do not update their software. Internet hackers dismiss the actions of script kiddies as unskilled.[36]

White Hat Vs. Black Hat

The current fashion for describing hackers is to use a new set of terminology recognizing the "gray" areas of determining malicious hacking. Thus, "white hat hacker" describes an "ethical" hacker. A gray hat hacker is someone who typically behaves in an ethical manner, but sometimes violates accepted ethics. Finally, a black hat hacker is a "malicious" hacker (i.e., a cracker or computer criminal using hackerlike methods).

WHITE HAT HACKERS   "White hat" is a term used to describe an ethical hacker. The term "white hat" was needed because so many former or "reformed" hackers entered the computer security field. Eventually, computer science graduates employing hackerlike methods also spurred the need for the term. The reality existed before the label. There was a long and lively debate about hiring "former" hackers. Other examples of white hat hacking include the following:

- Software testing by manufacturers
- Independent verification of software function and security
- Reverse engineering
- Training

"Tiger teams," a term borrowed from the military, described a hacker or team of hackers hired to "test" the defenses of an organization. These white hat hackers follow a strict code of loyalty to their employers. The use of tiger teams is based on the theory that "only a hacker can beat a hacker." There is a great deal of common sense to the notion of testing defenses with the types of attacks used by an enemy. Several computer security/risk management companies have security services units that actually have white hat hackers on their rolls. A short list includes the "A" list of the field: Team CMYRU, KPMG, Kroll, Computer Associates, Gartner Group's, ICSA Labs (antivirus division of Tru Secure), and Cambridge Technology Partners.

GRAY HAT HACKERS   A gray hat hacker is someone who typically behaves in an ethical manner, but sometimes violates accepted ethics. The term "gray hat" came into usage to describe a usually ethical hacker who sometimes indulged in illicit activity. A typical gray hat is a penetration tester who would not attack a client, but hacks and intrudes recreationally. A gray hat may also occasionally violate the hacker ethic against hacking for profit (other than being paid to do penetration testing for a willing client). A typical contemporary interpretation of the hacker ethic usually includes the following elements:

- Do not profit from intrusion.
- Do not intentionally harm a computer system.
- Attempt to inform a system administrator of security flaws.
- Hackers are not bad guys; computer criminals are bad guys.

BLACK HAT HACKERS   A black hat hacker is essentially a cracker or malicious hacker. The term "black hat" does not apply to all computer criminals. Only network intrusion and other "hacker-like" activities committed in conflict with hacker ethics qualify as black hat activities. At first the term was not used by hackers (malicious or otherwise), but it has since been used by some hackers to describe themselves. In fact, individuals within the hacker community tend to think that a black hat hacker is someone with a good deal of skill over and above that of script kiddies.[37]

Hacktivists

Recently, there has been an increase in the political activity of self-identified hackers. Hackers have combined to challenge the treatment of their peers by the government.[38] The common characteristic of hacktivists is the use of hacker skills and attitudes to convey a political message.[39] Because of the emergence of cheap computer technology and Internet connectivity around the world, hacktivists have virtually unlimited access to cheap or free computing power and nearly boundless information. For example, members of a hacktivist group called the Electronic Disturbance Theater developed an attack tool called FloodNet that used a DoS attack method. This tool was used against the Pentagon as well as other government and business targets as a means of protest against their activities and policies.[40]

Internet-based resources are often turned toward political ends among hacktivists rather than standard goals of the hacker subculture. In many cases, the normal facilities of the Internet

---

BOX 4.3
Penetration Testing

Penetration testing is looked upon with suspicion by hackers because it is a little too close to law enforcement. Penetration testing is an acceptable use of skills by older hackers as long as they don't develop too comfortable a relationship with law enforcement. It seems to violate the hacker ethic against hacking for profit. Some hacker purists won't do it. However, free penetration testing is unquestionably a prosocial activity to hackers.

The business ethic of a tiger team is based on survival. Loyalty to the company hiring the team is essential to ever being hired again.

- Information discovered during the testing must not be disclosed to anyone but the employer.
- Only intrude where invited, otherwise you become a "bad guy."
- Where the methods are exactly the same, only the intention separates good guys from bad guys.
- White hats often even associate with black hats to keep current.

serve hacktivists better than hacker files and tools. For example, e-mail communication enabled supporters of the notorious computer hacker Kevin Mitnick to be in touch with him after his arrest and until he was released from prison. Web sites serve as platforms for publicizing political causes. They do not have to be hacked when access is so cheap and easy. Because so many of the activities of hacktivists are entirely legal, they are among the most accessible of hacker types.

THE ORIGINS AND HISTORY OF HACKING

Now that we have discussed the variations that exist within the hacker subculture, it is critical to consider how these various groups came to be. Examining the history of hacking gives significant insight into the problems and origins of the term "hacker." The Massachusetts Institute of Technology (MIT) claims a tradition of the use of the word before computer hackers existed. The word "hack" had long been used to describe the elaborate college pranks that MIT students would regularly devise. These "hacks" ranged from benign (hiding the incoming university president's office door with a bulletin board) to elaborate (building a full-sized replica police car on top of a domed building complete with working light bar and a ticket for parking illegally).

Among early MIT hackers, a hack was "a project undertaken or a product built not solely to fulfill some constructive goal, but with some wild pleasure taken in mere involvement."[41] When one of the early MIT computer hackers used the term "hacker," "there was serious respect implied. [T]o qualify as a hack, the feat must be imbued with innovation, style, and technical virtuosity."[42] The limitations of the hardware available made this creative problem solving necessary for the earliest computer hackers. "To top [a] program, someone else might try to do the same thing with fewer instructions—a worthy endeavor, since there was so little room in the small 'memory' of the computers in those days . . . This could most emphatically be done by approaching the problem from a whole new angle that no one had ever thought of before, but that in retrospect made total sense."[43] Thus hacking was most closely associated with creative, unorthodox problem solving to overcome the limitations of early computers. At that time, computers only existed in major universities, business research parks, and government installations. People with access to computers had a tremendous investment in not harming the few computers available. Thus, a hacker, in the classical sense, is someone who has mastered the art of programming to the point that he or she can simply sit down and "hack" in a program that works.

Hacking Changes

This conception of the hacker continued into the 1960s when the computer moved from universities into military applications. However, a shift occurred as a consequence of the turbulent social climate of the 1960s, as well as the Vietnam War. Military applications angered many programmers of the day, despite their work being funded largely by the military and federal government.[44]

Programmers' beliefs began to take shape in a series of ideals forming part of the core of hacker culture. Specifically, "hackers" of this period believed information should be free to all to understand how things work and can be improved. This notion formed the centerpiece of a series of related ideas called the hacker ethic that were documented by Levy in his book *Hackers*,[45]

1. Access to computers—and anything which might teach you something about the way the world works—should be unlimited and total. [p. 40]
2. All information should be free. [p. 40]
3. Mistrust authority—promote decentralization. [p. 41]

4. Hackers should be judged by their hacking, not bogus criteria such as degrees, age, race, or position. [p. 43]
5. You can create art and beauty on a computer. [p. 43]
6. Computers can change your life for the better. [p. 45][46]

This ethic guided the actions of hackers and formed the roots of the present hacker culture. At this point, hackers were viewed as skilled computer users. However, a subtle shift began to occur in the 1970s with the development of "phone phreaking." This involved tampering with phone technology to understand and, in some cases, control telephone systems. Phreaking allowed individuals to make free calls to anyone in the world by controlling telephone system switches.

This became notorious because of a man named Cap'n Crunch (John Draper), who blew a giveaway whistle found in a box of cereal into his phone receiver.[47] The whistle created the perfect 2,600 MHz tone that, at the time, was used to connect an individual to long-distance lines. This simple toy opened a new area of technology for individuals to explore and exploit, particularly those interested in computers and hacking. Also during the late 1970s, the first personal computer bulletin board system (BBS) was created.[48] A BBS, which is essentially an online system, allowed individuals to post comments and information. In turn, others could read and respond to those posts. Thus, hackers could come together online to share and discuss information and interact socially.[49] However, the real impact of these developments would be felt during the next decade.

The Criminalization of Hacking

From the 1950s through the 1970s, hackers never worried about breaking computer laws; there were none. The new generation that usurped the word hacker was defined—almost from the beginning—by crime. During the 1980s, a new breed of computer user challenged the hacker ethic. Because of changes in technology and society, more individuals had access to computer technology. Specifically, IBM's new stand-alone "personal computer" brought computer technology to a new generation and into more homes than ever. Modem technology, which connects computers to other computers and networks via telephone lines, also improved. This equipment allowed individuals with personal computers to connect to other dedicated computer users. As a result, the exploration of computer networks was now possible for individuals outside of university and business settings.[50] Modems also increased the number of individuals online and changed the shape of the computer underground through the emergence of BBS dedicated to hacking. Budding hackers shared detailed information about systems they explored and bragged about their exploits. The boards also allowed hackers to form groups with private networks and create password-protected boards to keep out the uninitiated and maintain privacy.[51]

Warez d00dz also developed during this time, finding ways to share and break copyright protections. These hackers already had innumerable justifications to try to break the copy protection. "Software is too expensive." "We only copy software we wouldn't buy anyway." "We only do it to try out new programs." It is a "backup copy in case the disk becomes damaged." During this period, warez d00dz created BBS as a way to share files with others who they trusted, because they were breaking the law and at risk for discovery and closure with arrest for the system operator. Warez sites could also be overwhelmed quickly. Leeches download only, and do not contribute. Leech time was wasted access to a scarce resource (i.e., the warez board). Thus, elite warez boards remained cloaked in secrecy. Unlike elite hacker boards, information was not distributed through the community.[52]

The 1983 film *War Games* introduced the general public to the rather unexplored world of computer hacking. The film suggested that young males with computers could break into any computer system in the world and wreak havoc without anyone ever knowing. This film and its message had a significant influence on a new generation of computer users.

An additional change to the hacker community occured in 1986 with the introduction of a brief text called *The Conscience of a Hacker*, also referred to as *The Hacker Manifesto*. A member of the notorious hacker group Legion of Doom (LOD), named "The Mentor," wrote this text.[53] The author railed against adults, law enforcement, and schools and evoked the angst of young hackers exploring network from home computers. They did not have the same support that hackers in the 1950s and 1960s experienced and worked in isolation. As a result, their experiences were vastly different and espoused in this work. The following excerpt is taken from the end of the manifesto:

> Yes, I am a criminal. My crime is that of curiosity. My crime is that of judging people by what they say and think, not what they look like. My crime is that of outsmarting you, something that you will never forgive me for. I am a hacker, and this is my manifesto. You may stop this individual, but you can't stop us all . . . .[54]

The Mentor also suggested hackers explore and seek knowledge even if that means breaking into or gaining access to otherwise protect computer systems. However, he stated that this should not make hackers criminals. The Mentor also encouraged hackers to use telephone systems without paying for the service because they are "run by profiteering gluttons." This unapologetic post derided the traditional hacker definition espoused in the 1960s, as well as the "Hacker Ethic." The document provided support for the increasingly criminal nature of hacker activities, thus affecting outsiders' perceptions of hackers and the attitudes of young initiates to the hacker community.

Within a few years, the manifesto became widely read, and computer users without real technical skill became interested in hacking. This caused a rift between hackers with malicious intent and those with an interest in exploring networks without breaking the law or violating privacy. The divide was also fueled by different beliefs, as represented in the hacker manifesto and the hacker ethic. In addition, malicious hackers became the focus of law enforcement during the mid- to late 1980s. High-profile hacking incidents took place, such as a battle between two hacker groups, the LOD and the Masters of Deception (MOD), whose attacks compromised personal computers, businesses, and telephone systems including AT&T.[55] The much-publicized arrest of a regional hacker group called the 414 Gang from Milwaukee (area code 414) also brought attention to the criminal aspects of hacking. This group of teenagers accessed secure computers in the Sloan-Kettering Cancer Center and Los Alamos military computers.[56]

One of the most famous cases of criminal hacking occurred during this time, involving the hacker Kevin Mitnick, who broke the law by accessing computer systems without permission. Mitnick intruded into a variety of private systems, stole proprietary software, and accessed voice mail computers at Pacific Bell. He was a fugitive from the FBI for two and a half years, during which time he engaged in identity theft to create fraudulent documents and illegally cloned cell phones to hide his location.[57] After his arrest in 1995, his prosecution was extremely controversial, as there were few legal precedents to guide the prosecution and a great deal of fear and concern over his ability. At one point, it was thought that he could cause a nuclear war by simply having access to a phone. Thus, his prosecution was a landmark for criminal hacking cases.

Challenges and Changes in Hacking

The emergence of criminal hacking in the 1980s and 1990s also saw a concurrent growth in original hackers from the previous generation who received recognition and disputed the criminalization of the word "hacker." Most of the original hackers had started their own high-tech companies or assumed leadership in research programs. The budding computer security community was also driven by the old-school hackers, along with the tech boom of the 1990s, which made many of them popular culture heroes. People working in the high-tech sector started to care about the early triumphs in information technology. It started to become more important to hackers to redeem the word hacker. Several factors contributed to this renewed interest:

- Increased computer use in the general population.
- Popularization of the Internet.
- Popular culture recognition and even reverence of nerds.
- Popular fiction like the *Cyberpunk* books and computer movies.
- The zealous promotion of computer media sources like *Wired* magazine.

The computer media wanted to prove their connection to the "wired world" by picking up speech patterns and opinions of the computer world's stars. Many of these stars were hackers. *Wired* magazine, recognizing the disputed use of the term *hacker*, pioneered the popular use of the term *cracker* through editorial policy. *Wired* tried to establish credibility among the important figures of the early computer culture by refusing to stigmatize the word *hacker*.

Despite their attempts, the notion of hacking as a crime continued on and was cemented by the mid-1990s, especially with the development of user-friendly computer systems and the Internet and World Wide Web. The slow but steady drop in the prices of computer technology also made the home computer ubiquitous. With access to the Internet and more powerful computers, hackers who wanted to learn needed only to bring up a Web page or use an online bookstore to gain access to information and resources. This facilitated the growth of unskilled hackers and script kiddies who were a significant divergence from the previous generations of hackers. New users also became interested in hacking with the release of the film *Hackers* in 1995.[58] This film's presentation of hackers helped cement the notion that hackers are criminals, as it featured overly styled misrepresentations of hacking and an emphasis on the destructive side of hacking.

By the start of the new millennium, most computers around the world were interconnected through the Internet, and sensitive financial and government information became commonly stored in accessible databases online. Financial services, social networking sites, and a wide range of new communications resources were made available to home computer users. As a consequence, the computer security industry was booming and the nature of computer hacking and attacks changed. Hackers in Russia, Romania, and China became more of a significant problem, especially for U.S. businesses, and the tools they used became increasingly complex and readily accessible for purchase through online markets.[59] These markets, discussed in detail in Chapter 6, are critical, as they have changed the nature of hacking by reducing the amount of knowledge required to attack secured networks. However, the old hacker ethic is still alive and well around the world in the computer security community and universities. The ethic is also evident in the growth of open-source software programs like Linux, where programmers collaborate to create programs that can be used by individuals around the world. Thus, the hacker community is now very segmented, with individuals engaging in legal and illegal hacks against all manner of targets around the world for curiosity, profit, fame, patriotism, or religious ideology.

BOX 4.4

The Open-Source Movement

Most software purchased today tightly restricts user access to the source code, or the human-readable version of computer programs. For example, the source code to Windows™ is a closely guarded trade secret of the Microsoft Corporation. When you purchase a copy of Windows™, you receive the computer-readable version of the code referred to as object code. You do not have access to the source code. Corporations can prevent some unauthorized use of their intellectual property and conceal security flaws of the software to would-be hackers by restricting access to the source code.

The open-source movement began in the late 1990s. The founders of the movement believe that software can be improved by allowing programmers access to the source code. The basic idea is that programmers will be able to read, modify, and improve the code through open access. Over time, these ad hoc revisions will rapidly transform the code and fix bugs in the program much faster than would be the case in the traditional closed model that relies on restricting access to the code.

The ideals of early hacker culture are alive and well within the open-source movement, where the best way to fix computer glitches is to rely on the creative and unorthodox problem-solving skills of individual programmers instead of corporate restrictions.

THE HACKER SUBCULTURE

In light of the diverse nature of skills, motives, and interests in the hacker community, it is important to consider how these individuals relate to one another and what drives their interests. As discussed in Chapter 3, there appears to be a subculture of hackers that provides justifications for behavior, information and skills to engage in hacking, and beliefs about the nature of their actions. This is true regardless of whether an individual engages in legitimate hacks (as per the hacker ethic) or malicious hacks and cracks (more in line with the hacker manifesto). The great difficulty in differentiating these groups lies in the fact that human behavior is dynamic and contextual. There is therefore no simple dichotomy between hackers and computer criminals.

As such, it is better to consider what structures the hacker subculture in an attempt to see how they relate to one another, what they value, and how their beliefs affect their behavior. Subcultural research suggests that the social world of computer hackers is shaped by five social norms: technology, knowledge, commitment, categorization, and law.[60] These structures appear to be consistent across place and time and have value for our understanding of the global hacker community and their actions. The following discussion will consider each of these subcultural norms using examples from the real world.

Technology

One of the most significant norms in the hacker subculture is the relationship between hackers and technology. Hackers possess a deep connection to computers and technology, which play an important role in structuring their interests and activities.[61] For example, many hackers report developing an interest in technology before or during adolescence.[62] Once they were given access to a computer, they spent their time becoming acquainted with its functions in a variety of ways. A hacker named Mack Diesel described his own experience, writing:

> I was, yeah, I was about four and [my mother] would take me up to school with her sometimes and they had a computer there. If I got bored, she would let me, uh, fool around with the computer, you know, to keep me occupied, and after a while I enjoyed playing around with it.[63]

Hackers also played video games and developed interests in the many different facets of computer technology. In fact, the growth of multiplayer computer games like Quake and CounterStrike helped to give hackers an interest in technology, as they would have to work to connect multiple computers together in a network to play with their peers. This gave them an appreciation for a variety of technical skills such as programming, software, hardware, and computer security.

The more time hackers spent familiarizing themselves with technology, the more their skill level increased. Whether on- or off-line, hackers discussed the need to understand the interrelated elements of computer systems, as a hacker's knowledge level directly relates to his or her ability and skill.[64] To meet the intense internal desire to understand computer technology, hackers often turn to online resources for help. In the 1980s, hackers commonly used BBSs, while the advent of the World Wide Web in the 1990s saw the development of Web forums. Web forums are online discussion groups where individuals can discuss a variety of problems or issues. They are composed of strings that begin when an individual creates a post within a forum, asking a question or giving an opinion. Other people respond to the remarks with posts of their own that are connected together to create strings.[65]

These resources are critical to increase a hackers' connection to computer technology. This was exemplified in the following comment from the forum poster Binkels: "Hacking allows people to learn more about computers. I am really into computers and try to learn as much as I can. I want to be a hacker to exploit systems/programs and using them to learn from and go further into my limited knowledge of computers." The urge to learn about computers and technology could be met through a variety of resources, especially Web forums. One user wrote:

> You might want to remember that forums are designed for people to ask questions, despite the fact that you can find almost anything on google. So if we all should just searched for things ourselves there'd be no forums.

Hackers can also ask questions about computers, hardware, software, and hacking in forums as a means to understand technology. For example, a hacker named g00fu5 wrote a post in a hacker forum demonstrating the importance of their interest in technology:

> Im planning on printing out a bunch of different texts to print out and take around with me so I can read them in my spare time. I was wondering if anyone could recommend any good texts that are actually worth printing out for me. I am printing out the SQL [programming language] white pages so far, but I need more. I am interested in just about anything hacking-related, but nothing stupid.

Thus, the forums emphasized hackers' significant interest in and desire to comprehend technology. Technology is also such an important component of the hacker subculture that it began to permeate the language of hackers in the 1970s and 1980s. Hackers in this period created their own dialect called eleet ('leet) speek or k-rad. In k-rad, numbers were substituted for visually similar letters.[66] Capital letters were freely and randomly used. For instance, "elite hackers" became 31337 HaKorZ. There is no definite pattern for the replacements; they are just inserted upon the whim of the writer. There are different reasons for 'leet speek. Foremost, much of the interaction between 'leeto hackers happened online. It required typing. Shortcuts and abbreviations became the norm. The use of numbers and other characters in place of letters is a reflection of the programs that hackers create. Because the development of computer programs involves symbols and characters, the incorporation of these components into speech reflect the value of technology in their communications. In fact, 'leet speek is still a common component of the hacker subculture and is used by individuals in hacker communities around the world.

Knowledge

Another important norm in the hacker subculture is knowledge. Being referred to as a hacker was a clear indication of an individual's understanding and skill since the development of the computer technology. In fact, the hacker identity is built upon a devotion to learn and understand technology. One hacker named MG defined a hacker as "any person with a sincere desire for knowledge about all things and is constantly trying to find it."[67] Hackers spent a great deal of time learning and applying their knowledge on- and off-line. Most hackers stressed that the learning process began with the basic components of computer technology. An understanding of the rudimentary functions of computers provides hackers with an appreciation for the interrelated nature of computer systems. Dark Oz explained his own learning experience with computers:

> You do this long enough, with many different technical projects, and you begin to really learn a lot . . . Once you learn the logic and how to "think" like a computer or programmer would, you can just guess at how things are working, based on existing knowledge.[68]

Developing a broad knowledge of systems, hardware, programming, and networking is extremely important to hackers because it influences their ability to hack. Though hackers can now find tools in forums around the world, they must understand how computers operate in order to effectively use these tools. In fact, the early computer hackers at MIT demonstrated their significant skill with computers by reducing the processing time of machines, which were very slow.

Forums and BBS also serve as repositories of information for hackers to access and connect with other hacker. However, it is important to consider that in the current hacker subculture, when an individual asks a question, he or she is often given a Web link that would answer the question. Users have to actively open links, read, and learn in order to find their answer. Tutorials, be they word documents or videos, can also be found and give detailed explanations on topics from programming to the use of hack tools. Hackers also make software programs available for others to download either for free or for pay to help them learn.

Hackers in the subculture today do not, however, mentor individuals in hacking skills. In fact, evidence suggests that most hackers do not have many real-world relationships with other hackers.[69] As a consequence, they must develop online relationships to learn, but these relationships do not lead to direct information on hacking. This sentiment was also evident in the following exchange from a forum when a poster asked for information to learn to hack:

STFUSER: ok im quite new to this and need some mega help i need to know the basics of this hacking [I am] on my quest to becoming elite so if someone can help and give me the info and tell me where i can get it [information on how to hack] from i would much appreciate it.

3NFOR3C3R: arrrrr how cute, seriously mate why would anyone want to go out of their way to help some random person hack computers?

H3H3:   Nah man, you want a teacher, you can pay lol [laughing out loud]. Besides that, read whatever you can get your hands on and understand the shit that you read.

The importance of knowledge is also evident in the growth of hacker conferences, or "cons." There are dozens of cons held in countries around the world, all focused on sharing information and spreading knowledge. There are several cons in the United States alone, including one of the most famous and long-standing in the world called Defcon. This three-day convention is held in Las Vegas and has operated since 1993.[70] The conference draws thousands of attendees and participants from around the world, including computer security professionals, law enforcement agents, attorneys, and hackers of all skill levels. The convention is open to the public and features panels directly related to technology and hacking. A wide range of topics are discussed every year, commonly including hardware hacking, phreaking, computer security, exploits, cryptography, privacy protections, and the legal issues surrounding hacking and piracy.[71]

The importance of knowledge is also evident at the conference, as hackers demonstrate their understanding of technology through hacking challenges and competitions held during the convention. For example, there is a contest called "Capture the Flag," where hackers compete against each other for 36 straight hours in teams to determine who has the greatest skill.[72] There are also contests in war driving, where hackers drive around the city trying to find the largest number of open wireless WIFI hotspots. Those who successfully apply their knowledge in the unique challenges at Defcon are acknowledged during an award ceremony at the end of the convention. Contest winners are announced on stage and distinguished for their achievements. Individuals are given a black conference admission badge and, in some cases, a black leather Defcon logo jacket. These items cannot be purchased, and the black badge provided the recipient with free convention admission for life. Since the convention badge design changes each year, the black badge stands out as a symbol of knowledge, achievement, and ability.

The importance of learning is also detailed in the program by the convention organizer, The Dark Tangent. He wrote, "I want a party where all like minded geeks and innovators can chill out and swap ideas."[73] Presenters provide new information to attendees along with tools, security tactics, and creative applications of existing products. Here, hackers place great value on the creative use of technology and spreading these innovations to others.[74]

Commitment

The elements that compose the normative order knowledge are also closely tied to the normative order commitment. Commitment is important because individuals must constantly study and practice hacking techniques in order to improve and progress. Those who are not willing to spend this time often wind up as script kiddies and are limited in terms of the attacks that they can complete. Commitment to hacking structures individual behavior through continued study and practice of hacking techniques. Forum posters indicate that it takes a tremendous amount of time to learn to hack. Wiggum wrote, "For me . . . the most important thing to have if u wanna be a hacker is to 'love it' and [be] ready to give your time to learn and master it." Another named Ashy Larrie also provided some insight:

> If you are just starting you might not have a clue what to learn, or what you should know. As for me, I just started reading texts for a long time . . . when I started I didn't understand most of what was said in the texts but just kept on reading, after awhile things become more clear and you get the idea of what hacking is all about. I think it's also better to find out yourself then if you would ask what is important to learn, because there are so many areas you do hacking in, and once you get the overall picture you can decide what interests you most at that moment.

While these comments echo elements of the order knowledge, the poster makes very distinct statements about the importance of commitment to learning. A commitment to learning and understanding computers and technology is needed to discover what topics a hacker finds truly interesting. In addition, continuous changes and improvements in technology compound the length of time required to learn. Thus, hackers must be committed to the continuous identification and acquisition of new information. A hacker named Mack Diesel emphasized the importance of commitment, saying, "the minute you feel you've learned everything is the minute you're out. There's always something new to learn."[75] Hence, hacker subculture places tremendous value on constant learning over time.

The order commitment also reflects the significant amount of effort applied to learn the tradecraft of hacking. Very skilled hackers spend constant and consistent effort in the process of learning and applying their knowledge. For example, a malicious software writer described the process he took to write one piece of code:

> This week has been terrible . . . not slept for almost three days . . . working on loadable kernel modules [for a rootkit]. During that time had to drink 8 cans of beer, 2 packs of cigarettes (which is a lot for me) to read the manual on the development of loadable kernel modules under the Linux kernel (collated all examples) OK, I finally decided to take sleeping pill after 2 and a half tablets . . . slept nearly 20 hours.[76]

The sheer amount of time and dedication he puts toward hacking is evident in his comments. Similar stories can be found across the hacker community.

In addition, a hacker's commitment to learning affected the quality of information he or she is given. This is evident in the forums, where posters who did not attempt to find an answer on their own before posting were berated. This was demonstrated in the following exchange:

SHArK0:   Hello . . . I was looking for some DoS [Denial of Service Attack] tools . . . I am wondering where I can find these at? Thanks.

CAPTAINMURPHY: If you can't even find a simple program, how do you expect you're going to have the patience to attempt a hack? I suggest this small piece of advice. Search again.

CaptainMurphy berated Shark0 for demonstrating such a lack of effort and gave him no information. This sort of exchange is common in the forums and reveals the relationship between a hacker's level of commitment and the amount of respect he or she is shown while online. If an individual does not prove that he or she puts forth effort to learn on his or her own, he or she is disrespected. This is most evident in the forums when hackers try to obtain information from others. The following exchange highlights the process:

HESHOPOLIS: Hi, I'm interested in the OpenSSL Exploit [a script to attack a system]. But I don't have a nix [Linux] system to test it on.

But I cant run it on a windows machine. Anyone know a binary?

Don't sta[r]t whit [with] that'juist [just] compile it crap of cource that doesn't work, you'd spend a year looking for all the includes.

Tnx.

THE MONKEY: If you can't even fucking compile someone else's exploits, think about actually learning what you're doing before you try doing it. It's clear you know very little about C, which means you probably have no clue how the exploit works, or even what it'll produce in the end. Get your head out of your ass, fuck off, and read a book.

T0MP3T3R5: Get off your dead ass and code your own exploits, you fucking script kiddie.

These comments plainly demonstrate hackers' stance on the importance of understanding how hacks actually work, which can only be gleaned through hard work and dedication. As such, Heshopolis was flamed, disrespected, and derogatorily referred to as a script kiddie.

Categorization

The ways individuals create and define the hacker identity constitutes the fourth normative order of hacker subculture: categorization. Commitment, knowledge, and technology clearly affect the way individuals construct their definition and meaning of the term *hacker*. However, there are common discussions in Web forums on how to define hackers and their motives. Posters spend considerable time explaining who and what is a hacker, which may be a consequence of the long-standing debate over the nature of hacking

Disputes over the nature of hackers and hacking allowed posters to define and differentiate themselves from others within the subculture.[77] The most spirited discussions in forums often center on how individuals define a hacker. One such discussion began because an individual asked "When did you start thinking you were a 'hacker'?" This post was a survey giving users options, including when they "used a port scanner [a tool that identifies the programs running on a target computer]," "used a lamer program with 'hacker tools,'" or "tried to download malicious scripts [programs including viruses and worms] and only ended up hurting yourself." The options available to posters accentuated behavioral measures or benchmarks in a hacker's development. Many users validated the use of such measures, arguing that once they performed a certain task or understood a complicated process, they could consider themselves a hacker. For example, the poster wa1st3d felt he would not be a hacker until he learned "some programming languages . . . fully understood Windows . . . and Linux [a computer operating system]."

At the same time, many individuals argue that there are attitudinal components that define a hacker, suggesting there are attitudinal components of their definition of "hacker." This includes a certain state of mind or spirit, as described by Brainiackk, who wrote, "the hacker seeks for knowledge, the unknown and tries to reach his own goals. That's the spirit." Curiosity and a desire to learn is an important part of most definitions of hacker, including the one by paranizoid who stressed, "In my opinion, a hacker is a person who is curious and enjoys exploring. Be that someones mind or someone's computer hard drive."

For some, the notion of "hacker" is an ideal to strive toward, primarily because of the knowledge required to become a hacker. The forum user M0thm0nst3rm@n explained:

> I think a real hacker never would call himself a hacker because no matter how much you know, you can't know everything and there's always more to learn. I don't consider myself a hacker, I consider myself a n00b but I hope to be something close to a hacker some day.

Hence, personal opinion significantly influences the forum users' identity and construction of the term *hacker*.

Individual conceptions also generate much of the discussion about what different types of hackers do and how this relates to their label or title. This is especially true of the ideology or behaviors associated with each type of hacker discussed earlier in this chapter. For example, there were many disagreements and discussions surrounding two of the main subtypes of hackers: white hats and black hats. Both are considered to be very skilled types of hackers who engage in different behaviors because of different ideologies. As the forum user j@ck0 indicated, "the black hats use their knowledge to destroy things. The white hats use it to build things." However, there was some disagreement over the malicious nature of black hat hackers. For example, kFowl3r responded to j@ck0's comments, suggesting:

> One thing about blackhats, its totally wrong that blackhats only use their knowledge to destroy . . . blackhats just hack . . . not like whitehats which aren't really hackers since they work against hackers, they build tools to stop people from breaking into systems etc.

These comments indicate that white hats are active in the computer security industry, securing systems from hacks. Black hats are more prevalent in the hacking community, identifying weaknesses and exploits for later attack. Beyond these concepts, arguments over the activities of black and white hat hackers appear to be based on personal opinion. This is apparent in the following exchange concerning the differences between black and white hat hackers:

TomServo: you seem to have a wrong view of blackhats dude . . . blackhats do audit [computer codes to identify program flaws] for sure . . . i dont think that a whitehat audits much and codes exploits [ways to attack a system], cuz . . . blackhats invent new exploitation tekneeqz etc we keep the scene going . . .

Crow: Imho [In My Honest Opinion] it's just a false statement that whitehats don't invent new exploitation teqs, it may be just the missing "slang" that makes you forget bout that.

The variation present in the meaning of black and white hat hackers illustrates the significance of individual opinion in the hacker experience online. Personal experience influences how they define themselves relative to other hackers. Labels may have specific connotations, but individuals can accept or reject that meaning. In turn, hackers form boundaries between themselves and others based on their definition of hacker. However, this sort of differentiation is not necessarily present off-line. This suggests categorization is relatively unique to the online experience of hacker subculture.

Law

The final social norm driving hacker subculture is law, because hackers regularly discuss the legality of hacking and information sharing in the real world and in cyberspace. Law emphasizes the influence of legal codes in structuring how hackers relate to individuals in and out of hacker subculture. Hackers have become acutely aware of the nature of the law regarding computer networks, because they may want to know if their hacks or related activities are legal, and if they should be performed. There is also a split between hackers who feel there is no need to break the law, while others view hacking in any form as acceptable.

Such competing perspectives can be found in Web forums, as noted in the following exchange. An individual asked for information on a password cracking tool and how to use it. Pilferer answered the poster's question and gave an admonition that was quickly contradicted:

PILFERER: You do understand that using these password crackers on machines which you don't own or have no permission to access is ILLEGAL?

LEETER: Illegal . . . . So is masturbation in a public place, but we don't get reminded of that every time anyone thinks about it do we? ;-)

In some cases, posters inquired about the legal ramifications of certain actions. For example, an individual asked if it is legal to use tools to examine other people's networks if they notified their Internet service provider. The poster received the following responses:

Z0R@K: Yes, ISP's [Internet Service Providers] can and will detect repeated scans . . . Yes it would be legal if you got permission from the person but your ISP will still not like it.

CLARENCE: That's untrue, depending where in the world you are then port scanning IS illeagle so be careful.

Legal matters are also regularly addressed at hacker conferences, including Defcon. For example, attorneys from the Electronic Freedom Foundation, a legal foundation supporting digital free speech rights and hacker interests regularly speak on the current state of law relative to computer hacking. There is also an annual panel titled "Meet The Fed," where individuals from federal, state, and local law enforcement agencies along with the intelligence community come together and allow members of the audience to ask questions on the law and hacking.[78]

However, concern over potential law violations appears to have little effect on hacker behavior. Hackers regularly provide information that could be used to perform a hack regardless of their attitude toward the law. This leads to a contradiction in the process of information sharing. If a hacker shares knowledge with possible illegal applications, they justify its necessity in a variety of ways. Hackers commonly state that they provided information in the hopes of educating others, as in this statement from a tutorial posted in one of the forums on macrovirus construction:

> This is an educational document, I take no responsibility for what use the information in this document is used for. I am unable to blamed for any troubles you get into with the police, FBI, or any other department . . . It is not illegal to write viruses, but it is illegal to spread them—something I do not condone and take responsibility for.

Even serious virus writers and sellers are aware of the illegal nature of their activities and note such information on their Web sites. One such Russian group made the following post concerning the tools that could be downloaded from their site, noting: "**Warning!** . . . all information on our site is given for exceptionally familiarizing purposes. We bear no responsibility for any use."[79]

Similar justifications were used at Defcon, especially when a presenter's content had rather obvious or serious illegal applications. An excellent example of this was in a 2004 presentation titled "Weakness in Satellite Television Protection Schemes or 'How I learned to Love The Dish.'" The presenter, *A*, indicated, "I will not be teaching you how to steal [satellite Internet connectivity] service, but I will give you the background and information to understand how it could be done." However, the second slide in his presentation included the message "Many topics covered may be illegal!" as well as the potential laws they may break by stealing service.[80]

This legal warning reduced the presenter's accountability for how individuals used the information he provided. He simply shared his knowledge on satellite systems and television service. If someone used the information to break the law, *A* had clearly described the laws they could violate by engaging in these actions. Just as with the warning in the macrovirus tutorial, he justified sharing information that could be used to engage in illegal behavior, stealing satellite service, as part of the pursuit of knowledge.

Nevertheless, some hackers do not condone the exchange or supply of overtly illegal information. In some forums, hackers eschew posting blatantly illegal content and forcefully explain their rationale. For example, an individual proclaimed himself, "the kind of hacker police really hate" and posted someone's credit card information. One of the senior users posted the following comments in reply:

> Not only do the police hate you regardless if its good or bad to card (btw its bad), someone should delete it because it IS illegal and this is an open forum Go away.

Others, however, actively encourage the exchange of illegal information, as in markets where hacked personal information is sold. For example, an individual who sells stolen credit cards advertised his service stating:

> !!! Hello Everyone. I want to offer great things for your needs from Me—Official Dump [Stolen Bank Account] Seller !!!
>
> 1) Dumps from all over the world Original Track 1/Track 2
>
> 1.1) EUROPE Dumps Track 1/Track 2
>
> > Europe and the rest of world (Following countries are not included: Swiss, Spain, France, Italy, Turkey, Germany, Australia)
> >
> > Visa Classic, MasterCard Standard—$60 per 1 dump
> >
> > Visa Classic, MasterCard Standard (Swiss, Spain, France, Italy, Turkey, Germany, Australia)—$70 per 1 dump

Visa Gold | Platinum | Business, MasterCard Gold | Platinum—$100 per 1 dump

Visa Gold | Platinum | Business, MasterCard Gold | Platinum (Swiss, Spain, France, Italy, Turkey, Germany, Australia)—$120 per 1 dump

1.2) USA Dumps Original Track 1/Track 2

DUMPS Visa Gold | Platinum | Business | Signature, MasterCard Gold | Platinum, American Express, Discover
Dumps with Name,Address,City,State,Zip,Phone—$100 per 1 dump
Dumps with Name,Address,City,State,Zip,Phone,SSN and DOB—$120 per 1 dump
DUMPS Visa Classic, MasterCard Standard
Dumps with Name,Address,City,State,Zip,Phone—$80 per 1 dump
Dumps with Name,Address,City,State,Zip,Phone,SSN and DOB—$90 per 1 dump

1.3) CANADA Dumps Original Track 1/Track 2

Visa Classic, MasterCard Standard
    Amount: >10<50—$19.5 per 1 dump
    Amount: >50<100—$14.5 per 1 dump
    Amount: >100—$12.5 per 1 dump

Visa Gold | Platinum | Business, MasterCard Gold | Platinum
    Amount: >10<50—$34.5 per 1 dump
    Amount: >50<100—$32.5 per 1 dump
    Amount: >100—$30 per 1 dump[81]

Individuals appreciated his service, and noted the quality of the data, making comments such as "great info!" and "wonderful service!"

The dichotomy of information sharing present in hacker subculture stems from the differences in hacks and cracks. Some feel cracking activities are unacceptable, while others feel it is perfectly justifiable. Forums designed for legitimate nondeviant hackers are less likely to contain illegal information. Other forums, whose audiences are interested in criminal hacks and illegal activities, can contain a great deal of illicit information. It may be difficult for law enforcement agencies to quickly assess the content of a forum, and identifying something illegal can draw investigations when the participants have not actually broken the law. Thus, limiting the amount of illegal information traded in the forums reduces the risk of law enforcement intervention.

In much the same way, law enforcement interest in hackers and hacking influences the way hackers relate to others in and out of the subculture. This is particularly evident at Defcon because of their Spot the Fed contest, which is referred to as "the ever popular paranoia builder," by asking, "Who IS that person next to you?"[82] To play, anyone who feels an attendee is a federal agent can alert one of the convention organizers and claim that they have "spotted a fed." The potential "fed" is then brought on stage before the crowd and asked a series of questions about their life and job. If the person is, in fact, a federal agent, both the fed and the spotter receive T-shirts to commemorate the experience.

There are regular "spot the fed" moments during the convention, and it is a Defcon tradition. The game informs attendees about the presence of law enforcement and influences the way individuals relate to one another during the convention. Attendees are much more careful about discussing illegal activities or sharing information in the open. Spot The Fed also creates and reinforces the boundaries between hackers and law enforcement. While the game is "all in good fun" and performed in a tongue-in-cheek manner, attendees often take second glances at those who do not blend in with the crowd. Openly questioning individuals about their lives clearly indicate who is a hacker and who is not. The answers provided by federal agents give hackers information about government agencies and agents. Also, the public spectacle produced from a "spotting" ensures attendees may recognize the differences between hackers and law enforcement. Thus, hackers take steps to limit their exposure to law enforcement agents on- and off-line. Computer hackers also delineate the boundaries of their subculture by fostering an antagonistic relationship between themselves and law enforcement.[83]

Summary

There are important reasons to understand the hacker subculture when considering computer crime. The fundamental differences in motivation from computer criminals require a categorically different approach to controlling hacking-related crime. Understanding the way hackers define themselves and the history that inspires them can be an important tool to predicting their actions and gauging appropriate responses to criminal hacking. Hackers understand their history in distinct eras and often hold older hackers in high regard. Furthermore, hackers who have a strong connection to technology and demonstrable skill garner more respect than their peers with less knowledge.

Showing a sophisticated understanding of these issues can increase hackers' respect for law enforcement. This increased respect can cultivate connections and information that may be valuable in solving crimes. Prevention efforts can also benefit from properly gauging the audience. Script kiddies and black hat hackers will require a different approach from other hackers. Perhaps, most usefully, understanding the mental processes of justification in the hacker's language and beliefs gives law enforcement an upper hand when dealing with hackers. It may be one of the few advantages available to law enforcement.

Review Questions

1. Explain why hackers do not consider themselves to be criminals. How can someone break the law, but not feel deviant?

2. Explain the hacker ethic. Can individual hackers deviate from the hacker ethic? Do all hackers hold the same understanding of that ethic?

3. What is the hacker manifesto, and how does it compare against the hacker ethic?

4. How has the definition of hacking changed over the last 40 years, and what does this mean for hackers today?

5. Explain the influence of the media on the development of the hacking subculture. Do all hackers agree with the way the media handles hacking? Why or why not?

6. What values drive the hacker subculture, and how does it help us to understand the ways that hackers become involved in and continue to pursue hacking over time?

Endnotes

1. LEVY, S. (1984). *Hackers: Heroes of the Computer Revolution.* New York: Dell Publishing; DUFF, L., and GARDINER, S. (1996). "Computer Crime in the Global Village: Strategies for Control and Regulation—In Defence of the Hacker." *International Journal of the Sociology of Law* 24(2): 211–228; HAFNER, K., and LYON, M. (1996). *Where Wizards Stay Up Late: The Origins of the Internet.* New York: Touchstone.

2. ICOVE, D., SEGER, K., and VONSTORCH, W. (1995). *Computer Crime: A Crimefighter's Handbook.* Sebastopol, CA: O'Reilly & Associates; GOLLMAN, D.

(1999). *Computer Security.* New York: John Wiley & Sons, Inc.; PARKER, D.B. (1998). *Fighting Computer Crime.* New York: John Wiley & Sons, Inc.

3. CHANDLER, A. (1996). "The Changing Definition and Image of Hackers in Popular Discourse. *International Journal of the Sociology of Law* 24(2): 229–251.

4. HAFNER, K., and MARKOFF, J. (1991). *Cyberpunk: Outlaws and Hackers on the Computer Frontier.* New York: Touchstone.

5. FLOHR, U. (November 1995). *Bank Robbers Go Electronic.* Retrieved May 5, 2004 from the World Wide Web: *http://www.byte.com/art/9511/sec3/art11.htm*

6. LOPER, D.K. (2000). "The Criminology of Computer Hackers: A Qualitative and Quantitative Analysis." *Dissertation Abstracts International* 61(8), AAT 9985422.

7. SCHELL, BERNADETTE H., DODGE, JOHN L., and MOUTSATSOS, STEVE S. (2002). *The Hacking of America: Who's Doing it, Why, and How.* Westport, CT: Quorum Books.

8. FURNELL, STEVEN. (2002). *Cybercrime: Vandalizing the Information Society.* Boston, MA: Addison-Wesley.

9. RAYMOND, E.S. (August 13, 2003). *The Jargon File, Version 4.4.4.* Retrieved August 30 from the World Wide Web: *http://www.catb.org/∼esr/jargon/*

10. HOLT, THOMAS J. (2007). "Subcultural Evolution? Examining the Influence of On- and Off-Line Experiences on Deviant Subcultures." *Deviant Behavior* 28(2): 171–198.

11. ABBIE HOFFMAN was a political activist and founder of the Youth International Party ("Yippies"). He was one of the Chicago Seven, who went on trial after violence erupted at the 1968 Democratic National Convention in Chicago.

12. The Bell System was dominant, but there were much smaller local—and a few regional—companies.

13. *Ibid.*, p. 8.

14. *Ibid.*, p. 8.

15. HOLT, THOMAS J., and COPES, HEITH. (Forthcoming). "Transferring Subcultural Knowledge Online: Practices and Beliefs of Persistent Digital Pirates." *Deviant Behavior.*

16. HOLT, THOMAS J., SOLES, JOSHUA, and LESLIE, LYUDMILA. (2008). "Characterizing Malware Writers and Computer Attackers in Their own Words." The Preceedings of the 2008 Conference on Information Warfare.

17. STERLING, B. (1992). *The Hacker Crack-Down: Law and Disorder on the Electronic Frontier.* New York: Bantam Books.

18. *Ibid.*, p. 8

19. LITTMAN, J. (September 18, 1997). *Hacker Shocker: Project Reveals Breaches Galore.* Retrieved from the World Wide Web: *http://www5.zdnet.com/zdnn/content/zdnn/0918/zdnn0010.html*

20. 18 U.S.C. § 1029 et seq.

21. 18 U.S.C. § 1030 et seq.

22. WALL, D.S. (2001). "Cybercrimes and the Internet." In D.S. WALL (ed.), *Crime and the Internet.* New York: Routledge, pp. 1–17.

23. BECKER, H.S. (1963). *Outsiders: Studies in the Sociology of Deviance.* New York: Free Press.

24. LOPER, "The Criminology of Computer Hackers."

25. *Ibid.*

26. WILLIAMS, M. (2001). "The Language of Cyberspace." In D.S. WALL (ed.), *Crime and the Internet.* New York: Routledge, pp. 152–166.

27. MANN, D., and SUTTON, M. (1998). "Netcrime: More Change in the Organization of Thieving." *British Journal of Criminology* 38(2): 201–229.

28. PARKER, *Fighting Computer Crime*

29. BARRETT, N. (1997). *Digital Crime: Policing the Cybernation.* London: Kogan Page.

30. GOLDSTEIN, E. (June 13, 1993). "Hacker Testimony to House Subcommittee Largely Unheard." In J. THOMAS and G. MEYER (eds.), *Computer Underground Digest, 5.43.* DeKalb, IL: Editor. Retrieved February 26, 2000 from the World Wide Web: *http://venus.soci.niu.edu/∼cudigest/CUDS5/cud543.txt*

31. GOLDSTEIN, E. (1996). "Knowledge is Strength." *2600: The Hacker Quarterly* 13(4): 4–5.

32. CHANDLER, "The Changing Definition and Image of Hackers in Popular Discourse."

33. GILMORE, J. (June 4, 1999). "Crackers Do for Gov't What Critical Infrastructure Report Couldn't." *RISKS Digest* 20(43). Retrieved August 22, 2003 from the World Wide Web: *http://catless.ncl.ac.uk/Risks/20.43.html#subj5*

34. Honeynet Project (July 21, 2000). *Know Your Enemy: The Tools and Methodologies of the Script Kiddie.* Retrieved September 13, 2003 from the World Wide Web: *http://project honeynet.org/papers/enemy/*

35. *Ibid.*

36. *Ibid.*, p. 10.

37. *Ibid.*

38. TAYLOR, P. (2001). "Hacktivism: In Search of Lost Ethics?" In D.S. WALL (ed.), *Crime and the Internet.* New York: Routledge, pp. 59–73.
39. JORDAN, TIM, and TAYLOR, PAUL. (2004). *Hacktivism and Cyberwars: Rebels With a Cause.* New York: Routledge.
40. Ibid., p. 7.
41. LEVY, *Hackers.*
42. *Ibid.*
43. *Ibid.*
44. THOMAS, DOUGLAS. (2002). *Hacker Culture.* Minneapolis, MN: University of Minnesota Press.
45. LEVY, *Hackers.*
46. *Ibid.*
47. *Ibid.*
48. MEYER, GORDON R. (1989). "The Social Organization of the Computer Underground." Unpublished Masters Thesis. Retrieved December 29, 2003, from the World Wide Web: http://csrc.nist.gov/secpubs/hacker.txt
49. *Ibid.*
50. *Ibid.*, p. 8.
51. *Ibid.*, p. 48.
52. *Ibid.*, p. 8.
53. *Ibid.*
54. BLANKENSHIP, L. (1986). *The Hacker Manifesto.* Retrieved March 21, 2000 from the World Wide Web: *http://viaduct.custom.net/glitch/manif.htm*
55. SLATALLA, M., and QUITTNER, J. (1995). *Masters of Deception: The Gang that Ruled Cyberspace.* New York: Harper Collins Publishers.
56. STERLING, *The Hacker Crack-Down.*
57. SHIMOMURA, TSUTOMU. (1996). *Takedown: The Pursuit and Capture of Kevin Mitnick, America's Most Wanted Computer Outlaw-By the Man Who Did It.* New York: Hyperion.
58. *Ibid.*, p. 44.
59. FRANKLIN, J., PAXSON, V., PERRIG, A., and SAVAGE, S. (2007). "An Inquiry into the Nature and Cause of the Wealth of Internet Miscreants." Paper presented at CCS07, October 29–November 2, 2007 in Alexandria, VA; HOLT, T.J., and LAMPKE, E. (2009). "Exploring Stolen Data Markets On-Line: Products and Market Forces." *Criminal Justice Studies* 33(2); Honeynet Research

Alliance. (2003). "Profile: Automated Credit Card Fraud," *Know Your Enemy Paper* series. Retrieved June 21, 2005, from the World Wide Web: *http://www.honeynet.org/papers/profiles/cc-fraud.pdf;* THOMAS, R., and MARTIN, J. (2006). "The Underground Economy: Priceless." *USENIX:login* 31(6): 7–16. *Ibid.*, p. 3.
60. HOLT, "Subcultural Evolution?"
61. JORDAN, T., and TAYLOR, P. (1998). "A Sociology of Hackers." *The Sociological Review* 46(4): 757–780; TAYLOR, P. (1999). *Hackers: Crime in the Digital Sublime.* New York: Routledge.
62. HOLT, "Subcultural Evolution?"
63. Mack Diesel (personal communication, October 10, 2003).
64. *Ibid.*, p. 120.
65. *Ibid.*, p. 27.
66. *Ibid.*, p. 44.
67. MG (personal communication, April 5, 2004).
68. Dark Oz (personal communication, August 18, 2004).
69. HOLT, THOMAS J. (2008). "Lone Hacks or Group Cracks: Examining the Social Organization of Computer Hackers." In FRANK SCHMALLEGER and MICHAEL PITTARO (eds.), *Crimes of the Internet.* Upper Saddle River, NJ: Pearson Prentice Hall, pp. 336–355.
70. www.defcon.org
71. HOLT, THOMAS J. (2006). "Examining the Changing Nature of DEF CON Over the Last 14 Years." Presented at the Defcon 14 Convention, Las Vegas, Nevada.
72. *Ibid.*, p. 129.
73. *Ibid.*
74. JORDAN and TAYLOR "A Sociology of Hackers"; TAYLOR, *Hackers.*
75. *Ibid.*, p. 122.
76. *Ibid.*, p. 16.
77. *Ibid.*, p. 10.
78. *Ibid.*, p. 129.
79. *Ibid.*, p. 16.
80. *Ibid.*, p. 129.
81. HOLT and LAMPKE, "Exploring Stolen Data Markets On-Line."
82. *Ibid.*, p. 129.
83. *Ibid.*, p. 120.

CHAPTER 5

White-Collar Crimes

CHAPTER OBJECTIVES

After completing this chapter, you should be able to

- Describe how computer technologies have altered the ways in which embezzlement is committed.
- Describe how computer technologies have increased the opportunities to commit money laundering.
- Describe how computer technologies have affected the crime of corporate espionage.
- Describe how computer technologies and the increasing use of the Internet have affected identity and fraud crimes.

INTRODUCTION

Historically, the field of criminology has emphasized the need to explain the occurrence of what has commonly been referred to as traditional "street crime." Crimes such as homicide, rape, armed robbery, and aggravated assault have garnered a vast amount of public and media attention, and criminal justice policies have been designed mainly to counteract these personal violent crimes. Whether or not this emphasis has been due to the very real fear that these types of crimes engender in citizens or the media's constant fixation with the "gory details" such crimes produce has been a matter of some debate; what is clear is that the public's common perception of what constitutes "crimes" as well as who is the common "criminal" has been formed largely in relation to traditional street crimes.[1] As a result, crimes that do not fall under traditional definitions or those that are committed by persons who do not fit the public's common perception of the typical criminal have received much less attention.

Noted criminologist Edwin Sutherland was the first to highlight the above-mentioned disparities in the late 1940s. He attempted to describe and define a class of behaviors very different from those of traditional street crimes, including acts committed by corporate executives, corrupt politicians, and unscrupulous professionals. He defined these acts as "white-collar crimes" and suggested that they are largely ignored because the perpetrators of these offenses comprised society's elite—people with the economic wherewithal and status to shape the criminal law in their favor and avoid detection and punishment.[2]

This chapter will describe the ways in which the computer revolution has altered the techniques used to commit some of the most common white-collar offenses, specifically embezzlement, corporate espionage, money laundering, identity crimes, and fraud. The large-scale dissemination of computer and information technologies seems to have created greater opportunities for the white-collar offender, and law enforcement officials are now faced with the unenviable task of looking for loopholes in the ever-expanding technologies used to commit white-collar offenses.

EMBEZZLEMENT

Embezzlement has been defined as the unlawful misappropriation for personal use of money, property, or some other thing of value that has been entrusted to an offender's care, custody, or control. Embezzlement is essentially a theft in violation of a trust. As such, embezzlement has been recognized as a crime since English common-law traditions dating back to the fifteenth century.[3] The embezzler usually is engaged in some type of fiduciary relationship with the victim, either as an employee, guardian, or trustee. Traditionally, embezzlement has involved the physical theft of money or property by employees or others engaged in managing the assets of persons or organizations.

Embezzlement has been the subject of considerable research and debate in regard to both its definition as a traditional white-collar offense and the motivations behind embezzlement schemes. Although Sutherland specifically used embezzlement as an example in his early portrayal of white-collar offending, historically, the embezzler has not been a person of high social status. Rather, he or she has typically been a person engaged in managing the financial affairs of societal elites. Historically, the typical embezzler is a low-level financial institution employee, usually a female bank teller, engaged in stealing financial deposits directly from bank customers. In this regard, some have argued that the embezzler has more in common with the traditional street robber than the corporate executives or professionals originally highlighted by Sutherland in his depiction of white-collar offenders. So too, unlike most other white-collar offenses, embezzlement schemes are often carried out by individual offenders rather than by corporations and other organized entities. These disparities aside, most researchers have historically categorized embezzlement as a white-collar offense, probably because the offense involves a violation of professional trust in which deception rather than physical force is used to carry out the act.

Donald Cressey, in his classic embezzlement study *Other People's Money,* identified a four-step process that described the motivations common to his sample of convicted embezzlers. Prior to the commission of the crime, the embezzler often finds themselves experiencing financial problems that cannot be solved through legitimate financial means. The offender then identifies embezzlement as an avenue through which to alleviate his or her financial problems. The embezzler must also possess the technical knowledge necessary to carry out the embezzlement scheme. Finally, the embezzler will use "neutralization techniques" in order to overcome any lingering shame or guilt associated with stealing money that has been entrusted to their care. These techniques may involve the intention of paying the money back before anyone notices its absence or justifying the theft based on the belief that the "rich" individuals or organizations that have entrusted the money to the embezzler's care will not miss the funds. Freed from these considerations, the embezzler commits the theft in order to solve his or her financial problems.[4]

The advent of the computer age and the ubiquitous use of computers in the management, allocation, and tracking of both personal and business finances have transformed the methods used by embezzlers to misappropriate cash and/or property. Today, the computer provides the most available means to commit embezzlement, and knowledge relating to the manipulation of large-scale computerized financial databases has become the primary tool of the embezzler.

With regard to other computer crimes, embezzlement can be classified as a "computer-assisted" crime rather than a "computer-focused" crime. Computer-assisted crimes are those where the computer is used in a supporting capacity. The specific crime, such as embezzlement, predates the introduction of computers. In contrast, computer-focused crimes have emerged more recently as a direct result of computer technology (e.g., hacking).[5] Anderson has classified the modern-day embezzler as an "internal perpetrator," or an authorized user of computer systems who uses legitimate access to computer files to commit theft. Because embezzlers have been authorized to use computer systems and resources, they are among the most difficult computer criminals to detect and apprehend.[6]

While the crime of embezzlement appeared centuries before the computer revolution, the use of computer technology does seem to have altered both the commission of the act and the profile of those who embezzle. First, the traditional embezzler was often limited by the physical nature of the theft act. That is, there was a limit to how much cash and/or property the embezzler could actually steal, because the act involved taking and transferring cash or other material goods. Modern embezzlement schemes using computerized records often may not involve the physical theft of anything. The embezzler's take is predicated only on his or her abilities as he or she relates to the misappropriation of data files, and millions of dollars can be stolen with simple keystrokes.

Second, the advent of technologically driven financial management techniques may have narrowed the pool of potential embezzlers to those individuals who possess the specialized skills required to use computer information systems. In this regard, modern-day "technical elites" who steal from their employers and organizations may more closely resemble the societal elites originally identified by Sutherland as typical white-collar offenders. Indeed, more recent studies of convicted embezzlers seem to suggest that rather than experiencing financial problems, many technically elite embezzlers are simply motivated by a desire for a more affluent lifestyle.[7] Nonetheless, the examples listed below of recent embezzlement cases involving the misuse of computer technologies can be used to illustrate the widely varied nature of both the perpetrators of modern-day embezzlement and their victims, including private businesses, government agencies, and individuals:

- Thirty-six-year-old Daniel Gruidl of Minnesota pled guilty to computer fraud charges related to the embezzlement of funds from his employer, Vital Signs of Minnesota Inc. Gruidl felt that he was underpaid, so he simply used false passwords in order to log onto the company's computerized payroll system. He proceeded to give himself raises and bonuses that totaled over $108,000. The scam went undetected for two years.[8]
- Don McCorry worked as a senior financial manager in charge of government employee retirement accounts in Fairfax, Virginia. McCorry altered computer records of employee withdrawals from their retirement accounts by reassigning monies to his personal retirement account, labeling them "emergency" withdrawals in his own name. McCorry embezzled over $1.1 million over a four-year period. When he was arrested, investigators confiscated a Mercedes-Benz, a $50,000 art collection, a $100,000 wine collection, and 50 suits valued at $10,000 from his residence.[9]
- A computerized payroll glitch at a North Carolina hospital resulted in a hospital cook being paid $787 an hour over a three-month period. The cook failed to report the overpayment, stating that she believed the glitch to be a "gift from God."[10]
- Cleveland stockbroker Frank Gruttadauria defrauded 50 prominent business executives and investment clients over a 15-year period. He exaggerated the values of client investment

portfolios by altering computerized financial statements. Clients believed they had $277 million in assets, but their accounts totaled barely $1 million in actual value. One individual investor appropriated about $120 million to Gruttadauria; $60 million was actually invested, and the actual cash value of his holdings upon detection of the scam was $8,000.[11]

CORPORATE ESPIONAGE

Corporate espionage involves any theft of proprietary business information through spying or deception, particularly the theft of "trade secrets." Trade secrets encompass any proprietary information that produces value to a commercial enterprise because that information provides competitive advantages over business rivals.[12] The informational targets to be stolen through corporate espionage schemes are wide and varied, including detailed customer lists, product specifications, research and development data, computerized source codes, memoranda detailing corporate strategies, pricing lists, and technology and computer systems data.[13]

Corporate concerns regarding espionage and the theft of business secrets have grown over the course of the last two decades. Several related factors have combined to increase the occurrence of corporate espionage and heighten awareness of the problem. First, the corporate community's increasing use of information and computer technologies to conduct business has provided corporate spies easier access to valuable proprietary information. In particular, the ubiquitous use of e-mail as a means of intraoffice communication has made employee exchanges readily accessible to potential corporate spies who possess the technical expertise to crack such networks. In addition, global commerce has increasingly been conducted electronically over the Internet (i.e., "e-commerce"), which has created a wealth of accessible corporate data available to cyberspace hackers.[14] These factors have worked to make the theft of corporate information much easier. It is no longer necessary for corporate thieves to steal information physically, since most valuable corporate secrets usually exist solely in computerized form.

As a result of these factors, the incidence of and costs associated with corporate espionage have risen sharply. A recent survey by the American Society for Industrial Security (ASIS) estimates that Fortune 1,000 companies lost close to $45 billion to corporate spies in 1999 alone.[15] Indeed, some analysts estimate that losses from business espionage have doubled since the early 1990s. The average company detects 2.45 cases of corporate espionage per year, with each incident costing approximately $500,000. Technology companies appear to be particularly vulnerable. Fortune 1,000 tech firms report an average of 67 espionage attacks per year, costing these firms an average of $115 million annually.[16]

While the dawn of the information age has increased the use of spy tactics among domestic corporate rivals, global political and military trends have also played a role in elevating the costs related to corporate espionage. With the end of Cold War rivalries between the U.S. and Soviet militaries, nations have increasingly concentrated espionage efforts toward the theft of trade, rather than military, secrets. So too, the end of U.S.–Soviet hostilities helped to create a vast network of former military spies—individuals highly skilled in espionage tactics—available for corporate hire.[17] The result has been an increase in the use of corporate espionage by nations looking for competitive advantages for their domestic industries. The National Counterintelligence Agency estimates that U.S. businesses lost $44 billion to the theft of trade secrets by international spies between 1996 and 1997.[18]

Corporate spies can be divided into two distinct groups.[19] Most corporate espionage schemes are conducted by business "insiders," persons who have legitimate access to a company's computer networks, such as employees, information technology personnel, or corporate executives. Limited research suggests that up to 85 percent of all such schemes are carried out by these insiders, whose motivations extend from blackmail and monetary concerns to a simple lack of loyalty or job dissatisfaction.[20] The remaining acts of corporate espionage are performed by corporate "outsiders," or persons who crack into a corporation's computer data networks without any form of legitimate access rights. Outsiders may penetrate computer systems via the Internet or by gaining access to internal computer networks. Outsiders include domestic spies hired by corporate competitors, as well as foreign nationals hired by adversarial governments intent on gaining a competitive advantage over American firms. At the extreme, these types of spies may access proprietary information simply by entering the workplace facility and visually stealing computer passwords or gaining physical access to computer server rooms.[21]

Outside the realms of insiders and outsiders, the growing employment of independent contractors by large-scale corporations has created unique problems in regard to corporate espionage schemes. Independent contractors are individuals hired by a corporation to perform specific, limited jobs, such as database management, product introductions, or programming changes. These individuals (often referred to as "kites") more closely resemble temporary workers rather than full-time employees, and their resulting lack of loyalty and long-term commitment to the hiring corporation may make them vulnerable targets for information for competing firms. "Kites" may also be hired by competing firms because they have specific knowledge concerning competitor operations.[22]

Companies that have been victimized by corporate espionage schemes can pursue a civil action against the offending firm; however, civil suits often turn into lengthy affairs, and the invariable costs incurred through civil courts are prohibitive. The case involving Silicon Valley software firms Cadence Design Systems and Avant! Corporation provides a prime example of the painstakingly slow and costly process involved in resolving domestic espionage suits (see Box 5.1 below for a timeline of events surrounding the case and its eventual outcome).[23] The case originated with an internal investigation conducted by Cadence Design Systems in 1995.[24] Over the course of the preceding four years, several top Cadence executives had left the company to form a rival firm, Avant! Corp. Both companies write software code that helps computer engineers design silicon chips used in advanced computer systems. Cadence executives claimed that Avant! executives had stolen Cadence source code in order to develop software that was producing over $100 million in sales by 1996. The civil and criminal trials took eight years to resolve.[25]

In response to these concerns, as well as the belief that the problem of corporate espionage had grown with the increasing use of computers in the workplace, Congress enacted the Economic Espionage Act of 1996. Under the act, corporations who suspect that they are victims of espionage schemes may request an FBI investigation. If such an investigation reveals criminal wrongdoing, the U.S. Attorney's office of the Department of Justice can prosecute the offending firm for theft of trade secrets.[26]

The Economic Espionage Act outlines two separate offenses related to corporate spying. First, the act attempts to enforce espionage crimes originating from foreign governments and businesses by creating criminal penalties for those who steal, destroy, or knowingly receive stolen trade secrets that would benefit foreign governments. Individual offenders may be fined up to $500,000 and/or face a prison sentence of up to 15 years. Under this portion of the act, corporations may be fined up to $10 million. Second, the act enforces domestic espionage between competing U.S. firms by making the theft of trade secrets related to or included in a product involved in interstate commerce a federal crime. Individual offenders may be fined up to $250,000 and/or face a prison sentence of up to ten years. Under this portion of the act, corporations may be fined up to $5 million.[27]

BOX 5.1

Cadence Design Systems Vs. Avant! Corporation

June 1994   Avant! sales reach $39 million after former Cadence vice president Gerald Hsu joins three other former Cadence executives to head up Cadence rival Avant!

August 1995   During a routine site visit to an Avant! customer, Cadence engineers notice similarities between Avant! code and Cadence code that they had developed years earlier. Four thousand lines of identical code are identified, including grammatical and program errors.

December 1995   Santa Clara Co. district attorneys conduct a search and seizure at Avant! headquarters. Cadance files a formal civil complaint in U.S. District Court. The complaint contends that four Avant! executives conspired to steal trade secrets and copyrighted information over a three-year period.

April 1996   Avant! and six employees, including the chairman and chief executive officer, are indicted on criminal charges in Santa Clara County, California.

March 1997   Cadence fails in its attempt to obtain a preliminary injunction against Avant! intended to stop the sale of software allegedly pirated from Cadence source code.

July 1997   Judge stays the civil suit against Avant! in consideration of the pending criminal charges.

September 1997   Preliminary injunction granted against Avant! barring the company from selling software developed from allegedly stolen source code.

February 1998   Avant!'s chief financial officer resigns.

November 1998   Grand jury convenes to consider criminal indictment against Avant! employees.

December 1998   Federal judge extends preliminary injunction against Avant! barring it from selling newer version of software.

May 2001   Eleven Avant! employees and executives plead no contest to criminal charges related to trade secret theft. Individual fines range from $27,000 to $2.7 million.

July 2001   Avant! ordered to pay over $200 million in restitution and court costs to Cadence.

November 2002   Cadence agrees to settle all civil claims against Avant! and its employees in exchange for $265 million in damages. The companies agree to a reciprocal licensing agreement covering the software in question.

MONEY LAUNDERING

Money laundering is the act of concealing the source of assets that have been illegally obtained. The primary object in laundering is to hide the source and ownership of such funds through the creation of a seemingly legitimate history or paper trail. Like embezzlement, money laundering is an "old" crime whose opportunities have expanded greatly with the increasing use of technology in the marketplace. It is impossible to know the extent to which money laundering occurs; however, experts estimate that about $300 billion in cash is laundered each year. The amount of illegal money laundering associated with the drug trade alone is thought to be anywhere from $5 to $15 billion annually.[28]

Traditionally, money laundering was accomplished through three primary means: (1) Cash that was illegally obtained could be physically transported from its place of origin to a jurisdiction that had less stringent banking and reporting requirements. Although the money would eventually be "lost" in the eyes of law enforcement in this new jurisdiction, the act of physically moving cash from one place to another is time consuming, dangerous, and cumbersome for the launderer. (2) The launderer could quickly transform hard currency into legitimate real property, such as real estate, commercial interests, or personal luxuries.[29]

The problems with transforming illegally gained assets in this manner are twofold. First, the large-scale purchasing of property is ostentatious, and authorities may notice changes tending toward a suddenly lavish lifestyle. Second, many criminals may have difficulty spending all of their ill-gotten cash, given the exorbitant profits in some illegal enterprises (e.g., large-scale drug trading). (3) Launderers often turned to a method commonly referred to as "smurfing." Smurfing involves the division of large amounts of cash into smaller denominations so as to conceal its common origin. The launderer would enlist several persons to deposit relatively small amounts of cash into several different accounts scattered over a geographic area. In this way, the launderer could successfully avoid federal reporting requirements regarding large-scale cash deposits.[30]

The increasing use of technology, especially telecommunications and the Internet, has provided a wealth of new opportunities for the money launderer. Obscuring the origin and owner of large amounts of cash is now a keystroke away. In order to understand the impact that technology has had on money-laundering crimes, it may be useful to view the advancement of technology in this area in two distinct phases. During the 1960s and 1970s, governments, banks, and other financial institutions increasingly used telecommunications networks to move large amounts of cash.[31] These electronic cash transactions, or "electronic funds transfers" (EFTs), served to digitize the financial marketplace. Telephone lines and computer networks substituted for the physical transport of cash and other financial instruments.

Money is swiftly and easily moved both legitimately and illegitimately across these computerized networks. Currently, there are two primary cash transfer institutions. FedWire is the electronic payment network created by the Federal Reserve System. Over 250,000 transactions are performed on the system per day. CHIPS is a clearinghouse payment system created by private banking companies. This consortium moves over $866 billion per day.[32]

The electronic revolution that has occurred in the banking industry, especially the large-scale movement of cash in electronic forms, has made laundering easier. Because money transfers now involve electronic messages rather than physical cash, it is easier for the launderer to move money in a series of transactions over a short period of time. Smurfing can be accomplished by one individual at a keyboard rather than a large group of smurfs over a wide geographic area. So too money that can be moved electronically is also easier to integrate into the mainstream banking system.

While the introduction of telecommunications and computer technologies in the 1960s and 1970s served to increase the ease with which money could be laundered, the current explosion in e-commerce and the influence of the Internet may provide launderers even greater opportunities in years to come. The biggest concern for law enforcement officials is the recent introduction of anonymous electronic cash exchange systems, or "e-cash."[33] E-cash is digital money that may be exchanged over the Internet. It is an electronic replacement for cash. E-cash comprises an electronic series of numbers that have intrinsic value in some form of currency.[34] E-cash may be likened to the serial numbers located on hard currency, except in the case of e-cash there is no hard currency, only the related electronic numbers. Interest in the use of e-cash has grown in conjunction with the Internet, largely because it can be exchanged with increased speed and efficiency. Online businesses can also increase e-commerce profits through its use.

Authorities fear that the increasing use of such "cashless" systems may promote unique "cyberlaundering" schemes that are more difficult to detect and defend against. Researcher Mark Bortner describes a hypothetical scenario whereby the anonymous nature of e-cash and the ease with which it can be accessed through the Internet provides "cyberlaunderers" easy opportunities:[35]

> Doug drug dealer is the CEO of an ongoing narcotics operation. Doug has rooms filled with hard currency that is the profits from his illegal enterprise. This currency needs to enter into the legitimate mainstream economy so that Doug can either purchase needed supplies and employees, purchase real or personal property or even draw interest on his ill-gotten gains . . . Doug employs Linda launderer to wash the dirty money. Linda hires couriers ("smurfs") to deposit funds under different names in amounts between $7,500 and $8,500 at branches of every bank in certain cities . . . In the meantime, Linda launderer has been transferring these same funds from each branch and depositing the money with Internet banks that accept E-cash . . . Once the hard currency has been converted into digital E-cash, the illegally earned money has become virtually untraceable— anonymous. Doug drug dealer now has access to legitimate electronic cash.

Law enforcement authorities have several tools at their disposal to enforce money-laundering crimes. The oldest among these is the Bank Secrecy Act (BSA) of 1970. The BSA requires banks and other financial institutions to file records concerning suspicious financial transactions over $10,000 (e.g., large cash deposits, foreign bank exchanges, cross-border currency transports). In addition, the 1986 Money Laundering Control Act works to close certain loopholes in the BSA that were exploited by launderers in the past. Specifically, the Money Laundering Control Act requires banks and other financial institutions to report any suspicious banking transactions (including possible "smurfing" schemes) regardless of the monetary amount of any single transaction.[36]

Finally, the U.S. Treasury Department's Financial Crimes Enforcement Network (FinCEN) serves as a "central clearinghouse" for intelligence and information sharing on money laundering.[37] FinCEN's main objective is to provide law enforcement agencies the analytical tools necessary to identify and prosecute money-laundering cases. FinCEN uses two primary avenues to accomplish this goal. First, FinCEN provides direct case support to over 150 local law enforcement agencies, and coordinates efforts with the International Association of Chiefs of Police (IACP), the National White-Collar Crime Center (NWCCC), and the National Association of Attorneys General (NAAG). This support specifically involves developing linkages from the various aspects of money-laundering cases so that prosecutions can occur. Second, FinCEN provides secondary support to local law enforcement agencies in the form of training, office space, and database research access. FinCEN officials have termed this support a "platform approach" to solving money-laundering cases, whereby federal resources are used to aid local law enforcement efforts directly.

Over the course of the last 13 years, FinCEN has provided law enforcement and regulatory agencies over 50,000 analytical case reports involving over 200,000 money-laundering suspects. In recognition of the increasingly "borderless" nature of "cyberlaundering," FinCEN also spearheads efforts to promote international cooperation in the fight against laundering. FinCEN develops these international partnerships through Financial Intelligence Units (FIUs), or centralized money-laundering analysis agencies, located across the globe.[38] These FIUs appear to be of increasing importance, given the inherently global nature of international terrorist attacks and terrorist organizations' vital interest in maintaining adequate monetary resources in order to foster new terrorist networks and fund future terror attacks.

Internet fraudsters have also begun to use these systems to their advantage to engage in money laundering and fraud. In 2007, a company called e-gold Ltd. was indicted in the U.S. federal court system on four counts of money laundering.[39] The company allowed individuals to make and receive payments through the transfer of gold ownership. Their payment system and structure were popular among a variety of fraudsters and led the United States to prosecute the operators of e-gold on charges of money laundering and fraud.[40] The CEO of e-gold, Douglas Jackson, pled guilty and negotiated a plea bargain for his crimes, and the company has subsequently changed its payment and system processes to conform to federal statutes.[41]

IDENTITY THEFT

The recent emergence of identity crimes as a primary public and law enforcement concern can be viewed as indicative of the more general patterns of growth we have witnessed in computer crimes during the course of the past several decades. The exponential growth in the incidence of identity theft can largely be attributed to the creation of opportunities that are directly linked to technological and commercial advances. These advances have produced an alarming rise in the fraudulent use of individual information such as Social Security numbers, dates of birth, and credit card numbers by thieves who are intent on using this information for personal gain, and they have forced law enforcement agencies to redirect scarce resources in order to mitigate the threat.

Statistical trends reveal the feverish pace of growth in identity theft crimes. Experts estimate that personal losses related to identity theft reached $745 million in 1997 alone, a figure that represents a 68 percent increase in losses tied to identity theft over only a two-year span.[42] Credit thieves victimize approximately 1,000 individuals per day, and national estimates indicate that 350,000–500,000 persons annually experience monetary losses connected to identity crimes.[43] Trans-Union Corp., one of the three primary credit-reporting bureaus, indicates that about two-thirds of all consumer inquiries to the company's fraud division in 1997 involved possible identity theft crimes, or over 43,000 complaints per month.[44] In 1999, the Social Security administration received over 62,000 allegations involving the misuse of Social Security numbers alone.[45] These explosive growth patterns are clearly beginning to strain law enforcement resources at the federal level—identity theft has been the primary charge in over 90 percent of all arrests made by the Secret Service's Financial Crimes Division since the mid-1990s. Losses related to closed identity theft cases by the Division topped $248 million in 2000, with potential losses tied to other reported cases nearing $1.5 billion.[46]

These trends can partly be attributed to the increasing use of Social Security numbers as personal identifiers. Social Security numbers, rarely referred to by those under retirement age decades ago, are now used as a means to conduct a wide range of business transactions, most notably the opening of new lines of personal credit. The use of Social Security numbers as personal identifiers, however, has not been limited to credit transactions. We are now asked to include the number on an ever-increasing array of forms, including medical records, motor vehicle driver's licenses, and educational and employment records—some car dealers will even ask for it prior to allowing a customer to test drive a vehicle. Obviously, theft opportunities increase in relation to the number of times that consumers are required to use Social Security numbers as personal identifiers by commercial and governmental enterprises.

Moreover, growth trends in identity theft have strongly paralleled the advent of "e-commerce," or the use of online technologies to conduct both consumer-based and business-to-business transactions. Today's consumer—ardently pounding out keystrokes and "surfing" commercial Web sites—is far more likely to be asked to provide his or her Social Security number at his or her virtual "checkout" than was the more traditional pedestrian shopper of previous decades.

Identity thieves use a variety of methods to steal personal information. Heading up the list of low-tech means is "dumpster diving," or rummaging through private or commercial trash receptacles in search of discarded bills or preapproved credit applications.[47] Other low-tech methods include the direct theft of mail, which may include a veritable treasure trove of personal information contained on bank statements and unwanted telephone calling cards. Some thieves even complete change of address forms in the name of unwitting victims in order to divert and more easily access personal mail. "Shoulder surfing," or eavesdropping on conversations and cash transactions that involve the disclosure of personal identifiers, provides an avenue for low-tech thieves who are unwilling to steal documents outright.[48]

While these theft techniques provide opportunities for everyday thieves, more organized and technologically based methods have been used by sophisticated thieves intent on stealing mass quantities of personal information. These schemes may involve hacking information from corporate databases used for online transactions or the bribing of employees who have internal access to customer identifiers. The loss of sensitive personal information is costly, considering estimates from 2007 found that businesses in the United States lost over $5 million due to the theft of confidential electronic data by hackers and computer attackers.[49] One of the most noteworthy and significant mass compromises in recent years affected customers of the TJX corporation. A small group of hackers compromised an internal database and stole at least 94 million customer credit card accounts, which financial agencies estimate caused as much as $1 billion in damages.[50]

Once personal identifying information is obtained, thieves can ransack a victim's financial status and destroy his or her credit history with frightening ease. For example, they may be able to open a new credit account using stolen Social Security numbers, names, and date of birth. The victim, of course, is left with the unpaid bills and delinquent accounts. Depending on the amount of personal information stolen, thieves may even be able to create entirely new bank accounts in your name, writing "hot" checks that are eventually traced back to the victim's credit history. Others have been victimized by thieves who have established wireless phone service, bought cars and other expensive consumer goods, and filed for bankruptcy under assumed identities in order to avoid paying past due accounts (see Box 5.2).[51]

Identity thieves have also developed black markets online where stolen personal information can be sold and resold to individuals around the world. Evidence suggests that Internet Relay

---

BOX 5.2
Recent Identity Crime Prosecutions

- Federal agents arrested a former employee at a Long Island software company who allegedly originated a crime ring that eventually cost consumers $2.7 million. The suspect sold the credit reports of over 30,000 people, including names, Social Security numbers, and other credit information, to black market identity thieves who used the information to fraudulently obtain a wide variety of consumer goods. Each victim's credit history was sold for only $30.

- A defendant was recently convicted in federal court for fraudulently obtaining the names and Social Security numbers of high-ranking military officers from internal government Web sites and using the information to apply online for credit cards and other lines of credit. He was sentenced to 41 months in prison and ordered to pay over $186,000 in restitution.

- A former temporary employee of an insurance firm was convicted for using policyholders' bank account information to deposit over $764,000 in counterfeit bank checks.

- Seven defendants were recently convicted in an identity theft–drug smuggling scheme. The suspects used stolen Social Security numbers to garner employment and identification documents that were used to facilitate the smuggling of heroin and methamphetamine from Mexico. A number of the defendants also used their stolen identities to claim earned income tax credits on IRS tax forms.

Chat, or IRC, channels and Web sites operate for hackers to sell significant volumes of data obtained through database compromises and other means. These Web-based resources exist to sell credit card and bank accounts, PIN numbers, and supporting customer information obtained from victims around the world in lots of tens or hundreds of accounts.[52] Stolen credit and bank accounts are referred to as "dumps" within these markets, and the individuals who participate are referred to as "carders."[53] Financial accounts in carding markets are sold at very low prices for as little as $1.30 in some cases.[54] Individuals could also buy accounts obtained from countries around the world, suggesting that identity theft and fraud have no boundaries.

Carding markets also facilitate real-world identity theft and fraud, as individuals offer cash out services to obtain physical money from electronic accounts. In addition, individuals can buy skimming devices that can be attached to an automatic teller machine or point of sale terminal.[55] These devices capture and store the magnetic stripe data from debit and credit cards and steal data from unsuspecting individuals. Finally, individuals sell passports, drivers' licence, and financial records within these markets, thereby allowing individuals to more efficiently engage in identity theft in the real world. Box 5.3 details a significant case in the investigation of carding groups. In general, carding is a significant problem, because the criminals who frequent these markets can quickly and efficiently engage in credit card fraud and identity theft without any technical knowledge or skill.[56]

Federal law enforcement agencies and the criminal justice system have begun to respond to the increasing threat posed by identity thieves through new legislation and consumer awareness programs. In 1998, Congress passed the Identity Theft and Assumption Deterrence Act. The law makes it a federal crime when someone

> Knowingly transfers or uses, without lawful authority, a means of identification of another person with the intent to commit, or to aid or abet, any unlawful activity that constitutes a violation of federal law, or that constitutes a felony under any applicable state or local law.[59]

Violations of the law may be punishable by up to 15 years in prison. While the act clearly signifies a growing recognition of the costs associated with identity crimes, the impact of these and other laws aimed at curtailing identity theft may be largely symbolic for many of those victimized. The reality is that identity crimes remain extremely difficult to prosecute once detected. A large number of cases are detected too late for officials to investigate adequately. These cases are extremely labor intensive and often require collaborative effort on the part of federal, state, and local law enforcement agencies for successful prosecution. So too, the actual monetary losses involved in many individual cases of identity theft may be considered too small for dedication of a large amount of prosecutorial resources.[60]

BOX 5.3
Prominent Carding Market Cases

CASE #1: The ShadowCrew opened a Web site in 2002 and developed a brisk trade in credit cards, financial information, and identity documents.[57] Over one million credit cards were said to have been sold through their site, and there were over 2,000 registered members. Their Web site was taken down on October 26, 2004, by the U.S. Secret Service and various police agencies around the world, and the homes of 28 members of the group were raided. Subsequently, 12 individuals arrested pled guilty to charges ranging from computer fraud and abuse to document fraud and conspiracy. The leader of the group, 32-year-old Andrew Mantovani, received 32 months in a federal prison camp for his role in this carding group.[58]

Given the difficulties inherent in detecting and prosecuting identity crimes, many experts believe that the establishment of consumer awareness and monitoring programs may be the most viable avenue toward thwarting the growth of identity theft. To this end, the Federal Trade Commission (FTC) has established the identity theft clearinghouse. The clearinghouse collects identity theft complaints and provides victims referral information and other resources aimed at helping them restore their credit history and financial status. The clearinghouse has also established a hotline for consumers who believe they have been victimized in an identity crime.[61]

INTERNET FRAUD SCHEMES

The Internet has increasingly been used as a vehicle for interpersonal communications, research, consumer spending, and business-to-business transactions over the course of the last decade. This growth has provided the public with previously unparalleled opportunities for personal and economic advancement and has created entire new industries in the process. These advances, however, have also produced fresh opportunities for fraud and abuse online. Interestingly, many fraud schemes committed over the Internet are simply new takes on old themes—chain letter hoaxes, confidence schemes, and bait-and-switch con games that are now performed over an electronic medium rather than in person or over the telephone. Whether in old or new form, it is clear that the increasing use of the Internet has given rise to an alarming growth in fraudulent schemes. According to the official reporting rates of the NWCCC, consumer complaints concerning online fraud have risen from 16,838 in 2000 to over 75,000 in 2002, over a 400 percent increase in just two years.[62] These Internet fraud schemes encompass a wide range of offenses, including financial institution fraud, investment fraud, communications fraud, and confidence schemes. This section will briefly define and describe the first three above-mentioned types of Internet fraud, as well as discuss various types of confidence schemes in more detail.

Financial institution fraud involves attempts to conceal the truth from deposit and lending institutions so as to gain monetarily.[63] Examples of financial lending institution fraud include credit/debit card fraud and identity theft. Credit card fraud is one of the most widely reported Internet frauds, and identity theft has become a primary concern for law enforcement personnel and the public alike (see Chapter 10 for a discussion concerning enforcement efforts against identity theft). Investment frauds are "deceptive practices involving the use of capital to create more money," including traditional stock market investment schemes and pyramid business schemes designed to defraud individual consumers, all of which can be conducted online.[64] Communication frauds involving new and different forms of technology have skyrocketed through thefts of wireless phone codes and other satellite communication devises.[65]

While all types of Internet fraud have experienced recent growth, frauds that involve a breach of personal trust, or what have been traditionally referred to as confidence schemes, may be among the most widely practiced and familiar to the general public. These schemes now typically use e-mail communications or online sites as a primary medium rather than the mail or telephone. The most widely perpetrated Internet confidence schemes include online auction fraud, the Nigerian "419" fraud, chain letter hoaxes, and what are known as "urban legends" passed along through electronic mailings.

Online auction fraud is the most widely reported type of Internet fraud by a large margin. Sixty-four percent of all reported Internet fraud is auction fraud. The Internet Crime Complaint Center (IC3) received over 30,000 auction fraud complaints in 2001. Losses related to online auction fraud surpass $4,000,000 annually.[66] The IC3 has also received an increase in the number of reports of auction fraud over time, and the average loss per complaint was $610.[67] Individuals and/or businesses participating in online auctions can be defrauded in several ways. The most prevalent form of online auction fraud is nondelivery of goods. In most cases, the victim of nondelivery has very little recourse if payment for the item has already been received by the would-be seller. Most online auction buyers do not have a physical address or description of the perpetrator. Because of this, nondelivery of goods is one of the most commonly reported forms of auction fraud.[68]

Sellers may also purposely misrepresent the item to be auctioned in terms of its quality or characteristics. This can be accomplished through simple item descriptions or the altering of item pictures. "Shill bidding" is the use of intentional fake bidding on the part of the seller in order to artificially inflate an item's auctioned price. Finally, "fee stacking" occurs when the seller adds hidden charges to the cost of the item prior to delivery, most often through inflating the shipping cost. The costly nature of these schemes is detailed in Box 5.4, which provides excerpts from case summaries provided by the IC3 of two of the most extensive schemes recently investigated by federal law enforcement authorities.[69]

Another highly publicized online fraud scheme has been dubbed the Nigerian 419 scheme by authorities. Since its origination in 1989, the online e-mail letter scheme has cost individuals and businesses an estimated one billion dollars globally. The scheme is named "419" after the relevant Nigerian criminal codes that are involved. The scheme encompasses numerous different e-mails forwarded by Nigerian nationals in which the correspondence outlines nonexistent opportunities for recipients to receive Nigerian government funds in exchange for advance fees.[70] The following is an excerpted summary of the content of these fraudulent e-mails detailing the scheme from Interpol.[71]

The letters explain that the money is from delayed approved contract payments by the Nigerian administration to certain companies or individuals who have abandoned their claims. The letter alleges that the present military government is now paying these claims. The signatories claim to be acting as middlemen and request that the victim supply signed and stamped blank company letterheads and invoices together with detailed account information so that monies can be transferred in advance of payment in order to pay taxes and bribe relevant officials in charge of the supposed proceeds. Obviously, no money is ever received, resulting in a total loss of bank deposits from the victim.

BOX 5.4
Prominent Online Auction Fraud Cases

CASE #1   The CATCH Task Force successfully prosecuted Raj Trivedi for victimizing more than 700 individuals throughout the world with his Internet fraud scheme of advertising high-tech products, accepting payment, and then failing to deliver the merchandise advertised. Losses from these frauds were over $992,000. Trivedi victimized consumers who went to his Web site to purchase electronic equipment (e.g., computers and camcorders) that Trivedi advertised on the auction Web sites eBay, uBid, and Yahoo. In March 2002, Trivedi was sentenced to three years in prison and ordered to pay restitution to his victims, who averaged $1,200 in individual losses.

CASE #2   The case against Teresa Smith of Massachusetts represents one of the largest online auction fraud schemes on record. Smith was the subject of over 300 individual complaints stemming from frauds occurring from April 2001 through October 2002. Her scheme was simple: She would defraud her victims by selling a computer, requiring them to pay up front, and then not sending any of the auctioned merchandise. Smith then refused any type of refund request. During the investigation it was discovered that Smith had spent the victims' money on living expenses, a new vehicle, and advertising costs associated with the scheme. Smith would change her online identity any time complaints were reported against her. The scheme was finally detected after investigators uncovered over $800,000 in fraudulent proceeds. Smith was sentenced in 2003 to nearly five years in prison for her crime.

The IC3 received over 16,000 complaints about the scheme in 2008 alone. Largely as a result of this scheme, Nigeria ranks second behind only the United States in losses associated with Internet fraud schemes.[72] Victims in the United States lost an average of $1,650 due to these schemes, which are one of the more costly forms of fraud according to the IC3.[73]

Another costly form of Internet fraud is **phishing**. Perpetrators of phishing schemes attempt to lure or "hook" potential victims to fraudulent Web sites for the purpose of gathering sensitive personal information. Phishing attacks involve the distribution of e-mails that appear to be from a legitimate financial institution or credit card company. The text of the message usually states that the recipient's account has been compromised or requires maintenance. The e-mail then asks the potential victim to log into his or her financial accounts through a Web link contained in the phishing e-mail. The link appears to take the victim to the Web site of a legitimate financial institution, but actually redirects his or her browser to a fraudulent Web site created by the criminal. The fraudulent link contains a spoofed Web page that mirrors the legitimate Web site of the financial institution. The best phishers take images and Web page designs directly from legitimate Web sites. The victim provides his or her bank account number, PIN, passwords, or other sensitive information. From here, the criminal can use the information to engage in credit card fraud or identity theft without the victim's knowledge. The IC3 has seen an increase in phishing schemes since 2004, and these types of schemes have quickly become one of the most common forms of internet fraud. The Gartner Group estimates the cost of phishing schemes in the United States during 2007 alone to be $3 billion. Box 5.5 contains a summary of recent research efforts designed to help Internet users detect phishing e-mails before the damage is done.

Once the recipient clicks on the link provided in the e-mail, he or she is taken to a spoofed Web page that mirrors the actual financial institution's site. The best phishers take the images and design directly from the originating business to ensure that they can fool as many victims as possible. At this point, the victim is asked to provide his or her bank account, PIN, password, or other information, which is then transmitted to the phisher in a variety of ways. From here, the criminals can use the information they collect to engage in credit card fraud or identity theft without the victim knowing this has occurred.[75] Phishing is a particularly costly form of fraud for both victims and financial institutions alike, as the Gartner Group estimates that phishing victims in the United States lost $3 billion in 2007 alone.[76] Additionally, the IC3 has seen an

BOX 5.5
Detecting Phishing E-mails

Criminals can easily duplicate the legitimate Web sites of financial institutions to perpetrate a phishing attack. Researchers at Carnegie Mellon University recently presented a method for detecting phishing e-mails and mitigating the costs associated with these attacks.[74] The researchers designed a system for detecting phishing e-mails that involves (1) extracting data contained in the phishing email and (2) collecting additional information from external sources. Their approach—referred to as PILFER—is designed to detect communication that is intentionally deceptive or intended to "trick" the users into believing that they are dealing with a legitimate financial institution. PILFER involves the use of several different types of information to detect phishing e-mails. These data include Web addresses, Web site domain names, the number of links present in the e-mail, HTML e-mails, JavaScript, and information gathered from existing spam filters. The researchers found that PILFER identified phishing e-mails with 99.5 percent accuracy. The research shows that it is becoming increasingly possible to detect phishing e-mails using a specialized filter such as PILFER. Future detection strategies will need to continue to develop, as the nature and character of phishing attacks evolve over time.

increase in phishing reports since 2004, making it one of the more common forms of Internet fraud.[77] Chain letter hoaxes and "urban legends" comprise another highly publicized and common form of Internet fraud. Chain letter hoaxes over the Internet are simply online versions of age-old schemes designed to perpetuate the forwarding of e-mails. Often, these letters ask the recipient to forward the e-mail message to as many people as they can in exchange for a specified sum for each forwarded e-mail.[78] Chain letter hoaxes are typically less costly than other forms of online fraud, because the recipient is simply duped into believing that he or she will receive compensation that is not forthcoming. These hoaxes have included claims that prominent businesses will compensate recipients for forwarded e-mails, including Microsoft, Outback Steak House, Victoria's Secret, Newell Company, Nokia, Old Navy, and McDonalds, among others.[79] These claims are *never* true, because currently there is no software in existence that is capable of tracking the number of times that an e-mail is forwarded and then subsequently compiling a report back to a central tabulator.[80] So-called urban legends are myths designed to create a generalized panic among e-mail recipients. These messages typically entail grandiose claims of impending danger arising from commonplace activities. Box 5.6 details some of the more common urban legends currently circulating online. Rest assured, none of the claims are true.[81]

BOX 5.6
Common Online "Urban Legends"

Needles on Gas Pumps

Some persons have been affixing hypodermic needles to the underside of gas pump handles in the Jacksonville, FL area. These needles appear to be infected with the HIV virus. In the Jacksonville area alone, there have been 17 cases of people being stuck by these needles over the past five months. We have verified reports of at least 12 other cases around the country . . . Evidently, the consumers go to fill their car with gas, and when picking up the pump handle get stuck by infected needles . . . IT IS IMPERATIVE TO CAREFULLY CHECK THE HANDLE OF GAS PUMPS EVERY TIME YOU USE ONE!

Cyanide-Laced Deposit Envelopes

I hesitate to be an alarmist, but if anything like this happened to one of my family or friends I would not be able to forgive myself for not passing this along . . . A woman died recently from licking the deposit envelope at a Bank of America ATM. It was laced with cyanide. Investigators stated that they went back to the ATM in question and found six other envelopes in the slot . . . Please, I implore you to use extreme caution when using those envelopes. The radio station advised that you should first spit on the envelope, and then close it . . . I know this sounds gross, but better gross than DEAD.

Poison Perfume Samples

I was sent an e-mail at work about someone walking up to you at a mall parking lot and asking you to sniff perfume they are selling at cut-rate prices. This isn't really perfume but ether, and you will pass out and they will take your wallet and all of your valuables. This is not a prank e-mail. This is true! I could have very well been a victim. PASS THIS ALONG.

Rat Feces

A stock clerk was sent to clean up a storeroom at his work place. When he got back there, he was complaining that the storeroom was really filthy, and that he had noticed dried mouse or rat droppings in some areas . . . A couple of days later, he started feeling like he came down with a stomach flu, achy joints, and headache. He went to bed and never woke up. Within two days he was ill and weak. His blood sugar count was down to 66. He was rushed to emergency where he suffered from complete organ failure. He died shortly before midnight . . . There is a virus that lives in dried rat droppings (much like Hanta virus). Once dried, these droppings are like dust and can be easily digested. ALWAYS carefully rinse off the tops of any canned foods or soda . . . A family friend recently died from drinking a can of soda!

The Computer Fraud and Abuse Act (CFAA) has become the primary vehicle for the prosecution of Internet fraud crimes. The CFA was initially enacted by Congress in 1984, primarily as a means to protect classified information contained on government computers. The scope of the CFA was expanded in 1986, and again in 1996. The 1996 amendments to the act worked to incorporate *all* computers that are involved in interstate and/or foreign commerce.[82] Essentially, the CFA covers most fraudulent business practices that are conducted over the Internet.

Summary

This chapter has defined and described how the growth in computer technologies has affected five major criminal offenses: embezzlement, money laundering, corporate espionage, identity crimes, and fraud. The traditional crimes of embezzlement and money laundering have clearly become more prevalent, and modern technologies have increased opportunities to commit both crimes. In terms of embezzlement, the computer has allowed individuals increased access to funds manipulation and has eliminated problems related to the material bulk of moving large quantities of cash. Money laundering is now easier because of two primary reasons: (1) electronic funds are easier to conceal while maintaining anonymity, and (2) the advent of "cashless" banking systems such as e-cash has made detection of such crimes much more difficult.

In addition, computer technologies have created a wide array of new avenues to the pilfering of corporate secrets, including trade technologies, research and development strategies, and customer lists. Computerized corporate data are easier to access, and the prevalent utilization of electronic mail in business environments has given corporate thieves expanded opportunities. So too the end of the Cold War has created a cadre of former spies who can provide foreign firms the skills and expertise necessary for stealing domestic trade secrets.

Finally, the traditional crime of fraud has taken on new forms as a result of the information revolution. In particular, the Internet has increasingly been utilized as a platform to perpetrate fraud, especially through carding, online auction schemes, financial institution frauds, and the transmission of "urban legends."

Review Questions

1. Identify and describe the similarities and differences between corporate espionage offenders who are "insiders" and those who are "outsiders."
2. What is the Bank Secrecy Act of 1970? How has the advent of computer technologies created ways around this act?
3. What is phishing? How does phishing fit into the problem of identity theft?
4. What are "urban legends"? How have these "legends" changed over the course of the last two decades?

Endnotes

1. REIMAN, J. (1995). *The Rich Get Richer and the Poor Get Prison.* Boston, MA: Allyn & Bacon.
2. SUTHERLAND, E. (1940). "White-Collar Criminality." In G. GEIS, R.F. MEIRER, and L.M. SALINGER (eds.), *White Collar Crime: Classic and Contemporary Views.* New York: Free Press, 29–38.
3. GREEN, G.S. (1997). *Occupational Crime,* 2nd ed. Chicago, IL: Nelson Hall.

4. CRESSEY, D.R. (1953). *Other People's Money: A Study in the Social Psychology of Embezzlement.* Glencoe, IL: Free Press.

5. FURNELL, S. (2002). *Cybercrime: Vandalizing the Information Society.* Boston, MA: Addison-Wesley.

6. ANDERSON, J.P. (1980). *Computer Security Threat Monitoring and Surveillance.* Fort Washington, PA: James P. Anderson Co.

7. *Ibid.,* p. 3.

8. FIEDLER, T. (June 24, 1999). "Man Admits Helping Himself to Raises; Embezzlement Trial is the First Computer Fraud Case to be Heard in Minnesota." *Star Tribune* (Minneapolis, MN).

9. GLOD, M. (November 23, 2002). "Ex-Fairfax Official Gets 14 Years in Theft." *Washington Post.*

10. KANE, D. (November 24, 2002). "Millions Vanish Through Theft, Embezzlement at North Carolina Agencies." *Knight Ridder/Tribune Business News.*

11. MURRAY, T.D., and CANIGLIA, J. (February 16, 2003). "Broker's Victims Start Over; Gruttaduria's Investors Still Hurting, Rules Not Changed." *Cleveland Plain Dealer.*

12. HUDSON, J.E., III. (October 4, 2002). "Trade Secret Theft Threatens Everyone with Corporate Espionage Escapades." *Houston Business Journal.*

13. ROBINSON, S.W. (2003). *Corporate Espionage 101.* SANS Institute.

14. KONRAD, R. (September 21, 2000). "Leaks and Geeks: International Espionage Goes High-Tech." *C/Net News.Com.*

15. *Ibid.,* p. 14.

16. *Ibid.*

17. *Ibid.*

18. *Ibid.,* p. 12.

19. *Ibid.,* p. 13.

20. *Ibid.*

21. *Ibid.*

22. *Ibid.*

23. BOWMAN, L.M. (July 19, 2001). "Avant Ordered to Pay $182 Million." *C/Net News.Com.*

24. SWARTZ, J. (April 16, 1997). "Felony Charges Halve Avant's Stock." *The San Francisco Chronicle.*

25. BURROWS, P. (June 15, 1997). "A Nest of Software Spies?" *Business Week.*

26. *Ibid.,* p. 14.

27. *Ibid.,* p. 12.

28. LYMAN, M.D., and POTTER, G.W. (2000). *Organized Crime.* Upper Saddle River, NJ: Prentice Hall.

29. *Ibid.,* p. 28.

30. *Ibid.*

31. GRABOSKY, P.N., and SMITH, R.G. (1998). *Crime in the Digital Age.* New Brunswick, NJ: The Federated Press.

32. *Ibid.,* p. 31.

33. BORTNER, R.M. (1996). "Cyberlaundering: Anonymous Digital Cash and Money Laundering." Presented as a final paper at the University of Miami School of Law.

34. *Ibid.,* p. 33.

35. *Ibid.*

36. *http://fincen.gov*

37. *Ibid.,* p. 36.

38. *Ibid.*

39. Department of Justice (2007). "Digital Currency Business E-Gold Indicted for Money Laundering and Illegal Money Transmitting." United States Department of Justice.

40. *Ibid.,* p. 37.

41. *Ibid.*

42. LEASE, M.L., and BURKE, T.D. (2000). "Identity Theft: A Fast-Growing Crime." *FBI Law Enforcement Bulletin* 69(8).

43. *Ibid.,* p. 40.

44. HOAR, S.B. (March 2001). "Identity Theft: The Crime of the New Millennium." *USA Bulletin.*

45. *Ibid.,* p. 42.

46. *Ibid.*

47. *Ibid.,* p. 40.

48. *Ibid.,* p. 42.

49. Computer Security Institute (2007). "Computer Crime and Security Survey." Retrieved March 2007 from *http://www.cybercrime.gov/FBI 2006.pdf*

50. GOODIN, D. (2007). "TJX Breach Was Twice As Big As Admitted, Banks Say." *The Register.* Retrieved March 27, 2008, from *http://www.theregister.co. uk/2007/10/24/tjx_breach_estimate_grows/*

51. Excerpted from HOAR, "Identity Theft."

52. FRANKLIN, J., PAXSON, V., PERRIG, A., and SAVAGE, S. (2007). "An Inquiry into the Nature and Cause of the Wealth of Internet Miscreants." Paper presented at CCS07, October 29–November 2, 2007 in Alexandria, VA; HOLT, T.J., and LAMPKE, E. (2009). "Exploring Stolen Data Markets On-Line: Products and Market Forces." *Criminal Justice Studies* 33(2); Honeynet Research Alliance (2003). "Profile: Automated Credit Card Fraud." *Know Your Enemy Paper* series. Retrieved June 21, 2005, from *http://www.hon eynet.org/papers/profiles/cc-fraud.pdf*; THOMAS, R.,

and Martin, J. (2006). "The Underground Economy: Priceless." *USENIX:login* 31(6): 7–16.

53. *Ibid.*, p. 49.

54. *Ibid.*

55. *Ibid.*

56. *Ibid.*

57. Parizo, E.B. (2005). "Busted: The Inside Story of 'Operation Firewall.' " *Security News.* Retrieved January 18, 2006, from *http://searchsecurity. techtarget.com/news/article/0,289142,sid14_gci11 46949,00.html*

58. *Ibid.*

59. Federal Trade Commission Bulletin (February 2002). "Identity Theft: When Bad Things Happen to Your Good Name." See *http://bulk.resource.org/ gpo.gov/hearings/106s/69821.pdf*

60. *Ibid.*, p. 41.

61. *Ibid.*, p. 47.z

62. IC3 2002 Internet Fraud Report (2003).

63. *Ibid.*, p. 50.

64. *Ibid.*

65. *Ibid.*

66. IC3 Internet Fraud Report (2008).

67. *Ibid.*, p. 66.

68. *Ibid.*

69. *Ibid.*

70. Professionals Against Confidence Crimes (2003). "Interpol Warning: Nigerian Crime Syndicates Letter Scheme Fraud Takes on New Dimension." See *http://stopcon.org/index.html*

71. *Ibid.*, p. 56.

72. *Ibid.*, p. 50.

73. *Ibid.*, p. 67.

74. Fette, I., Sadeh, N., and Tomasic, A. (2007). "Learning to Detect Phishing Emails." Proceedings of the 16th Annual International Conference on the World Wide Web, Banff, Alberta, CA.

75. *Ibid.*, p. 74

76. Rogers, J. (2007). "Gartner: Victims of Online Phishing Up Nearly 40 Percent in 2007." *SC Magazine.* Retrieved January 2, 2008, from *http:// www.scmagazineus.com/Gartner-Victims-of-online- phishing-up-nearly-40-percent-in-2007/article/ 99768/*

77. *Ibid.*, p. 66.

78. *http://www.scambusters.org*

79. *Ibid.*, p. 59.

80. *Ibid.*

81. *Ibid.*

82. *GigiLaw.Com* (2001). "The Expanding Importance of the Computer Fraud and Abuse Act."

CHAPTER 6

Viruses and Malicious Code

CHAPTER OBJECTIVES

After completing this chapter, you should be able to

- Identify and distinguish the various types of viruses and malicious code.
- Understand the differences between the differing types of viruses, including file viruses, boot viruses, macroviruses, and network viruses.
- Understand the differences between a virus and worm. Additionally, understand how a worm operates in comparison to a virus.
- Understand the definition and operation of a Trojan horse and how it is different from a standard virus.
- Describe adware and spyware, and the controversy concerning whether or not these types of programs are in fact viruses.
- Describe and understand other types of malicious code and attacks, including denial-of-service attacks and blended threats.
- Describe and understand the true threat posed by viruses, the extent of the virus and malicious code problem, and virus hoaxes and their effect on computers and productivity.
- Understand who the virus writers are and why they write viruses.

INTRODUCTION

There is perhaps no other area of computer crime that creates more fear, misperceptions, and attention than computer viruses. The immediate popularity of personal computing, rapidly developing technology, and a general lack of oversight and regulation have combined to create the concomitant development of software and malicious programs as well. None of the first personal computers (PCs), early versions of disk-operating software (DOS), or first networks were designed with security in mind.[1] As a result, law enforcement, virus security experts, and network managers continually play catchup with an ever-growing list of viruses and malicious code. Computer security is a multibillion industry, increasing in value every year. The market for virus protection software, firewalls, and computer security expertise is estimated at $4 billion and relies on the same fears that drive many to purchase home security systems.[2] The question is, how serious is the virus problem, and what is really necessary to deal with the problems viruses and other types of malicious code present? Indeed, in the years preceding the turn of the century, virus hype definitely outpaced virus damage. However, in recent years, several high-profile worms have caused millions of dollars of damage to numerous businesses and PC users. The type and scope of malicious software has also increased significantly in the past few years, creating a structure for all manner of computer attacks, which some refer to as "crimeware."[3]

Initially, viruses were spread primarily through floppy disks, with the infections being spread by infecting multiple computers via the same diskette. Today, viruses and other types of malicious code are primarily spread over the Internet through a variety of mechanisms including e-mail, e-mail attachments, downloadable files, Web pages, newsgroups, peer-to-peer file transfers,[4] instant messaging (texting),[5] digital pictures, and several other techniques and tactics.[6] The Internet was designed for the rapid propagation of data, making no distinction between good or bad data.[7] As such, viruses and other types of malicious code take advantage of the very conveniences and features that make the Internet so appealing. The true cost of viruses is unknown; estimates range from very little true damage to wild estimates claiming that viruses cost billions of dollars annually. A recent survey of security experts from the government, private industry, and universities revealed that 46 percent had experienced some type of security breach in the prior year, and 26 percent of those entities experienced ten or more attacks in a single year.[8] Though this is less than half of all reporting entities, the losses they face from malicious software and hacking are over $11 million.[9] Nonetheless, there is no centralized database that collects information on the damage that viruses cause.

At the outset, it is important to note that this chapter is not designed to provide the reader with substantial technical knowledge concerning viruses or virus prevention and computer security. It is simply an overview of the types of viruses, malicious code, and security problems that exist, with some relevant examples and some material on the investigation and prosecution of virus writers. This chapter focuses almost exclusively on common computer systems and windows-based viruses that the casual and neophyte reader will be familiar with. Viruses and malicious code can infect other operating systems and hardware, but that is beyond the focus of this chapter. Finally, this chapter is not written for expert computer users or experts in the virus writing and virus prevention fields. Instead, it offers a layman's approach, designed for people unfamiliar with the complexities of the virus problem.

Although no reliable estimate exists, there is probably no other area in computers where more time, energy, and resources are spent than on antivirus protection. This has led to the creation of the pseudo–virus expert, a person who proclaims expertise in office workgroups around the world, claiming that he or she knows about viruses and how to prevent them. Most commonly, this is the person who can download patches and update antivirus software, with little real knowledge of viruses. There are many reasons behind this so-called expertise; the most prominent reason is the "false authority syndrome," so aptly described by Rob Rosenberger, a well-known virus expert (see Box 6.1). Hence, the author of this chapter wants to make it perfectly clear that he is no virus expert and wishes to avoid false authority syndrome at all costs. Instead, the author, like most people who express legitimate concern about viruses and malicious code, is a student of the virus industry. This chapter provides a nontechnical look at viruses and malicious code and is designed to give the readers the knowledge of viruses they need to be discriminating about what they hear, read, and learn about this area. Often there is more bark than bite in most of the viruses that plague our computers.

BOX 6.1
Computer Viruses and "False Authority Syndrome"

The following account is from Rob Rosenberger, a virus expert and myth debunker concerning what he terms "False Authority Syndrome."

True Story

A couple of years ago I dropped by the Software Etc. store in Fairview Heights, Illinois, just to browse. Another customer had come in before me and told an employee about a problem with his video monitor. The employee warned the customer that he had contracted a newly discovered computer virus, which he proceeded to describe in great detail.

I interrupted the employee. "Sir, you have it completely wrong. That virus doesn't exist. It's the latest hoax."

"Oh, no," the employee replied. "We've got e-mail reports from our sales headquarters telling us to keep our eyes open for it."

To which I countered, "Some upper-tier sales manager has been duped and is telling you BS. McAfee Associates and others have issued public statements dismissing that virus as a hoax. What you've described simply cannot be done by any virus. Period."

I then turned my attention to the customer. "Stop listening to this guy. You don't have this magical virus he's describing because it simply doesn't exist. You have some other problem with your video monitor." What credentials does this salesman hold in the field of computer viruses? He may have flipped burgers at a McDonald's restaurant two weeks ago, for all we know.

Most people who claim to speak *with authority* about computer viruses *have little or no genuine expertise.* Some virus experts describe it as "False Authority Syndrome"—the person feels competent to discuss viruses because of his job title, or because of his expertise in another computer field, or simply because he knows how to use a computer.

I want you to question the credentials of anybody who talks about computer viruses. Indeed, I want you to question my credentials in this field!

The U.S. Air Force highlights the concept of False Authority Syndrome in *Tongue & Quill,* their official publication on effective writing:

> "*Nonexpert opinion* or assumed authority— Don't be swayed (or try to sway someone else) based on the opinion of an unqualified authority. The Air Force is chock-full of people who, because of their position or authority in one field, are quoted on subjects in other fields for which they have limited or no experience."

(As this Air Force publication notes, False Authority Syndrome can attack people in all fields of expertise.)

Computer salesmen, consultants, repairmen, and college computer teachers often succumb to False Authority Syndrome. In many cases a person's job title sounds impressive, but his or her job description at most may only include references to vague "computer security" duties.

People without impressive job titles suffer from false authority syndrome, too. A user who contracts a virus, for example, will often turn around and confidently tell other people how to avoid them. He or she may even rise to the position of "office virus expert."

False authority syndrome plays on two important desires. First, people genuinely like to help others; second, they like to feel in control of their computers. Users easily succumb to the effects of false authority syndrome when driven by these natural desires.

"Marcello," a typical user who took a hoax for real, posted a message on CompuServe warning users not to read any messages with "Good Times" in the subject line (lest they contract the so-called Good Times virus). Ironically, Marcello *used* the words "Good Times" in the subject line of his own warning message!

At least one virus expert sent Marcello a playful reply telling him to "stop infecting people" with the Good Times virus. Confronted with details about the hoax, Marcello replied, "Thank you for your help, and I'm sorry, because I was duped, but anyway I was worry [sic] about my computer and a lot more from [sic] my job."

So-called "Office Virus Experts"

A rule of thumb: The first employee attacked by a computer virus will quickly rise to the position of office virus expert. "Trust me, I know what I'm talking about. I've *been* there."

Sadly, managers often overlook more competent people when naming office virus experts. The guy who practices safe computing is nobody, but all hail the jerk who barely survived an attack.

Experts Believe *ILoveYou* Cost $2.7/$4.7/$6.7/$8.7 Billion

Legend: Experts around the world believe the ILoveYou virus in May 2000 caused $2.7 billion, $4.7 billion, $6.7 billion, or $8.7 billion in damages. *Reality:* Computer Economics, Inc. concocted the first three estimates as a publicity stunt during the peak of *ILoveYou* hysteria. They concocted the fourth estimate after the hysteria died down. *Reason experts are duped:* No statistically accepted metrics exist to gauge virus costs—and no statistically valid data exist to gauge worldwide virus proliferation. Therefore, any cost estimate is as good as any other cost estimate. *Fallout:* The antivirus industry can cite yet another plausible-sounding estimate.

Conclusion

I don't want to dispel any particular computer virus myths someone may have told you—that's not my goal here. Rather, I want you to *question a person's expertise* if he or she claims to speak with authority on computer viruses. This way we can prevent all the "blind leading the blind" techno-babble. And we can reduce the number of people who believe all the myths out there.

In summary:

• Most people have little or no expertise in the field of computer viruses.
• People with little or no expertise often fall prey to false authority syndrome.
• False authority syndrome contributes significantly to the spread of fear and myths about computer viruses.

Visual Developer editor Jeff Duntemann sums it up best: "If people exercised greater discretion in who and how and to what degree they place their trust, we would know more as a community—and we would know it better. There would be fewer paths for bad or phony knowledge."

Source: http://vmyths.com/fas/fas1.cfm

Most virus writers and attackers are opportunistic and like other criminals choose to attack systems at their weakest and most vulnerable points.[10] The significant growth of computer technology, the diverse number of computer operating systems available, and the increasing number of mobile computing devices like iPhones and Blackberrys make it easy for hackers to find attack points in most all computer users. In fact, the SANS Institute created a list of the top ten cyber threats for 2008 to help organizations and security experts identify the most likely attack points in the wide-ranging computer world. The list is contained in Table 6.1 and depicts the consensus of opinion of security experts from the government and private industry. SANS claims that an overwhelming majority of successful attacks occur in this area, ranging from attacks through Web sites to malicious software to faulty or infected computer hardware.[11] This chapter reviews the nature of viruses and other types of malicious code through an examination of what these programs are and their effect on infected systems. An examination of the threat posed by viruses, real and imagined, is undertaken with a particular emphasis on the ultimate effect viruses and malicious code have on society. This chapter will explore who the virus writers are and why they write viruses in the first place, and review investigative procedures and prosecution of virus writers—and all of the difficulties faced by law enforcement in this area.

**TABLE 6.1   The SANS Institute Top Ten Cyber Threats
for 2008**

1. Increasingly sophisticated Web site attacks that exploit browser vulnerabilities
2. Increasing sophistication and effectiveness in botnets
3. Cyber espionage efforts by well-resourced organizations to extract large amounts of data for economic and political purposes
4. Mobile phone threats, especially against iPhones, Google's Android phones, and voice over IP systems
5. Insider attacks
6. Advanced identity theft from persistent bots
7. Increasingly malicious spyware
8. Web application security exploits
9. Increasingly sophisticated social engineering to provoke insecure behavior
10. Supply chain attacks that infect consumer devices

THE LANGUAGE OF MALICIOUS SOFTWARE

Before discussing viruses and malicious software, it is important to discuss some of the vocabulary surrounding viruses, antivirus detection, and their impact. As such, several terms and issues associated with this area must be discussed prior to the coverage of the subject matter in this chapter. To begin, viruses and malicious code must be understood from several perspectives and variables, the most important of which is the potential damage that viruses and malicious code can cause. Damage can include triggered events that cause computer operations to be disrupted, clogging or disrupting e-mail or network operations, deleting or modifying files, accessing and sharing confidential information, performance interference and degrading, compromised security, and damage to the computer's software and hardware.[12] As such, many viruses and malicious code are graded based on the potential damage they can cause and their overall impact on computer operations at the individual level and across the world.

In a similar vein, the level of vulnerability or exposure is an additional defining characteristic of viruses and malicious code. Vulnerabilities include the ability of an attacker to execute commands on a victim's computer or network, the ability to access data on a remote system, the ability to take control of a system and assume another's identity, and the ability of the attacker to deny service to legitimate traffic on a given system or systems.[13] These are essentially the weak points in a piece of software that allow attackers use to propagate a virus or engage in some type of malicious attack. In turn, hackers identify these vulnerabilities in various systems and create exploits, or programs that attack known weak points to gain access to and facilitate hacks and compromises. For example, firewalls and certain types of code like ActiveX controls, Java, and JavaScript have flaws that make it difficult to protect vulnerable systems.

Computer systems and software can be graded in terms of their exposure to vulnerabilities. In making assessments of how secure or unsecure a system or computer is, exposure assessments describe a state of operations that are not universal vulnerabilities as well as how exposed a system is to a potential attack. The degree of exposure is determined by how easy it is for an attacker to conduct information gathering on a system, how easy it is to hide attack activities on a system, how easy it is to access a system and compromise its operation, and how many points of entry or security holes are present in a given system. In other words, exposure refers to the potential problems or security holes that are present that would allow an attacker to exploit the vulnerabilities described above. For instance, Trojan horse-type attacks could be accomplished through a worm, which would then open a security hole in the system that would allow the attacker access to the system. The Trojan would then block off further attempts to enter the security hole and cover its own tracks on the system.[14]

In addition to the vulnerabilities, exploits, and exposures described above, there are numerous terms used in describing viruses and their potential impact. The most common term used to describe how a virus is operating and the effect it is having is listing the virus as "in the wild." The "wildness" of a virus measures the extent to which a virus is spreading among computer users and systems. This measurement includes the number of infected independent sites and computers, the geographic distribution of infection, the ability of current technology to combat the threat, and the complexity of the virus. The true number of virus infections and malicious code attacks can never be ascertained with any degree of reliability and validity. However, several firms and independent organizations propagate lists of the most active viruses and the number of reported infections. One such list utilizes a Delphi technique (a survey and analysis of experts) to ascertain the number of viruses that are in the wild and that are most damaging. Viruses in the wild are those that are spreading as a result of normal day-to-day operations on and between the computers of unsuspecting users. Further, to make the list, two or more virus experts must report problems with the virus.[15] The March 2009 Wildlist reported 451 viruses currently in the wild; however, as is the case with most computer statistics, this number changes almost daily.

VIRUSES AND MALICIOUS CODE

Viruses and malicious code are simply programs and, like any other program, are designed for a specific function. A virus or malicious code program is written for a variety of noncriminal purposes including advertisements, jokes, and political messages. However, less humorous and more malicious intentions include destroying data and information, information acquisition and identity theft, surreptitious control of a remote machine, or the shutdown of a legitimate business or Web site. The virus program delivers a payload; this is part of the virus program that delivers the malicious intent or other device. The virus is executed by some type of payload trigger, which causes the virus or malicious code to deliver its contents or execute its commands. The trigger can be something the user does, such as opening an e-mail attachment or downloading a file; it can be triggered by some event such as a date or condition on a computer; or it can self-execute based on code written into the virus program. Early viruses were simple code, but recently viruses have become increasingly sophisticated and written to avoid detection. Some viruses are encrypted, which is a method of scrambling or encoding data to prevent reading or tampering with the data. The level of encryption and the strength of the encryption have increased substantially in recent years. Only individuals with access to a password or key can decrypt and use the data, and this allows the virus to hide itself from virus scanners—that is, the encrypted virus jumbles its program code to make it more difficult to detect. Some viruses also use "stealth," making them appear not to exist on a machine or hide their tracks from scanning software. Like a cyber Cold War of sorts, virus detection software writers and virus writers engage in a never-ending battle to stay one step ahead.

The development of virus construction tools by virus writers allows a larger number of less sophisticated computer users to write and create viruses. A virus construction set is a utility program intended for creating new computer viruses. Virus construction sets allow generating of source code of the viruses, object modules and/or infected files themselves.[16] Another tool developed by virus writers known as a mutation engine allows viruses to change their code each time they infect a new machine. Known as a polymorphic virus or malicious code, these programs do not have any constant section of code. In most cases, two strains of the same "polymorphic" virus will not have a single coinciding element of code. A polymorphic virus can change its pattern when it replicates, avoiding detection by simple virus scanning techniques. Viruses are also polymorphic if they cannot, or can but with great difficulty, be detected using the so-called virus masks or indicators; in other words the scanner looks for parts of nonchanging virus-specific code. The virus changes in two main ways: by encrypting the main code of the virus with a nonconstant key with random sets of decryption commands or by changing executable virus code.[17]

The type of encryption or operating algorithms used in a virus can vary substantially. The technical complexity of this area continually increases and changes. One area of interest is termed the *terminate and stay resident* (TSR) capability of the virus. This essentially means that the virus is able to leave itself in system memory, intercept some events, and in the process run infecting routines on files and sectors of the disk. Resident viruses stay in memory and are active until power down or until operating system reboot. Nonresident viruses do not infect computer memory and are active for a limited time only. Some viruses leave small parts in the memory, which do not spread the virus; these viruses are considered nonresident.[18] Resident viruses are active regardless of whether or not the infected program is running and remain viable until the next reboot, even if all the infected files are deleted from disk. It is also largely impossible to get rid of such viruses by restoring all the files from distribution disks or backup copies: The virus simply remains active and infects the newly created files. This is true for some boot viruses as well—even formatting the disk doesn't necessarily remove viruses, as they will continued to infect the disk repeatedly after formatting.[19] Hence the TSR capability of the virus is an important factor in classifying and determining the potential seriousness of a given virus.

Another feature of the operating algorithm of a virus is the use of stealth algorithms. Stealth allows the virus to remain hidden on a system and cover its tracks during and after the infection process. Yet another operating algorithm that can be used to grade or distinguish a virus is the use of self-encryption and polymorphism. These are used to make the virus detection and removal procedure as complicated as possible.[20] Polymorphic viruses are exceedingly difficult to detect, and they have no permanent signatures, that is, none of their code fragments remain unchanged. Often, a comparison of two samples of the polymorphic virus will yield few, if any, similarities in the code of the virus, making it impossible to program an antivirus solution. This may be achieved by encrypting of the main body of the virus and making modifications to the decryption routine.[21]

The destructiveness of a virus ranges from virtually harmless to extraordinarily dangerous and malicious. Some viruses have no real effect on the operation of the computer or the data and information stored on the computer; their payloads consist of some message being displayed or silly program being run. Other viruses can seriously disrupt the operation of the computer, rewriting commands, altering normal system operation, and changing boot routines and other malicious commands. Additionally, some viruses intentionally target the information and data on a system, resulting in lost data, data destruction, erasure of vital information in system areas, even inflicting damage to hardware.[22]

History and Development

There is a great deal of controversy surrounding the origins of computer viruses: who is responsible for creating the first computer virus, and who can claim responsibility for discovering and eliminating the early viruses. One author contends that the first viruses (although no one called them that at the time) appeared in the late 1960s and early 1970s on early versions of Univac and IBM machines.[23] Occasionally, on the mainframes in operation at that time, programs appeared that cloned themselves, occupied system resources, and lowered the productivity of the system. These programs, known as "rabbits," did not copy themselves from system to system and remained strictly local phenomena, mistakes or pranks by system programmers. The first incident, which may be called an epidemic of "a computer virus," happened on a Univax 1108 system. The virus called "Pervading Animal" merged itself to the end of an executable file. However, the first recognized versions of what could be termed the *modern virus* appeared on early PC machines in the middle to late 1980s, correlating largely with the enormous growth of the PC industry.

The earliest viruses infected boot sectors and floppy disks, performing such functions as playing Yankee Doodle Dandy on the speakers and deleting letters in documents.[24] Early viruses were extraordinarily easy to detect when compared with the viruses of today; each virus contained recognizable code that became known as the virus' signature. Once the signature was detected and identified, antivirus software could then be programmed to detect, isolate, and eliminate the virus.[25] The first vastly spread virus was a bootable virus called "Brain,"[26] which spread via floppy disks.[27] The virus was created in Pakistan by brothers Basit and Amjad Farooq Alvi. They left a text message inside the virus with their name, address, and telephone number. According to the authors of the virus they were software vendors and wanted to know the extent of piracy in their country. Unfortunately, their experiment left the borders of Pakistan.

The first counterpunch by virus writers was to encrypt the code within the virus, thus hiding their signatures by writing them in indecipherable code.[28] In order to complete the infection, the encrypted virus needed to return to its original state in order to replicate and infect. The decryption routine written into the virus could be identified and used as a virus signature, allowing detection by antivirus software.[29] MtE (MuTation Engine) is the first known polymorphic generator. It was released in 1991 and shocked antivirus researchers with its very complex polymorphic algorithm.[30] Polymorphic routines still encrypted the virus, but the encryption routine was randomized by a mutation engine.[31] The first polymorphic virus appeared in the early 1990s and was known as "Chameleon,"[32] but polymorphic viruses became really serious with the introduction of the "Tequila"[33] virus in April 1991.[34] The polymorphic virus took off two years later. A host of these viruses spread with the help of the burgeoning Internet.

Several things combined to aid the spread of viruses: the rapid growth of the Internet, the rapid growth and availability of PCs, the availability of the polymorphic engine, and the availability of virus creation tools that first hit in July 1992. The first viral code construction set for IBM PC compatibles was called Virus Creation Laboratory (VCL).[35] This set allows the user to generate code to produce viruses. The program used a Windows™ interface and a menu system that allowed the virus writer to choose virus type, objects to infect (COM and/or EXE), presence or absence of self-encryption, measures of protection from debugging, inside text strings, and an optional ten additional effects.[36] The created virus can then use a variety of means for infection by adding its body to the end of file, replacing files with its body destroying the original content of a file, or becoming companion viruses.[37] The introduction of the polymorphic engine and the VCL automated and simplified the virus-writing process so that any teenager with a computer and a cause could write a virus.

At the end of 1992, the first virus specifically designed for Windows™ was released.[38] With the release of Windows 95™, the first "virus epidemic" was soon to follow (in 1996) with the widespread release and propagation of macroviruses. The Concept[39] virus was an innocuous virus that spread very rapidly and was a wake-up call for Microsoft and the antivirus industry.[40]

The main problem with trying to give the exact definition of a virus is that virtually all the unique features of a virus—such as incorporating with other objects, stealth behavior, potential danger, and potential for spread—may be found in other nonvirus programs.[41] A second difficulty is that viruses are operating-system and software-system specific.[42] One author maintains that it is only definable through the specification of several necessary conditions. For example, a code's ability to produce copies of itself, to incorporate itself into other files and systems (networks, files, executable objects, etc.), and further contaminate other systems is a necessary condition to be able to define it as a computer virus.[43] Some authors claim that viruses are a form of artificial life possessing all of the properties of a live organism. They can propagate, adapt themselves to different environments, and self-transmit in an effort to move and relocate.[44] Ironically, legendary computer guru Peter Norton announced that computer viruses did not exist, declaring them to be mythical.[45]

Mobile code is a code that can be transmitted across a network and executed on the other end of a transmission. It may be created using one of numerous mobile code systems, including Java, ActiveX, safe Tcl, Visual Basic, Visual Basic for Applications (VBA), and scripting.[46] Mobile code has become quite routine on most Web pages and is also used in a growing number of Internet-capable programs. The positives of mobile code can be turned against the user and used in an attack that is quite difficult to detect.

Viruses

The classification or categorization of computer viruses and malicious code is ongoing. There is some disagreement concerning the exact terminology used and what is and what is not considered a virus or malicious code. Nonetheless, there is an active attempt by several antivirus vendors and the federal government to have some standard classifications of viruses and other types of malicious code. Viruses can be categorized based on the environment they operate in, the operating system they are targeted at, the type of encryption and operating algorithms used, and their destructive capabilities.[47] Other types of malicious code include worms, Trojan horses, adware or spyware, logic bombs, denial-of-service (DoS) attacks, and blended threats. This list is not necessarily complete, nor is there universal agreement on the exhaustiveness and mutual exclusivity of the list. Nonetheless, the list does comprise the majority of the types of viruses identified in the current literature.

Viruses operate in four primary environments: file viruses, boot viruses, macroviruses, and network viruses.[48] File viruses infect their targets in several ways: as a parasite, as a companion, or through file system–specific features known as link viruses. File viruses use a particular operating system to propagate, and they can infect virtually any type of executable file. These viruses can overwrite the contents of a target executable with its own code, destroying the original contents of the files. This method is the simplest and results in system failures and other problems because the infected file simply stops working. As such, these are relatively easy to detect and remove. Parasitic viruses also change the contents of the infected files, but they latch onto the file and leave it operational. Kaspersky (2003) contends that these types of viruses include "prepending" viruses (saving themselves at the top of file), "appending" (saving themselves at the end of file), and "inserting" (inserting themselves in the middle of file).[49] The insertion methods vary as well, by moving a fragment of the file toward the end of file or by copying its own code to such parts of the file that are known to be unused ("cavity" viruses). Companion viruses do not change the infected files; instead, they clone the target file so that when run, the companion virus runs instead of the original file. Link viruses, like companion viruses, do not change the physical contents of files, but when an infected file is started, they "force" the OS to execute their code. This is achieved by modifying the necessary fields of the file system.[50] Viruses can also infect other areas of a computer, including compiler libraries, object modules, and source code; however, these types of viruses are extraordinarily rare.

Boot viruses attack either the boot sector of the system, the master boot record (MBR), or change the system pointer to an active boot sector. Gap boot viruses infect the boot sector of a floppy disk and the boot sector or MBR of a hard disk. Boot viruses operate based on the algorithms of starting an operation system upon power on or reboot—after the necessary hardware tests (of memory, disks etc.) the system loader routine reads the first physical sector of a boot disk (A:, C:, or CD-ROM, depending on the options in BIOS Setup) and passes the control to the virus. In the case of a diskette or CD-Rom infection, the virus attacks a boot sector, analyzes the operations and boot routine of the computer, and substitutes the virus code in the place of the normal operating code. In the case of a hard disk target, the target is a boot sector on the hard disk. The virus passes control from the computer to virus in that particular sector. Upon infecting the disk, the virus in most cases moves the original boot sector to some other sector of the disk. If the virus size exceeds the size of the sector, then the target sector will contain the first part of the virus, the rest of it placed in the other sectors.[51] Diskette infecting is accomplished when the virus rewrites the original boot sector code with its own code. Hard disks can be infected when a virus writes itself over the MBR code or the boot sector code of the boot disk (C: drive, usually) or modifies the address of the active boot sector in the disk partition table.[52]

Macroviruses are most commonly associated with common business software and infect documents, spreadsheets, databases, and presentation files. Macroviruses take advantage of macrolanguages built into common systems of business software, most notably Microsoft Office™. Macroviruses transfer themselves from one infected file to another within a given system and cross over to other systems, typically via attachments or shared files. Macro functions within a file or processing program can operate without user intervention. Macroviruses generally use an automacro present in the file, or use a standard system macro (associated with some menu item) that has been redefined, or the macro of the virus is pulled automatically after a certain key or key combination has been pressed. If a Word document is infected, when opening it, the program calls the infected automatic macro and then executes the virus code. If the virus contains macros with standard names, they take control after a user executes the corresponding menu item (File/Open, File/Close, File/Save, etc.). If some symbol of the keyboard is redefined, the virus activates itself only after the corresponding key has been pressed.

Most macroviruses contain all of their functions as standard macros of the software program they infect. However, there are viruses that use the techniques of hiding their code and keeping their code as a nonmacro entry. For example, when activated, a Word macrovirus will move the macro code into the common macros contained in the program with the help of the macro editor contained in the program. The virus then creates a new macro, inserts its own code inside the macro, and then saves this macro with the code in the document. On exit from Word the global macros (including the macros of the virus) are automatically saved to a DOT file of the global macros (this file is usually called NORMAL.DOT). The next start of the Microsoft Word™ editor activates the virus at the moment when Word loads the global macros; in other words, immediately.[53] The virus then redefines one or several of the standard macros and then intercepts the commands of typical file operations. When routine commands are executed, the virus infects the currently open file. To do this, the virus converts the file to the template format and then saves its macros, including the automacro to the file. For example, once the virus infects the macro called File/Save, then every DOC file becomes infected. If the File/Open macro becomes infected, then the virus records itself into the file when it is being read from the disk.[54]

Network viruses attack the networks themselves or e-mail systems of the networks in order to spread themselves. With the advent of HTML, Active X, and Java code and the ability to send attachments, the thought was that only by executing the attachment could a user get an infection. Macroviruses and other sneaky tricks demonstrated that even nonexecutable files could infect a user's machine via e-mail, yet it was still assumed that simply reading e-mail could not infect a system. Recent viruses and worms demonstrated, however, that simply previewing e-mail is enough to trigger an infection.[55] Network viruses make extensive use of networking protocols and capabilities of local and global access networks to multiply. The main operating principle of the network virus is its capability to transfer its code to a remote server or workstation on its own. Network viruses also are capable of running their code on remote computers or at least "pushing" users to run the infected file.[56] Network viruses essentially spread themselves on a computer network, and as a rule, like companion viruses, don't change files or sectors on disks. They infiltrate computer memory from the network, calculate and record network addresses of other computers, and then send copies of themselves to the network addresses.

Worms

Computer viruses have progressed from urban myth to annoyance to major threat. However, even with all the damage that computer viruses have done, they pale in comparison to what we have seen and have yet to see from the computer worm.[57] A computer worm is also a piece of software that copies itself elsewhere. However, unlike a virus, it does not attach itself to, or modify, other files. The worm is a stand-alone piece of code; although it may need to use another program to spread, it does not change that program in any way. The term *worm* is taken from the book *Shockwave Rider* and refers to a self-replicating piece of code (called the "tapeworm") created by a character in that book.[58] In contrast to a traditional virus, a worm is a program that makes copies of itself from one disk drive to another, or by copying itself using e-mail or another transport mechanism. The worm may damage and compromise the security of the computer. It may arrive in the form of a joke program or software of some sort or may be spread through e-mail and networks without much active user intervention. These programs spread in a computer network and, similar to virus companions, don't change files or sectors on disks. They penetrate the computer's memory from a computer network, calculate network addresses of other computers, and send their own copies to these addresses. Worms sometimes start files on the system disks, but generally can't apply themselves to computer resources (with the exception of main memory).

The first known Internet worm was the Morris worm. This worm crippled the Internet for several days in 1988 by exploiting buffer overrun flaws common in several pieces of software. A buffer overrun occurs when a program does not check the length of an input string against the amount of memory it has available to store that string. If the entered string is too long, then it overwrites other memory in the computer. In the case of the Morris worm, the string contained garbage data, followed by instructions for the computer to send the same message to other available machines. The worm was supposed to spread slowly, and in a controllable fashion, but, due to a bug in the code, it spread much faster than anticipated. This brought about the first large-scale DoS condition on the Internet itself. An infected machine could have its resources entirely controlled by the worm in as little as one hour. The courts were not impressed by Morris' actions, and sentenced him to three years' probation, 400 hours community service, and $10,050 in fines.[59]

BOX 6.2
The Melissa Virus

The Melissa virus first appeared on the Internet in March of 1999. It spread rapidly throughout computer systems in the United States and Europe. It is estimated that the virus caused $80 million in damages to computers worldwide. In the United States alone, the virus made its way through 1.2 million computers in one-fifth of the country's largest businesses. David Smith pled guilty on December 9, 1999, to state and federal charges associated with his creation of the Melissa virus and was sentenced in 2002. Smith admitted spreading the Melissa virus, which infected more than one million PCs in North America and disrupted computer networks in business and government.

Prosecutors noted that the Melissa virus demonstrated the danger that business, government, and PC users everywhere face in our technological society. "Far from being a mere nuisance, Melissa infected computers and disabled computer networks throughout North America. There is a segment in society that views the unleashing of computer viruses as a challenge, a game. Far from it; it is a serious crime."

"Computer criminals may think that they operate in a new frontier without boundaries, where they won't be caught. Obviously, that's not true," said investigators. "We've responded by breaking down traditional borders among federal, state, county and local law enforcement. In this case, it helped us to make an arrest in less than a week." Attorney General Janet Reno stated, "This plea is a significant marker in the Justice Department's efforts to stop computer crime. In light of society's increasing dependence on computers, the Department will vigorously investigate and prosecute computer crimes that threaten our computer infrastructure."

Smith admitted in state and federal court that he created the Melissa virus and disseminated it from his home computer. Smith acknowledged in his federal plea agreement that the Melissa virus caused more than $80 million in damage. He was eventually sentenced to 20 months in federal prison followed by three years of supervised release, 100 hours of community service, and a fine of $5,000 and was prohibited from accessing a computer of any kind. He said that he constructed the virus to evade antivirus software and to infect computers using the Windows 95™,

Windows 98,™ and Windows NT™ operating systems and the Microsoft Word 97™ and Word 2000™ word processing programs.

According to Paul Zoubek, Director of the state Division of Criminal Justice, the Melissa virus appeared on thousands of e-mail systems on March 26, 1999, disguised as an important message from a colleague or friend. The virus was designed to send an infected e-mail to the first 50 e-mail addresses on the users' mailing lists. Such e-mails would only be sent if the computers used Microsoft Outlook™ for e-mail. Because each infected computer could infect 50 additional computers, which in turn could infect another 50 computers, the virus proliferated rapidly and exponentially, resulting in substantial interruption or impairment of public communications or services. According to reports from business and government following the spread of the virus, its rapid distribution disrupted computer networks by overloading e-mail servers, resulting in the shutdown of networks and significant costs to repair or cleanse computer systems.

Smith described in state and federal court how, using a stolen America Online account and his own account with a local Internet service provider, he posted an infected document on the Internet newsgroup "Alt.Sex." The posting contained a message enticing readers to download and open the document with the hope of finding passcodes to adult-content Web sites. He acknowledged that each new e-mail greeted new users with an enticing message to open and, thus, spread the virus further. The message read: "Here is that document you asked for . . . don't show anyone else ;-)."

Opening and downloading the message caused the Melissa virus to infect victim computers. The virus altered Microsoft word processing programs such that any document created using the programs would then be infected with the Melissa virus. The virus also lowered macro security settings in the word processing programs. The virus then proliferated via the Microsoft Outlook™ program, causing computers to send electronic e-mail to the first 50 addresses in the computer user's address book.

Source: http://www.usdoj.gov/criminal/cybercrime/meliinfo. htm

In sum, a worm is self-propagating malicious code program that does not necessarily require user intervention to spread. Unlike a virus that requires a user to run a program or execute a command, a worm self-propagates and infects systems in a very short period of time. The Code Red worm infected more than 250,000 systems in just nine hours on July 19, 2001.[60] Some worms include built-in DoS attack payloads or Web site defacement payloads, while others have dynamic configuration capabilities. However, as noted by the CERT® Coordination Center, the biggest impact of these worms is that their propagation effectively creates a DoS because of the huge amounts of scan traffic that the worm generates.[61] Additionally, worms cause a great deal of collateral damage, such as crashing routers, overloading networks, and creating meaningless and repetitive tasks for the computers they infect.[62]

Trojan Horses

A Trojan horse is commonly an unauthorized program contained within a legitimate program that performs functions unknown (and probably unwanted) by the user.[63] Trojan horses typically masquerade as something desirable, a joke program, a legitimate software program, or some other type of executable file that the user wishes to install and run. Just like the Trojan horse of history, however, there is a hidden purpose and program hidden within the desirable file. The hidden program typically waits for some computer event to occur, a date to be reached, or some other type of trigger, and then delivers its payload.[64] The hidden payload can open a backdoor for the virus writer, destroy files or disks, or simply display a message of some type. In the case of an attachment, as the user executes the file, the infection occurs simultaneously and silently. The Trojan horse is a program that neither replicates nor copies itself, but causes damage or compromises the security of the computer. In many cases, a legitimate program has been altered by the placement of unauthorized code, the Trojan horse, within legitimate code.[65] Typically, an individual e-mails a Trojan horse to you. However a growing number of attacks are accomplished through port scanners looking for installed Trojans by attackers who did not install the Trojan themselves. In other words, it is possible to conduct scans for Trojans in a systematic fashion and then exploit the security holes uncovered through the scans. There is a variety of ways that a Trojan can be installed on a user's computer, including via ICQ chat, Internet relay chat (IRC), attachments, actual physical access to a machine, a Web browser or e-mail program, and file sharing.[66]

BOX 6.3
Could Your Computer Be a Criminal?

PCs hijacked to send spam, serve porn, steal credit cards

by Bob Sullivan
MSNBC

July 15—One thousand home computers hijacked and used to serve up pornography. Perhaps tens of thousands co-opted by the "SoBig" virus, many of them turned into spam machines. Hundreds of other home computers loaded with secret software used to process stolen credit cards. If your biggest computer crime fear was lost or stolen files, think again: Someone may be using your PC to commit crimes.

A curious spam mail went out and disappeared without much fanfare on June 25. Playing on a familiar prank, the e-mail urged recipients to visit "Windows-update.com" and download a security fix for their computers. Those who fell for the ploy were tricked into downloading a Trojan horse program. The malicious software steered the victim computer into an Internet Relay Chat room, where a computer criminal playing the part of the Pied Piper awaited to issue instructions to the now enslaved PC.

Joe Stewart, senior intrusion analyst with Lurhq Corp., played along with the Windows-Update spam. For one hour that day, he was in the chat room, too. And during that hour, he watched as about 800 PCs were drawn in. There, the hacker loaded them with more software, a small "bot" program which could be used by other chat room members. But what for?

Hiding Behind Innocent PCs

Internet credit card thieves have a major barrier to cross when they sell stolen card numbers: "Hot" cards become "cold" very quickly, as victims get wise and call to cancel their accounts. No one wants to pay for stolen credit cards that have been canceled. So the thieves have written a number of automated programs, or "bots," that quickly verify the validity of a credit card number. One such bot simply checks to see if a supplied account number follows the mathematical formulas designed by credit card companies to prevent random account numbers from being used for fraud, called a "checksum." Windows-Update.com victims had this checksum bot placed on their machines, ready for use by an eager credit card thief looking to test out stolen numbers.

Only one machine would be used at a time, Stewart said. The moment one "bot" computer was disconnected, presumably by a victim who discovered the problem, another was ready to take its place. But each PC that was used in the scheme was an unwitting accomplice to credit card fraud.

"Maybe you don't think you have anything on your machine worth stealing," Stewart said. "Well, you do. Your bandwidth and your disk space."

For years, computer intruders have had their fun at the expense of innocent computer users by seizing control of their machines. Such zombies were a central part of the the the first famous major Internet attacks, which knocked Web sites like Yahoo.com and CNN.com off-line in 1998.

But such attacks have for the most part been limited to pranks until just recently, when a new spate of malicious computer programs with obvious criminal intent have been unleashed. More and more, experts say, these are for-profit pranks.

"We're definitely seeing a paradigm shift," said Richard Smith, the well-known computer sleuth who last week helped uncover a widespread scheme that turned about 1,000 PCs into an elaborate system that served up porn Web sites. "There's a real problem here. With hijacked computers, there's a lot of bad things you can do with them. I think we're just at the beginning."

Beware of Geeks Bearing Gifts

At the core of the problem is the type of computer virus known as a Trojan horse. It takes its name from the well known Greek myth, and functions much the same. Trojan horses sneak onto a victim's computer by appearing to be something benign, like a software update. Unlike the Melissa and LoveBug worms, Trojans don't spread themselves far and wide, and they don't call attention to themselves. These programs simply lie quietly on victims' computers, but now those computers are at the beck and call of the Trojan author.

Five years ago, hacker groups like the Cult of the Dead Cow released Trojans with names like "Back Orifice" to much fanfare, but they were often used just to perform spooky tricks like opening and closing victims' CD-ROM doors. This new batch of Trojan writers have far more serious crimes in mind, Smith said.

"It seems to me that when the (music industry) starts going after people, they will just start storing songs on other people's computers. And what if there's kiddie porn stored on someone else's computer?" Smith said.

The Trail Gets Cold

Using an army of hijacked computers to commit crimes or send out spam obscures the computer criminal's tracks effectively—and rotating rogue programs among the machines makes shutting down criminal operations tricky for Internet service providers. Smith actually discovered the porn ring when he was investigating a "phishing" e-mail, a note sent out, which appeared to be a request from PayPal.com for users to update their password information on a Web site. The site was actually controlled by people intent on stealing the data.

Such "phishing" e-mails are common now, and the corresponding Web sites are normally shut down within hours when investigators like Smith complain to the Web host provider. But this site stayed up for days because its location was constantly changing—from one innocent victim's computer to another.

"I got an IP address for it, but the host didn't know what was going on, and finally I said, 'Oh my God, it moved.' It is much harder to do anything about this. The hacker gained a week on us," Smith said.

Another disturbing fact about the new wave of programs: "They are simple and small, and nearly impossible to spot with an untrained eye," said Oliver Friedrichs, senior manager at Symantec's Security Response Team. "The hijackings will likely go unnoticed by victims who aren't running up-to-date antivirus software and personal firewalls," he said.

"When this thing is running, you're really not going see it on your system," he said.

Spam, Virus, Hacking Worlds Converge

"The trouble really started when the worlds of spam and computer viruses began to converge," said Mark Sumner, chief technology officer at antivirus firm MessageLabs Inc. For years, virus writers were content to just get attention by causing a nuisance. But now, some have discovered that clever virus programming can be profitable—by enabling spammers to hide their trails and send out e-mail from hijacked computers, for example.

"There's never been any money in writing viruses but now there's the potential of commercial gain," Sumner said.

The SoBig virus, first released in January, probably ushered in this new era of Trojan horse programs. "From the start," Stewart said, "it was designed to enable spammers to sneak their e-mail software onto unwitting home users' computers who have high-bandwidth connections to the Internet." SoBig is now in its fifth iteration, the most recent released on June 24, the same day as the Windows-Update spam. The coincidence has some researchers, including Smith, thinking that all these Trojan horse incidents might be related—that the SoBig virus was used both to hijack PCs for spam and for serving up porn.

But even if one group is behind the recent spate of incidents, consumers should be aware that virus writers will likely seize on this new way of doing business, experts say. Whatever is successful in the computer underground world is immediately imitated.

"The possibilities are growing as to what your machine can be used for," Stewart said. "The likelihood that people will encounter (Trojan horses) is pretty high. Whether they infect you or not depends on the computer user."

Source: http://www.msnbc.com/news/939227.asp

Trojan horses can be viruses or remote control programs that provide complete access to a victim's computer and, as such, are one of the most accessible weapons that hackers use to conduct attacks.[67] If a certain type of Trojan horse is installed and initialized on a system, that computer is now completely open to anyone who knows to connect to it using the Trojan horse as a server.[68] The person responsible for the initial installation is not the only person who can be privy to the knowledge that a Trojan horse resides on the target computer; there are port scanners designed to find remote control Trojans already planted on systems.[69] Therefore, anyone who utilizes the port scanner and finds the installed Trojan horse can have access to the victim's computer or system. A remote-controlled Trojan is not a traditional virus; it is a self-contained program designed to invisibly execute commands issued from a remote user.[70] Trojans work by utilizing a client part and a server part. When the victim (unknowingly) runs the server on its machine, the attacker will then use the client to connect to the server and start using the Trojan.[71] Most Trojans use autostarting methods, so even when you shut down your computer, they're able to restart and give the attacker access. New autostarting methods and other tricks are discovered all the time, ranging from "joining" the Trojan into some executable file that is often used like explorer.exe to modifying the system files or the Windows Registry.[72]

Perhaps the most popular and widely used Trojan horse is the Backdoor Sub Seven Trojan.[73] Upon a successful installation, the Sub Seven Trojan allows a remote attack virtual control over an infected machine. This Trojan comprises distinctly separate programs that work to overtake the victim's computer. The first program is called the Sub Seven server and is run on the targeted computer to allow the attacker to connect to the victim and gain access to the computer. The editserver portion of the Trojan defines the characteristics of the infection and determines whether to notify the attacker when the victim computer is online. This part of the program also allows the attacker to monitor and change the settings through which the attack occurs. In other words, the attacker can connect to the victim's machine and install a different configuration of the Sub Seven server that uses alternate ports, different techniques for autostarting, and allow the attacker free access to alter and control the victim's system.[74] Once installed and operating, attackers can initiate a variety of attacks, including the ability to restart Windows, reversing mouse buttons, recording sounds from the microphone attached to the compromised machine, record images from an attached video camera, change desktop colors, opening/closing the CD-ROM drive, record screen shots of the victim's computer and turn the victim's monitor on and off.[75] The attacker can also obtain characteristics of the hardware and software installed on the compromised machine and access stored information on the computer, including passwords and other personally identifying information. Finally, the Sub Seven Trojan installs a port redirector and the port scanner that allows an attacker to hack into other systems by configuring ports on an already-infected computer to point to new targets.[76]

The program Sub7 is a very well-known Trojan around the world and can be found in hacker Web sites in most any country. Because it is so widely available, it is no longer as useful as it once was and is primarily used by less-skilled hackers. A number of Trojans exist that have similar functionality, were created in Russia, China, and Turkey, and are available for download or purchase through the hacker community. For example, the Trojan Pinch is a widely used tool among Russian hackers and was created by an individual named Coban2k; an interview with him is provided in Box 6.4. The tool was initially sold for profit, but became so successful that hackers began to release its source code to the public and use it on their own. The program itself was designed to steal passwords from over 33 different programs on a single computer, and send those files to the user through a number of different means.[77] The program can also collect characteristics of the

---

BOX 6.4

Interview With Coban2K

INTERVIEWER: Tell me about yourself.

COBAN2K: From the very early childhood through my father surrounded me with computers and there I had a passion which then turned into a profession. Obsession with computers. I am 21 years old, learning in the Department of Mathematics.

INTERVIEWER: Let's talk now about your most famous project—Pinch. Tell me how it happened. Had difficulty with writing code?

COBAN2K: First Pinch was one of my first projects at the assembler, created solely for myself. Pinch was similar to a project established in Ld-Team which I was in at the time of the creation of Pinch. Since variants of the tool were sold by

others and sales fell it was decided to make the program open source. The version was written for two weeks and then drafted for several months written by just one person for profit.

INTERVIEWER: What would be the logical end of the project? Will Pinch continue to be open source?

COBAN2K: The logical end of a project can come only if there is additional deciphering of all possible projects. Pinch is open source, but commercial hackers convert the code to conceal people who are afraid of losing customers.

Sources: http://www.hackzona.ru/hz.php?name=News&file=article&sid=3978 and http://www.xakep.ru/post/32451/default.asp

hardware and software installed on the compromised machine and turn the infected system into a launch point for other attacks and Web surfing. Pinch can also hide itself completely, clean and kill the Web browser, and be used as tool to connect multiple infected machines into a bot network so that all machines can be commanded remotely from one point.[78]

The useful nature of this program has led to its multiple variations, which have been sold and used by a number of hackers and groups. In fact, two Russians made approximately $16,000 selling this tool to other hackers. Their actions led to over 4,000 PCs being infected by one variant of Pinch, with compromised machines in the United States, Brazil, China, and the United Kingdom on computers that were running antivirus software.[79] The pair was arrested by Russian police in December 2007 and were jailed and fined for their actions.

With this in mind, the problem of Trojans cannot be overstated.

There are numerous types of Trojans, and similar to viruses, there is no universal agreement on the naming and categorization of all of the types. Danchev (1999)[80] lists several types of Trojans, including the following:

- *Remote Access Trojans*—These are probably the most common, as they give attackers the power to do more things on the victim's machine than the victim possibly could, even while sitting in front of the machine. These Trojans can give the attacker complete access to a victim's computer as well as access to files, passwords, data, etc.

BOX 6.5

Disgruntled UBS PaineWebber Employee Charged with Allegedly Unleashing "Logic Bomb" on Company Computers

A disgruntled computer systems administrator for UBS PaineWebber was charged today with using a "logic bomb" to cause more than $3 million in damage to the company's computer network and with securities fraud for his failed plan to drive down the company's stock with activation of the logic bomb. Roger Duronio, 60, of Bogota, N.J., was charged today a two-count Indictment returned by a federal grand jury, according to Assistant U.S. Attorney William Devaney.

The Indictment alleges that Duronio, who worked at PaineWebber's offices in Weehawken, N.J., planted the logic bomb in some 1,000 of PaineWebber's approximately 1,500 networked computers in branch offices around the country. Duronio, who repeatedly expressed dissatisfaction with his salary and bonuses at Paine Webber, resigned from the company on February 22, 2002. The logic bomb Duronio allegedly planted was activated on March 4, 2002.

In anticipation that the stock price of UBS PaineWebber's parent company, UBS, A.G., would decline in response to damage caused by the logic bomb, Duronio also purchased more than $21,000 of "put option" contracts for UBS, A.G.'s stock, according to the charging document. A put option is a type of security that increases in value when the stock price drops. Market conditions at the time suggest there was no such impact on the UBS, A.G., stock price.

PaineWebber promptly reported what had happened to government investigators and the U.S. Attorney's Office, and has been helpful and cooperative in the investigation by the U.S. Secret Service's Electronic Crimes Task Force. "Cybercrime against financial institutions is a significant issue," Christie said. "Although the damage was contained in this case, the potential for catastrophic damage in other cases is always there. We will prosecute cyber criminals and put them in prison."

The Indictment alleges that, from about November 2001 to February, Duronio constructed the logic bomb computer program. On March 4, as planned, Duronio's program activated and began deleting files on over 1,000 of UBS PaineWebber's computers. It cost PaineWebber more than $3 million to assess and repair the damage, according to the Indictment.

As one of the company's computer systems administrators, Duronio had responsibility for, and access to, the entire UBS PaineWebber computer network, according to the Indictment. He also had access to the network from his home computer via secure Internet access.

Duronio is charged in Count One of the Indictment with securities fraud, which carries a maximum penalty of 10 years in federal prison and a $1 million fine. He is charged in Count Two with Fraud and Related Activity in Connection with Computers. That charge carries a maximum prison sentence of 10 years and a fine of $250,000 or, alternatively, two times the gain made by the defendant or the loss suffered by the victim.

Source: http://www.usdoj.gov/criminal/cybercrime/duronioIndict.htm

- *Password-Sending Trojans*—These Trojans attempt to steal all of the cached passwords and also look for other passwords entered on a computer while the victim is online and then send them to the attacker's e-mail address, which in most cases is located at some free Web-based e-mail provider.
- *Keyloggers*—These Trojans log the keystrokes of the victim and then let the attacker search for passwords or other sensitive data in the log file. Most of them come with two functions like online and off-line recording and can be configured to send the log file to a specific e-mail address on a daily basis.
- *Destructive*—The only function of these Trojans is to destroy and delete files. They can automatically delete core system files (e.g., dll, .ini or .exe files). The Trojan can be activated by the attacker or sometimes works like a logic bomb and starts on a specific day and at a specific time.
- *DoS Attack Trojans*—The main idea is that if you have 200 users infected and start attacking a secondary victim simultaneously, this will generate a great deal of traffic (more then the victim's bandwidth, in most cases), and access to the Internet will be shut down. A variation of this Trojan is the mail-bomb Trojan, whose main aim is to infect as many machines as possible and simultaneously attack specific e-mail addresses with random subjects and contents that cannot be filtered.
- *Proxy/Wingate Trojans*—These Trojans turn the victim's computer into a proxy/wingate server (zombie) available to the whole world or to the attacker only. It's used for anonymous Telnet, ICQ, IRC, Internet access, etc., and also to register domains with stolen credit cards and for many other illegal activities. This gives the attacker complete anonymity and the chance to commit crimes from a remote computer. If caught, the trace will lead to a victim's computer and not the attacker.
- *Software Detection Killers*—Some Trojans will kill ZoneAlarm, Norton Anti-Virus, and many other popular antivirus/firewall programs designed to protect users. Once they are disabled, the attacker will have full access to your machine, to perform some illegal activity, use your computer to attack others, and often disappear.

Adware and Spyware

Although not technically viruses or malicious code, adware and spyware have become a frequent topic of debate in regard to privacy concerns on the Internet. Adware and spyware are programs that can be contained in e-mail attachments, downloaded as part of another software program, or downloaded from a Web site. Adware is a type of program that is essentially a pain to the user that manifests itself in several ways, including changes to the browser, redirecting startup pages on the Internet browser, replacing the search function within the browser, and generating pop-up ads and frames that can be difficult to delete or shut down. Spyware programs are applications that send information via the Internet to the publishers or programmers for marketing purposes without obvious notification to users.[81] Spyware can send a variety of information about the user's computer hardware, software, browsing habits, and other personal information to the host marketer or programmer. Spyware is typically installed in addition to some other type of functional software, more often than not downloaded software that is distributed as freeware. The software operates independently of the spyware and is the visible and useful component of the downloaded package. Spyware serves as an information gatherer, which maintains, monitors, and sends user and/or computer information in the background.[82] Some programs that get installed as companion software, technically not spyware, can cause a great deal of frustration for the user—especially if the user chooses to uninstall the companion software or spyware. Programs have been known to replace the searching engine function in the Internet browser, directing the user to their own preferred Web sites. Spyware can also lead to annoying pop-up ads that users have difficulty disabling.

Spyware typically takes advantage of the fact that many software users do not read the end user license agreement (EULA) or fine print during installation. If they did, they would see legal disclaimers and permissions to share information and install the spyware. As noted by Post (2002), spyware EULAs are worded in such a way that they contain so much information and disclaimers that the average person can't understand what the software and spyware does and doesn't do.[83] Further, the data that are gathered are not specifically identified and how the data are going to be used is not specifically spelled out. Many people, upon finding out that they installed the spyware and were not really aware of it, feel that the spyware is malicious. The real fun starts when a user attempts to uninstall the spyware and programs that they downloaded. Often, the entire hard drive has to be scrubbed and the operating system reinstalled because the downloaded program made numerous and complex changes to the computer. As a result, now spyware killer software as well as Internet security software are available that allow you to monitor and deter adware and spyware. Another way spyware is installed is through the use of cookies. A cookie is a file that contains information about a program, a Web site, the user, or the user's computer. Cookies enable faster browsing and, when they are from a legitimate Web site, can be beneficial to the Web site and the user. However, in the case of some spyware, the cookie contains uniquely identifiable data, such as the user's name, computer specifications, installation version, and other personally identifying information that the user might not wish to share.

Denial-of-Service Attacks

A DoS attack uses multiple systems to attack one or more victim systems or Web sites with the intent of denying service to legitimate users wishing to log on or utilize the attacked server. In essence, the attack sends phony requests to the server, overloading it and preventing legitimate traffic. The degree to which the attack is automated, or self-sustaining and replicating, dictates how rapidly the attack denies service to the server or Web site. These attacks are remarkably effective due to the interdependency of computers and security on the Net and due to the limited resources of the Internet.[84] The attack tools are increasingly being distributed through "zombie" machines that are compromised on university campuses. In the week of February 7, 2000, several distributed denial of service (DDoS) attacks on several prominent

Web sites, including Yahoo!, E*Trade, Amazon.com, and eBay were launched. In these attacks, multiple computers are instructed by a rogue program to bombard the target site with nonsense data. This bombardment soon causes the target site's servers to run out of memory and thus cause it to be unresponsive to the queries of legitimate customers.[85] As described in the box item, these attacks can be used in a coordinated fashion to attack and destroy businesses and antispam companies.

Blended Threats

Blended threats combine the characteristics of viruses, worms, Trojan Horses, and malicious code with server and Internet vulnerabilities to initiate, transmit, and spread an attack. By using multiple methods and techniques, blended threats can rapidly spread and cause widespread damage. Recent blended threats have launched DoS attacks, defaced Web servers, and Trojan horses planted on machines for later use in future attacks. The blended threat spreads through multiple methods; the infection routine can vary as well. These threats can scan for vulnerabilities in a system (such as buffer overflows, HTTP input validation vulnerabilities, and known default passwords to gain unauthorized administrative access), exploit the vulnerabilities, and then use the machine to further spread the attack. The attack spreads within human intervention and attacks systems and networks from multiple points, attempting to infect executable files, change the access rules for the machine, make numerous registry changes, and further exploit the machine into harming other machines and extending the attack.

Blended threats exploit one or more vulnerabilities as they infect a system and may perform additional network attacks such as a DoS against other systems.[86] The essence of a blended attack is the multiple payloads and multiple targets that are part of the virus' programming. Many experts predict that blended attacks will increase in the near future. Examples of a blended attack are bot programs, which enable an attacker to compromise and infect multiple computers at once. Bots are distributed by hackers through Trojan horse programs or other methods to infect a computer system.[87] Once a machine is infected, the code then installs a bot program, making the machine a "zombie." This means that the computer can now receive commands and be controlled by another user through IRC channels, which are real-type communications enabled over the Internet.[88] The IRC bot program then surreptitiously contacts a preprogrammed IRC channel to wait for commands from the bot operator. Multiple machines that are infected with this malware will contact the channel, creating a botnet, or network of zombie machines.

Botnets can reach very large sizes and may include thousands of machines, enabling bot operators to engage in a variety of different acts. Zombie machines can be used to covertly distribute bulk e-mail that can be used to enable fraud and phishing attacks. Botnets can also be used to perform DDoS attacks or validate stolen credit card numbers, enabling identity theft on a rapid and large scale. Finally, botnets can be used to rapidly distribute new viruses and malware across the Internet. Thus, bots constitute a significant threat to computer users around the globe. In fact, zombies and bots cost U.S. businesses over $2.8 million in 2007 alone.[89] Bots can also act as a force multiplier for computer attackers by leveraging the power of thousands of systems to their needs. At the same time, they allow attackers to conceal their identities behind common computer users who may be unaware that their machines are involved in cybercrime incidents. Finally, bots act as a versatile attack platform, enabling all manner of cybercrime.

BOX 6.6
Spam Block Lists Bombed to Oblivion

"Bad guys have broken out the nuclear weapons," victim says

by Mike Brunker
MSNBC

September 24—Denial of service attacks by "zombie armies" of compromised computers have put two more spam-blocking lists out of business, adding to the body count in what one victim described as an "all-out war" raging in cyberspace.

The Operators of the Monkeys.com and Blackhole.compu.net "block lists"—used by Internet service providers and businesses to filter out incoming spam before it reaches end users—both announced this week that they are abandoning the services in the face of distributed denial of service attacks (DDOS) that have targeted antispam sites offering the lists this summer.

"It just wasn't feasible to run this (list) and make ourselves a large target anymore," said Bill Larson, network administrator for the Tennessee-based Internet Service Provider Compu-net Enterprises.

In withdrawing from the field of battle, they join *Osirusoft.com,* which announced earlier this month that it would no longer host the Spam Prevention Early Warning System, also known as SPEWS.

Other block list providers, including SpamCop.net, Spamhaus.org and the Spam & Open Relay Blocking System (SORBS) also have reported being subjected to increasingly intense DDOS attacks from thousands of compromised computers known as "zombies."

Mysterious Forces Behind Attacks

The "zombie army" is being marshaled by mysterious opponents of anti-spam forces who use virus-infected e-mail and hacking techniques to take control of machines from unknowing users, most of whom haven't taken the precaution of installing firewalls or anti-virus software to protect them from intruders.

Ron Guilmette, who operated the Monkeys.com block list for more than a year and a half before shutting it down Monday night, said in a news group posting announcing the list's demise that he had "underestimated both the enemy's level of sophistication, and also the enemy's level of brute malevolence."

Guilmette, of Roseville, Calif., told MSNBC.com on Wednesday that his mail, Web and DNS servers were bombarded by data packets directed at Monkeys.com from "more than 10,000 machines" in DDOS attacks that lasted for 10 days beginning on August 19 and then resumed again late last week.

He said that while his "small fry" operation was more susceptible than some of the bigger lists like SPEWS and Spamhaus, none of the antispam services are impervious.

"All of these services are now under criminal attack, which is premeditated and financially driven," he said. "It's all-out warfare and the bad guys have broken out the nuclear weapons."

In the case of Compu-Net, Larson said he made the decision to cease operating the list not because of a DDOS attack, but because of an escalating case in which someone was forging company e-mail addresses on spam, causing many thousands of messages to "bounce" back and threatening to overwhelm the company's e-mail servers.

Threats to Servers, Selves

In addition to the bounced e-mail, Larson and other members of Compu-Net staff were forced to handle a flood of abuse complaints from people who wrongly believed the company was spamming them and deal with "threats against ourselves, our servers and our Internet connection," he wrote in a posting to the news.admin.net-abuse.e-mail (NANAE) news group.

And he feared that the DDOS attacks that have targeted other block list operators would be next.

"As an ISP, if we got hit by a denial of service attack that lasted a week or 10 days, we would be out of business," Larson said, explaining the decision to cut and run.

Earlier this month, the cyberattacks forced Joe Jared, who had been hosting the Spam Prevention Early Warning System, also known as SPEWS, at his Osirusoft.com Web site, to suddenly pull the plug on the popular but controversial block list.

Jared's action blocked access to the SPEWS.org Web site, though mirror sites with the list continued to operate, enabling network administrators to reconfigure their systems to query the alternate sites.

Other block lists, which are used by Internet service providers and businesses to filter out the majority of incoming spam before it reaches the end users, have come under siege from DDOS attacks this summer. The bombardment of massive amounts of data has intermittently prevented subscribers or users from gaining access to lists at Web sites of SpamCop.net, Spamhaus.org, Monkeys.com and the Spam & Open Relay Blocking System.

Attacks More Systematic, Intense

DDOS attacks have been used against antispam sites before, but this summer's onslaught appears to be more systematic and intense than anything seen before.

"There's not much doubt in my mind that the various attacks are the work of the same person or organization," Julian Haight, president of Seattle-based SpamCop.net, which has been under attack intermittently since mid-July, told MSNBC.com earlier this month.

While it's not clear who is behind the campaign, suspicion has focused on renegade spammers, who have an obvious motive.

"These block lists have become more and more effective as they've become focused, so they've started to hit home," said Jesse Dougherty, director of development with software solution provider ActiveState.

The block lists have alienated some in the Internet community by blocking users who have nothing to do with spam, either accidentally or, in the case of SPEWS, as a deliberate tactic aimed at pressuring Internet service providers to crack down on spammers on their networks. But because the attacks are targeting multiple sites rather than just one or two, most experts say spammers are more likely culprits.

"It has been suggested to me that the person (behind the attacks) could be a site that I've erroneously blamed for spam, but given the amount of resources being put into it I'd certainly vote for the spammer," said Haight.

An Extra $30,000 on Bill

Haight, who said that SpamCop was knocked off line periodically in the early days of the attack in mid-July, said it will cost about $30,000 this year to pay for a content distribution network capable of withstanding such assaults.

Britain's Spamhaus.org also has been able to withstand steady attacks that began more than $2^1/_2$ months ago, chief executive Steve Linford told the Boston Globe earlier this month.

"We're usually under attack from 5,000 to 10,000 servers at once," Linford was quoted as saying. "They're extremely large attacks that would bring down just about anything."

Some security experts, and many in the anti-spam community, believe that spammers have been behind recent viruses that have placed malicious "Trojan horse" programs on vulnerable computers, creating the network of "zombies" that can be remotely ordered to launch such attacks.

And while there is no hard evidence, some believe that the "sobig" family of viruses may be recruiting for the zombie army.

Guilmette, the former provider of the Monkeys.com block list, said the electronic bombardment of his site began "at 11:27 p.m. Pacific Time on Aug. 19, which coincidentally or not was the same day that sobig.f started to make the rounds."

Big ISPs Seen as Culprits

While the escalating attacks have the antispam community up in arms, there is no indication that law enforcement yet considers them to be serious.

"I went to my local police and I had to twist their arms just to get them to take a report," said Guilmette, adding that he called his local FBI office and left a message but was never called back.

But the longtime spam fighter said he bears more of a grudge against big ISPs like AT&T and UUNet, because they are in a better position to halt the attacks.

"If *www.whitehouse.gov* had been under attack for 10 days, you can bet your ass that the big providers would have gone to the lower level ISPs and asked them to shut off the machines that were part of the zombie army that was doing the attacking," he said. "In my case they told me all I could do was try to ride it out and hope for the best."

_____

Source: *http://www.msnbc.com/news/959094.asp*

EXTENT OF VIRUSES AND MALICIOUS CODE ATTACKS

Every six months, Symantec produces the *Internet Security Threat Report*, which provides an update about Internet threat activity, including network-based attacks, a review of known vulnerabilities, and highlights of malicious code. Their report suggests that the number of malicious software threats spiked in 2008, with over 1.5 million new malicious software signatures being created that year.[90] This was a 60 percent increase over 2007, suggesting that malicious software has become a significant part of the digital crime arsenal. The types of attack have also changed, as the majority of computer users are being compromised by malicious software hosted on a Web server, which compromises a system through their Web browser.[91] This type of attack has increased because of the huge number of Internet users and the small number of Web browsers that exist. By identifying common vulnerabilities in a browser, an attacker can compromise millions of machines with greater ease and efficiency than a virus or worm.

Additionally, attackers appear tremendously focused on acquiring information and data that can be used to steal money. In fact, the majority of malicious software tools found in 2008 stole user information or contained keystroke logging software that could steal bank information and other sensitive information.[92]

The report noted the following trends:

Attack Trends

- The United States was the top country of attack origin in 2008, accounting for 25 percent of worldwide activity.
- The education sector accounted for 27 percent of data breaches that could lead to identity theft during this period, more than any other sector and a slight increase from 26 percent in 2007.
- The financial sector was the top sector for identities exposed in 2008, accounting for 29 percent of the total, an increase from 10 percent in 2007.
- In 2008, the theft or loss of a computer or other data-storage devices accounted for 48 percent of data breaches that could lead to identity theft and for 66 percent of the identities exposed.
- Symantec observed an average of 75,158 active bot-infected computers per day in 2008, an increase of 31 percent from the previous period.
- The United States was the location for the most bot command-and-control servers in 2008, with 33 percent of the total, more than any other country.
- The United States was the country most frequently targeted by DoS attacks in 2008, accounting for 51 percent of the worldwide total.

Vulnerability Trends Highlights

- Symantec documented 5,491 vulnerabilities in 2008; this is a 19 percent increase over the 4,625 vulnerabilities documented in 2007.
- Eighty percent of documented vulnerabilities were classified as easily exploitable in 2008; this is an increase from 2007, when 74 percent of documented vulnerabilities were classified as easily exploitable.
- Of any browser analyzed in 2008, Apple® Safari® had the longest window of exposure (the time between the release of exploit code for a vulnerability and a vendor releasing a patch), with a nine-day average; Mozilla® browsers had the shortest window of exposure in 2008, averaging less than one day.

- Mozilla browsers were affected by 99 new vulnerabilities in 2008, more than any other browser; 47 new vulnerabilities were identified in Internet Explorer, 40 in Apple Safari, 35 in Opera™, and 11 in Google® Chrome.
- The top attacked vulnerability for 2008 was the Microsoft Windows® Server Service RPC Handling Remote Code Execution Vulnerability.

Malicious Code Trends Highlights

- In 2008, the number of new malicious code signatures increased by 265 percent over 2007; over 60 percent of all currently detected malicious code threats were detected in 2008.
- Of the top ten new malicious code families detected in 2008, three were Trojans, three were Trojans with a backdoor component, two were worms, one was a worm with a backdoor component, and one was a worm with backdoor and virus components.
- Trojans made up 68 percent of the volume of the top 50 malicious code samples reported in 2008, a minor decrease from 69 percent in 2007.
- In 2008, the proportional increase of potential malicious code infections was greatest in the Europe, the Middle East, and Africa region.
- Malicious code that targets online games accounted for 10 percent of the volume of the top 50 potential malicious code infections, up from 7 percent in 2007.

Spam Trends Highlights

- The most common type of spam detected in 2008 was related to Internet- or computer-related goods and services, which made up 24 percent of all detected spam; this was the second most common type of spam in 2007, accounting for 19 percent of the total.
- Symantec observed a 192 percent increase in spam detected across the Internet, from 119.6 billion messages in 2007 to 349.6 billion in 2008.
- In 2008, 29 percent of all spam recorded by Symantec originated in the United States, a substantial decrease from 45 percent in 2007, when the United States was also the top-ranked country of origin for spam.
- In 2008, bot networks were responsible for the distribution of approximately 90 percent of all spam e-mail.[93]

As noted in this section, some malicious software can cause widespread damage and affect thousands of networks and machines. Undoubtedly, the greatest cost is loss of work hours and time spent patching systems, not to mention productivity lost from everyone having to chat and e-mail their friends about the latest threat. Even so, a growing number of experts and publications raise the idea that viruses, for the most part, are more hype and hoax than actual malicious threat. For example, perhaps the largest virus hype to date concerned the Michelangelo virus in the early 1990s. In the lead-up to March 6, 1992 (Michelangelo's birthday and the supposed date of the virus payload release), the media coverage and doomsaying about the virus was so intensive that millions of people around the world refused to turn on their computers at all for the entire period around March 6. McAfee claimed at the time that anywhere "from 50,000 to five million" computers were infected, a statement that was far from the truth.[94] The airwaves were flooded with supposed virus experts predicting the shutdown of governments and business worldwide. In the end, relatively few machines were infected, and the virus eventually lived on to become urban legend. The hype of potential viruses and the damage that people believe viruses can cause feeds into the larger problem of virus hoaxes.

BOX 6.7
E-mail Hoaxes

SEND THIS TO ALL OF YOUR FRIENDS, DO NOT DELETE THIS MESSAGE, IMPORTANT ALERT. These are but a few of the opening lines of many e-mails commonly received daily via the Internet. Most of these messages are relatively harmless, but some have a more sinister purpose. Some people think that many of the scams and hoaxes are new, when they are classically old schemes being perpetuated in a new format, cyberspace. To most, these are harmless annoyances that quickly find their way into the cyber trash bin. The undeniable cost is lost productivity and time spent on sifting through the increasing volume of these junk e-mails, typically referred to as spam. There is a growing body of information on the Internet concerning spam and e-mail hoaxes. In general, these e-mails can be grouped into five general categories: spam, chain mail, hoaxes, virus hoaxes, and fraud.

Spam

Spam is the generic term [also called unsolicited commercial e-mail (UCE) and junk e-mail] for any e-mail that is sent to a large group of people, typically as an advertisement or other solicitation. If your e-mail address falls into the hands of a "spammer," you will undoubtedly receive ever-increasing unsolicited advertisements. Most spam is easily deleted and is simply annoying. There are several Web sites with detailed information on spam, federal legislation, and other problems with these e-mails:

> *http://do-not-spam.com/*
>
> *http://spam.abuse.net/*
>
> *http://members.aol.com/e-mailfaq/e-mailfaq.html*
>
> *http://www.cauce.org/*

Chain Mail

This is simply traditional chain letters that have found a new medium. If you believe in good or bad luck, you can forward these to your friends. These are increasing because forwarding them is relatively easy using e-mail.

Hoaxes

There are almost too many hoaxes to document. Some of the more popular ones involve people spending $250 for a cookie recipe, having their kidneys removed while they sleep, and receiving cash awards and gift certificates by forwarding e-mail. There is no way for a company to track who you send e-mail to, and they are not giving away free computers, vacations, or cash. Check out these hoaxes at the Web sites listed below.

> Information on medical hoaxes:
>
> *http://www.quackwatch.com*
>
> Department of Energy's Web site for debunking myths and legends:
> *http://ciac.llnl.gov/ciac/CIACWelcome.html*
> Offers current information about hoaxes being propagated on the Internet: *http://urbanlegends.about.com/culture/urbanlegends/library/blhoax.htm*
>
> Entire Web sites dedicated to urban legends: *http://www.urbanlegends.com/*
>
> *http://www.nonprofit.net/hoax/hoax.html*
> *http://www.snopes.com*

Virus Hoaxes

> *We are spending much more time debunking hoaxes than handling real virus incidents.*
>
> *The U.S. Dept. of Energy Computer Incident Advisory Capability (CIAC)*

We have all received well-intentioned e-mail warnings about some virus that is possibly the worst ever found. Many people simply delete these messages. Others forward the e-mails on in the chance that this virus could be a real threat. E-mail hoaxes promote fear. They make you pause. They waste your time. They scare some people into not using technology to its fullest extent for fear of contracting a dangerous virus. Virus hoaxes are defined as deliberate or unintentional e-mail messages warning people about a virus or other malicious software program that simply doesn't exist.

Most hoaxes contain one or more of the following characteristics:

- Warnings about alleged new viruses and their damaging consequences
- Demands for the reader to forward the warning to as many people as possible
- Pseudotechnical "information" describing the virus
- Bogus comments from officials: FBI, software companies, news agencies, etc.

One of the better ones forwarded concerned a virus that was "infecting all digital cellular phones" and that I shouldn't answer any phone calls that caller-id couldn't track or I would get the virus. In short, there are numerous hoaxes that are propagated concerning viruses. In fact, there is more worry about viruses than is necessary. Rob Rosenberger maintains an excellent informational Web site on viruses, hoaxes and real, and offers sound advice concerning them at *http://www.vmyths.com/*

Symantec's Web site for virus hoaxes: *http://www.symantec.com/avcenter/hoax.html*

McAfee's Virus Hoax Center: *http://www.mcafeeb2b.com/asp_set/anti_virus/library/hoaxes.asp*

F-secure Corporation Web site: *http://www.datafellows.com/virus-info/hoax/*

Fraud

Bank Failures, Mergers, and Takeovers: A "Phish-erman's Special"

If the recent changes in the financial marketplace have you confused, you're not alone. The financial institution where you did business last week may have a new name today, and your checks and statements may come with a new look tomorrow. A new lender may have acquired your mortgage, and you could be mailing your payments to a new servicer. Procedures for the banking you do online also may have changed. According to the Federal Trade Commission (FTC), the nation's consumer protection agency, the upheaval in the financial marketplace may spur scam artists to phish for your personal information.

Phishers (pronounced "fishers") may send attention-getting e-mails that look like they're coming from the financial institution that recently acquired your bank savings and loan or mortgage. Their intent is to collect or capture your personal information, like your credit card numbers, bank account information, Social Security number, passwords, or other sensitive information. Their messages may ask you to "update," "validate," or "confirm" your account information. For example, you may see messages such as the following:

We recently purchased ABC Bank. Due to concerns for the safety and integrity of our new online banking customers, we have issued this warning message . . . Please follow the link below to renew your account information.

We recently acquired the mortgage on your home and are in the process of validating account information. Please click here to update and verify your information.

During our acquisition of XYZ Savings & Loan, we experienced a data breach. We suspect an unauthorized transaction on your account. To ensure that your account is not compromised, please click the link below to confirm your identity.

The messages direct you to a Web site that looks like the actual site of your new financial institution or lender. But it isn't. It's a bogus site whose purpose is to trick you into divulging your personal information so the operators can steal your identity and run up bills or commit other crimes in your name.

Source: http://www.ftc.gov/bcp/edu/pubs/consumer/alerts/alt089.shtm

Virus Hoaxes

There is a variety of Internet and virus hoaxes. Hoaxes are spread and believed by unsuspecting users for a variety of reasons. Gordon, Ford, and Wells (1997) note that in all the hoaxes they examined, the hoax was far more interesting and popular than the reality behind the virus or hoax. Perhaps the most common reason hoaxes are believed is a blind trust in authority. As noted previously, false authority syndrome can lead some people to proclaim themselves as virus experts. Often, well-intentioned users forward these bogus warnings to everyone in their address book. Additionally, virtually every workgroup has a "techie" person that many people go to with computer-related problems and technical questions. If such a person chooses to spread a hoax, or even if the hoax comes from a friend of the user, it is believed without much investigation or question. As some true virus experts note, this problem is magnified in the cyberspace environments, where little thought is given to authentication of sources: If you proclaim yourself to be an expert loudly and often enough, you are often accepted as such.[95] Another reason hoaxes can spread rapidly and become believable is the excitement generated by being the first person to e-mail everyone that a new and threatening virus is out there and feeling that you are performing a public service by notifying everyone. Even bright, well-reasoned people can be drawn in by an effective hoax. As Barnum so adequately noted, there's a sucker born every minute. Other reasons include a general lack of skepticism, a desire for attention and recognition, and a lack of knowledge concerning viruses and computer systems.

Authoring a virus hoax takes relatively little technical skill other than good salesmanship. However, the hoax can be as costly as or costlier than an actual virus. It is estimated that virus hoaxes could cost an organization as much as a genuine virus incident.[96] One source claims that a virus hoax could cost as much as $41.7 million.[97] The cost of a virus hoax is difficult to determine, but clearly the hoax could result in loss of productivity for those "affected" by it, in increased network traffic from people spreading the hoax, and in damage to systems by those who erroneously delete files off their system, resulting in increased tech support time to repair the damaged systems.

Spotting a virus hoax is relatively easy in some ways, as they tend to have several commonalities. Several virus experts conclude that most hoaxes:[98]

- Contain a warning message about a virus or some other malicious code.
- Are usually from an individual, occasionally from a company, but never from the cited source.
- Warn not to read or download the supposed virus and preach salvation by deletion.

BOX 6.8
A Variety of Virus Hoaxes

Virus Hoaxes began to emerge in the late 1990s and will continue as long as people believe them and forward them to other users. The Web site of leading antivirus software and computer security firm McAfee Inc. provides a list of close to 100 virus hoaxes that have appeared on the Internet. The threats contained in these hoax e-mails cover a wide range, including those that involve cell phones, screen savers, holidays, jokes, and news on prominent citizens, political figures, and world leaders. According to these selected hoaxes, opening infected e-mails that contain any of the following subject lines will result in a permanent erasure of your entire hard drive:

- "Help"
- "A Moment of Silence"

- "Osama Vs. Bush"
- "Osama Bin Laden Hanged!"
- "Invitation"
- "Got You!"
- "Work"
- "Happy New Year!"
- "Special Offer"
- "It Takes Guts To Say Jesus"

Note: *List and description of virus hoaxes available at* http://www.mcafee.com

- Describe the virus as having horrific destructive powers and often the ability to send itself by e-mail.
- Usually have many words in caps and exclamation marks.
- Urge the reader to alert everyone they know and forward the e-mail along.
- Seek credibility by citing some authoritative source as issuing the warning.
- Claim the source says the virus is "bad" or has them "worried."
- Seek credibility by describing the virus in baseless technical jargon.

VIRUS WRITERS AND VIRUS EXPERTS

Numerous authors have attempted to characterize virus writers and elaborate the reasons why people write and spread viruses. One train of thought contends that virus writers go through a progression from students and schoolchildren to young adults and college students to professional virus writers. At each stage, the destructive capability of the virus and the technical expertise of the writer increases.[99] In this theory, the motivations for virus writing also change from recognition from peers and experimentation, progressing to revenge and social notoriety.

The virus writers and those who wish to write viruses have a variety of resources from which to learn their trade and propagate viruses. There are numerous virus-maker journals, newsletters, bulletin boards, and Web pages devoted to virus writing and virus creation tools.[100] Sarah Gordon, currently at Symantec, has consistently taken a more conciliatory view. In a survey of virus writers, she claims that:

> . . . The virus writer has been characterized by some as a bad, evil, depraved, maniac; terrorist, technopathic, genius gone mad, sociopath. This image has been heightened not only by the media, but by some of the actions of the virus writers themselves. Public communications from the writers, in the form of echo-mail messages, often seem to indicate they are intent on doing as much damage as humanly possible. Their electronic publications have in the past reinforced this, and the very fact that they release viruses may seem to confirm it: These people are bad. [But it can be argued that] this is a gross oversimplification of the situation, and that the virus writing aspect of these individuals is not sufficient to characterize them into one group simply labelled "unethical people."

Most virus writers obviously have numerous justifications and rationalizations for why they choose to write viruses. Not all experts agree on the seriousness of the virus problem, with many noting that most viruses are relatively harmless and easily removed.[101] Trojan horse programs allow those without a comprehensive understanding of multiple operating systems, networking concepts, and programming languages to routinely attack remote systems. The largest group of attackers, comprising over 95 percent of the attacker population, is referred to as "script-kiddies," individuals with limited knowledge of operating systems and networks.[102] This group doesn't write code or create viruses; instead, they use precompiled programs like Trojan horses to do the work for them, which afford the attackers access to other computers to pilfer files, change settings, or launch DoS attacks.[103]

It must be noted, however, that the motives for malicious software creation have changed among some hackers. Over the past few years, malicious software creation has shifted from curiosity, damage, and revenge motives to a significant profit motive. In fact, some researchers use the term *crimeware* as a reference to the programs and tools that facilitate fraud and computer

BOX 6.9

Interview with a Virus Writer—Inside the Mind of Dark Avenger

by Sarah Gordon

About three years ago I was introduced to the man known as Dark Avenger. Having just purchased a PC, and finding myself the proud owner of not only the PC but of the Ping-Pong virus as well, I found my way to the Fidonet virus echo. Watching the information fly back and forth, suddenly there appeared a new name—Dark Avenger. I was intrigued by his style and the hype surrounding him. At some early point of participation in the forum, I commented that I would like to have a virus named after me, hoping to draw his attention. Had I understood at that time quite what viruses actually entailed, I would not have made that statement. As I talked with antivirus researchers and product developers, I began to understand the issues. I also talked to virus writers. Having a background in juvenile corrections, I found their attitude typical of youths in crisis. Their response to public mail demonstrated the attitude so prevalent in interaction between rebellious teenagers and authority figures. Their private mail (which I have not and will not disclose) resembled the private conversations I'd had when counseling in a one-on-one situation: frustation, anger and general dissatisfaction followed by small glimpses of conscience—often resulting in a decision to at least consider the consequences of their actions. Some, like their more traditional counterparts, never made it to that final stage, but at least we had some stimulating discussions. I've had, and continue to have, detailed conversations with virus writers, focusing on the reasons behind their misdirected creativity.

Time passed, and still Dark Avenger continued to haunt me. Why had he not responded to me like the majority of virus writers? Despite several failed attempts to contact him, he remained elusive.

Enter the MtE

With the release of the now-infamous Mutation Engine, I found Dark Avenger had indeed noticed me. The demo virus which accompanied the engine contained the text: "We dedicate this little virus to Sara Gordon, who wanted to have a virus named after her." Many people asked me about this, and I became quite accustomed to people assuming I knew Dark Avenger personally. The fact of the matter is, at that time, he was still a mystery. How could I explain to people that I "knew" him, yet had never spoken with him? I'm not a programmer, yet I knew him from looking at his viruses. I have no formal background in computer science, but I could understand what he was doing and how he was feeling, despite some people arguing that there is no such thing as "instinctive hacking." Few people believed me at that point; yet the fact is, at that time, I had never spoken with him directly.

When I learned Christopher Seeley was talking on a semi-regular basis to someone identified by both Alan Solomon and Vesselin Bontchev as Dark Avenger, I sent him a message to pass on to (dav). The message was written slowly and laboriously in Bulgarian, and I briefly stated that I would like to ask him some questions.

His response came quickly. I immediately recognized the author as the creator (not necessarily distributor) of the viruses attributed to him. We exchanged several electronic messages, routed through various gateways. Eventually—with the assistance of various intermediaries—I was able to speak "live" (or at least electronically) with Dark Avenger.

Since that time we have exchanged many messages, this interview being an edited compendium of our messages and conversations taking place over a five-month period. He agreed to allow me to ask him these questions, and I agreed to allow him to remove any questions or responses he was not comfortable answering or making public.

Who is the Dark Avenger? Many people have asked me: "Is Vesselin Bontchev the Dark Avenger?"; in fact, one of the reasons I became so intent on finding the Dark Avenger was to learn the answer to this question. I can state unequivocably that the Dark Avenger is not Vesselin Bontchev. Neither is he a crazed technopath, nor a maniac intent on destroying the world. He has very little in common with the usual crop of virus writers I have talked to. He is, all in all, a unique individual.

August 1992

SARA GORDON: Some time ago, in the Fidonet virus echo, when you were told one of your viruses was responsible for the deaths of thousands, possibly, you responded with an obscenity. Let's assume for the moment this story is true. Tell me, if one of your viruses was used by someone else to cause a tragic incident, how would you really feel?

DARK AVENGER: I am sorry for it. I never meant to cause tragic incidents. I never imagined that these viruses would affect anything outside computers. I used the nasty words because the people who wrote to me said some very nasty things to me first.

SG: Do you mean you were not aware that there could be any serious consequences of the viruses? Don't computers in your country affect the lives and livelihoods of people?

DA: They don't, or at least at that time they didn't. PCs were just some very expensive toys nobody could afford and nobody knew how to use. They were only used by some hotshots (or their children) who had nothing else to play with.

I was not aware that there could be any consequences. This virus was so badly written, I never imagined it would leave the town. It all depends on human stupidity, you know. It's not the computer's fault that viruses spread.

SG: It is said many people working for the government and companies in Bulgaria had computers at that time. Isn't this correct?

DA: I don't know who said that, but it's not true. Actually, at that time, most of the people in Bulgaria did not even know what a computer was.

SG: Did you have access to modems at that time? Did you ever make use of virus exchange systems to send your viruses? I've seen your name on some of the mail coming from those systems.

DA: At that time, I did not have access to a modem. At that time there were no virus exchange systems, I think. I've been on some of them, but that was much later. I never made any "use" of them, I was just fooling with them. I've been on almost no VX systems using that name. If you saw it somewhere, probably it was just some impostor, not me. When I have called any of them they (the sysops) insist I have written many more viruses. It's very difficult, when you're (dav) [Dark Avenger] and you upload a virus, to make out that you didn't write it.

SG: Did you ever call the virus systems using your real name?

DA: Not a real name but a name that sounded like a real person.

SG: Why didn't you ever contact me?

DA: I did. I left you a message once. Well, it was not to you, but I put something in it for you.

SG: Yes, I remember that one. Something about: "You should see a doctor. Normal women don't spend their time talking about computer viruses." I answered it, if you recall?

DA: Yes. You said: "I do not want to be a normal woman, at least not in Bulgaria."

SG: Yes, but why didn't you talk to me directly?

DA: I didn't know you wanted to talk to me. Why didn't you send me mail?

SG: I was afraid of you. Anyway, why did you dedicate that virus to me?

DA: You said you wanted it.

SG: People have wondered why you wrote your first virus. Why did you write it and do you have any regrets about it?

DA: I wrote it because I had heard about viruses and wanted to know about them, but nobody around me could tell me anything. So I decided to write my own. I put some code inside it that intentionally destroys data, and I am sorry for it. I started working on it in September 1988.

SG: Couldn't you have asked someone who had a virus to show it to you?

DA: I knew nobody who had a virus. In fact, I think that at that time, nobody in Bulgaria had one.

SG: Where did you hear about viruses? What in particular caught your interest?

DA: There was a magazine called *Computer for You,* the only magazine in Bulgaria at that time. In its May 1988 issue there was a stupid article about viruses, and a funny picture on its cover. This particular article was what made me write that virus. Of course, this was not the first time I heard about viruses. I was interested in them, and thinking of writing one a long time before that. I think the idea of making a program that would travel on its own, and go to places its creator could never go, was the most interesting for me. The American government can stop me from going to the U.S., but they can't stop my virus.

SG: It has been stated by Valery Todorov that he wrote his first virus, WWT, because he was curious as to whether he could write one or not, but that he wrote his second virus because Vesselin Bontchev (often called the Number One Enemy of Dark Avenger) gave him the idea. Did you get any ideas from other people's viruses? Have you ever written a virus with someone else?

DA: No, but for someone else, yes.

SG: For who?

DA: For you.

SG: How do you feel about the destruction of data?

DA: I think it's not right to destroy someone else's data.

SG: If you think that, then why did you put destructive code in your viruses?

DA: As for the first virus, the truth is that I didn't know what else to put in it. Also, to make people try to get rid of the virus, not just let it live. At that time, I didn't think that data in PCs could have any great value.

SG: Do you mean the data in PCs in Bulgaria is of no value?

DA: As I said (or did I?), at that time there were few PCs in Bulgaria, and they were only used by a bunch of hotshots (or their kids). I just hated it when some asshole had a new powerful 16 Mhz 286 and didn't use it for anything, while I had to program on a 4.77 Mhz XT with no hard disk (and I was lucky if I could ever get access to it at all).

Actually, I don't know why I'm saying all this. The real answer is: I don't know. And I didn't care. I also don't care very much now, I'm afraid. I just want the other people to leave me alone. The weasel (Vesselin Bontchev) can go to hell.

By the way, if you really think you should not break any laws, you can start by purchasing MS-DOS, or turning off all your computers permanently. First law of computer security: Don't buy a computer. Second law: If you ever buy a computer, don't turn it on.

SG: Don't you feel responsible if someone else uses one of your viruses to cause actual harm to a person's machine?

DA: No. If they wanted to cause harm, they wouldn't need my viruses. They could simply type "format c:" or something else that is much more effective.

SG: How can you say this? By writing and distributing the viruses, making them available, you do provide people with the idea and the means, in the same way you were initially provided. By doing this, your actions affect innocent users.

DA: The innocent users would be much less affected if they bought all the software they used (and from an authorized dealer) and if they used it the way they are allowed to by the license agreement. If somebody instead of working plays pirated computer games all day long, then it's quite likely that at some point they will get a virus.

Besides, there's no such thing as an innocent user, but that's another subject.

SG: What about the fact that you're giving people the idea, by creating such clever viruses?

DA: Ideas are not responsible for people who believe in them. Or use them. Or abuse them. Also, I didn't write them to "provide" anybody with anything. The weasel is the one who "provides." I just wrote them for fun. I couldn't care less for all the suckers who see/use them. They were not supposed to make such a big mess.

SG: Still, you have provided them with an insidious weapon. Don't you feel that by providing them with such clever computer tricks, you are contributing to hurting the innocent users?

DA: I don't provide nobody with nothing. The weasel provides.

SG: How does he provide?

DA: He just "provides." That's one of his favorite words. I don't want to talk or think about it.

SG: What do you think about the new crop of virus writers, like Falcon/Skism and nUkE?

DA: They are kids, most of whom seek fame (and achieve it easily with the help of a-v people). Most of them are not good at programming viruses at all.

SG: Well, at least that is some point you and the a-v community agree upon. You have achieved a certain amount of "fame" yourself. How does it make you feel when you see your name in magazines and mail? How do you feel when you see your viruses "defeated" by antivirus programs?

DA: I wrote the virus so it would be killed, like I said. It was not supposed to do all this. I like seeing my name in magazines and in messages. I used to read all the messages about me, but I like it most when I see it printed somewhere. And I liked it a LOT seeing my things in Western a-v programs. First time I saw McAfee Scan was about version 5.0 or so. I liked it a lot. I was just excited, happy.

SG: Where did you get that name, Dark Avenger?

DA: I didn't really "get" the name. I mean, I didn't call myself that. I put those words in the virus and someone else (we both know who) said it was written by the Dark Avenger. He's the one that made me be the Dark Avenger, that name. I didn't use the name until after he called me that. That phrase itself came from some old song from a long time ago, and not from an Iron Maiden song, like some people have said. In many ways, I suppose you could say he made the Dark Avenger.

SG: How long do you think you will continue writing viruses?

DA: I don't. I never planned it.

SG: You misunderstood the question. Are you going to continue writing viruses?

DA: I don't know. It depends on what will happen to me.

SG: What do you mean?

DA: I mean, I will not normally write/spread any destructive or virus code, unless something extraordinary happens. Well, not if they put me in jail. If they do, and I ever get out, I will not be in a mood for programming. It is not/was not a crime to write the viruses, so I don't think this should happen. I just am not interested in writing them now.

SG: Do you know the difference between right and wrong?

DA: Why do you ask me this? In American movies, at the end, always the good guy gets the money, the girl and the applause, and the bad guy gets in jail or something. But in real life, it's not clear who is good and who is bad, and who gets what. It's not black and white. The only thing that is for sure is that good people always lose.

SG: Have you ever considered making an antivirus product, other than the fake doctor.exe which is actually a virus?

DA: I have considered it many times, but antivirus products are as useless as viruses. As for doctor.exe, it's not fake, it really does the job as it says it does.

SG: Why do you say they are useless? Don't you think they help protect users from common viruses?

DA: The users spend much more money on buying such products and their updates rather than on the losses of data damaged because of viruses. The a-v products only help the users to empty their wallets. Besides, viruses would spread much less if the "innocent users" did not steal software, and if they worked a bit more at their workplace, instead of playing games. For example, it is known that the Dark Avenger virus was transported from Europe to the U.S.A. via some (stolen) games.

SG: But viruses have now spread far beyond games. Most viruses are known to come by other routes.

DA: Sure they spread beyond the games. Still, I've never found a virus on any original disk from a package I bought from Borland International.

SG: But I got my first virus from commercial software! Don't you remember my telling that story?

DA: Not from Borland International. Some places you get a virus, some places you don't.

SG: It is said that your fellow Bulgarian, Vesselin Bontchev, did many things to provoke the virus writers. Did he provoke you?

DA: This is quite true, and I don't think he ever denied it. If he did, it would be a lie. There are a lot of people in Bulgaria who know it and can confirm it, but I don't think this was a big contribution to virus writing—his viruses were pretty worthless. He is not a good programmer.

SG: Do you feel that conditions in your country really help create virus writers as was stated by Bontchev in his "factory" paper? What can you tell me about the conditions in your country that contributed to your writing your first virus?

DA: I don't think the conditions in my country help create virus writers any more than conditions in any other country in Eastern Europe. Not after a certain person we both know left the country. As for my first virus, it had nothing to do with that.

SG: What contribution could "a certain person" have made to assist you (or anyone) in writing a virus? Don't you think that the conditions affecting the economy and computer technology of your country have indeed contributed to the overabundance of virus writers coming from former Eastern Bloc countries?

DA: His articles were a plain challenge to virus writers, encouraging them to write more. Also they were an excellent guide how to write them, for those who wanted to, but did not know how. It never said that he himself wrote some.

SG: According to some people, the story of viruses being such a big problem from Bulgaria begins with: "Soon hackers obtained a copy of the virus and began to hack it . . . some were optimized by hand. As a result, now there are several versions of this virus that were created in Bulgaria—versions with infective length 627, 623, 622, 435, 367, 353

and even 348 bytes." It is said many young people brought Bontchev viruses in those early days.

DA: Sure they did. Do you know the viruses vhp and vhp2?

SG: I think I may have heard of them.

DA: I think you don't want to know about this. I will send you a copy of a book that will tell you all about it. You don't want to hear it, and most of all you don't want to hear it from me.

___

Source: http://www.research.ibm.com/antivirus/SciPapers/ Gordon/Avenger.html

attacks.[104] For example, Trojans that steal passwords like Pinch can be considered crimeware, along with botnets, which can be used for spam and phishing. The problem of financially driven hacking and malicious software is amplified due to the growth of markets for malicious software and stolen data, as outlined in Chapter 5. These markets provide access to highly sophisticated malicious software and resources to facilitate computer attacks, such as spam lists and credit card data.[105] Selling products in malware and carding markets means that individuals no longer need to understand how computer technology works to engage in sophisticated forms of digital crime. For example, an individual named Corpse sold a Trojan called Nuclear Grabber in multiple markets that enabled individuals to engage in phishing schemes with little to no technical knowledge.[106] The tool, costing $3,000, came with preloaded images of 12 international banks and spam message scripts to draw in potential victims. He also offered real-time support for his customers in case they should experience problems, much like a legitimate computer service. Similar products can be found in markets across the globe, along with malicious software that can support other tools, like polymorphic engines and binding tools that can combine one piece of malicious software like a Trojan with other programs or images to improve their payload activity.

Additionally, individuals who sell products in malicious software and carding markets must have their products and tools reviewed and receive feedback from their buyers.[107] For example, individuals called "testers" in these sites receive products from malware writers and actually attempt to use them to recommend whether or not others should buy their products. The review process acts as a sort of vetting process for the seller and gives potential buyers some knowledge of the person and their products. Reviewers would describe the quality of the information or service sold, as well as any problems or difficulties in utilizing the product. This process was exemplified in the review of a seller who offered a Trojan designed to steal funds from an electronic payment service called e-gold:[108]

> It is a very cool program that has been tried in a very critical environment and it runs undetected. Kaspersky and NOD32 (Norton) gives no alerts what so ever. The program is also conveniently small (under 100 KB).What the program does are once the victim logs on to his/hers e-gold account from Internet Explorer it highjack's the session and sends all the e-gold to a pre-specified account. How it looks is once the victim has clicked submit on the e-gold login page, the IE window disappears and the program continues to perform the transfer of funds hidden from

the victim. One possible flaw is that it only works on Internet Explorer. But that being the major web browser in use I don't see it as a big problem. The creator was very nice and had a lot of patience with me while I was doing the review. He provided me with a copy of his program set to send funds to an e-gold account of my choosing. He also answered all my questions and concerns very professionally. I think you will all find him easy to deal with. I recommend that win32.grams should be given verified vendor status.

This sort of positive review would help buyers to understand whether or not they should purchase these tools. These examples demonstrate that malicious software is now becoming a professional industry that goes beyond our previous understanding of the hacking and malware community. Taken as a whole, there is a significant need for continuous research to understand how malicious software creators' behaviors change with time.

Summary

Several virus thinkers have projected what the future will hold for virus writing, virus detection, and virus prevention.[109] Many of the predictions made during the early 1990s did indeed come true, particularly those that predicted that future viruses would be more polymorphic, have better encryption, and be better able to spread rapidly.[110] Their observations can be characterized into a few, relatively tight categorizations. The first prediction is that we will continue to have problems with polymorphism, mutations, and as-yet undescribed features of future viruses that will confound virus prevention experts and software.[111]

Malicious software can flourish and cause the most damage in an environment "friendly" to their existence. A friendly environment is one with a vulnerable operating system, one with complete documentation on the operating system, and the overall popularity of the operating system in the computer world.[112] In other words, security holes in a system can be manipulated to the extent that a malware writer understands the operating system and can exploit the holes and the code of the system. Once that code is exploited, the degree of damage inflicted and the nature and extent of the outbreak is determined by the popularity of the operating system—the number of potential targets. For example, for a virus to be successful, it must be able to spread. If only a small number of people used the targeted software or operating system, then the population available to infect is small as well, and the virus cannot spread.

It is important to note that computer security is always dependent on the weakest link in the chain. Security on the Internet and intranets is highly interdependent, and exposure to a potential attack is contingent upon the security, or lack thereof, of other parts of the network. This can be exploited through what is termed an "asymmetric" attack, which involves numerous distributed systems launching an attack against a single victim.

It is also important to note that there is an increasing number of dedicated infrastructure attacks. The interdependency of systems connected to the Internet used to carry out day-to-day business is ever growing and increasingly being relied upon by a variety of businesses, governments, and other operations. These types of attacks fall into four categories: DDoS, worms, attacks on the Internet Domain Name System (DNS); and attacks against or using routers.[113] DoS attacks and worms have been described. The attacks on Internet DNS would focus on disrupting or perverting the data and connectivity of the Internet systems that translate domain names to IP addresses. These attacks can result in a redirection of a user to a site determined by the attacker, compromised data on their servers, DoS, and co-optation or takeover of the domain itself.[114] Routers are specialized computers that direct traffic on the Internet rapidly. These systems could be used as an attack platform, to deny service, and to exploit the trust connection that may exist between routers to speed up service.[115] In sum, any of the attacks described in this chapter could lead to denial of service, compromise of sensitive or personal information, misinformation, and an extreme economic impact, largely from lost revenue and the time and resources necessary to recover.

Review Questions

1. What is the difference between a virus and other types of malicious code?
2. What are the most common types of viruses?
3. What variables are used to distinguish and classify viruses?
4. What is a Trojan horse? What are the various types of Trojan horses?
5. What is a worm? How do worms differ from traditional viruses?
6. What is a denial-of-service attack? How do these attacks work?
7. What are virus hoaxes? Why are the hoaxes sometimes more dangerous than an actual virus?
8. Describe the type of person who would write a virus.
9. Describe how the creation of malicious software is changing due to varying motives?

Endnotes

1. STEPHENSON, PETER. (2000). *Investigating Computer-Related Crime: A Handbook for Corporate Investigators*. Boca Raton, FL: CRC Press.
2. Computer Security Institute (2007). *2007 CSI/FBI Computer Crime and Security Survey*. San Francisco, CA: Computer Security Institute.
3. Avinti (2006). "Protecting Corporate Assets from E-mail Crimeware." *Avinti, Inc.* Retrieved April 20, 2007 from *http://www.avinti.com/download/market_background/whitepaper_email_crimeware_protection.pdf*
4. Refer to the Symantec website for articles and research relating to virus threats on personal computers, peer-to-peer networks, instant messaging, and other electronic devises: *http://www.symantec.com/norton/security_response/index.jsp*. See also the blog by Eric Chien (2009): *http://www.symantec.com/connect/blogs/eric-chien*
5. Ibid.
6. Ibid.
7. *Ibid.*, p. 2.
8. *Ibid.*
9. *Ibid.*
10. GRANT, I. (2008). "Sans Institute Reveals Top 10 Cyber Threats for 2008." *ComputerWeekly.com*.
    Available on line: *http://www.computerweekly.com/Articles/2008/01/14/228890/sans-institute-reveals-top-10-cyber-threats-for-2008.htm*
11. *Ibid.*
12. *http://cve.mitre.org/*
13. *Ibid.*
14. *Ibid.*
15. WELLS, JOE. (2003). "PC Viruses In-the-Wild— September, 2003." Available on line: *http://www.wildlist.org*
16. KASPERSKY, EUGENE V. (2003). *The Classification of Computer Viruses*. Bern, Switzerland: Metropolitan Network BBS Inc. Available on line: *http://www.avp.ch/avpve/classes/classes.stm*
17. *Ibid.*
18. *Ibid.*
19. *Ibid.*
20. *Ibid.*
21. *Ibid.*
22. *Ibid.*
23. KASPERSKY, EUGENE. (1999). "Computer Viruses— What Are They and How to Fight Them?" Available on line: *http://www.avp.ch/avpve/entry/entry.htm 1-1*
24. *Ibid.*

25. Symantec Corporation (2003). "Internet Security for the Web: Protecting Enterprise Networks from Malicious and Inappropriate Web-based Content." Available on line: *http://enterprise security.symantec.com/content/knowledgelibrary. cfm?EID=0*

26. This virus infects the boot-sectors of floppy-disks during access to them. Location on a disk is in a free cluster which the virus marks as BAD (pseudo-bad clusters). An infected disk gets a new volume label, "(C) Brain." The virus uses a stealth mechanism—when you look at the boot-sector of the infected disk, it shows the unchanged boot-sector.

27. KASPERSKY, "Computer Viruses—What Are They and How to Fight Them?"

28. Symantec Corporation, "Internet Security for the Web."

29. *Ibid.*

30. MtE (MuTation Engine) is the first known poly-morphic generator. It was released in 1991 and shocked antivirus researchers by its very difficult (for 1991) polymorphic algorithm.

31. Symantec Corporation, "Internet Security for the Web."

32. These are not memory-resident harmless poly-morphic viruses that affect .COM-files by using the "Vienna" algorithm. They are encoded and use two interesting algorithms. The first algo-rithm realizes the property of a polymorphic virus, due to which two strains of the virus would not coincide with high probability even in one byte. The main body of the virus is encoded depending on the timer (1000000h=16777216 variants), and the decoder is selected from more than 3,000,000,000,000,000,000,000 variants (the decoder length is 39 bytes). The second algorithm fairly successfully complicates the virus tracing—it performs dynamic en/decoding of the virus codes using INT 1 and INT 3.

33. These are memory-resident harmless stealth polymorphic multipartite viruses. They write themselves at the end of .EXE files are executed or closed. These infectors hit MBR on execu-tion of infected files, save the old MBR in the last sectors of C: drive and reduce its size in the Disk Partition Table. The viruses infect RAM on a reboot from the infected MBR only. They hook INT 13h, 1Ch, 21h. According to their internal counters, the viruses display a colorful picture (Mandelbrot fractal set) and the message:

```
Execute: mov ax, FE03 / INT 21.
Key to go on!
```
After executing this instruction, the viruses display:
```
Welcome to T.TEQUILA's latest pro-
duction.
Contact T.TEQUILA/
P.o. Box 543/6312
St'hausen/Switzerland.
Loving thoughts to L.I.N.D.A
BEER and TEQUILA forever!
```

34. KASPERSKY, "Computer Viruses—What Are They and How to Fight Them?"

35. The virus constructor utility VCL.EXE (Virus Creation Laboratory) seems to be the most well known virus creation tool. This constructor can generate source assembler files of the viruses, the OBJ modules and infected master files. VCL con-tains the standard pop-up menu interface. By using VCL menus, it is possible to choose the virus type, enable or disable self encryption, anti-de-bugging code, internal text strings. It also is possi-ble to choose up to ten effects which are called upon virus execution. VCL-based viruses can use a standard way of infection (they append their code to the files while infecting them), they can overwrite the files, or use companion technology. The main properties of VCL-viruses are:
    - They are non-memory resident
    - They scan the subdirectory three or the current directory of the current drive while infecting the files
    - They are appending to COM files, or create new COM files or overwrite COM and EXE files.

    Source: http://www.avp.ch/avpve/constr/vcl.stm

36. KASPERSKY, "Computer Viruses—What Are They and How to Fight Them?"

37. *Ibid.*

38. *Ibid.*

39. This is the first WinWord virus found "in the wild." The virus contains five macros: AAAZAO, AAAZFS, AutoOpen, PayLoad, FileSaveAs. It infects the files that are SaveAs'ed (FileSaveAs). These are the text strings in the infected document:
```
see if we're already installed
iWW6IInstance
AAAZFS
AAAZAO
```

```
That's enough to prove my point
and other. The WINWORD6.INI on
infected   system   contains   the
file:
WW6I=1
```

On the first execution of the virus code (i.e., on the first opening of the infected file), the MessageBox appears with digit "1" inside, and "Ok" button. *http://www.avp.ch/avpve/macro/word/concept.stm*

40. KASPERSKY, "Computer Viruses—What Are They and How to Fight Them?"
41. *Ibid.*
42. *Ibid.*
43. *Ibid.*
44. *Ibid.*
45. *Ibid.*
46. Symantec Corporation, "Internet Security for the Web."
47. KASPERSKY, *The Classification of Computer Viruses.*
48. *Ibid.*
49. *Ibid.*
50. *Ibid.*
51. *Ibid.*
52. *Ibid.*
53. *Ibid.*
54. *Ibid.*
55. CLARKSON, MICHAEL. (2002). Beating the Superbug: Recent Developments in Worms and Viruses. GIAC GSEC Practical (1.4) SANS Institute: Information Security Reading Room. Available on line: *http://www.sans.org/rr/*
56. *Ibid.*
57. Symantec Corporation, "Internet Security for the Web."
58. CLARKSON, "Beating the Superbug."
59. *Ibid.*
60. CERT Coordination Center (2003). "Overview of Attack Trends." Available on line: *http://www. cert.org/archive/pdf/attack_trends.pdf*
61. *Ibid.*
62. *Ibid.*
63. DANCHEV, DANCHO. (1999). "The Complete Windows Trojans Paper." Frame4 Security Systems. Available on line: *http://www.frame4.com*
64. Symantec Corporation, "Internet Security for the Web."
65. DANCHEV, "The Complete Windows Trojans Paper."
66. *Ibid.*
67. CRAPANZANO, JAMIE (2003). "Deconstructing SubSeven, the Trojan Horse of Choice." SANS

Institute Information Security Reading Room. Available on line: *http://www.sans.org/rr/*
68. DANCHEV, "The Complete Windows Trojans Paper."
69. CRAPANZANO, "Deconstructing SubSeven, the Trojan Horse of Choice."
70. *Ibid.*
71. DANCHEV, "The Complete Windows Trojans Paper."
72. *Ibid.*
73. CRAPANZANO, "Deconstructing SubSeven, the Trojan Horse of Choice."
74. *Ibid.*
75. *Ibid.*
76. *Ibid.*
77. HOLT, T.J. (August 7, 2007). "The Market for Malware." Paper presented at the Defcon 15 onference, Las Vegas, Nevada.
78. *Ibid.*
79. LEYDEN, JOHN. (2009). "Pinch Trojan Lives on After Authors' Convictions." *The Register.* Available online: *http://www.theregister.co.uk/ 2009/02/05/pinch_trojan_toolkit/*
80. DANCHEV, "The Complete Windows Trojans Paper."
81. POST, ANDRÉ. (2002). "The Dangers of Spyware." Symantec Anti-Virus Research Library. Available on line: http://www.symantec.com/avcenter/ whitepapers.html
82. *Ibid.*
83. *Ibid.*
84. CERT Coordination Center, "Overview of Attack Trends."
85. HOLDER, ERIC. (2000). "Internet Denial of Service Attacks and the Federal Response." Statement of Eric Holder, Deputy Attorney General of the United States Before the Subcommittee on Crime of the House Committee on the Judiciary and the Subcommittee on Criminal Oversight of the Senate Committee on the Judiciary on February 29, 2000. Available on line: *http://www.usdoj.gov/ criminal/cybercrime/ ccpolicy.html#mv.*
86. CHIEN, ERIC, and SZÖR, PÉTER. (2002). "Blended Attacks Exploits, Vulnerabilities and Buffer-Overflow Techniques in Computer Viruses." *Virus Bulletin Conference.* Available on line: *http://enterprisesecurity.symantec.com/content/ knowledgelibrary.cfm?EID=0;* GORDON, SARAH. (2003). "Virus and Vulnerability Classification Schemes: Standards and Integration." Symantec Security Response. Available on line:

http://enterprisesecurity.symantec.com/content/ knowledgelibrary.cfm?EID=0

87. BACHER, PAUL, HOLZ, THORSTEN, KOTTER, MARKUS, and WICHERSKI, GEORG. (2005). *Tracking Botnets: Using Honeynets to Learn More About Bots.* The Honeynet Project & Research Alliance. Retrieved July 23, 2006 from *http://www.honeynet.org/ papers/bots/*

88. *Ibid.*

89. *Ibid.*, p. 2.

90. Symantec Corporation (2009). "Symantec Internet Security Threat Report: Trends for 2008." Available on line: *http://eval.symantec. com/mktginfo/enterprise/white_papers/b-white paper_exec_summary_internet_security_threat_ report_xiv_04-2009.en-us.pdf*

91. *Ibid.*

92. *Ibid.*

93. *Ibid.*

94. GORDON, SARAH, FORD, RICHARD, and WELLS, JOE. (1997). "Hoaxes & Hypes." Presented at the 7th Virus Bulletin International Conference in San Francisco, California, October 1–3, 1997. Available, on line: *http://www.research.ibm.com/antivirus/ SciPapers/Gordon/ HH.html*

95. *Ibid.*

96. GROCOTT, DARREN. (2003). "Virus Hoaxes—Are They Just a Nuisance? SANS Security Essentials GSEC Practical Assignment Version 1.2e." SANS Institute Information Security Reading Room. Available on line: *http://www.sans.org/rr/*

97. *Ibid.*

98. GORDON, FORD, and WELLS. "Hoaxes & Hypes"; GROCOTT, "Virus Hoaxes—Are They Just a Nuisance? SANS Security Essentials GSEC Practical Assignment Version 1.2e."

99. KASPERSKY, "Computer Viruses—What Are They and How to Fight Them?"

100. *Ibid.*; PEARSON, DAVID. (2003). "Psst . . . Hey Buddy, Wanna Create a Virus? SANS Institute Information Security Reading Room." Available on line: *http://www.sans.org/rr/*

101. DUCKLIN, PAUL. (2001). "Is Virus Writing Really That Bad?" Presented at the Fourth Anti-Virus Asia Researchers (AVAR) Conference 2001, Hong Kong, November 2001. Available on line: *http://www.sophos.com/virusinfo/ whitepapers/virubad.html.*

102. CRAPANZANO, "Deconstructing SubSeven, the Trojan Horse of Choice."

103. *Ibid.*

104. FRANKLIN, J., PAXSON, V., PERRIG, A., and SAVAGE, S. (2007). "An Inquiry into the Nature and Cause of the Wealth of Internet Miscreants." Paper presented at CCS07, October 29–November 2, 2007 in Alexandria, VA; HOLT, T.J., and LAMPKE, E. (2009). "Exploring Stolen Data Markets On-Line: Products and Market Forces." *Criminal Justice Studies* 33(2); Honeynet Research Alliance (2003). "Profile: Automated Credit Card Fraud," *Know Your Enemy Paper* series. Retrieved June 21, 2005, from *http://www.honeynet.org/papers/pro-files/cc-fraud.pdf*; THOMAS, R., and MARTIN, J. (2006). "The Underground Economy: Priceless." *USENIX:login* 31(6): 7–16, 3.

105. *Ibid.*, p. 77.

106. *Ibid.*

107. *Ibid.*, pp. 77, 109.

108. HOLT, and LAMPKE, "Exploring Stolen Data Markets On-Line."

109. BONTCHEV, VESSELIN, (April 1994). "Future of Viruses." *Virus Bulletin.* Available on line: *http://www.virusbtn.com/old/OtherPapers/Trends/*; KASPERSKY, "Computer Viruses—What Are They and How to Fight Them?"

110. BONTCHEV, "Future of Viruses."

111. KASPERSKY, "Computer Viruses—What Are They and How to Fight Them?"

112. *Ibid.*

113. CERT Coordination Center, "Overview of Attack Trends."

114. *Ibid.*

115. *Ibid.*

CHAPTER 7

Sex Crimes, Victimization, and Obscenity on the World Wide Web

CHAPTER OBJECTIVES

After completing this chapter, you should be able to

- Understand the nature of victimization that can occur in cybercrime.
- Describe the groups affected by cyber exploitation, bullying, stalking, and obscenity.
- Describe the offenders who typically prey on victims in cyberstalking and exploitation cases via the Internet.
- Understand the law and legislation in the areas of cyberstalking, cyber exploitation, and pornography.
- Describe the Supreme Court cases that have recently been decided concerning federal efforts to target cybercriminals and protect children online.
- Understand and describe the issues with pornography online, child pornography, and child exploitation facilitated by the Internet.
- Understand the ways that the sex trade, such as prostitution and sex tourism, has changed as a consequence of the Internet.
- Understand and describe the difficulties faced by law enforcement in detecting, investigating, and prosecuting cases of cyberstalking and cyberexploitation.

INTRODUCTION

The Internet allows for communication across national and international boundaries. Not all of this communication is for benign purposes. The ease of use and perceived anonymity that the Internet affords has created the opportunity for certain criminals to exploit, stalk, and commit sex crimes electronically. Further, the nature of crimes committed electronically takes on a different character and presents unique difficulties for law enforcement. For example, physical contact or close proximity does not need to occur for a person to become a victim or for a crime to be committed. A child can be threatened, coerced, intimidated, and exposed to questionable material from offenders anywhere in the world. The crimes that are committed frequently involve multiple victims and offenders and cross national and international boundaries. In sum, the use of the Internet for exploitation, stalking, and obscenity has grown substantially in the past 20 years.

The driving force behind this growth is the vast profit that can be made selling pornography on the Internet. More disturbing is that sexual predators have found their way onto the Internet and have found it to be the perfect tool for exchanging child pornography, trolling for victims, and arranging meetings and tours for sexually deviant behavior. Sex rings of pedophiles have been uncovered that exchange numerous sexually explicit pictures and videos of children. In some high-profile cases, sex rings have been used to transport children across the world for sexual purposes—many times these networks are maintained via the Internet. In addition, pedophiles are using the Internet to arrange meetings with children and have been known to travel hundreds of miles for these meetings. This chapter surveys the nature of exploitation, stalking, and obscenity on the Internet, paying particular attention to the different character these offenses take on when committed over the Web. For every one of the crimes and problems discussed in this chapter, there are numerous victims involved. The primary focus of this chapter is on the offenders who commit these crimes, the nature of the offenses, and insight into the reasons why they occur. The aim of this chapter is to provide greater exposure of these types of offenses and offer enough information that the casual reader, computer scientist, and law enforcement officials can work to curb the victimization described. Effective prevention, enforcement, and investigation of the offenses described here necessitate a more complete understanding of the etiology of the offenses and offenders described.

NATURE OF EXPLOITATION ON THE INTERNET

The exploitation of people for sexual and other purposes is nothing new, but the use of the Internet to facilitate these crimes is a recent phenomenon. The explosion of pornography, exploitation attempts, and crimes facilitated by the Internet have caught politicians and law enforcement completely off guard. Some would argue that warnings went unheeded, others that regulation has come far too late, and still others that any regulation over Internet use is a violation of free speech and the free exchange of ideas. However, few would argue that that the use of the Internet for exploitation and other offenses is a productive and ethical pursuit. People can be victimized in a variety of ways online; the focus of this chapter is primarily on sexual victimization and stalking. The primary targets of such crimes are almost exclusively children and women, even though, as will be noted below, women stalking men via the Internet is not all that uncommon. Internet sex predators victimize people by enticing them through online contact for the purpose of engaging them in sexual acts; by using the Internet for the production, manufacture, and distribution of child or other sexually deviant pornography; by using the Internet to expose youth to child pornography and encouraging them to exchange pornography; and by enticing and exploiting women and children for the purpose of sexual tourism (travel with the intent to engage in sexual behavior) for commercial gain and/or personal gratification.[1]

Estimates of the number of children affected by online crime, child exploitation and abuse, and other Internet-related crimes vary considerably. One estimate puts the number of children who are prostituted in the United States between 100,000 and 3 million.[2] The numbers of children involved in pornography and sex trafficking also are uncertain and probably severely underestimated. Computer sex offenders frequently roam chat rooms and post sexually explicit material on the Internet to make contact with young children and teenagers. Initial victimization may be indirect and limited to showing a child pornographic sites or initiating sexual conversations in a chat room, by e-mail or instant messages. More aggressive predators will spend time developing close relationships with vulnerable children. Eventually, they may introduce them to photographs of children engaging in "normal" sex with adults, send them gifts, and contact them by telephone. Typically they will try to gain their trust, alienate them from their family, and eventually try to set up a meeting where the child will be victimized. Some online sex offenders have gone so far as to send plane tickets to children to fly across the country to meet them.[3]

Women are also targeted by online predators and other criminals. Many would argue that pornography itself is a victimization or objectification of women. As discussed in this chapter, women are frequently the targets of physical stalkers and are at greater risk of being the victim of a cyberstalker. Additionally, women report feeling higher levels of violation as the result of being stalked, threatened, or harassed online. Certain factors make some groups more vulnerable than others to online victimization. First, and most obviously, regular use and access to a computer

---

BOX 7.1
Keeping Children Safe

The Internet has become a boon to those who disseminate sexually explicit material, and this revolution in online content has made it much more difficult to keep children safe from the threats posed by child pornography and online sexual predators. Surveys sponsored by Internet Filter Review show that young males aged 12–17 may be the largest consumers of Internet pornography, and the average age at which they are first exposed to pornography on the Internet is 11.[1]

Studies show that child pornography is one of the fastest growing businesses online. One researcher estimated that there may be up to one million sexually explicit pictures of children on the Internet.[2] Research conducted by the Internet Watch Foundation found that the number of observed child abuse domains increased from 3,433 in 2004 to 10,656 in 2006.[3] Their research uncovered some more startling facts on the explosion of child pornography on the Web:

- The United States is home to 54 percent of all known child abuse domains.

- Images that depict the worst type of abuse—including sadism, penetration by animals, and penetrative sexual activity involving children and adults—has become the primary driver of growth in demand for Web sites that depict child abuse.

Mainstream online photo album services popularly used to share pictures with family and friends are increasingly being used to store images of child abuse.

[1] MAAHS, J., and LIEDERBACH, J. (2007). "Surfing for Porn: Obscenity and the Internet." In C. HEMMONDS (ed.), *Current Legal Issues in Criminal Justice: Readings*. Los Angeles, CA: Roxbury.
[2] HENLEY, J. (September 1, 1996). "The *Observer* Campaign to Clean up the Internet: Hackers called in as Cybercops to Drive out Porn." *Observer*.
[3] *Internet Watch Foundation* (2006). Annual Report. Available at *http://www.iwf.org*

with Internet capability is necessary to being victimized. The axiom that it is only a matter of time before you see something on the Internet that is pornographic or offensive holds true, and in many cases, first exposure is accidental. Older children tend to be at greater risk because they often use the computer unsupervised and are more likely to engage in online discussions of a personal nature. People that actively participate in chat rooms, trade e-mail messages, and send pictures online are also more likely to be victimized.

Many people simply use the computer at work, and correspondence is limited to e-mails between colleagues and friends. However, a growing number of people spend countless hours using Internet chat and posting to Internet discussion groups. Again, it is only a matter of time before such people cross paths with a victimizer. Troubled or rebellious teens who are seeking emancipation from parental authority can be particularly susceptible to Internet predators. Many sex offenders are well versed in the dynamics of teenage difficulties and know exactly what to say to a troubled teen to get them into a vulnerable position. All adolescents struggle with sexuality, and the Internet provides them with a seemingly anonymous and nonthreatening mechanism to ask questions and explore issues of a sexual nature. The problem is that often the teen has no idea who is on the other end of the wire. Most teens feel that victimization is unlikely and that they are safe talking online. Finally, single people have flocked to the Internet in growing numbers looking for companionship and relationships. While many professional online dating services exist, many people encounter someone in a chat room or as the result of some other type of Internet conversation. Seeking the thrills romanticized in the film *You've Got Mail,* these people set up meetings and make themselves vulnerable. While it is likely that most of these interactions are relatively safe, it is also a growing medium for pedophiles and sex offenders to lure their victims off the computer and into a compromising position.

Incidence and Prevalence of Youth Victimization Online

The potential for victimization online is probably much higher than most people think. As noted throughout this text, there are numerous ways in which people can experience some type of loss, including fraud, viruses, and malicious destruction of data. However, several areas of cybervictimization are becoming increasingly common, yet severely underreported and under investigated, including unwanted or unintended exposure to obscene or pornographic material, harassment, threats, and cyberstalking. To date, there is no central clearinghouse for the collection of data on the numbers of these types of victimizations. One of the more comprehensive examinations of these issues is the Youth Internet Safety Survey[4] conducted by Finkelhor, Mitchell, and Wolak and sponsored by the National Center for Missing and Exploited Children. The survey, conducted in 2000 and 2005, measured several areas of problems that youths reported being exposed to while surfing online, including the following:

- *Sexual solicitations and approaches:* Requests to engage in sexual activities or sexual talk or give personal sexual information that were unwanted or, whether wanted or not, made by an adult.
- *Aggressive sexual solicitation:* Sexual solicitations involving off-line contact with the perpetrator through regular mail, by telephone, or in person, or attempts or requests for off-line contact.
- *Unwanted exposure to sexual material:* Without seeking or expecting sexual material, being exposed to pictures of naked people or people having sex when doing online searches, surfing the Web, opening e-mail or e-mail links.

- *Harassment:* Threats or other offensive behavior (not sexual solicitation), sent online to the youth or posted online about the youth for others to see. Not all such incidents were distressing to the youth who experienced them.
- *Distressing incidents* were episodes where youth rated themselves as very or extremely upset or afraid as a result of the incident.[5]

For the purposes of our discussion, we will focus on the results of the 2005 wave of the study and consider how the results changed from wave to wave. In the 2005 research, a nationally representative sample of 1,500 youths, ages 10–17, who use the Internet regularly were interviewed. The results indicated that approximately one in seven children sampled received a sexual solicitation or approach over the Internet in the past year, which was a decline from the 2000 wave, where approximately one in five children were approached. This good news suggests that children may be more aware of the risks they face from interacting with strangers online. Unfortunately, the proportion of children who received aggressive sexual solicitations, where an individual asked to meet them somewhere, called them on the telephone, sent regular mail, money, or gifts stayed the same during this period. One in 33 received such a solicitation, and this figure increased among young girls.

Additionally, one in three children experienced unwanted exposure to pictures of naked people or people having sex in 2005. This was an increase from 2000, where approximately one in four were exposed to such material. In addition, 83 percent of the materials youths were exposed to happened while surfing the Web. This is argued to be a result of an increase in the number of children online every day, increases in high-speed Internet connectivity, and increasingly aggressive marketing of sexual materials via the Web.

The number of children who were threatened or harassed online also increased, from 1 in 17 in 2000 to 1 in 11 during 2005. This may again be a result of an increase in the amount of time that young people spend online. Additionally, youths appear to be more unkind or rude to others while online. Approximately one in four youths reported making rude or nasty comments to someone while on the Internet during 2005, and one in ten harassed or embarrassed someone they are mad at while online.

Although the respondents reported high rates of victimization, less than 10 percent of sexual solicitations and only 2 percent of unwanted exposures were reported to authorities such as a law enforcement agency, an Internet service provider (ISP), or a hotline. Further, less than one-quarter of youths who encountered a distressing sexual solicitation told a parent; however, 42 percent of those reporting an unwanted exposure to sexual material did tell a parent. There appears to be increasing appreciation for harassment among youths, as over 40 percent of those who experienced harassment reported this to their parents, though 10 percent reported the incident to law enforcement.

Given the significant increase in exposure to pornography and harassment, it is important to consider how parents use protective software programs to keep their children safe while online. Surprisingly, there has been an increase in the number of parents who have filtering or blocking software on home computers. In 2000, approximately one-third of parents had some sort of protective software, whereas in 2005 more than half had such a program installed. Thus, this raises some difficult questions about the utility of such programs to reduce exposure to pornographic content and harmful communications.[6]

The results from this research can be viewed in a number of ways. Although the percentages may seem at first glance to be relatively small, the researchers extrapolated estimates of the number of victims based on the sample drawn in the survey. The results of this extrapolation are presented

TABLE 7.1   Population Estimates and Confidence Intervals for Online Victimization of Youth

Online Victimization	Regular Internet Users (%)	95% Confidence Interval	Estimated Number of Youth[a]	95% Confidence Interval[a]
Sexual Solicitations and Approaches				
Any	13	12–15%	3,220,000	2,970,000–3,720,000
Distressing	4	3–6%	990,000	740,000–1,490,000
Aggressive	4	3–5%	990,000	740,000–1,240,000
Unwanted Exposure to Sexual Material				
Any	34	32–37%	8,430,000	7,930,000–9,170,000
Distressing	9	8–11%	2,230,000	1,980,000–2,730,000
Harassment				
Any	9	7–10%	2,230,000	1,730,000–2,480,000
Distressing	3	2.5–4%[b]	740,000	620,000–990,000

Estimates and confidence intervals are based on an estimated number of 24,780,000 regular Internet users between the ages of 10 and 17.

[a]Estimates and confidence intervals are all rounded to the nearest 10,000.

[b]This percent was not rounded so the lower bound of the confidence interval could be shown.

Source: WOLACK, JANIS, MITCHELL, KIMBERLY, and FINKELHOR, DAVID. (2006). *Online Victimization of Youth: Five Years Later.* Washington, DC: National Center for Missing & Exploited Children.

in Table 7.1 and reveal that between 2.9 and 3.7 million youths between the ages of 10 and 17 received a sexual solicitation or approach online. This is a decline from 2000, when between 4 and 5 million youths received such a solicitation. Another 7.9 to 9.1 million were exposed to unwanted sexual material, which is a significant increase from 2000. Finally, between 1.1 and 1.7 million were harassed online in 2000, though this number increased to 1.7 and 2.4 million in 2005. The authors note that the survey suggests that youths encounter a substantial number of offensive episodes, many of which are distressing and most of which are unreported.

The survey also reported demographics regarding the types of youths that were targeted for sexual solicitations and approaches. The research reported the following:

- Girls were targeted at almost twice the rate of boys (70 percent vs. 30 percent), but given that girls are often thought to be the exclusive targets of sexual solicitation, the sizable percentage of boys is important.
- More than three-quarters of targeted youth (81percent) were aged 14 or older, and this group experienced 75 percent of distressing incidents.
- Almost all (86 percent) were persons the youth originally met online.
- Adults were responsible for 49 percent of sexual solicitations and 49 percent of the aggressive solicitations.
- Most of the adult solicitors were reported to be aged 18–25. About 9 percent of all solicitors were known to be older than 25.

TABLE 7.2   Risky Online Behavior (*N* = 1,500)

Risky Online Behavior in the Past Year	All Youth % Yes
Posting or Sending Personal Information or Pictures Where Anyone Could See It	
Real Name, Telephone Number, Home Address, or School Name	34
Age or Date of Birth	45
Picture	18
None of the Above	44
Sent Personal Information to Someone Met Online[a]	
Real Name, Telephone Number, Home Address, or School Name	11
Age or Date of Birth	23
Picture	9
None of the Above	39
Online Sexual Behavior	
Talked Online About Sex with Someone the Youth Never Met in Person (*n* = 77)	5
Went to X-Rated Sites on Purpose (*n* = 199)	13
Downloaded Sexual Images Through File-Sharing on Purpose	2
Used Screen Name That Was "Sexual In Any Way"	1
Posted or Sent Sexual Picture of Self	0.1
Made Rude or Nasty Comments To Someone Online (*n* = 425)	28
Used Internet to Harass or Embarrass Someone Youth Was Mad At (*n* = 129)	9
Downloaded Pictures, Videos, or Movies Through File-Sharing Program	15
Had People on Instant Messaging "Chat List" Youth Did Not Know in Person	35

[a]Only asked of youths who said that they talked online with people they did not know in person (*n*=645).

Source: WOLACK, JANIS, MITCHELL, KIMBERLY, and FINKELHOR, DAVID. (2006). *Online Victimization of Youth: Five Years Later.* Washington, DC: National Center for Missing & Exploited Children.

- Juveniles made 43 percent of the overall and 44 percent of the aggressive solicitations.
- Males made 73 percent of the solicitations and approaches.
- Women account for a small percentage of the aggressive (16 percent) or distressing (7 percent) solicitations (16 percent).

The Youth Internet Survey has consistently found that a larger number than might be expected of offensive experiences on the Internet are being perpetrated on youths. Although the majority of solicitations do not result in a more serious offense, the sheer number of such encounters is alarming. Although many youths simply ignore such affronts, a significant percentage is severely distressed by the incidents. Complicating things is the fact that the overwhelming majority of these offenses and innuendos go unreported to authorities or the parents of the child.[7] The problems that youths experience online could be exacerbated by the youth engaging in other risky behavior, especially harassing or being mean to others online. Recent research has found that there is a significant connection between individual involvement in risky behavior and risk of harassment.[8] Finally, the belief by many that such online offenses are not serious adds to underreporting and lack of attention being paid to these victims.

Cyberbullying

In addition to harassment and sexual exposure over the Internet, young people are also at risk of experiencing cyberbullying. There is no consistent definition for this behavior, though the National Crime Prevention Council defines cyberbulling as "when the Internet, cell phones or other devices are used to send or post text or images intended to hurt or embarrass another person."[9] This can include the use of text messages via cell phone, as well as e-mails, instant messaging, and other Web-based services to annoy or otherwise hurt someone's feelings. Some even use social networking sites like MySpace and Facebook as a means to post pictures or messages about another person without their knowledge or consent that could be embarrassing or hurtful.[10]

Bullying is distinctive, as it occurs among juvenile populations only, whereas the same actions among adults constitute harassment or stalking.[11] In addition, cyberbullying is different from real-world bullying, as the perpetrators can reach their victim at all hours, day or night. Thus, a victim may find it hard to get away from their bully and find some relief. There are several potential reasons as to why young people use the Internet as a means to engage in bullying. Online communications and text messaging allow bullies to hide their identities and easily contact their victims. Furthermore, some may feel that it is easier to say something mean or hurtful via e-mail than in person.

BOX 7.2
Growth in Cyberbullying

A recent study conducted by the Pew Research Center indicates that cyberbullying among online teens is now common. The research project involved a telephone survey of teens and parents and a series of focus group discussions with teens. The Pew Internet & American Life Project reported a number of alarming trends and statistics.[1]

- About one-third of teens who use the Internet report having been a target of annoying and potentially menacing activities, including the receipt of threatening messages, having rumors spread about them online, or having an embarrassing picture posted to the Web without permission.
- Teens who use social networking sites were more likely to report being a victim of cyber-bullying. Nearly 40 percent of survey respon-

dents who reported using these sites also indicated that they had experienced some form of cyberbullying online.
- Girls aged 15–17 reported more victimizations than did boys and/or younger teens.

Senior Research Specialist Amanda Lenhart offered comparisons between traditional bullying and newer cyberbullying problems online, "Bullying has entered the digital age . . . Now, with a few clicks, a photo, video or a conversation can be shared with hundreds via email or millions through a website . . . "[2]

---

[1]LENHART, A. (2007). "Pew Internet & American Life Project." Data Memo, June 27. Pew Research Center. Available at *http://www.pewinternet.org*. Accessed September 9, 2009.
[2]*Ibid.*, p. 5.

Though cyberbullying is a recent development, several studies have found that juvenile populations have experienced high levels of bullying victimization. Studies in the United States have found that as much as 50 percent of youth have experienced bullying.[12] One survey of approximately 2,000 adolescent Internet users found that approximately one in five youths had experienced some form of cyberbullying during their lifetime.[13] This includes a range of problems, including receiving an e-mail, instant message, or MySpace post that made them upset, or being made fun of in a chat room. Girls appear to be slightly more likely to be bullied than boys; whites appear more likely to be bullied, followed by multiracial children, Hispanics, and African Americans. Most victims of cyberbullying often find they are not bothered by the event, though some report experiencing negative emotions as a consequence. In particular, individuals who are bullied may feel angry, frustrated, sad, or scared. Victims are often bullied by their current or former friends or individuals they go to school with. Few children are, however, harassed by strangers or individuals they know online.[14]

The issue of cyberbullying is complicated and may often go unnoticed by parents and teachers. Victims often do not report their experiences, much like with other forms of sexual harassment or contact. Most will talk about their experiences with their friends, though some tell their parents.[15] However, few victims will talk about their experiences with teachers or law enforcement. This may be because victims can avoid certain Web sites, delete or block offensive e-mails and chat identities, or not answer a phone or text message. This may also help to account for why victims often are not bothered by the bullying experience. It is clear, however, that the increasing number of cyberbullying events make this a troubling problem that requires attention from parents and law enforcement.

STALKING VIA THE WORLD WIDE WEB

Stalking is most often defined as the willful or intentional commission of a series of acts that would cause a reasonable person to fear death or serious bodily injury and that, in fact, place the victim in fear of death or serious bodily injury.[16] Stalking laws have changed recently in response to greater knowledge about the crime being generated through research. Originally, many statutes had a narrow definition of stalking that included a specific intent requirement.[17] However, many states have reformulated their laws to broaden the definition of stalking to include repeated behavior that is harassing, communicating, or nonconsensual communication. In addition, many states have adopted a "general intent" requirement, rather than a specific intent requirement, which allows prosecutions for implied threats and threats that may or may not be considered "credible."[18] Some definitions also take into account the receiver's reactions to the communications, including any reaction that would cause a reasonable person to fear for his or her personal safety, to fear bodily injury or death to himself or herself or a related person, to suffer substantial emotional distress, or to become seriously alarmed, terrorized, or tormented by the behavior.[19]

Many stalking laws are broad enough to encompass stalking via e-mail or other electronic communication, defining the prohibited conduct in terms of "communication," "harassment," or "threats" without specifying the means of such behavior. A more specific definition of cyberstalking would be the use of the Internet, e-mail, or other electronic communications device to stalk, threaten, or harass a person. Other states have specifically defined stalking via e-mail within their stalking or harassment statute. For example, California recently amended its stalking law to expressly include stalking via the Internet.[20]

The true numbers of cyberstalking incidents are unknown, but recent estimates suggest these behaviors appear to be on the rise, particularly among young people and college students due in part to frequent Internet use among this population.[21] For example, research by Finn found that approximately 15 percent of a sample of college students had experienced online harassment.[22] Similarly, Holt and Bossler found that 18.9 percent of students at a large southeastern university had been harassed at some point within the past year through a chat room, instant messaging service, or in Internet relay chats (IRCs).[23] Evidence from the National Crime Victimization Survey's Supplemental Victimization Survey (SVS) found that approximately one in four stalking victims experienced cyberstalking via e-mail or instant messaging.[24] Additionally, 1 in 13 victims was tracked via electronic monitoring tools, such as computer spyware, digital cameras, and GPS technology.[25]

Dynamics and Nature of Stalking and Cyberstalking

The traditional conception of the crime of stalking involves a stranger following some unsuspecting female and showing up for repeated interactions with the person. This conception has been reinforced in popular film in such movies as *Taxi Driver* and host of serial killer movies. However, the true dynamics of stalking have extended far beyond this traditional conception and new definitions, and laws have expanded the meaning dramatically. What makes this area of law difficult to enforce is that it is often difficult to distinguish between dangerous stalking behavior and relatively benign harassment or puppy love. Police officers investigating such crimes are as replete with true stalking stories as they are with false reports and overestimations of the dangerousness of the behavior. Many cases of stalking do not even rise to extreme levels of violence or harassment.[26] Nonetheless, all forms of stalking should be taken seriously, as they represent a fundamental threat to a person's physical and psychological well-being.

Stalkers have been known to use binoculars, telescopes, cameras equipped with "long lenses," video cameras, hidden microphones, the Internet, public records, and accomplices (both witting and unwitting) to keep track of the whereabouts and activities of those they target.[27] Cyberstalking is simply the electronic form of stalking, where the harassment or threats are directed via the Internet typically using e-mail, chat rooms, bulletin boards, or even Web pages. Most often, due to the distance between users and the anonymity of the Internet, this behavior will not escalate into physical harm, but this does not mean that the pursuit is any less distressing.[28] A recent survey of stalking victims reported that stalkers employed the following tactics most often:

- Followed or spied on the victim (24.5 percent).
- Made unwanted phone calls (62.5 percent).
- Sent unwanted letters or left unwanted items (30 percent).
- Showed up at places the victim was present (22.4 percent)
- Leaving unwanted presents (9.1 percent).[29]

Stalkers, by their very nature, want a relationship with their victims. They want to be part of their victims' lives. And, if they cannot be a positive part of their victims' lives, they will settle for a negative connection to their victims. It is this mindset that makes them not only stalkers but also dangerous. Thus, virtually all stalking cases involve behavior that seeks to make either direct or indirect contact with the victim.[30]

Most people using electronic forms of communication are much more brazen than they would be face to face; such is the case with cyberstalkers. The medium encourages people to interact in ways in which they would either be too embarrassed to do in person or in ways in which they feel they might not be caught. This is most likely due to the perceived anonymity of the Internet

BOX 7.3

Man Convicted of threatening Federal Judges by Internet E-mail

Carl E. Johnson, 49, of Bienfait, Saskatchewan, Canada, has been convicted on four felony counts of sending threatening e-mail messages via the Internet to federal judges and others. The convictions were announced following a seven-day trial before U.S. District Judge Robert J. Bryan, in Tacoma, Washington. Johnson was convicted of one count of Retaliating Against a Judicial Officer, one count of Obstructing Justice by Making a Death Threat Against a Judicial Officer, and two counts of Transmitting Threatening Communications in Foreign Commerce. The first three charges were based on death threats posted to the Internet naming two federal judges based in Tacoma and Seattle. The fourth charge was based on an e-mail threat sent directly to Microsoft Chairman Bill Gates. Johnson was acquitted on one count of Obstructing Justice.

In announcing his verdict on Tuesday, April 20, 1999, Judge Bryan stated that he had "no doubt" Johnson was the author of three threatening messages sent over the Internet. Although Johnson had used anonymous remailers and forged e-mail address information in an attempt to disguise his identity, Judge Bryan found that the government's technical evidence proved Johnson's authorship. In response to the defense contention that the statements constituted "free speech" protected by the First Amendment to the U.S. Constitution, Judge Bryan ruled that the messages were "serious expressions of intention to do harm," and thus "clearly over the line" of protected speech.

The guilty verdicts are the culmination of a two-year investigation by U.S. Treasury agents into anonymous threats posted on the Internet and a scheme to assassinate government officials known as "Assassination Politics." As the testimony and evidence at trial showed, the assassination scheme was first promoted by James Dalton Bell, of Vancouver, Washington, who had proposed to murder IRS employees, had gathered a list of IRS agents' names and home addresses, had contaminated an IRS office with a noxious chemical, and had experimented with other toxic and dangerous chemicals, including nerve agents. Johnson had corresponded with Bell about Bell's "Assassination Politics" concept via Internet e-mail. After Bell's arrest, Johnson vowed in an Internet e-mail message to take "personal action" in support of Bell. On June 23, 1997, Johnson anonymously posted a message on the Internet suggesting that specific sums of money would be paid, in the form of electronic cash, for the deaths of a Federal Magistrate Judge in Tacoma, Washington, and Treasury agents involved in the Bell investigation. Additional threatening messages linked to Johnson continued to appear on the Internet in the months that followed, and Johnson set up a World Wide Web page with a partial prototype of the "Assassination Politics" scheme.

Johnson also issued a death threat to several Judges of the U.S Court of Appeals for the Ninth Circuit, again through an anonymous e-mail message. The government was able to identify Johnson as the author of the threatening messages and the Internet assassination Web page through a variety of technical means. In the case of the Ninth Circuit judge's death threat, Treasury agents were able to link the unique characteristics of an encrypted digital signature on the threatening message to encryption "keys" found on Johnson's computer.

Treasury investigators received assistance in the case from Canadian law enforcement agencies who were investigating Johnson for his Internet activities and an unexploded gasoline bomb found in a courthouse in Estevan, Saskatchewan. The trial featured testimony from officers of the Royal Canadian Mounted Police and Canadian Customs, as well as the Canadian Internet Service Provider Sympatico and Canadian telephone company Sasktel. Computer experts from the Treasury Department and Portland Police Bureau also testified.

Johnson was sentenced to 37 months of imprisonment on four felony counts of sending threatening e-mail messages via the Internet to federal judges and others. The retaliation and threatening communication counts carried a possible maximum penalty of five years in prison. The obstruction of justice count carries a maximum penalty of ten years in prison. Johnson also faces additional charges in Canada in connection with the bomb found in the Canadian courthouse.

Source: http://www.usdoj.gov/criminal/cybercrime/Johnson.htm

and also because people talking to one another online are far away from each other physically.[31] Because individuals can mask their identity and remain relatively anonymous when using the Internet, linking the harassment to one individual is difficult and time consuming. Several programs and other techniques exist that can mask the IP (Internet Protocol) address of a person, making it difficult to trace the source of a given communication. Further, anonymous remailers and Internet providers who guarantee user anonymity also complicate any investigative process.

Cyberstalkers employ a variety of tactics online, most commonly sending unsolicited, hateful, obscene, or threatening e-mail or instant messages, and harass the victim whenever they are online in chat rooms.[32] With newsgroups and social networking pages, the cyberstalker can create postings about the victim or start rumors that spread virally. Cyberstalkers may also set up a Web page(s) on the victim with personal or fictitious information or solicitations to readers. Another technique is to assume the victim's persona online, such as in chat rooms or social networking pages for the purpose of sullying the victim's reputation, posting details about the victim, or soliciting unwanted contacts from others. Video- and photograph-sharing sites can also be used to send and create media that disparages their victim. The Internet can provide, both for free and at a cost, a wealth of information about anyone, including their address, phone numbers, e-mail addresses, their neighbors and friends' information, their housing information, credit reports, and personal identifying numbers and passwords. More complex forms of harassment include mail bombs (mass messages that virtually shut down the victim's e-mail system by clogging it), sending the victim computer viruses, or sending electronic junk mail (spamming).[33] Several interesting cases have been documented involving cyberstalking, including the following:

- In the first successful prosecution under California's new cyberstalking law, prosecutors in the Los Angeles District Attorney's Office obtained a guilty plea from a 50-year-old former security guard who used the Internet to solicit the rape of a woman who rejected his romantic advances. The defendant terrorized his 28-year-old victim by impersonating her in various Internet chat rooms and online bulletin boards, where he posted, along with her telephone number and address, messages that she fantasized about being raped. On at least six occasions, sometimes in the middle of the night, men knocked on the woman's door saying they wanted to rape her. The former security guard pleaded guilty in April 1999 to one count of stalking and three counts of solicitation of sexual assault. He faces up to six years in prison.
- A local prosecutor's office in Massachusetts charged a man who, utilizing anonymous remailers, allegedly engaged in a systematic pattern of harassment of a coworker, which culminated in an attempt to extort sexual favors from the victim under threat of disclosing past sexual activities to the victim's new husband.
- An honors graduate from the University of San Diego terrorized five female university students over the Internet for more than a year. The victims received hundreds of violent and threatening e-mails, sometimes receiving four or five messages a day. The graduate student, who has entered a guilty plea and faces up to six years in prison, told police he committed the crimes because he thought the women were laughing at him and causing others to ridicule him. In fact, the victims had never met him.[34]

Characteristics of Stalkers and Their Victims

Most stalkers are typically male (87 percent), white (80 percent), between the ages of 18 and 35 (50 percent), of average intelligence, and earning above-average incomes.[35] In contrast, rates of stalking victimization suggest that women are more likely to be stalked than males. Additionally, individuals aged 18–24 were most likely to experience stalking. Additionally, whites and blacks were more likely to be victimized. Divorced or separated women faced higher rates of stalking victimization, followed by single and married people. Finally, those living in lower-income households were more likely to be stalked than those in higher-income brackets.[36] The research in this area indicates that the majority of stalkers and their victims (72.5percent) had a personal relationship before the stalking began. The majority of these cases involved spouses or partners or had a dating relationship. Nearly 18 percent of stalkers were acquaintances or coworkers of the victim, while only 16.9 percent were complete strangers.[37]

Evidence from a study examining cyberstalking cases in New York City found that offenders were largely male (80 Percent), white (74 percent), and an average of 24 years of age, though 26 percent were juveniles.[38] Additionally, females (52 percent) were slightly more likely to be victims than males. They were also predominately white (85 percent) and of an average age of 35 years. Specific profiles or categorizations have been developed as the result of the study of this phenomenon.

Several categorization schemes exist for classifying stalkers,[39] and the behavior of each type varies to a certain degree. Comprising the largest group of estimated stalkers (47–60 percent), simple obsessional stalkers typically involve a victim and a perpetrator who have a prior relationship. The motivation behind this may be coercion to reenter a relationship or revenge aimed at making the life of the former intimate uncomfortable through the inducement of fear. Many simple obsession cases are actually extensions of a previous pattern of domestic violence and psychological abuse. The only difference is that the abuse occurs in different surroundings and through slightly altered tactics of intimidation. Thus, the dynamics of power and control that underlie most domestic violence cases are often mirrored in simple obsession stalking cases. This category of stalker is thought to be the most dangerous, and this is the most likely category of stalking to result in murder. Thirty percent of all female homicides were committed by intimate partners, and domestic violence victims run a 75 percent higher risk of being murdered by their partners.

The second largest category of stalkers (43 percent) is the love obsession type, where no prior relationship exists between perpetrator and victim or they are casual acquaintances. Often, the stalker identifies the victim through the media or the Internet. Usually, stalkers in this category seek to establish a personal relationship with the object of their obsession—contrary to the wishes of their victims. Love obsession stalkers tend to have low self-esteem and often target victims whom they perceive to have exceptional qualities and high social standing. These stalkers seek to raise their own self-esteem by associating with those whom they hold in high regard. These types of stalkers are also often suffering from some type of mental disorder or defect. They frequently target celebrities; several famous cases include that of Madonna and Jodie Foster. Often, love obsession stalkers are so desperate to establish a relationship—*any* relationship— that they "settle" for negative relationships, explaining why some stalkers are willing to engage in destructive or violent behavior in an irrational attempt to "win the love" (more likely the attention) of their victims.[40]

A third category is referred to as erotomaniacs, meaning that the stalker believes that the victim is in love with them. By definition, erotomaniacs are delusional and, consequently, virtually all suffer from mental disorders—most often schizophrenia. This category was the least frequent (less than 10 percent) and differed from the previous two in that these offenders were more likely to be females stalking males. Erotomania stalking cases often draw public attention because the target is usually a public figure or celebrity. Like love obsession stalkers, erotomaniacs attempt to garner self-esteem and status by associating themselves with well-known individuals who hold high social status. While the behavior of many erotomaniacs never escalates to violence, or even to threats of violence, the irrationality that accompanies their mental illness presents particularly unpredictable threats to victims. Perhaps the best-known case of erotomania stalking involved a series of incidents perpetrated against the popular late-night talk show host David Letterman. This woman, first found hiding in Mr. Letterman's closet, believed she was his wife. On numerous other occasions she was caught trespassing on his property. With her young son in tow, she once scaled the six-foot wall surrounding Letterman's property. On another occasion, she was arrested while driving Letterman's stolen car. When questioned by police, she confidently stated that her husband was out of town and that she was going grocery shopping so she would have dinner ready for him upon his return. Despite the treatment she received during her many involuntary stays at a mental institution, she eventually took her own life.[41]

Another, recently developed, category is the vengeance or terrorist stalker. Vengeance/terrorist stalkers attempt to elicit a particular response or a change of behavior from their victims rather than seeking a personal relationship with them. When vengeance is their prime motive, stalkers seek only to punish their victims for some wrong they perceive the victim has visited upon them. In other words, they use stalking as a means to "get even" with their enemies. Most commonly this type of behavior involves fired employees or political stalking (as in the case of some antiabortionists).

Traditional stalkers and cyberstalkers have several similarities and differences. The similarities primarily involve the motivations for stalking and the demographic and relational characteristics of the offense.[42] In essence, the stalker is motivated by a desire to get close to the victim, control the victim, or punish the victim in some way. The major difference is that while off-line stalking necessitates a closer proximity to the victim, cyberstalking can occur from across the nation or the world. Electronic communications technologies make it much easier

---

BOX 7.4

KC Man Indicted for Cyberstalking

Shawn D. Memarian, 28, of Kansas City, was charged in an indictment returned under seal by a federal grand jury on Thursday, May 8, 2008. That indictment was unsealed and made public today upon Memarian's arrest and initial court appearance. The federal indictment alleges that between July 15, 2006, and September 1, 2007, Memarian engaged in a course of conduct consisting of malicious postings to MySpace, Facebook, Craigslist and other Internet social sites in which he caused the personal identity information of Melissa Sandfort—including her home address—to be publicly displayed.

Memarian had been served with a restraining order forbidding contact with Sandfort. The indictment alleges that the intent of the malicious postings was to place Sandfort in fear of death and serious bodily injury. Memarian allegedly posed as Sandfort and distributed Web site invitations to visit Sandfort's residence for sexual gratification.

The indictment also alleges that Memarian sent malicious e-mails to Sandfort, threatening her with death and serious bodily injury, which caused substantial emotional distress to Sandfort. Wood cautioned that the charge contained in this indictment is simply an accusation, and not evidence of guilt. Evidence supporting the charge must be presented to a federal trial jury, whose duty is to determine guilt or innocence. This case is being prosecuted by Assistant U.S. Attorney John E. Cowles. It was investigated by the Gladstone, MO, Police Department and the Federal Bureau of Investigation.

Source: http://www.cybercrime.gov/memarianIndict.pdf

for a cyberstalker to encourage third parties to harass and/or threaten a victim (e.g., impersonating the victim and posting inflammatory messages to bulletin boards and in chat rooms, causing viewers of that message to send threatening messages back to the victim "author"). Finally, as noted previously, cyberstalkers are much more likely to be brazen than off-line stalkers because of the anonymity of the Internet and the lack of close proximity.[43]

Law Enforcement and Legislation Targeting Stalking

California was the first state to enact stalking legislation (in 1990), and today all 50 states and the federal government have antistalking statutes. However, a recent report notes that less than one-third of the states' antistalking laws explicitly cover stalking via the Internet, e-mail, pagers, or other electronic communications.[44] Nonetheless, many experts feel that existing stalking laws would cover the crime if committed using the Internet or other electronic means. Yet certain types of cyberstalking would most likely fall through the cracks and escape prosecutions. Currently, several federal laws cover the crime of stalking, but several of the statutes are not specifically targeted at cyberstalking. One such statute makes it a crime to transmit any communication in interstate or foreign commerce that contains a threat of injury.[45] This statute does not cover harassment offenses meant to annoy someone. A portion of a telecommunications law makes it a crime to annoy, abuse, harass, or threaten any person via electronic or telephone communication.[46] The Interstate Stalking Act[47] makes it a crime for any person to travel across state lines with the intent to injure or harass another person and, in the course thereof, place that person or a member of that person's family in reasonable fear of death or serious bodily injury. The problem with this law is that it probably would not directly apply to cyberstalking cases. Again, the existing law would most likely apply to cases of cyberstalking, although it would be prudent to be more specific about the crime in future legislation.

Additionally, there are pieces of legislation being added to state statutes around the United States concerning cyberbullying, largely as a consequence of the Megan Meier case. Meier committed suicide after receiving mean messages via the social networking Web site MySpace. She befriended a teenage boy named Josh Evans, and they developed a relationship that Evans terminated, stating that the world would be better off without her. In reality, Evans was a fictitious identity created by Lori Drew, the mother of one of Megan's friends.[48] Drew created this identity as a means to humiliate Megan as retribution for slighting her daughter. The subsequent development of legislation has attempted to decrease the likelihood of such an event happening again. The first state to directly deal with cyberbullying is California, which passed a law in January 2008 giving school administrators the power to discipline students for bullying other students on- or off-line.[49] In fact, principals and administrators can suspend or expel a student who engages in cyberbullying. There is no federal legislation in place as of yet, though a bill was proposed in the U.S. House as a direct result of the Megan Meier case that is currently still in review.

Cyberbullying and stalking is expected to increase as computers and the Internet become more popular. An Assistant U.S. Attorney reported that in two recent cases of e-mail harassment, he asked an FBI agent to confront the would-be harasser. Upon advising the cyberstalker that such behavior might constitute a criminal offense, both stalkers ceased their harassment.[50] Perhaps the greatest problem surrounding these offenses is the lack of enforcement and attention. Investigators and law enforcement agencies are relatively ill-equipped to deal with cyberbullying and cyberstalking for a variety of reasons. First, and most prominent, is the lack of reporting on the part of victims. Again, many people report that they do not think what has occurred is a crime or that they doubt the ability of law enforcement to do anything about the crime.

BOX 7.5
New State Cyberstalking Law

On April 1, 2001, amendments to the Michigan criminal stalking law were signed that make it illegal for a person to post a message through an electronic medium, including the Internet, if the sender intends to make the victim feel terrorized, frightened, intimidated, or harassed, and the action causes the victim to suffer emotional distress or feel terrorized, frightened, intimidated, or harassed. Violations of the law constitute felonies and can carry prison sentences of up to two years or fines of up to $2,000. The new law also provides more stringent penalties, up to five years in prison and $10,000 in fines, if the message is a violation of a restraining order, injunction, or condition of release.

Source: Office of Victims of Crime (2002). *National Victim Assistance Academy.* Washington, DC: Office of Justice Programs. Available on line: *http://www.ojp.usdoj.gov/ovc/assist/nvaa2002/chapter22_2sup.html*

Second, most law enforcement agencies are not trained to recognize the serious nature of these crimes and to investigate such offenses. Unfortunately, some victims have reported that rather than open an investigation, a law enforcement agency has advised them to come back if the cyberstalkers confront or threaten them off-line. In several instances, victims have been told by law enforcement simply to turn off their computers.[51] In the case of bullying, victims can find a variety of ways to avoid their bully.

Finally, even if reporting were higher, the overwhelming majority of law enforcement agencies are ill-prepared to deal with cyberstalking because of lack of resources, lack of investigative tools, and lack of trained personnel. Most large law enforcement agencies now have computer crime units, with extraordinarily busy police officers staffing them. Additionally, cyber evidence processors in local law enforcement agencies and the federal government are already overbooked and understaffed.

OBSCENITY ON THE WORLD WIDE WEB

The issue of what is obscene has been debated in the court systems of the United States for a long period. The growth of the Internet has forced the Supreme Court to revisit this slippery issue that lives somewhere between community protection and freedom of speech. The players are the same: on one side, governmental officials and politicians looking to regulate a sexually oriented industry that they feel is linked to a whole host of other, more serious, problems, and on the other side, free speech activists, the American Civil Liberties Union, and those who seek to profit from pornography. It is an old battle. The new battlefield, however, presents unique problems and questions for the American legal system. In the past, pornography, especially the seriously hardcore, the bizarre, and the illegal kind, was kept relatively out of sight and required that purveyors visit a sexually oriented business, purchase the materials in person, or order them via the mail or over the phone. In terms of monitoring, the government had a relatively easy job of tracking and preventing illegal types of pornography from being circulated in the United States. The Internet changed all of that and essentially made pornography, even the hardcore and illegal stuff, widely available to the general public.

The old questions of what is and what is not obscene became somewhat secondary in this new battle over the ability of the government to restrict what is posted on the Internet versus free speech.[52] Interestingly, the battle has focused on what both sides of the argument would agree is a problem—child pornography and access to pornography by children. The difference between the two sides lies in the proposed remedies. It is fair to say that neither side would allow child pornography to be shared, posted, or disseminated. However, adult access became the issue in several Supreme Court cases that examined a variety of federal law passed regarding the access of children to the Internet and the ability of government to regulate the Internet. The government's position has consistently been that the onus of regulation is on ISPs and the people and businesses who wish to post, sell, or disseminate pornography. Laws were passed that mandated that ISPs had to monitor and regulate certain types of pornography, especially child pornography. Further, anyone who wished to sell or promote pornography had to assure that children were not accessing the material or face federal charges.

On the other side, the onus is placed firmly on the individuals and the parents of the children. In short, it is up to the individual to self-regulate access, and it is up to parents to assure that children do not access the materials. As is typical, the law ended up squarely in the middle. The prosecution of Internet-related child pornography and luring cases is increasing. The Department of Justice has found that prosecution of these cases has increased by 10 percent every year since 1995. Many of these cases are international in scope.

Laws and Legislation Protecting Children Online

Over the past decade, several laws have been proposed and adopted to deal with the issues of child exploitation on the Internet; some of these laws are reviewed in this chapter. For example, the Child Protection and Sexual Predator Punishment Act of 1998 specifically addressed the issues of online victimization of children. The law prohibits the transfer of obscene material to minors, and increases penalties for offenses against children and for repeat offenders. Furthermore, the act amends the Child Abuse Act of 1990 by requiring online service providers to report evidence of child pornography offenses to law enforcement agencies.[53] In 1994, the U.S. Congress extended the Mann Act by enacting the Child Sexual Abuse Prevention Act.[54] This act empowers the Justice Department to penalize U.S. citizens traveling across state or national borders to engage in sexual activity with children.[55] The production of sexually explicit depictions of a minor for importation into the United States is also prohibited.[56] Additionally, a child sex tourism provision was added to the 1994 Violent Crime Control and Law Enforcement Act that makes it illegal for a U.S. citizen or permanent resident to travel in interstate or foreign commerce with the intent to engage in sexual acts with a minor that are prohibited under federal law in the United States. This provision applies even if these acts are legal in the destination country.

There are numerous state laws that prohibit the possession, manufacturing, distribution, and sale of child pornography. In many instances, simple possession is a felony. U.S. federal law on child pornography[57] outlines the prohibited behavior and law concerning the distribution and possession of child pornography.[58] The majority of child pornography offenses are covered by federal law in a number of statutes[59] and prohibit the production, sale, transmittal, and possession of child pornography. Additional federal law covers child luring[60] and the transportation of children for sexual purposes.[61] The same statute prohibits traveling for sexual purposes in the United States and abroad. The publication or posting of any information relating to a child for sexual purposes is also prohibited.[62] This statute would apply any time a child predator communicates online with another child predator and provides personal information about a minor under 16 for criminal sexual purposes.

Federal law on the sexual exploitation of children[63] prohibits people from using children in the production of sexually explicit material. The law also targets parents who allow or force their children to participate in the production of child pornography.[64] The law also prohibits the exchange of child pornography between people and prohibits the publication of advertisements seeking or offering child pornography.[65] Violations of this law are punishable by 10–20 years in prison for first offenders, 15–30 years for second offenders, and not less than 30 years for anyone with two or more prior offenses.[66] Additional federal law prohibits the transportation or transmittal, reception, distribution, and possession of child pornography.[67] Violation of the portion of the law relating to transportation, transmittal, and distribution carry a maximum sentence of up to 15 years, but a prior conviction carries a mandatory minimum of five years up to a maximum of 30 years in prison. The possession of child pornography carries a maximum sentence of five years with a mandatory minimum of two years to a maximum of ten years for prior offenders. This law has an affirmative defense provision that requires that a person possessed less than three matters of child pornography, took reasonable steps to destroy the materials, and promptly reported the matter to law enforcement officials.[68]

The Child Online Protection Act (COPA) prohibits anyone by means of a commercial Web site from knowingly making a communication that is "harmful to minors" available to those under 17 years for commercial purposes. The prohibited material includes pictures, writings, or recordings that are obscene, or that the average person would find, with respect to minors, appeals to the prurient interest; depicts sexual activity in a patently offensive way; and lacks serious literary, artistic, political or scientific value. The offense is a misdemeanor authorizing up to six months' imprisonment and a $50,000 fine for each violation. In addition, the attorney general is authorized to collect a $50,000 civil penalty for each violation.[69]

In 1998, Congress enacted the Protection of Children from Sexual Predators Act (PCSPA) of 1998, which established new criminal offenses, amended existing statutes, and provided for enhanced penalties. Three new offenses or definitions of offenses were created:

1. *Use of interstate facilities to transmit information about a minor:*[70] Prohibits the use of the mail or facility of interstate or foreign commerce to transmit information about a minor under 16 for criminal sexual purposes.[71] This statute is in response to a case from Illinois, where an individual posted a nine-year-old girl's name and telephone number on the Internet, indicating that she was available for sex. The individual initiating the transmission can be fined, imprisoned up to five years, or both.

2. *Transfer of obscene materials to minors:* Prohibits the use of the mails or a facility of interstate or foreign commerce knowingly to transmit, or attempt to transmit, obscene materials to minors under 16.[72] The individual transmitting the materials may be fined, imprisoned for ten years, or both.

3. *Definition of sexual activity:* Defines criminal sexual activity to include the production of child pornography.[73] Previously, several cases presented for federal prosecution could not be charged because the individual either transported a minor or traveled to meet a minor to produce child pornography, but not for sexual activity.

The new laws also enacted attempt provisions to several laws,[74] increased penalties for several child sexual offenses,[75] made prosecution for child sexual assault possible for imported child pornography,[76] and increased and expanded sentencing for child sexual offenses.[77] The legislation also imposes the death penalty if the death of a child results from the offense,[78] allows for civil forfeiture relating to these offenses,[79] and places an affirmative responsibility on ISPs to report child pornographic offenses.[80]

The U.S. Supreme Court has had the opportunity to review several cases involving child pornography and legislation designed to protect children online. In *Reno v. American Civil*

Liberties Union,[81] the Court examined two provisions of the Communications Decency Act of 1996. The first part criminalized the knowing transmission of "obscene or indecent" messages to any recipient less than 18 years.[82] Another section of the act prohibited the "knowing" sending or displaying to a person under 18 of any message "that, in context, depicts or describes, in terms patently offensive as measured by contemporary community standards, sexual or excretory activities or organs."[83] The Court decided that these two provisions of the Communications Decency Act, specifically the "indecent transmission" and "patently offensive display" provisions, potentially violated the free speech portion of the First Amendment. The Court specifically noted that the act lacked precision of definition, a requirement when justifying the restriction of free speech. The Court noted that the government has an interest in protecting children from potentially harmful materials; however, the Communications Decency Act attempted to pursue that interest by suppressing a large amount of speech that adults have a constitutional right to send and receive. Of particular interest was the analysis the Court made regarding what could be done in this area. Specifically, the Court concluded that the burden the act placed on free speech was not justifiable, given that currently available filtering software is a reasonably effective method by which parents can prevent their children from accessing material that the parents believe is inappropriate.

In *Ashcroft* v. *Free Speech Coalition*,[84] the Supreme Court reviewed provisions of law aimed at child pornography, specifically virtual child pornography. The ability of users to "morph" or alter images and to literally generate virtual pornography led the U.S. government to add a provision to the Child Pornography Prevention Act (CPPA) of 1996. The new additions to existing child pornography laws now included computer-generated imagery depicting or conveying the impression that a minor is engaged in sexually explicit conduct.[85] An additional section of the new law prohibited production or distribution of materials pandered as child pornography, even if it was not involving actual children. The Supreme Court decided that these two sections were unconstitutional and overbroad. The Court noted that the CPPA was inconsistent with existing jurisprudence regarding obscene material. The act placed an affirmative burden on anyone who might be charged to prove that the material under questions was not child pornography, either because it was fake or because the actors in question were indeed adults. Taken together, these two decisions effectively invalidated two major pieces of legislation regarding obscenity online; Attorney General Ashcroft complained that the Court had dealt a severe blow to the ability of law enforcement to fight child pornography.

The next major case the Court would decide examined provisions of the COPA. The COPA legislation was a specific attempt by Congress to address the free speech concerns raised in the *Reno* v. *ACLU* case discussed above. In *Ashcroft* v. *American Civil Liberties Union*,[86] the Court noted that unlike the Communications Decency Act, COPA applies only to material displayed on the World Wide Web, covers only communications made for commercial purposes, and restricts only material that is harmful to minors.[87] In addition, Congress placed a three-part obscenity test in COPA that drew on a previous Supreme Court decision.[88] The Court, although refusing to examine the overbreadth issue because of a technicality, concluded that COPA's reliance on "community standards" to identify what material "is harmful to minors" does not by itself render the statute substantially overbroad for First Amendment purposes. Finally, and most recently, the Court concluded in *United States* v. *American Library Association*[89] that the provision of the Children's Internet Protection Act requiring libraries receiving federal assistance to have filtering software was not unconstitutional. The Supreme Court also referred the case back to district court for trial, where it was again found unconstitutional and subsequently killed when the U. S. Supreme Court refused to hear the case again.

In response to the Supreme Court decisions, Congress enacted the Prosecuting Remedies and Tools Against the Exploitation of Children Today Act (PROTECT Act) of 2003,[90] which included a wide variety of provisions relating to the exploitation of children. The PROTECT Act strengthens existing U.S. law by increasing imprisonment penalties to 30 years for convicted sex tourists, criminalizing persons or organizations that assist or organize sex tours, and better enabling federal prosecutors to convict offenders by modifying burden of proof requirements. In addition, the new law establishes parallel penalty enhancements that apply to the production of child pornography overseas. The PROTECT Act is a wide-ranging bill pertaining to the investigation, prosecution, and punishment of offenses relating to children and pornography. The PROTECT Act also provides criminal penalties for users of innocent-sounding domain names if the owner knowingly uses the domain name to link to sexually explicit material. If a Web site's domain name deceptively draws people to sexually explicit material, the operator could be imprisoned for up to two years. The sentence is increased to four years if the domain name is intended to attract minors to the material. In addition, an offender of either provision can be fined up to $250,000.

PEDOPHILIA AND CHILD PORNOGRAPHY

Child pornography can be defined simply as depictions of children in a sexual act or in a sexual way. Most policy makers and researchers conclude that this applies to anyone under 18 years. Child pornography contains the same types of sexual activities as those depicted in adult pornography, except that the media contains images or descriptions involving children, children and adults, or children and animals or objects.[91] A narrower definition of child pornography would limit the concept to mean only images depicting sexual acts between real children and other children, adults, or some other sexual depiction. Broader definitions would include depictions of children that are sexually suggestive, drawings of children engaged in sexual acts, sexually graphic writings involving children, cartoons suggesting sex with children, and so on. Although certain forms of art and writing fall into a gray area subject to debate, clear visual depictions of children engaging in sexual conduct are child pornography and unilaterally prohibited. One study by the Justice Department found a history of child pornography in three mainstream pornographic magazines, *Playboy, Penthouse,* and *Hustler.*[92] The study found between 6,000 and 9,000 (depending on definitional criteria) child images in the three magazines, most involving sex or violence.[93] Of these depictions, 29 percent involved nudity or genital display, 20 percent genital activity, 16 percent sexual contact with an adult, 10 percent the use of force, and another 10 percent killing or maiming.[94] Regardless of the definition, child pornography is a serious issue with long-term implications for the offender and child victims, which has come to the forefront recently because of the Internet.

There is currently no accurate statistical source that reports the extent of or numbers of arrests involving child pornography. One recent estimate noted that at any given time, there are, on average, around one million sexually explicit pictures of children on the Internet. In just one week in December 1995, 5,651 messages about child pornography were posted on just four electronic bulletin boards. Included in these messages were over 800 graphic pictures of adults or teenagers engaged in sexual activity with children between eight and ten years of age.[95] In 2004, the Internet Watch Foundation found 3,433 child abuse domains, and then in 2006 there were 10,656.[96] These statistics indicate there is still a child pornography "industry" working internationally that produces materials for sale and consumption. Various sources estimate that child pornography comprises anywhere from 5 percent to 10 percent of the pornography trade, resulting in profits in the billions.[97] Other sources conclude that the extent and profit estimates of the child porn industry are grossly exaggerated.[98] A search on the Internet reveals that there are numerous Web sites that insinuate child pornography, a substantial number of newsgroups that concern child pornography, and a wide variety of writings and other material concerning how to access child pornography. The most common forms, if a broad definition is used, are altered pictures and stories relating to sexual contact with children—both of which were extremely easy to find and document. More thorough investigation and monitoring reveal that child pornography is commonly posted to several newsgroups and can be accessed at some personal Web sites internationally.[99]

Child pornography exists for reasons similar to other forms of pornography; there is a demand for such materials. In contrast to other forms of pornography, there is little discussion of child pornography being a victimless crime or a protected form of free speech. It is fair to assume that very few people would advocate the ready availability and use of child pornography. Child pornography is clearly an abhorrent and unconscionable act to the vast majority of people; however, to the pedophile the collection and use of child pornography is a source of pride, fantasy, and sexual gratification. Child pornography is used by the pedophile to feed and create sexual fantasies, lower the inhibitions of a child who they are planning to molest, and blackmail a child into remaining silent.[100] In addition, the pedophile uses child pornography as a profit device and in barter with other pedophiles to add to their collection or access other children to victimize.[101] The supply side of the child pornography trade largely consists of pedophiles willing to molest children as well as possess child pornography. As Campagna and Poffenberger[102] note, the single most distinctive characteristic of habitual child molesters is a compelling interest in collecting child pornography. Habitual child molesters categorize their collections in a sophisticated and elaborate way and typically possess a variety of child pornography in several media, including computer files, videotapes, magazines, amateur pictures, books and novels, drawings and art, and several others.[103] The pedophile also typically keeps an annotated journal or diary to record molestations and other details of their crimes. Once apprehended, the pornography and diary become invaluable evidence for prosecution. To the child molester, their child pornography collection is equated with valuable family heirlooms and investments, as the collections can be traded between pedophiles and used as payment for child prostitution.[104] This underground system used to be maintained through group associations, mail, and telephone; today, the Internet serves as the primary mechanism.

There exist, unfortunately, several national and international organizations dedicated to pedophiles and child sexual exploitation. The links between members in these organizations serve as a communication network for the exchange of child pornography. The North American Man/Boy Love Association (NAMBLA) advocates sexual and emotional relationships between adult males and underage boys. NAMBLA has chapters in many large U.S. cities and publishes a variety of print media for its members (estimated anywhere between 500 and 1,000 in 1988).[105] NAMBLA also has a Web site and annual meetings. Undoubtedly the membership, or at least those willing to access the Web site, has grown with the expansion of the Internet. Another such organization is the Lewis Carroll Collector's Guild, which publishes the newsletter *Wonderland* four times a year. *Wonderland* is a collection of articles and advertisements than promote interest in photographs and artwork pertaining to nude children on the premise that no exploitation is involved.[106] Several other organizations can be found on the Internet and have been documented by law enforcement officials. The common theme of these organizations is the promotion of sex and children. They are also undoubtedly useful for pedophiles to establish connections with others interested in their questionable practices.

BOX 7.6

The North American Man/Boy Love Association (NAMBLA)

NAMBLA stands for the North American Man/Boy Love Association. They are an organization devoted to furthering what they depict as consensual relationships between men and boys. The *NAMBLA Bulletin* describes their mission and their purpose:

"We speak out against the oppression endured by men and boys who love one another and support the right of all people to consensual intergenerational relationships. Throughout most of Western history, man/boy love has been the primary form of homoeroticism, and it is this love for which NAMBLA stands. . . . We insist there is a distinction between coercive and consensual sex. Laws that focus only on the age of participants fail to capture that distinction . . . Differences in age do not preclude mutual, loving interaction between persons anymore than differences in race or class . . ."

Source: NAMBLA Bulletin (2005) Issue 25.3 (September): 2.

The U.S. Customs Service initiated an investigation of the Wonderland group, eventually executing search warrants in 31 cities in the United States and cooperating with international law enforcement, leading to searches and warrants in 13 different countries. At the time, Customs officials noted that it was the most extensive ring of child pornographers ever uncovered, involving as many as 200 suspects around the world, 34 of them in the United States. All of the suspects were members of a perverse network trading in images depicting everything from sexual abuse to the actual rape of children. One of the requirements for membership was a stockpile of several thousand images of graphic child pornography. Customs agents tracked these suspects through cyberspace, sifting through a maze of Internet providers, servers, files, and screen names. The case resulted in numerous arrests and seizures of computers and other digital evidence. Such cases challenge the patience and capabilities of law enforcement due to the extensive distances between the conspirators and the difficulties associated with sifting through and processing digital evidence. In testimony before Congress, Deputy Assistant Attorney General Kevin V. Di Gregory stated:

> The trafficking in child pornography by computer users has, in some ways, challenged the progress of nearly eighty years of aggressive child pornography investigation and prosecution. Whereas by the early 1990s the Government had largely eradicated the cottage trade within the United States for this material and distribution was typically limited to trading or sharing between individual pedophiles who actually knew each other, today computer technology has reinvigorated both the commercial and non-commercial distribution of obscene child pornography. This reinvigoration means that child pornography produced in the 60s, 70s, and early 80s is now being re-released and distributed to an audience the size of which pedophiles could not have envisioned ten or twenty years ago. Additionally, the ability to mass market child pornography with little or no overhead to huge populations has created an environment where pressures for new material exist. This demand, unfortunately, is being met by new material from sources which include the Pacific Rim, Mexico, and South America. Our investigation has also resulted in the discovery that substantial amounts of written obscenity containing graphic descriptions of torture, bondage, and rape of children are being posted and distributed on the Internet and on private on-line systems. As the World Wide Web continues to grow, we expect that obscene visual images consisting of fantasy drawings

or computer-generated images featuring similar themes of child sexual and physical abuse will also be created and made available for distribution. Obscene material, both written and visual, which can be used to seduce, lure, or train children to perform certain acts, must be highlighted and punished differently.

The fact that there really is no way to gauge how extensive the exchange of child pornography is on the Internet underlies perhaps the most serious problem—that law enforcement is only finding the tip of the iceberg in terms of the actual extent of this problem. As high-profile prosecutions began to occur in the late 1990s, the message to pedophiles and purveyors of child pornography was that anonymity was not assured on the Internet. As a result, efforts to conceal their presence, secure their connections, and encrypt their files have become more prevalent in recent years. Therefore, the job of law enforcement in this area has become increasingly difficult.

The "New" Child Pornographers

In the past, child pornography took the form of pictures, magazines, and videotapes—many homemade and collected over long periods of time by pedophiles. Pedophiles now use the Internet for four primary purposes: trafficking child pornography, locating children to molest, engaging in inappropriate sexual communication with children, and communicating with other pedophiles.[107] In the past, the distribution and sharing of child pornography was through clandestine newsletters or tightly controlled networks,[108] whereas today the networking and distribution is online.

In the summer of 1996, a U.S. federal grand jury indicted 13 individuals from the United States and three from Australia, Canada, and Finland, charging them with orchestrating and participating in an online molestation of ten-year-old girls. The defendants took part in real-time photo shoots where they typed messages requesting photos of the girls in certain poses, while one member shot photos with a digital camera and transmitted the photos back to the group. The defendants were members of the Orchid Club, a private, online child pornography group that shared sexually explicit images and videos of girls as young as five. To be a member of the Orchid Club, members had to know the password to access photos and online chat sessions. Initiation to the club required a potential member to describe a personal sexual experience with a child. After the molestation, members allegedly asked that the camera be aimed at the girl's pubic area and then inquired about traveling to Monterey, California, to molest her themselves.

As noted by Lanning and Burgess,[109] child pornography collectors take great pride in their collections, sometimes numbering in the thousands of pictures, magazines, or videos. In a recent arrest by the U.S. Customs Service, a computer was seized that contained well over 100,000 images of child pornography.[110] The images were catalogued and filed by age, gender, hair color, sex act, and several other variables. Customs officials estimated that it took endless hours of work to enter and develop the file structure containing the images. In the past, the distribution of such a collection would take endless hours of photocopying, film developing, or video processing. If done commercially, it was relatively easy to track the source. Today the individual with the 100,000 images could easily upload the files to the Internet through a variety of mechanisms and methods and distribute them to the masses in a matter of hours. These images could then be downloaded and saved by anyone and redistributed at a later date.

Posting child pornography via Web pages has been curtailed substantially over the past decade; however, the distribution via e-mail, newsgroups, bulletin boards, file-sharing sites, file transfer protocols (ftps), and other direct connect mechanisms continues. The development of inexpensive video recorders and Web cameras has made it very easy for individuals to create high-quality movies of child pornography. Software programs like Photoshop and scanners also allow individuals to create images of child pornography from drawings or legitimate photographs. In addition, advanced encryption programs and software are now readily available and make detection even more difficult. These facts inevitably lead to the conclusion that the computer and the Internet are facilitating child pornography and changing the nature of manufacturing, distributing, and collecting it.

Unlike other forms of obscenity or pornography, child pornography laws are actively prosecuted. As noted in the U.S. Attorney General's *Report on Pornography*,[111] substantially more federal cases are prosecuted involving child pornography than for violating federal obscenity laws. The enforcement of child pornography laws is complicated by a variety of factors, including detection, distribution networks, and the definition of child pornography itself. Detecting child pornography is difficult, as those who actively possess and/or distribute the material take great pains to conceal their crimes. Many times the pornography is not discovered until after the person has been arrested for a far more serious sexual offense involving a child, at which point the child pornography is used as evidence but not likely to be prosecuted separately.

The Internet has made detection and prosecution all the more problematic. In the past, distribution networks were characterized as "cottage industries," where child pornography was exchanged between pedophiles.[112] Today, the Internet has produced what is currently being called a "global cottage industry." The formal publication and distribution was produced internationally outside the United States, and law enforcement considered the domestic production of materials under control.[113] Child pornography in the United States was described as primarily amateur photographs and videotapes being produced by pedophiles and exchanged through informal networks.[114] These conclusions must now be considered outdated given the extent and nature of law enforcement activities currently on the Internet. A secondary issue involves the definition and nature of the material itself.

Lanning and Burgess[115] identified several types of "sex rings" that were used by pedophiles to produce child pornography, victimize children, and prostitute children. Once detected, these rings involved multiple children and, on occasion, several adults. Usually participants in these rings use large hard disks, digital satellite links, cable modems, and the most current encryption technology to communicate and distribute child pornography over the Internet.[116] Agents and local law enforcement personnel go into chat rooms, news groups, and Internet relay channels assuming fictitious screen names to document and engage individuals trading in or posting child pornography.

There have been various law enforcement operations to deal with the problem of child pornography creation, distribution, and ownership. Operation Cheshire Cat, a joint investigation between the Customs Service and the English National Crime Squad, involved over 100 members of a major pedophile ring that operated in 21 countries. There are numerous state statutes involving obscenity; the test for obscenity is determined by local community standards. Between October 1, 1997, and July 31, 1998, customs officials had arrested 183 individuals on new charges, convicted another 189 individuals, and returned 181 indictments on cases involving the possession, manufacture and/or distribution of child pornography. Additionally, Operation Predator was developed in 2003 as a joint investigation with the recently merged Immigration and Customs Enforcement (ICE), the FBI, and other agencies to reduce the number of pedophiles operating online. This operation has led to more than 10,000 arrests and 5,000 deportments from the United States for foreign nationals involved in child pornography and sex crimes.[117] Additionally, the FBI developed a program called Innocent Images, which operates in conjunction with the National

Center for Missing and Exploited Children. This program provides training for law enforcement agencies and operates undercover operations to catch child predators online. As of 2007, the Innocent Images Unit has opened more than 15,500 cases, leading to more than 6,100 arrests.[118] This program also has international relationships with law enforcement agencies in 12 countries and has produced 2,000 leads related to child porn and predatory behavior.

Moving from Pornography to Molestation

The theoretical link between child pornography and child molestation has been researched and debated by several experts.[119] The evidence is mixed, though there are some revealing statistics. One survey found that of 42,000 sex offenders, 42 percent reported the use of pornography either immediately prior to or during commission of the act.[120] Although much of the research in this area is limited and of questionable methodology, the "best" research finds harmful effects of pornography exposure.[121] One field study found that between 77 percent and 87 percent of convicted child molesters used pornography to stimulate themselves, to lower the inhibitions of the child victim, or to teach the child to model the activity in real-life sexual encounters.[122] A recent national study found that individuals arrested for the possession of child pornography are regularly "dual offenders," in that they molest children and possess child porn. In fact, one in six cases that began with investigations or allegations of child pornography possession resulted in an offender who had also attempted to sexually victimize children.[123] Thus, there is a link between child pornography and sex offending, though it may be a correlate or risk factor than a causal factor and needs more research.[124]

A review of the current research and literature on child pornography and the link to child molestation reveals that child pornography is one of several potential facilitators in the crime of child molestation or sexual abuse.[125] We cannot determine at this point whether viewing child pornography produces the impulse to molest children initially or whether child pornography is obtained to satisfy or heighten an already present desire to sexually abuse children. Odds are that both of these statements are true to some extent. Child pornography has been found to stimulate the impulse, provide fantasies, and stimulate pedophiles.[126] Some people are particularly vulnerable to the influence of exposure to pornography, but this exposure in and of itself does not cause their sexually aberrant desires or acts.[127] Importantly, however, several research studies have found that as a group child molesters are more aroused by sexual stimuli that depict children than any other forms of pornography.[128] They use child pornography prior to and during their actual assault[129] as a stimulus and as a tool to entice children into the act.

Sexually abusing children is most commonly assumed to be a learned behavior that has important ties to the Internet and the distribution of child pornography. There are a range of user groups, Web forums, and chat rooms where individuals who are interested in developing relationships with children can identify and talk with others who share their interests.[130] These sites provide a way for pedophiles to come together to validate their sexual interests, share information about their habits, and find support for their behaviors, much like the computer hacker subculture discussed in Chapter 4. Exchanges between individuals provide information on the ways individuals become interested in relationships with children, and how to justify these behaviors. For example, online communities often use the term *child love* to refer to their attractions, rather than the term *pedophile,* which they perceive to be a derogatory and stigmatizing clinical term that does not adequately account for their behaviors.[131]

In fact, an examination by Jenkins found a subculture of child pornography exists that expresses several beliefs and concepts to its members.[132] Those involved in the exchange and consumption of child pornography communicated the dangers they face from a variety of law enforcement agencies and others along with the need for computerized tools to obfuscate and remove data from their computers. They provided information on tools to encrypt their hard drives, secure their collections of child pornography, and hide their Web searches from others. They also discussed how previous societies like feudal Japan and ancient Rome encouraged sexual relationships with children.[133] Some even argued that their interests make them a minority group that deserves legal protection, as in the NAMBLA example provided in Box 7.6. Thus, some individuals with sexual interests in children feel that there should be a social movement for child love to make their behaviors accepted.[134]

With this in mind, a noted clinical psychiatrist in testimony before Congress outlined the role that child pornography plays in the development of a pedophile.[135] Pedophiles are sexual in nature, highly addictive, compulsive and repetitive, and very difficult to treat; self-control and self-discipline don't stop them. The overwhelming majority of pedophiles use child pornography to stimulate their sexual appetites, which they masturbate to and then later use as a model for their own sexual acting out with children. Over time the use of child pornography desensitizes the viewer to its pathology; no matter how aberrant or disturbing, it becomes acceptable and preferred. Some also use it to seduce children into engaging in sexual acts with them. When they introduce it to children, the suggestion is that this is normal behavior and many other young people, like themselves, also use it and do these things. Pedophiles often trade, lend, or sell the pictures they make of young people nude and having sex through an informal network. The pedophiles use pornography during masturbation and eventually become at risk of conditioning themselves into sexual deviancy. In time the "high" obtained from masturbating to pornography becomes more important than real-life relationships. It makes no difference if one is an eminent physician, attorney, minister, athlete, corporate executive, college president, unskilled laborer, or an average 16-year-old boy. All can be self-conditioned into deviancy. The process of masturbatory conditioning is inexorable and does not spontaneously remiss. The course of this illness may be slow and is nearly always hidden from view. It is usually a secret part of the person's life, and, like a cancer, keeps growing and spreading. It rarely ever reverses itself and is very difficult to treat and heal. Denial on the part of the addict and refusal to confront the problem are typical and predictable.

The presence of child pornography creates the potential of many types of harms in the community in creating sexual predators or pedophiles and, later, their victims.[136] Eventually, the sexually addicted male may move into actual molestation, which is recorded and used for further fantasizing and reinforcement.

In conclusion, pedophiles use child pornography for several reasons:

- For personal sexual stimulation
  - Child pornography provides a powerful erotic stimulus to achieve sexual arousal, relive prior sexual acts, visualize fantasies, and focus attention during masturbatory manipulation when alone.
- To reduce the inhibitions of the child
  - After a child's initial shock, a molester will point out that the children and adults in the pictures are enjoying their mutual sexual activities and that "lots of kids do it; pictures don't lie." The perpetrator can then convince the child that it is normal for children to be sexually active with adults, and their fears are unfounded.
- As an instructional tool
  - Pornography is used literally as a textbook of visual instruction to educate children to perform specific sex acts.

- For barter, trade, or sale
  - Transactions may be for money, pornographic materials, or information about how to gain sexual access to children.
- To blackmail the child
  - "Silence is golden when a child has been abused," according to one molester. In addition to silence, a child may be required to recruit siblings or friends for the molester. Many times children are told that they will be ridiculed, disbelieved, or reprimanded by their parents and police if anyone finds out what has taken place. A pedophile knows how to put a heavy burden on the child to bear the blame if his family is broken up and he's taken away, or his parents break up, etc., if the incident ever becomes public.

The pedophile uses a combination of deception, desensitization, and psychological conditioning to lure potential child victims into a sexual molestation relationship. Before any sexual advances are made, the molester generally befriends the child through the use of rewards such as food, toys, movies, or money. This first step of becoming close to the child is part of an elaborate nurturing process leading to a friendly and trusted relationship between the pedophile, the victim, and oftentimes the parents or guardians of the child. Once the relationship is established, the door to sexual abuse and molestation is open. Most pedophiles do not use force or intimidation, but a long-term approach, to gain the confidence of the child.

The molester has such success with children because he communicates with them at their emotional and psychological level. He plays their games, speaks their language, and even likes their toys. In the course of grooming potential victims, each pedophile develops a somewhat unique modus operandi, leaving behind valuable evidence for investigators. Often the investigation in such cases reveals that the pedophile's victims were approached in a similar way and the process leading to the abuse followed a similar pattern. Such evidence is crucial for successful prosecution of the pedophile at a later trial.

The molestation process follows a typical pattern known as the cycle of victimization. First, adult pornography is casually shown to a target child in an effort to raise the child's curiosity level and provide a sex education of sorts. The child is often surprised and bewildered by the images in men's magazines, but the molester explains that these images demonstrate that this kind of behavior is normal and acceptable.

A number of children testified before the 1986 Attorney General's Commission on Pornography that what their molester showed them was to demonstrate that this was what "all big boys and girls did." Once the molester has used adult pornography to convince the child that sex is acceptable, even enjoyable, for children, more deviant forms of pornography are introduced to further the learning process. Actual or simulated child pornography is shown to convince the child that other children regularly participate in sexual activities with adults or peers. Simulated child pornography includes pictures of youthful-looking adults dressed up and acting as children or computer-generated images of children involved in sexual activity. These images can be real or created out of the imagination of a computer user; either way they have the same devastating effect on the children who see them. Continued exposure to pornography lowers the inhibitions of the child to a point where he or she allows the molester to kiss and touch him sexually. Eventually, if successful, the seduction process progresses to more explicit activity between the child victim and adult or other children, using the pornography as an instructional tool.

Once the desire is initiated in the child to view pornographic materials and once the pedophile realizes that the child will not tell that he or she has seen the material, the process of molestation progresses into the next level. The child is now exposed to increasingly more graphic pornography, typically depicting children engaging in sexual acts with each other or with adults. Inevitably, questions about the acts being portrayed would arise to be readily answered by the pedophile. The pedophile would then begin to demonstrate that the sexual acts feel good and aren't wrong for the child to engage in. It is often at this point that the child victim is photographed, innocently at first, but eventually progressing to nudity and sexually explicit types of pictures. The attention garnered on the victim is especially damaging if the child has needs for attention and love that are not being fulfilled by his or her family or friends. Such children are particularly vulnerable to a pedophile's advances.

CHILD MOLESTATION

According to law enforcement statistics, there was an estimated 78,188 child abuse cases in 2003.[137] However, the true number of actual child sexual abuse cases is much higher. A telephone survey of 2,000 children between the ages of 10 and 16 revealed that 3.2 percent of girls and 0.6 percent of boys had suffered, at some point in their lives, sexual abuse involving physical contact. If one infers that those statistics can be generalized to the rest of the country, children have experienced (but not reported) levels of victimization that far exceed those reported.[138] Most child molesters are able to molest numerous children before they are caught and have only a 3 percent chance of being apprehended for their crimes. Statistics show that boys and girls are at nearly equal risk for abuse, and almost a quarter will be molested sometime before their eighteenth birthday; however, less than 5 percent will tell someone. The overwhelming majority of child victims are abused by someone they know, or a family member. In general, most molestations are perpetrated by adolescent males, but older pedophiles, though fewer in number, molest in greater numbers and with greater frequency.

Child molestation or exploitation can be defined as any sexual behavior or activity that is abusive or nonconsensual toward a child or a sexual behavior that is specifically prohibited by state or federal law. Various states have differing definitions and age limits in their statutory rape laws and concerning the age at which a person can voluntarily consent to sexual relations. Some states define a specific age, such as 16, to enumerate the point at which a person can voluntarily consent to sex. Others include an age-range difference, such as three years, up to a certain age where a person can consent to sex. For example, a 16-year-old could consent to sex with an 18-year-old but not anyone over the age of 19. While statutory offenses comprise a substantial portion of sexual offenses, largely unreported, the more important area concerns the molestation and exploitation of children by adults and strangers. Fondling, oral sex, simulated or actual intercourse, exhibitionism, taking sexually explicit pictures of children, showing sexually explicit material to children or having sex in front of a child are all considered child sexual abuse. In such cases, the sexual contact is between a child that cannot voluntarily consent to sex and someone in a position of power or trust. The sexual relations are concealed by the abuser through denial, secrecy, and threats to the child. Such cases are the primary focus of this show.

In a stunning study, Abel et al.[139] recruited and interviewed 561 nonincarcerated pedophiles and child molesters. Their findings revealed the following:

- A total of 291,737 "paraphilic acts" were committed against 195,407 victims under the age of 18.
- The five most frequently reported paraphilic acts involved criminal conduct:
  - Nonincestuous child molestation with a female victim (224 of the 561 subjects reported 5,197 acts against 4,435 victims).

- Nonincestuous child molestation with a male victim (153 of the 561 subjects reported 43,100 acts against 22,981 victims).
- Incest with a female victim (159 of the 561 subjects reported 12,927 acts against 286 victims).
- Incest with a male victim (44 of the 561 subjects reported 2,741 acts against 75 victims).
- Rape (126 of the 561 subjects reported 907 acts against 882 victims).

The remaining 16 categories included a wide range of paraphilias, which may or may not have involved coercion. The first five categories included a total of 64,872 acts. The total number of subjects and victims cannot be determined since the categories are overlapping (i.e., many subjects reported multiple paraphilias and hence were recorded in multiple categories). This study and other estimates based on victimization studies and self-report crime studies paint a much darker picture of the true extent of sexual assault and child molestation in the United States.

The Problem of Child Sexual Abuse

David Finkelhor developed a four-part model that enunciates how a sex offense occurs between an offender and a child victim. He argues that each part must occur for an offense to take place.

1. *A potential offender must have some motivation to sexually abuse a child.* The potential offender must feel some form of emotional congruence with the child, sexual arousal with the child must be a potential source of gratification, and alternative sources of gratification must be unavailable or less satisfying.
2. *Any internal inhibitions against acting on the motivation to engage in sexual assault must be overcome.* For example, alcohol or drugs may be used in order to lower inhibitions against sexual offending. This may be combined with the knowledge that society often shows greater tolerance toward those who commit crimes while under the influence of substances.
3. *Any external impediments to acting on the impulse to abuse must be overcome.* Inadequate care or supervision by a parent or guardian can provide an opportunity for an offender to act.
4. *Avoidance or resistance by the child must be overcome.* This may involve enticing an emotionally deprived child into accepting inappropriate attention, or overt coercion to achieve domination of the relatively powerless child.

A voyeur or exhibitionist is motivated by a sexual desire for exhibitionist behavior toward children, perhaps as a preliminary step to approaching children or as part of some fantasy. Care or supervision by a guardian is overcome through the exhibitionist exposing themselves to children with their parents or in the presence of other children. There is little, if any, need to overcome resistance; as is often the case, the sexual stimulation comes from the reactions of the children involved. In contrast, the incest, molestation, and rape offenders achieve their goals through different mechanisms. The incest offender is motivated by sexual desires and uses the already established power relationship to offend within their own family. These offenders reduce inhibitions through alcohol or drugs frequently; in fact, most offenses between a parent or guardian and their child occur while under the influence of a substance. Additionally, incest offenders victimize children while capable guardians are out of the house, discreetly at night, or when the child is vulnerable. Resistance by the child is overcome through coercion, lying, or through extra attention, leading the child victim into submitting and even welcoming some sexual advances. However, the relationship between the offender and victim is always based on power and control, and not voluntary or consensual relations, when the victim is under the age of consent.

Offenders typically select their victims in one of two ways: preselection involving a certain type of child, or a child that they know or through opportunity. Each of these types of offenders has different characteristics discussed previously. Investigators should recognize the differences between a situational child molester and a pedophile. A situational child molester is generally a socially inadequate, inhibited, and introverted individual with low self-esteem. They frequently have a substance abuse problem and will deny any involvement in the molestation. There are numerous categorizations of child molesters, but there are four generally recognized types. The first is the *regressed* child molester. This subtype usually leads the most stable life, preferring female victims. Oral and vaginal intercourse is their goal. They tend to always keep a "stable" of potential victims in various stages of seduction. The second type is the *morally indiscriminate* child molester, who frequently exhibits multiple paraphilias and a desire to experiment sexually. They frequently interact with others who share similar desires and will network in attempts to find victims. The third type is the *inadequate* child molester. Their sexual desires vary, but always revolve around a perceived inadequacy in their lives or their inability to mesh socially with other adults. These offenders can progress into serial killers, substituting child murder for the sexual aspect of their offenses. The molestation, in many cases, is driven by a need to "get even" with some perceived injustice experienced by the molester. Finally, the *sexually indiscriminate* molester does not necessarily specialize in a certain type of sex or sexual partner, but will try anything and everything. The difference between this type and the others is the gratuitous use of pornography and the high victim total when eventually apprehended. Table 7.3 depicts the differences among the four types.

Pedophiles attracted to teenage boys might have their homes decorated the way a teenage boy would. This might include toys, games, stereos, rock posters, and so on. The homes of some pedophiles have been described as shrines to children or as miniature amusement parks. In

TABLE 7.3   Characteristics of the Situational Child Molester

	Regressed	Morally Indiscriminate	Sexually Indiscriminate	Inadequate
Basic characteristics	Poor coping skills	User of people	Sexual experimentation	Social misfit
Motivation	Substitution	Why not?	Boredom	Insecurity and curiosity
Victim criteria	Availability	Vulnerability and opportunity	New and different	Nonthreatening
Method of operation	Coercion, force, younger victims	Lure, force, or manipulation	Involved in existing activity	Exploits size, advantage
Pornography collection	Possible	Sadomasochistic detective magazines	Highly likely, varied	Almost certainly, varied

Source: Deviant and Criminal Sexuality (1993), 2nd edition, NCAVC, FBI Academy.

addition, virtually every pedophile has access to and a collection of child pornography. Molesters also test and desensitize children by telling dirty jokes, talking about sexual things, and engaging in nonsexual physical contact like back rubs, wrestling, hugging, and horseplay. This behavior generally starts long before sexual touching and serves to normalize contact and trust.

Many molesters work just as hard to seduce and manipulate adults as they do to trick children. Most pedophiles think out, far in advance, plans and tactics to use to reduce the likelihood that a child will report the offense. Separate tactics and justifications are used to allay the fears and inquiries voiced by adults. Many have elaborate denial routines and are extremely adept at lying and convincing people that the child is mistaken or has misinterpreted the interactions. Investigators must be extremely adept at interviewing children and at working the investigation with the adult guardians, if available. A common presumption is that children will not lie or make up stories about molestation, but several cases in the recent past have demonstrated that pressure by social workers has led some children to make up stories of sexual assault. Investigators must be wary of putting words in the child's mouth and leading them to conclude that they were molested. A common tool is to use anatomically correct dolls to allow children to show exactly what happened. The use of these dolls and other tactics should be done only by a trained investigator familiar with the rule of evidence in these cases and the correct use of investigational tactics when dealing with children.

PROSTITUTION AND THE SEX TRADE

One of the emerging issues surrounding sex and the Internet is the increasing use of Web sites and online resources to facilitate the sex trade. Though most prostitution occurs in the real world, the Internet has become an important resource for sex workers and their clients.[140] This is due in part to the fact that advertising and discussing the illegal sex trade online reduces the risk of detection and arrest from law enforcement. This has particular importance for escorts and prostitutes who use the Web sites as a means of advertising their services. Hundreds of escorts advertise their services across the country through Web sites such as The Erotic Review and BigDoggie.[141] These spaces allow sex workers to post pictures of themselves, describe their services, and interact with clients. This has a significant benefit for sex workers as they reduce their likelihood of arrest or detection by law enforcement. Also, these Web sites allow sex workers to more carefully select their clients, travel to meet them, and charge more for their services.

Relatedly, the clients of prostitutes, often called johns, have also come to rely on the Internet, because they can interact with others and discuss their experiences with prostitutes without fear of arrest or social embarrassment.[142] Individuals who pay for sex often face significant shame if they are caught and are unlikely to talk about their activities with others in person. The Internet, however, offers an opportunity for anonymous communications with others who share their interest in paid sexual encounters. Thus, a number of Web sites have emerged that exist only to link johns together to talk about the sex trade.

The discussions in these sites regularly revolve around reviews of street prostitutes, escorts who advertise online, strip club workers, and other sex workers. Their reviews regularly address the sexual acts they engage in, the location where the sex act occurred, and the relative safety of the place, as well as costs for services.[143] Johns also elaborated on sexual encounters with escorts in their posts, complete with physical descriptions of the prostitutes, their attitudes, and any critiques about their performance during the act. The reviews can be extremely detailed, including use of condoms during sex acts and the johns' beliefs about the sex worker's cleanliness.[144] For example, the following is a post from a forum for individuals in Chicago, Illinois, that provides a review of two escorts who advertise online:

NOT AS ADVERTISED AND MAJOR UP-SELL

I had a bad experience with Eros under "Chicago GFE Escorts." I guess it's another reminder to RTFF and only go with recommended contacts.

I do NOT recommend Nikki. She was significantly overweight compared to the pictures, and the person who showed up wasn't anything close to the girl pictured. I let myself get carried away with her major up-sell pitch. Another reminder to stay cool headed.

I do NOT recommend, Aspen. It may have been the same person pictured a while ago, but as of now she seemed strung out and anxious to pay the rent. She confided that the last guy she went to sent her packing because she "wasn't what he expected." I can see why.

"Escort" is an overstatement for these women.

These accounts also provide some insight into the characteristics johns seek in prostitutes, noting "girlfriend experiences" (GFE) as the ideal. GFE occur whenever the woman is enthusiastic about the sex act and makes the john feel special, as though they were in a "consensual non-commercial relationship."[145] The following post provides a review of an online escort who provided such an experience for the john:

After about an hour of email replies we finally agreed [and] negotiated on the phone for 200 and funny part about it is I tried to get cash on ATM and damn machine spitted out only 120 just my bad luck.

Went to her place what I saw was a heaven sent angel. 20 yrs old definitely non pro. Probably one of those girls just needed money for shopping. She lives with her parents I was a bit paranoid I'm sure her parents doesn't know she does this. And of course parents are at work!

Anyway here's the climax of the story. I apologized to her that we agreed on the price that my atm only spitted out 120 and she said u don't have to pay me 200 just give me a hundred I thought I had died and went to heaven.

This girl was such a beauty she gave me [oral sex] for about 2 minutes while I was . . . caressing her smooth skin of course total gfe. Foreplay went for about 5 minutes got so damn horny started with the missionary with my damn bad luck came in probably less than 3 . . . minutes. Gave her some excuses that I haven't done it in months. lol she said it was ok and even asked me if I wanted to relax for a few minutes and try it again. stupid me just told her no its ok just got cleaned up went home.

I asked her how I can get hold of her again she said just send her email since she kept calling me on a block number. I'm planning to send her email again tomorrow since its pay day and I'll ask her if she will agree on giving out her email and I'll share this heaven sent.

In turn, johns give higher reviews and recommend sex workers who can provide GFE. As a whole, the quality, quantity, and detailed information provided by johns through forums may increase prostitution rates by facilitating sex work.

Sex Tourism

Another facet of the sex trade is sex tourism, which is a loosely defined practice that encompasses several sexually related practices, some legal in certain countries and some illegal. In many instances, visitors to foreign countries utilize legal brothels and other sexually oriented businesses that are illegal in their home country. In other instances, the visitors use services that are illegal in both countries. Finally, a growing practice is for typically wealthy Westerners to travel specifically to certain countries to procure sexual services of adolescents or to be set up with children for sexual purposes. In sum, sex tourism is the practice of men (there are virtually no known cases of women engaging in this practice) from Western countries visiting developing or third world nations for the purpose of engaging in sexual activity that is illegal in their home country or that they don't want to be discovered committing in their home country. Often, the sexual desires of these tourists are for adolescents, for children, or for a paraphilic or strange sexual encounter. Sex tourism has been growing over the last several decades, with the highest prevalence occurring in Southeast Asian countries, particularly those with long histories of sexually oriented businesses.

A recent report by the International Labor Organization found that 1.39 million people are forced into commercial sexual exploitation, and up to 50 percent of these individuals are children.[146] United Nations Children's Fund (UNICEF) also offers staggering statistics on this problem:

- Approximately 12,000 children in Nepal are trafficked for commercial sexual exploitation to brothels in Nepal, India, and other countries.
- There are between 28,000 and 30,000 children under the age of 18 who are used in prostitution in South Africa.
- There are at least 244,000 women and children who are part of the commercial sexual exploitation trade in the United States.
- There are between 400,000 and 500,000 child prostitutes in India.
- Debt bondage—paying off loans given to their parents or guardians—is often the reason young girls enter prostitution in India, Nepal, Myanmar, Pakistan, and Thailand.[147]

The sex trade in many countries involves young boys who are offered to European, American, and Asian tourists, sometimes as part of vacation packages. Estimates are that 20,000–30,000 of Sri Lanka's child prostitutes are boys who are "rented" to tourist pedophiles. Several other countries are known for tolerating an active sex trade of young boys, including the Dominican Republican, Haiti, Egypt, Morocco, and Tunisia.[148] It is important to note that children are also forced into commercial exploitation in the United States.

Recent research attempted to account for the ways that children are forced into the sex trade. This study found that pimps scout bus stations, malls, and other locations looking for girls who appear to be runaways seeking help.[149] The pimps then attempt to befriend them and give them gifts and food in exchange for sex. As the pimps develop a relationship with the girl, they convince her to engage in sexual acts for money with other men. They may also threaten or blackmail the girl into sex. In some countries, contractual relationships are developed between traffickers and parents, where the child's earnings are given back to the parent in small amounts. Children may also be given drugs or forced into isolation as a means of keeping them from running away or trying to get out of the trade. Box 7.7 provides a detailed continuum on the process of abuse and commercial exploitation.

The growth of sexual tourism is often attributed to a Western military presence that has increased the demand for sex workers and sexually oriented businesses. However, recent research shows that many other factors contribute to the sex tourism practice and industry. The sex tourism industry has become an important source of income for many nations, supporting weak economies

BOX 7.7

Continuum of abuse and commercial exploitation

Adult family member or friend sexually abuses the child.

    Adult abuses the child regularly.

        Abuser seeks other children.

            Photographs/videos shared via Internet.

                Photos/videos sold via Internet.

                    Family members or friends pimp children.

                        Children kidnapped, sold for prostitution and sex tourism.

Source: ALBANESE, JAY. (2007). *Commercial Sexual Exploitation of Children: What Do We Know and What Do We Do About It?* Washington, DC: National Institute of Justice.

and aiding in putting money in the hands of governmental officials and law enforcement officials. Thus, eliminating the industry is difficult without the cooperation of the countries where the tourists travel. Without international agreement and implementation of certain standards dictating the way these businesses are owned and operated, it is unlikely that a change in practice will occur. Nonetheless, several attempts have been made in recent years to change the way that the world views the practice of sexual tourism. Both the United States and the European Union have passed laws making it illegal for citizens to make use of these types of services when underage children are involved. In the future, the elimination of the child sex tourism industry as well as increased awareness and care for adult sex workers who are forced into this line of work need to be addressed.

Of the 160 pedophiles and sex tourists arrested up to 1994, 25 percent were American, 18 percent German, 14 percent Australian, 12 percent British, and 6 percent French. Estimates of the number of children involved in the worldwide sex trade vary. The UNICEF contends that one million children at any one given time are involved in prostitution in Asia alone. End Child Prostitution in Asian Tourism (ECPAT) assesses the value of the prostitution industry to be $5 billion. These appraisals, whether completely accurate or, at least, reflective of educated guesses, bespeak the extent that children are actually affected by sex tourism.[150] Estimates of child prostitutes in South Asia, which are difficult to come by, place the number for Bangladesh at 10,000; India, 400,000–500,000; Pakistan, 40,000; and Sri Lanka, 30,000.[151]

It has been suggested that men are more likely to travel to an Asian nation because they do not speak the same language and therefore all human attributes are obliterated to hide the identity of the girl. Because there can be no verbal communication, the customer does not have to explore the girl's past or even know her name.[152] This situation allows for a completely confidential exchange in which the consumer gets what he paid for and has no connection to the encounter once it is complete.

The Internet is a primary facilitator of the sex tourism industry.[153] It allows for quick and easy access to a number of different destinations and options at a range of prices. These excursions are usually offered in packages in which the men can travel for a desired period of time. For example, in India these trips can be as short as 24–48 hours, during which time sex tourists can experience sexual encounters with a number of different women.[154] In 1999, Philipine Adventure Tours (PAT) of California advertised their tourist package on the Internet. For $1,645, tourists would receive roundtrip airfare, hotel accommodations, and a guided tour of bars where they could purchase sex from prostitutes who were working in bars as entertainers.[155] The Internet allows for men freely to search available destinations and to make choices based on desire and the potential for pleasure. The Internet contributes to the tourism industry and the hidden identity of sex workers through its display of women and children as toys and entertainment. The most dangerous type of person who may retrieve this type of information from the Internet includes pedophiles, who want nothing more than to use and exploit children to fulfill their sexual fantasies and desires.

Although little research exists on how tourists find their way to these hotels and brothels abroad, clearly the Internet has led to an explosion of interest in this area. The process typically begins with the viewing or exchanging of pornography on the World Wide Web, via newsgroups or via ftps and file exchange software. Many sex offenders and pedophiles report on sex rings or clubs that they have encountered on the Internet. The clubs routinely trade pornography. Some also provide services in the way of information and the procurement of sex workers for interested parties willing to pay for their visits. The exchange of information revolves around known hotels where sexual services can be obtained, bars or nightclubs where contacts can be made, or sex clubs and brothels where these people can go for services. The process a sex tourist goes through to be trusted by the club or ring prior to gaining the information they need is unclear. In some cases, the sex club or brothel will advertise in the newsgroups, via e-mail, or even posted directly to the Web (deviant sexual services and sex with children is not commonly advertised or posted). There are reports that child sex rings are shuffling children between pedophiles for sex in these countries and even in the United States. The price for admission to the club or sex ring is often photographs of the potential member engaged in a sexual act with the children.

The Process of Sex Tourism

The sex tourist encounter is rather typical. The sex tourist is usually male, most likely either from Europe or North America. Some of the perpetrators are pedophiles, but most are "respectable" doctors, lawyers, servicemen, and teachers—many with children of their own.[156] Sex tourists are generally divided into two groups: preferential abusers and situational abusers. Preferential abusers, the pedophiles, have clear and definite sexual preferences for children, while situational abusers generally have not planned to have commercial sex while abroad, but took the opportunity when it presented itself. Most of these perpetrators tell themselves that there is no abuse or harm occurring to the child because the child has actively "chosen" that "profession." They also assume that because the child has "chosen" prostitution, the child consents to and ultimately benefits from sexual relations with adults, and that commercial sex is a way to help children out of poverty. Many of these perpetrators believe that the victims are inferior people and thus they have little problem with or remorse about exploiting them. Steinman[157] outlines an interview with a sex tourist to Latin America:

> "On this trip, I've had sex with a 14-year-old girl in Mexico and a 15-year-old in Colombia," says a 65-year-old retired Orlando schoolteacher. He talks about his trip, on the condition of anonymity, in a ramshackle casino in downtown Tegucigalpa. For three months this winter, the divorced grandfather traveled Latin America, visiting brothels. He sees nothing wrong with having sex with teens. "I'm helping them financially," he says. "If they don't have sex with me, they may not have enough food. If someone has a problem with me doing this, let UNICEF feed them. I've never paid more than $20 to these young women, and that allows them to eat for a week." Sexual tourists attempt to delude themselves that they commit no wrong by telling themselves that Latin American cultures are less sexually inhibited and sexually freer than

Western societies. They rationalize this by maintaining that "girls in these countries are portrayed as grown up and sexually experienced at 14 already, and that there is no stigma attached to prostitution." Many of these perpetrators enjoy the anonymity of traveling abroad, which releases them from social constraints that they would feel in their home countries. Child sex tourists persuade themselves that in another country, normal social and moral restraints can be discarded, along with the belief that one will not be held responsible for his behavior. It is within these circumstances that child sexual exploitation thrives.

The tour can be self-initiated by the sex tourist with the aid of the Internet and sales brochures. It is common that many of them will hear about certain hotels or bars where such services can be procured, usually through word of mouth or via the Internet. Other tourists utilize the services of a procurer or facilitator. Procurers and facilitators are simply the pimps who provide the services, capital, and resources that make sexual trafficking of children both a feasible and lucrative industry. Some of the procurers are former child prostitutes who "climbed the ranks" within the industry.[158] Facilitators, while often not directly involved in the child prostitution transaction itself, expedite the victimization process. The facilitator might be a recruiter, a parent who sells his or her child into prostitution, a landlord or motel owner who permits the activity to occur on his or her property, or a sex tour travel agent. Transporters also move children throughout a region, importing and exporting them in order to facilitate the sex trade. These sex tour travel agents publish brochures and guides that cater to sex tourists. The brochures emphasize the youth of prostitutes at these advertised destinations. In 1999, there were over 25 businesses in the United States that offered and arranged sex tours.[159]

Thailand, the Philippines, Sri Lanka, and Taiwan are the countries traditionally connected with child sex tourism, and all have serious child prostitution problems. Prostitution of a massive nature involving children originated in Thailand and the Philippines in the late 1960s, during the Vietnam War. In Thailand, Burmese women and girls as young as 13 are illegally trafficked across the border by recruiters and sold to brothel owners. In the Philippines, many children are tricked into prostitution after their parents sell them to recruiters with the promise of legitimate work in the city. The Philippine government has calculated the number of child prostitutes in the Philippines at 50,000.[160] During the late 1970s and early 1980s, pedophiles from Europe and North America found a Shangri-La for sexual activity with minors in Thailand and the Philippines. More than half of the sex tourists overall are pedophiles, and approximately one-third of them are North American or European.[161]

Currently, tourist agencies actively campaign to entice travelers to visit their countries for sex with "young women." Although agents running these tourist organizations deny that child prostitutes are involved, investigations by reporters illustrate that is untrue. For example, Russell Herman, a U.S. Citizen, ran a sex tourism business online from Thailand.[162] He ran a Web site offering to facilitate tours where he would introduce customers to young women between the ages of 18 and 24. ICE agents conducted an undercover investigation and arranged for a tour from Herman, which involved traveling to four brothels containing young women between the ages of 12 and 17. These women were prostitutes, many of whom were illegally brought into Thailand and, in some cases, padlocked inside the brothels. Herman was arrested and pleaded guilty to charges of sex tourism in a U.S. court. Some agencies go as far as to compose travel guides delineating the laws of countries patrons visit and explain how prosecution for sex tourism in those countries is avoidable. Patrons' willingness to travel to engage in sexual activity with children clearly shows that the child sex industry will continue to thrive, especially if ignored.[163]

As growing international attention has increased public awareness of the prevalence and dangers associated with sex tourism, prosecution against sex tourists and owners of such establishments have also become more prevalent. Many of the recent cases that have been successfully prosecuted have been against older men who engage in child sex tourism. For example, in 1996, Michael Clark, a British citizen, was convicted of inducing child prostitution and sentenced to over 16 years in prison. Clark organized sex tours and provided minor children for the pleasure of sex tourists in the Philippine cities of Olongapo and Angeles. The Philippine court also ruled him to be deported after serving his sentence, and he has been barred from ever returning to the Philippines.[164]

In 2002, a businessman of Dallas, Texas, was convicted of having traveled out of the country to engage in sexual conduct with minors. Nicholas Bredimus traveled to Thailand where he sought the companionship of young girls and boys, photographed himself engaged in sexual conduct with the children, and took explicit photos of young boys. Bredimus was sentenced to six and a half years in prison, a $30,000 fine, and three years of supervised release following his sentence, during which time his access to children and the Internet were closely monitored.[165] The author had the opportunity to interview Mr. Bredimus prior to his sentencing for these crimes and can offer the following description of the offense.

Mr. Bredimus was a well-known and well-liked software designer and airline consultant in the Dallas area. The details of his background in sex offenses and how he obtained the knowledge of the sex tourism industry are still sketchy. However, he was able to arrange several visits to Thailand, where he obtained sexual services through a procurer. Mr. Bredimus also obtained fake passports, which he used to leave the country from a vacation in Hawaii. On the particular trip that he was convicted for, he left Hawaii, traveled to Japan, and then to Thailand. Once in Thailand, he made his way to a border town (on the border with Burma) called Mae Sai, where he arranged for his procurer to rent two adjacent hotel rooms and then asked that young boys aged 10–15 be brought to one of the rooms.

The procurer met with a bellman at another hotel known to be a sex tourist location and helped the procurer round up six boys aged 11–14. Each of the boys was paid approximately $22 for their services. He systematically examined each of the boys, rejecting one of them for having a deformed toe, and each boy was ordered to shower prior to being led into the room that Bredimus occupied. In his room, he had set up his laptop and a digital video camera and had a still digital camera with him. Each boy was led in systematically and ordered to undress. Mr. Bredimus was in his underwear and proceeded to molest the boys while filming each encounter with the video camera on the tripod and taking pictures with the camera. The level of sexual assault increased over the course of the event, with Bredimus eventually inserting his finger into the anus of one of the boys who cried out in anguish. One of the boys left the hotel and alerted the police that a Westerner was in the hotel molesting young boys. The Thai police knocked on the door and eventually had to force their way into the room. They stopped Mr. Bredimus as he was attempting to erase the images on the camera and video camera. The Thai police seized his equipment and arrested him. He was able to bond out for $13,000; incredibly, the Thai police returned his laptop to him, as they were unable to crack the password on the computer.

Mr. Bredimus fled the country with another phony passport, eventually returning to Hawaii. The case would never have come to light had it not been for the work of Fight Against Child Exploitation (FACE), a Thai-based organization that alerted U.S. officials to the crimes.

American law enforcement officials then went to Thailand to interview the police and victims, and eventually brought charges against Mr. Bredimus in the U.S. District Court in Dallas. This case is one of the first in the United States where a child sex tourist has been successfully sent to prison. It also demonstrates the extraordinary difficulty in dealing with crimes such as these that occur abroad.

ISSUES IN THE INVESTIGATION OF INTERNET EXPLOITATION, CYBERSTALKING, AND OBSCENITY

Numerous challenges and obstacles exist to effectively enforcing and prosecuting these types of cybercrimes. First, there are numerous, and overlapping, law enforcement initiatives that target them. There is already a problem: Overlapping effort, overlapping jurisdictions, and a general lack of funding and priority dedicated to such crimes are pronounced. Second, the cybercriminal of today is elusive, largely anonymous, and often likely to be operating in a jurisdiction outside of the United States. Finally, there are several evidentiary issues and problems in the prosecution of these crimes that make it more difficult to gain a conviction.

Law Enforcement Initiatives

The primary federal agencies that have been combating this type of crime are the FBI, the ICE, the Postal Inspection Service, the Department of Justice's Child Exploitation and Obscenity Section (CEOS), and the National Center for Missing and Exploited Children (NCMEC).[166] In 1995, the FBI initiated Innocent Images, which is a proactive, intelligence-driven, multiagency investigative initiative. It serves as the clearinghouse and coordinating body for all FBI investigations that involve child exploitation or child pornography and has led to thousands of arrests. As mentioned earlier, ICE also formed and runs Operation Predator, which develops leads about and receives and coordinates undercover operations against international child pornography and child sexual exploitation rings.

The National Center for Missing and Exploited Children (NCMEC) produced a Cyber Tipline for leads about child sexual exploitation.[167] Mandated by Congress, the Cyber Tipline allows individuals to report online (and via a toll-free number) incidents of child luring, molestation, pornography, sex tourism, and prostitution. Since March 1998, the Cyber Tipline has received over 500,000 reports of child exploitation and pornography.[168] The Postal Inspection Service has conducted thousands of cases related to child exploitation, molestation, and pornography. Their investigations of child molesters reveal that these offenders are using computers increasingly, along with the mail, to find potential victims, to communicate with other criminals, and to locate sources of child pornography. In fact, 95 percent of all the Postal Inspection Service's child exploitation cases involved both computers and physical mail.[169] The undercover operations include the placement of contact advertisements in sexually oriented publications, written contact and correspondence with subjects of investigations, development of confidential sources, and, more recently, undercover contact with suspects via the Internet.

The CEOS of the Justice Department has taken an active role in training federal prosecutors to handle child crime cases that were once mainly handled by local jurisdictions. The section has sponsored several training seminars for federal prosecutors on the issues of child pornography, exploitation, trafficking, and sex tourism. In addition to these operations, many law enforcement agencies of the federal government have begun to seek partnerships with corporations and local law enforcement to target cybercrime. These partnerships are frequently called electronic crime task forces, and seek to coordinate efforts and eliminate overlap.

Overlapping Jurisdictions and Duplication of Effort

The government currently has numerous operations dedicated to child pornography and additional units and operations targeting obscenity in general.[170] As is the case with other areas of law enforcement, a problem exists with overlapping jurisdictional boundaries and duplication of effort between agencies. Two examples cited in a recent report on cybercrime highlight the problems of overlapping effort:[171]

> Some state and local law enforcement agencies also have been frustrated by jurisdictional limitations. In many instances, the cyberstalker may be located in a different city or state than the victim, making it more difficult (and, in some cases, all but impossible) for the local authority to investigate the incident. Even if a law enforcement agency is willing to pursue a case across state lines, it may be difficult to obtain assistance from out-of-state agencies when the conduct is limited to harassing e-mail messages and no actual violence has occurred. A number of matters been referred to the FBI and/or U.S. Attorney's offices because the victim and suspect were located in different states and the local agency was not able to pursue the investigation.

Cybercriminals can cross national or international boundaries at will via a computer, and information and property can be easily transmitted through communications and data networks. As a result, law enforcement agencies are forced to try to work with local officials, foreign governments, and other agencies of the federal government—something that they have been quite reluctant to do in the past. As one report noted, a law enforcement official could secure a search warrant for a computer in the United States and, as a result of the search, remotely access a computer in Canada, which irrespective of the warrant is potentially a crime in Canada. Further, certain cybercrimes that are illegal in this country are perfectly legal in other countries (i.e., gambling, prostitution, and underage sexual relations). As a result, Congress has passed some laws that make certain offenses a crime regardless of whether they are legal in the host country. Additionally, the ICE agency has developed relationships with foreign law enforcement agencies through Operation Predator, including Australia, Denmark, Finland, Japan, the Netherlands, Liechtenstein, New Zealand, Norway, Sweden, Switzerland, and the United Kingdom. These relationships have led to the arrest of more than 1,900 individuals worldwide.[172]

Identification of Suspects

We all tend to enjoy the feeling of anonymity that the Internet provides, allowing us to conduct business and communicate without fear of "somebody listening" to our personal communications. Individuals who actively collect pornographic materials share information and resources on methods to hide or minimize the likelihood of detection. Several Web services offer free anonymous e-mail and Web accounts along with proxy tools that hide the actual location of a computer. Further, it is quite difficult to trace some communications over the Net, especially with the availability of access on numerous college campuses and Internet cafes. Many criminals assume the identity of someone else to conduct their online crimes, such as theft of e-mail addresses and hacking into someone else's computer to conduct business (making that computer a zombie). Another service provided by some ISPs are mail servers that purposefully strip identifying information and transport headers from electronic mail. By forwarding mails through several of these services serially, cybercriminals can make the message almost completely anonymous. The sending of anonymous communications is thus relatively easy for the criminal and makes it difficult for law enforcement to identify the suspect responsible for the crime.

Issues with Evidence and Detection

The problems of evidentiary collection and analysis are fully discussed in Chapters 11 and 12; however, a few problems in this area deserve mention. As you are aware, computer data are easily destroyed, deleted, or modified. The discussion of the morphing of images and the purposeful alteration of material has already reached the Supreme Court. Further, the technical capability to collect, preserve, and analyze such evidence is not widely distributed in the law enforcement community. Finally, the fact that people can use their computers to conduct both lawful and unlawful activities or to store both contraband and legally possessed material presents another significant issue.[173] Termed *commingling,* one computer can be used in multiple fashion, by multiple users, and be connected to multiple other machines. As such, investigations would naturally have to cross boundaries, invade computers that were not necessarily involved in the criminal act, and involve people who might be upset at the intrusiveness of the investigation.

Enforcement of the laws against child pornography often leads law enforcement officials to use sting operations over the Internet to catch pedophiles and find child pornography. As such, issues of entrapment have been raised by civil rights groups. In one case, postal inspectors posed as an organization that dealt in sexual freedom and hedonism. They seized several mail lists of individuals in raids of pornography distributors. Then they sent out a sexual attitude questionnaire and a membership application to people on the mail list. The suspect completed and mailed in the sexual survey with his membership fee, noting that he would like to receive additional material and that he was interested in sexual depictions of pre-teenagers. He was then mailed another survey and a list of "pen pals" who shared his sexual interests. The suspect began corresponding with one of these pen pals, an undercover postal inspector. Over a period of 27 months, the suspect received "two sexual attitude surveys, seven letters measuring his appetite for child pornography, and two sex catalogues."[174] He was assured in the mailings that the materials were completely legal. Over the course of the investigation, he corresponded eight times with the inspectors and eventually ordered the magazine "Boys Who Love Boys" from a Postal Service catalogue and a set of sexually explicit photographs of young boys from a Customs Service brochure. Upon verifying that the man had received the magazine, postal inspectors searched his home, found the illicit magazine, and arrested him for receiving it through the mail in violation of federal law. At trial, the man raised two defenses. First, he argued that he had been entrapped as a matter of law, but the court found sufficient evidence of predisposition to submit the issue to the jury. Second, he asserted that the government's conduct was outrageous, thus violating his due process rights. The jury rejected his defenses and found him guilty of knowingly receiving through the mail sexually explicit material depicting a minor. He appealed his conviction to the Eighth Circuit, which affirmed the trial court, holding that the government's actions did not constitute entrapment or outrageous governmental conduct, despite the government's lack of reasonable suspicion to target the man as a predisposed consumer.[175]

Summary

This chapter reviewed the nature and dynamics of exploitation, stalking, and obscenity on the World Wide Web. A variety of victimizations can occur online, many that are similar to their real-world counterparts. In particular, the nature of the victimizations included threats, obscene comments and intimations, and exposure to obscene and threatening materials, including pictures and other media. Most often, children and women are the primary targets of those who would commit cyberstalking and exploitation over the Internet. Young people report relatively high rates of victimization while online, and many youths report exposure to sexually oriented and obscene material that they did not wish to view. Most commonly, white males between the ages of 18 and 35 make up the majority of the offenders. Similar to most criminal victimizations, the victim and the offender had some type of prior relationship before the stalking or exploitation occurred. However, the percentage of stranger-on-stranger victimizations online was higher. Children are most commonly victimized online through unwanted exposure to sexually related material, sexual solicitations and approaches, harassment, bullying, and other distressing incidents. The rates of these types of offenses are larger than most people would think. Children rarely report such incidents to their parents or other authorities.

The laws and legislation targeting online stalking, exploitation, and obscenity are in their infancy, with many of these laws being challenged in the court system. The Supreme Court of the United States has had the opportunity to hear several cases regarding cybercrime laws. Many of the same issues involving noncybercrimes are being heard by the court. Many of the laws were overturned for being too vague and sweeping with too broad of a stroke. The federal government has responded with the passage of new laws and refinements of the old laws in an attempt to regulate and control content on the Internet, particularly the access of children to objectionable content. These types of crimes also present unique difficulties for law enforcement, including lack of expertise, lack of resources, and difficulty in tracking and prosecuting offenders. Cyberspace offers greater anonymity for offenders and permits offending to cross-state and international boundaries, making prosecution increasingly difficult. In the future, local law enforcement agencies are likely to see increased reports of cyberrelated cases of stalking, exploitation, and exposure to unwanted materials.

Review Questions

1. What are the various types of exploitation that can occur over the Internet?
2. What are the characteristics of the typical victims of Internet exploitation crimes?
3. What are the characteristics of the typical perpetrators of Internet exploitation crimes?
4. How common is it to become the victim of an Internet-involved crime in the area of exploitation or stalking?
5. What is cyberbullying, and how is it different from real-world bullying?
6. What is cyberstalking?
7. What types of offenses can occur that could be defined as cyberstalking?
8. What are the primary types or categories of stalkers?
9. What are the primary federal laws that target Internet exploitation?
10. What are the major Supreme Court cases on cyber exploitation?
11. How prevalent is child pornography on the Internet?
12. How do pedophiles and other child exploiters use the Internet to commit their crimes?
13. What role does child pornography play in child molestation?
14. How has the Internet changed the landscape of prostitution and the sex trade?
15. What is sex tourism?
16. What are the roles of the various law enforcement agencies in the area of cyber exploitation?
17. What are the primary challenges that law enforcement agencies face in investigating cyber exploitation?

Endnotes

1. Office for Victims of Crime (2001). *Internet Crimes Against Children.* Washington, DC: U.S. Department of Justice.

2. Youth Advocate Program International (1998). "Children for Sale: Youth Involved in Prostitution, Pornography and Sex Trafficking." *Youth Advocate Program International Report Vol. 3, No. 2, Summer.* Available on line: *http://www.yapi.org*

3. Office for Victims of Crime, *Internet Crimes Against Children.*

4. FINKELHOR, DAVID, MITCHELL, KIMBERLY J., and WOLAK, JANIS. (2000). *Online Victimization: A Report on the Nation's Youth.* Washington, DC: National Center for Missing and Exploited Children; WOLAK, JANIS, MITCHELL, KIMBERLY, and DAVID FINKELHOR. (2006). *Online Victimization of Youth: Five Years Later.* Washington DC: National Center for Missing and Exploited Children.

5. *Ibid.*

6. *Ibid.*

7. *Ibid.*

8. HOLT, T.J., and BOSSLER, A.M. (2009). "Examining the Applicability of Lifestyle-Routine Activities Theory for Cybercrime Victimization." *Deviant Behavior* 30(1): 1–25.

9. *http://www.ncpc.org/newsroom/current-campaigns/cyberbullying*

10. HINDJUA, SAMEER, and PATCHIN, JUSTIN W. (2009). *Bullying Beyond the Schoolyard: Preventing and Responding to Cyberbullying.* New York: Corwin Press.

11. *Ibid.*

12. *Ibid.*, p. 13.

13. *Ibid.*, p. 14.

14. *Ibid.*

15. *Ibid.*

16. Office of Victims of Crime (2002). *Strengthening Anti-Stalking Laws.* Washington, DC: National Institute of Justice. NCJ 189192.

17. *Ibid.*

18. *Ibid.*

19. *Ibid.*

20. Under California law, a person commits stalking if he or she "willfully, maliciously, and repeatedly follows or harasses another person and . . . makes a credible threat with the intent to place that person in reasonable fear for his or her safety, or the safety of his or her immediate family." The term "credible threat" includes "that performed through the use of an electronic communication device, or a threat implied by a pattern of conduct or a combination of verbal, written, or electronically communicated statements." "Electronic communication device" includes "telephones, cellular phones, computers, video recorders, fax machines, or pagers." Office of Victims of Crime, *Strengthening Anti-Stalking Laws.*

21. HOLT and BOSSLER, "Examining the Applicability of Lifestyle-Routine Activities Theory for Cybercrime Victimization," p. 12.

22. FINN, JERRY. (2004). "A Survey of Online Harassment at a University Campus." *Journal of Interpersonal Violence* 19(4): 468–483.

23. *Ibid.*, p. 12.

24. BAUM, KATRINA, CATALANO, SHANNAN, RAND, MICHAEL, and ROSE, KRISTINA. (2009). *Stalking Victimization in the United States.* Washington, DC: National Institute of Justice.

25. *Ibid.*

26. ZONA, M.A., PALAREA, R.E., and LANE, J.C. (1998). "Psychiatric Diagnosis and the Offender–Victim Typology of Stalking." In J.R. MELOY (ed.), *The Psychology of Stalking: Clinical and Forensic Perspectives.* San Diego, CA: Academic Press.

27. Office of Victims of Crime (2002). *National Victim Assistance Academy.* Washington, DC: Office of Justice Programs. Available on line: *http://www.ojp.usdoj.gov/ovc/assist/nvaa2002/chapter22_2sup.html*

28. PETHERICK, WAYNE. (2003). *Cyber-Stalking: Obsessional Pursuit and the Digital Criminal.* Court TV Crime Library. Available on line: *http://www.crimelibrary.com/criminal_mind/psychology/cyberstalking/1.html*

29. *Ibid.*, p. 21.

30. *Ibid.*, p. 33.

31. *http://www.mcafee.com/anti-virus/parents/contributors.asp*

32. PETHERICK, *Cyber-Stalking.*

33. Office of Victims of Crime, *National Victim Assistance Academy.*

34. Attorney General to the Vice President (1999). *1999 Report on Cyberstalking: A New Challenge for Law Enforcement and Industry.* Available on line: *http://www.usdoj.gov/criminal/cybercrime/cyberstalking.htm*

35. TJADEN, P., and THEONNES, N. (1998). *Stalking in America: Findings from the National Violence*

Against Women Survey. Washington, DC: U.S. Department of Justice, National Institute of Justice; Office of Victims of Crime, *National Victim Assistance Academy.*

36. *Ibid.*

37. *Ibid.*

38. D'OVIDO, ROBERT, and DOYLE, JAMES. (2003). "A Study on Cyberstalking: Understanding Investigative Hurdles." FBI Law Enforcement Bulletin 10-17.

39. See, for example, ZONA, M.A., SHARMA, K.K., and LANE, M.D. (1993). "A Comparative Study of Erotomanic and Obsessional Subjects in a Forensic Sample." *Journal of Forensic Sciences* 38: 894–903; GEBERTH, V.J. (October 1992). "Stalkers." *Law and Order*, pp. 138–143; WRIGHT, J.A., BURGESS, A.G., BURGESS, A.W., LASZLO, A.T., MCCRARY, G.O., and DOUGLAS, J.E. (1996). "A Typology of Interpersonal Stalking." *Journal of Interpersonal Violence* 11(4): 487–503; ZONA, PALAREA, and LANE, "Psychiatric Diagnosis and the Offender–Victim Typology of Stalking"; MULLEN, P.E. (1997). "Erotomanias: (Pathologies of Love) and Stalking." *Directions in Mental Health Counselling* 7(3): 3–15; and PETHERICK, *Cyber-Stalking*; Office of Victims of Crime, *National Victim Assistance Academy.*

40. Office of Victims of Crime, *National Victim Assistance Academy.*

41. *Ibid.*

42. Attorney General to the Vice President, *1999 Report on Cyberstalking.*

43. *Ibid.*

44. *Ibid.*

45. 18 U.S.C. 875(c).

46. 47 U.S.C. 223.

47. 18 U.S.C. 2261A.

48. CATHCART, R. (2008). "MySpace Is Said to Draw Subpoena in Hoax Case." *The New York Times.*

49. SURDIN, ASHLEY. (2009). "In Several States, A Push to Stem Cyber-Bullying." *The Washington Post.* Accessed *http://www.washingtonpost.com/wp-dyn/content/article/2008/12/31/AR2008123103067.html*

50. Computer Crime and Intellectual Property Section (CCIPS) (2000). *The Electronic Frontier: The Unlawful Conduct Involving the Use of the Internet: A Report of the President's Working Group on Unlawful Conduct on the Internet.* Washington, DC: Department of Justice. Available on line: *http://www.usdoj.gov/criminal/cybercrime/unlawful.htm*

51. Attorney General to the Vice President, *1999 Report on Cyberstalking.*

52. *Miller* v. *California,* 413 U.S. 15, held that (1) obscene material was not protected by the First Amendment; (2) the proper First Amendment standards to be applied by the states in determining whether particular material was obscene and subject to regulation, were (a) whether the average person, applying contemporary community standards, would find that the work, taken as a whole, appealed to the prurient interest, (b) whether the work depicted or described, in a patently offensive way, sexual conduct specifically defined by the applicable state law, as written or authoritatively construed, and (c) whether the work, taken as a whole, lacked serious literary, artistic, political, or scientific value; (3) there was no requirement that the material must be shown to be "utterly without redeeming social value"; (4) the requirement that state law, as written or construed, must specifically define the sexual conduct as to which depiction or description was proscribed, provided fair notice as to what public and commercial activities would bring prosecution, and (5) obscenity was to be determined by applying "contemporary community standards," not "national standards"—there thus having been no constitutional error in instructing the jury in the instant case to apply state community standards.

53. Public Law 105-314: The Child Protection and Sexual Predator Punishment Act of 1998, October 30, 1998.

54. (Child Abuse Act), 18 U.S.C. 2423(b).

55. 18 U.S.C. § 2423(b) Travel with intent to engage in illicit sexual conduct. A person who travels in interstate commerce or travels into the United States, or a United States citizen or an alien admitted for permanent residence in the United States who travels in foreign commerce, for the purpose of engaging in any illicit sexual conduct with another person shall be fined under this title or imprisoned not more than 30 years, or both. (c) Engaging in illicit sexual conduct in foreign places. Any United States citizen or alien admitted for permanent residence who travels in foreign commerce, and engages in any illicit sexual conduct with another person shall be fined under this title or imprisoned not more than 30 years, or both.

56. 18 U.S.C. § 2260.

57. Title 18 Part I, Chapter 110, Section 2252.

58. Child Pornography Prevention Act 18 U.S.C. § 2252A.

   (a) Any person who

   (1) knowingly mails, or transports or ships in interstate or foreign commerce by any means, including by computer, any child pornography;

   (2) knowingly receives or distributes

   (A) any child pornography that has been mailed, or shipped or transported in interstate or foreign commerce by any means, including by computer; or

   (B) any material that contains child pornography that has been mailed, or shipped or transported in interstate or foreign commerce by any means, including by computer;

   (3) knowingly reproduces any child pornography for distribution through the mails, or in interstate or foreign commerce by any means, including by computer;

   (4) either

   (A) in the special maritime and territorial jurisdiction of the United States, or on any land or building owned by, leased to, or otherwise used by or under the control of the United States Government, or in the Indian country, knowingly sells or possesses with the intent to sell any child pornography; or

   (B) knowingly sells or possesses with the intent to sell any child pornography that has been mailed, or shipped or transported in interstate or foreign commerce by any means, including by computer, or that was produced using materials that have been mailed, or shipped or transported in interstate or foreign commerce by any means, including by computer; or

   (5) either

   (A) in the special maritime and territorial jurisdiction of the United States, or on any land or building owned by, leased to, or otherwise used by or under the control of the United States Government, or in the Indian country, knowingly possesses any book, magazine, periodical, film, videotape, computer disk, or any other material that contains an image of child pornography; or

   (B) knowingly possesses any book, magazine, periodical, film, videotape, computer disk, or any other material that contains an image of child pornography that has been mailed, or shipped or transported in interstate or foreign commerce by any means, including by computer, or that was produced using materials that have been mailed, or shipped or transported in interstate or foreign commerce by any means, including by computer, shall be punished as provided in subsection (b).

   (b)

   (1) Whoever violates, or attempts or conspires to violate, paragraphs (1), (2), (3), or (4) of subsection (a) shall be fined under this title or imprisoned not more than 15 years, or both, but, if such person has a prior conviction under this chapter, chapter 109A, or chapter 117, or under the laws of any State relating to aggravated sexual abuse, sexual abuse, or abusive sexual conduct involving a minor or ward, or the production, possession, receipt, mailing, sale, distribution, shipment, or transportation of child pornography, such person shall be fined under this title and imprisoned for not less than 5 years nor more than 30 years.

   (2) Whoever violates, or attempts or conspires to violate, subsection (a)(5) shall be fined under this title or imprisoned not more than five years, or both, but, if such person has a prior conviction under this chapter, chapter 109A, or chapter 117, or under the laws of any State relating to aggravated sexual abuse, sexual abuse, or abusive sexual conduct involving a minor or ward, or the production, possession, receipt, mailing, sale, distribution, shipment, or transportation of child pornography, such person shall be fined under this title and imprisoned for not less than two years nor more than ten years.

(c) It shall be an affirmative defense to a charge of violating paragraphs (1), (2), (3), or (4) of subsection (a) that

(1) the alleged child pornography was produced using an actual person or persons engaging in sexually explicit conduct;

(2) each such person was an adult at the time the material was produced; and

(3) the defendant did not advertise, promote, present, describe, or distribute the material in such a manner as to convey the impression that it is or contains a visual depiction of a minor engaging in sexually explicit conduct.

(d) Affirmative Defense. It shall be an affirmative defense to a charge of violating subsection (a)(5) that the defendant

(1) possessed less than three images of child pornography; and

(2) promptly and in good faith, and without retaining or allowing any person, other than a law enforcement agency, to access any image or copy thereof

(A) took reasonable steps to destroy each such image; or

(B) reported the matter to a law enforcement agency and afforded that agency access to each such image.

59. 18 U.S.C. § 2251; 18 U.S.C. § 2256.

60. 18 U.S.C. § 2422.

61. 18 U.S.C. § 2423.

62. 18 U.S.C. § 2425.

63. 18 U.S.C. § 2251.

64. 18 U.S.C. § 2251(b).

65. 18 U.S.C. § 2251(c).

66. 18 U.S.C. § 2251(d).

67. 18 U.S.C. § 2252.

68. 18 U.S.C. § 2252(c).

69. 18 U.S.C. §§ 1301, 1302.

70. 18 U.S.C. § 2425.

71. *Ibid.*

72. 18 U.S.C. § 1470.

73. 18 U.S.C. § 2427.

74. An attempt provision was added to 18 U.S.C. 2422(a), Coercion and Enticement and 18 U.S.C. 2421, Transportation generally.

75. The Act clarifies that in 18 U.S.C. 2422(b), Coercion and enticement of a minor, coercion can be through use of the mail, or any facility of interstate or foreign commerce, and increases the maximum sentence to 15 years.

76. The Act amends 18 U.S.C. § § 2251(a) and (b), Production of Child Pornography by expanding the jurisdictional reach of the federal child pornography production statutes. The existing statute required the knowing transportation, transmission or distribution of the child pornography. The amendment creates a jurisdictional element similar to the possession, receipt, and transmission statutes which are violated if the individual, e.g., possesses child pornography that was made with materials (e.g., the paper, the computer, the diskettes, the camera) that had been transported in interstate or foreign commerce. The amendment thus increases the possibility of federal prosecution for the direct abuse of the child in the production of child pornography.

77. The Act increased the maximum statutory penalty for the following offenses: 18 U.S.C. § 2422(a) [from 5 to 10 years], 18 U.S.C. § 2422(b) [from 10 to 15 years)], 18 U.S.C. § 2423(a) [from 10 to 15 years], and 18 U.S.C. § 2423(b) [from 10 to 15 years]. In addition, an individual convicted of 18 U.S.C. § 2244 involving a victim under the age of 12 can receive double the maximum statutory penalty, under the new Section 2244(c).

78. Death Penalty. If a minor under the age 14 dies as a result of the commission of an offense under 18 U.S.C. § § 2251, 2422, or 2423, the defendant may receive the death penalty under a new provision, 18 U.S.C. § 3559(d), Death or Imprisonment for Crimes Against Children This provision was added, in part, to increase penalties for "snuff" films involving minors.

79. Criminal forfeiture, under Section 2253, and civil forfeiture, under Section 2254, are now available for offenses under 18 U.S.C. § § 2251, 2251A, 2252, 2252A, 2260, 2421, 2422, and 2423. Civil remedies, under Section 2255, are now available for offenses under the aforementioned statutes and Sections 2241(c), 2242, and 2243. See below under "Forfeiture Provisions." The forfeiture provisions should provide incentives for increased investigative work by local, state, and federal law enforcement in all cases involving child pornography, luring and transportation of minors, and trafficking of women and minors for prostitution cases. The civil remedy provisions may be useful in providing relief for victims.

80. The Protection of Children from Sexual Predators Act amends the Victims of Child Abuse

Act of 1990 (42 U.S.C. 13001 et seq.) to require on line service providers to report evidence of child pornography offenses. The measure also amends 18 U.S.C. § 2702(b) of the Electronic Communications Privacy Act of 1986 to create an exception to the general statutory bar against a public provider's voluntary disclosure of customer communications to third parties.

81. 521 U.S. 844 (1997).

82. Title 47 U. S. C. A. § 223(a)(1)(B)(ii).

83. Title 47 U. S. C. A. § 223(d).

84. 535 U.S. 234 (2002).

85. 18 U.S.C. § 2256.

86. 535 U.S. 564 (2002).

87. 47 U.S.C. § 231(a)(1).

88. *Miller* v. *California,* 413 U.S. 15 where obscene material is judged based on: (a) whether "the average person, applying contemporary community standards" would find that the work, taken as a whole, appeals to the prurient interest, (b) whether the work depicts or describes, in a patently offensive way, sexual conduct specifically defined by the applicable state law, and (c) whether the work, taken as a whole, lacks serious literary, artistic, political, or scientific value.

89. No. 02-361 (2003).

90. Public Law No: 108-21. The PROTECT Act Prohibits: (1) making a visual depiction that is a digital image, computer image, or computer-generated image of, or that is indistinguishable from an image of, a minor engaging in specified sexually explicit conduct; (2) knowingly advertising, promoting, presenting, distributing, or soliciting through the mails or in commerce, including by computer, any material that is or contains an obscene visual depiction of a minor engaging in sexually explicit conduct or a visual depiction of an actual minor engaging in such conduct; (3) knowingly distributing, offering, sending, or providing to a minor any such visual depiction using the mails or commerce, including by computer, for purposes of inducing or persuading a minor to participate in an illegal act; and (4) knowingly producing, distributing, receiving, or possessing with intent to distribute a visual depiction of any kind, including a drawing, cartoon, sculpture, or painting, that, under specified circumstances, depicts a minor engaging in sexually explicit conduct and is obscene, or depicts an image that is or appears to be of a minor engaging in such conduct and such depiction lacks serious literary, artistic, political,

or scientific value. Allows as an affirmative defense to the charge of virtual child pornography only that: (1) the alleged pornography was produced using only actual persons all of whom were adults; or (2) the alleged pornography was not produced using any actual minors.

91. OSANKA, FRANKLIN M., and JOHANN, SARA LEE. (1989). *Sourcebook on Pornography.* Lexington, MA: Lexington Books.

92. REISMAN, JUDITH A. (1994). "Child Pornography in Erotic Magazines, Social Awareness, and Self-Censorship." In DOLF ZILLMAN, JENNINGS BRYANT, and ALTHEA C. HUSTON (eds.), *Media, Children, and the Family: Social Scientific, Psychodynamic, and Clinical Perspectives.* Hillsdale, NJ: Lawrence Erlbaum and Associates, pp. 313–326.

93. *Ibid.*

94. *Ibid.*

95. HENLEY, JOHN. (September 1, 1996). "The Observer Campaign to Clean up the Internet: Hackers Called in as Cybercops to Drive Out Porn." *Observer.*

96. *http://enough.org/inside.php?id=2UXKJWRY8*

97. *Ibid.*

98. SCHUIJER, JAN, and ROSSEN, BENJAMIN. (1992). "The Trade in Child Pornography." *Issues in Child Abuse Accusations* 4(2): 55–107.

99. SEVEL, JAMES. (1999). U.S. Customs Service Agent, Cyber Smuggling Center. Personal interview.

100. LANNING, KENNETH V., and BURGESS, ANN W. (1989). "Child Pornography and Sex Rings." In DOLF ZILLMAN and JENNINGS BRYANT (eds.), *Pornography: Research Advances and Policy Considerations.* Hillsdale, NJ: Lawrence Erlbaum and Associates, pp. 235–258.

101. *Ibid.*

102. CAMPAGNA, DANIELS S., and POFFENBERGER, DONALD L. (1988). *The Sexual Trafficking in Children: An Investigation of the Child Sex Trade.* Dover, MA: Auburn House Publishing.

103. *Ibid.;* LANNING and BURGESS, "Child Pornography and Sex Rings."

104. *Ibid.*

105. CAMPAGNA and POFFENBERGER, *The Sexual Trafficking in Children.*

106. *Ibid.*

107. DURKIN, KEITH F. (1997). "Misuse of the Internet by Pedophiles: Implications for Law Enforcement and Probation Practice." *Federal Probation* 61(3): 14–18.

108. *Ibid.*

109. LANNING and BURGESS, "Child Pornography and Sex Rings."

110. SEVEL, U.S. Customs Service Agent, Cyber Smuggling Center. Personal interview.
111. U.S. Attorney General's Office (1986). *Final Report of the Attorney General's Commission on Pornography.* Nashville, TN: Rutledge Hill Press.
112. *Ibid.*
113. *Ibid.*
114. *Ibid.*
115. LANNING and BURGESS, "Child Pornography and Sex Rings."
116. SEVEL, U.S. Customs Service Agent, Cyber Smuggling Center. Personal interview.
117. *http://www.ice.gov/partners/predator/index.htm*
118. *http://www.fbi.gov/hq/cid/cac/initiatives.htm#taskforce*
119. CLINE, VICTOR B. (1994). "Pornography Effects: Empirical and Clinical Evidence." In DOLF ZILLMAN, JENNINGS BRYANT, and ALTHEA C. HUSTON (eds.) *Media, Children, and the Family: Social Scientific, Psychodynamic, and Clinical Perspectives.* Hillsdale, NJ: Lawrence Erlbaum and Associates, pp. 229–248; LYONS, JOHN S., ANDERSON, RACHEL L., and LARSON, DAVID B. (1994). "A Systematic Review of the Effects of Aggressive and Nonaggressive Pornography." In DOLF ZILLMAN, JENNINGS BRYANT, and ALTHEA C. HUSTON (eds.), *Media, Children, and the Family: Social Scientific, Psychodynamic, and Clinical Perspectives.* Hillsdale, NJ: Lawrence Erlbaum and Associates, pp. 271–312; MALAMUTH, NEIL M., and DONNERSTEIN, EDWARD (eds.). (1984). *Pornography and Sexual Aggression.* Orlando, FL: Academic Press; MARSHALL, W.L. (1989). "Pornography and Sex Offenses." In DOLF ZILLMAN and JENNINGS BRYANT (eds.), *Pornography: Research Advances and Policy Considerations.* Hillsdale, NJ: Lawrence Erlbaum and Associates, pp. 185–214; OSANKA and JOHANN, *Sourcebook on Pornography*; U.S. Attorney General's Office, *Final Report of the Attorney General's Commission on Pornography.*
120. SHOWERS, ROBERT. (1994). "Research, Public Policy, and Law: Combination for Change." In DOLF ZILLMAN, JENNINGS BRYANT, and ALTHEA C. HUSTON (eds.), *Media, Children, and the Family: Social Scientific, Psychodynamic, and Clinical Perspectives.* Hillsdale, NJ: Lawrence Erlbaum and Associates, pp. 327–339.
121. *Ibid.*
122. *Ibid.*
123. WOLAK, J., MITCHELL, K., and FINKELHOR, D. (2003). *Internet Sex Crimes Against Minors: The Response of Law Enforcement.* Washington, DC: Office of Juvenile Justice and Delinquency Prevention.
124. CLINE, "Pornography Effects"; LYONS, ANDERSON, and LARSON, "A Systematic Review of the Effects of Aggressive and Nonaggressive Pornography"; MARSHALL, "Pornography and Sex Offenses"; OSANKA and JOHANN, *Sourcebook on Pornography*; SHOWERS, "Research, Public Policy, and Law."
125. CLINE, "Pornography Effects"; LYONS, ANDERSON, and LARSON, "A Systematic Review of the Effects of Aggressive and Nonaggressive Pornography"; MARSHALL, "Pornography and Sex Offenses."
126. *Ibid.*
127. MARSHALL, "Pornography and Sex Offenses."
128. CLINE, "Pornography Effects"; LYONS, ANDERSON, and LARSON, "A Systematic Review of the Effects of Aggressive and Nonaggressive Pornography"; MARSHALL, "Pornography and Sex Offenses."
129. MARSHALL, "Pornography and Sex Offenses."
130. *Ibid.*, p. 114; DURKIN, K.F., and BRYANT, C.D. (1999). "Propagandizing Pederasty. A Thematic Analysis of the On-Line Exculpatory Accounts of Unrepentant Pedophiles." *Deviant Behavior* 20: 103–127.
131. *Ibid.*
132. JENKINS, P. (2001). *Beyond Tolerance: Child Pornography on the Internet.* New York: New York University Press.
133. *Ibid.*
134. *Ibid.*
135. CLINE, VICTOR B. (1996). "Testimony on Child Pornography Prevention." U.S. Senate Judiciary Committee Hearing on S 1237, "Child Pornography Prevention Act of 1995," 10 AM, Rm 226, Dirksen Senate Office Bldg., June 4, 1996.
136. *Ibid.*
137. DOUGLAS, EMILY M., and FINKELHOR, DAVID. (2005). "Childhood Sexual Abuse Factsheet." Available on line: *http://www.unh.edu/ccrc/factsheet/pdf/CSA-FS20.pdf*
138. PRENTKY, ROBERT A., KNIGHT, RAYMOND A., and LEE, AUSTIN F.S. (1997). *Child Sexual Molestation: Research Issues.* Washington, DC: National Institute of Justice.
139. ABEL, G.G., BECKER, J.V., MITTELMAN, M.S., CUNNINGHAM-RATHNER, J., ROULEAU, J.L., and MURPHY, W.D. (1987). "Self-Reported Sex Crimes of Nonincarcerated Paraphilics." *Journal of Interpersonal Violence* 2:3–25.
140. O'NEILL, M. (2001). *Prostitution and Feminism.* London: Polity Press.

141. SHARP, K., and EARLE, S. (2003). "Cyberpunters and Cyberwhores: Prostitution on the Internet." In Y. JEWKES (ed.), *Dot Cons. Crime, Deviance and Identity on the Internet.* Portland, OR: Willan Publishing, pp. 36–52.

142. *Ibid.*

143. HOLT, T.J., and BLEVINS, K.R. (2007). "Examining Sex Work from the Client's Perspective: Assessing Johns Using Online Data." *Deviant Behavior* 28: 333–354; SOOTHHILL, KEITH, and SANDERS, TEELA. (2005). "The Geographical Mobility, Preferences and Pleasures of Prolific Punters: a Demonstration Study of the Activities of Prostitutes' Clients." *Sociological Research On-Line* 10(1). Retrieved October 10, 2005 from *http://www.socresonline. org.uk/10/1/soothill.html*; HOLT, THOMAS J., BLEVINS, KRISTIE R., and KUHNS, JOSEPH B. (2008). "Examining the Displacement Practices of Johns with On-line Data." *Journal of Criminal Justice* 36: 522–528.

144. *Ibid.*, HOLT and BLEVINS, "Examining Sex Work from the Client's Perspective."

145. *Ibid.*, p. 150.

146. International Labor Organization (2005). "A Global Alliance against Forced Labour: Global report under the follow-up to the ILO Declaration on Fundamental Principles and Rights at Work 2005." Report I (B), International Labour Conference 93rd session 2005, Geneva, 2005, pp. 12, 15.

147. *Ibid.*

148. *Ibid.*

149. ALBANESE, JAY. (2007). *Commercial Sexual Exploitation of Children: What Do We Know and What Do We Do About It?* Washington, DC: National Institute of Justice.

150. GIORDANELLA, HEATHER C. (1998). "Comment: Status of 2423(B): Prosecuting United States Nationals for Sexually Exploiting Children in Foreign Countries." *Temple International and Comparative Law Journal* 12: 133.

151. RAO, NINA. (1999). "Sex Tourism in South Asia." *International Journal of Contemporary Hospitality Management* 11: 96–99, University Press.

152. *Ibid.*

153. JEFFREYS, SHEILA. (1999). "Globalizing Sexual Exploitation: Sex Tourism and the Traffic in Women." *Leisure Studies* 18: 179–196.

154. RAO, "Sex Tourism in South Asia."

155. Captive Daughters (1999). "Sex Tours—A Learning Model." Retrieved from *http://www. captivedaughters.org/ByandAboutCD/CDdocume nts/cdfactsheet1.htm*

156. STEINMAN, KATHY J. (2002). "Sex Tourism and the Child: Latin America's and the United States' Failure to Prosecute Sex Tourists." *Hastings Women's Law Journal* 13: 53.

157. *Ibid.*

158. *Ibid.*

159. *Ibid.*

160. BEVILACQUA, ELIZABETH. (1998). "Note: Child Sex Tourism and Child Prostitution in Asia: What Can Be Done to Protect the Rights of Children Abroad Under International Law?" *ILSA Journal of International & Comparative Law* 5: 171.

161. *Ibid.*

162. Immigration and Customs Enforcement (March 2007). "Las Vegas Man Pleads Guilty to Sex Tourism." *http://www.ice.gov/pi/news/newsreleases/ articles/070309cleveland.htm*

163. GIORDANELLA, "Comment: Status of 2423(B)"

164. ABBUGAO, MARTIN. (October 1996). "Briton Child-Sex Tour Organiser Jailed for 16 Years." *Agence France Presse.* Retrieved from *http://www. vachss.com/help_text/archive/ sex_tourism_briton_jailed.htm*

165. Associated Press (November 2002). "Businessman Sentenced on Sexual Abuse Charge." Retrieved from *http://www.vachss.com/help_text/a2/n_ bredimus.com*

166. Computer Crime and Intellectual Property Section, *The Electronic Frontier.*

167. *www.cybertipline.com*

168. Computer Crime and Intellectual Property Section, *The Electronic Frontier.*

169. *https://postalinspectors.uspis.gov/ investigations/MailFraud/fraudschemes/ce/ CE.aspx*

170. *http://www.usdoj.gov/criminal/ceos/obscenity.htm*

171. Computer Crime and Intellectual Property Section, *The Electronic Frontier.*

172. *Ibid.*, p. 124.

173. *Ibid.*

174. PEREZ, CYNTHIA. (1999). "*United States* v. *Jacobson:* Are Child Pornography Stings Creative Law Enforcement or Entrapment?" 46: 235.

175. *Ibid.*

CHAPTER 8

Anarchy and Hate on the World Wide Web

CHAPTER OBJECTIVES

After completing this chapter, you should be able to

- Legally define a hate crime and describe how white supremacist groups use the Internet to spread their message of hate.
- Explain the relationship between left-wing groups and "special interest or single-issue extremist" groups.
- Describe ALF and ELF, and provide examples of each groups' recent terrorist activities in the United States.
- Describe some of the techniques that right-wing hate groups use to spread their propaganda.
- Discuss the primary issues associated with the USA PATRIOT Act, and list the four traditional tools of surveillance that have been expanded within the act.
- Explain the conflicting roles and activities observed within law enforcement pertaining to investigation versus intelligence gathering.

INTRODUCTION

The rise of the Internet over the last decade has paralleled some of the greatest milestones in communications history. Along with such great strides in bringing the world together, the frightening aspect of accessing information and propaganda that tests the very limits of the U.S. Constitution has arrived. With just a few keystrokes, an individual can have access to all forms of pornography, bomb-making instructions, and poison recipes and a plethora of extremist ideologies expressing everything from radical religious cults to clandestine organized crime groups. The Internet now makes it possible to view all sorts of material heretofore not easily found in the public venue. Many visitors to radical Web sites are shocked by not only the vast quantity of sexually oriented material but also the open advocacy of violence against specific groups of people. One of the more interesting multimedia promotions that are found on the Internet arises from the ashes of Nazism and the far right.

DIGITAL HATE

Right-wing extremism represents a movement that promotes whites, especially Northern Europeans and their descendants, as intellectually and morally superior to other races.[1] It is not coincidental that as these groups have grown in strength, so have the number of reported hate crimes. Hate crimes and hate incidents are major issues for all Americans because of their unique impact on victims as well as the community. Hate crimes are often very brutal or injurious, and victims are not only hurt physically but also are emotionally traumatized and terrified. Others in the community that share the same victim's characteristic may also feel victimized and vulnerable, posing a potential escalation in an attempt to retaliate for the original offense.

In the past, police officers have not been adequately trained to handle such incidents, treating them as routine assaults or vandalism. However, with new federal legislation has come the development of the National Institute Against Hate Crimes and Terrorism, which is located at the Simon Wiesenthal Center in Los Angeles. The institute provides training for teams of criminal justice professionals from the same jurisdiction to combat hate crimes. Their goal is to provide new strategic approaches to combating hate crimes based on a new understanding of the unique elements that differentiate them from other acts. The center has been highly successful, training a range of participants from law enforcement agencies across the country and providing an ongoing support center for follow-up communication, program evaluation, and professional development via Web site updates and videoconferences.[2]

Legal definitions of hate crimes vary. The federal definition of hate crimes addresses civil rights violations under 18 U.S.C. Section 245. A hate crime is a criminal offense committed against persons, property, or society that is motivated, in whole or in part, by an offender's bias against an individual's or a group's perceived race, religion, ethnic/national origin, gender, age, disability, or sexual orientation.[3] Most states have a hate crime statute that provides enhanced penalties for crimes in which victims are selected because of perpetrator's bias against a victim's perceived race, religion, or ethnicity. Some states also classify as hate crimes those in which a victim is selected based on a perception of his/her sexual orientation, gender, or disability. In some states, the passage of a hate crime statute has been very controversial, as politicians have debated the constitutionality of enhanced penalties based on a suspect's association with an extremist group, or the inclusion of homosexuality as a protected class.

White Supremacy, Hate, and the Internet

Many white supremacist groups have used the Internet to recruit potential new members and spread their message of hate. There are thousands of Web sites, social networking pages, and videos posted in file-sharing sites that can be attributed to extremist organizations that incite racial hatred and religious intolerance as well as terrorism and bomb making (see Box 8.1). One of the more popular of these sites is *www.stormfront.org,* which has over 135,000 members and thousands of posts every day.[4] More disturbing is the effort directed by many of these groups to attract young people into their ranks. Based in part on links to other social youth movements involving music and dress (e.g., skinheads, black cults, and heavy metal music), aggressive recruitment on college campuses and the development of Web pages, videos, games, and other materials designed to attract young people are now quite common. In fact, the stormfront Web site has a page on the popular social networking site FaceBook as a means to help recruit and connect members. Hate groups are even creating their own social networking sites, such as "New Saxon," which is a "Social Networking site for people of European descent" produced by the neo-Nazi group the National Socialist Movement.[5] In addition, white-power rock concerts are often sponsored by extremist groups such as the National Alliance and the World Church of the Creator. These concerts provide face-to-face opportunities for meeting and recruitment.

White supremacist groups have also created sophisticated computer games aimed at attracting teenagers. *Ethnic Cleansing,* the most high-tech game of its kind, encourages players to kill blacks, Jews, and Hispanics as they run through urban ghettos and subway environments. In the game, players can dress in Ku Klux Klan (KKK) robes and carry a noose. Every time a black enemy is shot, he emits a monkey-like squeal, while Jewish characters shout "Oy vey!" when they are killed.[6] Quite predictably, the game has spurred significant controversy between the media and game developers versus censor advocates. Very little can be done to ban the game since many other video games are designed to allow enthusiasts to create new levels and characters, while free software tools enable programmers to build new platforms.

These types of games and directed recruitment efforts have been effective tools in swelling the ranks of some extremist organizations.[7] According to one skinhead source, young people represent the future: "They are the front-line warriors in the battle for white supremacy."[8] In fact, white power groups in the United States became more active in 2008 and 2009 with the election of the first African American president, Barack Obama.

In fact, white power groups in the United States became more active in 2008 and 2009 as a result of the election of Barack Obama. The increase in supremacist activity has taken two different forms. On the one hand, many white racist groups responded to the election of the first African American president with disdain and even death threats. In October 2009, agents from the Bureau of Alcohol, Tobacco, and Firearms broke up a plot by two neo-Nazi skinheads to assassinate Obama and shoot or decapitate 88 African Americans.[9] On the other hand, some noted white power authorities believe that Obama's nomination and election will become a rallying point for their cause. David Duke, noted white nationalist and former Grand Wizard of the Knights of the Klu Klux Klan, described the Obama election as a "black flag for white America" and likened his nomination to the discovery of a serious medical problem, "Obama is like a big dark spot on your arm that finally sends you to the doctor."[10]

BOX 8.1
Resistance Records

Resistance Records is a racist recording label and Internet site that is part of the National Alliance. The National Alliance is a right-wing white supremacist organization founded by the author of the Turner Diaries, William Pierce. The National Alliance is one of the largest and most well-known racist organizations and has gone to great lengths to utilize the Internet. Resistance Records is constructed to appeal to the youth of America. The violent music and games on the site not only attract racist teens but also the mainstream punk/alternative crowd. The racist propaganda portrayed on the site and in the music and games will have some effect on the beliefs of the individuals who frequent the site at *www.resistance.com.*

TERRORIST EXTREMISTS FROM THE LEFT

The far right is not the only set of terrorists that pose a threat domestically. The traditional left-wing extremists were replaced in the 1990s by the right-wing ones as the most dangerous domestic terrorists, but subgroups of the left have developed that are potentially just as dangerous as the right and arguably more economically destructive.[11] A resurgence of anarchist groups, including those associated with Anarchist International, has dramatically increased since September 11, 2001. Most of these groups are relatively small and confine their activities to "rallies" against what they see as incursions of the government into the individual rights of people. Several "Black Bloc" rallies in protest of the USA PATRIOT Act and the increased security associated with terrorism prevention have been observed in several cities. However, unlike the anarchist groups of the 1960s (e.g., Weather Underground, Symbionese Liberation Army), there have been few violent acts attributed to these newly formed groups.

Those aspiring to extreme left movements are best observed in the modern ecoterrorists.[12] The FBI defines ecoterrorism as the use or threatened use of violence of a criminal nature against innocent victims or property by an environmentally oriented national group for environmental–political reasons, or aimed at an audience beyond the target, often of a symbolic nature.[13]

While these groups are definitely liberal and considered left-wing extremists, they are most often referred to as "special-interest or single-issue extremists."[14] Special-interest extremists are seen as different from traditional right- and left-wing extremists because they are not trying to effect a more widespread political change, but seek to resolve specific issues. These issues include animal rights and environmentalism on the left, and prolife, antigay, and antigenetic on the right.[15] In attempting to understand these groups, it is important not to be clouded by the political rhetoric of the left or the right. These groups attempt to change one aspect of the social or political arena through terrorism.[16]

Many special interest groups try to claim that they are not terrorist groups because they do not harm any animal, human or nonhuman, by their actions. Unfortunately, they often enjoy a sympathetic reception by many liberal affluent Americans unaware of the true actions of these groups. While in the United States, to date, no murders have been directly attributed to environmental activists, they have used intimidation tactics on those they see as enemies and have caused millions of dollars in damage. The FBI estimates that the Animal Liberation Front(ALF) and the Earth Liberation Front(ELF) have committed more than 600 criminal acts in the United States since 1996, which has resulted in damages that exceeded $43 million.[17] Unfortunately, other single-issue groups like those associated with the antiabortion movement have been very violent, having been responsible for the murder of numerous doctors and nurses that perform such operations.

Contrary to the claims of their partisans that ecogroups are not terrorists because they have not killed or injured any living being, making their acts mere vandalism and not terrorism, their use of arson and pipe bombs challenges their claims of innocence. It is also obvious that their intent is to influence policy by intimidation and coercion.[18]

Moreover, subcommittee Chairman Rep. Scott McInnis (R-Colorado) claims that "these are hardened criminals. They are dangerous, they are well-funded, they are savvy, sophisticated and stealthy, and if their violence continues to escalate, it is only a matter of time before their parade of terror results in a lost human life."[19] The loss of human life has already happened abroad, with the murder of Dutch politician Pym Fortuyn by an animal rights extremist.[20]

ELF and ALF

The ALF and the ELF are arguably the most central and active groups of liberal activism today. The ALF, established in Great Britain in the mid-1970s, is a loosely organized movement committed to ending the abuse and exploitation of animals. The American branch of the ALF began its operations in the late 1970s. Similar to the right wing's leaderless resistance, individuals become members of ALF simply by engaging in "direct action" against those who utilize animals for research or economic gain. Direct action is generally defined by the group as criminal activity, which is aimed at causing economic loss or destroying company operations. The ALF activists have engaged in a steadily growing campaign of illegal activity against fur companies, mink farms, restaurants, and animal research centers.[21] In fact, members of ALF were arrested by FBI agents in 2006 as part of Operation Backfire, which was an attempt to eliminate domestic terrorism. These individuals were responsible for acts of arson against meat-processing plants, lumber companies, and a ski center in multiple states over a five-year period.[22]

ELF emerged from a group called Earth First! This group developed in Arizona in 1980 after a series of acts of sabotage over the prior decade. Some of the first actions taken were in the early 1970s by University of Arizona students known as "The Eco-Raiders," who protested the spread of the city into the Sonoran Desert by vandalizing construction sites. In 1975, a fictional account of ecological saboteurs who chopped down billboards and plotted to blow up Glen Canyon Dam, called the *The Monkey Wrench Gang,* was published by Edward Abbey. Further, two homes built in the Tucson Mountains were knocked down by a hot-wired bulldozer in 1977. Subsequent acts, such as those performed by saboteurs who sawed through the supporting poles of four billboards just south of Tucson in 1979, toppling them, seemed to have been inspired by *The Monkey Wrench Gang.*[23]

In 1980, five radicals lead by Tucson resident Dave Foreman created Earth First! and began a nine-year campaign of civil disobedience and *monkey wrenching* (a term used to describe vandalism against active construction and lumbering locations). This was the group who started the practice of "tree spiking," or the insertion of metal or ceramic spikes in trees designed to damage saws and potentially injure workers.[24] The acts of tree spiking are exceedingly dangerous, as chainsaws buck back, often uncontrollably, against the user. In 1992, dissatisfied members who did not wish to abandon illegal actions when others wanted to mainstream Earth First! founded the ELF in Brighton, England. This group has gone on to claim responsibility for dozens of acts of ecoterrorism throughout the United States, starting in 1996. One of the more infamous examples of their acts was the $12 million in damages created when they set fire to a Vail, Colorado, ski lodge in 1998.[25]

ELF and ALF are similar groups committing similar acts, the difference being that one focuses on the environment and the other animal rights. Members of these groups consistently use improvised incendiary devices equipped with crude but effective timing mechanisms.[26] While the ALF and ELF are the driving force for the liberal/environmental terrorist groups, there are other attached groups that also commit illegal activities, as well as the groups that are legitimate and nonviolent.

As we stated in the preceding chapter, cyberterrorism is an issue that has gained much attention in recent years. This type of terrorism is seen as unlawful attacks or threats of attacks on computers, networks, and the information stored therein for the purpose of intimidation or coercion of a government or its people for the furtherance of a political or social goal.[27] Many officials fear that domestic terrorist groups will crack into important systems and create severe damage or steal classified information.

While the government has responded to this threat with the development of new legislation to combat it, such as the Cyberterrorism Preparedness Act of 2002 and parts of the USA PATRIOT Act, the Internet poses a much more serious and widespread issue in its ability to unite people and spread information.[28]

DOMESTIC TERRORISTS IN CYBERSPACE

The domestic terrorist groups that pose a threat in the United States are strongly entrenched in cyberspace. Neo-Nazis, animal rights groups, militias, Black Blocs, and hate mongers all have not only Web sites but clubs, posting boards, news groups, and all other types of Internet communities.

The danger the Internet poses with domestic terrorist groups is that it allows for a level of communication between separate groups that traditionally has not occurred. Also, it allows for wider recruitment. For instance, neo-Nazi skinheads around the world can talk in chat rooms, and right-wing groups, which in the past would not have interacted in the outside world, find camaraderie in cyberspace. This camaraderie will eventually solidify and pass out into the real world, where it will pose a threat of a larger, more united group. People who would never have gone to a skinhead rally or a People for the Ethical Treatment of Animals (PETA) demonstration now feel free to explore the Web sites of these groups and participate in their chat rooms in anonymity. Unfortunately, once they have become involved in these online communities, they are more likely to bring their participation out of cyberspace. These Internet sites pose many potential areas for concern.

Dehumanize, Desensitize, and Demonize

Several Web sites use images, music, games, and the like to spread their propaganda. By using these types of paraphernalia the groups can appeal to people who do not necessarily share their particular beliefs. Once a person is exposed to these ideas for a long enough time they begin to seem normal.

One of the more effective and therefore more dangerous techniques these sites use to dehumanize the "enemy" or desensitize the consumer toward violence is computer games that are filled with extremist beliefs. For example, the game Border Patrol allows players to shoot Mexicans attempting to illegally cross the border into the United States.[29] This new trend of racist, hate-filled computer games has gained much attention and concern. It is believed that exposure to the racist propaganda in the games coming into the mind under the cover of the action will serve to desensitize individuals to the horrors of hate that these groups preach. This follows from the idea that the youth of America have become desensitized to violence from more acceptable games, movies, and television. While the violence prevalent in modern media doesn't necessarily lead to violence by the consumer, it does seem that people are not as affected by the sight of true violence as they once were. This means that young people who play these games are not necessarily going to commit acts of hate and violence directly, but they may become less outraged when these acts occur in their own community. Vigilance and outrage against such acts of hate are necessary to eliminate these types of behavior in our communities.

As stated earlier, Resistance Records[30] has released one of the most advanced of these games. The game was released featuring an altered picture similar to the popular video game *Doom.* However, rather than killing monsters and other creatures, gamers kill ethnic minorities and Jews. *Ethnic Cleansing* was released on Martin Luther King Day with the slogan "Celebrate Martin Luther King Day with a Virtual Race War." The players can choose from KKK or neo-Nazi skinhead attire, roam the streets of New York murdering the "subhumans," that is, nonwhites, and their Jewish masters. The New York of the game has been destroyed by gangs of the subhumans who work under the control of the great Jewish Conspiracy. This game shows a world that has fallen to the extreme right's worst fear: the Jewish Conspiracy. At the end of the game, the player encounters the "end boss," who is characterized as Ariel Sharon. When he is defeated and dying, his last words are "Filthy White dog, you have destroyed thousands of years of planning."[31] This characterization further leads to demonizing the Jewish race, by showing them as "masters" who have been plotting for "thousands of years" to destroy the whites.

While this is not the first, and certainly not the only, racist game available, it is the most advanced. It was created using an open-source game program that allows for almost anyone to create a game simply by plugging in their ideas. In this manner, a person can take an existing game code and modify it to reflect the characters, backgrounds, sounds, and environment that the designer wants. By creating these highly interactive and attractive games, hate groups can spread their racist messages to thousands of unsuspecting players.[32] The importance of these more advanced games is that they have the ability to attract the serious gamer, someone who is not a racist, and not just the individuals who are already part of the racist right.

Resistance Records is a well-known racist music distributor. Music of different genres, but especially the punk/alternative types, are accessible through this company. Just like racist games, this type of music attracts people who are not active or even fringe racists. Exposure to racist propaganda and music again serves to dehumanize, desensitize, and demonize specific acts of violence against individuals based on race, ethnicity, or lifestyle. Music is a key resource among white supremacy groups, and more savvy groups have found ways to tap into youth markets to increase their recruitment. For example, the Resistance Record label signed and produced music by a number of groups featuring young artists or more pop-style music in the hopes of attracting young audiences to purchase and listen to the message of the artists.

Internet Cartoons

Besides computer games and music, many sites use cartoons to spread their ideas. One of the most widely distributed cartoons of the right is *Jew Rats*.[33] This is a computer program that consists of 14 cartoons that depict Jews as humanoid rats and African Americans with highly exaggerated features. The depiction of nonwhite individuals in this manner further, yet subtly, dehumanizes the target race or ethnicity, because their features are depicted in unattractive ways, as opposed to those caricatures that represent the Aryan ideal. The cartoons in *Jew Rats* depict many aspects of the Jewish Conspiracy put forth by the extreme right. The cartoons also show the Anti-Defamation League and the NAACP as puppets of the Jewish Conspiracy and thus set on the destruction of the white race. This type of propaganda is used to counteract and undermine the effect that these groups have in opposition to the racist right's doctrine. On most of the cartoon pages, there are links to propaganda and articles with such names as Jewish Communism, Jew Business Thugs, and Who really brought the slaves to America? These articles offer names of famous people who are the true "enemies" of the white race, as well as further explaining the beliefs that the racist right holds dear. *Jew Rats* not only dehumanizes nonwhites but also helps in demonizing the Jews by extolling the beliefs of the Jewish Conspiracy.

Additionally, the Internet allows individuals to self-publish their cartoons and videos. This provides an outlet for individuals who are not skilled artists but still interested in pushing their message out to the public. Web sites like YouTube allow individuals to make animated cartoons using simple programs, though the sites carefully monitor content to reduce offensive content. For example, a YouTube user whose racist content has caused his postings on the site to be taken down repeatedly has repeatedly created new user profiles or channels to post his material. In this case, the individual has created 64 channels so far.[34]

It is easy to find examples of hate propaganda, games, and cartoons of the extreme right on the Internet. Unlike radical environmentalism, racism is not considered hip or even politically correct. All racists are seen as evil or bad even when they are nonviolent and do not participate in hate crimes or other violent actions. On the other hand, even the environmentalists who commit criminal acts tend to be romanticized and seen as righteous. There is a tendency to paint liberal extremists as Robin Hood types. While there are no hordes of violent cartoons, songs, and the like, the environmental and animal rights activist (ELF and ALF) sites do employ propaganda-filled images. Unfortunately, they do not possess the same negative image and social stigma associated with overt racism and bigotry. The propaganda of PETA[35] and other noncriminal groups instill the ideas of resistance that can later lead to more extreme activism.

On PETA's homepage, there is an Internet link that is aimed directly at young people. There is a kids section devoted to promoting the PETA agenda through child-friendly content. For example, they provide free comic books that describe the lives of cows, chickens, rats, elephants, and other animals that spend their lives in captivity in zoos or feedlots and slaughter-houses.[36] They also provide "GRRR! Magazine," a youth-oriented publication featuring interviews with popular celebrities and their beliefs about how animals should be treated. There are also interactive games and music designed to promote their perspectives to young children.

A liberal mainstream site that is youth oriented is PETA 2.[37] PETA 2 appeals directly to teenagers with youth-oriented graphics that purport the ideas of resistance and revolution. There are numerous graphics on the PETA Web site that encourage violence in the name of protecting the animals. One graphic in particular depicts a bloody knife in a hand holding books and asks the viewer to "question authority" (http://peta2.com/). Other graphics blend pop culture icons with messages that it is all right to use violence to change the world. For example, there are images of popular fast-food chains, such as McDonalds, whose slogan has been changed to read "McCruelty, I'm hatin' it!" News on popular actors or bands who are vegetarians or environmentalists is also offered. They also provide links to FaceBook and MySpace pages for PETA that individuals can join. This site and the propaganda it conveys open the door and motivate people to go on to more active resistance by employing the same desensitizing and dehumanizing effect as the right's propaganda, yet it is more universally seen as legitimate. Any racist, antigay, or even prolife sites are seen as "criminal" in their own right even if they do not extol the righteousness of violence, while the left can be considered mainstream when they do not laud violence.

STORAGE AND DISSEMINATION OF INFORMATION

The ability of the Internet to store information and make it available to everyone is obvious. So it is little wonder that extremists, just as everyone else, utilize this ability. Many racist sites archive the sermons of different preachers, whether Christian Identity or other, who exemplify the beliefs that these groups hold paramount. For instance, anyone can find and download for free all of the sermons of Wesley Swift (one of the most influential right-wing extremists in our history and a primary developer of Christian Identity). In addition, there are sites that have online copies of the *Protocols of Zion* as well as the *Turner Diaries* and other racist books. *Turner Diaries* was found in the automobile of Timothy McVeigh when he was arrested after the bombing of the Alfred P. Murrah Federal Building in Oklahoma City, Oklahoma, in 1995. Before the age of the Internet, racists could only find these manuscripts at swap meets or meetings. Now even nonracists are likely to find these manuscripts on the Internet. A simple Google search reveals sites and locations dedicated to hate and bigotry. Some hate groups even offer guidelines on how to publish your own racist manuscripts and materials, as noted in Box 8.2

On the anarchist and left-oriented sites, such information as how animals are treated by certain organizations or groups or the merit of the vegan diet are easily available. PETA even

BOX 8.2

"How To Publish Your Own Literature"

by John Doe, USA Assoc. Director website: *http://usawhq.cjb.net*

The first step in having a visible presence and attracting new recruits is often getting your information into print. This can seem a daunting task and is often something that people half do but in fact it is quite straightforward to produce high quality publications. The thing is to start small, do a leaflet for instance to begin with for a large gathering and perhaps an eight-page newsletter to sell. I'll start by talking about leaflets.

WRITING: Writing an article or leaflet is never as difficult as it seems. Start off by jotting down a few facts you want to get across and two or three arguments you want to make. Have a look at articles on similar subjects for ideas and if it's a current issue at recent newspapers for facts. Write an introduction paragraph that will grab peoples attention. Try and make it current and saying something they don't know, a lot of people will just look at the first paragraph and unless it's interesting, won't read on. If you're really stuck leave this to the end. Then put together the facts and arguments you wish to make. Keep your sentences short and free of jargon. Keep your paragraphs short as well, three or four sentences. Each paragraph should make no more than one argument. Think about the people who will be reading it. How much knowledge can you assume they have about the subject? You're better off under-estimating this slightly than over-estimating it. Try and finish off on a practical note, perhaps telling people of a good Web site or advocating a particular set of tactics. Steer clear of cliches as endings unless that's the central point you're making.

Now you should have a draft article. Read through it a couple of times and make the following changes: Do you support your arguments with facts or reason or do they just sound like slogans? Have you expressed yourself in a straightforward manner or are some of your sentences convoluted and unclear? Do you repeat yourself or can you rearrange the order of the paragraphs so your argument flows more clearly? What is racialist about what you are saying? How can you emphasise your

racialism better within what you are saying without appearing demeaning? Is the overall impact positive and constructive or do you just appear to be giving out about what other people are doing? You'll find each time you re-read it you'll see a slightly better way to say things. This makes the difference between an interesting piece and a boring piece. Have a look at the editing part below for more things to watch out for.

EDITING: Writing can be the easy part, the hard part is giving your work to someone else to look at and correct or suggest amendments. But again, this is a vital part both because everyone reads things in a different way and they will spot odd-sounding phrases you won't, and also because we all make mistakes which other people can pick up on. In a new group the process of editing, if correctly handled, can make a big contribution to the political development of the group. When you're editing, be careful to respect the writer's work while pointing out problems you see with it. There's nothing wrong with making mistakes and sometimes they may be right. The editing group should be willing to discuss suggested changes fully. Keep editing and proofreading separate, there's nothing worse then having your spelling constantly corrected in a session that's meant to be looking at the political or factual content of your work. Note down exactly the agreed-upon changes and see if the sentences still make sense when they are put in. Your suggestion of a wording or a fact possibly could be better expressed by trying to suggest the alternative wording. Points to look for when you are editing: Do I agree with what the leaflet is saying? Is the leaflet convincing or do the arguments need expanding on and are more facts needed? Do we assume too much knowledge on the part of the audience? Are there irrelevancies which could be cut or boring bits which should be re-written? Is it positive and what message does it get across? Does it present a positive image of the movement and will it promote interest? Is it the right length for the available space?

PROOFREADING: Proofreading is one of those things that some people are good at and some people are useless at. But it's very important to do it as when you write something it can be very hard to see even very obvious mistakes. If you give out something with a lot of mistakes then that is what people will remember about it rather then its content. The edited text of a leaflet should always be proofread before it is produced.

LAYOUT: You may be lucky when it comes to layout and have someone with computer skills, a computer and a printer, in which case they will be able to use a package like Pagemaker or QuarkXpress to give you a very professional looking layout. If you lack these though, you can still do a lot with a typewriter, a sharp blade, letterset and some glue. If you can only use word processors you can still do a lot by mixing the techniques. First of all, in general you want to have a big headline, text in columns and a graphic. Don't try and squeeze too much text in or people won't read it. If you have access to all the computer skills and equipment then just go ahead and do it. If you don't, find some way to learn and get access, as it will make life much easier. Meanwhile, here's how it was done in the old days. If you only have partial computer access/skills then mix what you have with what's below for the best results (e.g. many people will not be able to computerize graphics, but can use the cut and paste method below). Get a piece of paper and with a light blue pencil rule out columns, margins, space for a headline and a graphic. Measure the column width and type your text so it is the same width (either on a typewriter or word processor). NB Light Blue pencil marks do not show up when you photocopy or print. Then with a sharp knife, cut out the columns and put them to one side. With graphics, try and get one that is just black and white if you are photocopying. Racialist magazines/papers are good sources. Build up a clipping library. If you have to use a photo, try and use one that has been screened (i.e. from a newspaper, you should be able to see that it is made up of many dots) and has a lot of contrast

in it. Otherwise you may end up with a black smear. Most photocopiers can be used to enlarge or reduce the photo to the size you require. A computer equivalent of a clipping file is to keep copies of all the good graphics you find on racialist Web pages and convert them into pics (mac) or bmps (pc) which most application will read. For a headline, either print one out in a big text size using your word processor or if you don't have one, use letterset. Letterset consists of rub on letters and can be bought in most art or stationary shops. It's a pain to use, but looks much better then a normal size type headline. Carefully rule out a guide line and rub the letters down along this line. Next stick your columns and graphic down in the space provided.

PRINTING/PHOTOCOPYING: Be careful to leave enough time to get this done before the event you intend to distribute the leaflet at. If you have access to cheap photocopying where you live, (try print shops near college campuses for the best rates) then this is normally the cheapest way to print up to 1,000 or so copies. Check out community centres, student unions and office workers for cheap/free photo-copying. Otherwise, you'll have to find a cheap printer. Generally, print shops are very expensive although they may be more willing to deal in short runs. Find out where other local groups get their stuff printed; there may well be a sympathetic print shop in town. Make sure you have given the printer clear instructions, that everything is well stuck down and that it will be ready in advance of when you need it. Arrange for someone to pick up the material as soon as it is finished.

DISTRIBUTION: Drop leaflets around record shops, libraries, bookshops or anywhere else where free newspapers etc. are left.

_____

Source: http://www.whitehonor.com/literature.htm

offers vegan starter packages free of charge to anyone who wishes one. Moreover, the sites offer advice and help on performing "legitimate" activist actions. PETA offers information on organizing demonstrations and spreading their message to anyone who is interested.

The Internet also allows groups to put their credos or mission statements where millions of people who would not have had the chance to see them before can now read them at the click of a mouse. One such credo that has found a home on the Web is that of the ALF[38]:

Because ALF actions are against the law, activists work anonymously, either in small groups or individually, and do not have any centralized organization or coordination.

The ALF guidelines are as follows:

1. TO liberate animals from places of abuse, i.e. laboratories, factory farms, fur farms, etc, and place them in good homes where they may live out their natural lives, free from suffering.
2. TO inflict economic damage to those who profit from the misery and exploitation of animals.
3. TO reveal the horror and atrocities committed against animals behind locked doors, by performing non-violent direct actions and liberations.
4. TO take all necessary precautions against harming any animal, human and non-human.
5. TO analyze the ramifications of all proposed actions, and never apply generalizations when specific[39]

The Internet also offers blueprints for violent criminal acts. For instance, along with the ALF mission statement above are the following instructions for how to send in information on any actions individuals perform against the "enemy."

If you are a member of an active A.L.F. cell, send us any clippings, or your own report, with date, time, place, and a few details about the action. Send your reports on plain paper, using block capital letters, or a public typewriter that many people have access to. Wear gloves at all times so your fingerprints are not on the paper, envelope, or stamp. Do not give your address, and don't lick the stamp or envelope; wet it with a sponge. Remember, you should expect that all of our mail and any other support groups' mail is opened and read by the authorities.

In fact, ALF offers a downloadable primer and detailed documents on "economic sabotage" among other items. Many of the sites also publish newsletters that glorify the beliefs and activities of the group. Newsletters offer articles, propaganda, letters, and more in one place with easy access. The Internet then allows many diverse people to take advantage of the product. Box 8.3[40] offers an example of the features offered in one such newsletter.

More dangerous are the sites that offer directions for bombs or other devices. The ELF site offers a large link on their home page to directions for the incendiary devices that are the ecoterrorist's trademark.[41] Many bombings in the recent past have been committed by people who obtained the plans for the device from the Internet. In fact, complete directions for building an incendiary torch revealing the same type of ignition device used in the arson of a Vale, Colorado, ski resort were found on the ELF site.

Other sites, such as Ka-Fucking-Boom.com, provide detailed instructions on bombmaking and ignition devices. While these Web sites are *not* associated directly with a specific group, they provide information that assists them in carrying out their mission of destructiveness and violence.

The home pages of many ecoterror sites have excerpts from letters sent in about individuals' actions and links to even more stories. As seen on the ALF site earlier, they offer descriptions on how to send in the information without being caught. Moreover, all of the sites make sure to tell people that they should not send in any information on acts that have not yet been committed.

BOX 8.3

Newsletter Feature for "Green Anarchy"

Green Anarchy #13 (Summer '03) is out now!
Issue #13 features:
"Youth Liberation: Burn the Schools and Destroy the Media," "The Rising of the Barbarians," "Between Analysis and Vision: Moving Beyond the Theory–Practice Dichotomy," "A Quest Among the Bewildered," "Thoughts on the City," "On the Sabotage of the Fine Arts," "Zero War—Total Liberation," "Decoding the Apocalypse of the Militant Left," "Green Amazon Economics 101," "The Doctor is Sick: Schizophrenia, Anti-Psychiatry, and Anarchism," "News from the Balcony," reprints from the finest of sources, updates from insurrections around the world, direct action reports, state repression and prisoner into (including a Break the Chains Conference Manifesto), reviews, letters, and much, much more! This one is 36 pages (our largest yet!).

Publishing Information on Potential Victims

Many sites also celebrate acts of violence. For example, many racist or antigay sites lauded the actions of those who killed Mathew Shepard. One site even claimed in a "memorial" to him that he "got himself killed" due to his "satanic lifestyle" and "will be in hell for all eternity." Another site claims that the convicted murderer of James Byrd is an "American Hero."[42]

While this praise of past actions is dangerous and deplorable, the most dangerous actions of these Web sites are when they place specific information about individuals on their sites. The most famous instance of this was the Nuremberg Files case.[43] The original Nuremberg Files offered extensive personal information about abortion providers such as pictures, work and home addresses, phone numbers, license plates, Social Security numbers, names, and birth dates of spouses and children. People are also asked to send in any information they have from pictures to videos on "the abortionist, their car, their house, friends, and anything else of interest." The site claimed that any information gathered would be used to prosecute abortion providers once abortion becomes illegal, just as Nazi leaders were prosecuted after the World War II. The 9th Circuit Court upheld the concept that this site was being used for a much more violent purpose and awarded the plaintiffs $107 million in damages.

The list of abortion providers reads like a list of targets for assassination: Names in plain black lettering were still "working"; those in gray letters were "wounded"; and those names that were "Str[uck]through" indicated doctors who had become "fatalit[ies]." The site was actually a list of people targeted for assassination. Within hours of the murder of Dr. Barnett Slepian in Amherst, New York, in 1998, his name was struck through, indicating that he had become a "fatality."[44]

The court found that the site's language and the strikethrough on the murdered person's names constituted a threat to others on the list. District Judge Robert Jones called certain language on the site "blatant and illegal communication of true threats to kill."[45] While the original site, with all of its trappings, is gone, many sites today host the Nuremberg files, just without listing the slain.

A similar site is the Stop Huntingdon Animal Cruelty (SHAC) Web site[46] (see Box 8.4). This site offers a map of the United States that can be clicked on to find information on those individuals or companies committing "crimes" against animals anywhere. Clicking over a specific area gives a list of all "offenders" in that area. It has the names, addresses, phone numbers, and e-mail addresses of companies that do business with Huntingdon as well as some names of executives or other employees. The homes and/or cars of some of the people whose names have

---

BOX 8.4

"Letters to the Editor" Invoking Action against the Huntingdon Life Sciences Corporation

---

Stop Huntingdon Animal Cruelty (SHAC)

The focus of SHAC is on Huntingdon Life Sciences, a firm that is involved in pharmaceutical testing. The smaller focus of the group may make them the most effective of the radical environmental and animal rights groups. The SHAC Web site reports on the actions of its supporters. For instance, the Web site publishes the letters sent in by activists. The following are just two of the letters that were published on the site with personal information x-ed out.

Received from Canadian activists:

CANADA JOINS THE FIGHT TO SMASH HLS!
        On July 28, 2003, about 25 Canadian activists joined in the fight to shut down HLS. Gathering in a major park in downtown Montreal, activists made speeches and handed out leaflets to hundreds of onlookers before taking over the street and marching to the offices of Sumitomo Canada.
        Once there, activists attempted to enter the building and had a rousing protest, complete with spray painted anti-HLS slogans and strategically placed stickers. Everyone entering and exiting the building was treated to a crash course on the atrocities supported by their neighbours in the Sumitomo suite. A whole slew of newspeople were educated as well, and the demo appeared on the 6 o'clock news of two major T.V. stations. The demonstration ended with a reminder to Sumitomo that until it severs all ties with HLS—
        "We will be back!"

Received anonymously:

WAKE UP CHIRON SCUM!
        We couldn't sleep on Tuesday night, so we decided to go see what one of our local Chiron scum was up to at 2:30 am. We knocked and knocked on the door of Linda Short (27 xxxx Ave. xxxxxxx, CA, xxx-xxx-xxxx) but she didn't answer. Go figure, she must have been fast asleep. We were really curious to know for sure, so we decided to use our trusty bullhorns to make sure she knew we we were outside anxiously awaiting her. We finally got the hint that she wasn't going to come out to visit with us, but our curiosity as to what she was up to got the best of us, so we decided to give her a call or two or three . . .
        Chiron when are you going to get it? Wake up and realize that we have tons of energy and we are determined. We know where you live and we're finding out more and more personal information about you every day. Ask yourself if can you take it. Stop doing business with Huntingdon Life Sciences!

---

been listed by SHAC have been vandalized. These people have also faced demonstrations outside their homes at all times of the day and night, received harassing telephone calls or e-mails, and, in some extreme cases, have been physically attacked.[47]

Unlike the Nuremberg Files, this site seems to understand what is and is not allowed under freedom of speech (for more on freedom of speech, see Box 8.5).[48] SHAC has faced multiple lawsuits, but they have always prevailed. Their knowledge of the law can best be seen in the following disclaimer that is linked to many places within the site:

> The SHAC USA Web site and eNewsletter, its hosts, designers, contributors, and sponsors, are not responsible for actions on the part of any individual which prove defamatory, injurious or prejudicial to the individuals or entities named herein, their families, or acquaintances. This publication is provided for informational purposes only, and is not intended to incite any criminal action on the part of its readers, visitors, or recipients.[49]

BOX 8.5
Freedom of Speech

The only lawful limitations on speech are as follows:

Obscenity. Obscenity is speech that (1) the average person, applying contemporary community standards, would find, taken as a whole, to appeal to the prurient interest; (2) depicts or describes in a patently offensive manner specifically defined sexual conduct; and (3) lacks as a whole serious literary, artistic, political, or scientific value.

Fighting words. Speech likely to provoke an average listener to retaliation and thereby cause a breach of peace.

Commercial speech. The government can ban deceptive or illegal commercial speech; any other regulation must be supported by a substantial interest to be achieved by restrictions, regulations in proportion to that interest, and a limitation on expression carefully designed to achieve the state's goal.

Incitement ("clear and present danger"). Speech that is intended and likely to incite "imminent lawless action," or where the speech presents a "clear and present danger" to the security of the nation.

Time, place, and manner. Content-neutral regulation of the time, place, or manner of speech that does not interfere with the message being delivered and leaves open adequate alternative channels of communication is permissible.

Libel/slander. Speech that is not only false but that the speaker was negligent to some degree in using. The level of negligence is raised to "actual malice" (knowing or reckless disregard for the truth of the statement) for all statements made about public figures.

It is widely acknowledged that the Internet poses challenges to traditional law, but many people have tried to impose regulation. Most of these regulations have fallen to the First Amendment. The Communications Decency Act and the Child Online Protection Act are both congressional acts that tried to place limits on any information that is considered harmful to children and that were held unconstitutional.

Another issue of First Amendment rights was the case against Yahoo in the French courts. Yahoo was found in violation of French law because they hosted Nazi paraphernalia in their online auctions. An American judge ruled that the French decision could not be enforced in U.S. courts because the First Amendment protects American companies from foreign laws that are more restrictive. The site that hosted the controversial material was on the American Yahoo server, and they can not regulate where people are when they view the sites. The French Yahoo site had always conformed to the French laws.

So, the open nature of the Internet and the First Amendment make regulations hard to implement. Many of the sites walk a fine line, but, with care, all sites, extremist or not, can continue to operate if they are careful to remain within constitutional protections.

Fund-raising

Fund-raising has also been helped by the Internet. The fact that millions of people are potentially exposed to numerous sites means that more potential donors will be reached than ever before. Many of the sites have information on how to send in donations. Some sites, like PETA, even allow for secure online credit card donations. Additionally, the SHAC group provides a list of individuals who have been arrested and imprisoned for their actions in support of animal rights.[50] They provide pictures and details of each person and links to Vegan Prison Support Group and ALF Support Groups who accept donations to provide direct or indirect financial and material support for these prisoners.

Besides donations, these groups also earn money through the selling of merchandise. For example, Resistance Records sells *Ethnic Cleansing* at $14.88. Other than the games and of course the music they release, they have a large online catalog of clothing, bumper stickers, and all other types of racist paraphernalia. Another source of income is through selling sermons, articles, or racists' books on their sites. While, if a person looks long enough, he or she can find free downloads of Wesley Swift's sermons, many more sites only offer them as mail-ordered hard copies. Somone can order a hard copy of lots of different types of works off these sites.

An example of a right-wing group that employs the Internet's fundraising ability is Kingdom Identity Church,[51] which offers many different products. To begin with, they offer an "American Institute of Theology Bible Course," which is a 12-lesson plan that costs $100 and upon completion gives the student a "Certificate in Christian Education." Moreover, they have audio- and videotape catalogs. The audiotapes, which are of sermons or lessons, are offered for a suggested donation of $3.50 per cassette. Similarly the videotapes that are proclaimed to be "professionally produced documentaries of our Christian Israelite heritage" have a suggested donation of $22. These are only an example of the products that this site sells, or more accurately, offers in exchange for donations. The only limit to the money-making abilities of these sites is in the imagination of the site designer.

TERRORISM, INTELLIGENCE GATHERING, AND THE USA PATRIOT ACT

One of the most controversial topics in America today focuses squarely on the emergence of domestic groups that express radical and extremist political thoughts on the Internet. Are these groups free to express their political opinions under the protection of the First Amendment without scrutiny or monitoring by law enforcement agencies? Certainly, the existence of controversial and inflammatory material on the Web has been safeguarded, including most forms of pornography and hate speech (refer to Chapter 7 for a discussion of the law and legislation surrounding this issue). This discussion focuses more on the role of the police to collect and analyze information (or intelligence) on groups expressing radical thoughts and ideas through their Web sites. Do the police have an inherent duty to collect information on individuals involved in the development of these types of Web sites in an effort to thwart or prevent violent crimes and terrorist attacks? Nowhere are these questions more openly evoked than in the passage of the new USA PATRIOT Act, and it is within this environment that we shall discuss the issues of privacy, freedom of speech and expression, and the right of society to be secure from future attacks.

A Short History of Intelligence in the United States

The framework for U.S. intelligence was created in a different time to deal with different problems other than terrorism. The National Security Act of 1947, which established the Central Intelligence Agency (CIA), envisioned the enemy of the United States to be nation-states such as the Soviet Union, China, and North Korea. The result was organizations and authority based on distinctions between domestic versus foreign threats, law enforcement versus national security concerns, and peacetime versus wartime.[52] The Federal Bureau of Investigation (FBI) was given responsibility for domestic intelligence and the CIA, the National Security Administration (NSA), and the Defense Intelligence Agency (DIA) were given primary responsibility for foreign intelligence outside the United States. During the politically active periods of the Vietnam War and Watergate, the roles between foreign and domestic intelligence agencies were further delineated and separated by executive and legislative initiatives (among these can be included the Privacy Act, the Freedom of Information Act, and the Attorney General Guidelines of Levi and Smith).

Domestic Intelligence and Policing

Law enforcement's primary focus was to collect evidence after a crime was committed in order to support prosecution in a court trial. This process is commonly called investigation and is reactive in nature. Previous to the passage of the USA PATRIOT Act, police intelligence activity had to focus on the development of probable cause that would justify other law enforcement and prosecutorial activities. In most incidents, a subject had actually to break the law or threaten to break established law before the FBI or other police agencies could utilize intelligence operations. The frustrating predicament in which the law enforcement community found itself was that law enforcement agencies could not act without probable cause, but at the same time were prevented from engaging in the activity from which that probable cause could originate.[53] The most critical point pertinent to the functions of domestic intelligence concerned the protection of civil liberties and constitutional rights of individual citizens, such as those that develop political inflammatory and radical Internet sites. The primary purpose of law enforcement is to protect the rights of all citizens through the objective enforcement of the law. This goal is seriously thwarted, as some question the ethical validity of covert intelligence operations against its own citizens. Such activities are violative of constitutional safeguards inherent in our democracy and could culminate in the formation of a police state.

Conflicting Roles

In contrast to the FBI and other police organizations, the CIA collects and analyzes information regarding national security in order to warn our government before an act occurs. The CIA is relegated to working *outside* the United States; agents have no arrest powers, and their activities are proactive in nature. The two roles of domestic versus foreign intelligence gathering and analysis are directly competitive in function. The FBI and other police agencies are restricted in sharing information with the CIA so as not to compromise future court action or abridge the civil liberties of U.S. citizens. Similarly, the CIA is reluctant to give information to the FBI (or other law enforcement agencies) for fear of having sources and methods of acquiring information being revealed in court.[54] Note the difference between investigation and intelligence in Box 8.6.

Defining Intelligence

Intelligence can be defined as information, which has been identified as relevant, collected, verified, and interpreted within the context of specific objectives. This necessarily includes that the information has been analyzed, classified, and distributed to policy makers, who utilize it toward the betterment of the country or the community.[55] Historically, the missing dimension in quality intelligence has been analysis. The transformation of raw data, whether acquired through human, technical, or

---

BOX 8.6

The Differences between Investigation and Intelligence

• *Investigation* Reactive; occurs after the event or incident Reports are generally open Sources are generally known and open Arrests are made based on evidence and facts	• *Intelligence* Proactive; information gathered before the event Reports are almost always closed Sources are confidential and closed Arrests are rarely made

open sources, must be collated, scrutinized, and processed accurately and in a timely manner. The ultimate goal of this analytic process is a finished product more intelligible, accurate, and usable than the data and information drawn upon to prepare it.[56] Placing this discussion in perspective, information collected by the FBI and other police agencies on individuals within groups that develop radical Web sites when no crime has been reported becomes intelligence data.

U.S. Intelligence Weaknesses

In the aftermath of September 11, 2001, several studies were conducted to assess shortcomings that may exist in our nation's ability to collect and analyze important intelligence information on terrorist groups. Several weaknesses were identified in counterterrorism efforts led by the FBI, CIA, and the National Security Agency. These included communication problems among agencies, a shortage of linguists, and a failure by these agencies to correctly analyze relevant intelligence information to potential terrorist threats. Several of the issues identified as potential problems existing within the U.S. intelligence community included the following: (1) a failure to place an emphasis on traditional human intelligence gathering and analysis and relying too much on technology tools such as spy satellites and expert system programs to gain intelligence advantages; (2) a failure to provide timely, accurate, and specific intelligence information to law enforcement agencies and U.S. policy makers; (3) an overly bureaucratic and decentralized structure (particularly within the FBI) that hindered counterterrorism efforts and the efficient use of intelligence information; (4) outdated and obsolete computer systems that were not compatible with other systems and unable to provide accurate and timely sharing of critical information nationally; and (5) overly restrictive guidelines and laws that hindered the effective use of informants and the general collection of intelligence information.[57]

These problems are particularly distressing, considering the effort to combat terrorism. The organized, clandestine, and destructive activities of terrorist groups uniquely confound both the gathering and analysis of intelligence information. Complicating this matter is the inability of policy makers to place the acts of terrorism within the scope of one jurisdiction. Are acts of terrorism crimes to be investigated by the FBI, or are they threats to our national security that fall within the purview of our military and national security agencies?

THE USA PATRIOT ACT

In an effort to clarify and improve these conditions and provide sweeping new powers to both domestic law enforcement and traditional intelligence agencies, President George W. Bush signed into law the USA PATRIOT Act on October 26, 2001. The USA PATRIOT Act (**P**rovide **A**ppropriate **T**ools **R**equired to **I**ntercept and **O**bstruct **T**errorism) changed over 15 different statutes with little or no external review. The law addressed not only terrorism and intelligence issues but also focused on more traditional money laundering, computer abuse and crime, immigration processes, and fraud. However, the most substantial part of the act is that it expanded all four traditional tools of surveillance used by law enforcement with significantly reduced checks and balances:

- *Wiretaps:* The surreptitious eavesdropping on a third-party conversation by wire, oral, or electronic communication. Usually conducted with a microphone receiver ("bug") on a telephone device; requires both a search warrant and a court order.
- *Search warrants:* A legal document signed by a judge directing police officers to search a specific area for a specific person or item of evidence/contraband. The document must be based on probable cause that a crime has occurred or is about to occur.

- *Pen/trap and trace orders:* Telephone call set-up information only is intercepted without individual communications. A "pen register" provides the law enforcement agency access to the numbers dialed from a subject's phone, while a "trap and trace" provides the incoming numbers to the subject's phone (like caller ID).
- *Court orders and subpoenas:* A court document signed by a judge that instructs the police to perform a specific task. A subpoena is a court order that commands a person to appear in court at a specified date and time to testify.

Law enforcement and intelligence agencies can now more easily and more surreptitiously monitor the Web surfing and communication of individuals using the Internet, conduct nationwide roving wiretaps on cell and line telephones, and build profiles on the reading habits of people visiting public libraries. Under the act, police can now force ISPs (Internet Service Providers—such as America Online, AT&T Worldnet, and Prodigy) to "voluntarily" hand over information on customer profiles and Web-surfing habits *without* a warrant or court order. This has a dramatic potential impact on the various radical groups and Web sites discussed here. Not only do the police have the legal right to monitor politically and socially extreme Web sites but also the ability to monitor those individuals that visit such Web sites!

The Reauthorized PATRIOT Act

In 2005, provisions of the PATRIOT ACT were to sunset, and Congress acted to review, reauthorize, and pass this bill. The revisions were passed into law by President Bush in March 2006. The roving wiretap provisions were maintained, though greater oversight was added to ensure that these powers would not be abused by law enforcement. The changes include judicial review and approval by the Director of the FBI or NSA, along with a more detailed application process to specify targets and actions. The provision that allowed library records to be subpoenaed was also removed to protect citizens, with the exception of electronic communications through the library. The original PATRIOT act also allowed law enforcement agencies to conduct covert, or "sneak and peek," searches in the homes of potential suspects without their knowledge or authorization. Since this was considered by some to be too extreme, the reauthorization was changed to limit the time when such a search could be conducted so as not to give unreasonable power to law enforcement. However, the ability to conduct surveillance against what are defined as "lone wolf terrorists" was increased to provide greater time to monitor a target. The definition of terrorism was also expanded to include receiving military-type training from a foreign terror organization and narcoterrorism and criminalizes the act of planning a terror attack against a mass transit system.

Constitutional Rights and the USA PATRIOT Act

The expanded scope and breadth of the act has raised concerns from a variety of sources.[58] Most agree that intelligence gathering and analysis has to improve in order to prevent future domestic and international terrorist attacks. However, some argue that the USA PATRIOT Act went too far. The act increases information sharing between domestic law enforcement departments and traditional intelligence agencies such as the FBI and CIA. In such a state, the line between intelligence gathering and public law enforcement becomes blurred. Critics are quick to point out the civil rights abuses that have occurred in the past whenever police agencies have become too involved in intelligence gathering. Most major cities, including New York, Chicago, Denver, and Los Angeles, have had relatively recent litigation aimed at limiting the role of the police in this function. The arguments focus on the collection of irrelevant private information of individuals (including Web-surfing habits and sexual orientation) to the profiling of individuals in minority communities. In one case, an intelligence officer in Portland, Oregon, developed boxes of information on over 500 community groups and over 3,000 well-known citizens of the city and stored them at his own residence. Over 20 years of police intelligence records were discovered by family members several years after the officer died. The dusty reports and pictures not only focused on private meetings and information on local politicians but revealed that the officer had himself been an active member of the John Birch Society, a right-wing organization often under scrutiny by governmental intelligence agencies.[59]

Some argue that the expanded role of police in intelligence gathering under the act will only provide a significant threat to the personal and civil liberties of all Americans and do very little to thwart terrorism.[60] In an extreme example of opposition to the PATRIOT Act, the government of Nova Scotia province in Canada passed a law called "The new Personal Information International Disclosure Protection Act."[61] This act was designed to protect their citizens from having any information provided through PATRIOT Act investigations and dictated punishments for failing to do so. The Reauthorized PATRIOT Act attempted to respond to these critiques by increasing judicial and managerial review, though many still think the laws afford too much power to law enforcement.

Summary

With the passing of the Homeland Security Act in late 2002, and its reauthorization in 2006, and the passing of the Reauthorized PATRIOT Act in 2006, it is clear that police will at least maintain a significantly new role in the fight against terrorism involving intelligence gathering, particularly using the Internet. This new role must be accompanied by vastly new training for law enforcement officers, defining the tactical, operational, and legal limits involving intelligence gathering and analysis.

The Internet offers people the ability to participate in or be exposed to all sorts of questionable material. Some of this includes politically and socially extreme Web sites developed by hate mongers, bigots, racists, and radicals. These can be experienced in the privacy of one's own home, no matter where they live. A person can download information, order products, or communicate with others without ever having to leave his or her home. Moreover, using the computer to explore and chat gives a person a feeling of anonymity that allows him or her to do or participate in things he or she never would in the real world. Most certainly, the freedom offered by the Internet allows for a continuation of extremist goals by reaching a wider audience and provides a means for easy excess to information, no matter how distasteful.

Review Questions

1. Legally define "hate crime," and explain why hate crime legislation have been so controversial in the United States.
2. What is *Ethnic Cleansing,* and why is it so controversial?
3. What are ELF and ALF? Explain their similarities and differences.
4. What are the primary purposes of right-wing hate Web sites that use images, music, games, and the like to spread their propaganda?
5. What are the "Nuremberg Files," and why were they important in setting legal precedence relating to communication on the Internet?
6. Explain and discuss the inherent conflicts associated with the police as intelligence gatherers.
7. List and discuss some of the weaknesses associated with U.S. intelligence in the aftermath of September 11, 2001.
8. What is the USA PATRIOT Act, and what are the four traditional tools of surveillance expanded with the act?
9. How has the Reauthorized USA PATRIOT ACT changed the legal definitions of terrorism and responded to critiques against the original law?

Endnotes

1. Simon Wiesenthal Center (1999). *"The New Lexicon of Hate: The Changing Tactics, Language and Symbols of America's Extremists."* Los Angeles.

2. For more information, visit the Nation Institutes Against Hate Crimes Web site: *http://www.wiesenthal.com*

3. Department of Justice and IACP (1999). *"Responding to Hate Crimes: A Police Officer's Guide to Investigation and Prevention."* Washington, DC: U.S. Department of Justice and IACP.

4. See *www.stormfront.org*

5. PARSONS, C. (2009). "Hate Goes Viral on Social Networking Sites." *Reuters. http://www.reuters.com/article/technologyNews/idUSTRE54C4KW20090513.*

6. GODINEZ, VICTOR. (March 14, 2002). "Hate Group Wooing Teens by Making a Game Out of Racism," *Dallas Morning News,* p. 2A.

7. TAYLOR, R.W., FRITSCH, E.J., and CAETI, T.J. (2002). *Juvenile Justice: Policies, Programs, and Practices.* New York: Glencoe/McGraw-Hill Publishers, pp. 518–520.

8. An interview with leader of the Texas Militia in Dallas, Texas (January 2000), reflecting many of the sentiments expressed by Tom Metzger, a leader of the White Aryan Resistance (WAR).

9. "ATF: Plot by Skinheads to Kill Obama is Foiled." *Associated Press.* October 27, 2008.

10. DUKE, D. (2008). "Obama Wins Demo Nomination: A Black Flag for White America." *The Official Website of Representative David Duke.* Available at *http://www.davidduke.com.* Accessed Septemeber 9, 2009.

11. JARBOE, JAMES F. (February 12, 2002). Domestic Terrorism Section Chief, Federal Bureau of Investigation. "The Threat of Eco-Terrorism." Speech before the House of Resources Committee, Subcommittee on Forests and Forest Health.

12. *Ibid.*

13. FREEH, LOUIS J. (May 10, 2001). Director, Federal Bureau of Investigation. "Threat of Terrorism to the United States." Speech before U.S. Senate, Committees on Appropriations, Armed Services, and Select Committee on Intelligence.

14. SMITH, BRENT L. (1994). *Terrorism in America: Pipe Bombs and Pipe Dreams.* Albany, NY: State University of New York Press, p. 125.

15. FREEH, "Threat of Terrorism to the United States."

16. SMITH, *Terrorism in America: Pipe Bombs and Pipe Dreams.*

17. JARBOE, "The Threat of Eco-Terrorism."

18. Center for the Defense of Free Enterprise (CDFE). "Ecoterrorism." *www.cdfe.org/ecoterror.hml*

19. SCHABNER, DEAN (February 26, 2002). "New Front on Ecoterror? Some Want to Target High-Profile Activists in Battle on Ecoterror." *ABCNews.com. http://abcnews.go.com/sections/us/DailyNews/ecoterror_support020226.html*

20. CDFE, "Ecoterrorism."

21. JARBOE, "The Threat of Eco-Terrorism."

22. Department of Justice (2006). "Eleven Defendants Indicted on Domestic Terrorism Charges." *http://www.usdoj.gov/opa/pr/2006/January/06_crm_030.html*

23. Off-Road.com. "A Short History of Ecoterrorism." *http://www.off-road.com/land/ecoterrorism_history.html* (viewed July 2003).

24. JARBOE, "The Threat of Eco-Terrorism."

25. Off-Road.com, "A Short History of Ecoterrorism."

26. JARBOE, "The Threat of Eco-Terrorism."

27. AYLWARD, KIM, DEHAVEN, CHAD, ROBINSON, WILL, and SMITH, BILL. (2003). "Cyberterrorism." *http://www.cob.vt.edu/accounting/faculty/belanger/sec/article5.ppt* (viewed July 2003).

28. *Ibid.*

29. *Ibid.,* p. 5.

30. Resistance Records. *http://www.resistance.com/* (viewed July 2003).

31. Anti-Defamation League (ADL). "Racist Groups Using Computer Gaming to Promote Violence Against Blacks, Latinos and Jews." *http://www.adl.org/videogames/default.asp* (viewed July 2003).

32. Anti-Defamation League (ADL). "Creating a Racist Computer Game—A Relatively Simple Task." *http://www.adl.org/videogames/game_creating.asp* (viewed July 2003).

33. "Jew Rats." *http://www.nsec-88.org/ruzne/jew_rats/jew-rats.zip* (downloaded July 2003).

34. *Ibid.,* p. 5.

35. People for the Ethical Treatment of Animals (PETA). peta.org (viewed July 2003).
36. PETA. www.petakids.com. (viewed May 15, 2009).
37. PETA 2. *peta2.com* (viewed May 2009).
38. The Animal Liberation Front (ALF). *Animalliberationfront.org* (viewed July 2003), or *DirectAction.info* (viewed July 2009).
39. *Ibid.*
40. Green Anarchy. *greenanarchy.org* (viewed July 2003).
41. Earth Liberation Front (ELF). *www.earthliberationfront.com* (viewed July 2003).
42. ADL. "Poisoning the Web: Hatred Online, Internet Bigotry, Extremism and Violence." *http://www.adl.org/poisoning_web/introduction.asp* (viewed July 2003).
43. See *Planned Parenthood* v. *American Coalition of Life Activists,* 41F. Supp 2nd, 1130 (D. OR 1999). This is a landmark First Amendment case involving a $107 million dollar award against antiabortion activists that branded abortion doctors as "murderers" and then crossed out their name when they were killed.
44. ADL. "Poisoning the Web."
45. SCHABNER, D. (May 5, 2003). "Interactive Ecoterror? Animal Rights Group Provides Target List in Anti-Lab Campaign." *ABCNews.com. http://abcnews.go.com/sections/us/SciTech/ecoterror030505.html* (viewed July 2003).
46. Stop Huntingdon Animal Cruelty (SHAC). *shacusa.org* (viewed July 2003).
47. SCHABNER, DEAN. (May 5, 2003). "Interactive Ecoterror? Animal Rights Group Provides Target List in Anti-Lab Campaign."
48. Electronic Privacy Information Center. "Free Speech." *http://www.epic.org/free_speech/* (viewed July 2003).
49. *shacusa.org*, Stop Huntingdon Animal Cruelty (SHAC).
50. *http://www.shac.net/features/prisoners.html*
51. Kingdom Identity Church. http://www.kingidentity.com/
52. DEUTSCH, J., and SMITH, J.H. (2002). "Smarter Intelligence." *Foreign Policy* 128: 64–69.
53. MOTLEY, J.B. (1983). *U.S. Strategy to Counter Domestic Political Terrorism.* Washington, DC: National Security Affairs Monograph Series 2: 62–70.
54. TAYLOR, R.W. (1987). "Terrorism and Intelligence." *Defense Analysis* 3: 165–175.
55. MCCARTHEY, S.P. (1998). *The Function of Intelligence in Crisis Management.* Burlington, VT: Ashgate Publishing.
56. GODSON, R. (ed.) (1983). *Intelligence Requirements for the 1980s: Elements of Intelligence,* revised edition. Washington, DC: National Strategy Information Center.
57. Summary of Classified Report to the U.S. Congress, House of Representatives Intelligence Subcommittee. (July 16, 2002). *Report on Intelligence Gathering and Analysis pre September 11, 2001.*
58. Electronic Frontier Foundation (October 31, 2001). "EFF Analysis of the Provisions of the USA PATRIOT Act." See: *www.eff.org/Privacy/Surveillance/Terrorism_militias/20011031_eff_usa_patriot_analysis.html*
59. "Terrorism Forces Renewed," *The Portland Observer,* September 25, 2002, p. 1.
60. *Ibid.*
61. GRANT, C. (2006). "Protection of Privacy Legislation Proclaimed." *http://www.gov.ns.ca/news/details.asp?id=20061115005.*

CHAPTER 9

Digital Laws and Legislation

CHAPTER OBJECTIVES

After completing this chapter, you should be able to

- Explain the intent and fundamental concepts of search and seizure law as it applies to digital crime.
- Identify situations where search and seizure is possible without a warrant and describe its limits.
- Describe the federal statutes that govern electronic surveillance in communications networks.
- Discuss the issues presented regarding the admission of digital evidence at trial.
- Identify and discuss the significant U.S. Supreme Court cases focusing on digital crime and evidence.

INTRODUCTION

In this chapter, law and legislation as it applies to the collection of evidence and prosecution of digital crime will be discussed. First, search and seizure law for digital evidence will be analyzed, including searches with warrants and numerous searches without warrants. Second, the major federal statutes governing the collection of digital evidence, especially electronic surveillance law, will be covered along with federal criminal statutes, which forbid certain types of computer crime. Third, issues related to the admission of digital evidence at trial, including authentication and hearsay, will be reviewed. Fourth, significant U.S. Supreme Court cases in the area of digital crime will be highlighted.

SEARCH AND SEIZURE LAW FOR DIGITAL EVIDENCE

Our current body of search law is the ongoing product of the interaction of legislation, case law, and constitutional law. Most of the search law discussed in this section applies to searches and seizures overall, not just those involving digital crimes and evidence. In fact, much search and seizure law has failed to keep up with the changes brought about by increases in digital crimes and the increasing need to collect digital evidence.

The Fourth Amendment states:

> The right of the people to be secure in their persons, houses, papers, and effects, against unreasonable searches and seizures, shall not be violated, and no warrants shall issue, but upon probable cause, supported by oath or affirmation, and particularly describing the place to be searched, and the persons or things to be seized.

As simple as this language may be, numerous questions may be raised by the specific details occurring in searches and seizures of digital evidence. In general, questions focus on whether or not an activity is a "search" and whether a search is "reasonable." The best way to ensure that a search is not "unreasonable" is to seek and obtain a warrant from a neutral, detached magistrate. In *Johnson* v. *United States*,[1] the U.S. Supreme Court stated:

> The point of the Fourth Amendment, which often is not grasped by zealous officers, is not that it denies law enforcement the support of the usual inferences which reasonable men draw from evidence. Its protection consists in requiring that those inferences be drawn by a neutral and detached magistrate instead of being judged by the officer engaged in the often competitive enterprise of ferreting out crime.

The key to understanding search and seizure law is to remember that the point is not to protect criminals; the point is to enforce a reasonable person's expectation of privacy. Criminals entering their home with the police chasing them do not receive sanctuary. Similarly, a guilty desire to hide something does not necessarily create a reasonable expectation of privacy. The Fourth Amendment protects persons evidencing an expectation of privacy; however, society must be willing to recognize that expectation as reasonable.[2]

A seizure of property occurs when there is some meaningful interference with an individual's possessory interests in that property.[3] In relation to property, a seized item deprives an owner of its use. On the other hand, a search is an attempt by law enforcement officers to obtain evidence. By definition, a search intrudes into a person's reasonable expectation of privacy.[4] Therefore, a search occurs, in a constitutional sense, any time there is a governmental intrusion into a person's reasonable expectation of privacy. An act as simple as opening a notebook and reading the contents in a suspect's living room changes the character of the interaction from simple observation to a search.[5] However, just because the police intrude into a person's reasonable expectation of privacy does not mean that the intrusion is unlawful. Several mechanisms are available to the police in which they can lawfully search a person or property and thus lawfully intrude into a person's reasonable expectation of privacy. In the following sections, these mechanisms will be discussed, including searches with warrants and searches without warrants.

Searches with Warrants

In order to obtain a search warrant, a law enforcement officer must show probable cause by reasonably establishing the following:

1. A crime has been committed.
2. Evidence of the crime exists.
3. The evidence presently exists in the place to be searched.

Further, the law enforcement officer must particularly describe the place to be searched and the evidence to be seized. Specific evidence of a specific crime must be named. General evidence facilitating a criminal act may be described by function. The investigator can search anywhere the named item(s) can be found. The judicial officer issuing the search warrant must be legally authorized to issue search warrants. Different jurisdictions empower different officers with this authority. Local policies and procedures should specify who has the power to issue search warrants. Furthermore, the judicial officer issuing the search warrant must have jurisdiction over the area to be searched.

Jurisdiction "is the power of the court to decide a matter in controversy and presupposes the existence of a duly constituted court with control over the subject matter and the parties."[6] When a transaction crosses state boundaries, typical in digital crime cases, jurisdictional issues may arise. A search warrant is only valid within the jurisdiction of the magistrate signing it. The degree of activity projected into a geographic area determines whether the doctrine of personal jurisdiction applies. If a criminal actor actively engages a victim, the local court may exercise personal jurisdiction over the actor. If the criminal actor simply provides information from a Web site, the victim's local court may not have grounds to exercise personal jurisdiction; however, local investigators are by no means ever prevented from engaging the assistance of remote law enforcement or courts to further an investigation.[7]

The remedy for a flawed search is most frequently suppression of the evidence obtained during the trial. This means that even the most clear-cut and self-evident material can be ruled inadmissible at trial. Some violations of statute may incur civil liability for the investigator, the investigator's department, or parent jurisdiction. An improper search and seizure is eligible for civil suit under 42 U.S.C. § 1983. The current implementation of the exclusionary rule is defined in *Mapp* v. *Ohio* (1961). The sole purpose of the exclusionary rule is to curb police abuse of civil rights. There is no common law expectation of the suppression of evidence improperly obtained. To invoke the exclusionary rule, the defendant must have standing; that is, the defendant must be the one whose rights were violated by the search.

The good faith doctrine provides one possible defense to accusations of a flawed search. If the investigator has a reasonable, bona fide (good faith) belief that the search conducted is based on a valid warrant, but that warrant is in actuality unsupported by probable cause, the fruits of the search are admissible. The reasoning behind the exclusionary rule is to deter police from misconduct, not to remedy violations of rights.[8] The exclusionary rule applies not only to evidence improperly obtained but also to evidence discovered using the improperly obtained evidence (i.e., derivative evidence). This is known as the fruit of the poisonous tree doctrine. Again, the rationale is to discourage the violation of citizens' rights by not rewarding such behavior.

There are two other defenses to the exclusionary rule that are related to one another. First, an independent source of the same information can redeem the evidence tainted by illegal search. Thus, if an illegal search—a forensic fishing expedition—reveals child pornography, the investigator may seek independent indication of the suspect's involvement in child pornography. A posting from a pedophile Web site may indicate the presence of evidence, but remain completely independent of the tainted source. Another potential defense is that the tainted evidence may lead to a short-cut, but would otherwise have been obtained (known as the inevitable discovery doctrine). For example, a coerced confession of possession of child pornography without a lawyer present would be suppressed, but a search warrant that was issued prior to the coerced confession could show the inevitable discovery of the materials. Since the materials would have been discovered if the process had continued, an illegal search does not immunize the evidence to discovery.

Searches without Warrants

Numerous exceptions exist to the general rule that searches must be conducted pursuant to a warrant. In fact, most searches conducted by the police do not involve a warrant (known as warrantless searches). Although numerous established exceptions to the warrant requirement exist and will be discussed in this section, it is best to be cautious in applying real-world analogies to the electronic world. Even if an officer believes they have a legitimate exception to the warrant requirement, it may still be worth stopping and seeking a warrant. Furthermore, the level of analysis required to obtain digital evidence can rarely be justified without a warrant; however, it may be appropriate to seize potential evidence to preserve it, while awaiting a warrant for the analysis. This section will discuss several warrantless searches.

STOP AND FRISK   A law enforcement officer has the right to self-protection during a brief interview by conducting a frisk of a citizen for weapons. A frisk is limited to a patdown of the outer clothing of the individual and can occur based on reasonable suspicion. Although it is possible to identify potential sources of digital evidence during the interview (e.g., a personal data assistant(PDA)or cellular phone), there is no clear justification, under the stop and frisk doctrine, to analyze such a device based on the logic of a stop and frisk (which basically only allows officers to look for weapons). However, if probable cause exists to believe evidence of a crime exists in the device, then further analysis should wait, pending a warrant.

A stop and frisk may be combined with other exceptions to examine content. For example, the plain-view doctrine can be used in association with data displayed by the device. Perhaps more useful is a trend in lower court cases allowing the preservation of perishable data under the exigent circumstances doctrine.[9] Warrantless searches of cellular phones and pagers have been allowed due to the possibility of incoming calls deleting evidence.

CONSENT SEARCH   When attempting to collect digital evidence without a warrant, consent searches are the most commonly used searches conducted by law enforcement. An officer can ask a citizen to consent (i.e., give permission) to a search of their person or property. Valid consent to search allows officers to search for any item within the scope of that consent. The courts apply a "totality of the circumstances" test to ensure that the consent was intelligently granted and free of coercion. Further, a suspect may revoke consent at any time, even during the search. The scope of the search is directly related to the consent given. Again, the totality of the circumstances will dictate the court's acceptance of searches that seem to exceed the scope of the consent.

An additional concern with consent searches is that the person giving consent must be legally capable of doing so. Briefly, these are persons with equal property rights (e.g., spouses, co-owners, or other employees using the same equipment); hosts during brief stays of a houseguest; employers, when it is clear by contract or policy; custodians of children (school officials, parents, etc.); or persons lawfully borrowing the property with access to the areas to be searched.[10] Some relationships have been defined by the courts to preclude legal consent. These include a spouse or co-owner specifically precluded from an area with reasonable precautions to prevent entry; a landlord (including hotel managers); an employer reserving an area for the exclusive and private use of an employee; or the host of a long-term guest with exclusive or private control over an area.[11]

Even if physical access to a space is granted, it does not come with the assumption of access to protected data. For example, if one spouse takes precautions to keep the other from using a computer (like a password or placing the computer in a separate room and denying access), or if a laptop is in the personal possession of a guest—even if left in an otherwise searchable room—a search of the data contained therein cannot be based on consent.[12]

EXIGENT CIRCUMSTANCES   The exigent circumstances doctrine allows law enforcement officers to search and/or seize evidence without a warrant if they have probable cause and there is some pressing need (i.e., exigent circumstance) to preserve evidence that is in danger of being destroyed or corrupted. The nature of digital evidence makes it subject to quick disposal and easy corruption. Encryption is another concern in making evidence unusable by an investigator. Once data are encrypted, the key can be almost instantaneously destroyed. The suspect may have another copy of the key somewhere nearby, but the location may be unknown to investigators. These very real dangers may justify warrantless searches under the proper conditions, but the burden of proving exigent circumstances falls on law enforcement.

Unless the computer, device, or network can be secured, it is unlikely that exigency will allow analysis; it will just allow for the seizure of the items. For example, the mobility of laptop computers makes them analogous to a vehicle. Investigators may seize the laptop without a warrant to prevent it from being taken out of their control, but it would require truly unusual circumstances to justify searching the contents without a warrant.

SEARCH INCIDENT TO ARREST   The Supreme Court has ruled that officers are allowed to search the person arrested for any weapons or for any evidence on the arrestee's person in order to prevent its concealment or destruction. Further, officers may also search areas within the arrestee's immediate control for the same purpose.[13] Like the stop and frisk, this exception could yield the physical container of evidence (e.g., PDA or cell phone), but would not justify analysis of the contents without exigent circumstances (e.g., batteries dying or new calls replacing numbers in memory).

PLAIN VIEW   The plain-view doctrine allows an officer lawfully to seize an item as long as certain requirements are met. In order to seize an item under the plain-view doctrine, an officer must (1) see the item, (2) be legally present in the area from which the item is viewed, and (3) immediately recognize that the item is subject to seizure. Since the officer is not conducting a search (i.e., the item is in plain view, and thus, there is no governmental intrusion into a person's reasonable expectation of privacy), the criminal nature of the item to be seized or observed must be immediately apparent to the officer (e.g., child pornography).[14]

Each of these requirements applies to the discovery and seizure of digital evidence, but it is possible that upon closer examination evidence not covered by a warrant will be discovered in plain view. For example, a search warrant may allow an investigator to search a hard drive for evidence of fraud. While the investigator is conducting the analysis, the officer discovers child pornography on the hard drive. The child pornography can be seized under the plain-view doctrine, since the three requirements discussed above have been met. As it applies to digital evidence, Orton states that it is important for investigators to not change the focus of their examination as a result of discovering a plain-view item. As an example, Orton states:

> [I]f a search protocol calls for examining all files sequentially on a computer, then every file may be examined . . . [I]f the search . . . calls for a key word search and an examination of the directory and file structure, but not the examination of each individual file, then the discovery of a possibly incriminating file name does not justify the opening of that file.[15]

If evidence is discovered in plain view while conducting another analysis, it is best to stop the analysis and seek a warrant based on the plain-view evidence.

The Supreme Court has examined the use of technology to achieve the "simple observation" contemplated by the plain-view doctrine. In *Kyllo* v. *United States,* the U.S. Supreme Court stated:

> Where, as here, the Government uses a device that is not in general public use, to explore details of a private home that would previously have been unknowable without physical intrusion, the surveillance is a Fourth Amendment "search," and is presumptively unreasonable without a warrant.[16]

This decision does not preclude technology in general use by the public. The decision allows technology not contemplated by the framers of the Constitution, but in common use, to define an expectation of privacy.

BORDER SEARCHES   In order to protect the government's ability to monitor contraband and other property that may enter the United States illegally, the courts have recognized the need to allow for border searches that are more intrusive than would be allowed in other locations. In at least one case, the court allowed a warrantless search of a computer disk for contraband computer files because the search was classified as a border search. In *United States* v. *Roberts,* customs agents believed that William Roberts was in possession of computerized images of child pornography. He was scheduled to travel from Houston to Paris on a particular day. On the day of the flight, the agents set up an inspection area in the Jetway of the Houston airport with the purpose of searching Roberts. After Roberts arrived at the inspection area, he was told by agents that they were searching for "currency" and "high technology and other data" that could not be exported legally. The agents searched Robert's property and found a laptop computer and six Zip diskettes. Roberts then gave the agents consent to search the diskettes, and several thousand images of child pornography were located. The Fifth Circuit Court of Appeals upheld the search.[17]

SEARCHES BY PRIVATE CITIZENS   Given that the Fourth Amendment only restricts the activities of government officials, the silver platter doctrine allows evidence collected by members of the public and presented to law enforcement to be admitted as evidence. Evidence presented to investigators "on a silver platter" is admissible as evidence at trial. For example, if a computer technician discovers contraband, investigators could use the contraband as a basis for further searches or as evidence in and of itself. In one case, the Court allowed a warrantless examination by law enforcement of the contents of a container already opened by a private company hired to transport the container. The scope of the search is limited to the scope employed by the private party. However, the fruits of a limited search may be used to obtain a warrant for a more complete search.[18]

FEDERAL STATUTES

Search and seizure law has developed incrementally as Congress and the courts have struggled to come to grips with criminal activity involving electronic communication. Because of this incremental development, the laws have built upon past concepts rather than attempting comprehensively to address the rapidly changing world of digital communication. This section discusses significant federal statutes that assist law enforcement in obtaining and seizing evidence related to digital crime. Most of the laws discussed were created for other purposes besides finding evidence of digital crime, but the laws have been adapted to include such actions by law enforcement. The focus of this section will be on federal statutes. It is important to note that states have laws that govern similar practices by law enforcement. Some state laws may place more restrictions on law enforcement than is required by federal statutes. For example, an exception to the wiretap statute discussed below is consent of one of the parties involved. This exception applies if the law enforcement officer is one of the parties communicating or has obtained prior consent from such a person. The exception authorizes the interception of communications when one of the parties to the communication consents to the interception. However, some states forbid the interception of communications unless all parties consent.[19] The federal laws governing electronic surveillance in communication networks as well as significant federal criminal statutes will be discussed in this section.

Criminal investigations involving digital crime frequently require electronic surveillance. As it applies to computer crimes, agents may want to monitor a hacker, a suspect's e-mail correspondence, or an individual sending or receiving child pornography via the Internet. Two federal statutes govern the practice of electronic surveillance in criminal investigations: Title III of the Omnibus Crime Control and Safe Streets Act of 1968 and the Pen Registers and Trap and Trace Devices chapter of Title 18. These statutes do not apply exclusively to criminal investigations involving computers, but more generically to traditional forms of electronic surveillance such as wiretapping a suspect's telephone. In general, the pen/trap statute regulates the collection of addressing and other noncontent information for wire and electronic communications. Title III governs the collection of actual content of wire and electronic communications.[20] As it applies to the Internet and e-mail, the pen/trap statute allows the government to obtain the addressing information of Internet communications much as it would allow the government to obtain phone numbers for traditional phone calls. However, reading an Internet or e-mail communication requires compliance with Title III.

The Pen/Trap Statute 18 U.S.C. §3121-27

The pen/trace statute regulates the collection of addressing information from wire communications. The statute takes its name from the now-obsolete physical devices attached to phone wires to perform this function. A pen register records outgoing numbers dialed from a phone. A trap and trace device records this information from incoming calls, similar to caller ID. The pen/trap statute allows the government to apply for a court order authorizing the installation of a pen register or trap and trace device so long as the information likely to be obtained is relevant to an ongoing criminal investigation.[21] This statute has been applied to include computer network communications, not just telephone communications (e.g., an Internet user account, an e-mail account, or an IP address). To obtain a court order for a pen/trap device, applicants must identify themselves, identify the agency conducting the investigation, and must certify their belief that the information likely to be obtained is relevant to an ongoing criminal investigation.[22] The court can authorize the installation and use of a pen/trap device anywhere in the United States. The order may authorize the use of a pen/trap device for up to 60 days and may be extended for additional 60-day periods.[23] Pen/trap devices are used more frequently by law enforcement than wiretaps.

The Wiretap Statute (Title III) 18 U.S.C. §2510-22

Title III regulates the collection of communication content. It was passed under Title III of the Omnibus Crime Control and Safe Streets Act of 1968 and provides the statutory framework that governs real-time electronic surveillance of the contents of communications (e.g., listening on a phone conversation). The statute prohibits a third party (such as the government) who is not a participating party to the communication from intercepting private communications between the parties using an "electronic, mechanical, or other device" unless one of several statutory exceptions applies.[24] In other words, communication content intercepted from a wire communication may not be used in court unless an exception applies. Title III contains dozens of exceptions, but the following seven exceptions apply the most frequently in computer crime cases:

1. *Interception pursuant to a Title III court order (wiretap order)* Title III permits law enforcement to intercept wire and electronic communications pursuant to a court order under 18 U.S.C. §2518. Approval from Department of Justice administration is required for the application. A U.S. District Court or Court of Appeals judge must then approve of the application. When authorized, a Title III order permits law enforcement to intercept communications for up to 30 days.[25] Wiretap orders carry more stringent standards than an application for a federal search warrant, with an annual reporting requirement by the Administrative Office of the U.S. Courts (AOUSC). This reporting requirement and explicit processes to minimize intrusion into subjects' privacy raises the procedural burden beyond that of a search warrant.

2. *The consent exception [§2511 (2)(c)-(d)]* This exception applies if the law enforcement officer is one of the parties communicating or has obtained prior consent from such a person. The exception authorizes the interception of communications when one of the parties to the communication consents to the interception. Some states forbid the interception of communications unless all parties consent.[26]

3. *The provider exception [§2511 (2)(a)(i)]* Employees or agents of communications service providers may intercept and disclose communication to protect the providers' rights or property. For example, system administrators of computer networks generally may monitor hackers intruding into their networks and then disclose the fruits of monitoring to law enforcement without violating Title III. This privilege belongs to the provider alone, however, and cannot be exercised by law enforcement. Once the provider has communicated with law enforcement, the computer trespasser exception may provide a basis for monitoring by law enforcement.[27]

4. *The computer trespasser exception [§2511 (2)(i)]* This exception allows victims of computer attacks to authorize law enforcement to intercept wire or electronic communications of a computer trespasser. In order to use this exception, the owner or operator of the computer must authorize the interception, the person who intercepts the communications must be lawfully engaged in an investigation, the person who intercepts the communications must believe that the content of the intercepted communication will be relevant to the investigation, and the interception should not acquire any communications other than those transmitted to or from the computer trespasser.[28]

5. *The extension telephone exception [§2510 (5)(a)]* This exception was originally designed to allow businesses to monitor by way of an extension telephone the performance of their employees who spoke on the phone to customers. Today, routine taping of all telephone calls made to and from a police station may fall within this exception as well.[29]

6. *The inadvertently obtained criminal evidence exception [§2511 (3)(b)(iv)]* Communication that is unintentionally obtained by the provider and that appears to relate to a crime can be released to a law enforcement agency. For example, a provider could report evidence of a fraud scheme to law enforcement if the provider inadvertently obtained such evidence.[30]

7. *The accessible to the public exception [§2511 (2)(g)(i)]* Intercepting unscrambled or unencrypted communication broadcast over public frequencies does not violate the wiretap statute. In addition, the language of this statute appears to permit the interception of an

electronic communication that has been posted to a public bulletin board, a public chat room, or a Usenet newsgroup.[31]

Electronic Communications Privacy Act (ECPA) 18 U.S.C. §§2701-11

The ECPA is an unusually complicated statute. It regulates how the government can obtain stored account information from network service providers such as ISPs. Whenever officers seek stored e-mail, account records, or subscriber information from a network service provider, they must comply with the ECPA. The stored communication portion of the ECPA creates statutory privacy rights for customers and subscribers of computer network service providers.[32] The wire communication portion of the ECPA affirms a higher level of protection for communication in transit. This recognizes the fact that electronic communication follows a store-and-wait model rather than a direct exchange model like the telephone system, but affirms a citizen's expectation of privacy in communication. However, once the purpose of communication is achieved (i.e., the recipient reads or receives it), it enjoys the lesser protection of any stored document. To achieve a functional distinction between these points, the ECPA creates two categories of computer service:

- *Electronic Communication Service (ECS):* An ECS provider is a company holding an electronic message in transit (e.g., an unopened e-mail on a mail server).
- *Remote Computing Service (RCS):* An RCS provider is a company that holds or processes the data of a customer (e.g., saving an e-mail that has already been read makes the server's owner an RCS. An RCS can also be any form of data warehousing).

Information to be obtained under ECPA must be specified as one of three categories, with each category enjoying progressively greater protection through procedural burdens on the investigator:

1. Basic subscriber information [§2703 (c)(1)(C)]:
   - Name
   - Address
   - Local and long-distance telephone toll billing records
   - Telephone number or other subscriber number or identity
   - Length of service and types of service
2. Records or logs pertaining to a subscriber [§2703 (c)(1)(A)-(B)]:
   - The contents of any relevant logs
   - All basic subscriber information
   - Cell site data for calls made
   - Destinations of outgoing e-mail
   - Any other noncontent records
3. Contents of communication [§2510 (8)]

Each category of the above-mentioned information requires a progressively greater showing of cause to obtain. The ECPA also defines five types of instruments that may be required to obtain such information: subpoena, subpoena with prior notice to service user, §2703(d) order, §2703(d) order with prior notice to service user, and search warrant.

1. Investigators can subpoena basic subscriber information. The legal requirements that must be met before issuing a subpoena are not stringent.[33]
2. Investigators can subpoena opened e-mail (and other stored electronic or wire communications in electronic storage more than 180 days) from a provider if they comply with

the notice provisions required by the ECPA. The notice provisions are satisfied by giving the customer prior notice of the disclosure. The notice can be delayed for 90 days if there is reason to believe that notification of a subpoena will have an adverse result (e.g., jeopardize a pending investigation or endanger the safety of someone).[34]

3. Agents need a §2703(d) court order to obtain most account logs and most transactional records. In other words, all relevant records (except the contents of communications) held by providers of electronic communications services and remote computing services can be obtained with a §2703(d) order.[35]

4. Investigators can obtain everything in an account except for unopened e-mail or voicemail stored with a provider for 180 days or less using a §2703(d) order combined with the prior notice provisions discussed above.[36]

5. Investigators can obtain the full contents of an account with a search warrant. ECPA does not require the government to notify the customer when it obtains information from a provider using a search warrant.[37]

It is also possible under certain circumstances for the service provider to voluntarily disclose account information to law enforcement. Nonpublic providers may disclose both contents and other records relating to stored communications. The ECPA imposes significant restrictions on voluntary disclosures by public providers, but exceptions do exist to the restrictions.[38]

USA PATRIOT ACT

The USA PATRIOT Act was passed in the aftermath of the 9/11 attacks and reauthorized by Congress in 2006. This treatment only considers the domestic provisions of the act. The PATRIOT Act is discussed further in Chapter 8. The foreign provisions can be applied to foreign operatives in the United States, but will generally not be applicable to domestic law enforcement. The act primarily updates and enhances surveillance procedures while maintaining the established distinction between content and routing information. The PATRIOT Act also:

- Permits the seizure of voicemail messages older than 180 days with a §2703 order (§209)
- Permits the seizure of voicemail messages less than 180 days old with a search warrant (§209)
- Expands the definition of "basic subscriber information" to include a more detailed length of service use, type of service use, dynamic IP assigned, and means and source of payment (§210)
- Permits emergency disclosure by public service providers to protect life and limb or regarding terrorism offenses (§212 & §505)
- Permits delay of required notice of the execution of a warrant if notice may result in the unduly delay of a trial (§213)
- Makes warrants and pen/trace orders national (§216 & §220)

Contrary to popular opinion, the USA PATRIOT Act does not change any of the procedural burdens previously placed on investigators when seeking information. In fact, the reauthorized PATRIOT Act has increased judicial oversight for the use of wiretaps and searches. From the highest burden to lowest, these are shown in Table 9.1.

TABLE 9.1 Burden of Proof Standards in the PATRIOT Act

Instrument	Procedural Burden
Title III interception order	Probable cause standard with explicit minimization and reporting
F.R.C.P. Rule 41 search warrant authorizing the search of physical premises and physical items Or ECPA search warrant authorizing search of "in-transit" data held by an ECS for less than 180 days	Probable cause standard
ECPA §2703(d) order Or ECPA §2703(d) order with notice	Specific and articulable facts showing reasonable grounds to believe that the records are relevant and material to an ongoing criminal investigation
Pen register and trap and trace device order	Relevant to a criminal investigation
Subpoena with notice, ECPA§2703(b)(1)(B)	Filed with the court
Subpoena with delayed notice, ECPA §2705	Notice may be delayed in successive 90-day periods "upon the written certification of a supervisory official that there is reason to believe that notification of the existence of the subpoena may have an adverse result."

Communication Assistance for Law Enforcement Act

The Communication Assistance for Law Enforcement Act (CALEA) was signed into law in 1994. Although telecommunications companies have been required, since 1970, to cooperate with law enforcement in conducting lawfully authorized electronic surveillance (e.g., wiretaps), CALEA requires telecommunications companies to modify the design of their equipment, facilities, and services to ensure that lawfully authorized electronic surveillance can actually be performed by law enforcement personnel.

Federal Criminal Statutes

There are also several federal criminal statutes that focus on computer crime. Three significant statutes will be discussed in this section, including the Consumer Fraud and Abuse Act, the Economic Espionage Act, and the Copyright Act.

THE COMPUTER FRAUD AND ABUSE ACT The Computer Fraud and Abuse Act was originally passed in 1984.[39] It has been amended multiple times, in 1986, 1994, 1996, 2001, and 2008. It is the primary federal statute targeting unauthorized computer use, primarily focusing on unauthorized access and theft of information from computers. It covers a broad range of acts and protects a range of computers that facilitate interstate and international commerce and communications. After several amendments, the act basically covers any computer connected to the Internet. For example, the act makes it a crime to access a computer without authority to obtain financial information from a financial institution or any information in possession of the government. Furthermore, another section of the act makes it a crime for anyone to cause the transmission of a computer program, information, code, or command that results in unauthorized damage to a protected computer.[40] Criminal actions covered by the Computer Fraud and Abuse Act include access to and transmission of government classified information, access to computers in or outside of the United States that are used in interstate commerce, intentional access of a government nonpublic computer, knowingly accessing and intentionally causing damage to a protected computer, intentionally accessing a computer without authorization and causing damage, and conspiring to commit a computer hacking offense.[41]

THE ECONOMIC ESPIONAGE ACT   The Economic Espionage Act was enacted in 1996. The primary purpose of the Economic Espionage Act is to impose criminal penalties on the theft of trade secrets. The trade secrets may be stored either physically or electronically. In order to be defined as a trade secret, the property must be economically valuable and the owner must take measures to protect it. In addition, in order to be covered by the act, the person who is stealing the trade secret must know that the theft will result in economic loss to the owner and a benefit to another person.[42] This act applies anywhere in the world as long as a U.S. citizen or company is the perpetrator. A recent alleged violation of this act occurred when a software engineer for Cisco Systems took a job with a competitor. The engineer was arrested for taking voice-over and optical network software designs contained on a CD from Cisco Systems.[43]

THE COPYRIGHT ACT   Copyright infringement has become a significant focus for law enforcement with the increased use of computers and the internet. Copyrightable property includes literary works, musical works, dramatic works, pantomimes and choreographic works, pictorial and graphic works, motion pictures and audiovisual works, sound recordings, and architectural works. Copyright infringement as it applies to computers typically involves software piracy but has recently focused on downloading music and video files. The primary criminal statute protecting copyrighted works is Title 17 U.S.C. §506(a). This act makes it against the law to willfully infringe upon a copyright for commercial advantage or private financial gain.

THE FAMILY ENTERTAINMENT AND COPYRIGHT ACT   Video-sharing services like YouTube and new piracy technologies like Bit Torrent have increased the global problem of piracy. As a result, the Family Entertainment and Copyright Act of 2005 was signed into law to increase the penalties attached to acts of piracy.[44] In particular, this law makes it illegal to record, photograph, or otherwise copy a motion picture or other protected work as it is presented or screened in a theater. This statute also criminalizes the distribution of copyrighted materials before they are released to the public for commercial profit. Thus, this makes it illegal to provide pirated copies of movies or music before they are officially made available in stores or theaters. This law also makes it illegal to create technologies that enable individuals to edit DVD movies on the fly. The intent of this part of the statute is to protect the content of an artist's creation in its original format from individuals who intend to alter the content in some fashion.

ADMITTING EVIDENCE AT TRIAL

In this section, issues related to admitting computer records and other digital evidence into trial will be discussed. Much of the discussion will focus on the Federal Rules of Evidence. Most federal courts that have evaluated the admissibility of computer records have focused on computer records as potential hearsay.[45] The courts have typically admitted computer records upon a showing that the records fall within the business records exception to the Federal Rules of Evidence 803 (6).

However, the evidentiary issues raised by the admission of computer records really depend on what type of computer records are being admitted as evidence. Computer records that contain text can typically be divided into two categories: computer-generated records and computer-stored records.[46] The difference depends on whether a person or machine created the record. Computer-stored records include documents that have been created by a person. Examples of such records that may be admitted as evidence include word-processing files, e-mail messages, and chat room messages. In comparison, computer-generated records contain output from computer programs that have not been manipulated by a person. Such computer-generated records include log-in records from ISPs, telephone records, and ATM receipts.[47] The evidentiary issues are typically different for these two types of records. For computer-stored records, the evidentiary issue involves a question of whether a person's out-of-court statement was truthful and accurate. In other words, using computer-stored records as evidence brings up the issue of hearsay. However, when the evidence involves computer-generated records, the question becomes whether the computer program that generated the record was functioning properly. This is a question of authenticity, not hearsay.

Therefore, the admission of computer records as evidence usually involves two issues. First, the government needs to establish that the computer records are authentic. Second, if the records involve computer-stored records created by a person, then the government must demonstrate that the person-generated records are not inadmissible hearsay.[48] The issues of authentication, hearsay, as well as the best evidence rule will be discussed in further detail.

Authentication

Before the government or a defendant can move for the admission of a computer record as evidence, the authenticity of the record must be proven first. The government must offer evidence "sufficient to support a finding that the computer record or other evidence in question is what its proponent claims."[49] In authenticating computer records, the witness must have first-hand knowledge of the relevant facts to which he or she testifies.[50]

Challenges to the authenticity of computer records often take one of three forms. First, parties may challenge the authenticity of both computer-generated and computer-stored records by questioning whether the records were altered, manipulated, or damaged after they were created. In challenging the admission of computer records, opposing counsel frequently alleges that computer records lack authenticity because they were tampered with or changed after they were created. Generally, the courts are skeptical of unsupported claims that computer records have been altered. Therefore, the mere possibility of tampering does not affect the authenticity of a computer record: Specific evidence that tampering occurred must be presented.[51]

Second, parties may question the authenticity of computer-generated records by challenging the reliability of the computer program that generated the records. The opposing counsel makes the argument that the computer-generated record may not be authentic because the program that creates the record contains serious programming errors. Often, the reliability of a computer program can be established by showing that users of the program rely on it on a regular basis during their ordinary course of business.[52]

Third, parties may challenge the authenticity of computer-stored records by questioning the identity of their author. Although handwritten records may be penned in a distinctive handwriting style, computer-stored records do not necessarily identify their author. For example, technology allows users to send effectively anonymous e-mails and chat rooms allow users to communicate without using their real names. Defendants frequently challenge the admission of computer-stored records of this nature by arguing that they are not the authors of the material. The key to establishing authorship of computer-stored records typically involves the use of circumstantial evidence.[53]

Hearsay

The hearsay rule exists to prevent unreliable out-of-court statements by people from influencing the outcomes of trials. Therefore, rules of evidence require that individuals making statements be placed on the stand and subjected to cross-examination. When a computer record contains the assertions of a person, the record can contain hearsay.[54] Before a court will admit the records, the court must establish that the statements contained in the record were made in circumstances that tend to ensure their trustworthiness. In order to accomplish this, the government typically fits the record within a hearsay exception such as the business records exception. The business record exception is the most common hearsay exception applied to computer records [Federal Rules of Evidence 803 (6)]. It states:

> *Records of regularly conducted activity.* A memorandum, report, record, or data compilation, in any form, or acts, events, conditions, opinions, or diagnoses, made at or near the time by, or from information transmitted by, a person with knowledge, if kept in the course of a regularly conducted business activity, and if it was the regular practice of that business activity to make the memorandum, report, record, or data compilation, all as shown by the testimony of the custodian or other qualified witness, unless the source of information or the method of circumstances of preparation indicate lack of trustworthiness. The term "business" as used in this paragraph includes business, institution, association, profession, occupation, and calling of every kind, whether or not conducted for profit.[55]

In applying this principle, courts have generally indicated that computer records can be admitted as business records if they are kept following a routine procedure to ensure their accuracy.[56] The hearsay rule is discussed further in Chapter 11.

The Best Evidence Rule

The authentication requirement and the hearsay rule are typically the two biggest issues encountered by prosecutors when seeking the admission of computer records as evidence at trial. Another issue that sometimes comes up is known as the best evidence rule. The best evidence rule states that to prove the content of a writing, recording, or photograph, the "original" writing, recording, or photograph is ordinarily required.[57] Prosecutors sometimes are concerned that a printout of a computer-stored electronic file may not be an "original" for the purpose of the best evidence rule.[58] The original file is a collection of 0s and 1s, while the printout is a result of manipulating the original file. However, the Federal Rules of Evidence have expressly addressed this issue. Federal Rules of Evidence 1003 states that if data are stored in a computer or similar device, any printout or other output readable by sight, shown to reflect the data accurately, is an "original."[59] Therefore, an accurate printout of computer data always satisfies the best evidence rule.[60]

SIGNIFICANT COURT CASES

In *Katz* v. *United States* (1967),[61] Katz made a phone call from a public phone booth. Federal agents placed a listening device in the phone booth but did not tap the line. They obtained incriminating evidence. Katz appealed. The government contended that the phone booth was a public place. The Court concluded that the Fourth Amendment protects persons evidencing an expectation of privacy; however, society must be willing to recognize that expectation as reasonable.

Perhaps most important for future electronic search and seizure law, the case hinged on the interception of communication content. In attempting to create a "technological workaround" to bypass statutory protections on telephone content (see Title III, discussed previously), the Court defined that the functional equivalent of an impermissible intrusion is an impermissible intrusion regardless of the actual route employed by the technology. Thus, constitutional protections apply to persons and expectations, not to physical locations or actual techniques. The functional presence of officers in a "private" space violates the reasonable expectation of privacy protected by the Fourth Amendment.

In *Florida* v. *Riley* (1989),[62] the Court allowed the use of aerial surveillance of arguably "private" spaces. It has long been established that police can observe private property from a public space; this is not considered a search. Thus evidence observed in an open field (even if it is on private property) carries no reasonable expectation of privacy. Technology has changed the vantage point of police observation. In *Florida* v. *Riley,* the Court decided that the government may use the "high place" of otherwise legal flight to observe illegal activity. This ruling opened observation flights over suspected marijuana fields. Perhaps most significantly, this ruling allowed a fundamental change in the notion of privacy that recognized changing technology.

Thus, the reasonable expectation of privacy is not static; it must adapt to technology beyond the intentions of the framers of the Constitution. The implications for electronic search and seizure are broad. The home, once the bastion of privacy rights, may contain a Web server with illicit materials. Viewing those materials does not constitute a search. Law enforcement officers may use a tool like a Web-based search engine and "invade" the Web server without violating a reasonable expectation of privacy.

Although searches usually implicate the Fourth Amendment, there is a precedent for First Amendment implications as well. In *Zurcher* v. *Stanford Daily* (1978),[63] police sought photographs of a student riot taken by a *Stanford Daily* photographer. In addition to defining search law, a relatively obscure circumstance was observed. The legitimate interest of the police in searching does not automatically override the substantial deference given to the press. The principles derived from the *Zurcher* case include the following:

1. A search is not unreasonable if items sought are not in the possession of the suspected criminal. The items sought must be reasonably expected at the place searched.
2. The search should not interfere with the execution of actions privileged by the First Amendment, particularly freedom of the press.

This principle was applied to computer search and seizure in the *Steve Jackson Games* (1993) case.[64] Federal agents tracking the theft of an electronic document related to the 911 system traced the document to an electronic bulletin board system maintained by Steve Jackson Games. Players of a conspiracy-paranoia game called *Illumination* exchanged messages about the game and sometimes about real life. Steve Jackson Games also used the system for internal development, e-mail, and newsletters. The Secret Service seized the entire physical system under a search warrant and did not return it for years. The company lost a substantial amount of business and customers and eventually claimed tens of thousands of dollars in damages. More fundamentally, the seizure unnecessarily deprived the company and gamers of a platform for speech and association.

Summary

In this chapter, law and legislation as it applies to the collection of evidence and prosecution of digital crime were discussed. The different types of searches available to investigators searching for digital evidence were analyzed, including searches with and without warrants. The major federal statutes governing the collection of digital evidence were reviewed. Many of these statutes focused on electronic surveillance of communications networks. Issues related to the admission of digital evidence at trial, including authentication, hearsay, and the best evidence rule, were reviewed as well. In addition, several significant U.S. Supreme Court cases that affect the investigation and prosecution of digital crime were discussed.

Review Questions

1. What types of warrantless searches can be conducted by investigators collecting digital evidence?
2. What are the major exceptions to the wiretap statute?
3. What are the major requirements established by the Electronic Communication Privacy Act?
4. What issues arise during the admission of digital evidence at trial?

Endnotes

1. *Johnson* v. *United States,* 333 U.S. 10 (1948).
2. *Katz* v. *United States,* 389 U.S. 347 (1967).
3. *United States* v. *Jacobsen,* 466 U.S. 109 (1984).
4. *Ibid.*
5. *Arizona* v. *Hicks,* 480 U.S. 321 (1987).
6. BLACK, H.C.,NOLAN, J.R., and NOLAN-HALEY, J.M. (1990). *Black's Law Dictionary,* 6th ed. St. Paul, MN: West.
7. CASEY, E. (2000). *Digital Evidence and Computer Crime: Forensic Science, Computers and the Internet.* San Diego, CA: Academic Press.
8. *United States* v. *Leon,* 468 U.S. 897 (1984).
9. *United States* v. *David,* 756 F.Supp. 1385 (D. Nev. 1991); *United States* v. *Romero-Garcia,* 168 F.3d 502 (9th Cir. 1999).
10. FERDICO, J.N. (1999). *Criminal Procedure for the Criminal Justice Professional,* 7th ed. New York: Wadsworth.
11. *Ibid.*
12. ORTON, IVAN. (2001). "The Investigation and Prosecution of a Cybercrime." In RALPH D. CLIFFORD (ed.), *Cybercrime: The Investigation, Prosecution, and Defense of a Computer-Related*
Crime. Durham, NC: Carolina Academic Press, pp. 71–121; *Trulok* v. *Freeh,* 275 F.3d 391 (4th Cir.).
13. *Chimel* v. *California,* 395 U.S. 752 (1969).
14. *Arizona* v. *Hicks,* 480 U.S. 321 (1987).
15. ORTON, "The Investigation and Prosecution of a Cybercrime," pp. 91–92; *Trulok* v. *Freeh,* 275 F.3d 391 (4th Cir. 2001).
16. *Kyllo* v. *United States,* 533 U.S. 27 (2001).
17. *United States* v. *Roberts,* 274 F.3d 1007 (5th Cir. 2001); U.S. Department of Justice (2002). *Searching and Seizing Computers and Obtaining Electronic Evidence in Criminal Investigations* Washington, DC: U.S. Department of Justice.
18. U.S. Department of Justice, *Searching and Seizing Computers and Obtaining Electronic Evidence in Criminal Investigations.*
19. *Ibid.*
20. *Ibid.*
21. 18 U.S.C. 3122(b)(2).
22. U.S. Department of Justice, *Searching and Seizing Computers and Obtaining Electronic Evidence in Criminal Investigations.*

23. *Ibid.*
24. *Ibid.*
25. *Ibid.*
26. *Ibid.*
27. *Ibid.*
28. *Ibid.*
29. *Ibid.*
30. *Ibid.*
31. *Ibid.*
32. *Ibid.*
33. *Ibid.*
34. *Ibid.*
35. *Ibid.*
36. *Ibid.*
37. *Ibid.*
38. *Ibid.*
39. 18 U.S.C. §1030.
40. *The Electronic Frontier: The Challenge of Unlawful Conduct Involving the Use of the Internet.* A Report of the President's Working Group on Unlawful Conduct on the Internet, 2000.
41. HILLER, J.S., and COHEN, R. (2002). *Internet Law and Policy.* Upper Saddle River, NJ: Prentice Hall.
42. *Ibid.*
43. *Ibid.*
44. 17 U.S.C. 110(11).
45. KERR, ORIN S. (2001). *Computer Records and the Federal Rules of Evidence.* Washington, DC: U.S. Department of Justice.
46. *Ibid.*
47. *Ibid.*
48. *Ibid.*
49. Federal Rules of Evidence §901 (a).
50. KERR, *Computer Records and the Federal Rules of Evidence.*
51. *Ibid.*
52. *Ibid.*
53. *Ibid.*
54. *Ibid.*
55. Federal Rules of Evidence §803 (6).
56. KERR, *Computer Records and the Federal Rules of Evidence.*
57. Federal Rules of Evidence §1002.
58. KERR, *Computer Records and the Federal Rules of Evidence.*
59. Federal Rules of Evidence §1003.
60. KERR, *Computer Records and the Federal Rules of Evidence.*
61. *Katz* v. *United States,* 389 U.S. 347 (1967).
62. *Florida* v. *Riley,* 488 U.S. 445 (1989).
63. *Zurcher* v. *Stanford Daily,* 436 U.S. 547 (1978).
64. *Steve Jackson Games, Inc.* v. *Secret Service,* 816 F. Supp. 432, 440, 443 (W.D. Tex. 1993).

CHAPTER 10

Law Enforcement Roles and Responses

CHAPTER OBJECTIVES

After completing this chapter, you should be able to

- Provide an overview of the roles and responses of federal law enforcement agencies concerning digital crimes and any interagency partnerships to deal with these offenses.
- Describe local law enforcement responses to computer crime.
- Identify the factors that have limited local law enforcement efforts against digital crime.

INTRODUCTION

The recent emergence of computer technologies and the growing threats created by digital criminals and terrorists have worked to produce a wide array of new challenges for law enforcement officials charged with protecting individuals, private businesses, and governments from these threats. In response, political leaders and police administrators have increasingly recognized the need to emphasize new priorities and foster new and innovative organizational strategies designed to counter the advent and continued growth of computer crimes.

This chapter begins with an overview of federal roles and responses as they relate to computer crimes. The discussion focuses on the responses and organizational initiatives recently enacted by prominent federal law enforcement agencies as well as the role of the Department of Homeland Security (DHS) in these efforts. The chapter concludes with a description of the ways in which local law enforcement agencies have joined the fight against computer crime. This chapter emphasizes the need to strengthen the capabilities of local agencies by identifying several factors that have thus far limited local law enforcement efforts.

FEDERAL ROLES AND RESPONSES

For the most part, federal agencies have spearheaded law enforcement efforts against computer crime because these agencies possess the technical expertise and political clout to garner significant financial and operational resources at the national level. These agencies have increasingly reorganized in an effort to channel resources directly at preventing digital crimes and apprehending computer criminals, including the creation of special sections within these organizations, the recruitment of new personnel who possess specialized technical expertise in this area, and the creation of new collaborative units that combine the resources of multiple agencies. Additionally, several agencies have developed partnership programs with other law enforcement agencies, private industry, and the public in an attempt to improve collaboration and cooperation to thwart digital criminals.

The Department of Justice

The U.S. Department of Justice (DOJ) was established in 1870. The organization is headed by the chief law enforcement officer of the federal government—the attorney general. The attorney general represents the United States in legal matters generally and gives advice and opinions regarding matters of jurisprudence to the president. In cases of extreme importance, the attorney general may appear before the U.S. Supreme Court as the federal government's representative attorney. Under the attorney general is a vast array of sections and organizational subunits designed to oversee the administration of justice on the federal level. These agencies include (1) the U.S. Attorney's Office, representing the federal government in court and prosecuting federal suspects; (2) the major federal investigative agencies, including the Federal Bureau of Investigation (FBI), the Drug Enforcement Administration (DEA), and the Bureau of Alcohol, Tobacco, Firearms, and Explosives (ATFE); (3) the U.S. Marshals Service; and (4) the U.S. Bureau of Prisons.[1]

The DOJ has stepped up efforts to respond to the legal threats posed by cybercriminals. The cornerstone of these efforts is the Criminal Division's Computer Crime and Intellectual Property Section (CCIPS). CCIPS began as the Computer Crime Unit of DOJ in 1991. This unit primarily prosecuted violations of the Federal Code covered by Title 18, Section 1030, of the Computer Fraud and Abuse Act. The scope of DOJ jurisdiction in such crimes was expanded with the enactment of the National Information and Infrastructure Protection Act of 1996. In accordance with this act, as well as the DOJ's recognition of the need to increase prosecutorial resources aimed at combating computer crimes, the department elevated the unit to section status in 1996 and adopted the moniker CCIPS.[2]

Currently, the section employs dozens of attorneys who focus solely on legal issues raised by computer and intellectual property crimes. CCIPS attorneys specialize in prosecuting crimes related to encryption, e-commerce, intellectual property crimes, electronic privacy laws, computer hacker investigations, and search and seizure cases involving computers. Members of the CCIPS section advise federal prosecutors on computer crimes cases, and CCIPS attorneys normally take the lead in litigating computer and intellectual property crimes on behalf of the federal government. In addition, CCIPS staff members comment on the legality of proposed computer crime legislation that is designed to mitigate computer crime threats. CCIPS works in close collaboration with the U.S. Attorney's Office in the prosecution of computer crimes. Finally, there is a subunit within CCIPS called the Computer Hacking and Intellectual Property (CHIP) unit. CHIP units focus on prosecuting computer hacking, fraud, and intellectual property cases. This specialized unit has proven highly successful and has been expanded multiple times to include 25 units across the country.[3] The CCIPS also has an Intellectual Property Task Force, which was created in 2004 as a way to improve prosecutions and guide cases against piracy and counterfeiting.[4]

While CCIPS primarily operates as a prosecutorial arm of the department, the section has also attempted to remedy the growing need for training and interagency cooperation. CCIPS attorneys conduct hundreds of training seminars every year for other federal attorneys in an effort to educate those prosecutors outside of the section in regard to relevant legislation and effective prosecutorial strategies for cases involving computer crime. They also offer training to law enforcement agencies and engage in diplomatic missions to build strong relationships between the U.S. and foreign law enforcement officials.

The Federal Bureau of Investigation

The FBI was established in 1908 as the investigative branch of the U.S. DOJ. The FBI carries a broad mandate that authorizes the organization to protect the United States from terror and foreign intelligence agencies, as well as to investigate any federal crime that has not been specifically designated to another federal agency. These broad legal areas can include civil rights crimes, violent federal crimes, organized crime and drugs, and financial crimes. The FBI employs over 13,075 special agents who operate out of the Washington, DC headquarters, 56 field offices, and over 400 satellite offices globally. The FBI plays an important role in the investigation of cybercrime. In fact, protection of the United States from cyber-based attacks and high-technology crimes is their third priority, behind terror and foreign intelligence. This suggests that cybercrime has become a high priority for investigation, over and above physical real-world crimes. The bureau's role in fighting computer crime is fourfold: (1) to capture the criminals behind serious computer intrusions and the spread of malicious code; (2) to stop online sexual predators who produce or share child pornography and meet and exploit children; (3) to stop operations targeting U.S. intellectual property; and (4) to dismantle national and transnational organized crime groups engaging in Internet fraud. The FBI is also leading the charge to investigate and prosecute cybercrimes.[5]

The bureau's Cyber Division works in tandem with the Criminal Investigative Division in the investigation of domestic threats generated by computer-related crimes. Typically, their caseloads focus on child pornography, followed by fraud, computer intrusions, and intellectual property theft. There are also 93 computer crime task forces across the country that provide a partnership between the bureau, federal, state, and local law enforcement agencies to better solve crimes.[6] A new program has also been developed called Cyber Action Teams, which have a small number of specially trained agents who are experts in malware and forensics.[7] These teams travel as needed to various spots around the world to assist in the investigation of computer intrusions and gather intelligence on threats and cybercrimes that threaten national security.

In addition, the FBI has developed and supports the Regional Computer Forensics Laboratory (RCFL) Program.[8] This is a partnership between the bureau, state, local, and federal law enforcement agencies within a geographical area. RCFLs provide computer forensic lab support and training programs in support of criminal investigations and the prevention of terror incidents. The first such RCFL was established in San Diego, California, in 1999.[9] The FBI then created a National Program Office in 2002 to oversee and facilitate the creation of other RCFLs around the country. There are 16 areas around the country, particularly in the Western, Southern, and Northeastern United States.[10]

In addition, the bureau has partnered with the National White-Collar Crime Center (NW3C) to operate the Internet Crime Complaint Center (ICCC or IC3). The IC3 provides victims of Internet fraud a mechanism to report suspicious online activities. The IC3 also provides other federal agencies a "central repository for complaints related to Internet fraud." The goal of the IC3 is to identify wider Internet fraud patterns and trends to aid in the enforcement of these crimes.[11] The bureau also works with the Computer Security Institute to produce an annual survey of cybercrime and computer security incidents in the private sector as a means of understanding the scope of the problems faced by individuals in this industry.[12]

The FBI has also developed relationships with private and public sector partners to improve their ability to protect computerized critical infrastructures.[13] The federal government owns and operates many of these critical infrastructure systems; these law enforcement agencies would be the primary responders in the event of a national crisis. Likewise, the private sector currently operates the vast majority of these systems, and private sector employees often have the greatest expertise in identifying and solving technical problems. Thus, the FBI developed the "InfraGard," program began in 1998 as a joint initiative of the DOJ and what was then the National Infrastructure Protection Center. This program is now housed in the bureau's Cyber Division, where there are approximately 86 chapters around the country with 23,000 members.[14] The program is designed to facilitate the exchange of information among academic institutions, the business community, and the FBI and serves as a prime example of the FBI's agenda for partnerships and interagency collaboration in the fight against cybercrimes.

The National Security Agency

The National Security Agency (NSA) bills itself as the nation's preeminent "cryptologic organization." In more familiar language, the NSA is primarily responsible for designing and maintaining computerized coding systems designed to protect the integrity of U.S. information systems.[15] It has also become the lead agency responsible for monitoring and protecting all of the federal government's computer networks from acts of cyberterrorism.[16] In direct relation to these responsibilities, NSA agents are also responsible for detecting and exploiting weaknesses in an adversarial country's computerized secret coding systems. Headquartered in Fort Meade, Maryland, the NSA has been providing the nation with "code-breaking" capabilities since these operations began against the Japanese in the Pacific theater of World War II. The NSA's role in providing information system security and information assurance has expanded with the parallel growth in computerized communications technology during the Cold War and the ensuing decades.[17]

The NSA's role in protecting classified computer data demands an eclectic mix of agents who specialize in a wide range of professional fields, including researchers, computer scientists, mathematicians, and engineers. Though much of the work of NSA agents remains secretive in nature, the agency's expertise in the area of information systems has led to a number of collaborative initiatives intended to improve information security research, knowledge, and expertise through the federal law enforcement system. For example, the NSA has recently created the INFOSEC Service Center designed to increase research initiatives concerning computer security by the federal government. The NSA has also helped to form the National Computer Security Center (NCSC), which is designed as an avenue to create partnerships among the federal law enforcement and intelligence communities.[18]

The NSA has also assumed an active role in providing information security training to both government and private entities through the National INFOSEC Education and Training Program. This program provides training for security specialists, including risk assessment, security design, and information security evaluation. Through these initiatives, NSA aims to provide government agencies and the private sector information system security expertise.[19] Additionally, the NSA works to provide information security through security tools, security products, threat warnings, analysis of attacks, and security bulletins.[20]

The Federal Trade Commission

The Federal Trade Commission (FTC) was created in 1914 primarily as a way for the government to "trust bust" or apply regulations ensuring a free marketplace for U.S. consumers and business enterprises. In this regard, the FTC enforces antitrust violations that could hamper consumer interests, as well as federal consumer protection laws against fraud, deception, and unfair business practices. The commission's primary enforcement mechanism is the Bureau of Consumer Protection, which is divided into seven divisions: (1) enforcement, (2) advertising practices, (3) financial practices, (4) marketing practices, (5) planning and information, (6) consumer and business education programs, and (7) privacy and identity protection.[21]

As the federal government's primary mechanism for protecting consumer markets, the FTC has been forced to apply its traditional enforcement tools in an increasingly computer-related marketplace. Consumers and businesses alike have grown accustomed to the exchange of goods and services through electronic mediums, especially the Internet. Indeed, so-called e-commerce generates hundreds of billions of dollars in revenue annually, making the Internet economy comparable in size to the energy, automobile, and telecommunications industries. In response to the growth of Internet commerce, the FTC attempts to minimize fraudulent and deceptive business practices that occur online and educate consumers regarding safe avenues to conduct e-commerce.[22]

The commission has been involved primarily in the enforcement of traditional criminal activities that now often occur online, including false marketing claims, credit card repair scams, financial pyramid schemes, and fraudulent business opportunity schemes. Since 1994, the FTC has brought hundreds of federal law enforcement actions against a variety of defendants based on fraudulent online services.[23] In fact, the FTC filed 38 actions in federal court from March 2007 through February 2008 and obtained 111 judgments and orders requiring defendants to pay over $240 million in remedies related to consumer fraud.[24] In addition to these traditional marketplace crimes, the commission has stepped up efforts to combat invasions of consumer privacy that occur online. The growth of e-commerce has resulted in consumers increasingly providing personal financial and medical information online, thus expanding the threat that this information could be used fraudulently through theft or other means. The FTC has brought 17 actions challenging companies on inadequate data security practices that leave sensitive consumer data vulnerable to compromise.[25]

The FTC has developed the Identity Theft Program, designed to provide assistance to local and federal law enforcement agencies attempting to curb the misuse and theft of personal information through online access. The program aids these agencies in enforcing the Identity Theft and Assumption Deterrence Act of 1998, which is a federal response to the widespread incidence of identity theft in recent years. The act emphasizes that personal information is increasingly used against individuals and businesses to commit fraud online. Under this act, the FTC was required to create a database of identity theft victim complaints, to provide useful information to consumers and educate them regarding protecting the use of personal information online, as well as to provide a means to refer victims of identity theft to law enforcement authorities. These mandates resulted in the creation of the *Consumer Sentinel,* which is a centralized database of identity theft complaints used to compile statistics regarding the incidence of identity theft.[26] This database contains over four million fraud and identity theft complaints, which can be searched by over 1,700 law enforcement agencies around the world to share information and develop case leads.[27]

The Postal Service

The U.S. Postal Service's widely known primary mission is to provide safe, affordable, and universal mail service to the nation. The nation's mail service delivery agency has also operated one of the country's oldest federal law enforcement agencies—the U.S. Postal Inspection Service—since 1830. Congress empowered the Postal Service to "investigate postal offenses and civil matters relating to the Postal Service." In order to accomplish this task, the U.S. Postal Inspection Service was established to perform "investigative and security functions essential to a stable and sound postal system." Thus, the two main functions of the U.S. Postal Inspection service are to provide businesses with a safe avenue for the exchange of funds and securities and provide private citizens a safe and secure way in which to transmit correspondence. The Postal Inspection Service employs over 1,500 agents nationwide, including approximately 650 uniformed postal police officers who monitor and inspect critical postal facilities.[28] These agents investigate and enforce over 200 federal laws covering the illegal and fraudulent use of the U.S. mail service.[29]

In terms of the investigation and prosecution of computer crimes, the U.S. Postal Inspection Service must frequently conduct joint investigations with other federal agencies, primarily because many types of computer crimes involve the use of the mail system to accomplish computer-related fraudulent activities or to transport materials related to computer crimes. In these types of cases, the jurisdiction of the Postal Inspection Service may overlap with that of any number of local or federal agencies, including the U.S. Secret Service, the FBI, and the DOJ. The U.S. Postal Service's primary concerns in the area of computer crime are identity theft, child exploitation and pornography, and electronic crimes.[30]

As detailed elsewhere in this volume, identity theft involves acquiring key pieces of someone's identifying information, including name, address, date of birth, and Social Security number in order to impersonate them. Under Title 18, Section 1028, of the U.S. Federal Code, postal inspectors share jurisdiction in these cases because they often involve mail that is stolen in order to obtain the above information. In addition, identity thieves will use computers in order to elicit bogus credit cards and checks from financial institutions through the U.S. mail. In response to these crimes, the U.S. Postal Service has instituted the Mail Theft Reporting System (MTRS). MTRS aims to identify patterns in mail theft across geographic regions as well as compile statistics relating to mail theft victims and monetary losses. In 2007 alone, postal inspectors arrested 2,071 suspects of credit card and identity theft offenses.[31]

The U.S. Postal Inspection Service also plays a key role in combating the production and distribution of child pornography. Increasingly, child pornography crimes have been classified as computer related because they often involve the use of the Internet in production and downloading of pornographic images. In fact, 95 percent of all cases of child exploitation involve both computers and physical mail.[32] Postal inspectors become involved when these computer-generated images are distributed through the U.S. mail. The primary legal vehicle to enforce these crimes used by postal inspectors is Title 18 of the U.S. Federal Code, Sections 1470, 2251, and 2252–2254; investigators have arrested 155 individuals related to these offenses.[33]

In addition, postal inspectors share jurisdiction in any electronic crime that involves the misuse of the U.S. mail. These crimes can include consumer fraud schemes that originate on the Internet through e-mail solicitations, since these crimes often eventually involve use of the U.S. mail in the delivery of fraudulent documents and/or fraudulently obtained currency. Among the most widely cited of these crimes is the Nigerian advance fee fraud letter and e-mail scam in which Nigerian nationals send letters and e-mails to U.S. citizens. The letters or e-mails invariably ask the recipient for some kind of fee as a precondition to the transfer of large amounts of money from Nigeria. American citizens have lost over millions of dollars due to these schemes. Thus, the Postal Inspection Service has developed resources to help combat these crimes, including a joint task force with the DOJ.

The Department of Energy

The U.S. Department of Energy (DOE) was created in 1977 in order to consolidate existing federal energy programs and activities. The DOE's main responsibilities include the administration of domestic energy production, the promotion of renewable energy resources, and the promotion of energy conservation and efficiency. The department has increasingly relied on computerized technologies to operate and administer the nation's energy-producing infrastructure. The growth in computer crime has created an increasing need to protect these critical infrastructure systems from both domestic and international threats. These threats can involve the introduction of malicious codes designed to interfere with the operation of energy production systems.[34]

In response to these threats, the Office of the Chief Information Officer at DOE provides a range of resources to provide timely information on cyber-security threats. This includes the management of the entire DOE cyber security program, including desktop and application hosting for employees.[35] In addition, the DOE-Cyber Incident Response Capability (CIAC) is an organization that provides the DOE with incident response, reporting, tracking, and security support. This includes incident-reporting capabilities, security bulletins, and software tools. The CIAC is also designed to enhance communications between the DOE and private contractors who use these energy systems so that critical infrastructures can remain protected from cyber attacks.[36]

The Department of Homeland Security

The preceding section describing the manner in which federal agencies are organized to combat computer crime discussed each agency in separate terms and characterized the strategies of any single agency as independent and separate from those of the other agencies involved in the fight against computer crime. The attempt to classify these agencies in independent fashion is intended not only to help the reader understand the different roles of each federal agency discussed, but may be viewed as an indication of the historically "piecemeal" nature of law enforcement actions at the federal level. Federal law enforcement agencies have a long history of failing to coordinate and cooperate not only in the relatively recent fight against computer crime but also with regard to a host of more traditional crime problems, including organized crime, the "war on drugs," and more general intelligence-gathering operations.

The cost associated with these disjointed federal law enforcement strategies became fatally and critically clear on September 11, 2001, when these domestic agencies collectively failed to detect and prevent the terrorist plot against the World Trade Center and the Pentagon. With the need for federal cooperation becoming abundantly clear in the face of such attacks, President Bush launched an initiative to create a cabinet-level department designed to improve information sharing among federal law enforcement agencies, consolidate a host of over 100 federal offices in these departments, and increase interagency coordination in the fight against domestic terror. The recently established DHS is the result of these efforts.[37]

DHS has a wide range of organizational components and has subsumed a number of previously discussed federal agencies under the DHS umbrella including the Directorate for National Protection and Programs, Directorate for Science and Technology, Directorate for Management, Office of Policy, Office of Health Affairs, Office of Intelligence and Analysis, Office of Operations Coordination, Federal Law Enforcement Training Center, Domestic Nuclear Detection Office, National Cyber Security Center, Transportation Security Administration (TSA), Customs and Border Protection, Citizenship and Immigration Services, Immigration and Customs Enforcement, the Secret Service, Federal Emergency Management Agency, and the Coast Guard.[38]

The agency now employs over 200,000 federal employees who have been transferred or subsumed from other federal agencies.[39]

The National Cyber Security Division (NCSD) of DHS is of significant importance in the fight against computer crime. The NCSD is housed within the Office of Cyber Security and Communications and opened in 2003 with the charge of protecting cyber infrastructure. Specifically, the NCSD has a twofold task: (1) to build and maintain an effective national cyberspace response system and (2) to implement a cyber risk management program to protect critical infrastructure.[40]

There are several programs in place to aid in the achievement of these two tasks, including the National Cyber Alert System, which offers a free subscription service to security alerts and tips to better protect systems and infrastructure. This system also allows individuals to report threats and incidents directly to DHS.[41] The Cyber Cop Portal program is also run through NCSD, which provides a Web-based resource for information sharing and collaboration between law enforcement agencies around the world. There are over 5,300 investigators who use this tool as a means to help capture computer criminals. The NCSD also manages the National Vulnerability Database that acts as a clearinghouse for information on software and hardware vulnerabilities. Individuals can access this database as a way to improve and automate computer security processes and compliance. There is also a Software Assurance Program designed to develop more secure software at the outset to minimize the number of vulnerabilities and therefore increase computer security.[42]

The umbrella of the NCSD also includes the US-Computer Emergency Readiness Team, or CERT. The US-CERT provides response support and defense against cyber attacks in the executive branch of government, as well as support for public, private, and international partners. The CERT provides information on new and existing vulnerabilities in all manner of computer systems, as well as resources to help patch and secure networks. They also offer security and threat reports and act as an information clearinghouse on cyber security matters.[43]

The NCSD also manages the National Cyber Response Coordination Group, which is composed of 13 federal agencies that respond to cyber attacks. This entity is designed to coordinate the federal response to a nationally significant cyber incident, operating through law enforcement, intelligence agencies, and the US-CERT.[44] The NCSD also coordinates the Cyber Storm exercise to assist in the protection of cyber infrastructure. This event takes place every two years and is an attempt to assess the capability of government, public, and private entities to respond to a national cyber incident. The Cyber Storm training exercise simulates attacks against multiple infrastructure resources to understand the procedures, processes, tools, and responses of agencies to such an attack.[45] These exercises are key to improving cyber security and incident response in the event of a serious threat to cyber infrastructure.

U.S. Immigration and Customs Enforcement

The U.S. Immigration and Customs Enforcement (ICE) agency is the largest and primary investigative arm of the U.S. DHS.[46] ICE is responsible for identifying and investigating weaknesses within the nation's borders, developing intelligence concerning threats, removing foreign nationals, and enforcing over 400 federal statutes. The agency was formed in 2003 as part of the Homeland Security Act and is the result of a merger of several federal agencies including the Customs Service, Immigration and Naturalization, the Federal Protective Service. ICE has approximately 15,000 employees in 400 offices in the United States and 50 offices around the world.[47]

The ICE agency plays a pivotal role in enforcing Internet-related crimes because of its responsibility to protect resources within the U. S. borders and the inherently international nature of cyberspace crimes. In particular, ICE operates the Cyber Crimes Center (C3), which has four subsections focused on child exploitation, computer forensics, cyber crimes, and information technology and administration.[48] The C3 also offers training for local, federal, and international law enforcement agencies.

The Child Exploitation Section (CES) exists to investigate producers and distributors of child pornography and abuse, as well as sex tourism. The CES operates in conjunction with international law enforcement agencies to investigate and prosecute these offenses. This section also coordinates Operation Predator, which is an ongoing multiagency international investigation of child exploitation and crimes against children. Operation Predator was developed in 2003 and has led to more than 10,000 arrests and 5,000 deportments from the United States for foreign nationals involved in child pornography and sex crimes.[49]

The Cyber Crimes Section (CCS) investigates and enforces laws pertaining to a wide variety of cybercrimes, including international money laundering, intellectual property rights violations, human smuggling, illegal exports, and arms trafficking. The CCS conducts undercover stings and investigations over the Internet and has conducted a variety of operations, such as Operation Apothecary, to arrest and prosecute the sale and distribution of counterfeit pharmaceuticals and controlled substances over the Internet.[50]

The Computer Forensics Section offers digital evidence recovery and analysis for ICE agents as well as other law enforcement agencies. In particular, they have 125 computer forensic agents (CFAs) who retrieve and analyze digital evidence as well as assist in the development of warrants for the seizure of digital evidence.[51] Forensic agents also provide expert testimony for cases in support of criminal investigations. The Information Technology and Administrative Section provides operational and technical services to support the other three arms of the C3.

The Secret Service

The U.S. Secret Service was created in 1865 to serve a dual purpose: to provide protective services to the president and other cabinet members and to safeguard the nation's financial payment system against fraud and counterfeit financial instruments. In the massive reorganization of federal agencies after 9/11, the U.S. Secret Service became a key entity within the U.S. DHS to combat computer crime. The agency's responsibilities have increased tremendously as a result of the revolution in computerized information systems and the growth of the Internet as a vehicle for financial transactions.

For example, the ever-increasing sophistication of computerized reproduction capabilities has expanded the potential for the production of counterfeit financial instruments. In addition, the development of Internet communications has facilitated the rapid communication of encrypted messages and financial fraud schemes using phony debit and credit card transactions and electronic funds transfers (EFTs). Finally, the agency's protection responsibilities in terms of special events have grown to include the safeguarding of computerized telecommunications and power systems integral to these events. The convergence of these related factors has thrust the Secret Service into the role of the federal government's primary law enforcement weapon against computer and cybercrime.[52]

The Secret Service's Financial Crimes Division is the agency's primary tool in the fight against computer crime. The division's main responsibilities include the enforcement of three high-profile computer-related crimes. First, the division is charged with identifying and investigating financial institution fraud (FIF). Since 1990, the Secret Service has been granted concurrent jurisdiction with the DOJ to investigate fraud committed against financial institutions such as banks and savings and loans. Primary FIF schemes include the creation of counterfeit financial instruments (primarily cash) through desktop publishing systems. Recent Secret Service investigations have pointed to large increases in the production of counterfeit corporate checks and negotiable instruments that have paralleled the advent of sophisticated desktop publishing systems and copying technologies. Title 18, Section 514, of the U.S. Federal Code was enacted in 1996 in order to stem the growing tide of phony cash and checks in circulation.[53]

Second, the Secret Service has primary jurisdiction in cases involving access device fraud. Access device fraud falls under Title 18, Section 1029, of the U.S. Federal Code (the "credit card statute") and involves the fraudulent use of credit card numbers, personal identification numbers (PINs), and computer passwords. In addition to these access device frauds, the Secret Service has increasingly investigated the theft of computer codes located within cellular phones that are used to track billing information. The Secret Service estimates that losses resulting from access fraud cases run into the billions; the agency arrested over 2,400 individuals for access fraud crimes in 1996 alone.[54]

Third, the Secret Service has primary jurisdiction in the investigation of general computer fraud relating to computers and computer systems of "federal interest." These computers can be used as instruments of crime through hacking or other means as well as tools to produce fraudulent negotiable instruments or store private account information. The Secret Service has recently trained over 1,200 agents in computer forensics designed to detect and investigate these crimes through the agency's Electronic Crimes Special Agent Program (ECSAP).[55]

The Financial Crimes Division houses the Electronic Crimes Branch, which specializes in detecting and investigating credit card and other access device fraud. The Electronic Crimes Branch provides computer equipment and technical assistance to special agents concerning lab analysis of computer-related evidence and storage equipment, the seizure of computerized evidence, and the administrative management of all computer-related investigations.[56]

In recognition of the Secret Service's primary role in combating computer and cybercrime and the need for interagency cooperation, provisions of the USA PATRIOT Act point to the development of a "network" of task forces that span federal jurisdictions. These task forces include federal, state, and local law enforcement agency personnel and have been primarily aimed at addressing the increasingly global nature of computerized financial fraud. Specific task forces have included the Metro Alien Task Force, the West African (Nigerian) Task Force, and the Asian Organized Crime Task Force.[57] The most successful task force developed has been the Electronic Crimes Task Force (ECTF), which brings together law enforcement agencies, as well as prosecutors, private industry, and academia.[58] The ECTF mission is to prevent, detect, and investigate attacks against financial and critical infrastructures. There are now 24 ECTFs around the country, which provide support and resources to help investigate electronic crimes.

STATE AND LOCAL ROLES

As the sections above indicate, the growing danger posed by computer crimes has clearly resulted in an increasing enforcement emphasis at the federal level. Indeed, the current struggle against international terrorist threats—culminating with the September 11, 2001, attacks against the World Trade Center and the Pentagon—seems to have galvanized national-level efforts to protect critical computer infrastructures at the federal level. The threats related to computer crimes, however, have also become a growing concern to law enforcement officials at the state and local levels. While federal officials employed by the myriad agencies detailed above seem to have successfully garnered both public and political attention concerning the need for resources aimed at addressing the computer crime problem, law enforcement personnel at the local level continue to encounter a host of issues that have hampered efforts to combat computer crimes effectively within their own jurisdictions. This section will provide an overview regarding what is being done to fight computer crime at the state and local levels of enforcement, with an emphasis on identifying the critical areas of need that have thus far limited efforts to combat computer crime at the local level.

The number of local, state, county, and regional computer crime task forces continues to increase, largely because these agencies have experienced more computer-related criminal activities within their jurisdictions, and citizens and private entities have become increasingly willing to report these activities to local law enforcement departments. For example, a recent survey of local law enforcement computer crime experts found that 80 percent of the respondents indicated a "measurable increase" in the reporting of computer and electronic crimes, especially traditional fraud and theft crimes using computer devices.[59]

At the same time, local officers may not have the capacity or understanding of computer crimes necessary to properly investigate these offenses. For example, the most pressing computer crimes enforced by these agencies appear to be those related to "harmful computer content," especially child pornography and exploitation, threatening communications, and stalking.[60] These types of computer crimes are followed in priority by computer-related frauds (e.g., online shopping schemes and EFT fraud), other technology-based crimes (e.g., encryption used to hide criminal activities such as drug trafficking), and computer hacking crimes. Higher-profile computer crimes, such as threats to critical national infrastructure systems, are rarely handled solely by local and state investigators because they often require federal expertise and resources.[61]

Despite the ever-increasing caseload of computer crimes, there appears to be a lack of recognition and support from upper-level management within local police agencies in terms of providing the resources necessary to counter these threats. The majority of these cases receive a low priority at the local level. The fact that computer crime cases have not received the necessary recognition and support from local law enforcement administrators has created several areas in which local level agencies must improve if computer crimes are to be effectively enforced.

Critical Needs at the State and Local Levels of Enforcement

Officers involved in combating computer crime at the local and state level must be supplied with an increase in resources and technology in order to fight computer crime more effectively. These areas can be broadly grouped into four "critical needs": (1) training, (2) equipment, (3) updated criminal codes designed to complement current enforcement efforts, and (4) resources for tapping federal expertise and equipment related to computer crime enforcement.[62]

The need for training appears to be paramount at the local level. Currently, most local agencies fail to provide any training in computer crime to patrol personnel. This lack of training at the entry level can have severe consequences in regard to prosecuting computer crimes, especially in terms of protecting computer crime scenes and collecting forensic evidence. An untrained patrol officer can easily inadvertently destroy computerized evidence if not trained in protecting such evidence.[63] Related to training needs at the entry level, most local departments do not possess the technical expertise needed to train those officers interested in becoming computer forensic specialists. Often, these officers must obtain specialized training from outside sources such as private industry or the federal government. Some researchers and administrators have cited the need for a national certification program aimed at producing more specially trained computer experts at the local level. Others have noted that the career path for "computer crime specialists" at the local level can often be limited, and career advancement within many local agencies would require reassignment to another priority division.[64]

The need for computer crime training appears to go hand in hand with the procurement of additional resources and equipment. While federal personnel have increasingly used the growing awareness of computer crime at the national level as an avenue for larger equipment expenditures, these dollars have largely failed to trickle down to the local level.[65] The resulting disparity in equipment between federal and local cyber cops can most clearly be seen in the inability of most local agencies to decipher encrypted computer evidence.[66] Surveys of local computer crime experts indicate that for those jurisdictions that currently have computer evidence laboratories, more than 50 percent do not have adequate capabilities to read encrypted evidence. Much of the problem related to lack of equipment can be traced to insufficient funding behind efforts to control computer crime. Many local experts have cited the need to use equipment that has been purchased personally because local departments fail to provide adequate resources from within the organization.[67]

As detailed elsewhere in this text, the explosion in computer technologies and communications has stymied legislative attempts to enact statutes that are current and can be applied to the use of these new technologies. In short, state laws have been largely unable to keep pace with technology. The gap evident between the pace of technological change and the enactment of legal codes has been especially problematic for computer crime specialists and prosecutors at the local level. For example, there are no legal mechanisms designed to allow the enforcement of subpoenas across state lines.[68] In the case of crimes that occur over the Internet, the lack of these mechanisms can effectively halt computer crime investigations at the local level. So too, severe differences exist across jurisdictions in terms of the definition of what constitutes an electronic crime. Some states continue to define many computer crimes as misdemeanor offenses, thereby reducing local law enforcement incentives to increase enforcement resources in this area.[69]

Finally, those officers who are active in the enforcement of computer crimes at the local level have cited a lack of informational resources that would enable them to easily utilize the extensive technical expertise and equipment resources that currently exist at the federal level. Currently, there is no comprehensive source of information containing a list of federal contact persons who could aid local investigators. Such a "guidebook" could include not only a list of prominent federal agents who are experts in the field of computer crime but also prominent computer forensic laboratories, forensic equipment available for local use, and federally approved equipment manufacturers to aid local agencies who are interesting in upgrading their computer crime resources.[70]

Summary

American law enforcement agencies have assumed a variety of roles and responses to the new and increasing threats posed by computer crimes and terrorism. This chapter has provided an overview of how a number of federal agencies have responded to these threats, including the Secret Service, the Department of Justice, the Federal Bureau of Investigation, the National Security Agency, the Federal Trade Commission, the Postal Service, Immigration and Customs Enforcement, the Department of Energy, and the Department of Homeland Security. These wide-ranging agencies have worked independently to adapt their specialized law enforcement expertise to these new problems. The federal government has increasingly recognized the need for these disparate agencies to collaborate in the fight against computer crime and terror. Moreover, local and state level law enforcement agencies have attempted to assume their own role in enforcing computer crimes. Although a relatively small number of these agencies have responded successfully to these threats through increasing funding and the formation of multiagency task forces, these agencies have largely been limited by several factors, most notably a lack of funds, personnel, and technology.

Review Questions

1. Which federal law enforcement agency has assumed primary responsibilities in the area of access device fraud, including the fraudulent use of credit card numbers, personal identification numbers, and computer passwords?

2. Which federal agency is responsible for the prosecution of computer fraud and abuse violations through the Computer Crime and Intellectual Property Section (CCIPS)?

3. Which federal agency investigates cybercrime and is currently responsible for the management of the InfraGard private/public partnership program?

4. What agency within the Department of Homeland Security is responsible for managing cyber-critical infrastructure?

5. What are some of the impediments to computer crime investigations at the local level?

6. What are some of the key needs in local law enforcement agencies to improve their response to computer crimes?

Endnotes

1. *http://www.usdoj.gov*
2. *http://www.usdoj.gov/criminal/cybercrime/ccpolicy*
3. *http://www.usdoj.gov/opa/pr/2006/June/06_ag_379.html*
4. *http://www.cybercrime.gov*
5. *http://www.fbi.gov/cyberinvest/cyberhome.htm*
6. *Ibid.*
7. *Ibid.*
8. *http://www.rcfl.gov*
9. *Ibid.*
10. *Ibid.*
11. *http://www.ic3.gov*
12. *Ibid.*, p. 12.
13. *http://www.nipc.gov*
14. ROTHSCHILD, MATTHEW. (February 2, 2008). "Exclusive! The FBI Deputizes Business." *The Progressive*. Retrieved March 1, 2009, from *http://www.progressive.org/mag_rothschild0308*
15. *http://www.nsa.gov*
16. NAKASHIMA, ELLEN. (January 1, 2008). "Bush Order Expands Network Monitoring: Intelligence Agencies to Track Institutions." *The Washington Post*. Retrieved on February 9, 2008, from *http://www.washingtonpost.com/wp-dyn/content/article/2008/01/25/AR2008012503261_pf.html*
17. *Ibid.*, p. 28.
18. *Ibid.*
19. *Ibid.*
20. *http://www.nsa.gov/ia/ia_at_nsa/index.shtml*
21. *http://www.ftc.gov*
22. SWINDLE, O. (September 11, 1999). "E-Commerce: Tomorrow's Economy—Taxing and Regulation the Old-fashioned Way." Remarks before the Georgia Public Policy Forum.
23. *http://www.ftc.gov/bcp/internet/cases-internet.pdf*
24. Federal Trade Commission (2009). "FTC Annual Report, 2008." Retrieved March 28, 2009, from *http://www.ftc.gov/os/2008/03/ChairmansReport-2008.pdf*
25. *Ibid.*
26. Federal Trade Commission (August 14, 2002). Seminar. "Attacking Identity Theft Together: Usable Tools for Law Enforcement." Dallas, Texas.
27. *Ibid*, p. 24.
28. *http://www.usps.com*
29. *Ibid.*
30. *Ibid.*
31. *Ibid.*
32. *Ibid.*
33. *Ibid.*
34. *http://www.doe.gov*
35. *http://cio.energy.gov/about.htm*
36. *http://www.doecirc.energy.gov/aboutus.html*
37. *http://www.dhs.gov*
38. *http://www.dhs.gov/xlibrary/assets/DHS_OrgChart.pdf*
39. *Ibid.*, p. 62.
40. *http://www.dhs.gov/xabout/structure/editorial_0839.shtm*
41. *Ibid.*
42. *Ibid.*
43. *Ibid.*
44. *Ibid.*
45. *Ibid.*
46. *http://www.ice.gov*

47. *Ibid.*
48. *Ibid.*
49. *Ibid.*
50. *Ibid.*
51. *Ibid.*
52. JACKSON, W. (2003). "E-Crime Squad." *Government Computer News* 22(2).
53. *http://www.ustreas.gov*
54. *Ibid.*, p. 2.
55. *http://www.secretservice.gov*
56. *Ibid.*, p. 4.
57. *Ibid.*
58. *Ibid.*
59. STAMNBAUGH, H., BEUPRE, D.S., ICOYE, D.J., BAKER, R., CASSADAY, W., and WILLIAMS, W.P. (March 2001).

"Electronic Crime Needs Assessment for State and Local Law Enforcement." *National Institute of Justice.*
60. *Ibid.*, p. 75.
61. *Ibid.*
62. *Ibid.*
63. *Ibid.*
64. *Ibid.*
65. *Ibid.*
66. *Ibid.*
67. *Ibid.*
68. *Ibid.*
69. *Ibid.*
70. *Ibid.*

CHAPTER 11

The Investigation of Computer-Related Crime

CHAPTER OBJECTIVES

After completing this chapter, you should be able to

- Explain and understand the search warrant application process appropriate to electronic evidence at a single-location crime scene.
- Identify hardware and storage devices potentially containing evidence of a crime.
- Explain and understand the legal standards and best current practices for the documentation of a single-location electronic crime scene.
- Explain and describe the best current practices for the collection, preservation, transportation, and storage of electronic evidence.
- Distinguish between single-scene, multiple-scene, and network crimes.
- Be able to communicate an understanding of network architectures and standards relevant to network investigations.
- Identify sources of assistance for multiple-scene and network operations.
- Identify categories of evidence and probable locations of that evidence.
- Broadly outline procedures for preserving and collecting network trace evidence.

INTRODUCTION

This chapter focuses on the current state of the field in computer crime investigations. The personnel available to an investigation will dramatically influence the type and scope of investigations that may be undertaken. Understanding the roles of and skills needed by such personnel is vital to planning appropriate investigations. Although there is no single policy or plan for investigations, this chapter presents an overview of investigations, with special emphasis on the process of the investigation. The chapter breaks investigations into three basic types: single-scene, multiple-scene, and network investigations. Each type of investigation requires different skills from personnel involved. Single-scene investigations require the skills found in trained law enforcement investigators. The skills used in a single-scene investigation form the building blocks of the more complex investigations. Thus, while building on single-scene skills, multiple-scene investigations require additional networking and coordination skills. Coordination of multiple searches at various locations is the realm of an experienced criminal investigator. The networking skills may be provided by a subject matter expert (e.g., a computer consultant). Finally, network crimes require the skills of multiple-scene investigators and outside expert assistance. Even the most computer-proficient investigator needs help from the companies that maintain the Internet to track a crime successfully through their servers. However, some degree of preliminary knowledge is required even to know where to start. Techniques for acquiring this type of information are presented in this chapter along with conceptual tools that allow an investigator to communicate with the Internet experts.

INVESTIGATOR ROLES AND RESPONSIBILITIES

The role of computers is growing rapidly in our society; law enforcement has lagged behind. The pervasive use of home computers has added another potential source of evidence to the over 54 million households with computers in the United States.[1] Many large law enforcement agencies have a dedicated electronic crime investigation capacity. Medium-sized agencies may be acquiring their first electronic crime investigation unit or attempting to cross-train detectives from traditional areas. Even the smallest departments encounter electronic crime, but do not have the capacity for a dedicated unit. Thus, the mission of police, from patrol officers to forensic specialists, depends greatly on their department's size and organization. Generally, the role and responsibility of police staff in electronic investigation is the same as their counterparts dealing with physical crime.

First Responders

First responders to a crime scene are often patrol officers. First responders would not normally attempt to complete an electronic search and seizure; however, they do benefit from an awareness of the procedure and, if given even basic training, may be better able to preserve a potential electronic crime scene for specialized investigators. First responders are not dedicated electronic crime investigators. They have many other responsibilities, including safety, security, and basic documentation of an event or scene. Further, patrol officers are often not given the time to conduct in-depth investigations; those are handled by detectives.

A well-trained first responder will control the human element of the crime scene first: tending to the injured, isolating suspects, and controlling onlookers. First responders are trained to avoid contaminating a crime scene or destroying physical evidence. As the prevalence of electronic evidence increases, first responders have naturally become aware of the need to protect and preserve it. For example, first responders who recognize that iPod, Blackberry, and personal digital assistants can carry sensitive evidence are able to retrieve and carefully handle these devices. Making first responders aware of potential digital evidence allows them to protect it in the same way they protect physical evidence.

Investigators

Electronic crime investigators are trained law enforcement officers or experienced investigators brought (sometimes unwillingly) into the world of electronic evidence. The basic skills required successfully to organize an investigation, establish the elements of a crime, establish the connection between the suspect and the crime, conceptualize and present the crime, and document the investigation are still needed in electronic crime investigations. In fact, many corporations seek computer investigators and security directors from the ranks of law enforcement rather than technical experts. Investigators must have enough technical skill to gather evidence, comprehend the crime, and communicate effectively with technical experts, but do not need extensive theoretical knowledge or daily experience with computer systems. That is not to say that highly skilled investigators are not desirable.

Forensic Analysts

In physical crime investigations and electronic crime investigations, the complex analysis of evidence is often left to forensic specialists. A detective or crime scene technician would not feel bad about not understanding the intricacies of laboratory DNA analysis. Although computer skills and knowledge are essential to the investigator, the essential skills of an investigator involve collection and preservation of evidence for further analysis. Technical experts conduct this analysis through computer forensic techniques. Special programs and procedures allow forensic specialists to compile evidence and present it to the court. Out of necessity, many computer crime investigators feel compelled to learn these forensic analysis skills. Many investigators become skilled computer forensic examiners, but have to devote a great portion of their time to learning the latest technologies and conducting the analysis instead of conducting their investigations. Forensic analysts provide efficiency through a division of labor and regular practice with their equipment and techniques. It is not uncommon for senior investigators to act as forensic analysts.

Private Police

Private police (usually corporate security or computer security investigators) are hired by corporations to secure the data assets of the corporation. Although they often cooperate with law enforcement, they have a fundamentally different mission. Corporate officers must always consider the good of the corporation. For example, a private computer investigator may be withdrawn from a case if the corporation decides that expending resources on such investigation will not be justified by the results.

Private computer security or investigative consultants are often brought in to review security incidents or suspected crimes. A small discrepancy can indicate a system failure or a major intrusion. In a famous case at the University of California, Cliff Stoll tried to reconcile a trivial accounting error and ended up discovering an attempt at international espionage.[2] It is not always obvious that a crime has been committed without further investigation. Since many crimes are committed by insiders, a security consultant also provides a check to the power of system administrators.[3]

Many corporations keep former police officers on staff to advise them when to call the police and when not to call. Although it is hard for many officers and investigators to understand such a decision or even consider it dereliction of a societal duty, many corporations do not want adverse publicity or fear the "seize everything" tactics of law enforcement once a crime is reported. The delays, staff time, and computing resource downtime created by an investigation may cause more financial loss than a break-in. In spite of the potential antagonism between the roles of private police and law enforcement, these groups often work together smoothly. Once a decision is made to report a crime, private police often act as liaisons between investigators and the corporate structure, insulating other employees from disruption and facilitating the efforts of investigators. A corporate security director not only will have access to the entire physical premises but will also be able to issue directives to corporate employees without the direct invention of management or company executives.

Subject Matter Experts

Technical expertise has a short shelf life. Many skills that were in great demand two years ago are now virtually obsolete. Using a subject matter expert is one way for an investigator to gain access to detailed knowledge on a highly specialized or uncommon topic. Although many investigators feel confident handling a Windows™ system, large, multiuser systems may present unknown challenges and opportunities for mistakes. Similarly, a complex network with unfamiliar technology may be beyond an investigator's skill level. If an investigator does not feel confident with the technology to be searched or seized, a subject matter expert with experience using that technology can provide invaluable insight.

A skilled investigator can often successfully conduct analyses on all but the most demanding cases; however, with the staggering complexity of some systems, it is not unreasonable for the investigator to turn to an expert in the system to be examined: its own system administrator. When electronic crime enters the network, investigators are forced to call upon the experts at Internet service providers (ISPs) and corporate information technology (IT) departments. Even the most skilled investigator cannot instantly fathom the processes and data structures of large information systems. Just as the corporate security director becomes the liaison with corporate employees, the system administrator becomes the liaison with corporate data resources. Of course, if the local system administrator is a suspect, this is not appropriate. In such cases, a subject matter expert familiar with that type of system can provide the necessary guidance.

BOX 11.1
Cyber Vigilantism

Cyber vigilantes are not part of the formal investigation process. They are private citizens not affiliated with law enforcement. There are two basic forms of cyber vigilantes. The first type, Online Neighborhood Watch, simply gathers intelligence and alerts police to unlawful acts. Some organizations, like the CyberAngels, also provide information to victims. The online watch groups do not take direct action against alleged perpetrators. The second type of cyber vigilantes takes more direct action. In some cases, retaliation simply turns the tables on the supposed offender.

[A] notorious spammer, Alan Ralsky, gave an interview in the course of which he mentioned his home in West Bloomfield, Michigan. The interview was posted on Slashdot, the leading geek website, and some enterprising reader found Ralsky's [physical] mail address in a database. Slashdot readers then subscribed him to thousands of catalogues, mailing lists, information requests, etc. The results, according to security expert Bruce Schneier, were devastating: "Within weeks he was getting hundreds of pounds of junk mail per day and was unable to find his real mail amongst the deluge. . . ."[4]

The most extreme examples include so-called hack-backs and posting personal information about pedophiles; unsubstantiated reports also indicate direct physical action may be taken against computer intruders. Hack-backs describe a wide range of illegal responses to intrusion attempts. Victim companies may use hostile code or denial-of-service attacks to disable their attackers. These retaliations may be directed at unwitting, intermediate sites used by attackers. In any case, such direct actions are just as illegal as the attacks that provoke them. Companies and individuals using such tactics are subject to civil and criminal penalties.

Online vigilantes also often pose as underaged girls and boys willing to talk about sex. Generally, it is not a crime to discuss such matters.

The crime occurs when the alleged pedophile takes action to meet supposed minors for sexual encounters. Law enforcement stings often use this technique to ensnare pedophiles. Some vigilantes assist law enforcement, but law enforcement officers generally discourage vigilantism. For one thing, individuals acting as "agents of the state" suffer from the same restrictions on entrapment and search as law enforcement officers. Online vigilantes may also commit crimes in their apparent zeal to ensnare pedophiles; many have been charged with possession of child pornography.

Aggressive cyber vigilantes often use public humiliation to punish would-be pedophiles and warn potential victims. They post the names and even physical addresses and pictures of adults discussing sex with vigilantes posing as children. Privacy advocates and attorneys retained by the targets of this form of cyber vigilantism claim that many targets never intended to meet a child for sex, just talk anonymously to someone else about their desires. Other "innocent role-players" claiming to have known they were communicating with adults are also ensnared by vigilantes.

SINGLE-LOCATION CRIME SCENES

Although the gamut of electronic crimes can span the global communication networks and cross many jurisdictions, single-location electronic crime scene search and seizure is the most fundamental skill-set of an electronic crimes investigator. Investigators specializing in other forms of crime possess a set of skills that adapts well to a fairly straightforward single-location electronic crime scene. This is because the single-location crime scene does not involve complex networking or the enormous storage capacity and complexity of network crime scenes.

SEARCH WARRANTS AND ELECTRONIC EVIDENCE

Criminal investigators must establish probable cause in an affidavit in application for a search warrant (also called a "warrant application"). The affidavit must specify that a crime has been committed, evidence of the crime exists, and the evidence presently exists in the place to be searched. Further, the affiant (the investigator applying for the warrant) must particularly describe the evidence to be seized. Specific evidence of a specific crime must be named or general evidence facilitating a criminal act may be described by function. Unless traveling through a network, electronic evidence must be stored in a container or medium. Single-scene crimes, by definition, do not involve networks. Thus, it is often useful to think of the storage medium (i.e., container) when planning a search. Each of the following containers of electronic evidence presents unique challenges and opportunities in the warrant application process.

Computer Systems

If an investigation requires the seizure of an entire computer system, the investigator should decide whether the computer itself is the target of the warrant or if the data on the computer are the target of the warrant. If stolen property is the target of the search, the contraband (i.e., the fruit of the crime) may require specific and particular description. When the data contained on the computer are the target, the magistrate signing the warrant will usually allow the investigator to describe the computer suspected of holding the evidence required by general function. It is fairly easy for a suspect to move information from one physical storage device to another. Even detailed investigations may be outdated by the time the warrant is served. Further, it is often impossible to specify precisely a physical computer when probable cause is established through network investigation; however, network identification or physical, premise location often meets the requirement that a warrant must particularly describe the place or person to be searched (i.e., particularity requirement).

External Storage Media

When data are the target of the search, the warrant should be written to allow seizure of electronic storage media found at the crime scene. Electronic storage devices come in a broad variety of physical sizes, shapes, and storage capacities. It may be impossible precisely to identify the storage medium of electronic evidence in a warrant. In this case, the broad function (i.e., electronic storage device) should be used. The smallness of these devices makes it possible to hide them virtually anywhere; a warrant may have to apply to a broader physical area than the immediate surroundings of a computer system. Common examples include compact disks (data CDs) hidden in the pages of books, data CDs hidden among music CDs (especially if music CDs are home reproductions), tiny Universal Serial Bus (USB) storage devices, and smart cards and Secure Digital (SD) cards that can be placed in a cell phone or digital camera hidden near a computer.

Handheld Devices

PDAs, iPods, iPhones, most cell phones, and other data devices are miniature computer systems designed to be highly mobile. They may be found virtually anywhere under the control of a suspect and may contain data storage comparable to a full-size computer of just a few years ago. Warrant applications should describe the function of the device and person carrying the device rather than trying to specify a physical location. Even though warrants must "particularly describe the place to be searched,"[5] the courts have recognized that must often occur at a time and place determined by the suspect. Warrants for such searches can describe the function of evidence thought to be in the possession of a person.

Other Electronic Devices

Many electronic storage devices do not fit a narrow definition of "computer" and may be excluded as evidence if not properly defined in a search warrant. Examples include, but are not limited to

1. Telephone answering machines and other electronic telephone equipment, including voice-over Internet protocol (VoIP) boxes.
2. Video game systems like an Xbox, Playstation, or Wii as well as digital video recorders (DVRs).
3. Access control devices such as security smart cards.
4. Credit card skimmers and magnetic stripe encoders.

5. Personal items such as digital watches with storage capacity, pagers, calculators with storage, and electronic calendars.
6. Digital cameras or digital sound recorders.
7. Webcams and any other recording devices.

The range of storage capacity in these different electronic devices ranges from a minute encryption key to a full-motion, DVD™-quality video.

Networking Equipment

In the course of a search, agents may come across networking equipment, or devices that allow multiple computers to be linked in a network. The significant growth of wireless Internet connections has made the likelihood of observing such equipment at a crime scene very high. Thus, individuals must be cognizant of this sort of equipment that constitutes a network, including modems, wired and wireless routers, network cards and USB drives, and Ethernet cables that link these devices together, along with other devices such as printers.

Executing the Search Warrant

Once a warrant is obtained, the details of the search may be finalized. A preliminary plan is often attached to the application for the warrant. If the warrant is signed as written, most of the details will already be in place. The magistrate issuing the warrant may place special conditions on the search; those conditions should be integrated into the plan. For example, a magistrate may not wish to interfere unduly with the First Amendment rights of a disinterested party holding evidence of a crime. The system operator of a Web site hosting discussions may choose not to voluntarily divulge details about users of the Web site. A search warrant may specify that police may seize evidence related to the crime described in the warrant, but may not seize unrelated discussions or interfere with the public forum for discussion found on the Web site. The search strategy would have to include both a way to keep the Web site open and specifically target discussions and logs relevant to the crime. Other considerations in the execution of a warrant include the conditions under which the warrant is to be served and coordination with uniformed officers, or even SWAT team members.

PRIORITY CONCERNS First and foremost, investigators must assess the potential danger to themselves. It is beyond the scope of this book to discuss planning an armed raid with a no-knock warrant versus a full-compliance search; however, officer safety should be a priority regardless of the expected level of compliance of the suspect. Some particular concerns lie in assessing the particular dangers of working with electronic equipment. Test for live voltage in wires before touching or wear insulative gloves if appropriate. Although there is often talk of booby raps in computers, this usually refers to methods for destroying data, not physical traps; however, in this age of enhanced homeland security, actual traps may be an issue. If the investigation involves terrorism, then additional concern should be taken in the planning and execution of the search.

SECURING THE SCENE Procedures for securing a crime scene typically include removing suspects, witnesses, and bystanders from the area to be searched. Technical assistance provided by a computer owner or the owner's designated operator may require their presence, but they should be supervised by an officer trained in the rules of evidence. Many system administrators happily comply with law enforcement requests, but do not understand the legal requirements of collecting evidence. To prevent inadvertent alteration of evidence or inadmissible collection techniques, an investigator should be present and understand the operations of the system administrator. It is preferred to have a resident expert in the system execute the commands rather than on-site experts. This allows for efficient testimony at trial. Sometimes a suspect may be allowed to assist in the collection of ongoing data or the dismantling of evidence seized; this is not common and should come only after careful consideration. Figure 11.1 provides a flow chart detailing the process of collecting digital evidence depending on the events of the scene and the computers and systems involved and their power state.

FIGURE 11.1   Collecting Digital Evidence Flow Chart

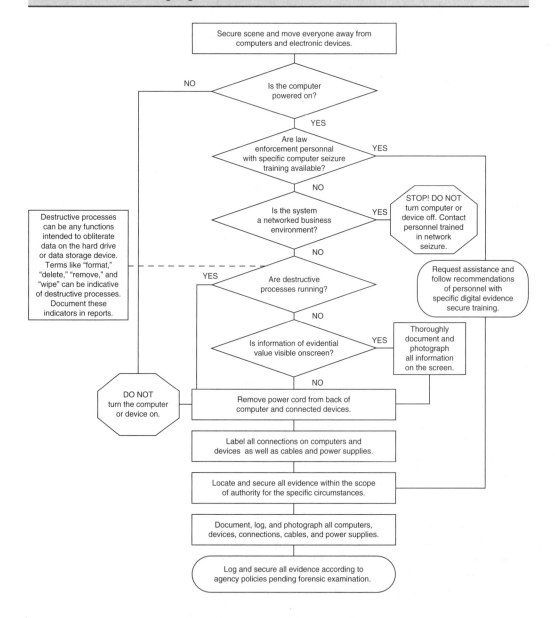

HANDLING ONGOING ACTIVITY   For the past ten years, the question that seems to get the most attention is what to do about an active computer. The one certain rule is: If it is off, leave it off. Various procedures are used to deal with computers that are running. The knowledge and experience of the investigator will have a lot to do with the decision of how to proceed. A first responder may have to be trained with very few choices; an experienced investigator or a subject matter expert accompanying the investigator may be able to interpret the situation with more finesse. Generally it is safe to leave a running computer on, but excessive hard drive activity, network activity, and the overall connectivity between devices and the Internet make it challenging to appropriately preserve evidence when the machine is active and online.

If the decision is made to turn off the computer, video or photographic documentation of activity should be attempted, if applicable, before shutting down a system abruptly. However, if there is enough reason to believe that it is necessary to shut it down, then it should be done at once. The best current practice is to remove the power cord from the rear of the computer and not use the power switch. Many switches activate a software command to power down. This command can be changed to alter data when the switch is used. Even old electrical switches can be modified to destroy evidence. It is also wise to make a note of the reasons leading to this decision as soon as possible after the computer is powered down. Many procedural questions that may arise later can be answered with a brief articulation of the facts leading to a good-faith decision.

Examining the Crime Scene

Safety is always the first concern, but a close second is the overriding concern of evidence collection: Do not alter the evidence. Any unavoidable alteration (e.g., packaging the evidence for transportation) should be documented so well that it can later be reassembled exactly as it was. After safety is assured, and the scene is secure, the entire scene should be photographed before altering it. If possible, lists and diagrams should be included with notes of observations. Particular attention should be given to the monitor screen, front of the computer, including indicator lights, wire connections, mouse and keyboard place, and screen saver status. An investigator should record in notes all actions taken and any changes observed on the monitor, computer, printer, or other peripherals that result from the search. The monitor is (1) on, (2) in sleep mode, or (3) off. The state of the monitor will decide which of the following situations apply:

1. If the monitor is on and a work product and/or the desktop is visible, photograph screen and record information displayed.
2. If the monitor is on and screen is blank (sleep mode) or shows a screen saver, move the mouse slightly (without pushing buttons). The screen should change and show work product or request a password. If mouse movement does not cause a change in the screen, *do not* perform any other keystrokes or mouse operations. Photograph the screen and record the information displayed.
3. If the monitor is off, make a note that it is off. Turn the monitor on, then determine if the monitor status is as described in either situation 1 or 2 above and follow those steps.

Once the scene is documented in its entirety, the process of collecting and preserving evidence can begin.

COLLECTION AND PRESERVATION OF EVIDENCE   All evidence collection activities may be later called into question by the defense. It is best to establish a written procedure and use it every time.

It is good to initial each step completed or note, in writing, why departure from the procedure was necessary. The following procedure is suggested by the National Institute of Justice.[6] An officer should

1. Photograph and diagram the connections of the computer and the corresponding cables. This step allows reconstruction of the system later if necessary.
2. Regardless of the power state of the computer (on, off, or sleep mode), remove the power source cable from the computer—*not* from the wall outlet. At this point, the question of whether to turn it off or not has been resolved; this procedure applies to collection, preservation, and transportation of evidence. If dealing with a laptop, in addition to removing the power cord, remove the battery pack. The battery is removed to prevent any power to the system. Some laptops have a second battery in the multipurpose bay instead of a floppy drive or CD drive. Check for this possibility and remove that battery as well. If dealing with a large multiuser system (e.g., a UNIX™ system), follow a safe shutdown procedure recommended by a subject matter expert.
3. Check for any outside data connection (e.g., telephone modem, cable, ISDN, DSL). If a telephone connection is present, attempt to identify the telephone number. The easiest way to do this is to connect a telephone and ask the operator to identify the number being used.
4. To avoid damage to potential evidence, remove any floppy disks that are present, package the disk separately, and label the package. If available, insert either a seizure disk or a blank floppy disk. This procedure prevents the magnetic heads of the floppy drive from damaging the disk in transit. Since CDs and DVDs are read by a laser and not by a physical read/write head, it is not required to remove CDs. In fact, there is no reason even to touch the CD drive when preparing a computer for transport.
5. Place tape over all the drive slots and over the power connector. This prevents accidental insertion of a disk or power cord. It also preserves the integrity of evidence in the drives.
6. To provide an additional level of security against confusion at the crime lab or during the sometimes lengthy storage, record the make, model, and serial numbers of the computer. This information is also required on a report generated from the seizure and on an inventory of seized items to be given to the owner.
7. Label all connectors and cable ends (including connections to peripheral devices) to allow for exact reassembly at a later time. Label unused connection ports as "unused."
8. Record or log evidence according to departmental procedures.
9. Recovery of nonelectronic evidence can be crucial in the investigation of electronic crime. Proper care should be taken to ensure that such evidence is recovered and preserved. Items relevant to subsequent examination of electronic evidence may exist in other forms (e.g., written passwords and other handwritten notes, blank pads of paper with indented writing, hardware and software manuals, calendars, literature, text or graphical computer printouts, and photographs) and should be secured and preserved for future analysis.

In fact, clear documentation is such a necessity that forms should be used to document in detail the equipment collected at a scene. Figure 11.2 provides an example of such documentation from the National Institute of Justice.

PACKING AND TRANSPORTATION OF EVIDENCE   If transport is required, package the components as fragile cargo. Actions taken should not add, modify, or destroy data stored on a computer or other media. Computers are fragile electronic instruments that are sensitive to temperature,

FIGURE 11.2   An Example of a Computer Evidence Worksheet

Computer Evidence Worksheet

Case Number: _____   Exhibit Number: _____

Laboratory Number: _____   Control Number: _____

Computer Information

Manufacturer: _____   Model: _____

Serial Number: _____

Examiner Markings: _____

Computer Type: Desktop ☐   Laptop ☐   Other: _____

Computer Condition: Good ☐   Damaged ☐   **(See Remarks)**

Number of Hard Drives: _____   3.5" Floppy Drive ☐   5.25" Floppy Drive ☐

Modem ☐   Network Card ☐   Tape Drive ☐   Tape Drive Type: _____

100 MB Zip ☐   250 MB Zip ☐   CD Reader ☐   CD Read/Write ☐

DVD ☐   Other: _____

CMOS Information   Not Available ☐

Password Logon: Yes ☐   No ☐   Password = _____

Current Time: _____   AM ☐   PM ☐   Current Date: _____ / _____ / _____

CMOS Time: _____   AM ☐   PM ☐   CMOS Date: _____ / _____ / _____

CMOS Hard Drive #1 Settings   Auto ☐

Capacity: _____   Cylinders: _____   Heads: _____   Sectors: _____

Mode: LBA ☐   Normal ☐   Auto ☐   Legacy CHS ☐

CMOS Hard Drive #2 Settings   Auto ☐

Capacity: _____   Cylinders: _____   Heads: _____   Sectors: _____

Mode: LBA ☐   Normal ☐   Auto ☐   Legacy CHS ☐

Computer Evidence Worksheet   **Page 1 of 2** humidity, physical shock, static electricity, and magnetic sources. Therefore, special precautions should be taken when packaging, transporting, and storing electronic evidence. To maintain chain of custody for electronic evidence, document its packaging, transportation, and storage. An investigator should

1. Ensure that all collected electronic evidence is properly documented, labeled, and inventoried before packaging.
2. Pay special attention to latent or trace physical evidence, like fingerprints or fiber samples, and take actions to preserve it. Testing for latent prints involves chemicals and dust, which may be harmful to electronic devices or storage media. Electronic evidence should be extracted before physical forensic examination. Specifically marking the evidence needing physical forensic examination will allow forensic analysts to avoid altering latent or trace evidence.
3. Pack magnetic media in antistatic packaging (paper or antistatic plastic bags). Avoid using materials that can produce static electricity, such as standard plastic bags or styrofoam "packing peanuts."
4. Avoid folding, bending, or scratching computer media such as diskettes, CD-ROMs, and tapes.
5. Ensure that all containers used to hold evidence are properly labeled. If multiple computer systems are collected, label each system so that it can be reassembled as found (e.g., system A—mouse, keyboard, monitor, main base unit; system B—mouse, keyboard, monitor, main base unit).
6. Keep electronic evidence away from magnetic sources. Radio transmitters, speaker magnets, and even heated vehicle seats are examples of items that can damage electronic evidence.
7. Avoid storing electronic evidence in vehicles for prolonged periods of time. Conditions of excessive heat, cold, or humidity can damage electronic evidence.
8. Ensure that computers and other components that are not packaged in containers are secured in the vehicle to avoid shock and excessive vibration. For example, computers may be placed on the vehicle floor and monitors placed on the seat with the screen down and secured by a seat belt.
9. Maintain the chain of custody on all evidence transported.[7]

STORAGE OF SEIZED EVIDENCE   The storage of seized evidence is as exacting a task as seizure and transportation. Above all, the evidence must remain unaltered until it is analyzed, and the continuity of the chain of custody must be maintained to prove it. Investigators in all but the smallest departments must turn evidence over to an evidence custodian. The evidence custodian is typically a ranking sworn officer. The custodian is then responsible for the evidence from that time until trial. When evidence is submitted for forensic analysis, the custodian delivers that evidence to the department's designated analyst (maybe another sworn officer, nonsworn employee, or off-site contract service). The evidence custodian obtains a receipt from the analyst. When the analysis is completed, the custodian receives the evidence and retains custody of the evidence until it is needed at trial. The evidence custodian maintains a secure area called an evidence locker to prevent general access to evidence stored therein. The custodian maintains logs of officers working shifts in the evidence locker. If officers are allowed to enter the locker, their entry is logged too; however, typically the custodian will bring evidence requested by officers or investigators to a window. That transfer is noted in the chain of custody, as is the return of the evidence. The chain of custody can be introduced and affirmed by calling the investigator, the custodian, and the analyst who examined the evidence.

The following procedure is suggested by National Institute of Justice and annotated with standard practices for all evidence.[8] Investigators should

1. Ensure that evidence is inventoried in accordance with departmental policies. This typically includes "marking" the evidence for later identification at trial. Without proper markings, one mass-produced computer is nearly indistinguishable from another. Investigators typically inscribe the metal case of the computer with their initials, the date, and case number—if possible. Containers can also be marked with indelible markers. Evidence tags can become separated from evidence, so actual marking is preferred.

2. Store digital evidence in a secure area away from temperature and humidity extremes. Protect it from magnetic sources, moisture, dust, and other harmful particles or contaminants.

3. Many electronic devices contain memory that requires continuous power to maintain the information, such as a battery or AC power. The most common example is the complementary metallic-oxide semiconductor (CMOS) battery that stores critical setup data for older computers. Data can be easily lost by unplugging the power source or allowing the battery to discharge. Collect and store the power supply adaptor or cable, if present, with the recovered device.

4. Potential evidence such as dates, times, and systems configurations may be lost as a result of prolonged storage. Since batteries have a limited life, data could be lost if they fail. Therefore, appropriate personnel (e.g., evidence custodian, lab chief, forensic examiner) should be informed that a device powered by batteries is in need of immediate attention.[9]

The basic police work involved in planning a search and obtaining a warrant are familiar tasks to investigators. Two key differences distinguish digital evidence from familiar physical evidence. First, electronic evidence must be contained in a physical medium. Since digital evidence can be copied flawlessly and frequently, there is no reason to limit a search to a single physical container. Anything capable of storing digital information may contain digital evidence. Second, digital evidence is fragile. A quick action by the suspect can erase digital information. Inadvertent mishandling of digital evidence can contaminate or destroy its evidentiary value. Specific procedures have been recommended by the National Institute of Justice to preserve the digital evidence for later analysis while maintaining its probative value. The ability properly to seek a warrant and execute a search forms the building blocks of more complex investigations.

Multiple-Location and Network Crime Scenes

Multiple-scene computer crimes are complicated by a number of factors beyond the standard single-scene seizure. Networked environments may contain evidence on multiple machines using multiple operating systems, in multiple physical and/or network locations, and in multiple jurisdictions. To further complicate search and seizure operations, current law enforcement practices, called minimization procedures, demand minimal intrusion to the operation of the network. Even the relatively few network experts in law enforcement may not be sufficiently familiar with a target network to extract evidence with sufficient legal integrity and not disrupt the operation of the target network. Officers skilled at single-scene seizures may feel overwhelmed at the thought of collecting network trace evidence. Fortunately, an investigator is not alone in attempting a multiple-scene or network investigation. Subject matter experts can be enlisted to guide investigators through unfamiliar networks. By concentrating on the purpose of investigation—the collection and preservation of evidence necessary to prove the elements of a crime and to connect the suspect to the crime—an investigator can coordinate the efforts of people with more technical knowledge. The investigator needs only the communication tools necessary to convey the purposes and precise needs of law enforcement to the local computer system administrators, who must often serve as guides in these unique environments.

DISTINGUISHING SINGLE-SCENE, MULTIPLE-SCENE, AND NETWORK CRIME SCENES   The distinction made is not based on technical differences, so much as functional differences for investigation. A single-scene crime involves only a single computer, for example, possession of child pornography or use of a computer to further a criminal enterprise. A multiple-scene crime involves more than one computer, with the possibility of an intervening network. Personal computers on wired or wireless local area network (LAN) can often be handled as several individual single-scene seizures. Additional complications include noting network connections and network identities for each machine. Data storage (i.e., network drives) can be spread across several machines on the network, but may be represented as a single unit to network users. In spite of the use of "network" technology, any geographically compact (same jurisdiction) crime scene under the administrative control of a single entity (one person, one corporation, etc.) is considered a multiple-scene crime. Network crime scenes would involve the Internet and any wired or wireless LAN or wide area network (WAN) that makes extensive use of dedicated servers, network or multiple-user operating systems (Unix™, Windows 2000 Pro™, etc.), or switching equipment. The presence of affected computers in multiple jurisdictions may also make it a network crime. The skill-set required to investigate this type of scene may exceed even a veteran investigator's ability. Further, an investigator may need numerous warrants or other legal search instruments (see ECPA in Chapter 9) to follow criminal activities. Cooperation from the companies owning the network resources can be the key to success. The need for such cooperation, either with ISPs or law enforcement agencies in other jurisdictions, distinguishes a multiple-scene crime from a network crime.

Identifying Network Architectures

Although there are numerous technical distinctions between different network architectures, investigators are not charged with maintaining these systems or understanding their full complexities. An investigator needs to know how to trace a transaction through the network and identify any potential sources of network trace evidence: latent signs of the transaction being traced.

INTERNET VS. INTRANET INVESTIGATIONS   The primary distinction of interest to an investigator is between Internet and intranet. An intranet is a WAN that uses a common addressing and transfer protocol suite called transfer control protocol/Internet protocol (TCP/IP). The key difference to an investigator is that an intranet is often administered by one authority; thus, it may be possible to get to a system administrator or system administration team and get definitive answers. Seeking technical assistance involves identifying the network administrator. This can usually be accomplished by looking up the domain registrant on a service like "whois" (see below).

The Internet is a network of networks owned and maintained by various private, corporate, and governmental interests. The only feature truly common to all of these various component systems is the use of TCP/IP. Seeking technical assistance involves identifying the ISPs involved. Steps taken to preserve Internet evidence must be quick. Routine logs are often quickly purged due to the huge volume of Internet traffic. If the network can be traced to a corporation, the corporate IT department may be of further assistance. Investigators may issue preservation letters (by fax, if speed is vital) to require service providers to retain relevant information. Preservation letters do not require a magistrate's signature; however, a warrant or lesser instrument may be required to obtain the evidence requested for preservation. In many cases, public ISPs cannot voluntarily release information to investigators.

Modeling Network Transactions

At the most fundamental level, all networks can be described with the Open Systems Interface (OSI) model. It is a standard used worldwide. By tracing the way each process of this model is completed, an investigator can slowly make sense of the most complex network environment. In general, the model proceeds from the most concrete, at layer 1 (e.g., a wire) to the most abstract, at layer 7. Abstraction makes a computer network more versatile because it can operate with many different purposes. Concreteness makes an operation easier to understand for exactly the opposite reason: It can only do one or a few simple tasks. For example, a wire can only carry electrical impulses from one end to the other. In a multiple-scene investigation, connected computers can often be identified by tracing the wire runs. At the other extreme, the applications (what we call programs, like MS Outlook™) can be used for a variety of purposes.

Beyond the traditional seven layers of the OSI model lie the even greater abstraction of human users (layer 8) and policies governing them (layer 9). Although the OSI model may seem very complex, it is actually a tool used by computer scientists simply to communicate about network functions. The seven layers of the model each serve a function in the transmission of data. The specific function of each layer is described in Table 11.1. An investigator familiar with the OSI model can communicate with system administrators using vastly different software. The investigator doesn't have to understand how each network component

TABLE 11.1 Layers of the Investigation

9. Policies	Human	The rules, policies, and management controls that govern the actions of users
8. User		The human being using the computer and network
7. Application		Provides direct interaction with the user (e.g., Netscape or Explorer)
6. Presentation	Application services	Standardizes data transmission formats (i.e., file types such as JPEG)
5. Session		Provides checkpoint, fall back, and encryption services (e.g., SSL)
4. Transport		Allows multiple simultaneous operations across a single network connection (e.g., TCP)
3. Network	Network services	Provides unique addressing for transmission across different networks (e.g., IP)
2. Data link		Assembles bits into packets, provides error correction, and flow control (e.g., Ethernet)
1. Physical		Provides a path for the transmission of bits (e.g., wires, fiber optics, and radio waves)

functions, only what happens to data in a network. This leaves the system administrator to sort out the details.

The addition of layers 8 and 9 emphasizes the role of human users and the policies that govern the network to investigators; they are not part of the worldwide standard. They originally stem from a joke about network breakdowns caused by user errors or corporate policies that inhibit network function, but investigators should keep in mind that all information transfer ultimately occurs because of a human operator or a policy that dictates it. Security flaws can also be examined with these additional layers. For example, insider crimes are the most common forms of computer crime. If an investigator suspects an insider, layer 8 reminds him or her to look into personal matters and backgrounds. Layer 9 reminds him or her to check company security policies to see who has access to the machines, both network and physical. It is easy to get stuck in the mode of assuming that a computer crime has a computer cause. The hacker trick of social engineering[10] recognizes that the most common weakness in computer security is the human operator, especially if the operator works in a large organization with complex policies (layers 8 and 9).

The application services are generally not retained in network trace evidence except for a few specific types of logs. These are the abstract services most directly under the control of the user—or in the case of a computer crime, the criminal. They can be encrypted and still function. However, key information, such as file names and sizes, might be retained and matched to a user.

The network services are most often tracked by system administrators, because they are necessary for proper network maintenance and function, but do not reveal private information without further investigation. Routine logs contain a wealth of information (discussed below) about network service transactions.

Locating Evidence

Local system administrators are the best source of information about network logging. Routine business records are not considered hearsay and are therefore considered admissible to court (see discussion of hearsay later in the chapter). Various security systems, commonly used by business, have logging features that may help detect anomalous activities. For instance, intrusion detection systems (IDSs) are designed primarily to log network traffic and examine it for known patterns indicating attacks. If the crime in question uses such a signature, the presence of an IDS can be of tremendous assistance to an investigator. Similarly, many firewalls—systems that block network traffic based on rules established by an administrator—have logging systems. For other cases, such as intellectual property violations, large volumes of apparently legitimate traffic might be ignored by an IDS, but show up in an administrator's log as an unusually large amount of network traffic (i.e., a usage spike). Administrators must plan for network growth and often track network usage statistics. They also manage network loads with a system of resource allowances reserved for each user (i.e., a user quota system). If a user exceeds his or her storage quota, even briefly, the administrator's log may note the event. In a final example, ISPs often keep logs of user activity to help predict demand and plan for growth as well as keeping logs for billing purposes. If a user dials into a "front" account under an assumed name, the dial-up record may record his or her actual telephone number.

All of this potential evidence is kept for various purposes on various machines on the network. It may be up to the investigator quickly to notify competent authorities to preserve the evidence. The great volume of log evidence generated in a typical business cannot be economically maintained for extended periods. Many logs purge after as little as 24 hours. Federal law (the Electronic Communications Privacy Act) allows a "preservation letter" to be sent to a company or individual with potential electronic evidence; it requires the responsible person to maintain the evidence pending further investigation.

Key Information for Locating Network Trace Evidence

The logs mentioned in the previous section use identifiers to match network transactions with the actual machines involved. These identifiers are often associated with a level of the OSI model. The identifiers are necessary for proper network function. With a few relatively rare exceptions, network communication is literally impossible without them; therefore, they will be present as latent evidence in network crimes.

MAC ADDRESS   The media access control (MAC) address is a unique hardware address associated with each network card or other network device. The MAC is used at layer 2 of the OSI model. Layer 2 is the data link layer; it is the most concrete electronic layer. MAC addresses are only used at the local network level. Network transactions that use TCP/IP usually strip the MAC address away from data. Therefore, MAC addresses are most useful in multiple-scene investigations using a single LAN. They may also help prove that a criminal had access from inside the victim's network.

The MAC address is usually reported in hexadecimal couplets. Hexadecimal is a numbering system that uses base 16 instead of the familiar base 10^{11} that we use for counting. Although an investigator does not need to know all of the intricacies of network addressing, recognizing the pattern of network addresses is helpful. Hexadecimal uses pairs of the characters 0–9 and A–F to represent 8 bits (also called a byte), for example, 00-AF-03-05-0E-B9. Contrary to common wisdom, MAC addresses can be changed with software configuration, so failure to match a MAC is not definitive proof that the computer was not involved in an incident.[12]

IP ADDRESS   The IP address is a unique address assigned to every computer on the Internet. Like all numbers used by computers, the IP address is a binary number made up of bits. Although an IP address can be found represented with hexadecimal couplets like the MAC address, the IP is almost always reported in the decimal-dot notation. "Decimal-dot" means four decimal elements (base 10, like we use to count) ranging from 0 to 255 separated by dots, for example, 192.168.0.0. Although many people recognize the decimal dot notation, they do not understand how it works. Because the decimal number represents 8 bits each, it cannot exceed 255. There are 2^8 (256) possible values for 8 bits. The maximum number that can be represented is 255 because computers start counting at 0, not 1. An investigator should know that any value over 255 cannot be part of a valid IP address. Thus, if a suspect reports an Internet address of 345.300.123.205, an investigator will know that it is false.

The IP is associated with transactions at layer 3, the network layer, of the OSI model. IP addresses are often dynamically assigned to computers when they start up. However, many computers, especially servers, use static IPs that do not change. The owner of a given IP can be determined through ARIN, the American Registry for Internet Numbers. Note: International investigations may require the use of the European and African authority RIPE[13] or the Asian authority APNIC.[14]

DNS   Domain name system (DNS) is a protocol that allows users to enter meaningful words instead of IP addresses to identify a computer. DNS is a helper service for layer 3 of the OSI model in TCP/IP systems. The Internet does not work on English words. To find a particular computer on the Internet, a user must have the IP address; as we saw in the previous section, these can be very difficult to decipher in their native form. To make it easier to use the Internet, the DNS was established to create a place to look up (also called resolving) the IP of a computer based on its human readable name.

BOX 11.2
Understanding IP Addresses

Understanding how IPs work can help an investigation. In this hypothetical example, a Web-based fraud scheme manipulates the way browsers interpret Internet addresses. The following URL will take a browser to eBay™, the leading Web-based auction site:

> http://pages.ebay.com/index.html?ssPage
> Name=h:h:home:US

The following URL will take a browser to the Web site of anyone with the $50 fee required to register a Web address:

> http://www.ebay.com@homeshoppingforyou.
> com

Without even registering a Web domain, the following URLs can provide access to a criminal's page from anywhere on the Web. By using these URLs from a Web page on a legally owned Internet address (called a "front" in fraud investigations), the criminal can claim ignorance of where the links go. The links below can easily be altered to lead to anywhere on the Internet without changing anything in front of the "@" sign.

> http://www.ebay.com@192.168.23.56
> http://www.ebay.com@%C0%A8%17%38

These URLs go to the exact same place. The IP address 192.168.23.56 (in decimal dot notation) is the same as %C0%A8%17%38 (in hexadecimal notation). Neither of the addresses will get a potential fraud victim to the real e-Bay site. All of the security used at e-Bay is useless if the customer never gets to the page. However, for the victim to reach the criminal, the address must point to a valid location on the Internet. The administrative details of that site may prove to be a rich source for search and seizure.

Thus, when you type in a Web address like www.eBay.com, your browser sends a request to a system of databases of domain names and matching IPs maintained by the Internet Corporation for Assigned Names and Numbers (ICANN) or its subset databases hosted throughout the Internet.[15] A reverse lookup is available to convert an IP to its human-readable equivalent.

PPP   Point-to-point Protocol (PPP) is most commonly used by modems that dial in to an ISP. PPP works at layer 2 of the OSI model, like Ethernet. Unfortunately, there is no equivalent of the MAC address used by Ethernet, because PPP connections are point to point. When there are only two computers involved in the connection, they do not need identifiers. Although the protocol itself yields little information, the routers that handle such connections often log useful information such as the account accessed and authenticated with a password and the times at the beginning and end of the session.

Collecting Network Trace Evidence

Due to various historic and legal problems with digital evidence collection,[16] it is the best current practice to minimize the intrusion of network investigations. Seizing a business's critical IT assets could easily do more harm to that business than the worst denial-of-service attack. Even lengthy downtime can cost the business substantial amounts. The seizure of evidence can be a significant deterrent to businesses reporting computer crime.

Minimization procedures have to be balanced against the needs of evidence integrity and the mission of law enforcement, but cannot be discounted automatically. Typically, if evidence is available from an existing backup tape or can be copied from an existing source without disrupting operations, it is acceptable. When a machine must be taken off-line, on-the-spot imaging is often used to collect evidence with minimal intrusion.

PRESENTING DIGITAL EVIDENCE AT TRIAL

Any reasonably experienced law enforcement official knows that police work does not end when a suspect is arrested and transferred to a jail custodian. Paperwork, reports, and possibly interviews with a prosecutor are as important as the investigation itself. Consider that an investigation is like writing a lengthy paper. The paper can be a masterful, witty, comprehensive coverage of the topic, but if you never hand that paper in, it is worthless. An investigation, no matter how well conceived and executed, is worthless if the case does not end in a successful prosecution. In fact, the quality of the investigator's report, credibility, and willingness to participate fully often influence plea bargains. If a case does go to trial, an investigator will be required to present the facts represented in the report or explain the procedures used to discover and collect evidence. The testimony of the investigator is often the bedrock of a case. Competent presentation and procedure are as vital to investigators as any technical skills. In fact, digital forensic examiners must be mindful of the fact that juries and judges may not necessarily understand the information that they are trying to present. As a result, examiners and attorneys should use simple analogies and define technical terms and events in as simple definitions as possible.[17] Drawings, figures, and cartoons that illustrate a point are helpful in communicating information to a broader courtroom audience.

Beyond simplicity in presentation, the rules of evidence require that the foundation for physical evidence be established with testimony; thus, evidence does not speak for itself.[18] The prosecution must establish when, where, and how the evidence was collected. The prosecution must also be able to establish that the evidence was not altered to prejudice the trial by either act (such as intentionally altering the evidence) or omission (such as allowing the evidence to be degraded or contaminated). Finally, the prosecution must also establish that the evidence collected conforms to the warrant or guidelines for commonly accepted warrantless searches. As the person responsible for these procedures, the investigator is the primary witness used to introduce evidence.

The Hearsay Rule

Black's Law Dictionary defines hearsay:

> Hearsay includes any statement made outside the present proceeding which is offered as evidence of the truth of matters asserted therein.[19]

It is fundamental to our system of justice that the accused be able to confront his or her accusers and offer evidence to rebut their statements. Witnesses must only testify to matters of which they have direct knowledge. This gives the accused a chance directly to confront and discredit statements made against him or her. According to the Federal Rules of Evidence (§§801–04), the hearsay rule excludes statements made outside of the ability of the accused to confront the person making the statement before the jury,[20] unless such statements fit one of several well-known exceptions.[21] The following section describes the most relevant applications of the hearsay rule to digital evidence-related testimony.

Using Notes on the Witness Stand

Investigators have large caseloads and must often wait months before testifying in a case. It is permissible to use case notes, journals, and logs created during the investigation to help the investigator recall fine details such as serial numbers, model numbers, and other minutia. The central question in the use of notes on the witness stand is whether the witness (i.e., the investigator) actually recalls the events or is relying on the notes entirely. If the witness uses notes to prompt memories of the events and recall details, it is known as "past recollection recalled."[22] Past recollection recalled does not violate the hearsay rule. The defense has a right to examine the notes and test the witness' memory before allowing the testimony. This test will establish the degree to which the witness has an independent recollection of the events.

If the investigator relies entirely upon the notes for any recollection of the events, it is known as "past recollection recorded."[23] Past recollection recorded does violate the hearsay rule. If the investigator does not recall the events of the case, the best the prosecutor can do is have the reports and notes read into evidence. If this is necessary, the entire contents of the notes become available. Many patrol officers use a spiral-bound notebook to record all kinds of information while at work and even at home. Investigators should avoid this and use loose-leaf sheets for a single case. There is a classic story about crime scene investigation where the defense noted missing pictures in a series. The officers were required to produce the negatives. Although the missing pictures did not provide evidence to clear the suspect, they did show one of the officers "posing" with the corpse. In a spiral-bound notebook with many cases and doodles, there are probably many such potentially embarrassing tidbits.

Business Records

It is an established exception to the hearsay rule that records or summaries created in the normal course of business (not specifically for law enforcement purposes) are not hearsay and are therefore admissible. "The courts generally have admitted computer records upon a showing that the records fall within the business records exception."[24] The Federal Rules of Evidence §803 (6):

> Records of regularly conducted activity. A memorandum, report, record, [etc.] made at or near the time by, or from information transmitted by, a person with knowledge, if kept in the course of a regularly conducted business activity, and if it was the regular practice of that business activity to make the memorandum, report, record, or data compilation, all as shown by the testimony of the custodian or other qualified witness, unless the source of information or the method or circumstances of preparation indicate lack of trustworthiness. The term "business" as used in this paragraph includes business, institution, association, profession, occupation, and calling of every kind, whether or not conducted for profit.[25]

The key to this section is that the "business process" be regular or routinized in such a way that the accuracy of the product may be assessed by the court. Failure to meet this standard does not mean that creating logs for law enforcement purposes is illegal. It does not even mean that such logs will be inadmissible. Other techniques can be used to admit such logs, but these methods are not covered in this book.

Presenting Best Evidence

Black's Law Dictionary states that the principle of best evidence

> requires that best evidence available be presented in lieu of less satisfactory evidence . . . This rule prohibits the introduction into evidence of secondary evidence unless it is shown that original document has been lost or destroyed or is beyond jurisdiction of court without fault of the offering party . . . [T]he basic rule

[is] as follows: "To prove the content of a writing, recording, or photograph, the original writing, recording, or photograph is required."[26]

The best evidence rule simply states that the court requires the original copy of evidence. Courtroom presentation is the ultimate purpose of collecting evidence. It does not make sense to store the original safely in a vault while using a (possibly imperfect) copy in the courtroom. Although best evidence is often considered to be the original copy, with digital evidence the original copy is inaccessible to human beings, because it is usually a series of magnetic zones on a hard disk. Courts have accepted printouts of the contents of a disk as best evidence. However, the contents of a disk are usually too large to print in their entirety. There is no technical basis to say that displaying information from the actual hard drive of the computer seized or the monitor seized along with it is any more likely to be best evidence than an exact digital copy displayed on a projector, paper, or other medium.[27] Subject to verification, a digital copy in a convenient form may be presented in court without violating the best evidence rule.

However, presenting a "live" demonstration of digital evidence on the accused's computer with the accused's monitor can have a powerful impact on the jury. Live demonstrations should be planned carefully and tested prior to presentation. Given the unpredictability of some technology, a video might be prudent and allowable under exceptions to the best evidence rule. For the convenience of the court, voluminous evidence may be presented in summary form. Federal Rules of Evidence §1006 states:

> The contents of voluminous writings, recordings, or photographs which cannot conveniently be examined in court may be presented in the form of a chart, summary, or calculation. The originals, or duplicates, shall be made available for examination or copying, or both, by other parties at reasonable time and place. The court may order that they be produced in court.

Similarly, if the process in question cannot be adequately represented in a printout, the court may allow alternate presentation.

Challenges to Forensic Analysis Strategies

Considering that digital forensic examinations depend in part on the use of software and technologies to examine digitial media, it is necessary to consider how these technologies can be challenged in court. The range of software and versions of programs that can be used may lead attorneys to attempt to discredit these tools and the subsequent analyses through *Frye* or *Daubert* challenges.[28] These two challenges were generated from legal cases and provide standards to assess the quality of scientific or methdological techniques used to find and develop evidence.

The first case is *Frye* v. *United States,* which provides a standard for scientific research that is commonly applied in state court.[29] In this 1923 case, James Frye was convicted of second-degree murder. He appealed his sentence on the basis that he confessed but later retracted his statement and was unable to present evidence concerning the accuracy of his admission through the use of an early version of a polygraph test or introduce an expert witness to testify on his behalf about the test. The appeals court who heard this case felt that the polygraph test in question did not have enough scientific support to be used as evidence in court, and the appeal was rejected. The *Frye* test was established as a consequence, stating that scientific techniques can be admitted in court if they are generally accepted within the relevant scientific community. This includes procedures, principles, or techniques that can be presented in a court case. This has significance for forensic examiners, as it suggests that evidence generated from nontraditional or untested strategies may potentially be deemed inadmissible in court, dependent on the judge's decision as to its general acceptance in the scientific community.

The second important case is *Daubert* v. *Merrell Dow Pharmaceuticals,* which created the *Daubert* standard used in federal courts, and in some state courts, concerning the presentation of expert testimony and evidence.[30] In this case, Merrell Dow Pharamceuticals was sued by a woman whose baby, Jason Daubert, was born with congenital disorders, including a lack of fingers and bones in the arm. During pregnancy, the mother took a drug produced by Dow that contained a chemical that was linked to a large number of similar birth defects in children across the globe. Medical tests presented by the plaintiff suggested that this product caused similar defects in animals, though evidence presented by scientists writing for Dow argued that medical tests in humans found no link to health risks during pregnancy. The court dismissed the case, arguing that Daubert did not provide sufficient evidence to support their argument. The case was appealed to the Supreme Court, but was not heard, and as a result the lower court decision stands and provides a standard for the presentation of evidence on the basis of admissibility of expert testimony based on (1) the relevance and (2) the reliability of evidence based off of the scientific techniques used to create it. In particular, there are four points of concern about the science used to produce evidence:

1. The scientific technique can be—and has been—tested.
2. The technique has been subjected to peer review and publication.
3. There is a known or potential rate of error.
4. The technique has been generally accepted by the relevant scientific community.

This again applies to digital evidence and the ways that it is acquired. Thus, it is important that examiners use well-regarded and well-tested standards for evidence development and examination in order to reduce the likelihood of successful challenges.

Chain of Custody

Black's Law Dictionary defines chain of custody as follows:

> In evidence, the one who offers real [physical] evidence . . . must account for the custody of the evidence from the moment in which it reaches his custody until the moment in which it is offered in evidence. [The] chain of custody is proven if an officer is able to testify that he or she took control of an item of physical evidence, identified it, placed it in a locked or protected area, and retrieved the item being offered [in evidence] on the day of the trial.[31]

The chain of custody is a legal document that records a history of who had the evidence and when. In the hypothetical example cited in *Black's Law Dictionary,* the chain is relatively simple. In a typical computer crime investigation, the chain of custody can be extensive. As more specialists (computer forensic technicians, subject matter experts, off-site laboratories, etc.) work on a piece of evidence, the chain of custody becomes more complex. Complexity is not necessarily bad, but it never helps establish evidence. For this and other reasons, departments and agencies have established evidence-handling procedures. At a minimum, these procedures include a list of anyone accessing the evidence with notations of time and place. They also include a notation of where the evidence was taken, if transported, and any changes, such as removing a piece for analysis. Digital information requires additional protection, and even more elaborate protections have been devised for it.[32]

The investigator seizing the evidence may be required to testify to the provenance of the evidence. This foundational testimony describes how the evidence was collected, where it came from, and what has happened to it since it was seized. An investigator can provide more effective testimony by using established procedures every time. The plan for conducting a search should include a designated custodian of evidence who will document and transport the evidence to maintain the chain of custody.

Expert Testimony

This section has focused on the presentation of the fruits of an investigation. Although there has been mention of subject matter experts, their contributions have been limited to assisting the investigator to produce a case. Experts undoubtedly play a role in helping the investigator gather evidence of the elements of a crime and may have opinions that help establish probable cause.

Summary

An investigator is charged with identifying that a crime has taken place, establishing the elements of that crime, and associating the crime with a suspect. The investigator must gather compelling evidence in a manner that allows it to be presented in court. If possible, an investigator should work with the prosecutor to understand the type of evidence specifically needed for the prosecutor's strategy. Even without direct input from the prosecutor (perhaps prior to the prosecutor's decision to take the case), an investigator must be able to understand the events constituting the crime. Several tools and procedures exist to help the investigator in this process. Unless the investigator has an unusually high degree of experience with computers, subject matter experts will play an important role in assessing the details of the crime. However, the primary burden of presenting a case to the prosecutor and eventually to the court falls on the investigator. Proper procedure and documentation guided by an understanding of the "endgame" in court will increase the odds of a successful prosecution.

Review Questions

1. Explain how labor is divided among professionals involved in the investigation of computer crime. Which role do you prefer and why?
2. Outline the process of preparing and executing a search warrant for electronic evidence. How does search and seizure of electronic evidence at a single scene differ from physical evidence search and seizure?
3. Explain the difference between single-scene, multiple-scene, and network investigations. In what ways do single- and multiple-scene investigations differ from network investigations?
4. Explain the procedures for securing digital evidence. After officer safety, what is the primary concern of the investigator during this whole process?

Endnotes

1. NEWBURGHER, E.C. (2001). *Home Computers and Internet Usage in United States: August 2000.* U.S. Census Bureau, p. 1.

2. STOLL, C. (1989). *The Cuckoo's Egg: Tracking a Spy Through the Maze of Computer Espionage.* New York: Doubleday.

3. STEPHENSON, P. (2001). *Investigating Computer-Related Crime.* Boca Raton, FL: CRC Press.

4. NAUGHTON, JOHN. (April 30, 2003). "Mailboxing clever," *Manchester Guardian Weekly.*

5. U.S. Constitution, Amendment Four.

6. Technical Working Group for Electronic Crime Scene Investigation (2008). *Electronic Crime Scene Investigation: A Guide for First Responders,* 2nd ed. National Institute of Justice (NIJ 187736). Washington, DC: National Institute of Justice.

7. *Ibid.*

8. *Ibid.*

9. *Ibid.*

10. Social engineering is basically lying to a person on the telephone or in person to get access to a desired resource (see Chapter 3 for a more extensive discussion).

11. This means that when we reach the highest individual digit (at the number 9), we then start to repeat digits (at 10). This is called base 10. Base 16 uses the following sequence before it repeats: 0, 1, 2, 3, 4, 5, 6, 7, 8, 9, A, B, C, D, E, F. The next number is 10 (think of it as 1 then 0, not 10). 10 in base-16 notation equals 16 in decimal.

12. STEVENS, W.R. (1994). *TCP/IP Illustrated Volume 1.* Addison Wesley.

13. RIPE (Réseaux IP Européens) is a collaborative forum open to all parties interested in wide area IP networks in Europe and beyond. The objective of RIPE is to ensure the administrative and technical coordination necessary to enable the operation of a pan-European IP network. (RIPE Web page: *http://www.ripe.net/ripe/index.html*)

14. APNIC is one of four Regional Internet Registries currently operating in the world. It provides allocation and registration services which support the operation of the Internet globally. It is a not-for-profit, membership-based organization whose members include Internet service providers, National internet registries, and similar organizations. APNIC represents the Asia Pacific region, comprising 62 economies. (APNIC Webpage: *http://www.apnic.net/info/about.html*)

15. This explanation greatly simplifies the DNS system, but accurately describes the general function. For an extensive discussion of DNS systems, see STEVENS, *TCP/IP Illustrated Volume 1.*

16. *Steve Jackson Games* v. *United States Secret Service,* 816 F.Supp. 432 (W.D.Tex, 1993).

17. Technical Working Group for Digital Evidence in the Coutroom. (2007). *Digital Evidence in the Courtoom: A Guide for Law Enforcement and Prosecutors.* National Institute of Justice. Washington, DC: National Institute of Justice.

18. The opposing side may waive the requirement of foundation by accepting the evidence without question of provenance (called stipulating).

19. BLACK, H.C., NOLAN, J.R., and NOLAN-HALEY, J.M. (1990). *Black's Law Dictionary,* 6th ed. St. Paul, MN: West Publishing.

20. It is part of the jury's job to assess the credibility of statements made. If a statement from an unreliable informant is repeated by an utterly reliable witness, the jury cannot properly assess the truth of the statement.

21. Federal Rules of Evidence §§ 801–04.

22. SWANSON, C.R., CHAMELIN, N.C., TERRITO, L., and TAYLOR, R. (2009). *Criminal Investigation,* 10th ed. San Francisco, CA: McGraw-Hill.

23. BLACK, NOLAN, and NOLAN-HALEY, *Black's Law Dictionary.*

24. KERR, O. (2001). "Computer Records and the Federal Rules of Evidence. *USA Bulletin. http://www.usdoj.gov/criminal/cybercrime/usamarch-2001_4.htm. United States Department of Justice.*

25. The Federal Rules of Evidence §803 (6).

26. BLACK, NOLAN, and NOLAN-HALEY, *Black's Law Dictionary.*

27. I do not advise arguing with a judge as to what comprises best evidence. Most courts can be convinced through expert testimony and there is sufficient precedent to allow the broader interpretation of "best evidence."

28. *Ibid.,* p. 16.

29. *Ibid.*

30. *Ibid.*

31. BLACK, NOLAN, and NOLAN-HALEY, *Black's Law Dictionary.*

32. SWANSON, CHAMELIN, TERRITO, and TAYLOR, *Criminal Investigation.*

CHAPTER 12

Digital Forensics

CHAPTER OBJECTIVES

After completing this chapter, you should be able to

- Outline and explain the process used to preserve the verifiable integrity of digital evidence.
- Suggest probable locations for particular types of digital evidence needed for various types of investigations.
- Explain how the storage system works in the computer.
- Describe, in broad detail, how information is stored on hard disks.
- Identify and explain hidden sources of information on a hard disk.
- Identify common storage media.
- Outline a basic universal procedure for examining removable storage media.
- Explain the basic logical structures of the hard drive and related magnetic devices.

INTRODUCTION

Forensic: "[b]elonging to courts of justice."[1] Although this chapter will deal with the technical details of computers and data storage, it will always be guided by the understanding that technical knowledge is secondary to the forensic analyst's ability to present technical information to the court. The various forensic sciences all share the role of bridging technical expertise with the courtroom process. Digital forensics can encompass many areas of inquiry. Civil court applications of digital forensics can include any aspect of computer science or information science. Information network analysis, source code analysis, and many other areas from civil litigation may eventually find their way into criminal investigations, but it is still fairly rare to see anything except storage forensics used in criminal court. However, recent trials involving virus writers indicate that criminal investigations may soon include some of these other areas.

The field of storage forensics covers the examination of information stored on a physical medium. A physical medium is a real-world object that may be inside the computer (e.g., a seized hard drive) or outside the computer (e.g., a floppy disk or CD). When information is stored on a physical medium, it is said to be "static." The fact that the information is static, or not moving electronically, distinguishes it from information on an active or "live" network. The examination of stored data[2] is often referred to as *postmortem* analysis because it is not on a live network. There is no functional distinction between the quality of evidence derived from a live network and from storage media, but the laws surrounding the collection and the collection procedures differ greatly. However, once the live data are stored, the forensic process is virtually identical.

THE BASIC PROCESS OF STORAGE FORENSICS

As with any other forensic operation, maintaining the continuity of evidence from the source to the final analysis product is the most important task of the examiner. The forensic analyst must have the ability to demonstrate the link between the seized drive, hereafter called the evidence drive, and the final analysis. Remember: The evidence exists on an unaltered original storage device (e.g., hard drive); analysis creates leads and summaries, not evidence. It may be necessary to demonstrate the process used to obtain the summaries and leads through documentation and, sometimes, even replication of the analysis. This section describes the best current practices to reduce uncertainty when presenting the results of an analysis in court. Unfortunately, the complex reality of investigations and forensic analysis does not always allow for the implementation of "best practices." For example, multiple-scene and network crimes do not always allow the seizure of the evidence drive. Anything short of best practices presents uncertainty in court, but does not signal the end of the investigation or preclude prosecution. Whenever possible, commonly accepted exceptions will be noted, but this section is primarily concerned with the most common situation found in law enforcement: a hard drive seized and in the possession of the analyst.

Some symbols will be used in this section to demonstrate visually the processes explained. These symbols are the standard flow chart symbols used to describe computer processes.

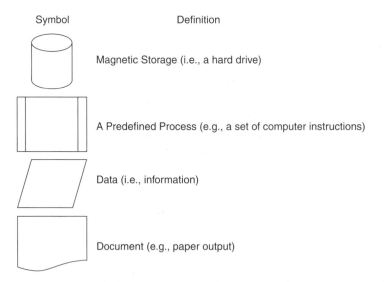

Symbol	Definition
	Magnetic Storage (i.e., a hard drive)
	A Predefined Process (e.g., a set of computer instructions)
	Data (i.e., information)
	Document (e.g., paper output)

FIGURE 12.1 Flow chart symbols and definitions used in this chapter.

PREPARATION FOR FORENSIC ANALYSIS

Some preparations must be made before any lab analysis is attempted. An analyst must be able to ensure that the result of an analysis comes from the evidence, not from contamination or error. The gold standard is that an analyst must be able to reliably reproduce any result from procedure notes and a copy of the original data seized.[3] Thus, the steps of an analysis should be documented. A successful practice is to have a standard procedure for types of evidence and document any modifications to this procedure, noting the reasons why they are necessary. Such procedures are designed specifically to prevent challenges to the analysis in court. Many computer experts could quickly determine several more efficient ways to collect and analyze information, but these alternative methods would not likely meet the standards and common objections found in criminal court. Beware of helpful computer experts that do not understand the mission of forensics. That is, evidence could probably be obtained without going through these procedures, but it would be more vulnerable to challenge if not completely useless in a criminal court.

It is also necessary to prepare an appropriate environment for the analysis. Using "clean," or verified, software tools with valid software licenses is an important first step. It can be embarrassing and expensive to have to admit to using illegal software. Lab equipment should be in working order. When new equipment is introduced, its function should be verified and documented in case later questions arise. One important early step is to obtain a "hash" value (like an electronic fingerprint) of the hard drive used for analysis (also called a bench drive). A program implementing the Message Digest 5 (MD5) is the most commonly used method of creating a hash. The process of hashing will be further explained later in this chapter. A hash of the blank bench drive will be used to verify that it is clean after an analysis.

A final preparation, often overlooked, is to verify the qualifications and skills necessary to explain the analysis in court. The information technology field is full of self-taught experts. While many of these "experts" are highly skilled, many are also frauds. Of those who are legitimate experts, many are incapable of a convincing (or in some cases comprehensible) courtroom presentation. The analyst conducting the analysis must be able to understand and explain the process of the analysis. It is dangerous for an analyst to be completely dependent on point-and-click tools combined with one-size-fits-all procedures.

Acquisition of Data

The forensic process described in this section assumes that the evidence drive is available to the examiner; however, an image can be obtained and authenticated in the field if circumstances require

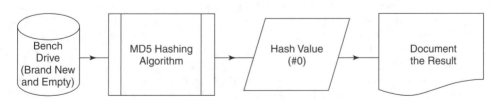

FIGURE 12.2   Before the first step of a new analysis, it is necessary to obtain a comparison value for the blank hard drive to be used in the analysis.

Note: These diagrams (steps 1 through 7) are explained throughout this section. Together, they describe, in order, a complete process. This process is easier to understand if you keep in mind that we need a way to verify that the drive analyzed has not been contaminated or altered since it was seized from the suspect (called the evidence drive).

it. Field acquisition is not the preferred method, because failure to maintain control of the evidence drive can also lead to problems in establishing the authenticity of the evidence in court. It is possible to obtain a written stipulation as to the authenticity of the evidence acquired. This is often used if a suspect wants the evidence drive returned prior to the end of the trial. If it is impossible to obtain a stipulation, the evidence is not necessarily inadmissible; it simply requires a greater showing that the evidence is authentic.[4] For example, a computer owned by an online publisher contains potential evidence. The magistrate signing the warrant places a special condition on the search that investigators use the absolute minimally intrusive search to avoid interfering with the First Amendment rights of the publisher. The suspect will not stipulate the contents of the search—having nothing to gain by doing so. The publisher's hard drive can be imaged and authenticated on the spot, but the seizure will be closely analyzed by the defense. Expert testimony as to the imaging process may be required.

Regardless of whether the image acquisition occurs in the field or in the forensic lab, different acquisition systems require different efforts to preserve the evidence drive. The acquisition usually runs from a specially designed forensic system. If the acquisition system uses the Windows™ operating system, acquisition should be performed against a hard drive with a write blocker installed (see Box 12.1). This technology helps to reduce the likelihood that the evidence contained on the system is not unintentionally altered in some fashion. Other acquisition systems use a true read-only mount of the file system (often not possible in Windows) with analysis proceeding from a drive mounted for read-only operations.

Authentication of Data

The prosecutor must be able to prove that the evidence presented or summarized in court came unaltered from the defendant. The digital forensic analyst has an easier job. The product of forensic evidence must be shown to be an authentic product of the evidence seized. There is a unique quality to digital evidence that allows it to be more easily authenticated than physical evidence. When evidence is seized, it can be summarized mathematically in a process called hashing (see Box 12.2). A hash is a unique numerical value calculated from the data in a digital file. No other naturally occurring file can have the same hash value.[5] A hash value (or, simply, hash) is essentially the "fingerprint" of the digital file. By comparing this fingerprint with a new

---

BOX 12.1

Unintentionally Altering Digital Evidence

Almost any action taken on a computer, even the simple act of starting it, alters potential evidence and gives the defense an avenue to attack the credibility of the analysis. Kruse and Heiser cite a statement from the Federal Law Enforcement Training Center (FLETC) that 400 files are altered in the start-up process of a Windows™ 9x machine and 500 files are altered in the start-up process of a Windows NT™ machine.

Several hardware write blockers are available to investigators. Once installed, the device absolutely prevents a write operation to the original evidence hard drive. In the Windows™ operating environment, the hardware write blocker is the only way to

be sure to prevent write operations. Unfortunately, if the seized hard drive requires specialized hardware device drivers, the hard drive may not work with a write blocker. Write block devices range in price from $70 to over $1,000.

Other operating systems, notably Unix™ or Linux™, allow hard disks to "mount" (i.e., be recognized by the computer) as "read only." This too absolutely prevents writing to the evidence drive. However, familiar Windows forensics packages may not be available for Unix™ systems.

Source: KRUSE, W.G., and HEISER, J.G. (2002). *Computer Forensics: Incident Response Essentials.* San Francisco, CA: Addison-Wesley.

BOX 12.2

The MD5 Hash

An algorithm is a process or procedure used to produce a specific result. A hashing algorithm takes a large body of digital information and produces a mathematical value, or "hash," that uniquely identifies the data, like a fingerprint identifies a person. A hash is quite small compared to the amount of data it represents. The most commonly used hashing algorithm is the MD5 hash created by Ron Rivest of RSA Inc. The odds of having two data sets, at random, that produce the same MD5 hash are calculated to be 10^{38} or a 10 followed by 37 more zeros. That is more time than the complete age of the universe, start to finish in seconds. An alternative algorithm called Secure Hash Algorithm (SHA) was developed by the National Institute of Standards and Technology. It provides greater security, but is slower.

fingerprint taken at each step of the analysis process, we can verify that the digital file being examined is a true and authentic copy of the original evidence.

The forensic analyst should calculate an MD5 hash of the evidence drive. The real work is accomplished by the software. All the analyst has to do is issue the command and identify the file to be hashed. The analyst can then compare this hash to a hash of any subsequent copies. If the hash matches, the copies are authenticated to the value of a single bit within a known (infinitesimal) probability of error. This authentication procedure should be performed and noted whenever an image is copied or loaded onto an analysis machine. As always, the analyst should document the results of the procedure. Documentation can be as simple as cutting and pasting the hash value into a computer log and noting that it is the same. This provides a basis of comparison that the evidence cited in the analysis has not been altered by error or intentional act.

Imaging of the Evidence Drive

With any seized system, it is important to create a working copy for forensic analysis. The best method is to create a bit stream copy (also called a mirror or image). A bit stream copy reproduces every bit of information found on the evidence drive. This method reproduces both active files and latent data. Active files are those files available to the user or created by the user. Word-processing documents, spreadsheets, text files, graphics, etc. are all considered active files. Unless the crime being investigated is fairly technical (e.g., hacking-related crimes), the bulk of evidence obtained will be from the active files. No special tools are required to access these files. A simple search for known keywords or fragments of file names (e.g., *.jpg, where * can be equal to any text) can provide positive results. Latent files are files that are not recognized by the operating system; thus, they do not show up on a list of files. The most common source of latent files is deletion. When most computers delete files, they do not actually erase the bits in the file; they simply allow new files to be saved to that space when it is needed. Until then, the file is left virtually intact. Recovery of deleted files will be discussed later in this chapter. Another type of latent data, accessible without extraordinary effort, is found in protected system files. These can be accessed by booting the computer from a floppy disk or boot CD. Most commonly, this includes that swap file or paging file used by Windows™ to simulate additional physical memory.

Logical copies, created with the copy command included with the operating system, do not reproduce latent data. Images can be created by readily available software with a hardware write blocker in place. Best current practices require the use of a write blocker because it simplifies courtroom presentation of the evidence. However, it is equally acceptable to boot from a CD or floppy and use an imaging program to produce a bit stream copy. Bootable floppies and CDs create a random-access memory (RAM) drive (storage to active memory, not the hard drive) and can be used to load larger programs that do not fit on a single floppy disk; thus, they do not alter

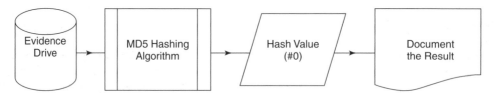

FIGURE 12.3 Step 1 is to verify mathematically the contents of the evidence drive. This value will prove that any future copies match the original exactly.

data on the hard drive. If possible, the image produced should be written to true, write-once media (e.g., DVD-R or CD-R), so that the copy cannot be altered; however, the size of modern hard drives makes even DVDs cumbersome to use.[6]

An image can be authenticated with an MD5 hash comparison and contains potential evidence that may be hidden from the operating system. The hash value of the archival image (#1) matches the hash of the evidence drive (#1). As always, document the results of the procedure. Documentation can be as simple as cutting and pasting the hash value into a computer log and noting that it is the same. This provides a verifiable record that the evidence has not been altered by error or intentional act.

The rule of best evidence requires that the original evidence, not a copy, be brought to court. However, the Federal Rule of Evidence 1001(3) allows unaltered digital evidence to be presented as a copy; thus the image of a disk is considered to be "best evidence." A comparison of MD5 hashes can verify that the data are unaltered. The data may even be mathematically compressed and retain their integrity. Compression simply reduces the size of a file for storage or transportation. There are many techniques used to compress data; one variety, called lossless compression, is not considered alteration. Lossless compression will produce the exact binary data as were compressed and can be mathematically and empirically verified to do so. The key is that the uncompressed version produces a hash value equal to the original.

Wiping the Analysis Drive

The analyst must ensure that the target area is free from contaminates of previous analyses. For example, analysis on a child pornography case may lead to loading pornographic images from the

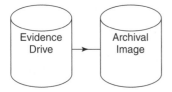

Step 2 is to create an exact "image," or bit-stream copy, of the evidence drive.

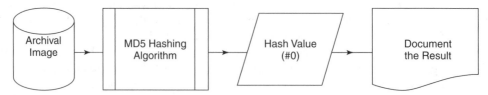

FIGURE 12.4 Step 3 is to verify that the image of the evidence drive is a true copy of the evidence drive. Note that the hash value produced (#1) is the same as the hash from the evidence drive.

image of a suspect's drive. If this material is not thoroughly wiped, it may be detected in a later analysis of another suspect's drive in a fraud case. To avoid having to explain this in court, it is best to establish a procedure that wipes both data and the space between data called slack space. By wiping the analysis drive before restoring the image, the analyst will be able to refute any claim that the drive was contaminated. Most common implementations of a wiping program meet the standards of Department of Defense Directive 5220.22—the DoD wipe (see Box 12.3).

After performing a suitable wipe, the results can be verified by hashing the blank drive and comparing the resulting hash value to the value of the blank drive. As always, document the results of the procedure. Documentation can be as simple as cutting and pasting the hash value into a computer log and noting that it is the same. This provides a verifiable record that the bench drive is not contaminated with evidence from a previous case.

Restoring

While small-scale, 4.7 GB or less, analysis can be performed from a DVD or other write-once medium, larger volumes of data can only be practically handled from a hard drive. Consider even a relatively

---

BOX 12.3

The DoD Wipe

The U.S. Department of Defense issued Directive 5220.22-M as part of its National Industrial Security Program. The directive sets security standards for Department of Defense contractors. The process, popularly known as a DoD wipe, is actually the standard used to "sanitize" a hard drive that contained data less than top secret. Although it is not absolutely necessary to use a DoD wipe, it has become a de facto standard; that is, the use of another technique would require explanation.

The use of the DoD wipe recognizes the potential of latent data to exist even after a drive is deleted or even formatted. Once the DoD wipe is performed, the hard drive cannot recognize latent data. Without extraordinary measures, the use of a DoD wipe places evidence beyond the reach of current law enforcement techniques, but recent advances with magnetic force microscopes and electron tunneling microscopes may change this some day.

Step 4 is to wipe the bench drive to be used when analyzing the archival image.

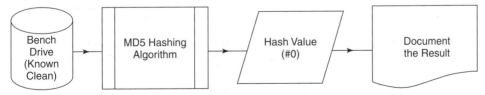

FIGURE 12.5   Step 5 is to create a hash of the clean bench drive and compare the value to the value of the drive when it was last known to be blank. Note that the hash value produced (#0) is the same as the hash from the blank bench drive.

small evidence drive at 20 GB. If completely full, it would take five DVDs to hold the contents. Each step of an analysis protocol (see the next section) must be performed five times, with the operator switching disks as needed. In addition to raw size, an internal hard drive has a much faster data transfer rate than any of the current removable media. Consider that to search a hard drive for one keyword, the entire contents of that hard drive must be read and brought into the computer's memory. Even a marginal speed advantage makes the restoration procedure necessary.

To perform forensic analysis of the data, they must be loaded onto a clean target drive or folder. When the image is loaded, it should be authenticated to verify that it is a true copy of the original.

Documentation can be as simple as cutting and pasting the hash value into a computer log and noting that it is the same. This provides a verifiable record that the evidence has not been altered by error or intentional act.

BOX 12.4

Size in Computers

Term	Value	Value in bytes	Volume in pages
Bit	1	1/8 byte	Less than 1 page
Byte	8 bits	1 byte	Less than 1 page
Kilobyte (KB)	1024 bytes	(2^{10}) bytes	About $\frac{1}{2}$ page
Megabyte (MB)	1024 KB	(2^{20}) bytes	About 500 pages
Gigabyte (GB)	1024 MB	(2^{30}) bytes	160-foot stack of paper

Understanding the scale of data handled in digital forensics is difficult. In one of the defining cases in data storage, Kevin Mitnick, accused of criminal hacking, possessed 9 GB of data when arrested. Prosecutors and the court refused to allow Mitnick access to a computer to view the evidence against him because of fears that he could cause damage or seek revenge.[7] Astronomical figures about the amount of paper needed to print that amount of potential evidence were used to justify not releasing it to Mitnick. To print all of the evidence would have required a stack of paper 1,440 feet tall.

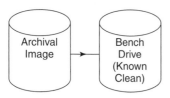

Step 6 is to restore the archival copy (from Step 3) of the evidence drive to a blank bench drive (from Step 5).

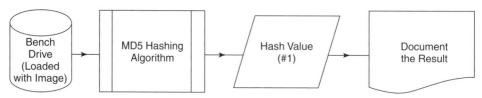

FIGURE 12.6   Step 7 is to authenticate the restored image by calculating an MD5 hash and comparing that hash value to the hash of the evidence drive. Note that the hash value produced (#1) is the same as the hash from the evidence drive (#1).

The Complete Process

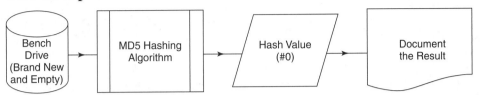

Step 1 is to verify mathematically the contents of the evidence drive. This value will prove that any future copies match the original exactly.

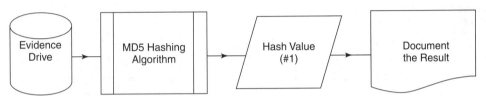

Step 2 is to create an exact "image," or bit-stream copy, of the evidence drive.

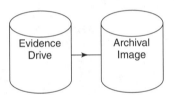

Step 3 is to verify that the image of the evidence drive is a true copy of the evidence drive. Note that the hash value produced (#1) is the same as the hash from the evidence drive.

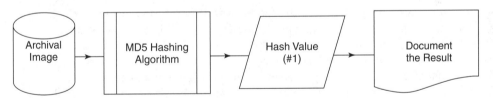

Step 4 is to wipe the bench drive to be used when analyzing the archival image.

Step 5 is to create a hash of the clean bench drive and compare the value to the value of the drive when it was last known to be blank. Note that the hash value produced (#0) is the same as the hash from the blank bench drive.

FIGURE 12.7 Summary.
(Before the first step of a new analysis) it is necessary to obtain a comparison value for the blank hard drive to be used in the analysis.

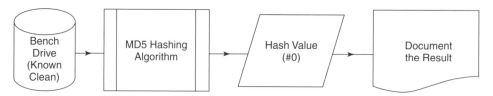

Step 6 is to restore the archival copy (from Step 3) of the evidence drive to a blank bench drive (from Step 5).

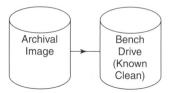

Step 7 is to authenticate the restored image by calculating an MD5 hash and comparing that hash value to the hash of the evidence drive. Note that the hash value produced (#1) is the same as the hash from the evidence drive (#1).

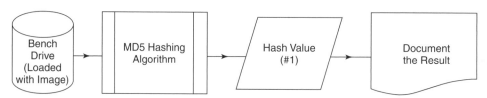

FIGURE 12.7 (*Continued*)

FORENSIC ANALYSIS

Computer forensics books often describe the identification of evidence in meticulous and exacting terms. In any given investigation, the variety of possible analyses is as broad as the evidence sought. Essentially, the analyst attempts to find information that is in itself incriminating (e.g., child pornography) or evidence that helps establish the elements of a crime (e.g., paper trail for a fraud case). When planning an analysis, the investigator and forensic analyst may wish to look for everything that might be incriminating. However, the fact is that overanalysis is as dangerous as underanalysis. Imagine an officer having to search every house and building in a neighborhood where a burglar has been reported. Ignoring the legal implications, it is too much work for an uncertain return. The officer might discover new crimes, but could become so busy with minutia that he or she would never complete the original investigation. The search warrant and original purpose of the investigating officer determine what type of evidence may be sought. This is not only a sensible strategy to limit a search, but exceeding the warrant may result in the evidence being ruled inadmissible in court. Further, a well-planned analysis can even be used to justify a plain-sight exception to the requirements of the warrant or the inadvertent discovery of a new crime. The plan can be used to demonstrate how the plain-sight viewing occurred.

The National Institute of Justice recently published the second edition of *Electronic Crime Scene Investigation: A Guide for First Responders.* The document is intended to assist state and local law enforcement and other first responders who may be responsible for preserving an electronic crime scene and for recognizing, collecting, and safeguarding digital evidence. Chapter 7, covers "Electronic Crime and Digital Evidence Considerations by Crime Category," provides likely

BOX 12.5

Common Evidence of Selected Crime Types

Child Abuse or Exploitation

- Video and still photo cameras and media
- Digital camera software
- Internet activity records
- Notes or records of chat sessions
- Web cameras or microphones

Computer Intrusion

- Network devices, routers, switches
- Handheld mobile devices
- Web camera(s)
- Lists or records of computer intrusion software
- Notes or records of Internet activity

Domestic Violence

- Mobile communication devices
- External data storage devices
- User names and accounts
- PDAs or address books
- Printed email, notes, and letters
- Caller ID units

Gambling

- Electronic money transfers
- Online banking software

- Sports betting statistics
- Customer information or credit card data
- References to online gambling sites

Theft

- Financial asset records
- Laminators
- Copies of signatures
- Check cashing cards
- Online banking software

Narcotics

- Handheld mobile devices
- PDAs, address books, and contact information
- GPS devices
- Blank prescription forms
- Forged identification
- Drug receipts

Source: National Institute of Justice (2008). *Electronic Crime Scene Investigation: A Guide for First Responders,* 2nd ed. Washington, DC: Office of Justice Programs.

sources of digital evidence for several different types of crime and the most productive avenues for forensic examination to investigators. Box 12.5 uses information in the guide to list the best sources of digital evidence for crimes that range from child abuse and exploitation to domestic violence.

Once an image is secured, it can be loaded onto a new hard drive and placed in the seized machine (while storing the original hard drive in a safe place). A basic examination can quickly be accomplished using the tools of the operating system. If there is reason to suspect a highly sophisticated user, this technique may be insufficient, but the vast majority of digital evidence will not come from a master hacker. It is possible that there will be no competent effort to hide evidence on the computer—not even so much as deleting it. A quick result in this case is infinitely preferable to an extensive analysis six months in the future. Further, directory structure and file-naming conventions can be used to associate a user with a particular piece of evidence discovered. A search of the active files through the operating system itself also produces the maximum chance of inadvertently discovering evidence of a new crime in plain view.

If simple techniques do not yield results, more extensive analysis techniques are available to the analyst. Regardless of the meaning of the information sought, all digital information is simply a pattern of bits. Discovering evidence becomes a process of matching a known pattern of bits, whether they form the first portion of a child pornography specimen (a picture previously known to law enforcement) or the name and Social Security number of an identity theft victim. By identifying the presence of the unique pattern of bits that corresponds to that decoded data, we can match the evidence drive with the illicit information.

THE FORENSIC ANALYST AS EXPERT WITNESS

After the completion of the analysis, the forensic analyst generates a report describing what evidence was identified, what elements of the crime it proposes to establish, how the evidence was identified, and finally, how and why any summaries of evidence were created. Depending on how the analyst was brought into the case, either the prosecutor or the investigator receives the report and decides to proceed with the case or not. Assuming that the analysis provides suitable evidence to proceed, the court process often takes a substantial amount of time, and the analyst proceeds with new work. Depending on the credibility of the report or the convincing nature of testimony in a deposition, the analyst's simple presence may be used to assist in plea bargaining negotiations. This does not invalidate all the work and preparation put into preparing the analysis for trial; quite the contrary, it means the evidence is so compelling that the defense does not want to risk a trial. If the case comes to trial and the analyst is called, he or she will have two duties. First, the analyst must testify to his or her direct experience. That is, the analyst may testify about everything from receiving the initial evidence to the final report. Given the time lag between analysis and testimony, this is where a routine set of well-documented procedures is most helpful. Second, the analysis may play the role of a technical expert, qualified to give summaries and opinions as to the meaning of evidence. The expert witness presents simplified explanations and abbreviations to the fact finder (judge or jury, depending on the trial). In essence, expert testimony allows the fact finder to make an informed decision without having to become an expert. In both roles, the forensic analyst should avoid partisan testimony. Independence and professional stature of the expert witness lend credibility that appearing to take sides would invalidate. It is typical for "opposing" expert witnesses to cooperate to determine facts and come to a satisfactory understanding of events and evidence.

To ensure the examiner's ability to demonstrate the link between the seized drive, hereafter the evidence drive, and the final analysis, the evidence drive itself must be maintained in the exact state it was in when it was seized. The best current practice in storage forensics usually involves creating an exact copy, hereafter image, of the seized drive. All analyses are performed on an image to avoid altering the original. The extra step of creating a copy for analysis is necessary because forensic analysis often changes the underlying data structures if performed on an active drive. While conducting the analysis, the forensic examiner must stay within the boundaries set by the original search warrant or consent of the evidence drive's owner/competent custodian.

COMPUTER STORAGE SYSTEMS

It surprises many people that we cannot simply identify where information is physically found on the evidence drive. Many forensic experts fall into the trap of explaining data structure with real-world analogies and are forced into explanations of the physical structures of computers. In recent years, the field of storage forensics has been complicated by the introduction of new hard drive technologies and rapidly growing storage capacities. These developments can be understood in the context of the two imperatives of hard drive manufacturers: storage density and speed (see Box 12.6).

BOX 12.6
Speed and Density

Storage density allows manufacturers to increase the storage capacity of hard drives. By packing more bits closer together, storage capacity has increased without the form factor (physical size) of the device increasing. Some of the physical differences in hard drives can be explained by the increasing density of information. For example, multiple platters allow more storage space. A denser magnetic medium means that individual bits can be written in smaller physical space and still resolved by new, more sensitive read heads. More precision means less space must be wasted between tracks of data arranged in concentric rings on the disk. Speed is a constant goal of storage manufacturers. The storage system of most computers is its slowest link. By increasing the speed of the hard drive, significant speed increases can be obtained for common tasks. The fastest part of the computer can only operate as quickly as the data and instructions can arrive. Computer architecture is designed to keep the most frequently used and most vital information in the fastest storage possible.

Volatile Storage Systems

The structures of computer storage can be divided into two parts: volatile and nonvolatile storage. The primary difference between these types of storage is that volatile storage is lost when the computer loses power. Thus, the decision to unplug a computer may lose the volatile or active memory. Volatile memory is difficult to access without special software and impossible to access without altering it. Such alteration can be explained in court, but does not come without risks.

PROCESSOR   Although not actually a storage system, the processor is the benchmark for speed and the organizing factor in nonvolatile storage. There has been a great deal of attention given to processor speeds ever since the first PCs. Today, the processor is by far the fastest part of the computer, completing operations over four billion times per second. To feed this incredibly rapid cycling of information, the storage system must bring large quantities of information at a relatively slower pace. Typical systems operate at 60 percent of possible throughput. Most systems spend substantial amounts of idle time; however, bursts of activity can use the full capacity of the processor's speed. Forensically, the processor is of little interest. Information in the processor is altered billions of times per second. Further, any information in the processor is completely inaccessible to human beings.

CACHE   All cache systems are volatile, which means that when power is removed, information held in RAM disappears. The Level 1 cache operates at speeds approximating the processor. Level 1 (L1) cache is built into the processor to reduce delays in getting information to the processor. Level 2 (L2) cache is often built onto the processor's daughterboard along with the control chip set that feeds information and instructions in and carries out operations based on the results. L2 cache is slower than L1, but holds more information. L2 cache serves as a buffer between L1 and the system's main memory (RAM). Forensically, the cache holds little interest, as it is inaccessible to the user.

MAIN MEMORY (RAM)   RAM[8] is the large reserve of information that supplies the processor through the cache systems. The bulk of the system's active data is held in RAM. Anything the user is doing, any open programs or files, will be in the RAM contents. Like cache, RAM is volatile storage. When the control systems predict the processor will need more data or must switch to a different task, the data are moved into the cache from RAM. When new processes are loaded or new data are requested by the user, the RAM draws information from the nonvolatile storage systems.

Forensically, RAM may be of some use. If software is already installed, RAM can be viewed by the user. All Unix™ systems provide a method to save RAM to a file with a process called a core dump. Windows™ systems require the use of special software called a hex editor to allow users to read RAM. Installing such software would undoubtedly alter the contents of the RAM and possibly purge them as well. If the computer uses virtual memory, a system that allows expansive, but slow, hard drive storage to substitute for RAM (see below), portions of the RAM contents may be saved on the hard disk in a file called a swap file or paging file. The swap file is normally inaccessible when the computer is running, making its contents latent data. Functionally, the swap file can be considered to be part of the RAM subsystem. In spite of the difficulties in accessing RAM, it can prove to be a treasure trove of useful data. Passwords, recently accessed files, and network settings may all be found in the contents of RAM.

Nonvolatile Storage Systems

Unlike previous components, the purpose of storage is not simply to convey data to the processor. Storage also maintains information when it is not needed or even when the power is removed from the system. Thus, storage systems are not volatile. Storage systems compromise between storing masses of information efficiently and allowing quick retrieval.

HARD DISK DRIVES   The hard disk is the primary storage device of most computers along with removable, peripheral systems such as DVD or CD-ROMs, floppy drives, and similar devices. Storage systems are far slower than RAM, cache, or the processor. Unlike the other systems, the hard drive relies on physical motion (usually a spinning disk and even slower read/write heads). All the other systems are solid state—no moving parts. All of their operations are electrical. Because hard disks must physically spin and physically seek locations to read and write, they will always be the slowest link in the information chain.

A few years ago, the lack of main computer memory (RAM) forced computers to crawl relative to today's computers. The biggest reason for this was that the lack of RAM forced computers to use the hard drive to trick the system into believing it had more memory through a system called virtual memory. More memory (even the slower, virtual memory) meant that larger files could be manipulated, more programs loaded, and more features could be built into programs. The tradeoff was overall system speed.

Hard drive manufacturers have found many ways to improve the initial performance of their products. Data structures optimize "seek times," thereby reducing the delay between the call for data and the hard drive's ability to retrieve the data. Multiple platters (disks) allow more than one read/write head to work at once. Faster spin speeds allow more data surface to pass under the read/write heads. The structures of the hard disk are the product of evolutionary search for speed and storage density. The rapid change in hard drive technology and competition between hard drive manufacturers make it exceedingly difficult accurately to describe the function of a given hard drive in all but the broadest terms. Forensic analysts should avoid using the physical and low-level structures of a hard drive to describe how data were obtained.

REMOVABLE STORAGE MEDIA   There are two broad classes of removable storage media: direct access and sequential access. Disk drives allow direct access storage. That is, they do not have stored information in sequential order like a magnetic tape or other sequential access device.

In direct access storage devices, the time required to access data is reduced, making retrieval faster. Tapes provide sequential access storage. Sequential access storage requires longer to fast-forward through unneeded data to find the data requested. This is analogous to selecting a scene with a DVD player versus fast-forwarding a VHS tape. Direct access devices need an index to locate information that may be scattered across the disk. The index holds a list of locations and the files currently residing in those locations. If portions of large files are scattered in many locations (fragmented), it takes longer to retrieve them, but still much faster than a sequential device. Sequential storage devices provide an attractive option for archival storage because of their low cost. Further, because tape drives are an older technology, they enjoy greater support in the proprietary systems of the non-Windows™ world.

Many different types of storage media are used today. An analyst must be able to identify correctly the equipment needed to acquire evidence from a seized storage device. Before any type of forensic operation can be completed, the analyst must be able to read the storage device. Fortunately, most modern drives have cross-compatibility (allowing them to read data written with other standards) and backward compatibility (allowing them to use older standards). Sometimes an analyst will be confronted with a storage device that is not standard. Fortunately, the device to read that storage device is often seized with the storage device. On occasions when it is not, the analyst might have to acquire a compatible device. An up-to-date knowledge of common storage devices and storage device readers will greatly benefit the analyst. One of the best ways to stay current with storage devices is simply to visit the local computer superstore.

Although there appears to be a bewildering array of storage media available, including flash drives, iPods, CDs, DVDs, and external drives, each contains essentially the same kind of information as contained by a hard drive. Procedures for examining this evidence are essentially the same, except for the acquisition.

FILE SYSTEMS

A file system is part of the computer's operating system. When a disk is formatted, it is imprinted with the structures used to control files. Several different systems have been developed to meet the growing needs of users for larger drives, greater efficiency, more speed, and security. This discussion focuses on the Windows™ family and its file systems. Although there are many arguments as to the superiority of operating systems, it is an indisputable fact that the Windows™ family of operating systems is by far the most common operating environment. It is almost certain that the majority of investigations will occur in the Windows™ environment.

The Windows™ family of operating systems can be divided into two groups. The Windows 9x series includes Windows 95 through Windows 98 and the follow-up Windows ME. All of these systems were designed to be consumer systems and do not seriously attempt to implement security. For example, the log-on password can easily be circumvented by hitting a conveniently close and clearly labeled "cancel" button. The other group is the Windows NT™ series, which includes Windows 2000™, Windows XP™, and Windows Vista™. Although Microsoft was not always successful, the Windows NT™ series attempted to improve security. Later versions contain some meaningful protection, such as Vista's™ User Account Control, which requires that the computer user authorize system procedures and processes. Of greatest forensic interest is the file system used. File allocation table (FAT) file systems provide the least security. The new technology file system (NTFS) has progressed and may prove difficult to examine in its latest incarnation.

The easiest way to identify the version of Windows™ on a booted machine is to examine the system properties or by entering the "ver" command at the command prompt.

Windows 9x	File System	Windows New Technology (NT)	File System
Windows 95	FAT 16	Windows NT 3.5	NTFS 3.5
Windows 95 OSR2	FAT 16/FAT 32	Windows NT 4.0	NTFS 4.0
Windows 98	FAT 16/FAT 32	Windows 2000	NTFS 5.0
Windows 98 Second Edition (Win SE)	FAT 16/FAT 32	Windows XP	NTFS 5.0
Windows Millennium (Win ME)	FAT 16/FAT 32	Windows Vista	NTFS 6.0

FIGURE 12.8 The Windows™ family of operating systems and associated file systems.

FAT: File Allocation Table

One of the characteristics of the FAT systems most useful to forensic analysts is that deleted files aren't wiped from the drive. Most people know that somehow deleted files can be recovered. The reason that works is the need for speed. To save time on unneeded operations, when a file is deleted, the file is not altered, except for a marker at the beginning. The only real change is that the FAT marks the clusters[9] used by the file as open or "unallocated." If no new data are stored to those clusters, the data can sit there intact for years. Even if new data are saved, they may not completely fill the unallocated space. This leaves fragments of the previous file in places that cannot normally be accessed. In the diagram below, full clusters of stored data are shown in gray. The dark gray portion at the end of one of the clusters represents space not used by the new file occupying this cluster. The dark gray cluster following it represents a currently unused cluster that may contain latent data from a previously deleted file. Both types of latent data are found in "slack space," disk storage space unused by active data, potentially containing latent data.

For forensic analysts, one problem with FAT32 systems is that MS-DOS cannot access FAT32. Newer versions of DOS have been modified to use FAT32. The DOS that underlies Windows 98 works well with the newer features of FAT32.

NTFS: New Technology File System

Windows NT™, 2000™, XP™, and Vista™ systems use NTFS. NTFS has numerous advantages over the FAT system, especially in terms of security. To the forensic analyst, the only difference is that DOS-based tools do not work. Some utilities have been created that allow DOS to read NTFS; for example, NTFS-DOS is freeware that allows DOS operations on an NTFS volume. Although NTFS implements a different method for dealing with files, it still has slack space and unallocated clusters that may contain old data. One of the primary advantages to users of NTFS is that it uses storage space more efficiently. This produces less wasted space between files. This wasted space has long been a treasure trove of supposedly deleted material for forensic analysis. Two other features of NTFS pose specific problems to forensic analysts.

DYNAMIC DISKS Dynamic disks manage disk space without partitions and offer numerous advantages to administrators, but are not compatible with previous versions of NTFS or other operating systems (including DOS). These volumes can be imaged, but can only be read with a Windows 2000™ or other compatible boot disk.

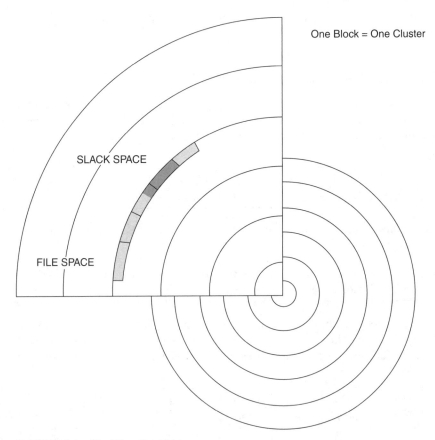

One Block = One Cluster

SLACK SPACE

FILE SPACE

FIGURE 12.9 File Allocation Table.

ENCRYPTING FILE SYSTEM (EFS)   The EFS presents a challenge to forensic analysis. If the machine is discovered in an operable condition (no screen saver and powered on), an investigator can use the Microsoft Management Console to create a key recovery certificate. It would also be possible to turn EFS off for each folder. Assuming that does not happen, there are other options. A centrally managed network using EFS will usually make the domain administrator the key recovery agent. Thus, a key may be available from the domain administrator. The initial seizure at the crime scene may include a floppy disk with the recovery key. Experienced users of encryption know how important it can be to keep an extra key around. Losing the only copy of an encryption key can make stored data useless.

A stand-alone machine makes the administrator the default key recovery agent. Achieving administrator access by resetting the administrator password or cracking the administrator password would make EFS completely transparent. No passwords are needed; simply being the administrator opens all the protections. Removing the Windows password file (SAM) resets the administrator   password. EFS cannot protect system files like the SAM. When restarting, the administrator password will be blank, but the administrator can still access the key to EFT. It is also important to note that the Enterprise and Ultimate editions of Vista System utilize a technology called bitlocker drive encryption, which can protect the entire operating system volume. This is a unique addition that provides a layer of protection not seen in previous version of Windows software, though it is a new component and may not be common in the larger population of home computer users.

APPLICATION: DEFRAGMENTING A DISK

When a disk is formatted for the first time, all of its clusters are open; there is no slack space. Reformatted disks can contain latent data, but it is not technically in slack space. When new data and programs are saved to the disk, they occupy clusters. Each cluster is represented by a number in the file allocation table.

0034	0035	0036	0037	0038	0039	0040	0041	0042	0043
used	used	used	used	used	used	used	used	used	used

When those files are move284d or deleted, the FAT de-allocates the clusters and makes them available for new files.

0034	0035	0036	0037	0038	0039	0040	0041	0042	0043
used	open	open	open	used	used	used	open	used	used

Over time, clusters are allocated and de-allocated. Files fit wherever there is space, or they are saved in several spaces. The file system tracks these fragmented pieces of file so the user has access to what appears to be a complete file. In this case, a new file needs three clusters to fit. It is placed in clusters 35–37.

0034	0035	0036	0037	0038	0039	0040	0041	0042	0043
used	new	new	new	used	used	used	open	used	used

When a file increases in size but there is no adjacent open cluster, the new cluster is saved in the nearest available cluster. In this case, the new file needs another cluster for newly saved material. It now occupies clusters 35–37 and 41.

0043	0035	0036	0037	0038	0039	0040	0041	0042	0043
used	new	new	new	used	used	used	open	used	used

This process goes on over time and slowly reduces the efficiency of the hard drive. To acquire all of the pieces of a file, the read/write heads must travel to several parts of the disk. Eventually, the delay becomes noticeable to the user and he or she defragments the drive. Using a utility program, the user frees up a large area of disk space and then saves fragmented files as continuous files. The process repeats until the disk is defragmented; however, as soon as new information is added to a file, the fragmentation process begins again. Some utilities track frequently changed files and give them a little buffer space during the defragmentation process.

EVIDENCE RECOVERY FROM SLACK SPACE

As noted above, the efficient operation of the computer's file system leaves both active data and latent data. Active data are available through the file system itself or through the methods described below. Latent data are not available through the file system; however, common tools can give analysts access to the data. The box item, examining the bits, describes one such tool called a hex editor. The hex editor can be used to examine intact files (active data) or deleted and obscured data (latent data) from the hard disk without interference from the file system. Thus, incriminating bit patterns (e.g., a victim's credit card number or a specimen from a child pornography image) can be discovered.

In this hypothetical example, an analyst has to prove that a suspect accessed data critical to a company and downloaded them using a security hole in the company's Web server. Investigators found a supposedly anonymous user in a chat room claiming to have secrets from the victim company. This led to the suspect and the seizure of his computer. A quick review of likely places on the image of the seized disk found nothing. Apparently the suspect had deleted the information or might have had it elsewhere. The analyst suspects that there may be evidence in the slack space that the suspect forgot to clear.

The analyst wipes the hard drive of a lab bench machine (called an analysis drive) and verifies it with an MD5. The hash of the analysis drive matches the hash taken when it was brand new and empty. He notes that fact in a bench journal on a separate computer.

The analyst applies the image to the analysis drive and verifies it with another MD5. The hash of the analysis drive now matches the hash taken from the suspect's drive and the hash of the image (because they are the same). He notes that fact in a bench journal on a separate computer.

From a bootable CD, he opens a freeware utility called *Strings*, which searches for text words embedded in a program. He looks for the company's name anywhere on the disk. He finds one hit in cluster 0040. The company includes its name in executable programs at the end. He notes that fact in a bench journal on a separate computer.

From a bootable CD, he opens a hex editor (see Box 12.7). Using the hex editor, he searches for unique patterns of bits found at the beginning of the program believed stolen. He finds a match in cluster 0034. He notes that fact in a bench journal on a separate computer.

The analyst must now recover as much of the program as possible to provide statistical certainty of the match. Some of the clusters have been overwritten. He creates the chart below to show exactly where the evidence came from. Each box is one cluster. Each cluster is labeled with

BOX 12.7
Examining the Bits

The interoperation of computers across networks and different operating systems has required the use of standard file systems. Typically, there are indicators at the beginning of a file (called a header) that inform the software of the file's characteristics. To read this information we need two things: (1) software capable of accessing the raw data and (2) a codex to allow us to interpret the raw data. The illustration below (labeled wtc-photo.jpg) depicts the initial bit-by-bit values of a picture of the World Trade Center. The hex editor allows an analyst to view every detail of the file.

Hex editors report binary information in "hexadecimal couplets" (on the left in the illustration).

Binary data, commonly understood as ones and zeroes (i.e., bits), is difficult for humans to interpret. Hexadecimal couplets are used to represent groups of eight bits—often called bytes. Two hexadecimal characters {0, 1, 2, 3, 4, 5, 6, 7, 8, 9, A, B, C, D, E, or F} can replace eight binary characters {0, or 1}. Once trained to do so, analysts find it much easier to make sense of this mind-numbing collection of 1–9 and A–F than an eight-times larger collection of ones and zeroes. Fortunately, most hex editors also attempt to translate the bits into text (on the right in the illustration). The photograph of the World Trade Center was produced with Adobe Photoshop 3.0™.

a number in the FAT. The original file was 112 kilobytes (112 KB). Unallocated clusters are marked in white; allocated clusters are markead in gray.

0034	0035	0036	0037	0038	0039	0040	0041	0042	0043

Cluster size = 16 KB

Cluster ID	Status	Used by file	Size of new file	Original file	Recoverable
0034	Empty		0 KB	16 KB	16 KB
0035	Used	M024MNFB.HTM	4 KB	16 KB	12 KB
0036	Used	M02505DE.CSS	2 KB	16 KB	14 KB
0037	Used	M1NSVN76.HTM	16 KB	16 KB	0
0038	Used	M1NSVN76.HTM	6 KB	16 KB	10 KB
0039	Empty		0 KB	16 KB	16 KB
0040	Empty		0 KB	16 KB	16 KB
					84 KB

By subtracting the amount of the new file overwriting each cluster of the original, the analyst calculates that about 84,000 bytes survived and can be matched to the missing file. The odds that that combination of bits occurred by chance alone are one to a number greater than the age of the universe in seconds; the analyst has a match. The analysts can now prove that the missing proprietary file was on the suspect's computer—even though the suspect tried to delete it. The presence of the fruits of a crime and motive (e.g., a disgruntled former employee) constitute the elements of a crime. Because his or her methods followed the best practices of the field, he or she will be able to present this summary of the evidence to the court in a convincing manner.

COMMERCIAL FORENSIC PACKAGES

The challenge of computer forensic examination lies in identifying, training, and equipping examiners to successfully complete their jobs. As a consequence, investigator fatigue and burnout can be a significant problem. Recent research with a sample of active forensic examiners found that more than half of the individuals contacted felt that they did not have the workforce to complete their tasks at work.[10] Furthermore, the examiners felt that their work would be challenged by others and that there are other ways to accomplish their jobs. One way to help to reduce these complaints and ease investigator stress is through the use of commercial forensic packages.

Modern forensic packages offer numerous advantages to the investigator, but also present pitfalls to investigators unsure of the fundamentals. To use these tools to their maximum benefit, the investigator must understand the way information is stored. Perhaps more important, to convincingly testify as to the proper use of these tools, the forensic examiner cannot be a passive observer of the analysis; he or she must plan and adapt the analysis based on an understanding of the technology and the specific legal requirements of the case at hand. A good forensics package must cover each of the basic forensic functions described in this chapter: importing data, hashing, wiping, imaging, and search capabilities.

Extended Analysis and Searching

All digital data are stored as a pattern of bits that tells the computer how to decode the patterns into pictures or text or other meaningful symbols. Computers cannot interpret symbols the way humans do. They can, however, match patterns of bits in storage to a sample provided by the analyst. In some cases, different encoding techniques are used. This means that the bit pattern used to represent the same symbol to the human user could be vastly different on different systems. For example, Unicode is used by Window NT/2000/XP™, and the IBM extended character set is used by DOS. This is another reason these two systems are incompatible. A forensic package must be versatile enough to recognize these common encoding schemes as well as the commonly used proprietary data storage formats. For example, Microsoft Outlook™ uses a proprietary database (called a DBX file) to store all of its e-mail. Without a third-party utility program, an analyst would have to install Microsoft Outlook™ to simply read seized e-mail. However, modern forensic packages have plug-ins that can decode proprietary file formats. Although freeware utilities are available to read Outlook DBX files, exporting data to separate utilities can be cumbersome and is prone to creating errors. Further, broad search protocols do not work unless the search software is aware of various encoding schemes.

Speed is a primary concern in searches run by forensic packages. When huge volumes of data must be searched, simple, one-at-a-time pattern matching would take too long. Forensic packages have routines that search for all the desired patterns at once. If a suspect's drive has 80 GB of data, that full amount of data must be run from the hard drive and into the processor for comparison. As previously noted, the hard drive is the slowest part of the storage system. Instead of bringing all of the information through the hard drive several times, forensic packages bring it through once and search for all of the terms indicated by the analyst programming the search.

The ability of a search to achieve results is called the power of the search. Beyond the recognition of encoding schemes, searches should be able to distinguish near misses caused by minor user errors. Simple search routines are very literal; if the searched data do not contain the exact phrase or combination of characters, the search will return negative results. Most people are familiar with the need for proper capitalization and spelling in some search programs. More powerful search engines can search from context, or with allowances for small errors. Powerful searches also allow the user to search for multiple terms, or small variations of those terms, at once. Modern forensic packages offer powerful and flexible search programs.

User Interface

Fatigue is a primary concern of forensic analysts. Huge backlogs of seized evidence are the rule, rather than an exception. Requiring an analyst to fight through uncomfortable menus to achieve simple tasks results in wasted time and repetitive, unproductive use of an analyst's time. Many forensic packages have pseudo-programmable features that allow an analyst to set up an analysis with a list of commands rather than requiring direct input at each step. Other interface features include common search term dictionaries. Thus, a standard search of threatening terms can provide the basic foundation for an analysis of a stalking case. These basic dictionaries can be enhanced with terms specific to the case from another list—names and addresses of suspects for example. Another key to a good forensic package is consistency of commands. Most of the features of a forensic package can be found in individual programs—many of which are freely available.

However, starting numerous programs and keeping track of the analysis requires much more effort. Further, each programmer of the freeware has his or her own notion of how commands operate. A forensic package has one consistent set of commands and menus to perform various functions on the data.

Centralized Report Writing and Auditing

A forensic analyst should be able to replicate every action that led to the discovery of evidence. A good forensics package should have the capability to track the analyst's actions to a log, so that productive procedures can be saved without requiring excessive notes. This may also include cataloging of key files for easy reference later. This log can form the basis for a more extensive report or simply be used as lab bench notes from the witness stand.

Validation and Support

A primary advantage to using a forensics package is that it has generally been validated by an external expert and used in standard practice. This saves an analyst from having to defend every tool used from attacks by the defense. As new versions of the package are released, they receive similar expert validation.

Support goes beyond the basic help-desk function. Forensic software vendors usually offer training to validate an analyst's skill and knowledge with the product. The credential provided by the vendor, upon successful completion of the training, is often a key validation of the analyst's skill.

When available, forensic packages will greatly increase the productivity of an analyst. The packages can be extremely cost prohibitive for some police agencies, however, as a site license for one program can cost thousands of dollars. At the same time, the wasted, salaried time of an analyst is worth considerably more to most organizations. In addition, the training provided by forensic package vendors can increase the productivity of an analyst by keeping him or her abreast of recent developments. A good package covers all the basics and helps keep the analysis organized and documented.

Summary

The basic process of digital forensic analysis is designed to present the elements of a crime in evidence from stored digital materials. In court, a forensic analyst will be asked to answer several questions about the evidence:

1. When restoring a backup to another machine, will it contain all of the files, no more and no less tha[n] were on the original?
2. Will the restored version's file be identical, faithful copies of the original?
3. Will [latent data] be faithfully reproduced?
4. Will the restored backup contain all the data, and only the data, on the original?

5. How do we know that our answers to these questions are accurate?[11]

By following the methods described in this chapter (especially the documentation), the analyst will be able to prove the answers to these questions. Other basic skills include a working knowledge of the devices used to store digital information and the tools required to analyze it. Computer forensics involves more that just computer knowledge; it also involves a detailed understanding of criminal law and the legal process.

Review Questions

1. Explain the process used to preserve the verifiable integrity of digital evidence. How does this ensure that data are preserved unmodified? How can an analyst show that the original evidence is unmodified?

2. Trace and explain how the hardware of a computer organizes and stores information for later retrieval from an active file being processed in the processor chip to a mass storage device (hard disk or removable storage). What is the trend in terms of speed in this progression of components? What is the trend in terms of size and capacity in this progression of components?

3. Describe in broad terms how the software of a computer organizes information for storage and later retrieval. Does this process yield any potential locations for latent digital evidence? Is latent evidence always intact? Why or why not?

4. What advantages are offered by commercial forensic packages? Are there any disadvantages to using them? If so, what are they?

Endnotes

1. BLACK, H.C., NOLAN, J.R., and NOLAN-HALEY, J.M. (1990). *Black's Law Dictionary,* 6th ed. St. Paul, MN: West Publishing.

2. "Data" is the plural form of datum. A single datum is one piece of information. Common usage allows discussion of data as a single grouping of information (e.g., "data is easily obtained"). This chapter uses data in this latter, common form.

3. STEPHENSON, P. (2000). *Investigating Computer-Related Crime.* Boca Raton, FL: CRC Press.

4. ORTON, I. (2001). "The Investigation and Prosecution of a Cybercrime." From *Cybercrime: The Investigation, Prosecution and Defense of a Computer-Related Crime.* Durham, NC: Carolina Academic Press.

5. It is possible, although complex to forge a file to produce a certain hash value, but it is extremely unlikely that the forged file could be confused with the original.

6. A single DVD can hold about 4.7 GB of data, but it would take more than 16 of them to hold the contents of a common consumer hard drive.

7. The underlying issue was that 1 GB of the data was encrypted and the prosecution did not want to release the data because they could not read it.

Mitnick refused to supply a decryption key based on his Fifth Amendment privilege against self-incrimination.

8. Random access memory (RAM) carries its name forward from the earliest days of computers. "Random access" distinguishes it from sequential access memory like a tape; this means that the processor can call for information located at any address in the RAM. In the 1960s, this was a tremendous improvement. Today, there are no other schemes for managing memory in common use, but we still specify "Random Access Memory."

9. Clusters are storage units that can be of several different sizes depending on how the file system on the hard drive is configured. They are the most accurate way to describe storage space on a hard disk.

10. HOLT, THOMAS J., and BLEVINS, KRISTIE R. (September 2008). "Examining the Stress, Challenges, and Experiences of Forensic Examiners." Paper presented at the annual meetings of the Southern Criminal Justice Association, New Orleans, LA.,

11. STEPHENSON, *Investigating Computer-Related Crime.*

CHAPTER 13

Information Security and Infrastructure Protection

CHAPTER OBJECTIVES

After completing this chapter, you should be able to

- Understand the concept of risk as applied to information security and infrastructure protection.
- Discuss the major principles of risk analysis.
- Identify and define the primary security technologies used to protect information.
- Discuss the various functions of firewalls, and identify their limitations.
- Define encryption, and discuss its use in terms of authenticity, integrity, and confidentiality.
- Identify and explain some of the security vendor technologies used today to secure information.

INTRODUCTION

Risk analysis will always be an art informed by science. We cannot know all possible outcomes and weigh them rationally. Risk analysis involves projecting the most probable outcome and allocating available resources to address that outcome. At the same time, a risk analyst must remember that assets (computers, networks, etc.) were purchased to fulfill a mission. If risk management strategies substantially interfere with that mission, then the assets are no better off than if they had been compromised through a security-related risk.

This section introduces the concept of risk by discussing several epochs of computer development. Each era presents its own risk and at least somewhat functional responses to that risk. Early decisions weighing the risk of computers not providing a useful function against potential or unknowable future security threats produced results that we still live with today. It is easy to criticize early decisions based on our knowledge of the outcomes, but even with hindsight, we may fail to see that the benefit provided greatly outweighs the harm. In fact, some decisions that have produced security vulnerabilities were absolutely essential to the basic functioning of computers and networks for their intended purposes.

MASTERING THE TECHNOLOGY AND THE ENVIRONMENT

In the earliest days of computing, before extensive networking and multiple user systems, the primary problem faced by users was the technology itself. During these early days, program-mers created the computer functions that we take for granted.[1] Early innovations included interactive operation (rather than batch processing and output), rudimentary networking, graphics, tools and utilities, and so on.[2] In many cases, the primary limitation was the capacity of the hardware. Limitations imposed by operating memory, storage, and processing speed each forced adaptations. The net effect was the absence of security. At the time, physical security (i.e., locked doors) was sufficient to protect computing resources. The primary concern of system architects was the expansion of useful function and overcoming hardware limitations. Although decisions made at this early point would later have negative effects on security, they were really unavoidable.

As technologies matured and found supporters in mainstream business, the computer moved from research platform to business tool. Complex software was created for business, and essential functions were transferred from armies of clerks to computer systems. Such moves were always in one direction. It is impossible to reemploy clerical staff and reimplement paper-based procedures once the existing system is gone. Further, the cost savings of computers make such a backward move unlikely. This placed new emphasis on availability of data and recovery from errors and disasters. Computer centers were created to concentrate technical expertise and provide a controlled environment in which to maximize the availability of computing resources. Innovations in fire suppression,[3] efficient environmental controls,[4] and administrative proce-dures (i.e., backup schedules) gave reasonable assurance against disaster.

The user was undeniably part of the computing environment. During this era, legitimate users were the primary human threat to computers. More harm was caused by failure to properly maintain systems and backup schedules than from intrusion or malicious intent. When malicious intent played a part, it was typically on the part of an insider.[5] Although there are documented cases of intrusion and loss, a much greater threat came from the relative scarcity of experts to operate and maintain systems. Once again, the operational need for availability was more pressing than security.

Personal Computers and Intruders

Although recreational system intrusion was not unknown in the previous era, it was largely restricted by access to computers. Few people had access, and fewer still had the skill to break through the rudimentary security on most systems. Those that did were often deeply invested in terms of time and resources spent to acquire that knowledge.[6] Recreational intrusion was a minor problem at best. The advent of the home computer in 1975 marked the beginning of the democratization of computing. It also marked the movement of hacking from the old-school era to the bedroom hacker era (see Chapter 4).[7] By the end of the 1970s, the restraint of peers and the investment in knowledge no longer provided reasonable protection against malicious users.

In this era, intruders sought knowledge and resources to continue their use of computers. Much of the literature is devoted to detailing the social connections or lack thereof among intruders and hackers.[8] Most pundits resort to the myth of the hacker as loner and contentious in interaction with other hackers.[9] An often-overlooked facet of the hacker culture is the need for information and resources. In the early era of intrusion, access to other computers required a phone connection, usually to a long-distance number. Thus, the search for access to resources and knowledge of how to exploit them dominated the vast majority of hacker interactions.

For the first time, intruders became a significant threat to routine computer use. Although efforts were made to secure computers, long-standing demands for the availability of computing resources and the expansion of computer capabilities simply eclipsed demands for security. Hollinger and Lanza-Kaduce provide one of the very few significant criminological works describing the efforts to supplement the computer industries' meager efforts toward security with law.[10] Various states and the federal government passed laws in the hopes of deterring would-be computer criminals and punishing those who were caught.

The Internet Explosion

The explosive growth of the Internet has been the subject of numerous books and articles in the popular press,[11] scholarly publications of general interest,[12] and works of technical research.[13] The dramatic influx of new users to computer networks has burdened both the technical infrastructure and the social cohesion of online communities.[14] The loss of social cohesion of the computer underground gave rise to script kiddies, low-skilled network intruders with little desire to pursue the traditional goals of hackers (see Chapter 4). At the same time, the influx of new users, also with low levels of skill, gave script kiddies and other larval hackers a rich field of targets. Unless a computer system holds particular interest (politically—like the World Trade Organization; technologically; or as a trophy—like NASA or the Pentagon), the most likely threat comes from script kiddies.

During this period, the amount of computerized data, such as bank records, personal information, and other electronic files, increased. Businesses and financial institutions store sensitive customer information in massive electronic databases that can be accessed and compromised by hackers. The increased use of online banking and shopping sites also allow consumers to transmit sensitive personal and financial information over the Internet. This created more attractive targets for criminals to engage in identity theft, fraud, and espionage.

In turn, the Internet increased the availability and proliferation of hacker tools and data and the professionalization of the hacker community. The recent emergence of malicious software markets and communities that engender the sale of stolen information as outlined in Chapters 5 and 6 makes it significantly easier for hackers to gain access to very sophisticated tools with little to no understanding of how they function. Such tools existed in the previous era, but were not as widely distributed or easily accessed. As a result, the global landscape of threats from hacking has changed dramatically, leading accomplished network intruders to offer their services for hire to unskilled hackers, terrorists, and organized crime groups. This has changed the way threats are perceived, though it is clear that the potential of the Internet to find and retrieve information from almost any jurisdiction has made it unlikely that a single nation's efforts could remove these tools from wide circulation. It is also undesirable to remove technical information from our networks; technological advancement depends on the open exchange of ideas.[15]

PRINCIPLES OF RISK ANALYSIS

Risk analysis is performed at many levels and with many degrees of detail. Risk analysis services are provided by Fortune 500 consulting firms like Deloitte & Touche, Ernst & Young, KPMG, and many others. Reports from a major risk analysis can cover every aspect of business and run into thousands of pages. Risk analysis may also be performed by small organizations or even individuals in the course of their businesses. Such informal decision making does not follow the comprehensive steps of the more elaborate analyses. Deciding where to draw the line on the depth of a risk analysis is an art with no clear standard. The principles of risk analysis presented here are broad, but examples are narrowly tailored to illustrate network security risks and remedies. Above all, this process shows that there is no single solution to security. The effort required to eliminate all risks (even if that is possible) would surely overwhelm an organization. All known factors relevant to an organization should be weighed so that a specific level of acceptable risk can be matched to a risk management strategy.

Assessment and Evaluation

The first step of risk analysis is to correctly assess and evaluate the existing information technology (IT) systems within an organization. Unfortunately, those who often conduct risk analysis studies tend to focus on external vulnerabilities and threats. Most losses of information come from inside the organization and through relatively simple security failures of existing information systems and networks. This assessment must include an evaluation of the organizational, managerial, and administrative procedures directly relevant to IT systems. Hopefully, the organization has and uses a well-developed and well-defined IT plan. This plan should include information relating to the acquisition and purchase of future IT equipment and systems, as well as a strategy for expanding information security parameters as the system grows or changes. Interestingly, most organizations have plans that represent large "bibles" of procedures and policies that sit on bookshelves (get dusty) and are rarely read or followed. Most managers and directors outside of IT fail to comprehend the complexity of information security. It is not simply the purchase of a new device or the implementation of a new password procedure, but rather an ongoing culture within the organization that reenforces security awareness and security protocols. Information and computer security must be a part of the everyday working culture of the organization. The information security plan is not just a written compendium of policies and procedures, but a living document that guides the organizational methodology for providing and improving information security. In this manner, the development of a specific risk analysis plan never really ends. New software and equipment acquisitions, new technologies, and new system requirements demand constant change and "tweaking" of the overall system, and hence, the security of the system as well. Similar to or part of an information resource management (IRM) plan, risk analysis highlights synergism and cooperativeness as well as overall improvement in information exchange through the use of new and varied technology and work processes.[16] This cannot be a haphazard experiment; it must be a well-thought-out plan implemented through a series of phases on a timely basis. Without such objectives in mind, existing IT resources flounder and security breaches proliferate. It should go without saying that constant training improves security knowledge and engenders security awareness within an organization. Training must accompany the development of any risk analysis or information security plan.

Executives must also be aware of a growing problem existing within information system security. Most executives are not highly information and computer technology literate. As such, they must rely on the technical advice and expertise of subordinates. This situation makes the executive vulnerable to "information security elites." Recognized and identified by a number of scholars during the technology boom of the 1980s, information security elites often gain control over others (influence) and resist control by supervisors.[17] This is often accomplished by occupying key positions whose competencies are essential to the overall success of the organization. In some cases, executives are almost held "hostage" by those who have the niche technical knowledge to understand specific information security systems. Information is critically important to an organization. Individual managers and personnel must have immediate access to secure and correct data as well as communication systems that link them to a global marketplace. This demand places the highest value on those who can assure both the quality and security of data and the information system. It also creates a potential environment for significant security loss and abuse. Who is monitoring those in charge of information security? For this reason, external reviews have significant advantages over internal assessments, particularly in the area of risk analysis.

Threats

The second important aspect of risk analysis is to identify the threats facing an organization. The single largest threat to an organization and its information security is from within. Many times, organizations suffer from key individuals intentionally stealing information or corrupting files. The vulnerability of the organization is extreme and as such, so is the loss. Additionally, in many instance of information security breaches from within, there is virtually no detection of an incident that has occurred. Many times, information is accessed, altered, stolen, or sabotaged without the organizational victim's knowledge—either the crime is covered up through the use of special programs or simply not detected in an audit.

Other than routine personnel and employment checks, incorporating solid hiring practices, and constant monitoring, very little can be accomplished to eliminate totally this type of threat. The most pernicious part of this threat is that it invariably leads executives not to trust their subordinates. It takes just one relatively minor problem from within for an executive to realize just how vulnerable the organization really is from this type of attack. Paranoia can become a problem; the breakdown of trust between executives and managers causes other significant personnel problems. Once again, frank awareness and training can help to instill the type of organizational culture required in today's information society.

Formal risk analysis also categorizes external threats with great detail and elaborate terms, especially after the events of September 11, 2001. Terrorism, sabotage, espionage, and criminal theft are real and comprise a bulk of the identified threats to an organization. Just as dangerous (and threatening) are the age-old issues presented by natural disasters, hurricanes, tornadoes, and earthquakes. Effective risk analysis should cover these types of standard threats as well. Interestingly, preparing for natural disasters often provides the type of secure information environment that thwarts insider problems and external attacks by people.

We are concerned primarily with risks and vulnerabilities to information systems and, as such, will focus our discussion pertaining to problems associated with these types of systems. These are usually summarized in terms of threats to information: integrity, authenticity, confidentiality, and availability. Threats to integrity are threats that actually alter data. Adding, moving, and deleting all change the integrity of data. These actions are also legitimate uses of data. The risk is that an unauthorized or unintentional action will cause a threat to integrity. To make matters more difficult, threats to integrity are not limited to malicious actions. Unintentional alteration (e.g., deleting a useful file) is far more common that malicious activity.

BOX 13.1

Complete Security Is Not the Complete Solution

Computer experts have long recognized that it is possible to make a computer completely secure. The steps are as follows: (1) unplug the network cable, (2) encrypt the data with strong encryption, (3) delete the encryption key and forget the password, (4) unplug the power, (5) lock the computer in a vault, and, finally, (6) cover the vault with concrete. This security procedure also makes the computer perfectly useless. For an asset to be worth protecting, it must have value. Most assets have value in the work they do for the business.

The recycling bin found in Microsoft™ systems is a risk management tool to avoid such unintentional deletions. It trades hard drive space and annoying pop-up dialogs, asking you to be sure before you delete, for a second chance to recover a file.

Authenticity is a more subtle concept, but it is related to integrity. In these terms, authenticity is the ability to trust the integrity of data. In broader terms, authenticity is the justified ability to trust. Data that cannot be verified or trusted are less useful than authenticated data, if not completely useless. Further, if an intruder is detected in the network, data may have perfect integrity (i.e., be unaltered), but if authenticity cannot be established, the organization cannot verify that fact. The data may as well be altered.

Confidentiality acknowledges that some information is more valuable if it is not publicly available. Confidentiality is treated more extensively in the section on encryption (below).

The final broad category of threat to information is availability. A denial-of-service attack can make information unavailable, but so can overly rigid security policies. What is the difference to the legitimate user who needs the information? Information systems exist to store, manipulate, and utilize data. When data are unavailable, the system's fundamental purpose is disturbed. Each of these categories of threat must be balanced against each other in an attempt to manage risk.

Cost-Effective Security

Risk management is predicated on the rational calculation of potential damage against certain damage of non-mission-related expenditure. The concept of risk management acknowledges that while it may be possible virtually to eliminate all risks, the resources expended to do so would greatly outweigh the potential gains.

With this in mind, computer security experts seek to optimize the balance between the intended function of the information asset (network, computer, etc.) and securing the asset from risk. Many strategies of risk management overlap. For example, protecting a system from natural disaster by maintaining a decentralized network also protects the system from local network outages or denial-of-service attacks on a single point of failure.

SECURITY TECHNOLOGIES

The primary purposes of risk analysis are to identify threats and then to provide recommendations to address these threats. Concerning information systems and technologies, the focus has historically been on protecting individual components such as software, hardware, and connected devices. While a hard drive can be replaced, the information contained on the hard drive may be irreplaceable, and its loss may be catastrophic to an organization. Here, more than in almost any other area of risk analysis and information security, an ounce of prevention is truly worth a pound of cure! Coupled with solid personnel hiring practices and an aware organizational culture, the following security technologies provide a sound base for information systems and networks.[18]

BACKUPS

Backups are the single most important security measure a company or individual can take. As noted above, most of the value of an information system lies in its information. In the event that threats to integrity, authenticity, or availability cannot be prevented, the information can survive risk actualization if a backup copy exists in a safe location. A backup is a copy of data. If data are lost, destroyed, or altered, the backup may provide the only way to recover the data. If there is reason to suspect that the integrity of the data was compromised, a secure backup provides a basis of comparison. If the suspect data match the backup (plus any expected changes), integrity has been restored. If alteration is evident, then the harm from compromised data has been isolated.

Mission-critical data (data that cannot be lost) is often protected with an instantaneous back-up as it is stored. A device called a redundant array of inexpensive disks (RAID) saves the data to two hard drives at once, making failure of a single drive less damaging.[19] Since RAID only makes two copies of the hard drive, regular backups are also necessary to protect against alteration.

Wireless Networks and Security

With the emergence of laptop and mobile computing has come the growth of wireless Internet access points, accessible by Wi-Fi connections. Wi-Fi connections are often synonymous with wireless local area networks, where machines can be connected to this network through the use of wireless network adapter cards.[20] Wireless networks are an especially vulnerable part of a network, as they can allow individuals inside of a network boundary if they are not secured. Thus, there are several steps recommended to secure wireless networks. Specifically, wireless routers and connections must be secured through the use of an encryption protocol like wired equivalent privacy (WEP) or Wi-Fi protected access (WPA).[21] These tools help to reduce the likelihood of theft of service or unintended access, as individuals will be unable to gain access to the network without the proper passphrase or network key. Wireless signal beacons that make individuals aware of the presence of a network can also be turned off. This will reduce the likelihood of individuals who attempt to compromise the network. There are also protocols that enable wireless routers to allow only known machines to access the network. This is accomplished through media access control, or MAC,

---

BOX 13.2
Case Study in Risk Analysis—Backup Schedules

Although there is no rule as to how often backups should be created, a good rule of thumb is to consider how much of the data you can afford to reproduce. When you exceed that point, create a backup. For example, a company pays people to enter data. A backup system capable of handling their demands costs $12,000. They have 120 employees making $10 per hour. They create a backup every 10 hours ($120 \times 10 \times 10 = 12,000$). The benefit is that they only pay for the backup system once, with small recurring costs for tape and a portion of an administrator's time. If they recover data from a ten-hour shift once, the system has paid for itself. If they suspect an intruder has tampered with the data, they can simply compare the data to a backup and restore the good data if necessary.

address filtering where the unique MAC address of each machine is kept on file, and those MAC addresses that are not recognized are unable to connect to the network.[22] Sensitive information and databases must also be secured and kept off of the wireless network in order to minimize the likelihood of an intruder gaining access. It is important to note, however, that wireless access points are extremely vulnerable to attacks, thus they can be a significant liability to network security.[23]

Firewalls

Another way individuals and organizations can protect their computer networks is by using firewalls. A firewall is a device or software that acts as a checkpoint between a network or stand-alone computer and the Internet. A firewall checks all data coming in and going out. If the data do not fit strict rules, they do not go through. In the past, firewalls were not widely used, since they could significantly reduce access from the protected network to the outside world. Firewalls have since improved greatly and are now relatively fast and easily configured by the user. Software development, combined with rapidly increasing computer-based crime occurring through interconnected networks, has led to the widespread use of firewalls.

A firewall is a tool to be used as part of a security strategy. It cannot protect a user from all threats. In fact, firewalls are a classic example of risk analysis. If the rules set in a firewall are too restrictive (i.e., more secure), then normal network functions may be impaired. Such impairment may make it impossible for users to conduct business—the whole reason for the network in the first place. If the firewall rule set is not restrictive enough, it may expose the network to an intruder. This critical balance is the primary problem with firewalls. A special administrator is often necessary for large corporate firewalls. This administrator constantly balances security versus business efficiency to configure the firewall rule set. New applications or new work zones force new rules for the firewall. For example, a sales force in the field may need access to the corporate network. The firewall must allow these users to penetrate the network while excluding unknown users. One solution (see below under "Encryption") is to allow a virtual private network (VPN) using encrypted data. Many early VPNs had difficulty penetrating firewalls because the firewall could not read the data headers (directions on how to deliver the data).

PERIMETER AND HOST-BASED FIREWALLS   The standard, corporate Internet firewall places a single barrier between the internal network and potential attackers. Servers that require public access (e.g., Web servers or mail servers) are placed outside the firewall to minimize penetration from the outside. Such servers, called "bastion" servers, have their own security measures. Like the curtain wall of a medieval castle, the firewall protects the interior, while towers, or bastions, provide hard defense points for contact with a threatening environment. This configuration places all of the defenses at the perimeter. If a malicious user attacked the network from within the "secure" area, there are no defenses. On the other hand, a single dedicated firewall can be built to handle a large volume of traffic without slowing the network.

A second layer of security can be provided with host-resident firewalls installed on machines within the secure perimeter. Host-resident firewalls are software programs installed on a computer. Clearly, there is an additional burden on every computer running such a program. There is also an additional cost for software and burden in administering host-resident firewalls. There is no requirement that all computers within a perimeter have a host-resident firewall. Particular resources within the secure perimeter may require additional protection. Using both types of firewall allows fine-grained control over network security. This means greater flexibility to manage risks. For example, a perimeter firewall might have to allow traffic into the perimeter due to use needs, but a host-resident wall could restrict such traffic on all computers except those that need access. Additionally, antivirus programs and other protective software should be installed on machines as a further layer of protection against attack.

PACKET FILTERING   One of the most basic functions of a firewall is to block certain traffic that may be harmful. One of the protocols that run the Internet, transfer control protocol and Internet protocol (TCP/IP), assigns numbers to computers called Internet protocol addresses (IP addresses). TCP assigns "ports" to each computer that allow different programs to communicate.[24] Imagine that each computer on the Internet is a hotel. Each hotel has about 65,000 rooms. The IP portion of TCP/IP identifies each hotel with a street address so that traffic can find it (IP address). The TCP portion of TCP/IP assigns room numbers so that traffic can go to the right place. Most of the higher rooms are not regularly used. Packet filtering allows a firewall to block traffic from a known bad location (a scruffy hotel in a bad neighborhood). It also allows the firewall to block traffic to a room that should be unused (which may indicate an unwanted "guest" in the hotel). The addressing information that is absolutely necessary for Internet communication is used to block potential threats. By using a firewall to block unused ports, many security threats can be eliminated. If the filtering rules are too aggressive, beneficial traffic may be blocked. Again, a security policy must carefully weigh the need for legitimate service versus security.

STATEFUL INSPECTION   Stateful inspection relies on another feature of TCP. To travel across the Internet, data are broken into smaller chunks called packets. IP addresses packets to find the right computer using the IP address of that computer. Each IP packet is an independent agent, finding its way across the Internet with the best guess of the shortest route. Sometimes packets take different routes and arrive out of order. These must be reassembled into the proper order before the computer can use them.

In addition to labeling ports, TCP reassembles packets by tracking sessions (a series of exchanges between computers). The TCP portion of each IP packet contains a sequence number that is based on a pseudorandom process negotiated between the two computers communicating in the session. Stateful inspection monitors these sequence numbers and other information to make sure that malicious data don't enter into a stream of legitimate data. This is most frequently done by denying an external attempt to open a session with a computer that is not a server. Packet filtering cannot block all traffic (or else the computer may as well not be connected to the Internet), but stateful inspection can be used to ensure that only information request from within the perimeter can enter.

NETWORK ADDRESS TRANSLATION (NAT)   Although technically not a security function, many firewalls allow administrators to use special reserved Internet addresses. All the machines inside the perimeter have these special addresses. These special addresses are not allowed on the Internet. To use Internet services, the internal machines start a session with the firewall server. The firewall uses NAT to assign an IP to that session, not to the internal machine. Going back to the hotel analogy, imagine a desk clerk with mailboxes. Data traffic goes to the mailbox and is then delivered to the guest. That way, no junk mail gets through; in this case, junk mail would be specially crafted attacks against an internal computer designed to bypass firewalls. A firewall with NAT stops these attacks because it moderates all communication from inside to the outside.

AIR GAPS   Air gaps are the ultimate in firewall network protection. An air gap is literally a separation between computers containing nothing but air. That is, the machine is not on the network.

Data have to be carried back and forth through the air gap by a person. The benefit to this is that no outsider can ever access the air-gapped machine. The downside is that no one on the inside can reach the air-gapped machine through the network. Air gaps are typically only used with the most sensitive data. Data carried to the air-gapped machine may contain malicious code like a virus, but the air-gapped machine is 100 percent immune to network attacks. Unfortunately many security equipment vendors label devices as air gaps when they actually connect to the network; these are "virtual air gaps." Absolute protection only occurs when there is no electrical connection—virtual air gaps do not fulfill this requirement.

Limitations of Firewalls

Firewalls are powerful and increasingly versatile tools for managing risks on a computer network; however, they are not *the* single solution to network security. Firewalls have to be managed to allow for growth in network function while maintaining the highest level of protection. This requires interaction between the firewall administrator and other users of the network. In large organizations, this interaction is formalized in a security policy. A security policy requires updates as situations change, and it requires auditing to ensure that users and management are complying with the policy. The security policy tells the firewall administrator how to balance risks when configuring the firewall. It also allows the security administrator to plan other layers of security, if necessary, to cover the holes in the firewall made necessary by legitimate network functions.

Firewalls cannot stop improper use of legitimate services. This is why bastion servers are placed outside the secure perimeter of the network. Servers exist to provide interaction with people and systems outside the company; however, many network attacks exploit flaws in server software to gain unfettered access to the computer running the server software. If the server was inside the firewall, such malicious traffic could enter the secure perimeter. If the server is compromised, then the attacker would have a base of operations to explore the inside network.

Firewalls exist as part of an overall security strategy. They are not magical talismans that protect the network from all harm. Many users believe that the firewall will protect them; however, as we have seen in recent e-mail-based viruses and worms (see Chapter 4), this is not always so. Users surfing the Web from inside a firewall are still vulnerable to exploits written into the Web pages they access. There are remedies for these security risks not handled by firewalls, but they all exist as part of an overall security strategy.

Encryption

Bruce Schneier defines cryptography as "the art and science of securing messages."[25] Messages can be any data. Encryption is a technique of securing data by scrambling the data into apparent nonsense, but doing so in such a way that the message can be recovered by a person possessing a secret code called a key. The requirements for a good encryption scheme include protecting the classic elements of computer security discussed above: authenticity, integrity, and confidentiality. Availability is generally not facilitated by encryption. Encrypting data has the inherent effect of confidentiality. This comes into play most often when confidential data must be sent through an insecure medium. An encrypted message (i.e., the scrambled message) can be stored or transmitted to another point with a reasonable expectation of security—even if the medium used to transmit it is not secure (e.g., the Internet). Integrity can be assured through a similar technique called hashing. Hashing produces a unique signature of the original data—like a fingerprint. At the other end of the transmission, a new hash is calculated on the data and compared to the old hash. If they match, the data have not been altered. A public key/private key system allows a user to authenticate data by matching a key—the only way to decode the data—with a well-known and publicly available key. This form of security is only as good as the secrecy of the key, but it offers a way to authenticate without being physically present (more about public key/private key systems below). Using these three techniques together provides a reasonable expectation that the message is private and unaltered.

To illustrate this process, imagine a check being mailed to a creditor. You create a transaction by filling in an amount to a preformatted check with all of your bank information already on it. You also fill in the receiver's name. You authenticate the instructions to your bank by signing the check. If there is any question as to who wrote the check, your signature can be checked against a signature card you filed when you opened the account. You place the check in an envelope to protect the confidentiality of your transaction. You then turn it over to the U.S. Postal Service and they deliver it. Evidence of tampering should be noticeable by the condition of the envelope. The elements of this transaction are as follows: authenticity—signature; confidentiality—envelope; and integrity—envelope. To conduct the same transaction over the Internet, you face different risks, but you still have tools to assist you.

To illustrate the online process, imagine that instead of writing and mailing a check, you log onto the bill payment section of your creditor's Web site. You enter your confidential bank information. Since you cannot sign a computer screen, you provide information that only you should know—a password. This password serves as your signature.[26] In the same way that your signature was verified by your presence in a bank with identification documents, your password is verified with identifying information when you start to do business with the online entity. Since only information is being exchanged, not a physical object like a signature on paper, confidentiality of your identifying information is imperative. The authenticity of your password is directly related to its confidentiality because anyone with the password would appear to be you. Both this information and the transaction details are protected with encryption. Finally, the integrity of the transaction details is guaranteed with a hash that accompanies the encrypted message. It is possible, although usually pointless, to blindly alter an encrypted message—a process called bit-flipping. A hash calculates a unique mathematical value for a message. When the message reaches its destination and is decrypted, a new hash is calculated. Any alteration of the message contents will cause the hashes not to match. The elements of this transaction are as follows: authenticity—password; confidentiality—encryption; and integrity—hash value. The transaction can be carried by the insecure Internet and retain a reasonable expectation of security.

A "reasonable expectation of security" does not mean absolute security. All encryption can be broken. "If the cost required to break an [encryption technique] is greater than the value of the encrypted data, it is probably safe."[27] The most essential feature of encryption is that scrambled data can be returned to a useful form by the data's intended user and cannot easily be returned to a useful form by others. Again, the concept of risk analysis can be applied to this security technique. The more valuable the information transmitted or the more determined a third party is to intercept the information; the more resources must be devoted to protecting it.

Encryption is used to store passwords on your home computer system and credit card numbers in "online wallets" and to secure e-commerce transactions. Modern encryption *can* be broken, but except for the most basic forms of encryption, like the encryption protecting Windows™ passwords, most criminals would find it immensely easier to look for other methods to get the data. While e-commerce may be protected as it crosses the Internet, credit information is often stored on unsecured computers at the merchant's site. It is important to remember that encrypted e-commerce data are decrypted at the other end. While e-commerce transactions are generally safe, few merchants have devoted the resources to securing their whole computer system.

USING PUBLIC KEY/PRIVATE KEY ENCRYPTION TO ENHANCE CONFIDENTIALITY   A public key and private key are parts of a matched pair of values. That is, they are mathematically related in such a way that no other value could be substituted for one of them. It is also impossible to predict the value of one based on the other. Thus, having access to a public key will not help an attacker (a person attempting to break the encryption). When a message is encrypted with one key, only the other can decrypt it. Thus, having access to a public key will not help an attacker decrypt a message encrypted with the public key. The idea of the key pair is that one key can be freely distributed while not compromising the other. When a key pair is generated, either one may become the public key. That does not need to be determined until it is actually distributed. Finally, having a document encrypted with either one of the keys does not necessarily help an attacker guess the key value used to encrypt it.

Public keys are often registered with a public key authority. Anyone wishing to send a confidential message to the key owner can use the public key to encrypt the message.

The resulting encrypted document can be sent across an insecure channel, like the Internet. The receiver simply uses the private key associated with the well-known public key to decrypt the message.

A malicious user intercepting the encrypted message cannot successfully decrypt the message with the public key.

The process of encrypting a document simply assures the recipient of the confidentiality of the document's contents.[28]

USING DIGITAL SIGNATURES TO ENHANCE AUTHENTICITY AND INTEGRITY   Another application of the public key/private key pair allows a user to authenticate a document with a "digital signature." Digital signatures use a hashing algorithm to create unique numeric value associated with the document. This value has two primary attributes. One, if the unaltered document is hashed again, it will produce the same hash value, and two, if the document is altered in any way, it will not produce the same value if hashed again. The problem with this method is that if the unencrypted original document is intercepted, it can be altered and a new hash value can be calculated based on the altered document and substituted for the old hash value. This means that the hash must be sent through a separate, secure mechanism or it must be cryptographically protected.

This is where the second step of the digital signature comes in. Once the hash value is calculated, it is encrypted with the sender's private key. Recall that having a document encrypted with the private key does not necessarily assist an attacker in trying to break the encryption or guess the key. To authenticate that the person claiming to have sent the message actually sent it, the signature is decrypted with the sender's public key. The sender's public key is known to be associated with the private key supposedly used to encrypt the message. If the signature decrypts properly, then the receiver knows that someone in possession of the supposed sender's private key sent the message; this is assumed to be the supposed sender.[29]

USING ENCRYPTION IN DAILY LIFE   Most users do not directly use tools that provide public key/private key encryption. Pretty Good Privacy (PGP) is one example of a common encryption package. It is commonly used to encrypt e-mail messages. In spite of the relative rarity of such encryption packages, most computer users today use encryption without knowing it. Web browsers have built-in encryption functions. Secure Web pages, such as shop cart checkout pages in e-commerce sites or any other secure information transfer page; use encryption to protect the transaction. This leads to an interesting problem with public key/private key encryption: It is very slow by computer standards. It is fine for small text files or very light graphics, but for wholesale secure transfer of information, it is simply inadequate. Symmetric key encryption is much faster, but it requires both parties to the transaction to have the same key; the key cannot be left unprotected to provide convenient authentication. The solution to this problem uses a hybrid of both symmetric key and public key/private key technology. A temporary symmetric key called a session key is generated for each data transfer "session." It is sent using a public key/private key exchange. The session key is simply information to be encrypted. Once both parties have the key, fast exchange of secure information is possible. As soon as the session is done, the session key can be discarded.

Encryption and hashing can be part of a risk management strategy to reduce threats to data authenticity, integrity, and confidentiality. The particular techniques discussed only indicate the possible uses of encryption. For example, a technology called IPsec (secure Internet protocol) utilizes cryptography to reduce threats to authenticity, integrity, and confidentiality of data as they travels on a network. IPsec is used to create secure cryptographic "tunnels" across the Internet so that eavesdroppers do not know where a packet is going after its next stop or what it contains. Without IPsec or similar measures, information traversing the Internet is vulnerable to even relatively unsophisticated eavesdropping attempts.[30] This and many other uses of cryptographic technology provide options to manage threats.

Password Discipline

The single greatest problem in computer security is password protection. Although there are some basic do's and don'ts, there are also sophisticated software programs that address the issue. Several approaches have been taken, including password-creation software, onetime password generators, and user authentication systems—like biometric devices. There is a variety of software programs that system administrators can use to in order to improve password security. Some programs force users to change their passwords on a regular basis, perhaps every month or few months, or even every week. Other programs automatically create random pronounceable passwords for users, such as "jrk^wud," which is pronounced "jerk wood." The user remembers that the ^ character is between two words. Such pronounceable passwords are subject to dictionary attacks by hackers, are easily remembered by users, and do not relate to user information (such as a child's first name or user Social Security number) that might be easily determined by an intruder. Other programs may force users to incorporate numbers, letters, and symbols into their passwords, making it more difficult to engage in dictionary attacks. When combinations of these protocols are in place, passwords are made even stronger, thereby increasing the overall strength of the network.

SECURITY VENDOR TECHNOLOGIES

SecurID, from Security Dynamics Technologies, Inc. is perhaps the most popular onetime password generator, with over three million users in 5,000 organizations worldwide. SecurID identifies and authenticates each individual user on the basis of two factors: (1) something secret that user knows—a memorized personal identification number (PIN)—and (2) something unique that the user physically holds—the SecurID card. Under this system, a computer user, when logging on, first types in his or her PIN. Then the user types in the number currently displayed on his or her SecurID card, which changes every 60 seconds. Each individual SecurID card is synchronized either with hardware or software on the computer system that the user is attempting to access. The result is a unique access code that is valid only for a particular user during a one-minute time period.

Kerberos is a program developed at MIT by the Athena Project. It is a leading network and data encryption system. Cygnus Support, a Mountain View, California company, has developed Kerberos-based user-authentication software—Cygnus Network Security (CNS)—that eliminates the need to use clear, unencrypted text passwords on a network. In this system, an individual user is given an encryption key to encrypt and decrypt Kerleros passwords, log-ins, and other computer system transactions. When this individual wants to access the network, he or she will send a message to the Kerberos server. This computer sends back an encrypted package that can be read only with that user's secret key. This package also includes a temporary encryption key good for only that session on the computer. To prove his or her identity, the user then sends a message coded in the temporary encryption key back to the computer. The Kerberos computer then acknowledges the user's identity by sending a second encrypted message to him or her, which can be decoded only by using the temporary encryption key previously sent to him or her.

Kerberos is just one program that utilizes encryption and password technologies. Many other programs also create encrypted sessions between the user's computer and the destination computer, thus protecting passwords and other sensitive information from cybercriminals and -terrorists.

Symantec, the maker of Norton Utilities, is also a world leader in information security technologies. Focusing primarily on Internet security issues, Symantec offers a variety of security monitoring plans, management services, best practices, proactive protection methodologies, and educational services for enterprises and home users. In a recent white paper distributed by Symantec, the authors eloquently point out that the Internet was developed primarily as an unregulated, open architecture.[31] This is an ideal environment for crime and terrorism where simply developed passwords may not be enough.

New technologies are altering the face of user identification. The use of tools such as digital fingerprint identification, retinal identification, and voice recognition greatly increases the accuracy of user identification, sometimes replacing passwords. In fact, a range of computers from various vendors are including some form of biometrics into the computer system, through the use of built-in cameras or fingerprint scanners. These features increase computer security by linking a user's unique physical attributes (those that do not change or cannot be easily altered) to known passwords or stored encryption keys. Biometrics do not provide absolute security; they make it increasingly difficult for intruders to guess passwords by adding another level of complexity to the password, but not making it harder for the user to remember the password. A retinal scan and a short password are effectively a 10,000–20,000–digit password. The longer the password is, the harder it is to guess.

Home Users

Cyber attacks have also focused on the home computer user. For instance, botnets infect and incorporate home computers into a broader network of compromised machines that can be used as a launch point for DDoS attacks, phishing, and spam distribution. The Conficker worm, for example, was discovered in November 2008 on a number of computers around the world. This worm spread over the Internet through vulnerabilities in Windows servers and systems and reportedly infected over nine million computers within a four-month period.[32] This worm is also a blended threat, as it propagates in a variety of ways and can be used to kill processes within the system and attack multiple components in any system.[33]

As a result, home users must also take computer security very seriously. It is important to note, however, that the use of antiviral programs is not enough to provide total protection for a system. Almost 25 percent of personal computers around the world that use a variety of security solutions have malicious software loaded into their memory, compared with 33.28 percent of unprotected systems.[34] Thus, many computers and individuals can be victimized despite the presence and use of antivirus and other protective software programs. Aside from the routine backups and use of antiviral software, home users must periodically conduct maintenance on their machines. Using the analogy of a car: A person buys a car and then performs routine maintenance such as oil changes, brake replacement, tune-ups, and the like as the automobile is used. Similarly, people who purchase new personal computers need to conduct routine maintenance on their machines by updating their antiviral software on a regular basis, checking reports from their operating system Web site, and repairing software glitches through provided "patches" offered by a number of credible sources.

The personal computer is much more like an automobile that needs constant care and upkeep, rather than an appliance like a refrigerator that is simply plugged into the wall and will continue to function without much maintenance. For the most part, this is a user-awareness problem demanding a significant shift in attitude and philosophy on the part of literally billions of home users. Fortunately, all of the major operating system companies (e.g., Microsoft™, Linux™) provide well-developed Web sites that offer the latest information on problems and remedies. Software fixes and patches often require simply a stroke of the key to download a specific file from the Web site. Then too, the Computer Emergency Response Team (CERT®) at Carnegie Mellon University maintains a well-developed Web site that tracks and reports trends in computer viruses.[35] Established in 1988, the CERT® Coordination Center (CERT/CC) is a center of Internet security expertise, located at the Software Engineering Institute, a federally funded research and development center operated by Carnegie Mellon University. This site should be regularly visited by all computer users.

Summary

We live in the "third wave" of the information society, and undoubtedly, abuses in information security resulting in computercrime and cyberterrorism will only grow in the future. Unfortunately, the losses suffered directly from these types of abuses may be only a part of overall economic devastation facing organizations. Indeed, the civil litigation resulting from loss of privacy, denial or loss of service from partner-type corporations, and loss of reputation and key executives may comprise a much more lasting and severe economic loss to victims of computer crime and cyberterrorism. In addition, the individual committing these attacks will no longer be the relatively uneducated "crook" of the past. He or she may well be a very sophisticated criminal, a greedy inside employee, or a highly motivated terrorist. To be sure, the attacker will be attuned to the intricacies of computer databases and the means to defeat information security systems within closed networks and open architecture systems like the Internet.

Risk analysis offers a continual strategy to assess and evaluate current systems and potential threats. The recommendations offered by risk analysis exercises often focus on the development of an aware organizational culture as well as the use of various security technologies: backup and redundant file systems, firewalls, encryption, and the use of passwords. There are no guarantees or immunities. Developing such programs only offers a first line of defense, as the computer hacker, vandal, or cyberterrorist is just one step behind in his or her ability to defeat the latest security measure. Information system security must be flexible, dynamic, and ever improving, characterized by an organizational culture that not only appreciates the issues associated with information security, but encourages and supports the types of work processes, upfront expenses, and awareness training consistent with change.

Review Questions

1. What are the major principles of risk analysis? List the common steps in developing a risk analysis strategy.
2. Define the following terms in relation to information security: integrity, authenticity, confidentiality, and availability.
3. What is a firewall? Identify and explain some of the functions of a firewall.
4. What is TCP/IP?
5. What are the limitations of a firewall?
6. What is encryption and hashing, and how are they used to secure data and information?
7. How does a digital signature enhance authenticity and integrity of data?
8. How are new security technologies altering the face of user identification?

Endnotes

1. HOLLINGER, R.C. (1997). *Crime, Deviance, and the Computer.* Brookfield, VT: Dartmouth Publishing Company.
2. LEVY, S. (1984). *Hackers: Heroes of the Computer Revolution.* New York: Dell Publishing; and HAFNER, K., and LYON, M. (1996). *Where Wizards Stay Up Late: The Origins of the Internet.* New York: Touchstone.
3. A fire in the data center was the ultimate disaster. Spraying water onto running computers would destroy them as surely as fires. A "dry" chemical called Halon™ and later CO_2 fire suppression systems were, and still are, used to protect data centers.
4. Computers generate large amounts of heat. Heat adversely affects the operation of computers when it builds up. Even the earliest computer required massive refrigeration systems and special floor-vent air conditioning systems. Failure of the air conditioner meant failure of the computer.
5. BLOOMBECKER, B. (1990). *Spectacular Computer Crimes: What They Are and How They Cost American Business Half a Billion Dollars a Year.* Homewood, IL: Dow Jones-Irwin; and PARKER, D.B. (1976). *Crime by Computer.* New York: Scribner.
6. LEVY, *Hackers.*
7. LOPER, D.K. (2000). "The Criminology of Computer Hackers: A Qualitative and Quantitative Analysis." *Dissertation Abstracts International* 61(8): AAT 9985422.
8. HAFNER, K., and MARKOFF, J. (1991). *Cyberpunk: Outlaws and Hackers on the Computer Frontier.* New York: Touchstone; SLATALLA, M., and QUITTNER, J. (1995). *Masters of Deception: The Gang that Ruled Cyberspace.* New York: Harper Collins Publishers; LITTMAN, J., and DONALD, R. (1997). *The Watchman: The Twisted Life and Crimes of Serial Hacker Kevin Poulsen.* Boston, MA: Little, Brown and Company; LITTMAN, J. (1996). *The Fugitive Game: Online with Kevin Mitnick.* New York: Little, Brown and Company; MUNGO, J., and CLOUGH, S. (1992). *Approaching Zero: The Extraordinary Underworld of Hackers, Phreakers, Virus Writers, and Keyboard Criminals.* New York: Random House.
9. SLATALLA and QUITTNER, *Masters of Deception.*
10. HOLLINGER, R.C., and LANZA-KADUCE, L. (1988). "The Process of Criminalization: The Case of Computer Crime Laws." *Criminology* 26: 101–126.
11. HAFNER and LYONS, *Where Wizards Stay Up Late.*
12. COMER, D.E. (1997). *The Internet Book,* 2nd ed. Upper Saddle River, NJ: Prentice Hall Inc.; and BAASE, S. (2003). *A Gift of Fire: Social, Legal, and*

Ethical Issues in Computing, 2nd ed. Upper Saddle River, NJ: Prentice Hall Inc.

13. HOWARD, J.D. (1997). *"An Analysis of Security Incidents on the Internet 1989–1995."* (Doctoral dissertation, Carnegie Mellon University, 1997). Retrieved July 13, 1999 from the World Wide Web: *http://www.cert.org/research/JHThesis/;* and LOTTOR, M. (January 1992). *Internet growth (1981–1991)* (Request for Comments 1296). Menlo Park, CA: SRI. Retrieved July 13, 1999 from the World Wide Web: *http://www.nw.com/ zone/rfc1296.txt*

14. HAFNER, K. (2001). *The Well: A Story of Love, Death and Real Life in the Seminal On line Community.* New York: Carroll & Graf.

15. Free Software Foundation (2001). *Why We Exist.* Retrieved March 15, 2001 from the World Wide Web: *http://www.gnu.org/philosophy/ philosophy.html*

16. The concept of an IRM plan was first introduced in the 1980s, as network systems first emerged. See CORBIN, D. (May 1988). "Strategic IRM Plan: User Involvement Spells Success." *Journal of Systems Management* 39(5): 12–16.

17. See KRAEMER, J., and DANZIGER, K. (January/ February 1984). "Computers and Control in the Work Environment." *Public Administration Review* 44: 32–42; and TAYLOR, R.W. (1989). "Managing Police Information." In D.J. KENNEY (ed.), *Police and Policing: Contemporary Readings.* New York: Praeger Press.

18. Much of this section has been adapted from TAYLOR, R.W., and LOPER, D.K. (2003). "Computer Crime." In C.R. SWANSON, N. CHAMELIN, and L. TERRITO (eds.), *Criminal Investigation,* 8th ed. New York: McGraw-Hill. See also SWANSON, C.R., CHAMELIN, N., TERRITO, L., and TAYLOR, R. (2009). *Criminal Investigation,* 10th ed. New York: McGraw-Hill.

19. RAID comes in many schemes. For other RAID configurations, see *http://www.whatis.com*

20. VACCA, JOHN R. (2006). *Guide to Wireless Network Security.* New York: Springer.

21. *Ibid.*

22. *Ibid.*

23. *Ibid.*

24. STEVENS, W.R. (1994). *TCP/IP illustrated: The protocols* (vol. 1). New York: Addison-Wesley.

25. SCHNEIER, B. (1996). *Applied Cryptography: Protocols, Algorithms, and Source Code in C,* 2nd ed. New York: John Wiley & Sons.

26. There are many other methods of on line authentication, including third-party trust-based relationships, token-based authentication, and challenge hand-shake mechanisms, but simple passwords (preshared secrets) illustrate this point well enough.

27. SCHNEIER, *Applied Cryptography.*

28. *Ibid.*

29. *Ibid.*

30. KAUFMAN, E., and NEWMAN, A. (1999). *Implementing IPsec: Making Security Work on VPNs, Intranets, and Extranets.* New York: John Wiley & Sons Inc.

31. GORDON, S., and FORD, R. (2003). "Cyberterrorism?" A white paper distributed by Symantec Corporation, Cupertino, California.

32. HIGGINS, KELLY JACKSON. (2009). "Storm Botnet Makes a Comeback." *Dark Reading. http://www. darkreading.com/security/vulnerabilities/showArt icle.jhtml?articleID=212900543*

33. *Ibid.*

34. PandaLabs (2007). "Malware Infections in Protected Systems." Retrieved November 1, 2007 from *http://research.pandasecurity.com/blogs/ images/wp_pb_malware_infections_in_protected_ systems.pdf*

35. See: *www.cert.org*

CHAPTER 14

Digital Crime and Terrorism

A Forecast of Trends and Policy Implications*

CHAPTER OBJECTIVES

After completing this chapter, you should be able to

- Identify the future trends and issues the criminal justice system will have to contend with regarding digital crime and digital terrorism.

- Be able to discuss the areas of computer crime victimization that are growing in both incidence and prevalence.

- Describe the impact that digital crimes and digital terrorism are likely to have in the future.

- Identify and understand the eight general forecasts that experts believe are likely to occur in the area of computer crime.

- Understand what response the criminal justice system and other governmental agencies should adopt to deal with future issues in digital crime and digital terrorism.

THE IMPACT OF COMPUTER CRIME: THE FUTURE IS NOW

Throughout this text, the authors have noted the significant problem of cybercrime and terror, the motives and actors involved, and diverse agencies tasked with investigation and prosecution

---

*Adapted from papers presented at the First Annual UNC-Charlotte Interdisciplinary Conference on Cybercrime, Charlotte, North Carolina, May 15–16, 2008, and CARTER, DAVID L. and KATZ-BANNISTER, ANDRA J. "Computer Crime: A Forecast of Trends and Policy Implications." Paper presented at the 2003 meeting of the Academy of Criminal Justice Sciences.

of these offenses. Taking this body of knowledge as a whole, it is important to consider how the landscape of cybercrime will look in the future. This vision is highly dependent on the ways that computer technology shifts and changes with time. Specifically, the hyperevolution of technology and networking that fuels e-commerce and communications are quickly co-opted or corrupted by cybercriminals. For example, growth of wireless local area networks (WLANs) has not only increased mobile computing but also has made networks easier to penetrate by outsiders. As noted in Chapter 4, hackers engage in war driving, where persons drive through a community with a wireless network card in a laptop computer activated in order to detect the presence of a wireless network.[1] The "war drivers" then attempt to access the network—often successfully—and use this as a portal to the Internet. Less scrupulous users will also attempt to penetrate the network's computers—essentially a "drive-by hacking." Interestingly, wireless networks are fairly easy to penetrate because they are frequently "open" with no security, apparently to make it easier for the network's users; of course, this makes it easier for the intruder also.

Another technological trend is the increased availability of wireless microintegrated and multifunction devices that have increased storage and networking capacity. The most common illustration of this is the integrated wireless telephone, personal digital assistant (PDA), with full Internet connectivity capability. Given the types of information often kept in PDAs—ranging from credit card numbers to passwords to Social Security numbers and various types of account and financial information—the ability to access this information using a combination of hacking and phreaking skills within the device's operating system by intruders is a threat to be reckoned with. These devices also provide mobile attack platforms, as they can download applications and utilities that can be used to engage in hacking. For example, the Apple iPod Touch has Internet connectivity and supports a variety of hacker tools, making it an excellent device to engage in covert mobile hacking from a coffee shop or private network. The presence of these devices, integrated with WLANs and combined with the growth of e-commerce and e-government, makes the probability of technological criminality even more pervasive.

Finally, there is a significant growth in the number of home computers using broadband access to the Internet. Generally speaking, whenever these computers are booted, they are connected to the Web, whether being used or not by the owner. Moreover, home computers are less likely to have security (such as a firewall), or if they have security, it is usually a form that is easier to penetrate. Hackers, using port scanners, can identify computers connected to the Web and can conceivably access personal and financial information. If, for example, a person manages his or her banking account and pays bills using a program such as QuickBooks, then the intruder could easily access those files and obtain a significant amount of information that could be used in frauds or other forms of identity theft. Essentially, the growth in capacity, speed, and ease of computerization and networking will also contribute to the speed of exploitation by offenders. The brief history of computer crime has shown that offenders are faster and more adaptable than law enforcement in using the technology.

With this in mind, this chapter will consider and explore the trends, needs, and issues related to cybercrime and terror in the future through the use of forecasts. The forecasts provided here were developed using inductive logic based on existing knowledge and trends within computer crime, criminal justice, and national security. Two important limitations to the forecasts are the lack of empirical data and the inability to be precise in anticipating incidents of computer crime. Forecasts of behavior—like weather forecasts—often lack pinpoint precision, but they can help prepare a response and minimize damage from a phenomenon. Using the small, but growing, knowledge of the incidence, methods, dispersion, character, and trends of computer crime, we can begin to make some assertions as to the future of computer crime and terror. The discussion provided here is not, however, based on scientifically categorized data, methodological controls, or rigorous analysis to explore the validity of typological constructs. In essence, the literature contains logical speculation and assumptions, but virtually no data or information collected and analyzed under controlled methods. It should be noted that these limitations are recognized by the authors, as is the problem of poor data sources and the lack of a uniform reporting system for computer-related crimes.

Other important factors limit the ability to analyze or collect valid and reliable quantitative data. One significant factor is the difficulty—and sometimes impossibility—of determining when a computer crime has occurred, for example, the undetected incursion of a system by a cracker or the undetected theft of intellectual property by an employee who copies files to removable media. Another factor is the tendency of businesses to not report computer-related crimes that have been detected. There are several reasons for this: In some cases, businesses view this simply as a "loss" or even an expense, but not a crime. In other cases, businesses hold the perspective that offenders will not be caught due to the difficulty of investigation, thus reporting the crime would be "wasted effort." Perhaps, however, one of the more fundamental reasons is the fear that publicity of computer crime victimization would undermine the confidence of the company's clients.[2]

THE FUTURE OF DIGITAL CRIME AND DIGITAL TERRORISM: FORECASTS

Based on the analysis of information collected in this study, the authors have developed eight primary forecasts related to computer crime.

FORECAST 1

The number of offenses reported to the police involving computers and electronic storage media will continue to increase substantially, requiring changing priorities for resource allocation, new training for line officers and investigators, new police specialties, and new knowledge for prosecuting attorneys and judges.

Perhaps a keyword in this forecast is "require." The number of police agencies with a high-tech or computer crime unit has increased significantly over the last few years.[3] In addition, prosecutors and judges are becoming increasingly well versed in computer crime and the unique law and vagaries inherent in these cases. That being said, it is unknown how well state and local law enforcement agencies are equipped to handle these offenses.

A recent study of forensic examiners found that they are regularly overworked and experience stress related to their work.[4] In fact, more than half of the individuals contacted felt that they did not have the workforce to complete their tasks at work.[5] The examiners felt that their work would be challenged by others and that there are other ways to accomplish their jobs. Additionally, examiners recognize that they need greater training to keep up with the rapid changes in computer technology.[6] Resources are always in demand within policing agencies, but computer crime units appear to suffer disproportionately at this point in time due to the various resources needed to appropriately image and analyze digital evidence (see Box 14.1).

A reasoned, analytic assessment documenting criminal incidents in a jurisdiction would give meaningful insight on which to make basic decisions. Ideally, a routinized data collection system—perhaps similar to the National Crime Survey managed by the U.S. Department of Justice, Bureau of Justice Statistics (BJS)—to include computer crimes would be a useful planning tool. Such a survey has been developed and implemented in the business community in 2005. The Bureau of Justice Statistics conducted the first National Computer Security Survey, drawing 7,818 responses from businesses around the country.[7] This study found that 67 percent of the businesses sampled experienced at least one cybercrime in 2005, with most of the sample experiencing a computer virus. Almost 90 percent of the respondents sustained some form of monetary loss, with most experiencing a loss of $10,000 or more.[8] However, only 15 percent of victimized businesses reported the event to law enforcement agencies. This suggests that businesses are still very unlikely to report a compromise or attack to law enforcement. Furthermore, it is important to consider that less than 25 percent of the businesses contacted actually participated in the survey.[9] Thus, there is a great deal of improvement needed in our understanding of the prevalence and incidence of cybercrime.

More useful, however, would be a system of collecting data on reported cyber offenses by jurisdiction. This would permit crime analysis for a better understanding of jurisdiction-specific offenses, offenders, and targets. As we have learned with predatory crime, deployment of personnel and resources is most effective when based on crime analysis. There is hope, however, in the National Incident-Based Reporting System (NIBRS), which is a national criminal incident–reporting system designed to replace the FBI's Uniform Crime Report (UCR).[10] NIBRS reporting collects data from local law enforcement agencies on each incident reported to police, including persons involved, property, weapons used, tools, and other information, which is then aggregated to provide general trend data. There is some value in NIBRS for the investigation of computer crime, as officers can indicate whether a computer is used as an object in the crime and whether offenders used computer equipment to perpetrate the offense. This is a significant step forward for the documentation of computer crime, though it is important to note that this system is not in use in many agencies across the nation. As of 2003, only 23 states were certified to provide data to NIBRS, and many of these were not fully compliant.[11] As a result, it may be some time before NIBRS data can provide insights into the scope of computer crimes nationwide.

Judicial, prosecutorial, and investigative officials as well as scholars and computer security specialists knowledgeable about cybercrime should perform a comprehensive review of criminal laws and procedure related to the unique character of computer crime. Additionally, hypothesized voids in a jurisdiction's penal code and anticipation of changes that may be required in response to technological evolution need to be conducted continually. Current computer crime laws will become dated or expanded as greater integration of computers, telecommunications, and entertainment networks occurs. For example, the recent suicide of Megan Meier, discussed throughout this text, demonstrated the ways that computer crime laws may be uniquely applied in prosecutions. Lori Drew, the woman responsible for the creation of the fraudulent MySpace account that sent Megan hurtful messages was prosecuted under the Computer Fraud and Abuse Act. Specifically, it was argued that she engaged in an act of unauthorized computer access because she violated the MySpace site's terms of service by creating a false account. Though the jury in this case found Drew guilty, many legal scholars have questioned if this is an appropriate use of the law, and the judge in the case has not yet rendered a decision.[12] Thus, this is an excellent example of the ways that laws are developed, challenged, and pursued in relation to computer crime.

Similarly, with more databases, information systems, multimedia, and integration software, defining criminal offenses, and even distinguishing what is criminal and what is civil, will become

BOX 14.1

Responding to Computer Crime

The following scenario will better describe the current situation: A business owner arrives at the office and discovers that locked filing cabinets have been broken into, and some documents have been destroyed and others stolen. The owner, suffering losses from both the forced entry, damage, and theft, calls the police, reporting a burglary. A patrol officer responds to take an offense report; a crime scene technician may be called to search for and collect physical evidence. In all likelihood, a burglary detective will conduct a follow-up investigation by reviewing the evidence, interviewing the victim, checking leads from the burglary's *modus operandi,* and perhaps checking with informants. The police have a defined response procedure with personnel fully trained to report and investigate the crime.

Now, assume the same business owner calls the police to report that the office computer has been hacked, and some files have been destroyed and others stolen. What would the police response be? The losses are essentially same, except that the first crime was physical, the second virtual. In the first case, the burglar may have used a crowbar on the door and the file cabinets; in the second case, the thief used only keystrokes.

When confronted with this scenario, one investigator said that many police departments would probably refer the victim to another agency. The investigator went on to say that he regularly received calls from victims outside of his jurisdiction saying they had been referred by another police department. These cases usually take a lower priority, which is likely to anger the citizen. What has made police agencies willing to respond immediately to a burglary, yet show hesitation and less than a full response to a computer crime? This is clearly inconsistent with the contemporary "customer-oriented" philosophy of community policing. Why should a virtual community be different from a physical community? Several factors apparently exist: Uncertainty of jurisdiction, lack of knowledge about computer crimes generally, and having a perspective that this is not a "real problem" are clear issues. Others include the lack of trained personnel who know the questions to ask and how to process a computer-based crime scene, the lack of knowledge and skill to analyze the computer forensically, and the lack of follow-up resources (such as informants) to "work" the case. While police officials would not consider denying a response to a burglary, they will deny a response to a computer crime.

more complex. Among other issues that may need to be reassessed are privacy issues, a redefinition of open records, changes in Freedom of Information law and processes, and new applications of liability law to law enforcement personnel.

New policies are needed to resolve questions of jurisdiction, the expenditure of resources in multijurisdictional investigations of network incursions, and multijurisdictional cooperation. Creative new policy areas must also be explored. For example, should a corporate computer crime victim be responsible for any costs of the investigation if the crime was due, in part, to inadequate computer security?[13] If so, how are these issues decided? Would the criminal justice system be better served if computer crime investigation and prosecution were privatized? Are state or regional computer crime units the best mechanism to deal with this problem? If so, how are they funded, and what are the boundaries of their jurisdiction? These and other policy issues must realistically be considered.

Training and expertise development obviously go hand in hand. At a basic level, during pre-service training related to criminal investigations, police officers need to be trained to regularly look for computers and removable storage media as evidence. They also need to know how to protect and collect cyber evidence as well as the elements of computer crimes and information needed in preparing reports of these offenses. At a more advanced level, training is needed for computer crime investigators—for example, understanding networks, tracing audit trails, dissecting telecommunications systems, tracing wireless transmissions, and associated other technical aspects that may be encountered. Similarly, if a police agency is large enough to have a crime laboratory, it is of sufficient size to warrant a trained computer forensic analyst.[14] Essentially, the model used to investigate and forensically analyze evidence for physical crimes should also be used for virtual crimes. Similarly, judges and prosecutors need to have training on the character and unique aspects of computer crime in order to handle these cases fairly and effectively.

With these aspects of training, necessary expertise will be developed. Police agencies might also consider some changes in personnel management. Is it better to take a trained investigator and teach him/her the technical aspects of computers and networking or to employ a computer expert and teach that person about law, investigation, and criminal case development? Maybe a hybrid model would be better wherein nonsworn computer specialists are hired as in-house technical consultants assigned to computer crime investigations. Another aspect of expertise may lead to computer crime prevention specialists. Since there are clear methods—both technical and behavioral—which can be used to prevent cybercrime, the investment of expertise in this arena may be a functional addition to other crime prevention initiatives. Each jurisdiction must evaluate its needs and follow the avenue that best serves its goals.

Training new personnel and developing new expertise obviously lead to resource allocation issues. In all likelihood, most agencies are not going to be given generous new budget lines to address these issues. Where will the money come from? Realistically, resources will have to be redirected from other departmental programs. Difficult questions of resource redistribution must be undertaken with careful study. In any such redistribution, there are issues that go beyond finances, including "turf," vested interests, and other crime concerns. Changing and rapidly advancing technology results in the need to keep training up to date, which can be quite costly.

The need to share expertise and resources in computer crime investigations appears inevitable for most law enforcement agencies. This sharing will likely extend beyond the interaction of government agencies and includes the need to work with the private sector. This raises some complicated issues related to the payment of expenses, privacy, and the parameters describing the types of cases and/or circumstances where external agencies and private companies are used. All aspects of these issues need to be fully explored and articulated in mutual aid pacts (where assistance between agencies is exchanged *quid pro quo*) and contracts (where financial reimbursement is provided.)

FORECAST 2

The largest computer crime problem affecting local law enforcement representing the largest number of victims and the largest monetary loss will be Internet fraud, including fraud via identity theft.

This forecast should not be interpreted as diminishing other forms of computer crime. In fact, the majority of computer crime cases investigated by local law enforcement are child pornography or exploitation related. However, given the current experiences and trends with e-commerce, online trading, and a virtual buffet of other financial schemes coupled with the growth of personal computing, it appears fraud is the offense most likely to touch the largest number of community members. A recent study by the Federal Trade Commission found that 8.3 million adults in the United States were victims of identity theft in 2005.[15] Additionally, consumers lost $1.2 billion due to fraud in 2007 alone, with average losses of over $300 per victim. Increasingly, local police agencies will receive complaints on these offenses with the expectation that reporting and an investigation will occur, just as would be the case of a noncomputer crime. As noted previously, most local law enforcement agencies are not able to comprehensively respond to and investigate Internet fraud case, due to the increased likelihood that the offenders reside in another state or nation.

With home Internet access becoming more common and more people using e-commerce resources to buy, sell, and trade money and goods, the probability of Internet fraud and identity theft has increased significantly. In fact, there have been several instances of large companies experiencing a mass compromise of data by computer hackers. The TJX Corporation lost over 50 million customer credit accounts due to hackers accessing a sensitive database in 2007.[16] In 2009, Heartland Payment Systems, Inc., a credit payment processing system, lost over 100 million credit and debit cards due to hackers using malicious software to steal data.[17] The huge volume of data obtained in both of these instances suggests that consumers around the world can be affected by fraud through little fault of their own. Furthermore, the growth of carding markets discussed in Chapter 5 allows computer criminals to buy and sell fraudulently obtained information and suggests that an individual can become the victim of fraud several times over.[18] Frauds—and other Internet crimes—will increase simply because the massive size of the Internet makes monitoring or spotting potential fraudulent schemes difficult. For example, the recent economic downturn has facilitated opportunities for fraud. The merger of multiple national financial institutions has produced confusion over what company holds an individual's account. As a result, phishers and fraudsters have begun to send fraudulent e-mails stating that the consumer needs to provide the acquiring bank with their account information in order to keep the account active.[19] Such threats are not unique, but rather emphasize the ways that the Internet enables fraudsters to dynamically act on changes and world events to victimize consumers.

Even with technological monitoring techniques of keyword targeting, the size and dynamic character of the Internet presents major barriers. These barriers are aggravated by the difficulty of transjurisdictional investigations and communications. A fraud scheme targeting Americans, and operated by American criminals, may have a Web site based in a country such as Myanmar, which has virtually no Internet monitoring and only casual relations with U.S. law enforcement authorities. This will hamper investigations, and U.S. authorities can do little except provide warnings to citizens.

Finally, it is relatively easy to create a fraudulent enterprise on the Internet with minimal cost. Even sophisticated malicious software tools can be readily purchased through online black markets to facilitate fraud, as discussed in Chapter 6. As a result, the range of people who can create a virtual fraud is quite broad. Moreover, the inability to readily determine the authenticity of claims or organizations helps further the fraud. Recently, a range of fraudulent e-mails were circulated, claiming to contain tax refunds from the Internal Revenue Service or tracking information from Federal Express or the Postal Service. These schemes caught a number of victims because of the issue of authenticity.[20] This is particularly true when the scheme is related to alleged changes in technology-related businesses, such as Initial Public Offerings (IPOs), new mergers, or new products. Technology businesses and stocks have been so profitable in recent years that many people feel a sense of urgency to complete a transaction while the opportunity is "hot." As a result, they frequently do not take the time to verify the offer's legitimacy. To further the appearance of legitimacy, the Web site may include fallacious quotes from recognized authorities and untrue statements of affiliations with respected businesses to lend further credence to the scheme's legitimacy.

The inherent character of the Internet and the expansion of the global economy, particularly related to technology issues, are fueling the growth of Internet fraud. The most effective tool for dealing with Internet fraud is prevention. The need to inform consumers of the potential for and character of fraud, notification of newly emerging fraud schemes, and precautions before investing or purchasing over the Internet are among the proactive approaches a local law enforcement agency may pursue. Delivery of this information could be from the police agency's Web page, creation of a listserv that describes newly discovered fraud schemes, and public service announcements. The Federal Trade Commission, FBI, the not-for-profit Anti-Phishing Working Group (APWG), and other entities are working to provide consumers with information to improve awareness of fraud. The significant point to note is that investigating Internet fraud is extraordinarily difficult, with a comparatively low rate of clearance. A comprehensive prevention strategy is the most efficacious approach to the problem.[21]

FORECAST 3

Virtual crimes against persons will increase at a faster rate compared with past years as a result of the significant expansion in networking, personal computing, and social networking sites. These hybrid crimes, which have coercive characteristics similar to those found in psychological warfare, will require new laws expressly to address the problem and new methodologies for investigation, prevention, and education.

Virtual crimes against persons encompass diverse behaviors; however, the common factors of these behaviors are (1) use of networking and (2) a manifestation of social-psychological dynamics. Networking is a key factor because this is the medium through which the behavior is facilitated, most frequently by e-mail but also through social networking sites like MySpace, video- and photo-sharing sites, bulletin board services (BBSs), and Web site postings (particularly hate and pedophilia). One survey by the Novell Corporation found that 50 percent of the respondents had received unwanted e-mail from a persistent sender. Thirty-five percent of the offending messages contained unsolicited pornography."[22]

The social-psychological factors take diverse forms. For example, cyberstalking and threats induce fear, while harassment can induce anger. Cyberbullying can produce depression, embarrassment, shame, or sadness. Hate messages can produce discriminatory behavior, and pedophilia can engender exploitation and intimidation. Interestingly, these behaviors are similar to the common law definition of assault. As a U.S. government report of the problem observed, "Make no mistake: This kind of harassment can be as frightening and as real as being followed and watched in your neighborhood or in your home."[23]

The manifestation of virtual crimes against persons is the product of several factors. First, virtual crimes against persons are easy and convenient. The offense may be committed immediately without leaving home, and gratification is instantaneous. The offender may also take action without physically confronting the victim. For instance, a person who posts a mean or hurtful message, picture, or video in a social networking site can harm another person without ever having to physically interact with them. In turn, they may gain status from people within their virtual social network.

In all likelihood there are people who have a propensity to commit a retaliatory act of some form, but do not because of reluctance to confront another physically. It is therefore probable that some of those people would act on that propensity through networking. In fact, a recent national study of youth found that children are experiencing greater levels of online harassment, largely from their peers, and are increasingly engaging in harassing behaviors themselves.[24] Thus, the problem of person crimes online is likely to continue to increase.

Just as the offense may be committed without confrontation, it may also be committed with relative anonymity. The anonymity is obviously sought to protect the identity of the offender, but anonymity can add to the victim's fear. There are various techniques that may be used to maintain one's anonymity in networked communications, the easiest of which is sending threatening or harassing e-mail through a Web site that obfuscates the SMTP audit trail.[25] Also contributing to the anonymity of these virtual offenses is the fact that there is no physical evidence of the crime, such as a fingerprint on the paper of a threatening letter or DNA from saliva on an envelope. Neither are there voice nor handwriting specimens from the offender that may be used as evidence. Consequently, developing a criminal case that can meet the burden of proof in court becomes challenging.

One of the potential factors factor contributing to the growth of virtual crimes against persons is the increasing loss of privacy that is occurring through online sources. When greater personal information is available about an individual, it is easier for an offender to locate them. Even more problematic is the fact that individuals voluntarily provide details about themselves and their lives through social networking sites. Facebook and MySpace are especially popular among young people, and a recent study found that a small percentage of youth share personal information, such as their name, address, or school name with others online.[26] Additionally, five percent posted images of themselves in underwear or a bathing suit, and 15 percent shared photos of their peers in similar states of dress. This simplifies the process of monitoring and tracking individuals on- and off-line.

Moreover, if an offender provides personal information about the victim in a harassing message—such as a description and license number of the victim's car, a Social Security number, or information about the victim's family—then a cyber assault can become even more frightening. As the prevalence of these crimes increase, they must be analyzed to determine the adequacy of existing law and policy to deal with them effectively. While they may not produce physical harm, the psychological damage, fear, and anxiety can be debilitating.

On a final note, the likelihood is strong that there will be an increase in "virtual workplace violence." A great deal of physical workplace violence appears to be retaliatory acts toward the organization and/or individuals who are perceived to have "wronged" the offender. It is clearly probable that employees with access to critical databases and/or information systems could vent their retaliation by the destruction of those files. Similarly, harassment and the creation of a hostile work environment can now be accomplished electronically.

Given the increasing threat posed by person-based computer crimes, legal structures must change to provide appropriate legal frameworks for prosecution. Though there are laws in place related to cyberstalking and harassment, increasing attention is being paid to bullying and the development of an appropriate legislative response. As discussed in Chapter 7, California passed a law giving school administrators the ability to discipline students for bullying other students on- or off-line.[27] Though this is the first legislation produced at the state level, legal scholars argue that others will adopt similar structures, and there may be potential federal legislation enacted. Thus, there is likely to be an increase in laws pertaining to person-based cybercrimes.

FORECAST 4

Computer hacker groups will emerge in developing countries around the world, increasing the threat of malicious attacks motivated by religion, politics, and money.

The basis of this forecast lies in the increasing penetration of Internet connectivity around the world, coupled with the characteristics of the hacker subculture and the increased access to sophisticated hacker tools. As of 2009, there are over 1.59 trillion Internet users around the world, with the greatest number in North America, Australia, and Europe.[28] These continents have a substantial number of developed nations, though developing nations are increasingly gaining access to the Internet. In fact, the Middle East, Africa, and Latin America have experienced between 800 and 1,000 percent growth in Internet connections since 2000.[29] These figures clearly illustrate the fact that soon most parts of the world will be online.

With this in mind, there is increasing evidence of hacker groups in emerging nations forming and connecting with others in the established world. This is accomplished because of the borderless nature of the Internet. An individual with an interest in technology in Turkey or Costa Rica can search the Web to find groups that share common interests. That interest may be in using certain types of computers, cracking specific types of systems, supporting a specific cause—such as opposition to government controls on the Internet—or simply a self-selected group who feel their hacking skills are greater than others and who hack into challenging systems as a demonstration of their abilities. In furtherance of their common interest, they share techniques and may even agree on a specific plan to accomplish their hacking goals.

As a consequence, strong and established hacker communities can support and improve the skills of emerging hacker groups through guides, tutorials, software, and other materials. These resources can rapidly accelerate the skill and ability of a hacker and make it much easier for these individuals to engage in malicious attacks. Additionally, the free exchange of information can also lead hackers in established communities to borrow and find tools in emerging communities. For example, a recent study found that hacker tools to automate denial-of-service (DoS) attacks made in Guatemala, Argentina, and Chile were being used and advertised in hacker Web forums in Russia and China.[30] Additionally, this study found that a binding tool created by a hacker in France was quickly adopted by hacker groups in the Middle East and China. The emergence of malicious software and stolen data markets also allow hackers to buy and sell tools that may be beyond their ability to create on their own. As a result, the globalization of hacking may prove to become a significant threat to networks around the world.

Given the diverse number of nations becoming active in the global hacker community, it is critical to consider how these hackers will use their skills. There is increasing evidence that hacker groups from Muslim majority nations are hacking to facilitate a religious or political agenda. For example, the publication of a cartoon satirizing the Prophet Mohammad in a Danish newspaper in 2005 led to a number of cyber attacks against different resources. By February 2006, Zone-h recorded almost 3,000 attacks against Danish Web sites, primarily by Turkish hackers. In addition, the al-Ghorabaa site coordinated a 24-hour DoS attack against *Jyllands-Posten,* the newspaper that first published the cartoons, and other newspapers in Denmark.[31] Other hackers may, however, be motivated by monetary gain and steal bank accounts and sensitive intellectual property in order to sell the information to others. Still others may have an interest in legitimate security applications of hacking and use their knowledge to benefit the larger community. It is important to note, however, that the variations in motivation will be difficult to discern based solely on country of origin.

As the hacker community expands around the globe, this will exacerbate the challenges faced by law enforcement agencies. Developing nations may not have laws in place against computer crimes, making prosecution unlikely and extradition complicated. The investigation, prosecution, and communication between law enforcement and intelligence organizations must also be better coordinated in order to effectively handle the changing landscape of threats.

FORECAST 5

Current organized crime groups, particularly those that are entrepreneurial, will increasingly adopt computerization as a criminal instrument.

Interpol defines organized crime as any enterprise or group of persons engaged in a continuing illegal activity that has as its primary purpose the generation of profits and continuance of the enterprise regardless of national boundaries.[32] Key factors in this definition with respect to the forecast are that organized crime groups are *entrepreneurial* and that they exist to make a profit. Just like legitimate businesses, organized crime groups have consistently used methods that will enhance efficiency and effectiveness to achieve profits. Many methods are illegal—such as use of violence, corruption, or fraud—yet legal methods are also used, such as stock investments, purchase of real estate, and other principles common to legitimate businesses for distribution and marketing of a commodity. Globally, the character of organized crime is evolving into this entrepreneurial model. Traditional images of organized crime as a "Mafia-like" entity are dated, not reflecting the vast amount of organized criminal activity occurring around the world today. To neither recognize nor respond to this change is to perpetuate a myth. Law enforcement agencies must be proactive in devoting resources and attention to organized crime as entrepreneurial criminal enterprise. Based on information collected in this study, there is documented use of computerization by organized crime groups in several areas (see Figure 14.1). As in the past, opportunistic organized crime groups will exploit any possible illegal avenues for increased profit.

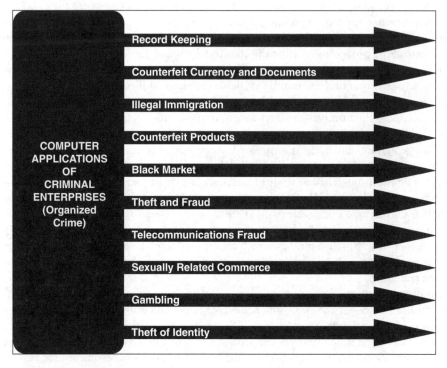

FIGURE 14.1   Uses of computers by organized crime groups.

RECORD KEEPING   Evidence by law enforcement and intelligence organizations have found crime groups keeping computerized records in a manner similar to businesses, using spreadsheets and databases. Records that have been discovered include contraband shipment schedules; income and expenses of contraband or commodities; databases of conspirators and "customers"; locations, account numbers, and status of monetary transactions (typically, money being laundered); records of monetary transfers and payments; databases and "status" of bribed or vulnerable officials; and database dossiers of officials, conspirators, and others in whom the crime group has an interest.[33]

COUNTERFEIT CURRENCY AND DOCUMENTS   Computer technology has provided a revolution in the counterfeit currency and document business. Because of color scanners, color printers, sophisticated word processing and graphics software suites, and computer-driven color photocopiers, successful counterfeiting has not only significantly broadened but has also become much more difficult to detect. As an example, at one point the U.S. $100 bill was the most frequently counterfeited currency in the world. With computerized counterfeiting, the global market was becoming flooded with counterfeit $100 bills (particularly Central and Eastern Europe). As a result, the U.S. Treasury changed the bill's design and incorporated a watermark (like most of the rest of the world's currency) and other security factors. It was announced by the Treasury Department that the new $100 bill was virtually impossible to counterfeit. Within a month of the new bill's introduction into circulation, good counterfeit copies surfaced in Eastern Europe. High-resolution color scanning of an original can even pick up the watermark and colors of fibers in the paper, which are, in turn, reproduced by high-resolution printers.

The same scanning process and graphics software are used for counterfeit passports. Counterfeiters maintain scanned masters of various passports in computer files and are then able to readily enter appropriate names, photographs, and identity information in the files to prepare a high-quality counterfeit.[34] Because the counterfeits are near the quality of legitimate documents and the process of creating the counterfeits is fast, the enterprise yields high profits. In fact, the online organized crime group the ShadowCrew sold identity documents through their Web forum as part of the resources available to engage in identity theft and fraud. In some cases, criminal enterprises offer a "package" to people who are illegally immigrating to Europe. One price includes the immigration documents, transportation, and an escort.

An additional technique in counterfeiting involves unique electronic devices and information to engage in fraud and theft. Specifically, hacker groups and computer fraudsters have begun to steal bank and credit account numbers, called dumps (outlined in Chapter 5). These dumps can be obtained online through a mass compromise, data breach, or phishing attack. This information can also be acquired in the real world through the use of electronic devices that capture the data obtained on a credit card's magnetic strip. These tools are called skimmers, as they skim information off of a card as it passes through the reader. In turn, the illegally acquired dumps can be placed onto blank plastic cards, called plastics, which can be used to make purchases in the real world. In fact, there are groups that sell counterfeit credit cards that have been printed and embossed to match the real thing.[35]

Another unique application of the technology has been found to make new certificates of origin and titles of stolen vehicles using the actual vehicle identification number (VIN) of the stolen auto. As with passports, master files of documents are scanned into a computer. They are then printed using the stolen vehicle's description and VIN along with the new "owner's" identification. Sophisticated auto theft rings operating from Poland to Morocco have used this method to ship luxury cars to the Mideast and Asia.

ILLEGAL IMMIGRATION   Evidence has indicated that organized crime groups previously involved mostly in black market smuggling have created new processes to smuggle immigrants into Western countries with "appropriate" documentation, typically for a substantial fee. While computers play a comparatively smaller role in these enterprises, they nonetheless help expedite the scheme through the use of such processes as logistics and arrangements via e-mail, computer-forged immigration documents, and general record keeping related to this enterprise.

BLACK MARKET   Outside of its illegal commodities and avoidance of licensing and taxes, the black market operates much like any business. It is market driven; requires suppliers, transportation, and distribution networks; has a payroll; must remain competitive; and is obliged to keep its customers satisfied in order to maintain repeat clientele. Because of similarities to legitimate businesses, organized crime groups involved in the black market have increasingly begun to operate much like legitimate businesses. Such an evolution has occurred in the creation of malicious software production, which is elaborated in Chapter 6.

Just as in any business, the black market needs to make its inventory descriptions known to both the "sales staff" and potential clients. Photographs, product descriptions, costs, inquiry processes, and related information for a wide variety of "commodities" have been found in computer files; in a few cases, the files are accessible through a restricted server or Web site. Additionally, some black market merchandise is increasingly available for order through the Internet (under the guise of a legitimate business), vastly expanding the enterprises' market, hence profits. In addition, computerization via networking provides increased anonymity to specific individuals in the criminal group.

COUNTERFEIT PRODUCTS   The extent to which "traditional" organized crime is involved in this area is debatable; however, there is strong evidence that such groups are strongly involved in the "marketing" and distribution of these products in what is referred to by Her Majesty's Customs and Excise Service as the "fakes trade." While skilled craft workers have been quite successful in designing and manufacturing counterfeit products, one area that was frequently relied on by customs and corporate security investigators was product logos and subtle design and coloration characteristics to distinguish licensed products from counterfeit ones. This too is changing because of computer technology.

As in the case of counterfeit currency and documents, criminal enterprises have been using color scanners and computer-driven color printers to scan legitimate logos, product tags, and such things as "jackets" and labels of videotapes, audio tapes, and software. Using the scanned images as masters, skilled printers are able to prepare these materials to legitimize the appearance of the counterfeit products. One corporate security director told the authors that while this process was an additional "wrinkle" for investigators to overcome, the intent of the counterfeiter was to make the product look more legitimate to the consumer. With packaging that makes the product appear authentic, the enterprise could sell more of their counterfeit products at higher prices and still undercut the legitimate manufacturer's sales.

SEXUALLY RELATED COMMERCE   New criminal enterprises have emerged, largely consisting of intelligent young entrepreneurs who are familiar with the capabilities and potential of computers as a tool for sexual commerce. While these emerging groups may not fit neatly into traditional definitions of organized crime, they nonetheless are ongoing enterprises that are frequently violating the criminal law in order to gain a profit. A problem exists, however, because many activities of these groups fall into the gray area of law. Some of their activities may be lawful in their country of origin but unlawful in countries serving their clientele. Because of these legal ambiguities and the fact that sexual commerce is viewed as being less serious than other forms of crime, comparatively little attention is given to these groups.

Using the Internet to arrange for prostitution is one of the more common enterprises. This includes not only logistical arrangements (i.e., appointments) but even payment by credit card using e-commerce protocols. The process is discreet and safer for both the "service provider" and "customer." In one case, a criminal enterprise using a server based in Amsterdam was arranging for prostitutes in both London and Frankfurt. Although the enterprise has been closed, it was difficult because of limitations inherent in dealing with multinational jurisdictions. One investigator stated that if the enterprise had been based in a non-European Union country, it would probably still be in operation.

GAMBLING   It is only natural that entrepreneurial criminals would turn to computerization—particularly the Internet—in order to expand their gambling operations and profits. A recent estimate indicates that online gambling revenues were $14.71 billion in 2005 alone.[36] While these amounts reflect largely legitimate gaming, there are complicating factors. For example, the gaming may be lawful in the location where the gambling is based but unlawful in the jurisdiction of some of its customers. With the potential profits to be reaped combined with low overhead costs and comparative anonymity afforded by the Internet, the likelihood of criminal involvement in gambling will grow significantly, particularly in those locations where taxes and governmental regulation can be avoided through corruption or intimidation.

At this point it appears that most unlawful computerized gaming operations—notably in North America and Asia—are not on the Internet but accessible via modem directly into a server (albeit using Internet protocols). However, accessibility to such operations is increasingly available through the Internet using virtual private network (VPN) access for security (largely from authorities) and to ensure payment for services. The expanded capacity for multimedia hardware and software is particularly fueling sites by enabling more effective simulation of video gaming machines.

Typically the user must "join a club" to be given access to the site for gambling. Part of the membership ruse is to pay "dues," which are used as bets. Most typically gamblers supply a credit card number wherein they can purchase "units" to wager—units are essentially electronic poker chips. In some cases, when a member joins and is given his or her personal identification number, he or she can then make a deposit—either by wire or money order—to a front company, which serves as the "bank" for the gambling operation. All bets and communications are then conducted via the computer link. When the gambler wins, he or she is typically given credits, which can be used for further wagers, or he or she can request payment, typically through the front company, which serves as a bank. Credit card "credits" are not used for two reasons: (1) The gamblers want their winnings quickly in a readily convertible form; and (2) it is feared that the issuance of too many credits to a given card number would raise questions leading to investigation. Interestingly, one investigator said that the financial transaction accounting procedures for unlawful gaming operations were typically quite accurate and reliable. The reason: The enterprise makes money from the "repeat business" of gamblers—if they cannot trust you, they will not bet their money.

IDENTITY THEFT AND FRAUD   As computers play a regular role in financial transactions, criminals are increasingly accessing them unlawfully to transfer funds, defraud, or steal information. The credit cards and financial information obtained through hacks and large database compromises detailed earlier are commonly being used to engage in identity theft and fraud.

Specifically, hackers sell the information they obtain to others, who in turn use the data to access bank accounts and steal money and make fraudulent purchases. The payment systems used to buy and sell these goods are also knowingly or unknowingly complicit in these acts of fraud.

Criminal groups also recognize that stealing intellectual property has merit because it is a valuable commodity. Organized criminals have learned how to market stolen information for high profits and substantially less risk than more traditional illicit commodity trafficking. Theft of information such as trade secrets, new product specifications, product pricing plans, and customer lists have proven to be highly profitable. The cost to a business competitor to pay for this stolen information is far less than original research, development, and marketing. Increasingly active in this arena are criminal enterprises in Japan, the United States, France, and Germany. While these transactions typically do not have the violence and emotional daring associated with more traditional organized crime activities, the economic toll can be far higher.

A third form of fraud facilitated by computers is related to insurance and medical payments. The Florida Division of Insurance Fraud has discovered fraud through altered computer programs that underreport insurance agency incomes. Medical and pharmaceutical overpayments through Medicare/Medicaid have also been fraudulently made in many ways through the altering of computer records and, more commonly, the use of shell companies billing the government for medical services, equipment, and pharmaceuticals. While these forms of theft net significant amounts of money, they typically are not products of broad-based organized crime, although they frequently meet the technical definition of a criminal enterprise. Such offenses are difficult to detect, investigate, and prosecute. Moreover, they engender little emotional outcry from the public. As a result, they offer little risk and high profits—an appealing combination of factors for the entrepreneurial offender.

TELECOMMUNICATIONS FRAUD   Telecommunications fraud is a particularly profitable area of computer-related crime that has many variations. Previously, individual criminal entrepreneurs committed these crimes, but they are increasingly being pushed out by organized crime groups because the profits are so high and the risk is so low. There are four types of telecommunications fraud in which criminal enterprises appear to be most involved. First is the theft of telephone credit card numbers, which can be gained by accessing computer records, some computerized voice mailboxes, and telephone billing files. Prime targets are large multinational corporations, because discovery of the fraudulent billings takes longer. The billing numbers are either sold "on the street" (using "pushers" in the same way as drug dealers) or, as is increasingly the case, sold to other crime groups for their use. In one case, stolen corporate telephone billing numbers from a U.S.-based multinational company were being sold to various drug trafficking groups, which in turn used the stolen numbers to make arrangements for drug transactions and shipments. Payment for the stolen numbers was cheaper than paying for numerous international calls, and it was more difficult for investigators to link the calls to their principal investigative targets.

The second type of telecommunications fraud, which has actually decreased, involves hacking into telecommunications "switches" (which are computers) for the purpose of routing calls and changing billing numbers. While individual hackers still break into switches, organized efforts to do this have largely stopped as a result of more aggressive security precautions by telecommunications carriers and comparatively little profit to be made.

The third area is the largest and fastest growing: wireless phone theft and fraud. This too was started by individuals and small groups but is increasingly involving organized crime groups. The process originally involved the capture of wireless electronic identification numbers (EINs) being transmitted from users' telephones. Using a device which detects and records the number, it could then be sold and programmed into a person's wireless phone. The number is typically usable for about one month before being detected as stolen. The fraudulent user would then need to purchase a new number.

Interviewees stated that because of the large number of wireless telephones in use and the ease with which a large number of EINs could be captured, the process became one of "assembly line theft."[37] Essentially, a "client" pays a flat fee and receives a new billing number each month, or whenever the number they are using is canceled.[38] The "service provider" typically also has the computer equipment to readily reprogram the client's cell phone. Averaging about $30 a month ($60 if a "new" telephone is also obtained) with several hundred clients in a "territory" and several territories within a given geographic area, the profits can add up quickly and, again, with minimal risk.

The fourth type—which has increased significantly—is where organized crime groups have compromised private automatic branch exchanges (PABX) of companies to use telecommunications services for their own benefit.[39] A PABX is the heart of a digital telecommunications system that can include a company's internal phone system, its wireless network, voice mail, e-mail, and internal data network. A criminal enterprise using this system can call anywhere in the world without costs. Moreover, using a compromised system makes it more difficult for investigators to gain a wiretap order or to follow a trail of telephone calls. The growth of phreaking tools available on the Internet and the digital integration of voice and text on servers make this form of telecommunications increasingly accessible. Thus, unlawful use of a PABX not only constitutes a real monetary loss to the victim, it makes investigations of organized crime groups more difficult.

FORECAST 6

Terrorist groups will increasingly use global networking as a tool to accomplish their goals. This includes use of the Internet for recruitment, surreptitious communications, and coordination purposes as well as attempting to use network access to critical infrastructure systems to strike for their cause via the creation of chaos, disinformation, and file destruction—cyberterrorism.

Generally, critical infrastructure components include (1) the continuity of government services; (2) information and communications; (3) banking and finance; (4) electrical power, oil, and gas production/storage; (5) water supply; (6) public health services; (7) emergency services; and (8) transportation. Not surprisingly, most of these services in developed countries rely, in varying degrees, on computerization.

Experts argue that al Qaeda and other Sunni extremists are improving their ability to conduct cyber attacks. In fact, a book published by Mohammad Bin Ahmad As-Salim stated that individuals should engage in electronic jihad through the use of discussion boards for media operations and hacking attacks to strike out and attack against Web sites and information related to American, Jewish, and secular Web sites.[40]

Beyond unlawful intrusions designed to disrupt computer systems, virtually all types of extremist groups—international and domestic—are relying on computers for everything from communicating to spreading propaganda to fund-raising. It is reasonable to conclude that increasing numbers of these groups will, as computer skills and opportunities develop, become involved in some aspect of cyberterrorism or terroristic support. In light of these facts, what are the implications for state and local law enforcement with respect to cyberterrorism? The challenge seems daunting for a local police agency, yet given the omnipresence of computer networking and the ease with which one may digitally traverse the global in nanoseconds, local police must accept this as a part of the challenge they face.

As a consequence, examples of cyberterrorist activity may include use of information technology to organize and carry out attacks, and support a group's activities and perception-management campaigns. For example, extremist groups participating in Jihad against the West have developed Web forums and sites to distribute manuals and tools for hacking and to promote and coordinate cyber attacks. There was also a failed attack billed as an "Electronic Battle of Guantanamo" against American stock exchanges and banks, which was canceled because the banks had been notified.[41]

Clearly, the human tragedy of cyberterrorism has not yet approached that of traditional (physical) terror attacks. Yet the damage to assets, resources, and the fundamental principles of life in an open society for those who rely on such systems is significant. Indeed, *a successful cyber attack can make people begin to question the sanctity, security, and reliability of critical institutions on which we have daily reliance.* The proper functioning of our government and our banking systems are two important examples. Had the "Electronic Battle for Guantanamo" been successful, there may have been a loss of trust in the financial industry and a mass withdrawal of cash, or a run, on banks. Should this occur the banking system could collapse. ATMs, credit cards, and checks could become worthless. Uncertainty about loans and investments would create chaos, and people would be pushed into a "survival mode." This would clearly lead to a growth in fear and possibly violence as people attempt to protect their assets.

A cyber attack would not need to be nationwide to generate such fear and lack of confidence in public institutions—the attack would only need to be publicized. Fear is irrational—a factor that terrorists rely on. If a cyber attack is successful, it can create chaos, which will translate to fear and eventual destruction of, or at least damage to, our critical infrastructure through distrust and failure to rely on institutions. Table 14.1 depicts different levels of seriousness of perpetrators committing similar types of Web intrusions. The legal implications based on motive,[42] as manifest by the character of the attacker, vary significantly.

TABLE 14.1   Characterizations of a Cyber Attack

Perpetrator	Intrusive Act	Legal Interpretation
Computer crackerHactivist	Compromise a financial services Web site to steal sensitive information	Computer fraud, unauthorized access
	Defaces Web page of private company to promote a political belief	Criminal mischief or destruction of property
Racist group	Defaces Web page of a minority organization with racial epithets	Hate crime; possibly ethnic intimidation
Organized crime group	Sends out spam for a small company with low stock price to artificially increase the value, then sell their shares at the inflated price, with contributions going to the crime group	Theft by a continuing criminal enterprise; possibly RICO violation
al Qaeda	Attacks multiple banking Web sites, web defacement to threaten future attacks against Americans similar to 9/11	Terrorism/terroristic threat

FORECAST 7

The character of espionage will continue to broaden into the arenas of information warfare, economic espionage, and theft of intellectual property.

A U.S. Department of Defense study on emerging threats to national security observed that the field of battle is increasingly moving away from political ideology and geographic control and toward economic issues.[43] The essence of national security is to maintain the homeostasis of a country's sovereign principles and socioeconomic health. In a global economy punctuated by multinational corporations and international dependence, this homeostasis is inextricably related to economic stability.

In making a link between cybercriminality and national security, the Director of the U.S. Defense Intelligence Agency (DIA) observed:

A growing array of state and non-state adversaries are increasingly targeting—for exploitation and potentially disruption or destruction—our information infrastructure, including the Internet, telecommunications networks, computer systems, and embedded processors and controllers in critical industries. Over the past year, cyber exploitation activity has grown more sophisticated, more targeted, and more serious. The Intelligence Community expects these trends to continue in the coming year.

We assess that a number of nations, including Russia and China, have the technical capabilities to target and disrupt elements of the US information infrastructure and for intelligence collection. Nation states and criminals target our government and private sector information networks to gain competitive advantage in the commercial sector. Terrorist groups, including al-Qa'ida, HAMAS, and Hizballah, have expressed the desire to use cyber means to target the United States. Criminal elements continue to show growing sophistication in technical capability and targeting and today operate a pervasive, mature on-line service economy in illicit cyber capabilities and services available to anyone willing to pay. Each of these actors has different levels of skill and different intentions; therefore, we must develop flexible capabilities to counter each. We must take proactive measures to detect and prevent intrusions from whatever source, as they happen, and before they can do significant damage.

We expect disruptive cyber activities to be the norm in future political or military conflicts . . . Such attacks have been a common outlet for hackers during political disputes over the past decade, including Israel's military conflicts with Hizballah and HAMAS in 2006 and 2008, the aftermath of the terrorist attacks in Mumbai last year, the publication of cartoons caricaturing the Prophet Mohammed in 2005, and the Chinese downing of a US Navy aircraft in 2001."[44]

Global networking adds an important dimension to this problem. John Chambers, president and CEO of Cisco Systems, a leader in producing networking hardware and software, stated, "The Internet levels the playing field between countries . . . regardless of size or political form of government, in a way that has never occurred before." Thus, the threat to national security is significantly increased as we move toward digital economies. This was demonstrated in a recent cyber conflict between Russia and Estonia in 2007. The removal of a war memorial in Estonia led hackers in Russia to engage in DDoS attacks against Estonian embassies, government, and commercial Web sites.[45] Financial and communications systems were knocked off-line, leading to millions of dollars in losses for the Estonian people. These attacks clearly demonstrate the interrelated nature of security and economics in the digital age.

Government policy in Malaysia, Thailand, and Singapore are expressly developing technology centers to become major economic sectors of the global e-economy. A number of countries—notably Japan, China, and France—provide government support to businesses based in their countries through assistance with the surreptitious acquisition of intellectual property. In fact, a coordinated series of attacks on government and private industry contractor systems in the United States occurred in 2003. The attacks, referred to as "Titan Rain," appeared to come from Chinese systems performed by very skilled hackers.[46] Evidence suggests they were able to steal massive amounts of files from NASA, Lockheed Martin, and Sandia National Laboratories in as little as 10–30 minutes, leaving no traces behind. Though little information is available about the content of the data accessed, this demonstrates that intrusions are a serious and very real threat to critical infrastructure and networked systems. Clearly, with the emergence of global networking and the digital economy, the greatest target threat for economic espionage is through cyber attacks on business networks rather than on government installations.

FORECAST 8

Criminals, terrorists, nation-states, patriots, and anarchists will increasingly use technology-based instruments and methodologies, which can surreptitiously capture data/information or destroy technological communications, information processing, and/or storage appliances.

Part of the forecasting process is applying inductive logic to known facts. That logic is based on evidence and the reasonable extension of that evidence to a future state. The authors emphasize this point in the current forecast in light of three important factors. First, all of the technologies discussed in this forecast currently exist—in some cases, for at least two decades or more—yet they were not readily (or even feasibly) usable by criminals or terrorists because of technological complexities and/or limitations. Second, the exceptionally rapid evolution of computer-related technology and miniaturization of hardware and components in the past few years is making these offensive weapons more accessible and easier to use. These factors, coupled with the fiscal resources of criminal enterprises and "wealthy" terrorists,[47] make the development and use of these offensive weapons more probable. Finally, the wide adoption of computers for communications, commerce, information distribution, and information management, and the integration of computer technology into everything from wireless telephones to automobiles, magnifies the potential impact electronic weapons can have on a business, government, or individuals.

Criminals will often take any step possible to gain an advantage over legitimate businesses and processes. For example, drug cartels have been found to use sophisticated weapons, surveillance devices, and intelligence techniques in order to maintain their competitive advantage in the drug trade, whether by undermining competition or attempting to corrupt officials. Since, as discussed previously, criminals are already taking advantage of computers and high-technology communications, it is reasonable to assume they will also adopt technologies that can surreptitiously capture information and/or incapacitate communications, surveillance, and information systems of government entities and businesses.

ELECTROMAGNETIC IMPULSE AND HIGH-ENERGY RADIO FREQUENCY[48]   The phenomenon known as an electromagnetic impulse (EMP) was discovered in the 1940s during the testing of nuclear weapons. Essentially, the EMP disabled electrical devices as a result of the massive electromagnetic field created by the nuclear blast. Research on this phenomenon led to the discovery that an EMP could also be produced by generating a high-energy radio frequency (HERF), typically by using a truck-sized device. The impact of a HERF electromagnetic emission is that any electronic "equipment can be irreversibly damaged or in effect electronically destroyed . . . and may require complete replacement of the equipment."[49] Not only are computers and peripherals subject to destruction by HERF, but so are " . . . radios, satellites, microwave equipment, UHF, VHF, HF, and low band communications and television equipment."[50]

The HERF effect is real, with substantial research on its development as an electronic warfare tool in the United States, England, and Russia and speculated research on it as a weapon in China. The research is not focusing on creating an EMP, per se, but on accurate targeting and miniaturization.[51] Indeed, there has been research in the law enforcement community on the use of HERF as a less-than-lethal weapon that could be used to disable fleeing vehicles. There has also been a wide range of experimentation—typically unsuccessful—by hobbyists in developing homemade, handheld HERF devices. The probability is high that functional and portable HERF devices will be developed in the short term. Just as weapons ranging from machine guns to surface-to-air missiles have found their way to organized crime groups and terrorists, so will HERF technologies. The destructive impact such weapons could have is evident, from disabling communications systems and computers in police cars to disrupting the computers of the New York Stock Exchange. The systems do not need to be hacked, nor does physical entry have to be gained—simply the transmission of a HERF is sufficient, which will not harm people but will destroy or disable every electrical device in its range from coffeepots to computers.

In addition to HERF, there is development of low-energy radio frequency (LERF) devices that are less damaging but can disrupt communications and data systems through "jamming" the signals. Whether used by a criminal to disrupt communications during a surveillance by a terrorist to disrupt air traffic control communications at a busy airport or by a speeder trying to disrupt radar, these devices could also have a significant impact.

Fortunately, research has also explored promising ways to minimize the effects of HERF and LERF attacks (such as encasing computers in a wire mesh shroud to absorb the RF signal). The point to note is that EMP weapons are on the horizon and will eventually be in the hands of criminals. Plans for protecting assets, preventing attacks, recovering from attacks, and investigating offenders must be developed.

COMPROMISING ELECTRONIC EMANATIONS AND TEMPEST/EMISSIONS SECURITY (EMSEC)[52]   The capture of compromising electronic emanations (CEE), which have been fully classified by the National Security Agency (NSA) for roughly ten years, permits the surreptitious capture of electromagnetic signals emanating from computers. Also known as Van Eck phreaking in the hacking/phreaking community, the system works by capturing the computer's keystrokes, which are transmitted to the display (monitor). Each character (or keystroke) emits a unique characteristic that can be received with the proper equipment. By capturing these emanations, whatever was displayed on the target computer can also be read on the equipment of the CEE user.

The use of such devices for surveillance and espionage is obvious. A person with CEE equipment may be sitting outside a building surreptitiously capturing information from a target's computer. Just as there are privacy concerns with this technology, there are also concerns when CEE technology reaches the hands of criminals. Beyond gathering confidential information—such as intellectual property—information could be used for blackmail, the basis for corruption, to undermine investigations and to identify confidential informants or undercover personnel.

The implications for abuse of this technology are pervasive. What is the potential for this technology to become available for criminals? According to intelligence and law enforcement personnel interviewed in both Europe and Asia, the potential is quite high. One high-ranking police official in Asia told the authors that his organization has learned that wealthy drug traffickers in a neighboring country of the Golden Triangle had gained access to CEE equipment. While being used by criminals, the police official stated that his agency did *not* have this technology.

Electronic filters and interference devices can be defenses to Van Eck phreaking. However, at present the CEE threat is not sufficiently severe to warrant widespread adoption of these defenses. Technological development of the systems and defenses are ongoing. Suffice it to note, there is a "dark side" to every technological development that will be exploited by criminals.

MALICIOUS SOFTWARE   Malicious software (or code) refers to viruses, worms, Trojan horses, logic bombs, and other "uninvited" software designed to disrupt a computer's operations or destroy files.[53] This software is widespread and widely available on the Internet, with new programs created regularly.[54] As noted in Chapter 6, malicious software is now sold and custom designed for individuals in online black markets, enabling participation in serious cybercrimes without the need for knowledge of computer systems. Bots, viruses, Trojan horse programs, and myriad other tools are all now a common component in computer and network attacks. What is more disconcerting is that these programs have shifted from demonstrations of curiosity and mischief to become tools designed to facilitate fraud, espionage, data theft, and network destruction.

In fact, one of the increasingly significant tools in the arsenal of attackers are spear phishing attacks. This form of malware involves sending a fraudulent, yet convincing, e-mail to a targeted individual within an organization who has a position of authority or access to sensitive systems. Unlike traditional phishing schemes, however, the message appears to come from within the organization or an individual in a position of authority to increase the likelihood that the recipient will open the e-mail. In addition, the message will request information from the victim and request the individual to download or open a keylogger, spyware program, or some other type of malicious software to surreptitiously gather sensitive information. Spear phishing is less likely to be used by hackers, but rather "sophisticated groups out for financial gain, trade secrets or military information."[55] The prevalence of spear phishing has increased drastically over the last few years; one study intercepted 56 attempts in January 2005 to over 600,000 in June of the same year.[56]

Malicious software has also been adapted by terror groups for the purposes of network attacks and destruction. The electronic jihad site al-Ghorabaa, for example, contained information on penetrating computer devices and intranet servers and stealing passwords, along with an encyclopedia on hacking Web sites and a 344-page book on hacking techniques.[57] Similarly, the forum Minbar ahl al-Sunna wal-Jama'a offered a hacking manual with details on infiltrating corporate and government networks, personal computers to steal information, and methods of intercepting sensitive information such as credit card numbers in transit.[58] Additionally, a hacker by the name of Younis Tsoulis, who used the handle Irhabi (Terrorist) 007, published a 74-page manual called *The Encyclopedia of Hacking the Zionist and Crusader Websites.*[59] This guide included instructions on how to hack and maintained a Web site that published details on vulnerable Web sites around the world. Toulis was arrested as a result of his actions and sentenced to ten years in prison for inciting terrorist murder on the Internet. These examples demonstrate that malicious software is a particularly effective weapon to cause damage, disrupt network operations steal data, and cause chaos and confusion. All of these effects would serve the goals of terrorists and criminals alike.

Summary

Organizations—public and private alike—must be made aware of the real threat posed by technology-related abuses and their impact on both crime and national security. One of the greatest challenges in this process is the willingness of organizations and people to be alert to changing criminal trends and devote resources to address emerging problems. As part of this change process, there must be development of new law and policy where voids exist. Policy should include regular development of both strategic and tactical intelligence as related to the integrated criminal and national security threats posed through computer crime and its evolution. Similarly, there must be a body of both civil and criminal law developed that expressly addresses the unique elements of cybercrime. This includes attending to the issues of transnational criminality and the ambiguities of attaching value to information and intellectual property. In addition, effective policy must address security, prevention, investigation, prosecution, and damage recovery of electronic property. There must also be a new standard of personnel development to ensure employees have skills necessary to deal with computer- and technology-related crime. These include knowledge of security issues, processes, and practices; investigative techniques; and the capacity to perform forensic analysis of electronic evidence.

Global crime issues require global strategies. In this regard, it would be advisable to have a transnational working group of police; national security; and relevant commerce, security, and regulatory groups to help guide efforts in the prevention, investigation, and prosecution of computer-related crime. Groups such as the Anti-Phishing Working Group and Infragard provide important assistance, though greater collaboration would improve the response from law enforcement, private industry, and academia. With the furious pace of technological development coupled with the global growth of e-commerce, networked computers are increasingly becoming as commonly used as the telephone. Dogmatism and traditional beliefs that "this is not a problem" must be set aside and replaced with an aggressive policy to address these trends.

To help remedy this dogmatism, there needs to be empirical data collection and analysis on computer criminality to define the problem more accurately, map trends, and fully understand the character of the offenses and offenders. National-level data collection has begun, and academic samples of computer crime offending and victimization are beginning to expand our understanding of these offenses. While exploration of hardware and software system protection is important, as is operational security of computers, research must go beyond this. Defining behaviorally based prevention, exploring the cybercrime equivalent of crime "hot spots," developing a catalog of best practices for investigation and prosecution of computer crime, and researching crime control methodologies in a fashion similar to predatory crime are all strategies where emerging research must focus. The National Institute of Justice and similar agencies have begun to produce such manuals, though constant updates are necessary to improve the law enforcement response to computer crimes. As with any forecast, neither a timetable nor certitude can be provided. A forecast is probabilistic; however, there is strong evidence supporting the evolution of cybercrime as described in here. A willingness by public officials to openly explore the feasibility of these forecasts is warranted.

Review Questions

1. What are the biggest problems facing the criminal justice system in the area of computer crime?
2. How is the hacker community changing with the spread of the Internet?
3. What types of computer crimes are going to become more prevalent in the future?
4. Describe the mechanisms and tactics terrorist organizations are likely to use in the future.
5. Which of the forecasts described in this chapter is most likely to come to pass? Which of the forecasts is least likely to come true? Why?

Endnotes

1. See *http://www.wardriving.com/* for a good understanding of the practice and the culture.
2. CARTER, D.L., and KATZ, A.J. (1999). "Computer Applications by International Organized Crime Groups." In L. MORIARITY and D.L. CARTER (eds.), *Criminal Justice Technology in the 21st Century.* Springfield, IL: Charles C. Thomas, Publisher.
3. BRENNER, S.W. (2008). *Cyberthreats: The Emerging Fault Lines of the Nation State.* New York: Oxford University Press.
4. HOLT, THOMAS J., and BLEVINS, KRISTIE R. (September 2008). "Examining the Stress, Challenges, and Experiences of Forensic Examiners." Paper presented at the annual meetings of the Southern Criminal Justice Association, New Orleans, LA.
5. *Ibid.*
6. *Ibid.*
7. *http://www.ojp.usdoj.gov/bjs/abstract/cb05.htm*
8. *Ibid.*
9. *Ibid.*
10. *http://www.ojp.usdoj.gov/bjs/nibrsstatus.htm*
11. *Ibid.*
12. ZETTER, KIM. (2009). "Judge Postpones Lori Drew Sentencing, Weighs Dismissal." *Wired.* Accessed May 29, 2009 from *http://www.wired.com/threatlevel/2009/05/drew_sentenced/*
13. There is precedence for charging fees and placing responsibility on citizens. For example, many jurisdictions charge fines or service fees for police responses to false burglar alarms. In another illustration, the Arlington, Texas Police Department does not dispatch officers to "gas drive-offs" at convenience stores because a prepay policy can prevent that crime.
14. The Tampa Division of the Florida Department of Law Enforcement (FDLE) has organized the computer forensic analyst in the Crime Laboratory section, treating it the same as other forensic evidence analysis.
15. Federal Trade Commission (2007). *2006 Identity Theft Survey Report.* MacLean, VA: Synovate.
16. GOODIN, D. (2007). "TJX Breach Was Twice As Big As Admitted, Banks Say." *The Register.* Retrieved March 27, 2008, from *http://www.theregister.co.uk/2007/10/24/tjx_breach_estimate_grows/*
17. VIJAYAN, JAIKUMAR. (2009). "Heartland Data Breach Could Be Bigger Than TJX's." *Computerworld. http://www.computerworld.com/action/article.do?command=viewArticleBasic&taxonomyName=security&articleId=9126379&taxonomyId=17&intsrc=it_bloglines*
18. FRANKLIN, J., PAXSON, V., PERRIG, A., and SAVAGE, S. (2007). "An Inquiry into the Nature and Cause of the Wealth of Internet Miscreants." Paper presented at CCS07, October 29–November 2, 2007 in Alexandria, VA; HOLT, T.J., and LAMPKE, E. (2009). "Exploring Stolen Data Markets On-line: Products and Market Forces." *Criminal Justice Studies* 33(2); Honeynet Research Alliance (2003). "Profile: Automated Credit Card Fraud," *Know Your Enemy Paper* series. Retrieved June 21, 2005, from *http://www.honeynet.org/papers/profiles/cc-fraud.pdf*; THOMAS, R., and MARTIN, J. (2006). "The Underground Economy: Priceless." *USENIX:login* 31(6): 7–16.
19. *www.fbi.gov*
20. *Ibid.*
21. A good source of information on Internet fraud schemes can be found at the National Fraud Information Center: *www.fraud.org/welcome.htm*. Information is also available through searching the U.S. Federal Trade Commission Web site: *www.ftc.gov*

22. National Criminal Intelligence Service (1999). *Project Trawler: Crime on the Information Highways.* An NCIS project report. London.

23. U.S. Department of Justice (1999). *Cyberstalking: A New Challenge for Law Enforcement and Industry.* A report to the Vice-President. *www.usdoj.gov/ag/cyberstalkingreport.htm*

24. WOLAK, JANIS, MITCHELL, KIMBERLY, and FINKELHOR, DAVID. (2006). *Online Victimization of Youth: Five Years Later.* Washington DC: National Center for Missing and Exploited Children.

25. The Simple Mail Transfer Protocol (SMTP) audit trail can give a wide range of information about the sender of e-mail: the sender's name, e-mail address, Internet service provider, e-mail client software, date, time, etc. There are Web sites which offer the service of hiding this information and sending an audit trail with e-mail which "can't be traced." For example, see *The Anonymizer, www.anonymizer.com*; *Hushmail, www.hushmail.com*; or *Disappearing Inc., www.disappearing.com*

26. PATCHIN, JUSTIN, and HINDUJA, SAMEER. (2007). "What Kids Do on MySpace." *Technology and Learning* 27(7): 7.

27. SURDIN, ASHLEY. (2009). "In Several States, A Push to Stem Cyber-Bullying." *The Washington Post.* Accessed *http://www.washingtonpost.com/wp-dyn/content/article/2008/12/31/AR2008123103067.html*

28. *http://www.internetworldstats.com/stats.htm*

29. *Ibid.*

30. HOLT, T.J. (2008). "Examining the Origins of Malware." Presented at the Department of Defense Cyber Crime Conference, Saint Louis, MO.

31. ULPH, S. (February 7, 2006). "Internet Mujahideen Refine Electronic Warfare Tactics." *Terrorism Focus* 3(5). Jamestown Foundation.

32. CARTER, D.L. (1994). "International Organized Crime: Emerging Trends in Entrepreneurial Crime." *Journal of Contemporary Criminal Justice* 104: 239–266.

33. SANDHU, H. (1999). "Underground Banking and Alternative Remittance Systems." *INTERPOL and Technology in Partnership.* London: Kensington Publications Limited.

34. The new European Union passport is particularly popular for counterfeiters.

35. *Ibid.,* HOLT and LAMPKE, "Exploring Stolen Data Markets On-line: Products and Market Forces."

36. BURTON, BILL. (2006). "14 Billion Profit Made from Net Gambling." *http://casinogambling.about.com/b/2006/03/05/14-billion-profit-made-from-net-gambling.htm*

37. A telephone does not have to be in use, but simply turned on, in order to emit the EIN.

38. Traffickers in stolen wireless telephones and number recommend that a stolen number not be used over one month in case it is being traced by investigators.

39. Federal Bureau of Investigation (1999). *CyberNotes* (3): pp. 1–13.

40. LEYDEN, J. (2003). "Al-Qaeda: The 39 principles of Holy War." *Virtual Jerusalem.*

41. ALSHECH, E. (February 7, 2007). "Cyberspace As a Combat Zone: The Phenomenon of Electronic Jihad." *MEMRI Inquiry and Analysis Series* (329). The Middle East Media Research Institute.

42. Motive is typically not an element (i.e., part of the *corpus delecti*) of a crime; hence, while it can be presented in court, it is not required. Nonetheless, demonstrating the motive can aggravate or mitigate the actual crime charged as well as the severity of the penalty.

43. When NATO began bombing Serbia in March 1999, Serbian hackers began a low-level campaign of harassment directed at the U.S. government and military groups involved in the NATO actions. The "Black Hand" hacker group and the "Serbian Angels" hacker group threatened to damage NATO computers in retaliation for the war against the Serbs. On March 29, the White House Web site was defaced by red letters reading "Hackerz wuz Here." It was speculated that anti-NATO activists were involved. On March 30, hackers damaged a NATO Web server, forcing it off line for a short time. *Information Security* (December 1999), p. 26.

44. *http://www.dni.gov/testimonies/20090212_testimony.pdf*

45. LANDLER, M., and MARKOFF, J. (May 29, 2007). "Digital Fears Emerge after Data Siege in Estonia." *The New York Times.*

46. THORNBURG, N. (2005). "Inside the Chinese Hack Attack." *Time.*

47. The wealth amassed by drug dealers has purchased a wide array of sophisticated technology and the services of people—frequently intelligence personnel from the security services of the former Soviet bloc countries—to use these technologies to further their enterprises and

avoid prosecution. Similar wealth has purportedly furthered terroristic acts, such as terrorism networks supported from Afghanistan by Osama Bin Laden.

48. The authors reinforce the point that our focus is on *behavioral applications* of the weapons discussed in this section. Details on the development and mechanics of the technologies are available from a wide range of sources.

49. Kopp, C. (1999). "The E-Bomb: A Weapon of Electrical Mass Destruction." A paper posted on the Web site of the Department of Computer Science, Monash University, Australia. *www.cs. monash.edu.au/~carlo/*

50. *Ibid.*

51. Miniaturization of a HERF weapon to a handheld size appears probable. As a comparison: A laptop computer that can be purchased by mail order today has more processing speed, more memory, and more diverse capacity (such as audio and video) than a state-of-the-art mainframe computer of 1980 which required an entire room with strict environmental controls to be housed.

52. Much of the information in this section is based on a confidential interview with two intelligence specialists—one from the United States and one overseas—familiar with this technology. The reader is also referred to the *TEMPEST Information Page* on the Internet at www.eskimo.com/~joelm/tempest.html, which contains a great deal of information released from the U.S. National Security Agency (NSA) through Freedom of Information Act requests.

53. Computer Systems Laboratory Bulletin (1994). *Malicious Software Information Bulletin.* Washington, DC: Computer Security Resource Clearinghouse, National Institute of Standards and Technology. *csrc.nist.gov/nistbul/csl94-03.txt*

54. For example, See Holt, T.J. (August 7, 2007). "The Market for Malware." Paper presented at the Defcon 15 Conference, Las Vegas, NV.

55. O'Brien, Timothy. (2005). "Gone Spear-Phishin'" *The New York Times.* Accessed May 4, 2008 from *http://www.nytimes.com/2005/12/04/business/your money/04spear.html?_r=1&ex=1157083200&en= 88dace68c6663bbb&ei=5070*

56. *Ibid.*

57. *Ibid.*

58. Pool, J. (October 11, 2005). "Technology and Security Discussions on the Jihadist Forums." Jamestown Foundation.

59. Jamestown (March 4, 2008). "Hacking Manual by Jailed Jihadi Appears on Web." *Terrorism Focus* 5(9). Jamestown Foundation.

INDEX

Note: Locators followed by 'f', 'n.' and 't' denotes figure, note number and tables respectively.